The
L/L Research
Channeling Archives

Transcripts of
the Meditation Sessions

Volume 8
October 20, 1985 to February 22, 1987

Don
Elkins

Jim
McCarty

Carla L.
Rueckert

Copyright © 2009 L/L Research

All rights reserved. No part of this book may be reproduced or used in any form or by any means—graphic, electronic or mechanical, including photocopying or information storage and retrieval systems—without written permission from the copyright holder.

ISBN: 978-0-945007-82-1

Published by L/L Research
Box 5195
Louisville, Kentucky 40255-0195

E-mail: contact@llresearch.org
www.llresearch.org

About the cover photo: *This photograph of Jim McCarty and Carla L. Rueckert was taken during an L/L Research channeling session on August 4, 2009, in the living room of their Louisville, Kentucky home. Jim always holds hands with Carla when she channels, following the Ra group's advice on how she can avoid any possibility of astral travel.*

Dedication

These archive volumes are dedicated to Hal and Jo Price, who faithfully and lovingly hosted this group's weekly meditation meetings from 1962 to 1975,

to Walt Rogers, whose work with the research group Man, Consciousness and Understanding of Detroit offered the information needed to begin this ongoing channeling experiment,

and to the Confederation of Angels and Planets in the Service of the Infinite Creator, for sharing their love and wisdom with us so generously through the years.

Table of Contents

Introduction 7

Year 1985 9
    October 20, 1985 10
    October 27, 1985 14
    November 3, 1985 19
    November 10, 1985 26
    November 17, 1985 30
    November 24, 1985 36
    December 1, 1985 40
    December 8, 1985 45
    December 15, 1985 49
    December 22, 1985 55
    December 29, 1985 57

Year 1986 61
    January 5, 1986 62
    January 12, 1986 68
    January 19, 1986 74
    January 26, 1986 78
    February 2, 1986 83
    February 9, 1986 89
    February 16, 1986 94
    February 23, 1986 99
    March 2, 1986 105
    March 9, 1986 110
    March 16, 1986 115
    March 23, 1986 118
    March 30, 1986 123
    April 6, 1986 127
    April 13, 1986 131
    April 20, 1986 135
    May 4, 1986 141
    May 11, 1986 147
    May 18, 1986 150
    May 25, 1986 156
    June 1, 1986 161
    June 8, 1986 168
    June 15, 1986 175
    June 29, 1986 182
    July 6, 1986 189

July 13, 1986	195
July 20, 1986	202
July 27, 1986	208
August 10, 1986	213
August 31, 1986	219
September 7, 1986	228
September 14, 1986	236
September 21, 1986	243
September 28, 1986	248
October 1, 1986	253
October 2, 1986	255
October 3, 1986	258
October 5, 1986	261
October 6, 1986	266
October 8, 1986	268
October 9, 1986	272
October 10, 1986	276
October 11, 1986	279
October 12, 1986	281
October 13, 1986	286
October 14, 1986	288
October 15, 1986	292
October 19, 1986	294
October 22, 1986	300
November 2, 1986	303
November 9, 1986	307
November 16, 1986	313
November 23, 1986	320
November 30, 1986	327
December 14, 1986	336
December 20, 1986	342
Year 1987	**346**
January 4, 1987	347
January 10, 1987	353
January 11, 1987	359
January 18, 1987	365
January 25, 1987	372
January 28, 1987	376
February 4, 1987	377
February 8, 1987	382
February 11, 1987	386
February 15, 1987	389

FEBRUARY 18, 1987	395
FEBRUARY 22, 1987	399

Introduction

Welcome to this volume of the *L/L Research Channeling Archives*. This series of publications represents the collection of channeling sessions recorded by L/L Research during the period from the early seventies to the present day. The sessions are also available on the L/L Research website, www.llresearch.org.

Starting in the mid-1950s, Don Elkins, a professor of physics and engineering at Speed Scientific School, had begun researching the paranormal in general and UFOs in particular. Elkins was a pilot as well as a professor and he flew his small plane to meet with many of the UFO contactees of the period.

Hal Price had been a part of a UFO-contactee channeling circle in Detroit called "The Detroit Group." When Price was transferred from Detroit's Ford plant to its Louisville truck plant, mutual friends discovered that Price also was a UFO researcher and put the two men together. Hal introduced Elkins to material called *The Brown Notebook* which contained instructions on how to create a group and receive UFO contactee information. In January of 1962 they decided to put the instructions to use and began holding silent meditation meetings on Sunday nights just across the Ohio River in the southern Indiana home of Hal and his wife, Jo. This was the beginning of what was called the "Louisville Group."

I was an original member of that group, along with a dozen of Elkins' physics students. However, I did not learn to channel until 1974. Before that date, almost none of our weekly channeling sessions were recorded or transcribed. After I began improving as a channel, Elkins decided for the first time to record all the sessions and transcribe them.

During the first eighteen months or so of my studying channeling and producing material, we tended to reuse the tapes as soon as the transcriptions were finished. Since those were typewriter days, we had no record of the work that could be reopened and used again, as we do now with computers. And I used up the original and the carbon copy of my transcriptions putting together a manuscript, *Voices of the Gods*, which has not yet been published. It remains as almost the only record of Don Elkins' and my channeling of that period.

We learned from this experience to retain the original tapes of all of our sessions, and during the remainder of the seventies and through the eighties, our "Louisville Group" was prolific. The "Louisville Group" became "L/L Research" after Elkins and I published a book in 1976, *Secrets of the UFO*, using that publishing name. At first we met almost every night. In later years, we met gradually less often, and the number of sessions recorded by our group in a year accordingly went down. Eventually, the group began taking three months off from channeling during the summer. And after 2000, we began having channeling meditations only twice a month. The volume of sessions dropped to its present output of eighteen or so each year.

These sessions feature channeling from sources which call themselves members of the Confederation of Planets in the Service of the Infinite Creator. At first we enjoyed hearing from many different voices: Hatonn, Laitos, Oxal, L/Leema and Yadda being just a few of them. As I improved my tuning techniques, and became the sole senior channel in L/L Research, the number of contacts dwindled. When I began asking for "the highest and best contact which I can receive of Jesus the Christ's vibration of unconditional love in a conscious and stable manner," the entity offering its thoughts through our group was almost always Q'uo. This remains true as our group continues to channel on an ongoing basis.

The channelings are always about love and unity, enunciating "The Law of One" in one aspect or another. Seekers who are working with spiritual principles often find the material a good resource. We hope that you will as well. As time has gone on the questions have shifted somewhat, but in general the content of the channeling is metaphysical and focused on helping seekers find the love in the moment and the Creator in the love.

At first, I transcribed our channeling sessions. I got busier, as our little group became more widely known, and got hopelessly behind on transcribing. Two early transcribers who took that job off my hands were Kim

Howard and Judy Dunn, both of whom masterfully transcribed literally hundreds of sessions through the eighties and early nineties.

Then Ian Jaffray volunteered to create a web site for these transcriptions, and single-handedly unified the many different formats that the transcripts were in at that time and made them available online. This additional exposure prompted more volunteers to join the ranks of our transcribers, and now there are a dozen or so who help with this. Our thanks go out to all of these kind volunteers, early and late, who have made it possible for our webguy to make these archives available.

Around the turn of the millennium, I decided to commit to editing each session after it had been transcribed. So the later transcripts have fewer errata than the earlier ones, which are quite imperfect in places. One day, perhaps, those earlier sessions will be revisited and corrections will be made to the transcripts. It would be a large task, since there are well over 1500 channeling sessions as of this date, and counting. We apologize for the imperfections in those transcripts, and trust that you can ascertain the sense of them regardless of a mistake here and there.

Blessings, dear reader! Enjoy these "humble thoughts" from the Confederation of Planets. May they prove good companions to your spiritual seeking. ☙

For all of us at L/L Research,

Carla L. Rueckert

Louisville, Kentucky

July 16, 2009

Year 1985

October 20, 1985 to December 29, 1985

Sunday Meditation
October 20, 1985

(Carla channeling)

I am Hatonn, and I greet you through this instrument in the love and the light of our infinite Creator. We are most grateful to be able to speak through this instrument, as we conditioned each instrument in the room and found that each felt somewhat fatigued and each wished to listen. We shall continue to make our presence felt for the practical aspect of continuing the good contact which we have with each instrument. However, we shall use this instrument at present.

There is not one within this domicile, and, indeed, we may say there is probably a paucity of those within what you call humankind who does not question the reason for all the difficulties of the incarnational experience. We would like to address this subject in yet another way this evening.

Each has a certain amount of compassion. Each has a certain measure of wisdom. That measure for most of those upon your planetary sphere is a very small percentage of the biases which collect about the mind and body complexes of each entity. And yet, the key to grasping the assessment of difficulties lies in gaining enough wisdom and addressing that wisdom with enough love. We shall come back to this point. We hope you will bear with us, for we are attempting to train this instrument to deliver unexpected information without fear. Therefore, there will be pauses.

Each of you has what seems to be a self, that self containing two hands, two feet, a face with mobile features, a torso that moves with more or less skill and gracefulness. This seems to be the self, my friends, and yet wisdom will tell you that it is not the self, for where in your arms or your legs, your face or your torso can you locate your self? It has been written within your holy work which is called the Bible that the Creator shall not allow any danger to befall His chosen people, not even a foot stubbed against a stone, so the one known as David writes. This is true, absolutely and completely. Therefore, you may ask, "Why am I continually stubbing my toe against rocks?" speaking often in terms of emotional discomfort rather than physical.

You are in this incarnational experience as one who views a movie. To consider that you are a portion of the movie is accurate, for each motivation and attitude that you are able to carve into positivity, joy and gladness raises the amount of light that you are able to receive and accept. However, the body which you inhabit is evanescent in the extreme, comparatively speaking, for you as a spirit are older than some stars and will outlive some stars. Consequently, that part of you which is infinite shall never have the foot dashed against a stone. It would be impossible, for your very nature is like that of the

Creator. However, you have chosen to dress yourself in flesh and dwell within this illusion so that you may experience a large number of seeming difficulties.

This brings us back to compassion, or love and wisdom. If the beginning of love is the acceptance of the self, the beginning of wisdom is freedom from fear, for what can happen to you? Should you be killed? That would not be astonishing, for each body shall die. Should you be hungry or cold? These things occur. What is your reaction to them? Should you fall into disharmony with a relationship with another? This frequently occurs. What is the reason for the discomfort this causes?

Difficulties, my friends, are what they seem in the illusion, and it is your challenge within the illusion to deal with as much love as possible with each difficulty. So you learn the lessons of love. So you see, in part, through an illusion. So, finally, you have no need any longer for this illusion.

We would pause at this time and work with each instrument, if each instrument wishes to receive conditioning. I am Hatonn.

(Pause)

I am again with this instrument, and we thank each for the privilege of sharing the vibration and love while we work with the conditioning. We do not mean to seem coldhearted or unhelpful about the difficulties which you face. We find in this instrument's mind fear due to upcoming surgery. We find in each mind some fear, the fear of pain, of dying, of losing a beloved relationship, of growing older. Many fears other than these are held, and yet to enumerate all those fears would not be any more helpful than to mention just a few. However, there is a measure of wisdom in each. We ask you to reach for it, and as difficulties, fears, doubts, worries overcome you, find that measure of wisdom that says, "The beginning of wisdom is freedom from fear."

Where can you go? You are in the creation. What if you are suddenly in a negative creation? No matter, my friends, for all does become One, so our teachers tell us. And then once again you are free to serve the Creator and turn again homeward to the heart of the creation, to become One, indeed, with the one great original Thought. Where is fear in a creation that has an absolute certainty of turning homeward in every seeming second that ticks by? Indeed, it would be most helpful in your incarnational experience if you can give praise to the Creator of your difficulties, and thereby remove your center of attention onto higher ground, shall we say, for you are able to see that each fear, each difficulty, and each doubt is a challenge, is a force, shall we say, against which each entity now has the opportunity to push in order to carve ever deeper the attitudes of thanksgiving, joy and love.

This does not mean that you become blind to what is occurring about you. It means only that you see what seems to be and you deal appropriately with that which seems to be within the context of the illusion, while maintaining your center, your focus of attention upon the love, the beauty, and the truth inherent in each moment. Rejoice in your difficulties, just as a servant may rejoice that he may serve his master, for your higher self designed and planned carefully that you might not waste a moment of time. Rest is given to the weary. There are calm stretches in incarnational experiences and these are healing times. And then once again will come the challenge. Use that challenge to polarize more and more effectively towards the love that is inherent in all of creation

We would now leave this instrument, for we find that this instrument, too, is fatigued, and shall yield the floor to our brothers and sisters of Latwii. We thank you for calling us to speak. We realize that some of what we say must of necessity repeat itself. But it is important to grasp the basics of living a growing spiritual evolution rather than living a static existence, spiritually speaking.

It is important that you remember and use the very first things we teach first, that is, meditation to center the mind upon love, to gentle the spirit, to put in order that which is disordered, to heal that which is wounded. And it is equally important that you move from meditation into your daily illusion, retaining the sense of no fear and the sense of your own worth. These are the beginnings, my friends. You may build from them, but without them you shall find your spiritual evolution to be comparatively slow. We are those of Hatonn. We leave you in the love, the light, and the balance of the infinite Creator. Adonai, my friends. Farewell. Farewell.

(Jim channeling)

I am Latwii, and we greet you, my friends, in the love and the light of our infinite Creator. We thank you also for asking our presence this evening. We are eager to begin with any question which might be available. May we ask for the first query?

Carla: I have one. There is a disease which is called AIDS. I wonder if you could comment on what the disease is caused by in the emotional sphere, why it hits certain segments of the population, or any other comment that you wish to make about this disease or disease in general.

I am Latwii, and am aware of your query, my sister. There are many facets to the query; we shall attempt to speak to the heart. There are various diseases, as you call them, at this time which are becoming more prevalent within various segments of your population. The disease that you have called AIDS is one which aids the, shall we say, entities so suffering or within the potential population of sufferers, in focusing their attentions and their affections upon a smaller and smaller circle of intimate friends, so that the ultimate goal is the paired relationship in which the evolutionary process may have its most full and efficient sway, shall we say.

It is, as you know, but a short time as you measure these things before the end of this great cycle of evolution upon your planet. The time, then, is short for those incarnate upon your planet to polarize in a fashion sufficient for the graduation. Therefore, there are many more, shall we say, training aids available for the acceleration of this process, the time being short. Diseases are one such method of focusing the attention upon a symbol of a generally shared difficulty.

Within the majority of your population at this time there is the continued exercise of the mated relationship and the mirroring effect that this relationship provides to each. There are, however, various minorities or subcultures within your larger culture which have not so focused the mated relationship, and have therefore not been able to bring to bear those lessons and services that lie latent within. Therefore, the disease called AIDS has reminded many within this community that there is not only greater safety of the incarnation within the mated relationship but there is also to the far-seeing eye a greater ability to complete the preincarnational plans for the lessons and services that will allow for the graduation.

May we answer further, my sister?

Carla: Yes, indeed. It seems like a gross infringement on free will, for one thing. The other thing is, how in the world can an AIDS sufferer learn about a mated relationship? It's over half the time a killer. The victim is not around long enough to retrain the mind and accomplish the mirroring effect of the mated relationship.

I am Latwii, and am aware of your query, my sister. To the first part. It is not correct that such diseases [are] foisted upon a certain segment of the culture, shall we say. These entities themselves have planned, with the aid of the higher self—if you will continue to excuse our continuous puns—that there shall be certain, shall we say, optional plans brought into existence when the need arises.

Now to the second portion of the query. One who has a definite, it would seem, length of life remaining, knowing that it shall die, as you call it, after this portion of time, knows that all succeeding actions shall carry more weight, for it does not usually wish to waste the opportunities that are remaining. Therefore, such an entity will view each relationship in which it partakes as that which is most treasured, and can in a very short portion of time learn that which was avoided or ignored in the previous portion of the incarnation.

May we answer further, my sister?

Carla: Well, just in one thing, and this has me puzzled, too. Heterosexual people have recently started getting herpes, which really encourages a mated relationship or the nunnery, one or the other, yet it's not a killer. Is the Creator somehow biased against homosexuals?

I am Latwii, and, my sister, we remind you that the Creator dwells within all portions of Its one creation. Therefore, those actions and energies set forth within any portion of the creation are those actions and energies that are considered by that portion of the creation to be appropriate for the goal of the eventual learning of love, to the sufficient degree that the graduation may be achieved. The severity of various diseases, therefore, is dependent upon the choices made upon the subconscious level with the subcultures thusly affected. It is to such entities that the honor and the duty of making such choices must remain.

May we answer further, my sister?

Carla: No, thank you.

I am Latwii, and we thank you, my sister. Is there another query?

Carla: Do you expect, then, that the new diseases will begin to show up more and more often as we grow closer to the end of the cycle?

I am Latwii, and this is quite correct, my sister. If you will review the medical literature of the previous decade, you will note the discovery of a variety of new diseases which have not appeared previously within the past centuries and have made their appearance only at the end of this great cycle.

May we answer further, my sister?

Carla: No.

I am Latwii, and again we thank you, my sister. Is there another query?

(Pause)

I am Latwii. We find that we have quickly exhausted the queries for this evening. We thank this group once again for inviting our presence, and we hope that our humble words have been of some small aid in this endeavor. We again ask for your forgiveness, but we could not resist one final pun …

Carla: May I ask one final question?

Ah! We have another query. My sister, please proceed.

Carla: Would you care to talk about anything?

I am Latwii, and we find that for this evening our service is that of the response to your queries. We have no axes to grind—they're all quite sharp.

L: I'd simply like to make the observation that if this is indeed your last statement, we would all affectionately bid you, "Adieu."

(Laughter)

I am Latwii, and we know when we have been bested. All our congratulations to the one known as L, and upon that note we shall finally bid each a farewell, and thank each for inviting our presence this evening. Adonai, my friends. Adonai. We are those of Latwii. ✣

Sunday Meditation
October 27, 1985

Group question: What opportunities are presented to an individual when an individual is in a disharmonious relationship with any other and what part do psychic greetings or attacks play in such a disharmonious relationship?

(Carla channeling)

I am L/Leema, and I greet you in the love and the light of the One Who Is All in All. We shall attempt to use this instrument as this instrument is suited to the deliverance of the question. However, we find that although this instrument is willing, it is quite fatigued. Therefore, we shall begin.

It seems to be a vast universe peopled with unimaginable numbers of suns and whirling galaxies that paint the sky with diamond drops. There seem to be enormous numbers of individuals even on one small planet that makes its way about an obscure star near the edge of the galaxy it inhabits. There appear in one person's mind to be many, many thoughts and ideas which range in great complexity from one subject to another. There appears in each idea that there are ramifications and considerations of various levels of thinking so that one who is more mature in years shall think differently upon the same subject than one who is young. All of these appearances are appearances of separation. In truth, there is one creation, there is one consciousness, and for each density there is one Thought. In your density you are seeking to know the thought of love, not intellectually or by any guidebook but rather from the inside out, from the heart outwards, through the mouth, through the ears, through the eyes. One who has the heart of love also has ears that hear with love; one who has a heart of love sees that which it passes before its gaze with eyes of love.

When it seems apparent that there is a lack of communication between two entities, that there are hurt feelings and insults, one must look to the love in the insult and the love in the hurt feelings, for both of these pains belong to the emotional self and are a distortion of love. We shall dwell primarily upon the self that is hurt, for the questioner is the party which has been injured.

One who is hurt is experiencing a distortion of love in that it is not being appreciated for the gifts that it gives. And yet, is the gift any less because it is not appreciated? Is the giving less pleasurable because compliments are not given? One with a heart full enough of love can give without need for compliment or thank-you or payment of any kind, emotional or financial, physical or spiritual. Therefore, the one who is hurt is working with an illusion which is that of separation, for why is there need for the creation to thank itself? Why is there need for consciousness to thank itself? And why is there the need for the subject of love to thank itself.

We urge those who are in pain because of being hurt by the speech or actions of another to take into meditation the unity of all that there is and so strengthen the will and deepen the faith in that unity of love that gifts can be freely given with no expectation of any kind that there may be a return or a reward. Imagine each gift that one gives as the arrow which is sent from the bow. It will find its target more and more purely as the giver gives with less and less expectation of any reward, but rather gives for the upwelling joy of the gift given.

As to the case of the one who insults another, again, one cannot insult oneself except by insulting another unless one consciously wishes to insult the self. Normally the illusion calls up for those who insult others a need to find and choose and pick out those things which it finds are lacking in the self. Therefore, in any insult, look to the reflection of that insult upon the giver of revilement and have compassion on a soul that is hurting itself unknowingly and is falling into a vortex from which it is sometimes difficult to emerge unscathed. Feel compassion and blessing and an upwelling of joy in aiding such an insulting and difficult entity, for this entity is in great need of stable, sturdy, calm and constant joy that ever radiates and can never be extinguished.

We realize that this is difficult to accomplish. If there were no challenges, why would one decide to enter into incarnation? Take your challenge up with joy when it comes to you and attempt to the best of your ability to offer the same constant love to those who wrong you and those who praise you. Cast a cold eye on the difference between the two, for all things are one and the love in all things must needs be found. This is the heart of the lesson of insult and emotional pain.

We would transfer the contact at this time in order that any questions that you may have can be answered. I leave this instrument, thanking it for its service. I am L/Leema.

(Jim channeling)

I am L/Leema, and we greet you again through this instrument. It is our privilege at this time to attempt any further queries which those present may have in ready for the asking. May we attempt another query?

Carla: Is there any more on the subject that I was unable to pick up because I was tired?

I am L/Leema. We feel gratified that we were able to utilize your somewhat fatigued instrument and provide the detail which we felt would be helpful for that particular query. We are not aware of any portion of our intention that was not transmitted through your instrument, and again we thank you for your service.

May we attempt any other query?

Carla: When you started channeling through this group, the channelings were longer. Have you been attempting to abbreviate your answers so that the group would not get restless?

I am L/Leema. This is in part correct, my sister, for we in the beginning of our contact with this group were not as familiar with the desires and practices which this group has for some portion of your time taken a nourishment and an enjoyment in. We were more prone to the detail within our speaking, that is, we sought to explicate as plainly as possible and utilize more of your descriptive phrases with the hope that we might achieve a greater clarity. We find that a portion of this group's time together is that which includes a greater variety than the long discourses upon our part would allow, that is, the speaking with a number of entities and the inclusion of this question and answer portion of the meditation. We feel that we are achieving a better balance, shall we say, between the main address of the evening and this variety which each has found helpful in its own seeking. The shorter discourses are perhaps also of value, for there is in this group the appreciation of the brevity and clarity rather than the extended discourse with numerous allusions.

May we answer further, my sister?

Carla: Not on that, but I do have a personal question. When we were having sessions with Ra, Ra mentioned in one session of the personal material that about two years ago there was an opportunity which my higher self had built into my being for leaving the incarnation at that time. There is some doubt as to the length of that period. It is my feeling that it has ended and if you could simply confirm that, I think that perhaps it would lay fears to rest on the part of the one known as Jim.

I am L/Leema, and we shall do our best to shed some light upon this topic without infringing upon the free will of any present. The phenomenon which was mentioned in the contact with those of Ra at the time which you describe was a feature which had been preincarnatively chosen and which had found at that point in your experience the possibility of once again becoming activated should your desire be for the leaving of the incarnation, as indeed this factor was utilized at a much earlier time within your incarnational experience. This is a factor which is ever ready to play its part, for it is the need of each third-density entity at some point in its gathering of experience to assess that experience with the overview that is only possible from the, shall we say, after-death and preincarnative state of awareness.

Thus, each third-density incarnation shall find its end by whatever means is appropriate. The times or time which is designated by each entity is not firmly set but is the product of a number of factors. The choice of an entity concerning its departure from this illusion is due in large part to that entity's subconscious feeling that it has accomplished that which it has come to do, shall we say. There are instances in which entities find a great deal of distress in the evaluation that the incarnation is falling far short of such lessons and occasionally an entity will decide to depart due to such a feeling that there must be a new beginning. There is, however, in your particular case the desire to continue with the service as well as the desire to continue with the lessons, for there is the determination that the former is more important than the latter, and, indeed, the latter has been in large part accomplished. Therefore we find that your own will is that factor which is most important in this situation, for your will is, shall we say, free to move without the burden of further agreements to be fulfilled.

May we answer further, my sister?

Carla: Just to clarify. Am I to understand then that when the Ra contact was through that that portion of work which I had laid out for my incarnation as a minimum had been accomplished? And therefore I was free to go?

I am L/Leema, and we tread somewhat close to the Law of Confusion but would suggest that this is not entirely correct. There were additional services and lessons. These continue in some respect.

May we answer further, my sister?

Carla: No, no, I didn't mean that that was it, I just meant that that was the minimum. I'm sure there's plenty more before I get to the maximum of what I can do to serve. Thank you.

I am L/Leema, and we thank you, my sister. We at this point shall apologize for the delay between the transmission of various words and concepts. We are attempting to work with this instrument in a somewhat different fashion than is our normal technique. We are working at a somewhat deeper level of meditation to transmit more closely the word-by-word technique. This instrument is willing and is more and more able to function in this manner but is somewhat apprehensive, thus our transmission may be somewhat broken, shall we say, this evening.

May we attempt another query?

N: It is said that the capstone of the great pyramid of Cheops was removed from Giza and the crystals were used for the lighthouse of the Alexander. How many feet were removed of what is now the top of the great pyramid at Giza?

I am L/Leema. We shall attempt response, though we find it somewhat difficult to measure that which was removed. The original capstone was composed of that substance known to your peoples as granite. The entities of the priesthood in the culture known to you as Egyptian after a portion of time desired to remove that crystallized rock structure, the granite, and desired to replace this substance with a more precious substance, shall we say, of the golden nature. We must pause momentarily.

(Pause)

I am L/Leema. We are once again with this instrument. There was the need in this instrument's mind to recover the recording machine which had been covered by the second-density creature. To continue with the capstone. The amount of the substance which was removed is relatively small in proportion to the entire structure's volume. Approximately one thousandth of the structure was in the form of the capstone and was thusly removed.

May we answer further, my brother?

N: I had more interest in the height than in the volume. Some say that it was approximately thirty-five feet and others say it was approximately thirty feet. But I was under the impression not only was it made of granite but it also had not just a crystalline structure but had actually refractive amorphous crystals for diffusing the light.

I am L/Leema. We find that the measurements given are more or less accurate according to the proportion. However, we find that the information concerning the, as you have termed them, the amorphous crystals, to be less than accurate according to our estimation, for the proper functioning of the pyramid at that point of the apex was permitted by a solid granite capstone that was not inclusive of other types of crystal which would interfere with its function.

May we answer further, my brother?

N: Well, then this capstone was pure granite as I understand it, and it was removed, and was the height of it approximately thirty feet? The pyramid is said to be at about 454 feet now and it was estimated it was 480 or 485 feet at its inception. And why was the capstone removed?

I am L/Leema. The height of the pyramid after the granite capstone was removed was again approximated by the replacement of the capstone of golden quality. The entire pyramid at this time within your continuum is lesser in all its measurements, for there has been over great passage of time the removal of a covering that was originally included with the pyramid's construction. There has therefore been the overall reduction in size of this structure since its original construction. The granite capstone was removed by those of the priest nature or calling at a much later date, shall we say, than the first construction of the pyramid. The reason for its changing in the capstone was that those called priests had at that time moved more towards the reserving of the use of the pyramid for those of royal blood or those of more powerful position in regards to the entire population of those known as Egyptians. Thus, as the pyramid itself and the teachings associated with it became reserved for the elite, this small group of entities felt that it would be more fitting for their station if the capstone of the pyramid were of a more precious metallic construction.

May we answer further, my brother?

N: Thank you. Can you tell me the approximate measurement of the original pyramid at Giza in our measurements?

I am L/Leema. We find some difficulty in giving the precise measure in your feet and inches manner. We are somewhat more able to approximate the type of measurement that would be based upon the volume or upon percentage. However, we shall attempt, if this instrument is willing, to transmit a more precise measurement. The entire structure was at its inception larger in each measure by approximately two feet. Thus, if one added a mantle, shall we say, two feet thick that would cover each exposed portion of the existing structure, one would closely approximate the original measurements of this structure.

May we answer further, my brother?

N: Well, I was primarily interested in the height but I knew that the limestone covering had been removed, and that approximately two feet, but I also knew that the capstone had a flat surface at the top and that there is about thirty feet missing from the original, but I didn't know exactly how much. But if you can't answer, thank you anyway.

I am L/Leema, and we appreciate your query, my brother, and find that the information which you have previously accumulated in regards to this structure is basically correct except as we noted for the purity of the granite existing without other crystals within it.

May we attempt any other query at this time?

Carla: Is there ever a time when it's better to hold your tongue than to be honest?

I am L/Leema. We find an interesting concept within this query. This query assumes that an entity within your third-density illusion can ascertain the, shall we say, sum total ramifications of its each and every act. Though many live the well-examined life and have learned well the lessons that may be presented in the day-to-day round of activities, there are few who can project the possibilities of what you call the future and how that future might be affected by a choice made in your present moment. It is rather the salient lesson and ambiance, if we may, of your illusion that entities work upon the lessons of love. Those lessons include the seemingly foolish giving of self without expectation of return, the movement within darkness with the faith that the love of the one Creator exists in each portion of that darkness without knowing any fact for sure and yet giving wholly of the self regardless of the not being able to know. Yet do entities learn the lessons of love.

It is, in our humble opinion, not possible for those within your illusion …

(Side one of tape ends.)

(Jim channeling)

I am L/Leema, and am once again with this instrument. It is not likely that any within your illusion will move much past the lesson of love. Thus the recommendation to each is that one give wholeheartedly the truest and best of one's treasures, that is, to give without consideration of return, and to give with the greatest intention to serve that one can find. If the intention is to serve and to see the one Creator within each portion of one's illusion, then that which you call honesty is highly recommended. It, however, is also true that if one does not wish to serve and moves in thought and action with self-serving motives or motives that are less than loving, yet and still shall there be the service, without perhaps the potential to polarize in the positive sense that desiring honesty with the hope of serving another would provide.

May we answer further, my sister?

Carla: Well, yes. What was at the heart of that question was my observation which I have pondered a lot lately that when a truth is withheld so that the other person can figure things out for himself, sometimes it's of more use to that person that you're trying to serve than the whole truth and nothing but the truth which can be very abrasive. And I am honestly puzzled as to sometimes which way to turn, whether to just allow things to go by and run their course or to step in with honesty and communication and somewhat abrasively work towards a solution, a difficulty for someone else.

I am L/Leema and within your comment, which is thoughtful, we perceive the possibility of service. To conceive of what shall be the course of action with too much emphasis upon thought, shall we say, is to proceed in a manner which does not include the spontaneity which is the great enabler of lessons and services within your illusion. To examine the actions so closely as to rob them of the natural spontaneity which wells up from your own deeper self, shall we say, is to put limitations upon the possibilities of the moment. Thus, when one is puzzled as to what to do or how to do it, it is best for the moment to do nothing and to once again move into the current of your existence and be somewhat taken by it and to allow the channeling of this current to move through your thoughts and your actions and to later examine the results in order that the fruits of these labors might be harvested. To attempt to visualize the fruits before the harvest frequently affects the harvest in a deleterious manner.

May we answer further, my sister?

Carla: No, she said spontaneously. Thank you.

I am L/Leema, and we thank you, my sister. Is there another query?

(Pause)

I am L/Leema. We find that the queries have come to their end, and we are extremely grateful to each for providing us with this opportunity to speak. Without your desire to query and your desire for our presence, we would have no beingness within your experience. It is a great joy and honor to share that beingness with you this evening. We move with you on that great journey. As each, we seek our source, and as each, we find it quite, quite close to home. We are those of L/Leema, and we leave you in love and light and blessing. Adonai, my friends. Adonai. ❖

L/L Research is a subsidiary of Rock Creek Research & Development Laboratories, Inc.

P.O. Box 5195
Louisville, KY 40255-0195

www.llresearch.org

Rock Creek is a non-profit corporation dedicated to discovering and sharing information which may aid in the spiritual evolution of humankind.

ABOUT THE CONTENTS OF THIS TRANSCRIPT: This telepathic channeling has been taken from transcriptions of the weekly study and meditation meetings of the Rock Creek Research & Development Laboratories and L/L Research. It is offered in the hope that it may be useful to you. As the Confederation entities always make a point of saying, please use your discrimination and judgment in assessing this material. If something rings true to you, fine. If something does not resonate, please leave it behind, for neither we nor those of the Confederation would wish to be a stumbling block for any.

CAVEAT: This transcript is being published by L/L Research in a not yet final form. It has, however, been edited and any obvious errors have been corrected. When it is in a final form, this caveat will be removed.

© 2009 L/L Research

Sunday Meditation
November 3, 1985

(Carla channeling)

[I am Hatonn,] and I greet you, my friends, in the love and the light of our infinite Creator. We greet and bless you, welcoming those who are new to this particular group and greeting old friends as well. It is a great privilege for us to be called to speak to you and we are extremely appreciative of your allowing us to share our humble thoughts with you that we may attempt to be of service.

Picture with me if you will the Earth upon which you now are situated rolling and spinning in the darkness. It is the night side of Earth upon which you look and there seems to be darkness within darkness as the eye seeks to fathom the dark sphere in the midst of the dark sky. Such, my friends, is the nature of your Earth sphere, not in the physical sense, as you would call it, but in those portions of your density which may be called spiritual or metaphysical.

Suddenly one small flare of light is seen. You know what that is, my friends. That is one entity whose will has been turned to offering the one love and the one light inherent in the one original Thought of our infinite Creator. What a glorious light in such a darkness may we see when one entity alone orients itself to the One.

When groups of entities meet together, the light blazes far, far brighter than by merely addition, for each gives each strength, clarity and purity of being, each giving unto each the gift of light. That is why your so-called light groups are crucial, always have been, and always shall be. They are centers, if you will, of focus for that which is lightest in all men to have a safe place to be vulnerable and to shine forth in the darkness.

We who have served with the Confederation of Planets in the Service of the Infinite Creator within your sphere of influence for some time as you call it have seen more and more and more lights glowing in the darkness. Their radiance is growing brighter and there are beginning to be networks formed, networks of light, traceries like lace encircling the darkened spiritual metaphysical planes of your Earth world. However, we do not want to emphasize overly much the function of the group, for each entity goes forth from the group and yet is still an entity holding as in the holograph all of the light of consciousness, all of the fresh and living radiance of the one original Thought.

We ask each of you to value yourselves, not because of anything you have done or will do, any grand thought that you have thought or will think, but because of your innate and inherent nature. It is your birthright to be the Creator, and it is your challenge to find that same Creator in all that you meet, whatever the outward circumstances, whatever the challenges of personality. It is a fine thing to sit in meditation and glow with the inner and living light of the one Creator. And yet we say to you, my friends, it is incumbent upon you insofar as you are able to turn from daily meditation outwards into your planetary sphere, wandering wherever you go, trailing the pristine and untouched light that you have received during meditation. Then you shall truly be radiant and those about you shall be blessed. It does not take a group in order to do this, although, as we said, when more than one person gathers in meditation, the strength of the meditation is increased far more than by simple addition.

We ask for your patience as we work with this instrument. We are giving word by word communication and therefore this instrument must wait at the most unlikely places. As far as we can tell this instrument's thoughts, this instrument is impatient and wants to know the story. Yet this instrument is the story and so are each of you.

Pretend for a moment that you are a small child. You walk along the path kicking pebbles and gazing at the leaves on the trees, catching acorns in your hand and feeding them to the squirrels. The sun of childhood's fall is warm and golden. The path grows circuitous as one gains in incarnational experience. It winds and turns and the golden sun of childhood seems to become sickly and wan under the bruising influence of experience. And yet this is in no way necessary. One may retain that golden childhood, one merely needs to surrender the bruises, the anger, the hurt and pain which have grown up around various circumstances and experiences which seemed quite negative. These experiences are a great deal like old and heavy clothing. They have become tattered; they have done their service and it is time to shed these garments and put on fresh linen and go forth into that golden sunlight once again.

We ask you to remember the lesson of the pearl. The oyster does not turn its back upon the gritty sand of experience; when sand irritates the inside of the shell a pearl begins to be formed. The irritation may continue, but the pearl grows more and more beautiful, more and more lustrous and full of light. Look ye therefore also to the gritty sand of your experiences, whatever they may be, for within that experience is love. And the fruit of that experience is crystallization and radiance if you but choose it.

We ask that you seek to know the truth, and if anything that we say to you rings false upon your ears, we ask that you forget it immediately and move on, for we are very fallible entities and would never ask you to believe that things that we say are implicitly true, for still we learn also, still we are corrected by experience, still we are refined by the refining fire of catalyst. Oh, radiant voyagers, shine for yourselves and for each other so that those about you may wonder at the love within the group and within each individual. I am known to you as Hatonn. I leave you glorying in the love and in the light of our infinite Creator. Adonai, my friends. Adonai vasu.

(Jim channeling)

I am Latwii, and we are also grateful to be asked to join your group, and greet each of you in the love and in the light of our infinite Creator. It is once again our privilege to attempt to respond to those queries which those present may offer in the service of all. May we then begin with the first query?

N: Yes. I was wondering, is there any way the vehicle of the mind/body/spirit complexes of the star seeds, light workers, and so forth in California, since there is supposed to be a catastrophe in the next two or three years—is there any way to channel their energies and themselves out of that area prior to this occurrence or will they have to go ahead with the harvest?

I am Latwii, and am aware of your query, my brother. You must look upon the occurrences of the daily round of activities, be they traumatic or trivial, as that which has been chosen by each for lessons and services that such occurrences offer. As each entity moves through the incarnational pattern there will be various events that will mark the entity's progress and offer opportunity that no other events could offer. Many of your people are concerned that various geophysical events shall end this or that incarnation prematurely and shall do so on a grand scale as has been spoken of in many teachings. This causes in many a fearful response and a desire to avoid one or another event. Yet we say to you, my brother, that for as long as an entity's lessons and services remain there is no power upon your planet that can remove this entity. And when an entity has completed those lessons and services chosen by that entity there is no power that can keep this entity. For the progression of evolution is that stream of beingness that moves ever onward and the ending of one pattern is the beginning of another.

May we answer further, my brother?

N: Well, I understood that particular point, and I wasn't referring to any specific or particular entity. It was just that I was thinking that there are so many extremely advanced light workers in California, and that the fact that during the decade they would be needed in other areas of the United States so significantly that it would be nice to have their expertise to help with the next decade, and as I said, I was not referring to any specific entity but I'm sure that they could be of help in other areas to those of us, many of us, who are not so far advanced to help with the harvest and enlightenment.

I am Latwii, and from your comments, my brother, we draw the heart of what we hope is your query. Please requestion if we have mistaken the query. There is the need upon the part of each seeker of truth to develop the concept that you may call faith, the faith that indeed those truths which bind us all as one indeed exist. And there is the need to develop the will to power the faith and to seek continually, and to know at the heart of one's being that all needs shall be met. Where there is the call for light, light shall respond in one form or another. If lights are removed in one location, they shall spring again in another.

May we answer further, my brother?

N: Thank you very much. I believe that *(inaudible)* channels master Kuthumi, and he mentions a term, "tensor" organization or "tensor" enlightenment. I wonder if you would elaborate on that particular terminology? Tensor orientation, I believe it is, t-e-n-s-o-r.

I am Latwii, and we must confess our own fallibility and ignorance, my brother. We have no knowledge of this concept. May we be of service in any other way?

N: Well, I have one other item. That is in reference to the Reiki healing. Reiki healing enumerates seven keys, and of course this is supposed to be a healing method that is approximately ten thousand or more years old and is a vibratory science. I wonder if you would elaborate on the seven keys of the Reiki healing?

I am Latwii, and though we have a basic grasp of your query and shall attempt response according to that grasp, we do not hope to cover this topic fully, for as with many forms of healing, there is much of the philosophy, shall we say, that accompanies the teachings. We shall attempt our understanding, small though it is.

With each of those centers of energy which have long been called chakras by those metaphysical students upon your sphere, there is a nature or essence or tone, if you will, which allows the entity so possessing these energy centers to utilize the love and light of the one Creator in increasingly intensified fashions. This love/light of the one Creator then enters the energy center system of an entity and allows this entity to pursue its preincarnatively chosen series of lessons and services in such and such a fashion according to the choices freely made. Within each energy center then there will be the distortion or bias or tendency to utilize this love/light in one fashion or another corresponding to the chosen lesson or service. Thus the white light of the Creator becomes reflected in various colors and biases that may be also seen by those attempting to serve as healers as a blockage of energy, for as the white light is reflected and diffracted it is in some degree blocked in order that a pattern of experience may develop.

If these blockages or biases go, shall we say, unnoticed and unworked upon for a prolonged portion of your time, there may develop within the entity that situation called disease. Thus there are within each entity the potentials for various lessons and services which can provide the opportunity to find balance and wholeness when attention is focused upon the bias or blockage. Without the proper attention and work in a conscious fashion upon these blockages, then the disease may call for the healer.

Those of the philosophy of which you describe seek in a certain fashion to discover the tone of each energy center as it would be heard and felt if the center were freed of all blockages. The tone of one in a diseased, as you would call it, configuration is then matched to that which may be seen as the ideal, the differences noted and various efforts are then made to bring the two into harmony, or more correctly stated, to remove the difference between the diseased tone and the ideal tone.

May we answer further, my brother?

N: Yes, thank you. I'm sure others have questions—that I don't tie up the floor, so to speak, and I do appreciate the answers—but it seems that an individual who is presented as a healer does so by just merely initiation, and this healing can be transferred to the patient irrespective of the healer or the "healee"? And it just seemed to be, I just wondered, they talk about seven keys of which are sort of mystical and I don't really understand it. I thought perhaps you could elucidate on the seven keys or the way to increase the speed of healing and so forth that we who are trained as the healers can accentuate the treatment of the "healees" or the patient?

I am Latwii, and am aware of your query, my brother. To begin, may we suggest that the healer, the one who has healed itself by the inner work that each seeker attempts, has no will in relation to one seeking the healing, for the healer is one who offers itself as a vessel or a channel through which the healing power of the one Creator may move. The healer then surrenders its will and stands aside. This type of healing requires upon the part of the one to be healed a desire to be healed and upon some level of its being an understanding of those lessons symbolized by that condition called disease. It is, however, possible for some who serve as healers and who yet retain a will that they may serve efficiently to achieve a temporary state of healing within the one to be healed. However, if the one to be healed has not requested the healing and has not upon some level of its being understood the lesson, the healing shall not long last for it does not have the foundation built for it.

May we answer further, my brother?

N: Well, thank you. That's the way I had always understood it. But they explain that the "healee" doesn't have to request it; it can be sent to other areas, and of course more advanced training will allow us to send it in increased speed, something like fourfold, and I thought perhaps you might elucidate on that particular method of increasing the rapidity of healing for those of us that have been so initiated along with the understanding that it is a down-spiraling as contrasted with Kundalini which is an up-spiraling of energy?

I am Latwii, and in our humble opinion, those seeking healing and its increased or speeded up effects may achieve such by increasing the meditative attention upon those areas needing the healing, and upon unraveling the riddle posed by the disease. The process of evolution for each portion of the one Creator is a function of the efficient application of free will and the choice to seek and to learn. There may be many techniques that one may perform that will serve as models in this process, be it healing or simply seeking the meaning to each portion of one's life, and such models may indeed be helpful. But that which powers the progress is the will and the faith of each seeker of truth.

May we answer further, my brother?

N: Thank you very much. I would like to relinquish the floor at this time. They explain that by further training you can accentuate the initiation that you already have of fourfold and that the healer does this, not the patient. If you have anything to add I'd appreciate it, but otherwise, thank you very much.

I am Latwii, and we appreciate also your comments, my brother, and feel that we have spoken as well as our small understanding will allow.

May we attempt another query at this time?

Questioner: Latwii, it has been said that the ascended masters and other light entities will converge or convene in Peru in January at Machu Picchu. Are you aware of such a meeting of light energies there at that time, and if so, can you speak if it would be beneficial to try to be there?

I am Latwii, and am aware of your query, my brother. We are aware that from time to time, as you call it, there is the convergence of those servants of the One upon certain levels of your experience within this planetary sphere. This convergence is not necessarily that which finds a place upon which to converge but is more usually a convergence which finds a vibratory frequency upon which to send those answers of love and light that respond to the calls and questions posed by the various portions of your peoples' population, be they conscious or unconscious calls for aid.

Thus, as the mass mind, as you may call it, of this planet's population turns its attention to one area or another within the great evolutionary journey, there is the need to provide …

(Side one of tape ends.)

(Jim channeling)

I am Latwii, and am once again with this instrument. To continue. There is then periodically the need to provide a sustenance or nourishment that is in response to the call of the peoples of your planet. This response then becomes available to all who seek and to each so seeking there is the unique opportunity presented that will allow the seeker to utilize this nourishment. The vibrational frequency of the seeking will determine that which is received. It is not, in our knowledge, usually necessary for those unseen servants of the One to meet at a place and to focus from that place the service that is called for. We, however, are not aware of all that occurs upon your planetary entity. We in our humble way seek to serve in a relatively small fashion and our point of viewing therefore is not one which seeks in the large scope of things to fathom each and every movement of light upon and within this planet's influence.

May we answer further, my brother?

Questioner: No, thank you.

I am Latwii, and we thank you, my brother. Is there another query at this time?

Carla: I have one just out of curiosity following up the Machu Picchu question. It isn't just there but in other places on the planetary surface that ley lines of energy and cosmic force converge. And I wondered if the ley lines are as they are because pyramids or other buildings have been built at those places or if the reason that those buildings were built was because of the high energy that could be felt in those places. Which came first?

I am Latwii, and am aware of your query, my sister. The ley lines, as they have been called, or grid lines of energy are set for the planet much as one's aura surrounds and informs one's physical vehicle. Thus, many from days of old have constructed various structures in concordance with these lines of energy in order that they might take advantage of the increased influx of the love/light of the one Creator at these points. It is at such points that the nourishment of which we spoke previously may enter into this planetary influence and then move whence called and find the mark of the seeker.

May we answer further, my sister?

Carla: No, that's very clear. Thank you.

I am Latwii, and we thank you, my sister. Is there another query?

N: May I ask about … there's a house that was built outside of Kenosha, Wisconsin in the shape of a pyramid. Is there any harmful effects to the individuals within this house, then, having the down-streamings of energy occurring even though this house may not be on a ley line, or what does occur?

I am Latwii, and am aware of your query, my brother. Within the structure known as the pyramid, that [is] a pyramid of the 76 degree apex angle, may be found a position known to your peoples as the King's chamber position. This is the position which from days of old has been utilized for healing. However, those who were responsible for the giving of this form to this planetary influence were of a naive enough nature to be unable to see the danger of this position within this structure to those who entered into this position seeking not healing and the desire to serve others as a result, but who entered this position desiring power, as you may call it, over others, and seeking to coerce others to serve the self. Thus, the danger to any entity residing within this King's chamber position is that the more disharmonious elements within one's being may become intensified and the entity may leave such a structure more rather than less distorted.

May we answer further, my brother?

N: Yes, thank you. The healing chamber which was then transformed into the King's chamber was about 33 to 40 percent elevated above the base of the pyramid. What about those, say, that were down close to the ground level, would it injure them? Would that energy be in focus? And I thought it was around a 51 degree angle rather than a 76.

I am Latwii, and am aware of your query, my brother. The angle of the apex of the so-called great pyramid at Giza is of the 76 degree measurement, and is the angle that creates the King's chamber position which can be deleterious to those residing therein. The location of an entity at any point other than the King's chamber position is not deleterious in this fashion.

May we answer further, my brother?

N: Thank you very much. Did the old pyramids, the great pyramid at Giza, didn't they enter that primarily from an underground … I know they have above-ground entrances, but didn't they enter it primarily from an underground tunnel?

I am Latwii, and this is correct, my brother. May we answer further?

N: Well, there are no external entrances I assume, on the pyramid itself. There are some pyramids in—some Mayan pyramids like Chitzenitza or Tatoum down south of Cancun, and they say that these are over a thousand years old. Would it be erroneous to suspect that they were in the vicinity of four to six thousand years of the great pyramid or are they truly much newer?

I am Latwii, and am aware of your query, my brother. The actual dating of a great number of these pyramid structures is much younger, shall we say, than those found within the land known as Egypt. However, the structures within the south and central American locations are the offspring, shall we say, of older structures found in the more remote locations of your South American continent, and these structures, then, are of roughly the same time origin.

May we answer further, my brother?

N: Do the pyramids such as Chitzenitza or Tatoum have healing chambers in them, and are they sealed to outside entrance except through an underground entrance, and do they have the same 76 degree lead in to the healing chamber?

I am Latwii. We find that there were various construction methods and various purposes utilized in the structures of which you speak, therefore some are of the 76 degree apex angle and others are not. Some were utilized for healing and initiation and others were utilized for what might be called the balancing of the energy grid system of this planetary sphere.

May we answer further, my brother?

N: No, thank you very much. I appreciate.

Questioner: I'd like to ask something. Am I to understand from what you said about the older pyramids in the Americas, in South and Central America, that there are older pyramids that are still yet—older and larger pyramids that haven't been found yet that are covered by the jungles? Is that correct?

I am Latwii, and am aware of your query, my brother. This is basically correct, for there have been civilizations within this portion of your planetary sphere for a great portion of what you call time. There were some of these civilizations which achieved the necessary harmony in the seeking as a civilization to be aided in that seeking by those from elsewhere, shall we say, who had the privilege of serving and answering the call, and did so in part by giving information as was given in the land known as Egypt, this information having to do with the time/space ratio complexes known to you as pyramids.

May we answer further, my brother?

Questioner: No, that satisfies that question. I want to ask, it has been imparted to me at some point that the mammals that we know as whales, that they think spherically, and that are able to transcend into the various densities through this spherical type of thought, and I'm wondering if their collective consciousness of the whale species now is trying to impart a message to us, and if the whale that has been named Humphrey outside of San Francisco, it is hoping to act as a catalyst for this message?

I am Latwii, and am aware of many portions of your query, my brother, and shall attempt in our poor fashion to respond. We are aware that there are species of beings upon your sphere other than the human that have achieved a state of consciousness which is somewhat more unified, shall we say, than is that state exhibited by the great majority of the human population. Some of these entities are known to your peoples as the whale and the porpoise. These creatures have proceeded upon their own path of evolution, and have achieved certain awareness of the unity of all things and have sought to demonstrate to those with the opened ear and eye the greater truths that are sought by all.

May we answer further, my brother?

Questioner: I guess my query is, by this display of unified conscious thought are they, by the whale known as Humphrey in California, is this mammal trying to open up more receptive humans towards this unity of consciousness?

I am Latwii, and am aware of your query, my brother. As the mystery is presented, it is hoped that the seeking will be intensified, thus within the bounds of mystery the lessons of love are eventually found.

We at this time note that this instrument begins to grow fatigued, and would suggest that one or two more queries find the end then to this session. May we ask for such a query?

Questioner: Yes. I'd like to ask you a question about as we're going through our lives and our interactions with people on the planet, how might we ourselves make ourselves more clear and able to be perceptive of the needs of those around us as we're living and seeing and being with each other?

I am Latwii, and am aware of your query, my sister. May we suggest that when one looks upon the daily round of activities, what immediately presents itself to the eye is not what remains to be found. The seeming disharmonies and distresses that one may find within one's experience are but the shadow of that which awaits. Then it becomes necessary, for one who seeks to be of service by sharing the love of the One with all about one, for such a seeker to penetrate the surface, the illusion, the outer shell of appearance. For within all experience, be it the most difficult or the most confusing or complex, there exists the love of the one Creator, whole, perfect and balanced. The more difficult it is to see such love, the greater the opportunity for growth.

Be then not so concerned with appearance and the first effects and impressions of interactions with those about you, but in your meditation look to the heart of the interaction. Find where love lives. Find then where love has sought to be known, and has perhaps for the moment gone unrecognized. Look to the heart of those who share with you in any degree a portion of their lives, for that which they share is love seen in many disguises. Do not let disguise fool you. It is there to teach and there is one lesson. That is love.

May we answer further, my sister?

Questioner: Yes. I'd like to know when we are in our lives amid some other brother who was doing rebirthing, and thus cleansing the nervous systems of the body/mind/spirit complex, and I wonder how we might maintain or through our thought further cleanse our nervous system, and thereby cleanse our being in the world?

I am Latwii, and am aware of your query, my sister. We shall speak to this query as our final response.

The entity that each is has encoded within not only the nervous system but within the entire system of energy centers those preincarnatively chosen lessons and services. When one discovers a certain distortion or imbalance within one's thinking and behavior, one may take this discovery into meditation and observe it carefully. The distortion may be allowed in the meditative state to expand and increase in intensity until it is beyond all reasonable proportions. Thus it finds its full sway within one's being, and all potentials to gather experience thereby are observed. One then may see the polar opposite quality planted as a seed within the being also within this meditative state. This opposite quality then may also be allowed to intensify beyond all reasonable proportions. The entity thus meditating may see then both qualities contained within its being, and may see these qualities as means by which the one Creator may know Itself through this entity's experience.

This entity may also see these qualities as means by which it may know the one Creator through its experiences. Without any quality of judgment then, the entity observes the wholeness of its being and fully accepts the self for containing these qualities. Thus, as acceptance within the being is increased, the ability of this being to learn the lessons associated with these qualities is enhanced. As the lessons become learned, the qualities are smoothed, shall we say, in such a fashion that the white light of the one Creator no longer needs be diffracted, and may in this regard at least remain until diffracted by another pattern of distortion which symbolizes lessons and services to be learned and offered. Thus is the life pattern pursued and the preincarnative choices completed.

We at this time find that we have approached the limit of this instrument's ability to continue to serve as an instrument in a relatively clear fashion. Therefore we must take our leave at this time of this instrument and we thank each present for allowing our presence and for requesting our humble service. We remind each that we are also quite humble and fallible seekers of truth. We do not claim any infallibility whatsoever. Take that which we have given and use it as you will; leave that which has no value. We leave this group at this time rejoicing also in the love and in the light of the one infinite Creator which resides in all. Adonai, my friends, we are Latwii. Adonai vasu. ☥

Sunday Meditation
November 10, 1985

(Carla had surgery on her wrist and hand this week.)

(Jim channeling)

I am Hatonn, and we greet you, my friends, in the love and in the light of our infinite Creator. Again it is with joy that we greet each of you and join your circle of seeking this evening. We shall attempt to work with this instrument in a manner which is novel for this instrument. We hope to be able to transmit our thoughts on more of a word by word basis, perhaps relying from time to time upon the phrase in order to aid this instrument in his development as an instrument. Therefore, we apologize in advance for any delays in the transmission.

This evening we should attempt to speak to a concern which each seeker of truth may discover upon the path of seeking. It is often a concern to such a seeker that there is no clearly discernible pattern of thought or constructed philosophy which serves all needs of any seeker. Each seeker wishes to proceed upon the evolutionary path as efficiently as possible, and as this journey is undertaken, there is the discovery that many philosophies exist concerning how best to travel. No matter how many sources the seeker may consult, there continue to be more and more aspects of this seeking and even divergent philosophies as to how best to proceed.

The concern, then, of many who consciously pursue their own evolution is, "What is truly of value at this moment in this process?" Adding to the concerns of such a seeker is the observable fact that for any such seeker there is the ever-changing experience and pattern of thinking that develops within the seeker over a period of time. Thus, at one point within the seeker's experience, the mind may be configured at quite a different fashion than it may later be found to be configured. Thus, there is placed before the seeker's attention the ever-changing nature of the resources which may inform the choices that a seeker makes. Yet within each is the nebulous though persistent feeling that there is an absolute essence, shall we say, which is at the heart of all philosophies. And it is quite often the heart's desire of the seeker to know this ultimate, shall we say, truth. Thusly desirous and propelled upon the journey, a seeker will find a multitude of reflections of that one image which as the holy grail, as it has been called, leads on and draws unto each seeker.

As you move within your own individual illusion, you are aware that there are patterns within your seeking. There are methods which seem to be more related, shall we say, or of a kin to you than any others. When you discover this feeling you may determine then that there has been a recognition upon some level of your own being for that which you seek in that which has come before your attention. This harmonious feeling or intuitive inspiration then becomes the great ally of the seeker of truth, for the mind of man can construct many magnificent structures of thought and philosophical expertise, shall we say, and if a seeker is left only with its intellectual evaluation of potential aids in its journey, then it is quite easy for a seeker thus limited to become confused when one philosophy sounds as good as another.

And, indeed, my friends, this may well be true, for each philosophy is a construction of a portion of the one Creator and thusly offers the essence in some degree of the one Creator to any who hold this philosophy. Yet, to be able to discern not with the intellect but with that feeling from within which wells up in spontaneous recognition of that which is most helpful at the present moment for the seeker is to rely upon a more trustworthy friend, shall we say, for these intuitive inspirations which well up from the deeper portions of one's being are in some fashion that which is sought or point the direction towards that which is sought. For at its heart, my friends, the process of seeking the truth is a process whereby one calls for a greater portion of the self and calls for this portion from the self.

It is the nature of a single creation that each portion or facet of the creation is contained within each individualized expression of that creation. You as such an individualized expression, then, when you seek, seek more of that which you are from your own self. Therefore, it is most helpful not only to analyze with the conscious mind that which is placed before one's conscious attention but then to also give over that thinking and analyzing at some point in order that the greater portion of one's own being may be allowed to move through the channel which you have created with your desire and make itself known in whatever fashion is recognizable and discernible to your conscious mind which propels your seeking.

Our message this evening is of necessity somewhat briefer than most, for the collective energies of this group this evening are somewhat lessened, and it is our discernment that it would be best that the briefer message be delivered. We shall therefore at this time take our leave of this group, thanking each wholeheartedly for inviting our presence, and we would ask that the proper discernment be applied by each to those words which we have given that you may further exercise that intuitive knowing which allows you to weave your way through the illusion which you inhabit on your journey of seeking. We are grateful to have been able to speak this evening. We are known to you as Hatonn, and we leave you in the love and in the light of the one infinite Creator. Adonai, my friends.

(Jim channeling)

I am Latwii, and we too greet each of you in the love and light of our infinite Creator. We too are aware that the energies of this group are somewhat diminished. We shall therefore spare this instrument of the necessity for the word by word communication, hoping that we might be able to spend more, shall we say, information with you as the time might be shortened. May we attempt our usual service of attempting those queries which those present may have use in the requesting? May we begin with a query?

L: I'd like to ask a question or perhaps ask for whatever you would care to offer to help me understand a facet of my life which seems that there are people who go away and then return, people whose influence seems to be potentially beneficial in some aspects, other people whose potential influence seems destructive. And it's almost as if each one is acting as a comet in its trajectory, and they disappear and they're out of my life and then come winging back in again and then they're gone again and then they come back again. What could you be able to offer to assist me in understanding this?

I am Latwii, and am aware of your query, my brother. We ask that you picture a tapestry which has many colors and is designed in such a fashion that the colors move in and out, each with the other, in somewhat of a rhythmic and yet somewhat of an irregular pattern. If one looks at any one point within the tapestry, one will note that there is a, shall we say, given set of colors, each in a certain relation with the others. If one follows two or more of these colors as they thread their way through the tapestry, one will note that there is a mingling from time to time and a departure of colors again from time to time.

So it is in the life of any seeker, for each of you, my friends, before the incarnation made general and specific agreements with many other seekers of truth. During the incarnational pattern, then, there will be the attempt to fulfill those agreements, to provide those lessons and services that were deemed a necessary part of the incarnation prior to its beginning. It may be that for a certain portion of what you call time there will unfold a relationship in some way or another with a variety of entities. Thus will your incarnational pattern unfold as the interaction between this grouping of entities creates the catalyst that offers the opportunity for the learning of certain lessons and the providing of certain services as a balancing function to the learning of lessons.

Thus does the pattern of one's life find a movement in and out of other selves who join in the rhythm of the learning and the serving. The specific nature of any one entity's relationship in your own pattern is of an unknown nature to any within the illusion. Thus, as one sees the appearance and disappearance of any entity or group of entities, one may assume in the general nature that there are those lessons and services which yet remain, for though there has been time and distance which has come between shared experience, yet there remains a certain affinity between these seekers of truth who have before the incarnation agreed to travel this incarnation in such and such a fashion.

As a small addendum to this response that we fear may have grown somewhat lengthy, we would also remind each seeker that what appears to the naked eye, shall we say, may not be in its essence in agreement with the appearance. Which is to say, it is difficult to discern the nature of any experience completely within your illusion, for what seems most helpful, happy and harmonious in one instance may not in truth yield the harvest of lessons that another situation which seems most traumatic, disharmonious and frustrating might yield, for it is within the bounds, shall we say, of the difficulty that the spiritual strength is put to the test.

This is a general description, but we hope can provide somewhat of an insight into the illusion which you inhabit, for truly it is an illusion, that which is not at its heart what it appears upon the surface to be.

May we answer you further, my brother?

L: No, that's given me quite a bit for thought. I appreciate it. Thank you.

I am Latwii, and we thank you, my brother. Is there another query?

N: Last week you said that the angle of a pyramid was 76 degrees for the healing chamber. But is the angle—I checked it, or at least the great pyramidal Giza, Cheops, was 51 degrees, 51 minutes and 14.3 seconds. How do you measure this 76 degrees for the healing chamber?

I am Latwii, and am aware of your query, my brother. The angle of 76 degrees and 18 minutes, approximately, is the angle of the apex of the so-called great pyramid at Giza, and is the angle which allows the formation of the King's Chamber, as it has been called by your peoples, and this location was the location used in days of old for the healing. Yet it is the position which has been suggested to be of a potentially dangerous nature for those entering it who are in any degree distorted towards the distortion of power of others, shall we say. The lack of purity in the desire to utilize this position can be further distorted by the apex angle that is greater than 76 degrees.

May we answer further, my brother?

N: There was an approximate thirty feet of top cap for the great pyramid. Was it ever put on? And if it was, what happened to it?

I am Latwii, and am aware of your query, my brother. This capstone, as it has usually been called among your peoples, was in place at the initial period of construction of this structure and was at a later time replaced with a capstone made of your granite material. This was itself removed at yet a later date by those many entities who sought to remove the outer portions of this structure for the purpose of constructing yet another structure.

May we answer further, my brother?

N: Well, thank you very much. Carla and I were talking about the Christ-like consciousness, that there was a book written that shows that there were fifteen or sixteen over the eons. Have there been that many? Or more? And was Jesus Christ the man reincarnated from other Earth entities previously, and if so which ones?

I am Latwii, and shall attempt response to this query by suggesting that there have been a larger number of entities upon your planet in its past who have achieved that state of awareness which has come to be called the Christ consciousness. The number of entities described in the book of which you speak is a number which has been given to a specific portion of your planetary surface, most notably that area of the desert known [as] Sinai. There has been, however, throughout other portions of your planetary surface, the gaining of the perspective, shall we say, which is known as the Christ consciousness. Various traditions, cultures and practices have been utilized over a great portion of your planet's third-density experience by various individuals who have sought the heart of the lessons of this illusion and have found in great part that heart of love within their own experience.

The entity known to your peoples as Jesus of Nazareth was an entity of this nature who had in previous incarnations achieved various levels of consciousness as a portion of its mission as what you would call a wanderer, and in this progression of incarnations sought to be of service in a manner which then was culminated in the incarnation of which you are aware. We are not able to utilize this instrument in giving names of the entity known as Jesus of Nazareth in its previous incarnations for there is a good deal of energy required to focus upon names not familiar to this instrument, and it is within the levels of what you would call trance that such energy is available for the retrieval of these names.

May we answer further, my brother?

N: No. Thank you very much.

I am Latwii, and we thank you, my brother. Is there another query?

(Pause)

I am Latwii. We are aware that we have been somewhat brief in our stay with this group this evening, but are most appreciative for each moment that we have been allowed to share. We thank each for allowing our presence and our words. We also remind each that our words are but our fallible attempts to be of service. Take those which have meaning. Leave those which have none. We shall leave you at this time rejoicing in that love and light which propels and guides us all in our seeking of the one infinite Creator. Adonai, my friends. We are those of Latwii. ☥

Sunday Meditation
November 17, 1985

Group question: What about guilt?

(Carla channeling)

I am L/Leema, and I greet you, my friends, in the love and in the light of the infinite Creator Whom we all serve in joy. And indeed it is a great joy to be here with you, to share these moments with you, to be in communion with that which makes each of you who you are, for that is the question that has come before us this evening.

There may seem to be many, many forces which operate upon the personality from without, those things the society would wish you to do, those things those about you would wish you to do. And yet when one asks for comment upon this subject, the comment must turn upon the subject of identity, for whom you listen to and what stress you feel is in the end a function of who you are, not what you mean to yourself.

Each of us is unique. This is not a uniqueness that is attempted, that is worked at, or that is in any way manipulative. Nor is it anything that can be manipulated, for your identity is one harmonious chord of being, unique in the whole creation, infinite in its beauty, and irreplaceable. And so you sit in circle within a dwelling place in meditation, each chord blending with each chord as the whole group becomes one identity, seeking the One which is not unique but which is limitless. That from which you are derived, shall we say, had no identity until It decided in the vastness of timelessness to experience Itself. And so you sit in meditation, far-flung bits of the Creator who have become unique. You experience each other—and the Creator experiences Itself.

We move now back into the area of illusion from which the question was asked concerning the pressures of "should" and "must" that are given one by those souls around one and by the society itself in its many forms. Perhaps it is easier now to see the illusion for what it is—many things impinging upon that which is unique. You who are unique cannot pluck this or that from you, for you have chosen the pressures, the musts, the shoulds, and all of the confusion that follows therefrom in order to further develop your uniqueness and thereby the infinite Creator's experience of Itself.

We realize that there is a need within the illusion to find a way of thinking about or dealing with these pressures. There are as many ways as there are individuals. One way which we might recommend to you is gentleness with yourself. If you can see yourself as that unique being that is not threatened by extinction by any force from without or from within, then perhaps you can see the possibility of offering to yourself the gift of gentleness, patience and kindness to the self by the self. Examine, if you wish, a pressure that is causing you anguish, pain and confusion. Turn it about in your mind, test it, allow the uniqueness that is you to impinge upon that illusion, and then with kindness and thanking the source of the pressure, the seeming pain, the seeming confusion, allow the self to sound its chord.

Perhaps it has been a difficult thing to hear your own beingness. This is understandable, my friends, for you do dwell within a heavy illusion. The heaviness of the illusion is not an error. There is a design which involves your becoming fuller, developing your uniqueness, accentuating certain qualities of being upon which you may have worked for many, many lifetimes. How could you develop without stimulus, even if that stimulus is painful? Look at the world with a kind eye, a gentle eye, a forgiving eye.

The world does not mean to hurt. The illusion is doing what it was intended to do, and you may move very quickly and confusedly so that you muddy that beautiful chord which is yourself, or you may stop and become gentled and thank the illusion for its pressures and its anguish and its pain. You shall not be victorious over it; you shall learn from it, and it shall learn from you. It is well to remember that the undifferentiated terms such as "society" and "family" and "church" are in fact parts of yourself which you have called to yourself in order that you may polish up that beautiful, harmonious, infinitely lovely identity, that you may develop and thrive without regard for life or death as you know it.

We know that this may be somewhat difficult to assimilate, for you are entities who dwell within bodies and who are impinged upon by what seem to be marvelously strong outer forces. Know, my friends, that all of those outer forces are portions of the creation which you have called to yourself for purposes of development. Know that you do not have to work at this development, you do not have to be a student of development. Indeed, the more active you are, the slower will be your going. Gentleness, patience and quiet are the balms of the identity as it waits and watches and loves and chooses.

Whenever the tangle of experience becomes heavy, take your fingers from the knot and rest. Rest within the infinite invisible world which is the creation. Rest, knowing that you do not have to be you by expressing or changing or doing anything. In meditation seek quiet, seek silence, seek that which is yourself—the one infinite Creator. And that which is you shall then have time to interact fully with the experiences you have had. You cannot be puzzled and be active and find change to be helpful. You can be puzzled and be silent and find that change, development and love bubble forth in good time and with messages for you that you would never have developed without the seeming pressures that are seeming to be so difficult.

We ask you to consider that you live within a house, a spiritual house, which has been constructed of illusion within illusion within illusion. There are many intellectual paths one may take at any time. There are many emotional paths one may take at the same time. There is one silence. There is one decision—to turn to meditation in patience, in kindness, and in gentleness and with no stress, for you have nothing to prove, you have nothing to gain or lose. You are as you are. And you will be as you will be because of your patience within the silence as you digest those things which you may have experienced. Never fear that you are cut off from yourself. It is in no way necessary that you fear this, for the louder the pressures from without may cry, the quieter you may get—and within silence all becomes love. And that which your higher self has planned for you to experience is experienced in love and without confusion. Can you do this of your own self within the illusion? The answer is no. If you need a quick answer, you may have to deal with the illusion. If you can find the infinite moment of silence, the work will be done infinitely better.

We celebrate you, my friends, each perfection, and the perfection of the group. And we thank you for requesting our presence, and for allowing us to be a part of those things which you may take into your silence, which you may patiently, gently and lovingly turn over and gaze at, and find further perfection in the gazing. May each of you have a grand adventure within yourself as you meet the illusion moment by moment.

We are known to you as those of L/Leema and we leave you now, resting, lingering within the beauty of each of you. We leave you in the love and in the light of the one infinite Creator. Adonai, my friends. Adonai. Adonai.

(Jim channeling)

I am Latwii, and we greet you in the love and light of our one Creator. We too are privileged to be asked to join your group this evening. We thank each of you for this honor. As always, we hope that we may be of some service by attempting to answer those queries which you present to us. Therefore, let us begin, if we may, with the first query.

J: Would you please speak about the idea of sacrifice?

I am Latwii, and we would ask if there might be a specific application of this concept that you would prefer us to focus upon, for it is a large concept?

J: Okay. It seems that the idea of sacrifice has been a response to the feeling or the experience of guilt in the way of expiation. It's just become pervasive in the human experience and in the individual, generally and specifically. So, just some thoughts about it.

I am Latwii, and we thank you for the further clarification. The concept of sacrifice as you have used it in its connection with the concept of guilt is as much of the illusion about you—that is, upon the outer appearance there are certain opportunities that present themselves in order that you might transform the outer into a much different concept or quality by your attention to it and your desire to learn from it.

When one feels the concepts of guilt and the concept of sacrifice that may be perceived as an effect, shall we say, or result of the guilt, [there] are the opportunities to transform the self, for when one has observed the situation within which guilt and sacrifice are felt and has penetrated more to the heart of the situation and has discovered that there is a purpose for these concepts within one's learning, one may then set about to discover that purpose.

As this process of discovery continues, and the layers of the illusion and the situation are peeled one after the other, one may discover that what seemed to be a sacrifice to another out of guilt may become a gift of love to a beloved portion of one's own being. This portion may have cried out in many ways that seemed harmful and hurtful to the self. Yet each cry was for love that would enable each to find that love not only within the illusion of the situation but within the heart of each entity's response to the other, for when there is a great seeming lack of love, there is being built a great potential for the fulfillment of love. The vacuum draws into it that which is sought.

May we answer further, my sister?

J: Thank you, no. Not right now.

I am Latwii, and we thank you, my sister. Is there another query?

Carla: I've been feeling lately as if I'm almost empty, kind of drifting. I imagine it's part of the experience I'm going through of not taking any medication for pain and so forth. What is the best thing for me to do in this situation? Continue with the affirmation that I went into the surgical experience with or attempt to think along certain inspiring thoughts or what would you suggest?

I am Latwii, and am aware of your query, my sister. We would not specifically guide you but would suggest that the words of those of L/Leema might be helpful in your situation. The gentleness with which one treats the self is a great aid in any situation in which one might find the self moving and experiencing. If the situation is difficult or mysterious and confusing, it is with the gentleness that one may view the self in refusing to demand that the self master the new situation quickly or at any set pace. If you give yourself the freedom to experience without expectations of structuring the experience so that a certain outcome results, then you provide yourself with the support that will allow you to move through a greater portion of your own being and it, in its own time, as you call for it, will reveal itself to you. All portions of one's experience teach and contain the treasures of the One. Confusion, mystery and even an emptiness call for certain fruits, and of these fruits you shall taste at the time that is appropriate.

May we answer further, my sister?

Carla: No, that was really helpful, thank you. I do have a question about sacrifice though, and this more following up on Judy's question. I've often thought of the concept of sacrifice as being a good thing, as being what we're learning in this illusion. In other words, we sacrifice every time we breathe; we sacrifice that part of our life. And whatever we do is a sacrifice of what effort it took to do it. And so when I think of sacrifice I think more in terms of Jesus' sacrifice of his entire being for the love of his fellow man. How can one free the concept of sacrifice from the concept of guilt?

I am Latwii, and am aware of your query, my sister. The concepts of which you speak are those which are well suited for the learning of love, which is the primary purpose for which you have gathered in this illusion. The guilt that one may feel is usually concerned with the concept of not having given enough of one thing or another to another being. Within your illusion, the things of the self, be they material or ideas of oneself, are carefully hoarded in order that one may have enough things and feelings of security. But when one …

(Side one of tape ends.)

(Jim channeling)

I am Latwii, and am once again with this instrument. His appreciation of the one known as Carla's predicament is heightened, for the left hand has learned a new lesson. To continue.

As one penetrates the outer shell of the illusion, one discovers that there is more than meets the eye, shall we say. The things are found to be of small value in the larger sense, for the seeker of truth discovers that all things change and move away, yet that which truly sustains the seeker and its journey is a force which is not captured but is freely given. That force is love and is available to all who call for it.

Thus, when one can give away all things, one then makes way for this force to move through the being, and it is then natural to give all one has at each moment to any who would call for the aid of one's being. Thus, the sacrifice becomes the honor, for there is no thing as important to one as loving another.

May we answer further, my sister?

Carla: No, thank you.

I am Latwii, and we thank you, my sister. Is there another query?

J: Would you please comment on the way I understood what you said about sacrifice? It seems to me that I heard you say that love and the willingness to give openly and freely in love then transforms sacrifice into just pure response, pure willingness to give, which is entirely different from the Old Testament attitude toward sacrifice, which was a sort of penalty that was required in order to pay a debt. Could you comment on that?

I am Latwii, and we shall do our best, my sister. The concepts of sacrifice and guilt with which we have been dealing this evening are primary concepts for any who seeks the nature of the process of evolution and how one may best move along this path. The finite nature of your illusion presents one with the situation which reproduces the illusion of limitation. Sacrifice is a limited concept, for one who feels that it is sacrificing moves within a limited perception of what is available to the self at all times.

The limitless love of the one Creator enables each entity at all times to experience and to be. By limiting one's awareness of this concept, many experiences become available that would not be available with the wider perspective. This is the nature of your illusion, and the reason that progress is possible in a rapid fashion within your illusion. For when one has worked long enough upon the concept of sacrifice and limitation and has through many, many experiences discovered that what is necessary is always provided, one discovers then that what was previously seen as sacrifice is a distorted perception which has allowed one to see the infinite nature of another, of a situation of the self.

This is not a quick process, my sister, yet it is one which teaches well, for that which is limited is seen to give way to that which is infinite, and that which is seen as the sacrifice gives way to that which is seen as another opportunity to give freely of the infinite love which is available to all at each moment.

May we answer further, my sister?

J: That was really helpful. Thank you. I have a question on another subject. When there is a person who is experiencing pain and fatigue and general depletion or really using up of vital energies, and others or another would like to somehow share strength and resource, is there any way that this can be done?

I am Latwii, and am aware of your query, my sister. We are somewhat unsure as how best to pursue the response, for there are many, many ways of transferring energy from one entity to another. The energy that enlivens each entity has been called the vital energy. This is a sum of the physical, mental and spiritual energy complexes of an entity. These complexes each then lend a portion of that energy which enables an entity to feel vital, alive and vibrant. The enhancing of the vital energies for one who is somewhat depleted may be approached from any of these three basic areas.

The spiritual energy system may be enhanced by any number of means which have as their common denominator, shall we say, the inspiration of the entity, as the narrower channel of influx is widened by song, reading, chanting, the visualizing of healing love being sent and surrounding the entity, and so forth.

The mental energy system may also benefit from the same procedures as well as the dialogue, shall we say, in which the one who has become depleted participates and exchanges the, shall we say, food for thought, and is nourished by those who provide the dialogue which also moves into the channel that feeds the vital energies.

The physical energy system is much aided by other techniques including the exercise, the nutrition, as of your foodstuffs, and the sexual energy transfers done with the intent of aiding the one depleted.

May we answer further, my sister?

J: No, thank you. That was very helpful.

I am Latwii, and thank you as well, my sister. Is there another query?

N: I have a sort of extension of the last question. There is a vibratory science of sound which was used in ancient China which has been rumored not only to heal but revitalize and reenergize individuals on not just the physical but the spiritual. The name of this ancient science is Shat Chai Mernis. Is there any way that you can channel information concerning Shat Chai Mernis or refer to material that can be read upon it or to an individual who may channel that information?

I am Latwii, and am aware of your query, my brother. We are somewhat limited in our ability to transmit specific information through this type of contact but can suggest that the use of sounds and colors is a specific means of utilizing the very, very general suggestions that we made concerning the revitalizing of the mind, body and spirit energy systems of one who has become depleted in the vital energies. The use of such sounds or tones is, in general, based upon the supposition that each energy system or center, when in a balanced or healthy, as you would call it, configuration vibrates at a certain frequency. The frequency then being reproduced in a somewhat artificial fashion is then used to aid the one depleted in a process of revitalization that first provides the model, shall we say, of the balanced center that the one depleted may then, shall we say, see the goal and be more able to harmonize one's own center with that goal.

The process is more complex in its application than this very simple description, for each seeker has a somewhat unique configuration associated with each energy center and therefore vary somewhat from the norm, shall we say, for each center.

May we answer you further, my brother?

N: Well, thank you. Does this in some way refer to Michael Helius' interpretation of an astrological variation for each entity as far as the sound vibration?

I believe that your statement is correct, my brother. For each branch of science, shall we say, that seeks to provide a means or blueprint by which the seeker may approach evolution there is the necessity for each branch or study to recognize the more subtle aspects of each entity that are not generally given in the more broad interpretations and applications of any philosophy or school of thought.

May we answer further, my brother?

N: I don't know about the sound vibrations but in Atlantis they did use the light vibration through various crystals to energize as well as to heal. Did they also use sound?

I am Latwii, and am aware of your query, my brother. We are aware of many uses of the sound vibrations by the entities who comprised the culture known to your peoples as Atlantis. This is correct, my brother.

May we answer further?

N: Is there anywhere that we can find a channel or seek a channel or an entity that might be able to enlighten us on the healing effects of sound vibration as well as the ability to energize the individual, through the mind, body and spirit complex—all three?

I am Latwii. We are unable to give the specific place or entity which might be so consulted, but we can assure you, my brother, that there are those within your culture who are quite adept at this practice. It is not that difficult to find such an entity if one perseveres.

May we answer further, my brother?

N: Thank you, no. I have looked, but I have not been able to find anyone who can enlighten me on Shat Chai Mernis. Thank you.

I am Latwii, and we thank you, my brother. We find that this instrument grows somewhat fatigued. We would therefore ask for another query or two, if they be somewhat short, as the final queries of the evening. May we attempt such a query at this time?

Carla: Well, I have a little one. I still feel L/Leema's presence, and that's the first time that L/Leema has lingered. I wondered if it was just her favorite group or if I wasn't complete in my channeling.

I am Latwii, and we find, my sister, that those of L/Leema have chosen to remain for a period of time in order that their vibrations might provide some aid to your own depleted energies which call for a certain nature or essence that is possessed by those of L/Leema.

May we answer further, my sister?

Carla: No, thank you.

I am Latwii, and we again thank you, my sister. Is there a final query for this evening?

A: I have an off-the-wall question. Please make your answer as short as you can. Out of curiosity, do entities mostly tend to reincarnate within their original racial complexes to work out karma, you know, racial karma, or are they free to hop in and out to whatever group would look like it would provide good balancing or good different experience?

I am Latwii, and am aware of your query, my sister. Though it is possible for any entity to incarnate within any group, be it race or sex or philosophical persuasion, it is most usually the case that each entity will gather about it those companions upon the journey. It is with these companions that one has traveled previously, shall we say, and has as a result been able to develop a certain ease or fluidity in the incarnational experiences that eases the evolutionary process, shall we say, once again. These groups also gather about them other groupings loosely held together, that serve the same function, yet upon the wider scale, therefore, the entities and groups find it helpful to continue as groupings throughout the incarnations that are found to be necessary in order that all might eventually learn the lessons set before each.

Thus, the groupings tend in the racial sense to remain as originally constructed. This, however, may result throughout the great span of time in one group inhabiting a certain racial configuration at one period of time and another racial configuration at another period of time. Thus, all avenues of learning become available to each seeker.

May we answer further, my sister?

A: No, thank you. That was very enlightening, and it's a pleasure to be with you all in person tonight.

I am Latwii, and we are also honored to be in your presence, my sister. We thank each for those queries offered, for by our humble attempts to respond, we learn more of the Creator in Its seeking and experiencing of Itself, and thus do we learn of ourselves. We thank each for inviting our presence and we shall leave this group at this time, rejoicing always in the peace and power and in the love and light of the one Creator. We are those of Latwii. Adonai, my friends. Adonai vasu borragus. ☥

L/L Research

L/L Research is a subsidiary of Rock Creek Research & Development Laboratories, Inc.

P.O. Box 5195
Louisville, KY 40255-0195

www.llresearch.org

Rock Creek is a non-profit corporation dedicated to discovering and sharing information which may aid in the spiritual evolution of humankind.

ABOUT THE CONTENTS OF THIS TRANSCRIPT: This telepathic channeling has been taken from transcriptions of the weekly study and meditation meetings of the Rock Creek Research & Development Laboratories and L/L Research. It is offered in the hope that it may be useful to you. As the Confederation entities always make a point of saying, please use your discrimination and judgment in assessing this material. If something rings true to you, fine. If something does not resonate, please leave it behind, for neither we nor those of the Confederation would wish to be a stumbling block for any.

CAVEAT: This transcript is being published by L/L Research in a not yet final form. It has, however, been edited and any obvious errors have been corrected. When it is in a final form, this caveat will be removed.

© 2009 L/L Research

Sunday Meditation
November 24, 1985

(Carla channeling)

I am Hatonn, and I greet you in the love and in the light of our infinite Creator. It is a great blessing to be with you this evening. We apologize for the delay but there were three entities all willing to speak to this group and beloved by this instrument, and the instrument had to wait while we elected whom was to speak. It was decided that I would have that honor and in all of our consciousness we thank you for requested information marginally better prepared by our social memory complex, as you would call it.

Before we speak upon the subject which hopefully would serve as some inspiration, we wish to answer an unasked question that is heavy on the minds of both who meditate this evening. We are aware that we have repeated many times that the group of three is the minimum group for a good contact. Were this an introductory meeting or at the other end of the scale, were this a contact which needed more protection than is consciously possible, the number two would not be satisfactory. Due to the introductory nature of the two who make up this contact and the considerable drive in both for purity in contact, the number two is satisfactory, although we encourage the continuing tuning throughout the meditation. For one times one is two—the multiplication of strength has begun but only begins to become noticeable with the third present. To substitute for the third presence, we suggest that you consider the words of the master who was known to your people as Jesus the Christ. He said that "Whenever two or three are gathered together in my name, I will grant what they request." Two such are gathered together in the name of the One, and we find the strength of the contact moderate but acceptable.

We would speak with you this evening about your portion as part of the one great original Thought. We would speak of the situation within the illusion and the situation when the illusion is dropped. In many of your people's equations, what is lost in the transition from the one original Thought to serving others within the illusion is the consciousness that all are one.

Where does it flee, this consciousness that we bring from sleep and manifest in our best moments? Where is it buried, this consciousness of the one original Thought, so that the lives are lived with the sensation of separateness and the lack of plenty? One great source of the entities of your planet's feeling apart from each other is the institution of trading various types of your money for those things which your body needs to survive.

There is that about money which is finite, in the heaviest illusory sense of that word. And indeed it does come through into the illusion as each entity pays its bills and ponders how to save, how to spend, and how to conduct one's business, that there is nothing left over, that the riches that one has coming to one are not aplenty but are a subsistence which one may work with with the budget and the planning. Indeed, this institution of the spending of money is one of very many ways that lead to separation.

And yet let us look at other ways as well. Yes, it is true that there are those within our city close to your dwelling place who are hungry this day, who do not have appropriate clothing for the chilliness of your present climate, who have found themselves unable to enter themselves into the society with enough success to produce money.

And, my friends, this is something that is likely to be somewhat of a growing experience as times become more confused and the society less stable. One does not have to look far to find ways to share one's money, for we shall tell you that there is a great liberation in the sharing of what in your illusion seems to be that which you need. It liberates an entity which is plunged into the illusion from the illusion, precisely insofar as the entity is giving great gifts with the desire to serve the one great Self that knows no separation. Yet there are many ways in which we plunge into the illusion, my friends, are there not? When is a smile stopped upon the face because an entity is plunged too far into an attitude of separation to be able to share joy with another? When is the young in experience shut off from the giver of that experience but when the giver of that experience is self-involved and feels that it would be too expensive to spend time in merely speaking?

You see in actuality, my friends, all those about you are cells of your body, living portions of your reality. To open one's heart, whatever the need, when done consciously, is a polarizing action, whether it is by the giving of money, the giving of time, the giving of attention or the giving of sympathy, you have much to share with those about you. You have many appropriate greetings for yourself. You have much room for love. And yet, can you do this for yourself? We assure you that unless the will is engaged, your experience of true sharing shall inevitably be blunted! For it is not something that is done mechanically, but from the heart.

Therefore, as always, we assure you that the process of service to others begins within as you groom and season your own personal reality with a thirst and a desire to serve. It helps within your illusion if some process of analysis is added to the thirst for service, for each has prepared a way in which to walk to be of service and clues are all about you, yet without the continuing process of prayerful meditation and of a daily focusing on the search for the one great original Thought and the consciousness it provides, your ambition to be a pure part of the body and vehicle for the Creator will be emaciated. How we encourage you to continue in your meditations and prayers, and then we encourage you to open the eyes and see within each day, each experience, not only the good that can come from that but the clues towards your own centering and your own greatest depth of being.

We realize that we speak to those who already meditate, but if anything, this makes our emphasis upon meditation the stronger, for there is the possibility of constant transformation. Guide your will, my friends, and witness the growing consciousness of the oneness of all entities, for, indeed, this consciousness is growing among your peoples and it will have its harvest of love, light and planetary transformation.

With all the vibrant energy that lies within your soul, my friends, love one another within the illusion and through the illusion by turning your will to the Creator and that great original Thought of love. We leave you now in that love and in that light. We reach out to you, cells of our own body, those of our own being. We are known to you as those of Hatonn. It has been a blessing to speak through this instrument and to share consciousness with you at this time. May we leave you in our love and laughter and joy and may we encourage your will to walk in the ways of seeking that your moments of joy may become more numerous and finally become connected that you may dwell in a river of joy and that you may bless those parts of yourself about you. Adonai, my friends. Adonai vasu borragus.

(Jim channeling)

I am Latwii, and we greet you in the love and the light of our infinite Creator. We too thank both present for requesting our presence. We are happy to be the third in this joyful company. We are aware that there might be a query or two that we could attempt and thereby provide our simple service. May we then entertain whatever queries might be upon the minds of those present?

Carla: Yes. I've been going through a time of drifting badly in spiritual terms. It isn't that I have found myself in the universe without a God or that I feel it necessary to take back anything that I believe, it is just that it all seems to impinge on my consciousness without causing me to become enthusiastic or to have a drive for more that I usually have. And I wondered if you could comment on this state and on its function in the transformation into a new Carla that I'm going through?

I am Latwii, and we are most happy to attempt the response which may be of some service in this regard. The condition of which you speak is one which is not common nor is it long lasting in manifestations, for the transformations which offer themselves to most seekers are transformations from one state of mind, shall we say, to another, with both states being of a relatively definite and well-defined nature. The experience that is now yours is that experience which might be likened unto the beginning movement as the mythical phoenix rises from the ashes, shall we say. As this beginning movement commences, the being which is to be is without definition. There is the seeming void or vacuum which shall eventually draw into it that essence which shall comprise the new being. However, your current experience is one which does not so much offer a definable quality needing only your acceptance, as it offers instead a quality or potential for quality or essence which you yourself shall determine.

This type of transformation is that related to the indigo-ray energy center, as it has been called by this group, in which the seeker is offered the knowledge of self as Creator, the knowledge of self as being of infinite worth. The self then as Creator has then as its first opportunity the creation of the self. That which you have been and that which you have desired provide some of the resources upon which you may draw for the creation of the new self. Within that which now exists are avenues and pathways of connection between that which you are and have been and the greater self, the one Creator which surrounds and supports you always. This resource, as you know well, is infinite in nature and waits only your request to give unto you those portions which you desire.

Now, as the Creator it is up to you, my sister, to desire. The function of the will is paramount in importance. What shall you desire? Who shall you be? How shall you be? For what reasons shall you be? No longer are these given as gifts or that with which you have been provided seemingly of another's choice, and with which you have journeyed for the years of your current incarnation. Now you shall be what you desire. What do you desire? That is your question, your challenge, and your opportunity. Thus the void, for the filling of this void is no longer a given, but is a response to your own efforts and to your knowledge of self as Creator.

May we answer further, my sister?

Carla: Is it still true that my higher self has work cut out for me to do and it's up to me to find that? Or have I done the things that I came to do, and now I'm free to do whatever else I wish? Which is it, if you can tell me that?

I am Latwii, and we find that the answer to this query is not an easy one, for it is not well-defined either. The higher self always provides the potential road map, shall we say. This map leads to the One. Many are the experiences upon the journey. One may before the incarnation map out a certain segment of this journey which it is hoped will be traveled during the incarnation. It may occur that the seeker covers this ground in good fashion and has, shall we say, new opportunities presented to it during the incarnation as the predetermined route has been traveled. In your particular case, my sister, we find that you have accomplished a great deal of what was your preincarnative desire. It is then in large part correct that you may now proceed in a fashion more congruent with your current conscious desires. Yet there is always the guidance and preparation for the journey made by the higher self in any event. Thus, both suppositions are in some part correct.

May we answer further, my sister?

Carla: Not on that topic. That's helpful. When one is in a situation where the will seems to be somewhat either extremely quiet or paralyzed, is this an organic part of this particular transformation? Should it be discouraged or accepted? By discouraged, I mean, should I be striving actively to come out of this state of mind or should I experience it until it's done with me?

I am Latwii, and we find that there are many factors, my sister, which influence this condition of the quieted will. The transformation and its opportunity of which we have previously spoken is one factor …

(Side one of tape ends.)

(Jim channeling)

I am Latwii, and we are once again with this instrument. The process of grieving for the lost, it would seem, loved one is another factor which has a great influence at this particular time upon your own being and exercise of will. These medications which are utilized with the hope of aid in this situation play a part as well. The surest path through this maze of influences, in our humblest opinions, is that which indeed seems to increase the lack of will. That, my sister, is to surrender the will but to surrender it to the desire to serve the one Creator in whatever fashion might be most appropriate for you at this moment.

To take the opportunity for each day's existence that is a gift and to give it over as a gift to the One and as a service to the One is to, at the heart, strengthen that faculty known as the will. And is this not a paradox? For one surrenders the will, and by doing so daily strengthens that which is surrendered. One receives the gift and gives it away and receives it yet again to be given away, and yet gifts of days continue.

May we answer further, my sister?

Carla: No, thank you. That's fine.

I am Latwii, and we thank you, my sister. May we attempt any further queries?

Carla: I have some, but I'll save 'em. Thank you very much.

I am Latwii, and, my sister, we thank you very, very much as well, for it is an honor to speak to even a small group. For it is not the numbers which count, but the desire to know. We don't really know very much, but we share all we have found and find that in return there is a great deal more presented to us in the same fashion of the giving of the gifts which are given to the self. Thus do we thank you and each present for giving us the gift of your questions and your desires to know the truth. We seek also that same truth, and find it in your seeking and in your questions. We hope that in some small degree you have found a portion of it in our replies. We speak as the One to the One. There are no errors in such a speaking, for each portion of the One draws to it that which it seeks. We are those of Latwii, and in joy we leave this small, happy group. We rejoice with you in your delight, in your joys, and in every happiness. Adonai, my friends. Adonai vasu borragus. ✻

L/L Research

Sunday Meditation
December 1, 1985

(Carla channeling)

I am Hatonn, and I greet you in the love and in the light of our infinite Creator. We paused with you, my friends, to enjoy the plangent silence of the harmony of this group and the haunting sound of your wind chime. As you remain warm and protected within your domicile, the harsh winds of winter begin to cause the environment about you to become less hospitable to your form of chemical life which you enjoy within this illusion.

There are times, my friends, when there are severe patterns of internal weather as well, for the illusion is as dense within the mind as it is without the mind unless steps which we have recommended time and again are taken. Let us begin with simple principles.

There is that which is unchangeable. This is not within your presence but this is what you seek. Yet upon the sphere which you call Earth, all that you see is changeable, and all that you see within yourself from time to time may seem to be all too changeable and undependable. If that which you seek is that which is unchangeable, then there must be tools which can be used within the illusion to find that kingdom of unchangeability which is findable within the illusion. These tools are the will to know and the faith to believe that grace, or kindness, cosmologically speaking, will offer you that which there is to know.

This instrument has experienced an ongoing series of lessons in the art of facing an illusion and accepting an illusion. Most of those upon your planet who seek will find periods wherein their will is not equal to the task of processing the catalyst which it has to process. When the force of will breaks down the illusion is complete, and many things may be distorted. Moreover, this process does not continue and then stop. It is steadily degenerative and is a bleeder of polarity in that that which consists of the worry, the fear, the apprehension, has the nature which subtracts positivity from an entity which harbors and continues to harbor the more serious of fears and apprehensions. This message is not for those who are still asleep, for those who sleep learn precisely from the catalyst which we are urging the seeker to consider facing with a renewed vigor of will. Those who sleep, having no consciousness of a need for will, react in a random manner, learning at a somewhat slow rate the lessons of love.

However, we speak to those who have already seized that path and named that path for their own, that path which leads towards truth. When one is overcome by the illusion it may well seem as if one is doing some violence to one's inner self by imposing upon it affirmations and meditations. This is to a certain extent worth some consideration. An entity which is experiencing catalyst may well wish to declare a period of examination of thoughts and behavior. During this time it is best to allow the self to be without influence from within or from without. We recommend this sort of analytical overview as taking no more than a period within one of your days. We do not recommend retaining the lack of affirmation, the lack of seeking, for the nature of the illusion can be seen and the poignancy of experience grasped within a relatively short time.

When the entity is convinced then that all that is observable has been observed, it is time for the entity to recall that which invigorated and enlivened the entity and sent it upon the journey in the first place, for it is easy to begin a journey but it is difficult to retain the energy of the journey until one has made a complete and irreversible choice of polarity. The fidelity of will is most important. Thus, we suggest to those whose head is bowed with some anguish, difficulty or pain, that the faculty of mind and observation be applied, but then the mind be cast back to the memory of joy and peace and love which is the frequent fruit of the seeker. This is the fuel which is internal and organic and not applied from without, which enables a suffering entity to make its own affirmations, to seek again its own silences, and to bring into being an entity built about the center of seeking.

We ask those who suffer to free themselves if it takes a day, a season, one of your years, or longer, for the self which is buried in the illusion which suffers without thought is opaque, and the love and the light of the infinite Creator shine not through opacity but through transparency. Turn and turn again and once again and always again to the seeking that has occupied your ideals, your desire for knowledge, and your seeking of love, for although you continue experiencing when sunk within the illusion, the processing of that experience is greatly slowed without the retaining and developing of desire. The need for desire, fresh each day, does not fall away when the student is not an introductory student. Indeed, the need for purer and purer seeking grows as the student begins to partake somewhat of that for which it seeks.

My friends, we speak for the most part for those who are beginning upon the path of seeking. We attempt within the clumsy confines of your language to identify terms to express inspiration that words cannot compass. And yet, there are few indeed among your peoples in third density which are able to sustain the keen point of seeking in a steady state over the period of an incarnation. Therefore, we speak to the most experienced and the most learned of seekers. The key to upsetting experiences is that they separate the experiencer from the seeker within. The experiencer is a small portion of the personality unless it is linked within the seeker within.

And so, my friends, when the air seems to grow dark and the winter of the soul sets in, know once again that all seekers are ever beginners and that the simplest of rules, if we may use that word, apply. Seek and seek and seek yet again. And do not feel that you have let yourself down when you have fallen away from the seeking wrapped up in overwhelming experience, but without judgment and without impatience, turn again to seeking. And from that seeking, from that meditation, from that inner silence, draw once again from the inexhaustible supply of love and joy. The kingdom which is all of love and joy awaits within you—but you must seek it.

We give you encouragement and sympathy, oh you who dwell within that which seems to be and yet is not. How very dim the light is and how very much there is to be seen as one seeks along a trail seemingly plunged in darkness—and yet this too is an illusion. Determine therefore to voice that within yourself which is your best, and persevere. Remember one difference between the beginning seeker and the seeker who has chosen his path. The beginning seeker may go from knowledge to knowledge, from system to system because this is the first step in seeking, to find the correct path for the entity who seeks.

But once the path has attracted the seeker, and the path has been taken by the seeker, that special and unique path which each seeker chooses alone, it is well to retain that path to the end of the incarnation. Developing, learning more, adding always to the depth of experience, but letting the intellectual mind and its limitations give way to the constant stream of acute perception which is available to one who seeks in fidelity along its unique path.

Cry your tears, my children, when tears are to be shed. But in the morning turn again and begin again. And know yourself as the eternal beginner. As we said, we are always with you if you request our presence, as are other principles and intelligences which wish to aid you. Ask and you shall receive help. Ask too of those about you who seek along the path. In communication with your fellow travelers, much of love and light may be generated. Communication then heals the will and enables faith. Therefore, seekers, love one another and witness the light to each other, for you are part of the Creator, experiencing Itself. And as you share yourself with others, others see that part of the Creator which you manifest. Let your being manifest that which is of the unchangeable. We are those of Hatonn and we leave this instrument in the love and in the light of our infinite Creator. Adonai, my friends. Adonai vasu borragus.

(Jim channeling)

I am Latwii, and we greet each of you in the love and in the light of our one infinite Creator. We thank this small group for calling for our presence. We are honored to be with you. As always, our task is a simple and humble one. We hope that we may offer a response to your queries that will point a direction that is helpful in your seeking. Thus, we will dispense with any further formalities and ask if we may begin with a query?

Carla: I ran across some information lately that suggested that AIDS is the latest of the diseases which have been thrown up by people's inability to make a decision for life. And I've heard other information which suggested that AIDS was the product of the kind of state of mind that goes along with promiscuity. I wonder if you could comment on both of those theories?

I am Latwii, and we find that there is good deal of correctness within the suppositions you have queried upon. The diseases that now begin to make their presence known among your peoples are, shall we say, last minute—we must use the word—"aids" that have the hoped for purpose of allowing those of your population who have the potential to polarize sufficiently for harvesting to do this and do it in a relatively short period of your time as you measure experience, for the great cycle of evolution which is now closing upon your planet, when completed, will then offer no more to your population, and many are those who now seek the graduation.

Thus, the various diseases which are cropping up in new form, and the intensification of many of your old diseases, has the purpose of aiding the harvest. Those diseases of the sexually transmitted variety, being in the realm of the mating relationship, are specifically designed to aid the evolutionary progress by suggesting to those thusly suffering their impact that the bond that is made between two that results in a traveling together and sharing of experience over a prolonged portion of your time is that kind of bond which will most efficiently aid in the evolutionary progress. Thus, those most frequently inflicted or struck with these diseases—and we speak of the AIDS and the genital herpes specifically—are those which have had some difficulty in making a choice, which at a deeper level of their own being they desire to make, but have found conscious difficulty in completing. Thus the training aid, shall we say.

May we answer further, my sister?

Carla: Not on that point. I'd like to ask about the harvest. We were on radio today, and talk of Earth changes and metaphysical changes came up. And it occurred to me, although I couldn't do anything about it within the scope of the broadcast, that we talk about the New Age as if it were all one thing, in other words, the planet changes and the people change. And I wondered if there were really going to be a finite day of judgment or if the entities leaving the planet at this time by death would be harvested one by one in simultaneous time rather than in our kind of time.

I am Latwii, and find that this query is one which touches upon information which has been previously transmitted in another form. We are having some difficulty with this instrument, for it is not in the proper depth of singleness in order to transmit our thoughts, therefore, we are having somewhat to round up the herd of thoughts and point it [in] one direction. We shall begin again.

The harvest, my sister, is underway and shall continue for a relatively significant portion of your time. There are those at this time who make the transition through the door of death and who enter no longer the third-density illusion, for their work within this illusion is complete. As your cycle continues to find its completion, there will be more and more of these entities who will by their own abilities be harvested and shall, with others from this planetary influence, be present for each succeeding harvest as the hosts of heaven rejoice [and] sing the praises of each soul so harvested, each soul then blending its voice and being in the heavenly choirs.

May we answer further, my sister?

Carla: Could you comment on suicide?

I am Latwii, and am aware not only of your query but of your concern. This subject is one which has many ramifications, as you would expect, for the taking of one's own life in a conscious fashion is but a most distorted means of making a transition from your current illusion to the next, for each entity within your illusion shall at some point leave it. The choice to leave shall be made in most cases on the subconscious level, there having been the completion of the tasks set out or sufficient completion to warrant such transition. In some cases there is the need to regroup, shall we say, for the lessons have become somewhat a heavy burden and there was perhaps the biting off of more than could be chewn—we correct this instrument—than could be successfully chewed. The word still sounds funny—we shall continue, nevertheless.

In the case of the suicide, the choice to leave the incarnation and the illusion is made upon the conscious level, yet is made with a consciousness which has become distorted by the difficulties which are presented to it. In most cases the taking of one's own life in such a conscious fashion cuts short that which remained full of potential, and therefore the entity so leaving finds the need within its own being to recommit itself to the illusion which was so abruptly left.

There are, however, again as you may imagine anomalistic circumstances under which the leaving of the incarnation even through this kind of means is undertaken as a, shall we say, lesson in itself, for any action may be appropriate with the proper motivation, and within your illusion it is most difficult to see any motivation clearly. Yours are the lessons learned in darkness, for as a small candle of light is lit, there is the ability to see small things with some difficulty but large things with little resolution. Thus, you carefully travel a dimly lit path and the forces that move about you move in darkness, and thus are you yourself moved by much which is unseen.

We cannot in this particular instance give you exact details concerning the one known as Don, the subject of your query and concern, for within this particular entity's own death there was implanted the hope for a continued growth, and this was carried out. The repercussions are understandably immense, yet within these repercussions lie a promise, the nature of which we may not describe but may affirm only its existence.

May we answer further, my sister?

Carla: No, thank you.

I am Latwii, and we thank you, as always, my sister. May we attempt another query?

Carla: Let me think back over the radio program this morning. …

(Side one of tape ends.)

Carla: … I had a kind of frustrating experience this morning talking on the radio because so many tendrils of thought were begun but could not possibly be finished successfully. And I guess the thing that stuck in my mind the most was a conversation I had with a born-again Christian who brought up the by-now familiar limitation, self-imposed, of Christianity to what was in the Bible and nothing else, and a prejudice against learning anything that is from a source other than the Bible. And I wondered if there is any better answer to someone with those limitations than the answer that his path is okay and yet there are others who cannot use that path and need another one. Is there a clearer or more compassionate answer that can be given either to the Christian or to the one who is listening who is not a Christian?

I am Latwii, and am aware of your query, my sister. We find that of itself the answers and the ramifications of these answers which you gave are more than adequate. It is helpful to remove one's desire to calm the mind of one who is concerned and agitated concerning your own point of view. One can only give what one has and our suggestion in this regard would only be to speak as you feel, to speak as you are, to speak as you live. All you have to give is what you are, how you feel, and what you seek. To speak as clearly and with as much compassion as you can in this manner is to do all that can be done. The means by which you are heard and the responses which are generated are not your responsibility. Allow those whose responsibility these are to exercise that responsibility as they will. To be concerned about how one is perceived presents a distortion in how one presents the heart of one's being.

May we answer further, my sister?

Carla: No. I think that's an excellent point, and I'm through, and I thank you very much. Nice to talk to you, Latwii.

I am Latwii, and we are most happy to talk to you, my sister. This evening, as has occurred recently, we have a small group with which to talk yet we are overjoyed that our words have a meaning here and that there is a desire to hear them. We hope that we have not overly taxed this instrument's ability to concentrate. When there is much on the mind, anything in addition tends to slide around within the confusion. We apologize for whatever distortions may have crept into our contact this evening, as does this instrument. However, with the best effort that can be given having been given, we shall take our leave of this instrument, blessing all who seek the One, those seen and unseen. Adonai, my friends. We are Latwii. Adonai vasu borragus. ❧

Sunday Meditation
December 8, 1985

(Carla channeling)

I am Hatonn. I greet you, my friends, in the love and in the light of our infinite Creator, and it is a great blessing for us to be able to make contact with you and to speak some humble words to you that may or may not have some significance to you at this time. We hope we may be of service to you and it is in that spirit that we speak, as always.

Outside your domicile at this time the trees stand dignified, stately, and without reserve in their winter's clothes of bark and root. The roadside shines pale in the dim light of your short day and your moon creates its special magic, shining luminously at this time of your year. All those things in your world of nature have gone home for their season of gestation and inner growth. Within the earth the slow process of transformation has begun. And that which is home to the seed and tree nurtures, heals and protects the delicate life within its mantle of soil.

And what of you? Each of you seeks a home. Let us go on a journey to find that most precious of all things.

Each of you came into the incarnation in a geographical place, and some call this place home, and yet the new consciousness of the babe does not hold the concept of home and geography. The place where one of you may grow up may seem to be home, a home to which you return from time to time, a home which still feeds you in some way. And yet most of you find that one cannot find home once one has left it. As one grows, one finds work to do and many find a home in work. Many find themselves relaxed and comfortable in the work situation as they are not when they enter the domicile in which they dwell. Many others as they are grown make homes for themselves and again attach themselves to geography. Your peoples may call this putting down the roots or settling down.

And then, finally, there are many who find homes with other souls along the path of seeking. And so it matters not where one is, for one has always the joy of the presence of the loved mate or friend about which to spin the home. We would like to take you further than this, my friends, in your search for home. We would like to take you into the smallest atom, to stand within that nexus of energy and to be given the eyes to see the path of creative power of articulated light. This is your home, my friends, this is part of your home.

We would take you with us away and further away, coming away from the planetary surface, moving towards that which you see as blackness. And as you move into what you call outer space and gaze back upon your beautiful planet, yours is now the larger view. You are a citizen of all that there is. And lest you think that geography has any lingering contact with home, let us bring you with us and fling ourselves all into unimaginable reaches of space and time, further than the largest of your telescopes can see, beyond the range of any human experience. You may fall into a planet of fire—and yet that is home. You may come upon a planet of ice as cold as absolute zero—and that is your home, your hospitable and welcoming home.

Now let us come back, slowly, so that you may see first your solar system and then the beauty of your planet. Let us walk among the streets of your cities and look into the faces of your people. Look into the eyes of the man who is poor and you see the light of home. Gaze into the eyes of a couple in love. You are still home. Exchange glances with one who rapes and murders and lives a dark life. You are still home, for you are a citizen of the creation. You are part and parcel of everything that there is. What must needs be stripped away from the concept of home is all concept of physicality, for home is that which is invisible to the physical eye and unknowable to the physical apparatus. Your metaphysical home is a thing of mystery and omnipresence. You cannot leave home—there is no home to find. All places are familiar and all souls a part of you. How then can you shape your mind to ignore all of those rational and sensible signals of experience which inform you of a chauvinistic love for geography, political ideology, or any of the other reasons you may choose a physical home?

We cannot see for you, and yet the silent ear and the closed eye hears and sees impeccably. Have you allowed your eye to see and your ear to hear this day, this day that is filled with all the joy that the word home suggests? We ask you to realize that that which is native to you, that which is part of you, that which is part of your life plan as devised by your higher self and offered as a feast for you, will come to you and will be your physical home. You may be fortunate in your geography, in your choice of mates, in your choice of professions, or in any of those ways which may make you find an identity or home.

And yet, until you look for a home, for that in you which is eternal, that in you which is most precious, and that in which partakes of the mystery of the one infinite Creator, you have not begun seeking your true home nor have you earned your citizenship in the creation.

And why should you look for a home that is so abstruse? May we say to you that it is, in our humble opinion, of utmost importance to place your consciousness where you feel you may find value in progressing and evolving spiritually.

We do not suggest that you cease seeking harmony in your geographical location, in your work, or in relationships. Rather, we suggest that overshadowing any of these considerations is the home of your soul or spirit. Many there are who would have no idea of what I say, and to those people, we say, "Enjoy your sleep. Wake up when you wish to wake up, and let no word of ours interfere with the pleasure of your dreaming." For seeking one's spiritual home means the discipline of transformation, a transformation in thinking which eliminates limitations and makes all things in creation one great gigantic being full of love, creative energy and thought whose consciousness is evolving and whose great heart is beating and will continue to beat infinitely. This is the eternal home of the spirit, and you shall see one end of the creation to the other, one refinement of understanding after another, and always desire shall power you. Desire to seek beyond the bounds of your physical illusion for your identity and for your sense of security and home.

As always, we suggest that the quickest and most efficient way to empower this desire to seek is meditation, and we encourage you to do that regularly, for there is much about which you may get excited within the illusion, but if your consciousness of yourself is that of a citizen of the creation, a co-creator with the One Who Is All, how can you then be so far removed by emotion from your home? The illusion may seem to take many homes away from you, but in reality you have never left home, you have merely veiled part of it from yourself so that you may come to an illusion and refine some lessons concerning how to love one another. And how shall you love one another, my friends? Freely and gladly, with a clear conscience and a pure heart. How wonderful that would be. The bare trees lean towards the whole creation in that love and the seeds beneath the sod sleep contentedly in that same love.

We have so much more consciousness than a tree or a seed. It is a question to ask oneself—why cannot we have the consciousness of purity which encompasses your natural life upon your planet? Lords of creation, you have been called, and like the lords, the gods, and other beings in your midst, you squabble and fight and do not see the Creator in each other and do not find a home in each other's hearts many times. Seek harder, my friends. Seek your home, for your identity and your home are one.

We would leave at this time, that our brothers and sisters may speak. We leave you in the creation, produced by extravagant free will, born of love, fashioned of light. We thank you and we leave you in peace, love and light, at home wherever you are and whoever you are. We are known to you as those of Hatonn. Adonai, my friends. Adonai vasu borragus.

(Jim channeling)

I am Latwii, and we also greet you in the love and the light of the one infinite Creator. It is again our privilege to join this group and we are eager to begin with any queries which those present may have value in the asking. We hope that we may serve in some small way this evening, my friends. May we accept the first query?

Carla: Okay, I've been thinking lately and especially today about making 1986 a special year in that I would make more special efforts during the year to do more transformational work and get a better idea of who I am and where I want to go. Could you comment on that and give any suggestions in general that you might find appropriate?

I am Latwii, and we are aware of your query, my sister. In the great search, each seeker shall find many ways to accelerate that journey. It is helpful from time to time to take a specific action that will have as its only goal the revealing of self to self, or as you have called it, the transformation of the small self into that which it truly is, the one Creator. The taking of time and the making of effort to construct a channel through which greater realizations might pour forth is most helpful to those who have consciously sought for a great portion of the life the truths that underlie all that which is known in your illusion as life.

The power behind such thoughts and actions is the power of your desire and your intentions, for by such desires are you moved in any direction according to the desire. As you have moved over a portion of time in a conscious fashion, it becomes more and more necessary for succeeding movements to be the product of further conscious choices. Thus, one who has consciously evolved over a period of time will find it difficult to maintain the progress without further conscious choice and the setting aside of such portions of time in order that such desire might be further defined and might further enhance the evolutionary process. That you choose is of primary importance. What you choose and how you choose to make this progress manifest is of secondary importance, yet is important in its own way according to your unique needs.

Thus, we can reaffirm the heart of your intentions or the desire to know the One and to serve the One in all is that portion of the seeking that is crucial and is that which is received that will be made manifest according to the strength of the desire, and as conscious attention continually focuses upon this desire, the seed shall be nurtured and shall produce the fruit. The fruit then shall further empower the journey as it nourishes the desire to know.

May we answer further, my sister?

Carla: Yes. The second part of the question had to do with the tools that one might use for making the seeking more manifest. To be more specific, although I don't know whether that helps or not, I was thinking about trying to write some things down on a regular basis, keep records of any important dreams, and any important thoughts, and maybe let a few automatic handwritings come through, and of course study the Sunday meditations and see how they're going. Could you suggest other tools or suggest tools that are especially efficacious?

I am Latwii, and my sister, we would suggest that for any who has such a desire as you have described, the utilization of the phenomenon of dreams is most helpful, for if it is known that during the time you call sleep that one may do work in consciousness, and if it is consciously sought, the dreams that one experiences can be utilized in order to enhance the waking process of learning and serving, for within the state of dreams one is able to receive information in a fashion which is unlike most forms of communication in that the communication may proceed through the subconscious mind and by certain configurations produced there reveal to the seeker those areas within the self which remain dark and mysterious and await the discovery and then shall become portions of a transformed being.

Within the dream state it is also possible to receive the aid of those which serve as guides and guardians for the incarnational self. These entities, as well as the subconscious mind, stand ready at all time, as you would call it, to lend assistance to the conscious seeker in direct proportion to the strength of the desire of the seeker to know. The assistance is usually given in a manner which the seeker is most familiar with, thus inspirations and ideas and hunches from time to time are experienced by one who seeks in a manner that does not consciously utilize the dreams. If these dreaming experiences are made available to the seeker through its own desire, communication can proceed from these sources in a much more, shall we say, rich and fulfilling manner.

May we answer further, my sister?

Carla: Yes. I had asked a friend of mine to go on this transformational journey with me and I wondered if there was more chance for polarization working with a companion than there is working alone or if it is all the same?

I am Latwii, and we find that it has been well said, my sister, that those who of like mind together seek shall far more surely find. That which one misses is more likely to be noticed by the other and vice versa. Thus, the old saying that two heads are better than one is surely true in any such endeavor, and we heartily encourage the joining of companions upon such a journey.

May we answer further, my sister?

Carla: No, thank you.

I am Latwii, and we thank you, as always, my sister. Is there another question?

(Pause)

I am Latwii. We find that the queries this evening are few. Yet we are not discouraged, my friends, for we know that the work that is done in any metaphysical sense is not measured in any ordinary terms. We thank each for inviting our presence this evening and we hope that we have provided some small measure of service. We, as always, suggest that one take the portion that has meaning and leave all that which has none from our words. We thank you again for your gracious and ever-present invitation to join you in your meditations. We shall be with you again. We are … [those of Latwii. Adonai vasu borragus.]

(Tape ends.) ❧

Sunday Meditation
December 15, 1985

(Carla channeling)

[I am Latwii, and] we greet you in the love and in the light of the one infinite Creator, and thank you for calling us this evening to your group. It is a privilege to share this meditation with you and to be able to attempt to be of service in our small way. We would share with you some thoughts upon the nature of that which you call judgment.

Once there was a boy with a wise father. This young man was eager to be of service and to show through his life the love and the light of the one infinite Creator. He questioned his father concerning all of the choices which presented themselves to him as he looked for the best way to be of service.

"Shall I go to be a soldier to protect my country and to stand for the ideals upon which our nation is founded?"

"That is a way to serve," answered the wise father. The young man thought. This was not a "yes" nor was it a "no," but as intensely as he questioned his father, his father would say no more.

"Shall I then be an athlete who can win the ears and the hearts of many because of my skill?"

"That would certainly be a way to be of service," said the wise father. And he would say no more.

"Shall I learn to play and sing music and share that gift, and as I gain in fame, serve the many who listen to the words of my songs?" asked the young man of his father. The answer was the same.

The well-intentioned son suggested as many ways to be of service as he could think of. The father was no more in favor of one way than another.

Finally, exasperated, the son said, "Well, then, shall I become a hobo, to walk along the streets and the roads of the country and the city and get my living by asking for money from strangers?"

"That would be a way to be of service," said the unruffled father.

By this time the son had become thoroughly upset. "I shall choose a life of crime," he said to his father. "I shall take what I wish, go whither I wish, and experience the freedom of being above the law."

"That is a way to be of service," came the answer from the wise father.

For many days the young man pondered what he knew to be a secret which he had not discovered and that was how best to be of service. He was capable of doing many things, but could not choose among them.

As the young man's life progressed onward, it shaped itself. The young man met and wed a young woman for whom he felt passion. Soon there were children and he found what job he could and worked very hard to support his family. The young man became a man in his middle years, still as dedicated as ever to serving, but unable to puzzle out what he should have done. It was a source of anguish to him, for he knew he was not a wise man, only a good man. He was unable to give his sons the dispassionate advice that his father had given him, for he did not understand his father's cryptic comment. But he questioned and continued questioning.

And as he grew in years, as his physical vehicle began to show the effects of the planet's turning around the sun time after time, he felt that he had begun to penetrate that which his father was attempting to tell him so many years ago. So he went to his father, who was by then an aged man, and he said to him, "My father, it has been the goal of my life to be of service, and yet of all the things that I thought of, all of which you said would be helpful to others, I did none. Instead, I did that which I did not comprehend or anticipate. And many things have occurred. And I believe now that I begin to understand that which you say."

"Very good, my son," his father said, "Please tell me so that I may bask in the reflection of my wisdom."

The son, never able to feel quite adult around his father, was suddenly bashful, for he was not sure, after all, that he had begun to understand.

"Well, father," he faltered, "I think I have found that service is something I cannot see."

"Very good, my son," said his father. "What else?"

"Well," continued the son, "I believe I have begun to see that I do not see very well."

"Very good, my son," said the father. "What else?"

The son mustered up his courage. "Father, I believe that I am of service, and that I cannot help being of service."

"Sit down, my son," said the delighted father, "for now we can talk together.

The son sat quickly, eager to listen to his beloved father unravel the riddle at last. The father pointed to the springtime flowers nodding in the breeze. "Which one of those flowers, my son, is not beautiful?"

"Oh, they are all beautiful," answered the son.

"And upon what do you base this opinion?" asked the father.

"The evidence of my eyes and my nose and my touch," said the son.

The father pointed to several flowers which had withered early.

"Do you find these beautiful?" the father asked.

"No," replied the son, "they are dead. They should be removed from the bed. I did not see them before."

"It is time for you to consider," said his father, "whether you are alive or dead. For if you are alive, you are as beautiful and fragrant and lovely to the touch as any other human that dwells upon the planet. You may be a great president and run a country well, you may inspire by writing or by the singing of songs and poetry you may inspire many. You may heal or you may feed your family. Or, indeed, you may do nothing. But if you are alive within yourself, if you question rather than accepting blindly, then you are precisely as beautiful as those who share your condition, your illusion, and your density."

My friends, it is most easy to judge yourself and others upon the basis of those things which you have accumulated within you which pass for knowledge among your people. And it seems, indeed, as if there is a striking variance among the great variety of peoples upon your planet, and so the illusion is intended to work. And yet because that which is metaphysical is by its very nature that which is unseen, there is no way to judge oneself or another upon the basis of opinion, for there is no knowledge from seeing the fruits of one's labor of what the intentions and the desires of the laborer are.

That which is action on the physical plane is illusory. That which is intended within the heart is of the spirit and is eternal. When you leave this particular incarnation, each of you shall gain a far wider viewpoint. You shall become what is now called your higher self, and shall dwell far more consciously within the Creator, and you shall judge yourself. You shall not look at the effects which you have produced within your environment, but rather at your state of mind and heart during the incarnational experience.

That, my friends, is why there is no judgment possible among peoples, and why there is acceptance of any road whatsoever that the seeker wishes to travel in order to enlarge its experience, for many are the experiences, yet one is the quest. Insofar as the quest is for light, for truth, for the one original Thought, just so shall one's steps spiral ever upward as service is given. And insofar as the seeker looks for the effect, just so shall he be pulled into the illusion and away from service.

We come not to give you answers as much as to encourage seeking. We have no dogma, although we do suggest meditation. We offer no structure except that structure which is builded by the student as a result of seeking. We do not want you to accept this or any material, and we take steps to remind groups such as yours that the last thing that we wish is to have our advice followed blindly. We want you to fight with this information, to question it, to doubt it, to work with it, and to make it your own.

Spiritual seeking is not a hobby, although many take it up as a hobby and go on to something else when enough time has passed that the hobby becomes tiring and progress slows. We hope instead that you will see the illusion as a hobby that you have taken on for a few of your years. There are many things to play with in this illusion, many variations upon the game of being a human being, as you call yourselves. And if you can look at your experiences as points in a game, each of which offers opportunities for questioning, fighting, tearing apart and working with the experience, this attitude is an helpful one.

We do not wish to denigrate the nature of incarnational experience, we merely wish to point out the nature of the illusion. Learn from your own questions. We attempt to tell you enough of the rules of the game called incarnation that you may have many clues and may form your own tools with which to deal with your experience within this illusion. And yet the instantaneous product that you are, that instantaneous vibration which shall be judged, is a product not of how you have bent and molded the illusion, but of how you have worked within yourself to produce a being that lives a life that is full of light.

The most apparently criminal of entities can choose under the press of experience to turn towards the light and seek and be far more zealous for the good than those who have never experienced living the darker life. Indeed, there is no situation which is not also an opportunity, not just on one level, but several. We do not wish for you to become indifferent to your illusion. That would spoil the effect of the illusion. We wish, rather, that you continue to question that which lies beyond the illusion, to ask and ask and ask again, for as you ask, it shall be given you. And only as you ask shall it be given you; that which is not asked for is seldom used.

We wish for each of you to find the deeper and deeper satisfaction within your internal existence. We wish for you to refine more and more your own ideals of love and beauty and service. But we do not wish to shape for you the life of mind and heart any more than the wise father would tell his son what path to take to be of service.

Picture if you will the stars and planets and comets and all the heavenly bodies racing with what seems to you incredible speed through incredible distances, hurtling through space. All is in motion, and yet all is in balance. This is a concept we would ask you to consider. We have suggested that it is a good thing to become a balanced entity, a clear channel through which love and light may flow, and yet we do not in any way wish to suggest stasis. Balance is not still, for you are never still, for the infinite consciousness of your mind and deep mind [breathes in] an infinite amount of time and space with movement.

It is not a wrong thing to seek the cave and become still and learn silence, and that is one path of service. Yet the son who loved a woman and had affection for his children and kept them as he would himself is of precisely as much service as the so-called holy man, if both hearts are equally full of the desire to serve and the continued questioning and discipline and refining of the way to serve.

We wish that your movements through this incarnation may be graceful, and that your hearts may be increasingly full of peace as that which you find in the illusion reflects to you that which is within each part of any illusion in the creation. And that is love.

Can you suspend your judgment? We believe you can. Do you wish to? What level of seeking do you wish to pursue? What have you pursued this day? What dreams lie within your heart and what attempts have you made to become clear within yourself? We speak to you but not for you. All the choices are your own. We offer you support and our love and encourage you to see that same love and support in all situations.

Any experience which masters the seeking entity to the exclusion of questions and further seeking is not helpful, or shall we say, is of a far more limited kind of helpfulness. We offer you not a structure, not a dogma, but what limited knowledge we have of what consciousness is and how you may seek to evolve that consciousness within yourself within this illusory incarnation. Use what you will and know that that which serves may bear fruit upon the physical plane. Or that same impulse may seem …

(Side one of tape ends.)

(Carla channeling)

… or that same impulse may seem to flounder and be useless.

There is that within you which is imperishable and which carries the traces of those energies of love and service to others. These shall not be judged within this illusion, although many attempt that judgment. Therefore, take courage and find each your own truth and then use the truth that you have found to seek and seek and seek again, and to forge for yourself a life that is its own teaching, that is an expression, inwardly speaking, of all that has been learned.

We hope you are a little uncomfortable with this message, for that which is physical dislikes change. And what we urge upon you is continual reexamination which encourages change, perhaps not change in the outside world of experience, but certainly change that is equally uncomfortable within the heart and the mind and the understanding that you may have of how things work, of who you are and of what service really is. May you seek in joy and may joy be added unto you, for the Creator laughs with great joy at every question, for so the Creator questions Itself and learns about the Creator.

The portion known as Latwii bids farewell to this group in order that our brothers and sisters of L/Leema may speak through the one known as Jim. We leave you in the creation of love and light. Adonai. Adonai, my friends.

(Jim channeling)

I am L/Leema, and we are grateful to greet each of you in the love and the light of our one Creator. We are pleased to be able to utilize this instrument in our attempt to be of service. We hope that we may serve by answering those queries which those present may find value in the asking. May we now attempt any such query?

Carla: Well, since no one is asking an important question, I'll ask a real dumb one. At the beginning of the meditation, I heard from Hatonn, Oxal and Latwii, and waited a considerable amount of time after I'd opened myself for channeling before I was able to tell which one was going to speak. Towards the end of the channeling, I again was feeling both Hatonn and Latwii. Who was talking? Was Latwii talking? And why was Hatonn there if Latwii was talking?

I am L/Leema, and we find that in this instance your ability to perceive the entities of Confederation known as Latwii and Hatonn was correct, in that those of Latwii were utilizing your instrument for the vocalizing of thoughts while those of Hatonn were providing a service by stabilizing, shall we say, the carrier wave or depth of your meditation in order that those of Latwii might utilize your instrument without undue fatigue, for their message was of some length and their normal effect upon your instrument is somewhat wearing.

Therefore, it was decided that those of Hatonn could aid best this evening by anchoring the contact in your instrument by somewhat stepping down the voltage, as you may call it.

May we speak further, my sister, upon this query?

Carla: No, that fits with what was happening inside my head. Thank you.

I am L/Leema. We are grateful to you, my sister. Might we attempt another query?

Questioner: Yes, I have a question. I spoke earlier of an experience I had during meditation, either a dream, a consciousness projection, or something in which I seemed to see what I perceived as a very large space craft. Could you comment on this? If this was a dream was this, indeed, basically the same as a projection? Your thoughts.

I am L/Leema. We find that with this experience you are entering into a realm of your own subconscious mind in which were present those elements necessary for the interpretation and initiation of a somewhat expanded mode of perception that you are currently in the process of utilizing for another type of resource upon which to call in your seeking of what is known as the truth.

As an entity proceeds along this journey of seeking in a sincere and diligent fashion, there are opened to such a one a variety of avenues which can provide the information in the precise fashion which the entity will understand and through which the entity may continue in its mode of seeking. Thus, this particular experience was but one of many which have the purpose of offering new opportunities for gathering experience and information that might prove helpful in answering those inner queries both asked and unasked.

May we answer further, my brother?

Questioner: I'm not sure if I completely understand. In other words, I believe you're saying that the experience that I had was the work of my subconscious or my higher self of commenting on the validity of the direction that my seeking has been taking? Because I definitely had some doubt about some of the material I was reading, even though at the same time I fully believed it was possible. So, are you saying that this was the way I had of telling myself, telling my everyday self that this was, indeed, one of many valid ways of proceeding along my path? I believe that was what you said. Is that correct?

I am L/Leema, and we find that you are in part correct. However, the experience of which you speak was not so much a verification of the information which you had recently read as the experience was itself an outgrowth triggered by that information, and an outgrowth which is in itself an outgrowth that is in itself a portion of your journey which is now opening before you in response to your continued desire to seek what is called the truth.

May we answer further, my brother?

Questioner: No, I think I understand. Thank you.

I am L/Leema, and we thank you, my brother. Is there another query?

Carla: I'd sort of like to follow up on that a little bit. Carl Jung suggested that UFO's were archetypical, and by that he meant subjective but projected. He felt that each archetype had some function. You speak as a UFO entity. If you are part of an archetype, what function does the visual UFO play? What function does it have?

I am L/Leema, and we find that you have asked a query which has many ramifications, for there is the experience of a phenomenon by many which is known generally as the UFO phenomenon. There are those who experience this phenomenon, or portions of it, in many unique ways and thus utilize this experience in fashions unique to the needs and perceptions of each who experiences it.

Those who move in service in the crafts which are perceived as UFO's are of many sources and natures. Many take the form or shape that is most easily perceived by the subconscious and conscious minds of those to whom they reach in service, and thus they are perceived in an outer fashion in a manner which shall cause the least distortion and trauma to those witnessing their presence. The message or service which is imparted is the portion of the experience of greatest import.

Again, this message may be perceived in many ways. As each entity is a portion of a greater mind that is archetypical in nature, each individual entity may utilize a portion of that mind or seek from a portion of that mind a message of the nature that matches their needs. Thus, various areas of one's mind or being, shall we say, may be seeking, and various deeper portions of that mind or being may respond in a fashion which seems to be external to the self, and, indeed, many responses to such seeking may be aided by entities external to the seeker.

Thus, there is a blending of response to a seeker's call that blends both the seeker and its perceptions with a greater portion of that same seeker and those who guide this seeker and who are drawn to it according to the nature of the seeker, what is sought, and those who respond.

May we answer further, my sister?

Carla: I'll have to read that one. Thank you.

I am L/Leema, we thank you, my sister. Might we attempt another query?

Carla: Not from me.

Questioner: Well, I have a couple of things I'd like to ask, but at this time I don't think I know clearly just what I want to ask, so I believe I'll put it off until another time.

I am L/Leema. We are happy and humbly so to have been able to speak with this small but vibrant group. We are hopeful that our meager attempts to serve have had some small success, and we again remind each that we do not have final answers. Our opinions and experiences are most fallible. Use those which feel the most helpful—leave the rest. We shall join you again. In joy we leave you. In love and in light we leave you. We are those of L/Leema. Adonai, my friends. Adonai.

(Carla chants a vocal melody.)

I am Nona. We send vibrations to the one known as R. We are with you in love and light. Adonai. ✽

Sunday Meditation
December 22, 1985

(L channeling)

I am Hatonn, and I greet you, my brothers and sisters, in the love and the light of the infinite Creator. My friends, we have received your calling and have attempted to communicate with the one known as Carla but have found that her physical vehicle's condition makes such a communication a poor effort toward service on our part, for we do not wish to further debilitate her vehicle through the stress of using her instrument for communication. We therefore are using this instrument, and we extend to the one known as Carla our gratitude for offering unselfishly the use of her instrument.

We of Hatonn realize that this time on your planet is one of both celebration and inspiration and that the collective subconscious of many of your race focus[es] upon the timelessness of giving and sharing. The simultaneous attentiveness toward the giving of that one you refer to as Christ in the past is recognized by your people. The giving of the present is celebrated in your customs for what you call the season and the contemplation of giving in the future all resound harmonically and attune your planet to a greater receptiveness than normal to those influences which characterize the polarity of service to others.

It is therefore not only a time of celebration upon your planet but among those who attempt to serve your planet as well. In giving, my friends, there is always a receiving, for such is the nature of your universe. We of Hatonn and the Confederation have attempted to share with those present and others for some time what little we had to offer in hope that our efforts might bear fruit for those of your group and for your planet. Our efforts in this direction were an attempt to be of service to yourselves and your brothers, yet my friends, we must acknowledge that an unexpected bounty has been reaped by those of us involved in this service through that love and light which yourselves and others have given in return to ourselves. For this, my friends, we are sincerely grateful. For the lessons which you have extended to us we are also quite grateful.

We of Hatonn would desire to speak more. Correction. We of Hatonn would desire to discuss this subject more fully, yet we do not wish to tire this instrument, as he is somewhat out of practice and we wish to avoid depleting his ability before allowing our brothers and sisters of Latwii the opportunity to communicate as well. For this reason, we shall now relinquish our use of this instrument that they also may be allowed with your permission to speak. In the love and the light of the infinite Creator, we are known to you as Hatonn.

(L channeling)

I am Latwii, and I greet you in the love and the light of the infinite Creator, and, my friends, we wish you all the joy and happiness that we ourselves feel this evening as we observe the changes which are occurring among the peoples of your planet as your date of celebration draws near. At this time we would like to perform our service of attempting to answer whatever questions you may offer. Is there a question?

(Pause)

I am Latwii. As there seem to be no questions forthcoming, we shall also bid you adieu, my brothers and sisters, in the love and the light of the infinite Creator. We are known to you as Latwii. Adonai, my friends. Adonai. ❧

Sunday Meditation
December 29, 1985

(Carla channeling)

I am Oxal, and I greet you in the love and in the light of the one infinite Creator. It is our privilege and our blessing to be called to you this evening, and we thank you for the opportunity to share a few thoughts with you.

This evening we would speak to you about that which you call time and space. It is difficult to approximate in your language the resonances of what these two words approximate, for we are speaking of that which is the material out of which your creation is made and that creative intelligence which creates that which is made. It is not unusual, we have found, that among your peoples time seems to pass more and more rapidly as one's incarnational experience builds up and that which is known as time passes. It must occur to many logical minds that the speeding of time is a kind of illusion within your illusion, for one cannot make mechanical objects such as your clocks that speed up the passage of time in concert with each person's subjective perception of time.

Time and space have a reciprocal relationship and are allegories or analogs of love and light. As these forces impinge upon each seeker's consciousness, they present to that seeker the possibility of experience. Indeed, another word for time is experience. It seems to be untrue that some moments contain more experience than others and, indeed, herein lies the crux of what we wish to impart to you this evening. When there is no distortion in space, each finite moment becomes a unified or cosmic moment and is a thing with the properties of timelessness. It is during timeless moments that experience is seated within the seeker.

Now, catalyst is given to each seeker moment by moment, and one need only look to your young souls to see what can be made of the catalyst of the moment. Children, being less used to the wasting of moments instinctually approach and perceive each piece of catalyst as that which will become experience. There is an overwhelming amount of catalyst in each moment. The fullness of catalyst available in each moment begins, as the child grows into what you call adulthood, to become more of a burden than a pleasure, and as one is overwhelmed by one's catalyst, one ceases to process it into experience. In other words, the space required to use one unit of time becomes distorted in a subjective sense so that the experience time offers buckles and bends and shrinks because that space with which time is inextricably paired has not room enough for the transformation of that which comes to the ear and eye and heart.

(Pause)

We apologize for the delay but this instrument was distracted for a moment and we wished to allow a deeper state of meditation [to] reoccur that our expressions might be clearer or, we should say, as full of clarity as language can form meaning.

When the seeker chooses consciously to use catalyst, space, that internal space which allows time to pass, is then of sufficient length to accept fully the catalyst and its possibility of being transformed into actual experience. When the seeker becomes bemused or distracted and partakes of the mundane, that seeker eliminates from conscious use much of the catalyst which the process of day-to-day living generates. When the seeker is read y to be conscious of the moment, that present moment being one with itself, that is, full of time and equally full of space, then the seeker has the opportunity to experience a timeless moment in which all time is one. Within this moment an infinite amount of work may be done in consciousness for the gradual transformation of the self into that being which each has the capability of claiming. Yea, it is part of your birthright. What is a birthright, my friends, but something with which you were born? A birthright is not something one is given partially or unevenly. Yet a birthright need not be used, just as an inheritance may not be claimed by an heir who does not wish to experience the having of money.

Let us again look at the small child who is greedy of his birthright, and who spends a significant amount of your time in the timeless present moment. In more and more of your young beings at this time, one is able to observe a heightened intensity of seeking and a more rapid translation of catalyst into experience which is seated within the heart. How does one become, then, as a little child? It is written in your holy work known as the Bible that unless one is as a little child, one cannot enter the kingdom of heaven. This statement is simplistic as regards that which is called the kingdom of heaven, but again, language fails to be adequate to meaning and so we must attempt to use words as well as we can.

This is a present moment. What is your catalyst, my friends? Time may be wasted. We listen through this instrument's ears and we hear this instrument's voice relaying concepts, some of which this instrument is unfamiliar with. We are aware of each vibratory complex which makes up each entity within this circle this evening. We hear the blessed sound of the furnace at work warming an otherwise frigid atmosphere. We find in each entity's mind much unprocessed catalyst. That is what each brings to time. When one seeks distraction from heavy catalyst, one puckers and ruffles the ratio between time and space and time is literally shortened in a subjective sense, for there is less space with which to match it.

We use the term space not only in a physical sense but in a metaphysical sense in which space is analogous to the spaciousness of one's point of view, or to put it another way, the room or area which is acceptable for using in the transformation of catalyst into seated experience. It is no wonder that so many of your peoples find time to move faster and faster. Nor is it a wonder that most entities are completely unaware of why this occurs. This is very understandable due to the fact that if one does not process catalyst in this present moment it will be carried over into the next discrete unit of time/space. If then the catalyst of the second discrete unit of time/space is also unused, the next unit of time/space is increasingly burdened with unprocessed catalyst and by the time one is counting one's years with dismay rather than pride most of your peoples have such a load of old unprocessed catalyst that to open oneself to the catalyst in the present moment is almost unthinkable, and it certainly takes a great deal of courage to begin to open to all the catalyst, old and new, which forms the catalyst of this discrete time/space unit of your incarnation.

There are very few—but it is notable enough that we mention this—who are so efficient in processing catalyst in the present moment that space begins to buckle inward under the burden of successfully approached and used catalyst. In that case, the entity who seeks will find itself in the creation in a true sense for the first time, for when time begins its full operation there is the possibility of spacelessness or the unity of all space. In this distortion lies a compassion which cannot be approached except by those few among your peoples who have used catalyst with a fervor and enthusiasm and a conscious knowledge of the probity of such an exercise.

We offer these thoughts to you this evening in hopes that as your time passes upon the face of your clocks, it may be used, appreciated and harvested by your heart. The activity of meditation is a great help in the reconciling of catalyst with the self and the claiming of that catalyst as part of the experiential self which enjoys incarnation at this time.

We hope that we have been of some small service to you this evening. We encourage you to discriminate for yourself. If our words have a sense which may aid you, then let that catalyst be used. It is for that purpose we attempt to serve. If that which we have to say does not appeal, we humbly ask that you drop all portions which disappoint or do not ring true.

In this instrument's mind is the first line of one of your popular songs, "Time is on my side." This is very true, my friends. May you use your time and find timelessness. And with that timeless understanding, may you then turn to that light which is space and manifest within that enlarged space that which is the harvest of your experience.

We are those of Oxal, and we leave now that our brothers and sisters may speak through another instrument. We leave you in the time and the space, in the love and in the light of the One that Is All. We leave you, knowing that it is impossible to leave you any more than we could leave ourselves, for you are our very selves and we yours. Thus, we cease speaking, yet are always as close to you as your desire would have it be. Adonai, my friends. Adonai vasu borragus.

(Carla channeling)

I Yadda. I greet you in the love and the light of our infinite Creator. We thank your group for calling us to you. We have missed the invitations and are happy to be with you. We not speak long but only a short bit of repartee. We look at conversation which each has had in recent past and we talk to you about the law. We are doing better with our accent, don't you think? Heh!

You are all lawyers, you people! Why are you so in love with laws? Do you think that if you obey all the laws of the land, all the laws of a … we must say another word—church. Do you think that if you obey the laws of your church, you will be a good person or one that is capable of advancing into some knowledge of the truth? My friends, there is no truth in that which is finite, for every law is made to be broken, and indeed laws are usually after the fact so that you have already broken the laws, and that is why the laws were made.

There is something called faith which defeats all laws. It is not in law but in faith that you are able to concentrate upon the business at hand. The business at hand is your spiritual development. The business at hand is seeking. The business at hand is learning. There is not motivation to learn in the law—you simply follow directions. This is a cookbook life, the law; take a little of Law Number One, take two tablespoons of Law Number Two, mix carefully with a batch of Laws Six, Seven and Eight and you will learn?! No, my friends—you will conform. There is a law for you and for you only. But this law is personal, intimate and can only be found as a product of the faith that there is a truth beyond all that you see and hear. Your path is your law. That which you deem correct is correct for you. Please do not think we are encouraging you to go out and manhandle some small child. This would be breaking the law of man but requires no faith whatsoever. So what requires faith, my friends? You do.

You close the cookbook. You shut up the mind and you wait in faith for that meaning and central beingness which will develop within you. Do you think to yourself that you do not have the equipment to have faith? Not so, my friends. You have all that is necessary.

We suggest that in your contemplations you look more and more to that within you which says against all visible and audible experience, "This is truth." We suggest that you continue and continue and again continue, for there is something which we might call grace which aids the heart more and more as seeking continues. With each step taken in faith the next step does not become easier in the sense that your pa …

(Side one of the tape ends.)

(Carla channeling)

I Yadda. We again with this instrument. She keep saying to us, "Do you come in the name of Christ?" We continue through this instrument. Taking one step in faith does not mean that the next step will be easier. However, it does mean that the experience of moving in faith will become something upon which one may count. The process is foreign to the everyday life, thus confidence must be built up little by little.

We thank you for inviting us, and we especially greet the one known as J, and leave you in the love and the light of the infinite Creator. Believe upon yourselves as you believe in the rightness of creation. Believe it will withstand all the deprivations which your peoples perpetrate. I Yadda. I, an imperishable being, leave each of you who are also imperishable beings. We do not leave you in law—we leave you in the process of faith. Adonai. Adonai.

(Jim channeling)

I am L/Leema, and am happy to greet each of you in the love and the light of the one infinite Creator. We have been having difficulty making contact with this instrument for it has been in somewhat of a deeper state of meditation than is its normal practice, and has had some difficulty in picking up our contact and making the necessary adjustment. We are happy to utilize this instrument to attempt to answer those queries which may be present.

May we now begin?

Carla: I have a question. In the Ra material the question was asked by the questioner having to do with what percentage of planets or people who are in the first density, second density and so forth through seventh. And Ra gave the answer that so many people were in first, second, third, fourth and fifth and stopped there and stated that the last part could not be given. Simple addition indicated that that last portion which could not be given was twenty-four percent of the total mind/body/spirit complexes in creation, and Don never followed up on why the information about this remaining number might have been withheld. Could you shed some light on that stricture? My supposition has always had something to do with spiritual gravity and the turning back towards the Creator so it would be difficult to count, but that's only a supposition. Any thoughts?

I am L/Leema. We observe the query and find that there are concepts involved which are difficult to describe. The nature of the journey is one of polarity. The positive and negative portions of the journey have expressions which are … we are having difficulty finding the correct terms. The manifestations of these choices are portions of your current experience. Some are available through the penetration of the outer portion of your illusion as a result of the seeker's own efforts. There is a blending of efforts in a fashion which is almost impossible to describe which occurs at the density of unity, so that the description, for all intents and purposes, is meaningless.

We apologize for the delays and difficulties in utilizing this instrument but find that its level of meditation is somewhat close to the trance level, and it is having some difficulty in maintaining a clear contact not only with our contact but with its own consciousness, shall we say. Therefore we suggest that this instrument be brought from its state and the meditation assume its completion. We are those of L/Leema, and we thank you for your patience. Adonai, my friends. Adonai vasu. ❧

Year 1986

January 5, 1986 to December 20, 1986

Sunday Meditation
January 5, 1986

(Carla channeling)

I am Hatonn, and I greet you in the love and in the light of our infinite Creator. It is a great privilege to be with you, and we thank you for that you have called us. We hope that our poor words have some use for you and encourage you to discriminate carefully so that that which is not of use to you may be dropped away, for though we have more experience than you, our experience is limited and finite. Therefore, we ask that our opinions be considered as fallible, for we are wrong sometimes. We do not know with the authority of the infinite Creator. Indeed, none of us who dwell in the creation and who still have individuality may know all of the infinite Creator, for we are but splinters of the one infinite Creator. Within each of us is all the knowledge which is contained in the one original Thought which is the infinite Creator. And to the extent that we are able to release our small identities with all their biases and opinions, just so to that extent are we holographs for the one original Thought. There are many questions my friends; there is but one answer.

As the seeker gazes down at the dusty road, at the dust that lies upon his feet and covers his sandals, he may well doubt that road and doubt the security and the promise of the journey of seeking. The staff which is intended to aid may become heavy and even those few belongings which the seeker has to carry with him begin to seem a great burden. And so the seeker sometimes removes himself from the dusty path which seems to go on forever. The seeker moves into a beautiful valley, well-watered and forested with pastures where spring the small animals and where the sweet flowers bloom. It is good for the seeker to rest in such a beautiful meadow and smell the beautiful scent of flower and bush and to rest beneath the nurturing and sturdy trunk of one of your trees. Because, you see, my friends, to go upon the journey is to become terribly vulnerable, it is to risk all for no obvious reward, for as you seek, so you shall be sought. As you polarize more and more towards the light, so your dedication to that light shall be challenged. The toll the journey takes upon the seeker is never the same from one seeker to another. And when the burden becomes too heavy, it is good that the individual seeker choose his own pasture and measure his own time of recovery.

It is acceptable and laudable for a seeker who has been overborne by experience not only to rest beneath the tree and smell the sweet smell of the wild flowers but also to fell great trees and dry the wood and build the cabin for shelter, for there is no shame in resting until the burden again becomes as nothing, and seeking fills the soul and mind and the will. It is not, shall we say, recommended that the seeker goad himself as if he were an ox or a mule, for the spiritual path is narrow and straight and the difficulty of walking that path is various for each entity. It is not a path to be walked when the will is not strong.

Let us then go to the cabin and gaze about its simple four walls. How restful and peaceful is the cabin that you build within your spirits, my friends, the household of your discontent and your pain. How healing it is that you have furnished for yourself the possibility of respite and redemption, for this search shall exhaust you not just one time, but many. Experience shall come upon you as a thief breaks into a house at an unexpected time. Yet no matter what the time, the seeker who has walked the path until his feet are dusty shall also have found his very own meadow, his very own place of healing.

There is a danger to the seeker within the resting and the healing, and that is that there is a temptation for a seeker to feel that the cabin and the meadow and pleasantness and rest are the end of the path of seeking. Indeed, we say to you that that which you know as the Kingdom of Heaven is often harsh and abrasive and may seem decisive, for as you continue urging yourself forward and experiencing the great joy of seeking the one original Thought …

We must pause.

(Pause)

I am Hatonn. I am again with this instrument. We apologize for the pause. The instrument is experiencing some pain and the state necessary for the transmission of these thoughts was not sturdy enough for our contact to continue in a clear manner. We shall continue.

As one seeks the one original Thought, there is the danger that one may decide that one has found what he has been seeking, and we say to you that in an infinite journey there are pauses between learning experiences, but never the full stop where one may lie back, rest upon one's laurels and say, "Now—now I understand. Now redemption is complete and all that I seek I have," for there is the next learning always.

We encourage you to comfort yourself when your journey is arduous and you need a place to rest. You have that within you and need only construct it in your mind. You may also with your mind and your will construct within your dwelling the tools for healing and for rebuilding the intensity of your faith that there is a path, that truth does exist, and that there is such a thing as love and the will to seek that which your faith tells you is there.

Although we speak in metaphor, we encourage you who seek to enjoy and praise the comrades that you shall meet along the way, for though each search is different and each soul has its own truth, beyond words and concepts there is the one original Thought which is love, which cannot be defined but which can be praised and shared, not by the words, but by the quality of silence between two seekers, for companionship lies between the words, the sentences, the talking, and the doing. Spiritual companionship lies in the resting that one silence may give to another, for all that there is is caught up in that silence and when another may share it, it is a wonderful thing.

Therefore, my friends, you are always alone and never alone. Always alone in that you are unique and so is your perception of the path of seeking and the truth that you seek. Never alone in that entities both incarnate and discarnate share the intensity of your seeking in their own seeking and are therefore closer to you than many of your thoughts, for silence is more intimate than any word.

We would encourage you to meditate and praise the silence within, for you truly are a holograph of all that is to be known. As you begin to trust the inward silence, as your mind becomes able to release and praise all the thoughts which race through it without holding on to them, you shall become more and more invested with that silence and with the truths which silence unfolds. This is not a short-term proposition, for one of your incarnations is a brief period during which one might do such intensive work. Judge yourself not then if you must pause by the way or even build a hut against the winter of your flagging faith and will. But live through those times, blaming not yourself and not the path, but realizing that this is part of the experience in an outward and manifested state, which, internalized as catalyst, will more and more inform your being. Rest as long as is necessary but do not allow your spirit surcease from silence, for as you wish to serve the Creator, so you must allow that silence which seats experience within the heart.

That is your one responsibility—to continue the seeking even as you are weak and weary and distraught, even as you lie upon your pallet within your hut and feel some blackness within you. Yet always we ask that you consider the possibility of completing each of your days with focused and articulate silence.

My friends, each of you came to this group seeking. The group has become one, and in the silence between the words of this instrument the fruits of that seeking are already available to you and physically felt by you in that the energy or what you may call prana of creative life flows now more quickly within your energy web. As you seek together, so are you the Creator which experiences Itself.

Shall we ask you to praise yourselves? To magnify your own glory? Indeed, that is what we would seem to be suggesting, for we say that you are the Creator. And yet, can the Creator praise the Creator? Yes, indeed, my friends. Such can be done and should be done, for you are all that is and all that is is within you and is to be praised and cherished. We would give thanks to you for that we have shared in your vibrational patterns. It gives us great joy to experience the beauty of each of you. It is especially joyful to us to visit groups such as yours, for we who serve the Creator cannot but rejoice at those sources of light which generate themselves within the planetary mist of indifference. You see, my friends, it is not that your planet is negative—it is that so many still sleep and are indifferent.

We are those of Hatonn, and we would leave this instrument at this time. May joy be yours as you travel your path. May dust cover your feet many times as you walk it, and you may always allow yourself the resting place when experience overwhelms you. You are always safe. But it is good to give yourself permission not only to seek forever forward, but to take your rest when you needs must heal some pain within. We leave you in the creation of love and light, for there is nowhere else but the silence of space and time, which is always and everywhere the present moment. Adonai, my friends. Adonai.

(Carla channeling)

I Yadda. I greet you in the love and in the light of infinite Creator. We have so much trouble with instrument who want us to say we come in the name of Christ. We always end up having to say, "Okay." But we always wonder, why not Buddha? Why not Mohammed? Why not some postman that we know of in Washington DC who is good to his children and gives away many Christmas presents to little children he does not know? All are Christ. All are perfect in consciousness. Yes—we come in the name of Christ, for we are the vibration which cannot be reached without going along the path of the Christ.

We not speak long but we come because we are called and we thank you. We speak to you of "why families?" There is that question in the group this evening.

You know, families sometimes difficult to be in, so why do you have them? Do you have them so you can have people that you like about you? No, my friends—many times people in family not like each other at all. So what is lesson? Why so important that you have those people that are true kin to you?

We say to you, it is to offer you a chance to learn duty and honor, for with family, you cannot say, "You are not family—go away!" No, my friends, you have to take care of each other. It may seem like a ridiculous thing but it is a great learning. If you can feel responsible for each other, then you learn service to each other, not because service is always fun, but because service is freedom. Service is your only freedom, for if you choose not to serve, then you have stopped your progress and are no longer "pohwerizing," *polarizing*—hah! We getting better—heh?!

Think it over, friends. Families are a pain in the neck. So why do you want a sore neck? Maybe to get your attention—heh? We leave you. We are joyful and leave you in "glate" joy for the night is full of light and the shadows are full of light. We Yadda. Adonai.

(Jim channeling)

I am Latwii, and we greet you in that love and light that our brothers and sisters of Yadda have left you in. We are also honored to be here and to be able to share our humble words of praise and thanksgiving with you. As always, it is our honor to attempt to serve by also answering your queries. We also remind you that our words are most fallible. We hope that you will take those which have value and leave those which do not. May we begin by asking for the first query?

C: Yes, Latwii. It still amazes me how something can be on your mind and be mentioned during the course of meditation. But family has been on my mind quite a bit here lately. Something has occurred with my family. Each year I experience a form of depression during the holiday season and usually afterwards I'm not that easy to get along with. But this year the feelings of the holidays were especially deep. It's almost as if I was just sort of numbed out to everything. And now for the first time in a long time my nerves seem like they're smoothing out and things are flowing smooth at this point. Can you enlighten me on what happened this time that's different from the times before?

I am Latwii, and am aware of your query, my brother. It has been noted within your culture that the season which is called your holiday season is one during which many find not the joy which the holidays are noted for but find instead a lack of joy and a sense of depression and despair. This is in general due to the fact that as our brothers and sisters of Yadda have mentioned, the relationships that you know with your family are relationships that exist for the purpose of growth, and growth most often occurs as a result of utilizing catalyst that may be of a difficult nature. Yet, if families can withstand the difficult times there is a strengthening that occurs of the individuals and the bonds between them. However, in your holiday season that is noted for its joy, it is likely that those suffering the difficulties within the family structures are more fully reminded that the joy of the season exists not in their experience, and [as] the joy of the season is advertised widely, the entity so disillusioned becomes constantly reminded that it has fallen short of that which is possible

In your particular situation, we may speak briefly and in general and may suggest that the difficulties that all face have been noted carefully by those within your close family, have been acknowledged openly and have been met with the full responsibility of each, thus there has been little taking for granted that which has been before. To clarify. As the difficulties have been acknowledged, there has been less opportunity to be disillusioned, for the light of truth has shined somewhat more clearly and the ability to respond to what is seen has been activated and each has thus taken strength from …

(Side one of tape ends.)

(Jim channeling)

I am Latwii, and am once again with this instrument. May we ask if we have answered your query sufficiently my brother?

C: Yes, it helps. It's … several years ago I became aware that I'm following along in a line of entities who have been trying to work out the same problem for years and years. I know my father has the same problems I've had and his father also. And just by feelings that I'm able to pick up, I know that A is also part of this line. I know that you can't assume a lesson for someone else, but I sure would like to get this line broken, and I appreciate yours and the help I receive from the other members of the Confederation. I have no question at this time—I just want to say thank you.

I am Latwii, and we thank you, my brother, for the opportunity to share our humble words with you, and would only comment that the difficulties one may encounter in the relationships in one's incarnation are more than one might imagine them to be in that there is contained within such seeming difficulties great opportunities to learn service and to give love, for it is not easy to love within the circumstances where one finds the misunderstandings passed on from person to person. Yet when one can break the chain of misunderstanding and bind all in love and compassion, one has used the opportunity provided by difficulty and has transformed that which lacked love into that which is full of love.

May we attempt any other query at this time?

Carla: Okay, just a little follow up on C's because nobody's jumping in. Is it because that we, our physical bodies, used to be second density and turned to the light for growth, that the dark days, the short days of winter are the most difficult for so many people or is this something that's cultural?

I am Latwii, and am aware of your query, my sister. We find that though there is some degree of correctness within your assumption, it is perhaps more accurate to look at the effect of the season upon your mental and emotional complexes as the root of the difficulties which many of your peoples suffer during the shortened and darkened season of winter. If one will observe the plant world in the time of your winter, the leaves from most trees have fallen, the sap has moved down into roots and there is a dormancy that approximates death in appearance.

There is a similar occurrence within the mind and emotion complexes of most of your population during this winter season in that the elements of nature, the wind, the clouds, the cold, and the snows tend to drive one's focus of consciousness deeper down within one's being in order that the introspective faculties might be awakened more fully to review the harvest of the season of learning just passed. As the harvest is frequently not understood and the seeming difficulties are easily discovered, one then on a most basic level becomes aware that there are those lessons not yet well learned remaining within one's being.

In many instances this awareness of lessons yet to be learned is upon the subconscious level if the entity has in some fashion in some time during its experience consciously ignored or removed the awareness of these lessons yet to be learned because it did not yet wish to face this responsibility. Thus, during the winter season of one's incarnation, the cycles of learning and seeking are enhanced by the driving of one's focus inward. When there is difficulty in meeting the lessons yet to be learned, the state of the mind tends to remain in the depressed condition not having fully processed the catalyst of the previous season, shall we say.

May we answer further, my sister?

Carla: Yes, just something that I thought of while you were talking about how this season mimics death. I was thinking about the fact that we celebrate the holy day or holiday of Christ mass or Christmas in the very darkest, almost precisely the darkest, within four or five days, day of the year. It's almost like the birth of Christ or Christ consciousness is the hope that comes after the little death of winter. And I was wondering whether the historical Jesus just happened on that date or whether it is placed at this point because it is more needed at this point of the year than any other point of the year. If that's the case, then it seems to me that one big problem that people have at this time of the year is that they're not paying any attention to the "holy" part of the holiday, and therefore they don't get the hope of the baby being born within them—there's a question in there somewhere, I think.

I am Latwii, and from the statements and the comments that you have made, we draw that which we feel is the query desired. Please ask again if we are mistaken. The birth of the one known as Jesus the Christ was planned for this season in order to present the symbol of birth and re-birth to those for whom this entity lived and died. The season of your winter is indeed as the small death, and may be again repeated in the meditative state where one looks within for the harvest of one's experience and seeks to find love where love was not. Thus, the experiences within one's incarnation which have seemed devoid of love may be transformed and born again when seen in the crystal-pure light of the Christed or Christened moment, the moment christened with love.

Thus, the one known as Jesus made entry into this illusion at the time of your year when the darkness of the season would represent the darkness of knowing, that is, the fabric of your illusion, and was born as a light unto your world as each may look within to that same light and see all experience within that light so that the love that gives birth to that light may be found in each experience thus christened.

May we answer you further, my sister?

Carla: No, thank you.

I am Latwii, and we thank you, my sister. Is there another query?

M: Latwii, my name is M. Is the Confederation aware of a planetary sphere named Kreeton, K-r-e-e-t-o-n?

I am Latwii, and am aware of your query, my brother. We find that although the query is simple in construction there is some difficulty in giving clear response, for within your people's culture there are various names given to various planetary bodies and we find that this name, Kreeton, is one name that has been used to describe a certain planetary influence of which we have some knowledge.

May we answer further, my brother?

M: Yes, Latwii. Of what density is the planetary sphere Kreeton?

I am Latwii, and feel that we may best answer your query by suggesting that this sphere is one with the activated densities of one through five, with the remaining densities in potential form, shall we say. May we answer further?

M: Yes, Latwii. Can you approximate a time frame in age of this planetary sphere Kreeton?

I am Latwii and am aware of your query, my brother. We find that giving this information in understandable terms is not within the limits of your language. For a planetary entity which has progressed to the point which this one has achieved, it is necessary to move through a great portion of timeless being before entering a great portion of what you would call time. Thus, our answer would be quite meaningless.

May we attempt another query, my brother?

M: No, thank you, Latwii.

I am Latwii, and we thank you, my brother. Is there another query?

M: Latwii, is the planetary Kreeton of a thought-form nature?

I am Latwii, and am aware of your query, my brother. We must respond by suggesting that it is of the same form of manifestation as are the planets within your own solar system. However, one must realize that all forms, be they planets or atoms, are a form of thought, the thought of the one infinite Creator. The use of the phrase, "thought-form" as we believe you intend it is more of the briefer duration, that created by a mass consciousness or the consciousness of individuals such as yourselves, and in this instance we would suggest that this planet is not of the briefer duration but of the more substantial manifestation.

May we answer further, my brother?

M: Latwii, approximately how far is the planetary sphere Kreeton in distance from the planetary sphere Earth?

I am Latwii, and am aware of your query, my brother. We find a difficulty in giving this information, for once again the means of measurement are most difficult to translate. The general means of describing distance among your scientific community would be the light-year or the distance that light would travel in one of your years. This distance is somewhat difficult to approximate and transmit through this instrument, for our contact is not of the precise nature that would allow an easy translation. The distance is roughly two hundred and forty thousand light years. We believe this is correct, however we are not adept at using your numerical system.

May we answer further, my brother?

M: No. Thank you so very, very much.

I am Latwii, and we thank you once again, my brother. Is there another query?

(Pause)

I am Latwii, and as it seems that we have exhausted the queries for this evening, we shall thank each profusely for offering not only the call for our presence, but the queries for our service. We hope that we have been of some small aid in the seeking for truth that each has brought this evening as the great gift. We shall be with each upon request in meditation in order to aid the deepening of that state. We leave this group at this time in the love and in the light of the one infinite Creator. We are those of Latwii. Adonai my friends. Adonai vasu borragus.

(Carla channeling)

I am Nona, and we come to offer our healing love and light. We would offer it for the entity known as R, and also for the far less serious but still significant discomfort of the one known as M. We also would be offering our presence to the one known as C and the one known as M because these entities have vibrational patterns which are very compatible with our contact. We bid you adieu in love and light.

(Vocal healing melody channeled through Carla.)

L/L Research is a subsidiary of Rock Creek Research & Development Laboratories, Inc.

P.O. Box 5195
Louisville, KY 40255-0195

L/L Research

www.llresearch.org

Rock Creek is a non-profit corporation dedicated to discovering and sharing information which may aid in the spiritual evolution of humankind.

ABOUT THE CONTENTS OF THIS TRANSCRIPT: This telepathic channeling has been taken from transcriptions of the weekly study and meditation meetings of the Rock Creek Research & Development Laboratories and L/L Research. It is offered in the hope that it may be useful to you. As the Confederation entities always make a point of saying, please use your discrimination and judgment in assessing this material. If something rings true to you, fine. If something does not resonate, please leave it behind, for neither we nor those of the Confederation would wish to be a stumbling block for any.

CAVEAT: This transcript is being published by L/L Research in a not yet final form. It has, however, been edited and any obvious errors have been corrected. When it is in a final form, this caveat will be removed.

© 2009 L/L Research

Sunday Meditation
January 12, 1986

(Carla channeling)

I am *(sounds like)* Ku-ohl[1]. We greet you in the love and in the light of the one infinite Creator. We are most gratified that we were able to make contact with this group through this instrument. We are those of the Confederation of Planets in the Service of the Infinite Creator and attempt to serve at this present, coming from the density this instrument calls wisdom or five. We wish to assert that we are eager to use this instrument and speak to this assemblage but that our thoughts are not to be taken as dogma but only as possible material for thought, as we intend to be accurate in our perceptions yet still we are in the process of learning and acquiring further densities that bring us ever closer to unity with the One Who Is All.

As we scan the energy webs about each of you, we find we are moved to speak this—we scan this instrument for an appropriate word—evening of service. You will have to be patient with us, as we have seldom worked in this manner with entities upon your planet. We shall begin.

Service to others is not an end product of meditation itself. Therefore, let us work with the concepts of what the darkness of meditation is. You may see yourselves as a mixture of earth—that is the vehicle and all of its elements—and water, not only that water which is the largest portion of your physical vehicle but also with the metaphysical waters of the deeper mind. When the seeker first decides to set his foot upon the path of finding out what is true, the seeker invites the great seed of consciousnesses, or should we say, levels of consciousness, and this water in turn vivifies and recreates the entity which is seeking. Therefore you are, metaphysically speaking, in darkness, and it is within this darkness that you seek knowledge of love, of light, and of unity.

Consider the earth that lies outside of your dwelling. There is water vapor always in the air about the earth. Deep rivers flow underneath the mantle of earth and spring forth often in unexpected places. When rains come upon the earth, the earth drinks thirstily, and so it is with the seeker. Much of understanding, if we may use this term, comes from the process of seeking within the darkness of inner vision and within the environment of water. This is seeking unmanifested. The only light which is visible metaphysically speaking to the seeker is paralleled by the light of the night sky, the stars, and the reflected light of the your planetary satellite. Metaphysically speaking, that star is called hope or faith. It is not a light which ameliorates the darkness but it is a

---
[1] The sound, "Ku-ohl," that was channeled resolved in subsequent sessions into the name of "Q'uo," which will be used throughout this transcript.

signal, a sign if you will, that light there is and light abundant.

This seeking is a matter of marshaling one's own will and focusing in a disciplined matter upon the seeking for truth, upon the finding of light. However, within this complex of seeking, there is no outward manifestation promised, no fruits must be born from such seeking. This is seeking unmanifested. There is a bridge between the darkness of hope, faith and will and the noonday sun of manifested service. That bridge is the surrender of the very will which the seeker has been marshaling and focusing, for in the attempt to be of service to others lies the implicit seeds of failure to be of service to others. The harder the seeker attempts to be of service, the less chance that seeker has of being led by inspiration to right service, that is, service that leads toward harmony and the feeling of kinship and unity with the one served.

It may seem a paradox that in order to manifest the glory and the joy which one has found in the darkness of inner silence, one must then give up all human opinion concerning situations, behaviors, activities and personalities to whom you wish to be serving. Yet it is surely true, and the full light of day dawns as the seeker sincerely and completely yields itself to grace, if we may use that term. Some call it quested consciousness, others call it right karma or destiny, but all of these words have connotations that suggest the lack of freedom of will and this we do not wish to suggest. You are perfectly free, each of you seekers, at all times to make each choice in each moment in each way that you wish. Yet to polarize involves manifested service.

We wish to convey also that we are not suggesting that there is a force completely outside of the seeker to whom one must yield control. The Creator is far closer than this—indeed the daylight is within the heart of the darkness. The difficulty is that words cause paradox and the deeper the understanding, the more plentiful the paradoxes.

Therefore, to sum. The seeker must begin seeking in darkness, and yet when the seeker comes from his sanctified ground and wishes to give glory back to the Creator which appears to the seeker in the guise of other entities, then it is that the seeker yields his conscious will, yields it utterly and completely to a higher knowledge, a higher wisdom, a higher compassion, and a higher intuition. One who has yielded and is moving in rhythm with the deep winds that play about the innermost self becomes touched with radiance, a radiance that is completely positive, a radiance that is the analog of your sun body, and in the radiance lies manifested service.

Therefore, worry not about how to serve. Instead, be disciplined as the earth and water within you become more and more articulated and the star of hope becomes ever more central in your inner sky. And when the moment comes for you to move from meditation to action, yield yourself again and again as thoughts come to you of service to that great fiery strength and surety that is the property of higher will.

Understand that this is a portion of yourself and that you are a portion of it but that it can be made available to your conscious self only by surrendering all hope of understanding and equally all fear of understanding, yielding further all hope of being of service and all fear lest you act wrongly.

My friends, we hope that we have been of some service to you this evening. We must leave this instrument, for we find that we have not sufficiently adjusted our vibrations to this instrument's somewhat delicate body complex. We thank you and praise the present moment that we share in the love and in the light of the One.

We are called Q'uo. This instrument does have but a portion of the name we are attempting to transmit, however the naming is never important. We come to you as one who accepts the challenge of Christ as this instrument has challenged us, so we gratefully say, "Yea." Dwell therefore in love and know that you are loved. Dwell in light and know that you shall be a light, and in that knowing, surrender. Adonai vasu borragus.

(Jim channeling)

I am Latwii, and we are overjoyed to be able to greet you, my friends, in that love and light of our one Creator. We thank you, as always, for inviting our presence. We are so happy to join you and hope that our humble service will provide some additional food for thought. We also have no dogma but only our gathered opinions to share with you. These we do so freely. May we then begin our service by asking if we may attempt to answer a query?

N: Latwii, can you tell me about the illness, schizophrenia?

I am Latwii, and am aware of your query, my brother. As with most cases of the mental imbalance, the condition of which you speak is one which, though having generally shared characteristics among those suffering its difficulties, is also one which contains the latitude for individual expression, shall we say.

To speak to the generalities, the entity suffering the schism or the division of the personality is frequently one which has faced a difficulty in a conscious fashion for a portion of time and has found that difficulty to be seemingly overwhelming. Therefore, as the entity continues to attempt to rectify the difficulty and finds less and less success but also more and more difficulty, it may be that this entity then will attempt to remove the difficulty by removing the portion of the memory which has dealt or attempted to deal with this difficulty whether it be with self or other selves.

After a portion of time, this sublimation or repression of memory concerning the difficulty surfaces again, for the entity in its deeper awareness is aware that this situation is yet unresolved. Therefore, there is gathered about the difficulty and the portion of the mind which has become responsible for it an energy field which attracts to this portion of the mind various traits or characteristics which then seem to become yet another personality. As many of these characteristics are, shall we say, borrowed or drawn from the primary personality of the waking consciousness, this personality also becomes somewhat disfigured or dysfunctional, for it no longer has a unified or coherent view through which the world and self are seen.

Thus, in such a breaking up of the personality there is the attempt to rectify a deeply felt difficulty which then is most usually noted by those about this entity in a—we scan for the correct word—clear and unmistakable fashion. Then the necessary counseling is usually necessary in order to aid such an entity in the rebuilding of the conscious personality.

May we answer further, my brother?

N: So it can be helped by counseling? And also you said a portion of the mind?

I am Latwii. Our reference to a portion of the mind was our attempt to indicate that when a difficulty for such a person has become overwhelming, one means of dealing with the difficulty is to move the difficulty and memory of it to another deeper portion of the mind—what may be called the upper reaches of the subconscious mind—in order that the conscious mind then be free of the constant stress and worry that has most likely developed in the one experiencing the difficulty without solution. The type of counseling or therapy which may aid this situation is again somewhat unique and various to each entity. However, it is usually most necessary that another entity who is familiar with this condition be utilized in the reintegration of the mind of the one suffering the, as it is called, schizophrenic condition.

May we answer further, my brother?

N: You said the upper conscious. Does this have anything to do with past lives?

I am Latwii. The cause is not easily determined, for it is again quite unique among the population of those experiencing this disorder. In some cases it is possible that the difficulty has its roots in previous incarnations and these roots then have by preincarnative choice been placed within the current incarnation with the hope that the lesson might be learned. The lesson may also be one which is of the current incarnation only, shall we say, realizing that all experience that all gathers about one is the result of previous lessons and desires.

May we answer further, my brother?

N: No. Thank you. That sure is scary.

I am Latwii, and we thank you for the opportunity to serve and can only add a note of comfort to suggest that all such difficulties may find their resolution at any time within an entity's experience when there is the desire to give and receive love by the entity in some portion of its being. At some point this balance of giving and receiving love shall be achieved in order that the balance of the mind might also be achieved.

Is there another query?

Carla: In my Christian belief system, there is the biblical statement that one is never given more than one can bear. That seems to be contraindicated by problems such as schizophrenia and suicide. Is this just another spiritual paradox or is the biblical statement untrue?

I am Latwii, and am aware of your query, my sister. Indeed there is the paradox, for each entity has the ability to carry those weights, shall we say, which are intended to produce a greater strength and therefore the ability to carry yet greater weights, if we may use this rude analogy.

The weights or lessons may take may forms. An entity may determine that within the upcoming, shall we say, incarnation there shall be a concerted effort to learn a lesson long past due, shall we say. Under these circumstances the lesson may be presented in an intense manner with the hope that the intensity of presentation will grasp the attention of the conscious mind and move it finally to the focus upon the lesson which will produce the desired fruits.

However, it may be that an entity, for one reason or another, refuses to utilize the talents and abilities that are indeed at its command. When one refuses for any reason to use those abilities that are within one's scope of being, then it is that such an intensity of learning may seem a weight too heavy to bear and the entity may be, shall we say, forced by its own reluctance to resort to what seems to be extreme measures of coping with the problem that it has devised for itself.

In the extreme case the entity may choose to stop its efforts during the incarnation by what you call the suicide. It may be that the entity stops short of this extreme response and takes, shall we say, somewhat of a breather and enters into the realms of the mental disjunction in order that the test that it has devised for itself may be put off, shall we say. There are lessons also in this area which await the entity so choosing. There are lessons in each area, for lessons cannot be escaped—they may be ignored for a time and may be dealt with in any …

(Side one of tape ends.)

(Jim channeling)

I am Latwii, and am again with this instrument. To complete our query. The lessons shall eventually be faced in way or another, in one incarnation or another. The means and time are of the choosing of the entity that has also chosen the lessons.

May we answer further, my sister?

Carla: I have heard it said—this is another question, not along the same lines. I have heard it said that schizophrenics have a tremendous creative power. This has been observed by various sober scientists. What's the source of this creative power?

I am Latwii, and am aware of your query, my sister. As we mentioned in our previous response to this topic, there is the relegation of a portion of the memory and the difficulty being faced to a portion of the subconscious mind with the hope that the problem, if moved deeply enough into the subconscious, will no longer trouble the conscious mind. However, with the schizophrenic individual this is not what occurs. The deeper awareness of the entity returns to the conscious mind that which was sent to the subconscious mind with somewhat of an aid, shall we say, presented to the conscious mind. That aid may be seen in general terms as some form of a channel or contact with the deeper portions of the mind reaching into the subconscious mind. This allows the conscious portion of the mind access to the more creative or imaginative portions of the deeper mind with the hope that this channel will allow the entity to find a, shall we say, creative solution to the problem which has overwhelmed the conscious mind.

Before this solution is achieved it is often the case that the creative nature of the subconscious mind is expressed in many other fashions. To those who are aware both of the physical, physiological and metaphysical nature of such a situation, these creative expressions are indications of the resources that have been made available to the conscious mind by the entity's deeper mind.

May we answer further, my sister?

Carla: No, thank you.

I am Latwii, and we thank you, as always, my sister. Is there another query?

Carla: I don't know how to put this so you could answer it … Let me try. The idea of community, a community that shares a common goal and common ideals, has been part of this group in its thoughts for some time. And in the last few months the coincidences of people writing us, calling us, or speaking to us about the feeling that now is the time to get on with community have just really piled up. And when the instrument and I were talking about the idea of community today, we got, if you count all of them through the day, three hawks and two silver flecks, which is the most array of spiritual coincidence I guess you'd say that we've seen in a long time. These are normally taken by us to indicate that we're talking about something that we should be paying attention to, that what we're talking about has some value. Could you comment in general on community as a way of service to others?

I am Latwii, and am aware of your query, my sister. We find that we may not speak in any specific fashion to this group, for there are confusions yet aplenty and must remain in the formative state, shall we say. It is well known by each present that the communion of seekers is the process in which each partakes. As this process of seeking and joining the wills of many in the seeking continues, it is of a self-generating nature, that is to say, that the seeking of each then is enhanced as is the ability of each to be of service to the other and to other selves that lie beyond the grouping of the community. Thus is the nature of any joining of minds and beings for any purpose. The being which is produced by the unified joining of efforts is one which is much greater than the sum of all those so joining. Thus is the seeking of the One and the serving of the One enhanced.

May we answer further, my sister?

Carla: What is the single greatest difficulty—spiritually speaking, not monetarily, we're aware of that—facing those who would wish to pursue the idea of community?

I am Latwii, and am aware of your query, my sister. We are not sure that we can pinpoint the, as you have called it, single greatest difficulty facing entities with the desire for community but can suggest that the inability to receive communication is a difficulty which is necessary for each in such a community to balance. Otherwise the communication is overbalanced in the giving as compared to the receiving. This is the result of the hardened position which is quite happy to spread its structures, and is not as happy to reform its structures.

May we answer further, my sister.

Carla: No. I'm familiar with resistance to change—it seems to be a part of everyone's life, in community or out. Thank you.

I am Latwii, and we thank you, my sister. Is there another query?

Carla: Are you familiar with the entity that I could get as "Q'uo," and if you are could you share with this instrument what the actual name might be or is it a transmission problem, regardless?

I am Latwii, and we are familiar with our brothers and sisters who have made contact this evening for the first time with this group. We are not able to utilize this instrument's mind for the transmission of the complete name as you would call it due to the limitations not only of this instrument's mind but of the type of contact which we are utilizing. The telepathic contact is one which is greatly limited to the mental familiarity, shall we say, of the one serving as instrument with the concepts in general and the language to be used specifically. Thus, if there is too great a quality of foreignness in either concept or word used to convey the concept to the mind of the instrument, then there is a kind of wall which cannot be penetrated by this type of contact. We apologize for being unable to move beyond this limitation.

May we attempt any other query, my sister?

Carla: No, thank you.

I am Latwii. May we attempt another query of any kind?

(Pause)

I am Latwii, and we find that we have exhausted the queries for this evening from this group, and we are overjoyed to have been able to speak a few words with each of you this evening. We thank you, as always, for the honor of blending our vibrations with your own, and we hope that you will take that which has value and leave that which has none. We leave you upon the winds of your winter season as they blow about the seeming barrenness of your environment, promising that there shall be warmer winds to follow as the seasons of experience move one after the other in the progression towards the one Creator. Adonai, my friends. Adonai. We are those of Latwii.

(Carla channeling)

I, Yadda, greet you in love and light of infinite Creator. We almost not get in this time because we have continuing difficulty with the challenging in name of name, that is, in name Jesus rather than in vibration of Christ or Christ consciousness. This instrument hard-headed on this point. However, we wished to give thanks to this instrument, as always, for the challenging and appreciate it even though it is pain in neck.

We wish to say greetings to the one known as J who call us at this time, and we only leave the thought with you that the naming is important and is not important. Is important to name those things which are precious because a name can be equal to the essential vibration of that which is dear. Naming unimportant because all names become trickier. Consider that you start out on your past meeting and say names to each other. Ah, but if man and woman like each other, soon they stop the name and make up the pet name and the nickname and the affectionate name. There go the so-called real name never to be seen again in the relationship possibly.

The essence of a thing is that which is its vibration. So, name important if it vibrates truly as you name yourself, feel your own vibrational system and know that that essence is your name and will be until the creation has coalesced and all become One.

We use name now to say farewell. We Yadda—but you can call us sweetheart. We leave you in love and light of the unnamed infinite Creator. May you vibrate with this allness and find joy therein. Adonai, my friends. Adonai.

L/L Research

Sunday Meditation
January 19, 1986

(Jim channeling)

I am Hatonn, and am privileged to greet each of you this evening in the love and in the light of our infinite Creator. We are most happy to be with you this evening, and offer our services in a joint effort in seeking the One who resides behind all mysteries of being. We thank you for inviting our presence this evening, and thank you doubly so for inviting the opportunity to exercise both instruments in the telling of a story. We delight in the sharing of our humble opinion by means of the story, for in such a manner may we point a direction with less chance of seeming dogmatic upon any point, for with the story comes the opportunity for each individual to interpret the story in an unique fashion, a fashion which shall have the most meaning and impact to that entity and to each so listening.

We would begin by suggesting to this instrument that as it attempts to regain the ability to speak without a beginning focus or query, it release from its mind all preconceptions as to what should be said, and thus emptied, speak those concepts which move through its awareness. It is as though in one sense this instrument were beginning for the first time to learn to talk. This is not so, but the rustiness, shall we say, needs the oil. We shall begin.

There was once a young man who was … we pause.

(Pause)

I am Hatonn, and we apologize for the delay which was requested by this instrument as it heard the sound which suggested to it that perhaps this small group would be joined by another. We shall continue. There was a young man who with some small experience in its life pattern, determined that while it was young in years and strong of body, it would make a journey out to the world about it and seek its fortune, for it observed in the small community in which it had been raised that life was ever the same, moving at the slow and steady pace, the cycles of days and seasons repeating one after the other with predictable movement. And this, though providing for a secure upbringing and grounding in certain ethics of work and devotion, was not sufficient to cause this young man to desire to remain within the repetitious cycles from which it was spawned.

Thus, the world that was unknown and the tales of this outer world that had come to this young man seemed a great attraction and promised to the yearning spirit within the adventures and the opportunity that would allow the young man to find its freedom and its purpose within the life. Thus, it left its community of friends and family, bade each a heartfelt farewell and with but few possessions for the road struck out upon that road with hopes of adventure and promise.

We shall transfer.

(Carla channeling)

The sun rose; the sun set; the sun rose again. The young man drove down roads large and small. He refrained from using the map, for his concept of freedom suggested no reliance on any plan, but rather the desire to be lead by the spirit of freedom. Days without number followed. Towns flashed by, forests, hills and plains. Finally, the lad fetched up at the shore of a great port. A great ship was hiring and the young man signed on board and they steamed off, he and a large crew and the cargo, bound for places with exotic names, faraway places that tasted and smelled of adventure.

We shall transfer.

(Jim channeling)

After but a short period of time, the young man had experienced the pleasures and the pains of the daily existence on the steamer and had accumulated experience within a handful of ports of call and had tasted of the unique flavor of each. As the days upon the ship continued to multiply and one port after another had been reached and investigated, the young man felt yet another yearning, for it was apparent to his adventurous nature that life upon the ship, though offering far greater excitement than the village within which he had been raised, was itself beginning to become somewhat repetitious. And the young man yearned to explore in depth one of the more exotic of the ports and to see what the citizenry and surrounding countryside of such a place might have to offer a young man such as he.

Thus, after deciding to make yet another journey, the young man did so and set out at the next port of call upon a journey which seemed most thrilling, for the land in which he found himself was one far different from any he had seen before. With the ocean at their feet, the mountains of this land rose majestically and their tops were circled with clouds that drifted down into valleys rich and lush with life and peopled with inhabitants that were most interesting and curious to this young man.

We shall transfer.

(Carla channeling)

The nut brown people of this land welcomed him, not as one would welcome a stranger, for in this land there was no concept of that word. He moved freely between settlements and sat at the feet of many men he considered wise and women whom he considered full of vision. He felt that he had never before been challenged, never before been sounded to the depths, for in this land there was no concept of philosophy except all of life. There was the concept that all things were holy and there was the most unexpected respect and manifestation of this ideal in the lives of those who dwelt in this lush land.

No longer in any vehicle, unbuffered from the winds of change, he weathered the elements and walked through valleys thick with fog, the fog curling and rising about him in wisps so that the sun shone golden and brilliant, refracted in a million tiny sparks. Within the gloom in the mist there revealed shadow trees—then, as he approached them, he could see the sturdy dignity of each tree. He felt enveloped by the nacreous glowing mist and each turn in his path showed him another glory. He puzzled over this, for had he not seen trees and fog and light in his own birthplace?

We shall transfer.

(Jim channeling)

He thought to himself that these experiences were not new, yet their effect upon him indeed was new, for now, for the first time in his young life, he began to ponder the meaning of the cycles and seasons that produced such simple miracles as trees, mountains and weather. Here in this far distant land, people moved according to a rhythm not unlike that which he had left in his home. They shared a dignity of being and purpose of life that was also not new to him. Yet whereas those friends and family which he had left seemed somewhat boring to such a young and energetic man in their regularity and predictability, the people of this land exhibited much the same qualities, it seemed, as the trees, to spark within this young man's heart and mind a response that was new to the young man. The response spoke of a center to seasons and cycles that went beyond the outer repetition of the daily round of activities and beyond even the seasonal reappearance of harvests, festivals and community affairs.

The young man wondered why he should travel so far and see things that in many ways were far removed and much more exotic than that which he had left in his home yet which upon close examination seemed so like his home, friends and family. And why here in this distant land did he now for the first time begin to notice the center of things, people, thoughts?

We shall transfer.

(Carla channeling)

It appeared to him that he must learn the language of this place more carefully and examine more carefully why this place had resonance for him, resonances that were missed and [he] could not find in places familiar and exotic.

At the next village he stopped the first person he saw. It was a young woman with glossy black hair and beautiful, glowing brown skin. Of a sudden he spoke to her, saying, "Can you tell me what it is that you know?" She smiled at him, her sloe eyes dancing, her lips quivering with suppressed mirth. "I do not know what you mean, my beloved brother," she said. "Wait a minute—wait a minute," said the man. "Why am I your beloved brother? I have not seen you—I have not spoken to you before in all my life." This was greeted with open laughter. "Are you not holy?" she asked. "Do you not need the water of life, of conversation, of communion?" "Yes, I do—I do," stammered the young man, "and I receive that here. But why?"

The young girl put down what she was carrying and went to the well close at hand. She carefully pumped him a cupful of water. "What do you see?" she said. He gazed at her. "Water," he said. She said quickly, "What sort of water?" He replied, "Water—mere water. Only water—in a cup. What would you have me say?"

We shall transfer.

(Jim channeling)

The young girl simply replied, "I would have you speak of that which you see, for to one the water in this cup may be mere water, good for quenching the thirst of the moment, and to another the water may be symbol of that which is greater than any moment and of that which gives birth to each moment, for within the water of life do we all not move and have our being? And does not the water that nourishes our physical bodies represent in a symbolical form the breath of life, the refreshing waters of spirit if you will, which are at the heart of all being?"

The young man thought upon these words and replied to the young woman that he had never looked at things like that before, that to him life was quite simple. "Water is water. A cup is a cup. A road is a road. And what I learn is what I experience."

The young woman replied, "If that is so, why have you come so far to do this simple thing which could have been done at any place that you found yourself? Indeed, one would never have to leave one's home for such experiences as those of which you speak."

Again, the young man thought. And he replied to the young woman, "But it seemed to me that there must be more than such a simple existence somewhere in this world. And if it did not exist in my home, then I would go and find it. And I thought perhaps I had found it here. Mayhaps I have. Yet now it seems to me that I have come a long distance in order to do a simple thing. Can you tell me why it is that seeing beyond the surface of things is easier for me here than it was for me at home? I do not understand."

The young girl replied, "The journey of seeking upon which you have set yourself is one which may take a good deal of time during which you may move from one place to another many times. Yet at some point, no matter where you find yourself, you will begin to look more deeply into your surroundings and eventually into your own desires for accumulating surroundings. In this way is your gaze sent outward to the world about you and then reflected back to you to the world within you.

"For you see, you seek not that which is other than yourself or far distant from yourself, but that which is within yourself. The world about you will help you in this journey by showing you that beyond the surface of appearance which beats at the heart of all creation. When you learn, as you have begun, to look beyond seasons and cycles and sameness and see what lies within these "things" of the world, you will find your quest lies not in things or places or people, no matter how far distant, exotic or interesting, but lies instead within your heart of hearts, for there, my brother, will you find the answers to your questions of why you live and how you do it.

"The world about you will show you what you are ready to see. The world within you will show you what is at the heart of all that which exists about you. And this, my brother, goes by many names, for each who seeks the answers to such riddles travels a journey much as you have traveled, yet accumulates a peculiar way of viewing the journey and the fruits thereof, and calls these fruits by familiar names.

Having made a portion of this journey myself and having recognized in you the qualities of the pilgrim, I share with you my name for that quality, and it is love that beats with a rhythm known to any heart and with a purpose of being known to every heart, yet veiled enough to require from each heart a desire to know more than the surface of things reveals."

The young man stood somewhat dumbfounded, yet aware also in his confusion that he had been touched by words and feelings from this young maid that made a kind of sense to him that quite exceeded description. And he determined at that point that he would return to the land of his youth and continue there the seeking which there had begun. And upon his return it was his pleasant discovery that the feeling of newness which he had obtained in distant lands remained with him, for now his eyes looked upon a new world, one no longer bounded by the surface of things and one which opened in promise in any direction that he gazed of providing a deeper taste of the rhythm and life inherent in all creation.

I am Hatonn. We are pleased to have been able to utilize both instruments this evening and most especially to have been able to use this instrument in a fashion to which it has grown unaccustomed. It has been helpful for this instrument to, shall we say, penetrate beyond the surface of its own abilities and find more treasures within. We feel that this instrument has grasped the greater portion of that which we wished to convoy, yet has in some degree omitted portions here and there that might have increased the richness and depth of illustration. We can only suggest that it would be helpful for this instrument to continue such, shall we say, undirected experiments in channeling.

We shall close this contact through the one known as Carla. We transfer.

(Carla channeling)

We share at this time some nuances of the tale so that the one known as Jim may grasp possibilities which may be experienced and shared with perseverance in this practice which we encourage and are most grateful for.

There is a land which is blessed as are its people with a sense of that which is holy. It is a land of mists and rivers, ocean and mystery-shrouded mountains. It is a land where feet touch earth, sole to soul. It is a bare-foot land, a touched land, a land loving and loved. It is a land which may be dreamed and from that dreaming a man may rise, awake for the first time to look beyond the dream of sameness. For is not every moment new? Is not every breath a new beginning and every out-breath the ending of what was?

Cycles there are, yet they are not the same, one upon another, any more than it is possible for one leaf to be like another or one snowflake to be identical to another. Once a dream has been given by grace, there is new vision of the spirals of infinite possibility. To be in touch with this vast infinity of possibility is to be in touch with the creative power of love. The young man may become an old man and die—die to his body and die to his personality, and yet remain awake in infinity, experiencing the water of forever and the joy of newness.

Thus, the story ends in foreverness, the story which is new, the message which is always the same yet ever spoken afresh. Love and love and love. We spoke three moments the same word and yet each ear heard three separate moments, each moment not a repetition but a new beginning. Breathe in the new, then, breathe out the old, and find joy in the newness of that which seems the same to those who sleep. See, taste, touch, hear and love that which is holy and know you then that you are in love with the universe and all that lies within it.

This we offer humbly through this instrument in order to encourage the one known as Jim to feel free to meander patiently and with perseverance while listening to the inner voice, for there is that within that instrument which is most eloquent. We encourage, as we have said, these workings and we thank the one known as Jim for opening himself to us in this manner. With a heart full of love for each, love made new each moment, and in the light of foreverness, we leave you. We are those of Hatonn. Are we ancient or are we new? We are—as are you. May you be blessed. Adonai vasu borragus. ☙

Sunday Meditation
January 26, 1986

(Jim channeling)

I am Hatonn, and greet this group in love and light. We are honored to be asked to join this group once again. It is through efforts such as this that our contact with the older instruments, shall we say, is strengthened and given new opportunities to develop in those areas which yet await the development.

We thank each present this evening for calling for our presence and humble words to aid in the seeking of those who have awakened to the need for seeking. This evening we are quite happy to agree upon the format and will speak a small story through each instrument. As always, we remind this instrument that it may speak as it feels the concepts moving into the mind without the fear of the break in contact, for the type of channeling which is now being experienced is somewhat at variance with what this instrument has become accustomed to. The answering of questions, or more precisely, the channeling of the answers to queries, when undertaken over a long portion of time to the near exclusion of this type of contact, tends to give somewhat of a false security to one such as this instrument, for it can be imagined by such an instrument that the channeling of answers to queries is a kind of channeling which can more easily be created by the subconscious, for it is frequently the case that this instrument feels a source of information within it exists for whatever query is presented. However, in this type of contact, this instrument has no idea of the concepts which shall be transmitted through its instrument, and must once again, as in the beginning of its experience with vocal channeling, open the mind and relax the analysis in order that the contact may proceed in a smooth fashion.

We have taken some extra time this evening to describe the process which this instrument has undergone in its channeling experience in order to enable it to gain somewhat in the confidence that this kind of contact can indeed succeed. We shall now begin this story.

Once, as most stories begin, there was a young woman who was quite sure of herself and of her abilities, for many had praised both her and her abilities throughout her young and developing years. She was able to converse easily with not only peers but with her elders upon subjects of a wide-ranging variety. She was one easily able to solve the new and unique problems of her immediate surroundings, the management of her personal affairs, her business affairs, and was one who found an easy comfort in the friends and social intercourse of friends and strangers.

This young woman, in the terms of her day, had success at her feet. Her efforts were easily rewarded.

The efforts were of the kind which one would expect the young and successful woman to take part in. The development of this young woman's mind was rapid and moved quickly from those areas of social acceptance and career successes to the more abstract in which the young woman began to question herself in her quiet moments as to why her life had seemed to unfold with such ease and comfort, for she observed many around her who struggled for but a fraction of what this young woman was able to reap in each area of her existence.

We shall transfer.

(Pause)

(Carla channeling)

I am Hatonn. We apologize for the delay. This instrument was attempting to be fastidious concerning the tuning and the challenging of spirits. This was especially difficult for this instrument at this time as there was a target of opportunity offered when the instrument received the message, "I am Ra." The instrument was pleased at the contact and at the same time requested that this entity leave, for it was forbidden that this instrument would channel that particular social memory complex without adequate protection. The contact was a negative contact pretending to be that which it was not. However, it took some of your time for this instrument to remove the unwanted entity and to open itself once again for our contact.

We would take this opportunity to offer our opinion that no matter how long it takes to be satisfied within one's mind as to the tuning and the nature of the contact, it is the most important part of the contact for the instrument, for those who have these words then made available to them may have words which can be trusted. If the initial work is not done, there is no trustworthiness in the contact and the integrity of the light source which [the] group represents is undermined increasingly with each failure to be patient with the tuning and the challenging of spirits as this entity and its cultures calls those of us who, though persons, are not human but dwell in other bodies and other time/spaces and with, shall we say, alternate modes of thinking and expression.

We shall continue with the story.

"It is not acceptable to me," said the young woman, "that there should be such disparity betwixt my good fortune and others' ill luck. Who am I to have been born under such a fortunate star? And how can I dispense justice where no justice is possible, for were I to change places with a poorer, less advantaged person, yet still I would learn and I would once again be fortunate, for it is within me to work and to learn. And yet these traits will not talk to me, thus it is not a virtue but a mere trick of nature that I am who I am."

These thoughts made the woman feel lonely and full of sadness. Lonely, for she had no teacher, for those who attempted to teach her did not move as quickly as she, thus she became the teacher and the teacher the pupil. "What a tragedy," thought she, "and how unfair that one is given opportunity upon opportunity, and yet to another that little which has been given seems to vanish."

We shall transfer.

(Jim channeling)

The young woman pondered for some time this unwelcome state of affairs. She wished within her own heart that there was some way that she could aid those she saw about her who were seeming to struggle for what came so easily to her, and in her experience it was soon apparent that what had been given to her seemed in a relative fashion to be greater than that which those about her enjoyed. Yet as she continued her own personal inquiry into the nature of her life and the lives of others, there were from time to time new thoughts and resources that came within her reach, bringing with them the possibility of the further refinement of those gifts which were hers. Soon she came to …

I am Hatonn. We apologize for the delay. This instrument is somewhat concerned that it has lost the thread of thought—and indeed it has.

Jim: I'm going to quit, Carla—it isn't working well.

Carla: Shall I just take it then? Are you in a good enough state to continue meditating?

Jim: Yes.

Carla: Okay.

(Carla channeling)

I am Hatonn. We are with this instrument, and although we may seem to dally, commenting overly as we tell this story, it is of necessity in our opinion that we thank the instrument known as Jim, for this contact has been threatened by those entities which would if they could desire to reduce this group's productivity or to pollute the messages promulgated. The instrument known as Jim has the integrity to recognize and state clearly the limits of his ability, and we may say that under difficult circumstances this entity was able to make some strides in improving confidence and clarity, two necessary prerequisites to helpful channeling.

We shall continue through this instrument with a story which may seem to have wandered a bit. However, the story is as an arrow, seeming to arc a bit, but coming to its target nevertheless.

Soon the young woman was granted the wish she did not know she had. Another young woman of a different creed and color was brought in to the company for which she worked. They both held the same office, and as high-ranking executives were called upon to function at a very high rate of competency. The black woman had qualities which the young woman recognized as being those qualities which she did lack. It was the first experience that she had had in being able to depend upon another upon an equal basis for the exchange of information. And so she carried to her friend and co-worker her ponderings about the unfairness of life, about her great good fortune and all the power she had and about others' lack of good fortune and lack of power within this illusion.

Her friend gazed at her long, smiling very slightly. "Girl," she said, "you are working so hard to pat yourself upon the back within the illusion that you have forgotten what power really is." "What do you mean?" asked the young woman. "Do you think power is equal to money? To position? To great intelligence?"

"Why, yes," replied the young woman. "That is the way the world measures power and that is why the world is so unfair."

"Now sit down," said her friend, "for I want to talk to you about power. What do you think of me?"

The young woman looked puzzled. "You are my friend and I trust you."

"Last week," said her friend, "I cut in front of another car when I was driving to work. I did not damage my car, but I did not stop to see if there was any damage to the other person's car. What do you think of that?"

The young woman pondered briefly and said, "That sort of thing happens all the time. I suppose I would have been tempted as you to move on since the damage was so slight."

"Then do you forgive me?" said the black woman.

"Do I forgive you?" said the young woman. "If you need to be forgiven, then, yes, I forgive you."

"Aha," said her friend. "Now you are exercising power. Do you forgive those who kill and are put in prison? Would you set them free today?"

"No, I wouldn't," said the young woman. "The streets would not be safe."

"Ah," said her friend, "You have not forgiven. And so, no matter what the fate and destiny of those who dwell within prisons not of their own making, they are bound in chains by your power, for if you do not forgive, then there shall be no forgiveness."

"I don't buy that," said the young woman. "What can my opinion be worth?"

Her friend smiled *(inaudible)*. "The hardness of your heart or its softness or compassion are all in all. There is no power for justice that is greater than your opinion which you hold within the silence of your own mind or heart. As you open your heart, so you exhibit power for that which is beautiful and good. As you harden your heart to beauty and sanctity of all that is alive, so your denial becomes law, binding those whom you would bind. Yours is the ultimate power—yours and mine and all peoples.

Dwelling upon your great good fortune will get you nowhere, literally, my friend, for you see that when you accept the illusion and look upon your life experience as a game in which one may win or lose, you then become imprisoned by that which is not. You are not fortunate because you have worked in many lifetimes before this one—you are distinctly unfortunate in that you have not yet grasped that which you planned that in this incarnation you would accomplish to increase the light upon this planet and to share compassion with all those radiant ones about you who, like you, shut themselves up in the darkness of intelligence and stupidity, winning and losing, and all the dualities by which men judge things fair when they have not gone within to find that which is."

For the first time in this young woman's life, she had fetched up against an idea that was almost impossible to fathom. "I am going to need some time to understand what you are saying," she said. "But you know, it rings clear to me that what you are saying has merit. There is fairness—the fairness must come from me within the privacy of my heart—is that what you are saying?"

Her friend smiled again, eyes twinkling merrily. "Do not forget," she said, "that within the illusion there are things which you have accumulated far beyond your need. Even within the illusion, radiancy of compassion may manifest itself by physical giving. I ask you only," she continued, "that it is within the heart that compassion resides and not within any action. It is only within the illusion that like actions are accepted as similar."

My friends, each of you is a being waiting and watching for a time when you may be acceptable so that grace may come to you and you may be the radiant and compassionate being that you seek to be. We encourage you to find inspiration before your attempt to manifest, for manifestations which come from one's sense of duty or from outrage at the injustice and unfairness which are apparent in that experience will be unable to share that which makes others joyful, the reason being that without the compassion and the joy within the heart, there is only a mechanical transfer of illusory objects from person to person.

It is easy to feel that some among your peoples have all the advantages and others almost none. It is well to remember that the fortune of each individual is illusory. Some who seem most fortunate had what you would call karmic situations in which they must face the seeming responsibilities and duties of this good fortune and face them not mechanically but from the heart. There are similarly many, many of your peoples seemingly born and living and with expectations of dying with almost no advantages who are working upon lessons of love which demand apparent adversity, for the shining of light in the darkness that is the building up of faith is a lesson of love in which the will is strengthened and the advantage which is so priceless spiritually and which is then chosen by the individual is that there is no false pride to overcome. Many are those seemingly poor who are untroubled by pride and therefore are untroubled by the illusion and whose faith and will move and move and move again ever closer to the goal of seeking the source of love and light which is the one unmanifest Creator whose mystery is shared by all.

We ask you to reconsider, if you need to, your good fortune. Use the intelligence which seeming good fortune may have given you to list that which is of the illusion and then find for the self that which is not of this illusion. And as your heart warms and becomes soft, radiant and giving, as you forgive, as you give up yourself, so shall your seeking produce great fruit.

(Side one of tape ends.)

(Carla channeling)

For love which is unmanifest does not have to be guarded or governed. The channels through which love may wind are everywhere. The only governance needed is the choice of the direction your eyes of compassion shall turn. And as all beings are one being, and as all beings are the Creator, unmanifest love made manifest through any means is love offered to the Creator.

May the reality of your good fortune shine upon you, and may you seek it with all that is within you. And if you are disheartened, we ask you to remember that you too are the Creator and you too must be the object of your forgiveness. You too are slave to yourself until you free yourself. You too are poor until you give yourself the coin of unbridled compassion. Rejoice and shout in the joy that is freedom, the true freedom of unmanifest love and of manifest service. You are in the Kingdom of Heaven within your heart, and yet you stride a planet and have the opportunity to manifest the giving, the forgiving, the freeing, and the spending of ineffable and infinite love.

We are most grateful to have been able to work intensively with the one known as Jim and to be able to speak through each instrument. We thank you that your desire to serve continues and we wish to affirm the spoken thought by the one known as Jim that fidelity of a perceived service, when lit by the compassion of the heart, is the cornerstone upon which all services and polarizations depend.

We leave you as we arrived, in the love and in the light of our infinite Creator. Go your way in peace. We are known to you as Hatonn. Our hearts touch yours in joy. Adonai, my friends. Adonai vasu borragus.

(Carla channels a healing melody.)

I am Nona. We greet and leave you in the love and light of the One Who Is All. Adonai. Adonai. ☥

Sunday Meditation
February 2, 1986

(Carla channeling)

I am Monka. We greet you in the love and in the light of the one infinite Creator. It is long since we have been called to your group, and we are full of gratitude that we are able to speak and share our being and our thoughts with you as brother to brother and sister to sister. We are one being and therefore words are clumsy, yet we shall use them as best we can. May we say that we appreciate this instrument's challenging of us. This instrument doubted that we were indeed Monka, for this instrument has heard tapes in which the contact was quite garbled. However, after three challengings, the circle of trust was completed between we who speak and she through whom we speak. The fastidiousness of this challenging tunes the contact more finely and clarity of channeling is far more possible.

It is our specialty within the Confederation to share our humble opinions upon the subject of those issues concerned with community and social responsibilities. Our planetary population had in your density and in the fourth density a very strong desire for harmony and thusly we became what has been called a social memory complex in late third density, which is the density and the period within that density which you now share.

There are many questions upon your mind at this time about not just the correct way to live, for this in itself has almost no meaning, as correctness is different for each individual, but rather the most spiritually propitious way to join in community and to relate to each others within a society. We can give you some guidelines, however we ask, as do all members of the Confederation, that you remember that we are fallible, that this contact is fallible, and that it is your responsibility to use the intellect and the power of discrimination, the gifts of an infinitely kind Creator, to distinguish that which you need from that which you do not need. Anything which you hear from any source whatsoever which is not helpful to you should be laid aside; perhaps you shall come back to it in the future and it shall make sense. Perhaps it is simply erroneous. In any event, there is a rhythm within each life, and within those tides of being information will come in a regularized manner. Trust the rhythms of information and of your own discernment.

The question of community is an extension of this suggestion. It is of primary importance that the deeper rhythms be acknowledged within those who have found companionship with each other. It is not chance or accident when two people meet and recognize each other. When this occurs it is not to be doubted—it is also not to be abused. Thus, the first hallmark of successful sharing of experience in community is that each, while acknowledging the deep currents which brought each together with each, shall also be aware of—even militantly aware of—the individual currents and rhythms which may express themselves as crosscurrents within a community or even as contrary tides at times. Freedom is the hallmark of successful community— freedom to be yourself, freedom of each to be himself and freedom to experiment, to make mistakes, to be at risk and to grow.

Upon other occasions through other channels we have spoken of that life which we enjoyed in fourth density. There was a need at the time at which we spoke for people to consider specific topics such as education, the use of money, and so forth. We do not find such concerns within this group's seeking for a sense of true community, and for this we are grateful, for topics such as we have just mentioned are the outward and visible signs of an inward and spiritual gift. It is the inward and spiritual gift that concerns each: how does one give of oneself freely and in joy, without diminishing the self and without diminishing those other selves over whom we may have undue influence?

That is a great concern and it is for this reason that we counsel the exaggerated respect for each freedom in spiritual seeking. May we say that which is obvious so that it shall not be left out when one is working with a group of people. It goes almost without saying that each shall attempt to be honest, forthright and of service to others. Since we understand that each of you has accepted this, we do no more than mention it.

We would ask you to consider, then, the deeper reasons for community. Events cause a message to be given both metaphysically and physically. The coming together of entities in order to form spiritual community is an event, and the manifestation that it shall have is caught up in the event itself. The event causes a message; the message is heard by those whom you do not know and can never know, and this message in turn allows transformation among others. Thus, we suggest to you that before joining together in community the overriding goals be grasped in a unified manner so that each, while unique, shares the goal with each other in the community.

Our second observation is this. Great ideas without the addition of perseverance, the sense of humor, the light touch, shall cause each self to draw upon the human, if we may use that term, resources. Even the use of words causes variation betwixt people so that understanding cannot be shared fully. If each brings a light and forms a community of lights, those lights together form a great light, a city of light, if you will, in the metaphysical sense. And yet if you expect to sustain that light by intellectual practice or by dependence upon logic alone, the light will lose its luster, it will dim and the darkness will overcome it. Thus, we suggest that the common goal never be taken for granted, but that some form or ritual for the remembrance of that goal and the surrender to that goal be at the very heart of community.

Community begins with one entity. This may be difficult to perceive at first. But each entity to whom we speak has had many and diverse incarnational experiences and each who grasps these ideas is therefore a digest or an amalgamation of many and sometimes conflicting experiential preferences, ideas, opinions and goals. Therefore, the first spiritually oriented community is you yourself. It is easiest in this context to see how easily the spiritual integrity may be shattered, the light may be dimmed and then put out because of dependence upon intellectual analysis alone without the contact with that infinite source of intelligence which is love and which is available from within in the silence of the heart. Community then springs forth in full flower with two, and many are the words that are spent in accomplishing clarity of understanding and the harmonizing of two unique entities into one community with common goals and with the desire to surrender the self to the higher self so that those goals which have been prepared for you to seek may be sought in peace and with efficacy.

Each of you has considered what it would be to surrender to a group larger than what this instrument would call the nuclear family. It is no different than the harmonizing of the self with the self, the harmonizing of one self with another self. However, it is, as entities are added to the community, both more and more important and more and more frustrating to communicate as clearly as possible and to come into harmony rather than agreement forced upon one by a majority while pursuing the common goal.

We would like to emphasize that while there is great potential for happiness as you call it, or joy, and for companionship in community, these states of the emotion and mind are transient and the pursuit of them in or out of community shall result in disappointment as the moments of joy depart. We suggest to you, therefore, the possible wisdom of surprising yourself by appreciating the joys that occur without attempting to retain that state of mind and emotion, for these swings in emotion are of the surface, for in happiness one is still oneself and even in human joy, if we may use that term again, the importance of this state of mind is that of the stone which causes ripples to pass in their circular, outward gyration. Happiness is with you and then gone. To expect community to supply one with happiness is unrealistic due to the nature of that emotion. We are not saying that happiness is to be scorned—it is to be savored. But to cling to one happiness is to lose another, as if laughing too long at one jest, one may fail to hear the next cause for laughter.

Rather, we suggest the discipline in community of whatever size of the regular sharing of two things most of all. The food and drink which is symbolic of so many other necessary foods—for the soul, for the mind and for the heart and of the coming together in meditation, in thankfulness and in praise for that which is, which has been and which will be always the same. In that is joy and the heavens are full of this joy. A large portion of your creation has never left that primal joy and dwells in infinite joy. May you be one. May you be one, my children—and may you love each other, serve each other and cause your events to serve as a message that will aid others who are seeking their own ways.

We are aware that there is much that we have left unsaid and are willing to take questions. However, we cannot use this instrument for this purpose. We therefore would attempt to make contact with another instrument in order that questions may be taken, not simply on community, of course, for there may be other concerns which you may wish to share at this time. We leave this instrument and are grateful for this instrument's willingness to challenge us, to accept us, and to serve as channel for us. We transfer now. We are Monka.

(Jim channeling)

I am Monka, and greet you again through this instrument in love and light. We thank this instrument for accepting our contact and would continue our efforts to be of service by asking if we might answer any queries which those present may have upon the mind at this time?

Carla: Just for purposes of identification, are you fifth density and did you work many years ago with a channel named Richard Miller?

I am Monka, and our level of seeking is that which is of light and is numbered five, as you noted. We have for a significant portion of your time attempted to contact various groups and channels within groups in order to provide our service. We were those who spoke through the one known as Richard in an attempt to provide information which was congruent with the call by that group and our ability to serve.

May we respond further, my sister?

Carla: Yes. In those channelings which I have listened to that were made in the fifties, you went rather systematically through how to bring up children, the use of barter instead of money, the nature of rapid transit in a more fully articulated technology, and so forth. In other words, you were describing not just a spiritual community within a planetary sphere, but an entire society. We do not wish to remold our society … I'll just speak for myself. I do not wish to remold our entire society, but rather to mold my life according to the highest spiritual plan which was intended. Is this difference or distinction an important point?

I am Monka. That which is sought is indeed that of importance, for as one seeks one shall find. To those who seek in a certain manner is brought the closest approximation possible from those that offer themselves in service. Thus, our experience in previous contacts with your peoples was one which sought to provide what we could within our range of abilities and to integrate this with what was sought by those whom we hoped to serve. Thus, we now find that our ability to be of service to this group is determined by the nature of seeking that we find within this group. Our services therefore will be of a different nature, relatively speaking, than previously were our services, and we appreciate the opportunity to offer what we have found in our experience in the fashion which the seeking of this group allows.

May we speak further, my sister?

Carla: Yes. I've wanted to ask this question for years. I know from the Richard Miller tapes that Monka is a social memory complex of Mars in the fifth density, although I don't think the Miller tapes said that—they did say that you were of Mars. And so you must have been in fifth density when the third density of Mars destroyed its own environment. What part could you play in that drama of your planetary sphere of third density, which you probably had some feelings about? What were you able to do, or was it simply something that you watched without emotional feeling of any kind, waiting to be of help, but not asked? I guess what I'm really asking, I want to clarify, is are you still sentimental about being of Mars, even though you've gone on?

I am Monka, and we find this query is one which is based upon somewhat of a misperception. This misperception dates back to the original contact that we made with the group previously mentioned in that when our identity was sought we attempted to give an approximation of the nature of our being. This nature is one which is closely associated with the, shall we say, guardianship of the influence of the planet known to your peoples as Mars. In your rituals of the …

(Side one of tape ends.)

(Jim channeling)

I am Monka, and we greet each again in love and light. In those traditions of your white magical rituals there is the influence of the planet Mars, as you call it, that is seen to have a part to play, shall we say. That part has been, for a great span of time, our part, for each portion of the creation is guided by many influences which serve much as do the parents within your own people's cultures. Thus, when speaking to the group in your previous times with which we first made contact, we attempted to identify ourselves in the manner of our role as guardians of the planetary influence known to you as Mars.

We attempted in that role to be of what service was possible as the population of that planet moved into its third-density experience, and through that third-density experience began to express the bellicose nature that was eventually to render that sphere uninhabitable by a third-density population, as you are aware. It was not our proper role to save that population from the tribulations that it chose for its experience but was instead to offer ourselves in whatever manner was congruent with the call for service of that planetary population. Thus, we guided where possible and sent light where possible and healed those wounds that we were asked to heal.

We are with this planet that is your home at this time because there are many from the planetary influence of Mars who now reside within this planet's influence and who now seek the ways of love with you upon your sphere.

May we speak further, my sister?

Carla: I hate to keep dogging the questions and answers, but what's your relationship, if any, to the entities of the vibration Yod-he-va-heh or Jehovah or Yahweh?

I am Monka, and our relationship is that of brothers and sisters within the Confederation of Planets in the Service of the One Infinite Creator. We have worked closely with these entities for a great span of what you call time, most especially in the transfer of souls from the influence you call Mars to the influence that is this planet's.

May we answer further?

Carla: One last thing and then I'll shut up. A very capable woman who has been in community for twelve years wrote a letter to Jim and me that we got this week, and she said from her experience that the three biggest problems in community were money, sex and children. Would you care to comment on that in any way …

L: *(Sotto voce)* Life.

Carla: … or just leave it—it doesn't matter.

I am Monka, and we would agree with the one known as L that these areas are those most frequently utilized by your peoples to generate opportunities for what you would call the spiritual advancement, for within these three areas, the identification of the individual self is given the opportunity to either learn the love and acceptance of those about it or to gather for the self as much protection from and control over other selves as possible. Thus, it is natural that when entities would seek to join each with the other in a closer relationship that those areas would be primary for growth potential.

May we answer further, my sister?

Carla: No, thank you.

I am Monka. May we ask for further queries?

L: How is the instrument doing?

I am Monka, and we find that this instrument is doing well with the type of contact that we have established, that being somewhat deliberate, and we find that this instrument can accommodate several more of your queries if that is acceptable to you.

L: You took the opportunity a moment ago to correct a misconception. Are there any other misconceptions you'd like the opportunity to correct, and, if so, would you trot 'em out now so we can get it straight for a change?

I am Monka, and though the invitation is most gracious and we warmly accept it and appreciate such an opportunity, we find that our service is most appropriately rendered by attempting to answer those queries which each may present to us, thus signifying that which is of importance in your own process of seeking. Our identity, for example, being that which was associated with the planetary influence of Mars, was not, in our humble opinion, a significant misperception, for it approached that which was in our view appropriate. All information which we shall share will approach that which is true. We remind each that we do not view ourselves as being infallible, thus we shall leave to each of you the determination of that which is important to you to query upon.

L: It's my understanding from the subject matter you covered earlier, that your—I was going to say "appearance" for lack of a better term—here tonight is partly the result of a desire within this group to develop themselves into a community. Would you give us—whatever you possibly can—your perspective on what our communal desires in that direction consist of?

I am Monka. If we perceive correctly the query that you have asked, we have been asked to describe the call which we have perceived from this group. We have observed within this group what might be termed a seed. It is one which has within its husk the desire to join with those of like mind, as you would say, and similar means of seeking the truth in order that these qualities might be enhanced, for each within the group is aware that the combined efforts of many can produce far more opportunities for individual growth and service to others than can the efforts of one or two. Thus, the desire has arisen and with those expressing such desire has created the call which we observed and are attempting to answer.

May we speak further, my brother?

L: I have no further questions. I thank you for your time and patience.

I am Monka. We thank you as well, my brother. May we attempt further queries?

S: Yes, Monka. I am studying a religious philosophy called Nichiren Vedaism [Buddhism] founded in Japan seven hundred years ago by a man named Nichiren Daishonin. His philosophy was a chant that we use called "Nam-myoho-renge-kyo," simply meaning "Everyone without exception has the potential to be a Buddha and life is eternal[2]." What I would like to know, my question is simply, can "Nam-myoho-renge-kyo," the chanting of "Nam-myoho-renge-kyo," open the gateway to intelligent infinity in the third-density experience?

I am Monka, and will attempt response to your query, my brother. There are more factors present than would at first glance seem apparent in the repetition of the chant of which you speak. Its specific wording is perhaps of least importance, though significant. The wording itself is that which the will of the seeker focuses the attention upon. When this focus of attention is one-pointed, as it is called, for longer and longer periods of time, the inner meaning or direction of the words becomes seated within the seeker's being, becoming then a resource upon which the seeker may call in any life experience.

It is the experience of the daily round of activities in an unified and balanced fashion that provides the seeker the increasing opportunity of unity with all creation or the contact with intelligent infinity, as you have called it. Thus, the chant itself is that which serves as catalyst or that which points the

---

[2] After sixteen years of studying the sutras, Nichiren Daishonin declared that the Lotus Sutra contains the ultimate Buddhist teaching: namely, that everyone without exception has the potential to be a Buddha and that life is eternal. Further, the essence of these teachings is contained within the sutra's title. As he says in one of his letters:

"Included within the word Japan is all that is within the country's sixty-six provinces: all of the people and animals, the rice paddies and other fields, those of high and low status, the nobles and the commoners, the seven kinds of gems and all the other treasures. Similarly, included within the title, Nam-myoho-renge-kyo, is the entire sutra consisting of all eight volumes, twenty-eight chapters and 69,384 characters without exception … Everything has its essential point and the heart of the Lotus Sutra is its title, Nam-myoho-renge-kyo." (*The Major Writings of Nichiren Daishonin*, Vol. 1, p.222.)

direction for the seeker. The mere repetition of such a chant is much like the push-up. It focuses the attention for the moment, yet the true value of such an exercise is the seating within the seeker's being of the concept to which the chant points and the providing of the seeker thereby with the means of manifesting this concept in each facet of its life experience.

May we speak further, my brother?

S: No, thank you very, very much.

I am Monka, and we thank you, my brother. May we attempt further queries?

Carla: Just a quick follow up. I've always been curious about whether certain words or sounds have a vibration which is unrelated to the person speaking the sound or whether the vibration of the sound is only energized by love?

I am Monka, and would respond by suggesting that both are true, for there are indeed certain vibrations of sound that are powerful of themselves. There are also entities who may speak any sound and imbue that sound with love and thereby give that sound power. There are also entities who may misuse, shall we say, any vibration of sound and degrade it to the point that it is robbed to a large degree of whatever power it may have contained.

May we speak further, my sister?

Carla: No, thank you.

I am Monka, and we thank you once again, my sister. We find that we may attempt another query or two through this instrument before it is too fatigued for the clear transmission of our thoughts.

(Pause)

I am Monka. We appreciate the concern that each has for the comfort of this instrument and would take this opportunity to thank each also for being of that nature that has allowed us to speak with you. We are happy to be able to give voice to our thoughts as a service to those with whom we walk the path of seeking. We shall join you again upon your request. Until that time, we shall join you in silence in the Allness of the One. We are known to you as Monka, and we leave you now in love and in light. Adonai, my friends. Peace and blessings.

(Carla channeling)

I am Nona, and greet you in the love and in the light of the Creator. We ask your patience as we vibrate for the healing of the one known as B. This entity is soon to dwell within the form-maker body and the angelic hosts are awaiting this entity with great joy. We are also called for the one known as J and the one known as G. We thank you for your patience as we know this has been a somewhat long meeting. We cease speaking through this instrument and leave you in love and in light. We are Nona.

(Carla channels a healing melody from Nona.)

L/L Research

L/L Research is a subsidiary of Rock Creek Research & Development Laboratories, Inc.

P.O. Box 5195
Louisville, KY 40255-0195

www.llresearch.org

Rock Creek is a non-profit corporation dedicated to discovering and sharing information which may aid in the spiritual evolution of humankind.

ABOUT THE CONTENTS OF THIS TRANSCRIPT: This telepathic channeling has been taken from transcriptions of the weekly study and meditation meetings of the Rock Creek Research & Development Laboratories and L/L Research. It is offered in the hope that it may be useful to you. As the Confederation entities always make a point of saying, please use your discrimination and judgment in assessing this material. If something rings true to you, fine. If something does not resonate, please leave it behind, for neither we nor those of the Confederation would wish to be a stumbling block for any.

CAVEAT: This transcript is being published by L/L Research in a not yet final form. It has, however, been edited and any obvious errors have been corrected. When it is in a final form, this caveat will be removed.

© 2009 L/L Research

Sunday Meditation
February 9, 1986

(Carla channeling)

I am Q'uo. I greet you in the love and in the light of our infinite Creator. It is a privilege to be allowed to share our thoughts with you at this time and we thank you and bless you with all our hearts. We wish to reassure especially the one known as C that our brothers and sisters of Hatonn are overshadowing this contact in order to aid this instrument especially in deepening the state of meditation to the appropriate level for our contact which is somewhat more narrow band, as you might call it than some. Because of this there will be the energy of Hatonn present in the room, and we trust each may use that vibration to aid in the clarity of meditation achieved by each.

We would speak with you this evening upon love. It will not seem at first as if we are talking about love, for what we wish to do is gaze with a clear eye at what many among your peoples call phenomena. The more obvious of these phenomena are those so-called occult arts of astrology, Tarot, and those who work within the trance state in inner level work as opposed to the work with those influences which are external to your planetary sphere.

We would not wish to discredit either the art itself or its reality, if we may use that term within an illusion. The energies or vibrations, much like waves upon a pond, which emanate from your whirling spheres, especially those relatively close to you, as you whirl about upon your island home, enter the planetary energy web at certain points which may be calculated by those with the bent and the time for such calculation. Further, these instreaming energies affect each entity upon the planet in an unique fashion. Therefore, there is validity in prophecy by astrology, nor would we wish to deny any other form of prophecy of a personal nature which an entity may find helpful.

However, we would like to examine the situation where one gives information and another receives it. The one giving information is doing so in one of several ways. By this we mean that it is not necessarily a sign of spiritual advancement, as this instrument would say, that one is able to use some means such as astrology or cards to tune in to the planetary energy web's emanations as they impinge upon an entity. It is rather an indication that such an entity as you may call psychic has in its past incarnations worked in these areas. One would not consider, for instance, a world-class pianist to be spiritually advanced, although the depth of emotions which such an artist may offer his audience may be a spiritual experience far too deep for words. Such transcendent talents are the result of more than one incarnation spent in the development of that particular characteristic.

"Phenomena" is another way of saying "things." It would be a poor argument indeed to debate the possibility that spiritual advancement is aided by things. We speak to you thusly because we are concerned to notice that there is within the community of those who seek the emphasis on knowledge of the near future, knowledge of one's past before birth—in other words, knowledge of things. The spiritual stance cannot depend upon any thing. It is, we feel, natural and comfortable that one with the talent for some sort of phenomenon to share it with those who request it. In this way such an entity is being of service to the best of his ability. But to live one's life as a seeker, dependence upon any thing outside the self is to have denied the self the greatest opportunity for learning that there is, and that is the untutored and unbiased circumstance. In other words, we suggest that it is one's instantaneous reaction or action to or in the face of circumstances wherein the great opportunity for spiritual evolution lies.

Let us look then not from the standpoint of the one who receives prophecy but one who generates it. Each within this room has generated spiritual material for the use of other seekers. Each therefore has accomplished a phenomenon known as channeling. We do not need to tell each of you that this in no way distinguishes any channel as one spiritually advanced because of its skill at being a channel.

Let us go further, now that we have considered both the one who receives prophecy and the one who generates it, and consider the things, the phenomena of the illusion in which you dwell. This instrument has spent a significant portion of its intellectual concern during the past twenty-four hours, your day, considering how much it desires to do a thing that will brand it as one who cares. This instrument has considered that it would be a valuable thing to do. That which this instrument wishes to do is to walk for the cause of peace for many of your months, and we say to this instrument and to all who feel that the great quest is best taken as a literal journey that neither this nor any other thing will necessarily make an entity progress spiritually or be in any way more polarized towards service to others or service to self.

To be more extreme, one may consider those who give all that they have to the poor, thus becoming poor. One may consider an entity who makes a great sacrifice in order that it may advance spiritually. The phenomena of your experience revolve about such insubstantial words as power, glory, money and so forth and because seekers dwell within a physical illusion of this certain type in which outer things are seen, a fruit is seen, but the originator or planter or cultivator are not. It is not surprising that entities wish to do things to both express and encourage spirituality.

We say to you that you must turn from the outside manifestations that meet your senses, turn from your own opinion of yourself, your own judgment of the fruits of your spiritual labors, and from any and all prophecy having to do with your probable future, and instead join the great darkness of the sea of mystery which surrounds and expresses the gateway to the spiritual progress. You cannot see or hear or feel or taste or smell anything in this darkness. You are, shall we say, without feedback as you progress upon a path that is narrow because it is only the span of footsteps—there are no things to carry. Why do you think the spiritual path is so narrow? If it needed to be wider it would be. It is your metaphysical feet touching the very stuff of spiritual reality that walk the path of the seeker. There is no luggage, there is no rest and there is no turning back. And so you walk on in darkness, each of you berating yourselves many times for your lack of spirituality.

How you people love phenomena. But within the darkness that is complete lies your heart, beating without sound, gleaning that light as you intensify and intensify your seeking to the point at which your inner beating heart is manifested as the star of hope, the beacon of faith. Can you then see? You can see the star. At that point that is all that you can see. It does not shed light upon your path but by your own seeking you have planted that which is no thing, but which is a symbol of light, the light that shall shine until there is no darkness, the light that is without time and without space. Footstep after footstep you walk on, lighted by a dim but very real star, a star kindled within your heart and within no other. Walk on in majesty, walk on in humility, walk on in trust, for you are not alone in this darkness, you are not alone upon this path and you are not beguiled or mistaken in seeking light. When you reach past the phenomena to touch your own heart, it is then that you have placed your feet upon the path.

Without this heart, all actions are without spiritual reality, all fruits are withered in the merciless glare of the spiritual sun. You see, the fruit does not become the plant which becomes the seed which is then sown. That is not the way of growth. And yet your peoples so often consider their spiritual path in just such a reverse manner, first looking at the fruits, wondering how to arrange them by asking for phenomena and working backwards to the heart that sows the seed.

What a treasure your hearts are when they love. I beg you to love. It does not matter that you do not love perfectly according to your own judgment, it does not matter that you do not love all the time. It matters that you see your inner state of love as the cornerstone of your existence, your seeking and your destiny, for this universe is one thing and one thing only—it is love, the creative love—the one original Thought is love. It is within your heart that this love is reproduced so that you become creative also.

And when you are creator, what shall you create? Do not be concerned, for you have planned, each of you, what your service shall be. And you have been given grace sufficient to enable you to do what you have planned. What thing is it that you shall do? Many are those who feel that they are of no spiritual worth because all that they do is work, love their children, and die. And yet we say to you that you may well have prepared this as your mission, as your lesson, as your offering of love. There are those who have come with larger missions, larger in the sense that more entities will hear of the fruits of their particular labors. This in no way distinguishes one love from another, one fruit from another. Insofar as each fruit or manifestation takes part in love, just so each fruit is equal, for unbounded love and limitless light are all that there is. And whether you extend love and light upon your little ones or upon some more dramatic object, you have loved—and love is all that there is.

We appeal to you to meditate without judgment of yourself or others, to accept phenomena as they enter your life, to use them, to be alert for them, for it is well to receive the many hints that you will give yourself concerning that which you are to be doing, that which you have planned for yourself to do. We earnestly implore you to grasp that this channeling is also a phenomenon, that our words are things. We cannot prove our love to you nor can we say it, and you must realize that our words are nothing but shadows flitting across the inside of your mind. They may be without worth for you and if so we ask you to discard them, to shrug them away and to move on. Our love for you is part of our spiritual path. Your love shall be yours.

May all that is true and beautiful in your mind and in your heart be of blessing to you. May you dream, may you seek, may you love and may you know that you are not alone. The sensation of the air touching the ears of this instrument is remarkable to us. The heartbeat, the dilation of the veins—this is all new to us. We are enjoying the experience of sharing this instrument's body.

Because we have had to move rather deeply into meditation with this instrument to use it, we shall continue speaking of what we sense through this instrument until we are certain that this instrument is at a good state of conscious awareness of the illusion. We find this instrument's mouth to be dry. We are experiencing a very noisy environment within the body and we find variations of surface temperature across the lower portions of this entity's physical vehicle. The energy is not apparent to this instrument as it breathes. It does not breathe deeply enough. It is capable of a great deal more of the deep breathing and it would be helpful for clearing out many impurities for this entity to practice such.

We believe we are now able to leave this instrument. It is reluctantly that we do so, for we speak rarely with your peoples. We thank this group for being of a nature which calls to us. We send our love to you and we leave you in that love and light which is the infinite Creator. We are those of Q'uo. Adonai.

(Jim channeling)

I am Latwii, and am very glad to be able to greet this group in love and light and to speak our few humble words of inspiration and the joy of being. We, as always, offer ourselves in an attempt to join with you in your seeking by attempting to answer queries which may have arisen as you seek. May we now begin that service with the first query?

Carla: I have a question that I've been pondering; I haven't figured anything out about it yet. It seems that some changes hit you over the head with a hammer and there's no getting away from the changes, there's no thinking about it—it's just something that has changed. It seems that other changes are completely within our conscious control.

How can one determine when one has thought about a change to the point where it's best to leave it alone?

I am Latwii, and if we have understood your query, we shall attempt response. For those who seek in a conscious fashion the steps to be taken upon the path, there are …

(Side one of tape ends.)

(Jim channeling)

I am Latwii, and we are once again with this instrument. To continue. For the entity who has consciously begun the journey of seeking there are points upon this journey at which time the placement of the foot is indicated by a sign, shall we say. This sign is that which is of the unconscious, shall we say. The greater being that each is and which has put the particle of itself which you call a person into the illusion which is your daily life then at various points may direct and indicate the most appropriate journey or step within a journey for the conscious seeker. This is in response to the seeker's desire to know. For as it has been written in your holy works, as one seeks, so shall one find, for the universe in which we each move and have our being is made of one thing—that is love, and by one entity—that is the Creator.

As the small self which is seeks, then, that which is sought is a greater portion of that which seeks. There is for each, then, guidance which may be sought with benefit in the seeking. The seeker at some point in its journey will find that the aids or indications thusly received may take on a more and more subtle nature in some cases. This is in order that the entity's own discriminating faculty of free will might be further enhanced. Thus, if one has for a great portion of its incarnation been used to receiving the, shall we say, two-by-four between the eyes as obvious markers along the path, it may be that less and less force is required to guide the entity, and the entity may well be better advised to look within its own being for that still small voice which when consulted gives the answers that are most appropriate for that entity at that time.

We apologize for a somewhat deliberate and involved response to your query, my sister, but we are attempting to work with this instrument in a somewhat variant fashion from the more conceptual techniques which we have employed in the past, as you call it.

May we answer further, my sister?

Carla: Well, I will give you specific information and see if you can add anything to what you've already said, realizing that it is often true that one can't get anything from us, specific questions, but I'll risk it because I'm really puzzling this one out. What you have said is very clear and it isn't convoluted at all as far as I'm concerned, in talking about making spiritual choices and hearing the hints and everything for yourself. In this situation there are two of us, myself and Jim, who have been talking about the possibility of forming a community for some years. For some reason, we have been talking about it far more intensely lately. The decision is a weighty one, is a heavy one in that it's sort of like buying a car or buying a home or having a child—you can only do it once or twice in a lifetime—you can't start something and then run away, at least not if you're Jim or me.

So what I see in Jim is that he is desirous of change but at the same time is of such a nature that the loss of solitude which even the most carefully run community would involve, could be a real life-threatening thing for him. In other words, we both feel the impulse towards change, and I am deeply questioning whether this is the right change because I am concerned for Jim. Neither of us knows whether to drop the thing for now or to go on thinking and talking about it. Sometimes we feel one way, sometimes we feel another. It's this situation that I'm trying to address. Can you be of any more assistance than you were to the general question?

I am Latwii, and am aware of your query, my sister, as we were aware of it with the more general form previously asked. We find that we may speak in general only and this is well for each must retain the full use of the free will in such matters. As one wishes to do that which is most appropriate within the incarnation in regards to being of service and to learning those lessons that are one's pattern, it is well to balance the great desire to accomplish these two goals with a lightness and lack of concern in order that one remain open to the influence of the creation about one, for it is sometimes the case with the over-serious seeker that it will try so hard to be diligent and correct in its movements and thoughts that it will develop a type of tunnel vision that is overly focused upon a matter to such a degree that the spontaneity and wide-ranging viewpoint suffer. These lighter and—we search for a word—more carefree characteristics are those which play an important role in aiding an entity's movement of intuition, for when one becomes overly dedicated to any particular thought or action, one then closes off certain helpful avenues of assistance that are open to those of the more balanced nature.

May we answer further, my sister?

Carla: No, thank you.

I am Latwii, and we thank you, my sister. We would ask if there might be another query.

Carla: Well, since you're about to close, I'll just throw this one in as an oddball question. The word "Belgium" has been rolling around in my head for the last few hours, and I wondered if you could tell me why, or in general, why words roll around in people's heads, if you can't tell me specifics. I have no emotional ties, any ties of any kind to Belgium.

I am Latwii, and am aware of your query, my sister. Consider, my sister, who has pulled the rug out from under the feet and the condition of the rug and its origin.

May we answer further, my sister?

Carla: The rug. I'll have to think about it. Thank you.

I am Latwii. We thank you, my sister, and would be happy to attempt any further queries that either present may have.

(Long pause.)

Carla: I get it! Thank you. Okay.

I am Latwii, and we shall at this time relinquish our use of this instrument. We are happy to have been able to speak to this group. This instrument is in the process of attempting to expand its ability to serve as an instrument and we are happy to work with it in this capacity. We hope that its desire and practice of this skill will allow us to speak in a fashion which is more nearly characteristic of our own nature, which is much more lighter and free-flowing than the somewhat rigid framework that this instrument provides us in the form of its mind. We leave each of you in the love and in the light of the one infinite Creator. We rejoice with you in that peace and in that power of Oneness. Adonai, my friends. Adonai vasu. ❧

L/L Research

Sunday Meditation
February 16, 1986

(S channeling)

I am Hatonn. I greet you, my friends, in the love and light of the one infinite Creator. We ask your indulgence, our brothers and sisters, for it has been some time that this instrument has channeled our words and we are grateful that she has been so cautious, for as each of you know, there are those times when the duplicity of vibrations has been mistaken. We are very grateful, and it is with much joy we join you this evening, for the love and the light which glows around you is as great a thing for us to behold as it is for each of you to feel.

Many things, my friends, have been happening upon your planet's surface, much growth of the light and its balance, for in all things, my friends, as each of you perhaps have heard many times in the past, there is a balance and must be that balance. And it is in this that many of your questions may be answered, for the times when doubts arise remember that for all of the darkness that seems to be happening within your illusion, there is that much light as well and it is within that light that each, if it be his choice, will dwell. For we have found, my friends, by our choice that in that light will each find much joy and peace, for in the path of service to others there is joy.

We would now transfer this contact, as this instrument is experiencing some difficulty in maintaining our contact. I am Hatonn.

(Jim channeling)

I am Hatonn, and we greet you again in love and light. We would like to thank the one known as S for offering herself as an instrument for our words. We are overjoyed that we have been able to make contact with an old friend. We rejoice at each opportunity to utilize one who wishes to serve as an instrument in the vocal channeling.

We would remind you, my friends, that each of you is an instrument, each of you serves the one Creator in a manner which is very like unto the phenomenon of vocal channeling as you call it, for each of you with your own unique abilities, interests and desires takes that gift of love which is yours each day and makes of it an offering that seems upon its surface to be merely another daily round of activities. Yet from the deeps of your own being and from reaches and resources far beyond that which you call your own identity, do you draw the inspiration and motivation to take that enabling force that you call love and form it into each thought that you think, each action that you complete and each word that you speak.

Thus do you, each of you, all of you, articulate that great unspoken thought that dwells ever present and ready to serve as the base upon which you stand, the palette from which you draw your colors, the canvas upon which you place them and the appreciation within each heart and eye that looks upon your creation. And thus do you provide glorification of the [One] Which dwells in all.

The particular type of channeling that you experience this evening as you gather together in your seeking is but one small form of articulation of the one original Thought that is love. We are privileged to partake in this offering with you, for in this participation do we also discover more about the one Creator and the means by which it may be manifested within your illusion. We spoke of doubt at the beginning of this contact and we would choose at this time to expand somewhat upon this concept, for if what we have just spoken has truth within it, then it must be asked by any seeker of that truth what part doubt plays and why it seems many times that doubt plays such a large part within the process of seeking and experiencing that each of you and your fellow beings experiences in your daily life.

Within the cultures of your peoples at the current level of development of technology, it would seem that much of doubt would have been erased from the daily life and experience of your peoples. For do you not have shelters to protect you from the elements? Are not the great majority of your peoples clothed and fed at least to a minimal degree? Do you not have relationships and means of communication with each other? Do you not have pursuits of work and leisure with which to focus your attention? Are there not within your culture areas in which each may find the potential of reward and satisfaction? Are there not many who speak of the one Creator and who provide paths by which a seeker may find that one Creator?

Yes, my friends, you and your peoples have all these things and more in great abundance and yet we would suggest that perhaps it is this very abundance of things, of ideas, of entities, of groups, of possibilities and opportunities that itself seems to provide the basis for much confusion and doubt. For with such great variety available in these areas of seeking of the mind, of the body, and of the spirit, how then does one decide in each particular instance what shall be the choice that is most appropriate for one at any time?

In your daily round of activities, from time to time you find the difficulty perhaps due to misunderstanding with one of your fellow beings. There is perhaps the intention of each entity to give of the self in a manner which is unique to the self. The gift perhaps finds little acceptance though the intention be relatively pure. Yet there is the disharmony, the accusation, the harsh and disharmonious words. Then, perhaps, there is silence, the heart being wounded, the mind being confused, the tongue then holds its peace. And the entity goes its way wondering to itself where was the missed step? How was it that one with the intentions one knows one had could give so freely and yet seemingly be so mistaken and misunderstood?

Yes, my friends, this is not an unusual occurrence; each of you has had similar experiences far more times than perhaps one cares to remember. And it returns again and again to the mind and to the heart, the wondering how can intentions be purely translated and communication made clear with those with whom one has contact on a daily basis? How can the relationships be smoothed and harmony be found and maintained? How can doubts be overcome and how can the next step be placed with surety on the path of seeking and sharing relationships each with the other?

We suggest to you, my friends, that it might be helpful if one can perhaps, only briefly at first, adopt a somewhat different attitude as one looks at the, shall we call it, metaphysical import or nature of one's daily life. When you experience the disharmonious relationship, the angry word, the cold and shriveled silence, that what you have is not so much the missed opportunity as a renewed opportunity for that which seems lost. Within your illusion it is not apparent in even the least degree that each is the Creator and that love binds all as one. Yet if you can within the heart of your being draw upon that realization and look upon each situation in which you find yourself with that point of view or attitude, you will see unfolding before you the limitless opportunities to discover love, harmony, peace and joy where there seems to be none or very little of these ideals which each shares.

For when you have experienced the smoothly functioning relationship and the either spoken or unspoken joy of sharing time, words and experience, you are living upon the fruit of a harvest that has been completed, and you now, as you view that which is disharmonious, may take what has been completed and move into a new experience, another opportunity to plant a seed of love, to nurture it with will and faith, with perseverance, with the kind gesture, the loving word, the respectful attitude, and watch that seed take root. It may be a great portion of what you call time before the seed sends a shoot into the light of your daily experience, and an even greater portion of what you call time before that plant of love bears fruit. Yet, is this not what each of you have come to do in some fashion within the incarnation that you now know?

That you have love and harmony a portion of the time with those about you can become an inspiration that motivates you, shall we say, to plant those seeds in areas that seem to have the most barren of ground, for it is [within] such seemingly barren soil that the greatest of opportunities may be found.

If you look upon the purpose of your incarnational patterns as not so much [for] experiencing love as for you to discover and nurture love where it has not been, then we suggest that you may find that the daily round of activities becomes far more acceptable within your sight, for if one becomes involved enough in the mundane nature of the world about one, it is far too easy to forget that the world about one is more the training ground than the, shall we say, finishing school, for there is the need and the opportunity to work the mind and the heart in the barren fields of your environment that these fields might become as the oasis and produce the life-nourishing waters of love that may then be offered freely to all about one.

Where you find yourself in your daily round of activities is where you have planted yourself, shall we say, in order that you might tend the field in the most loving fashion that you may. It is not so much the ability you may have to change those about you that is important as it is the ability that you have to look upon those about you in a new way, in a way which gives acceptance and love as freely as each of you is given the air you breathe, the ground that you walk upon and the experience that comes before you each day that you draw the free air into your lungs and each day that you find yourself once more moving in a world of seeming confusion, of endless choices and of seemingly multiple confusions and opportunities for misunderstanding. To be able to move one's own point of viewing from the mundane to the sacred, shall we say, is but a small step within one's own mental viewpoint, but one which can produce great changes in one's experience.

These changes, my friends, are those which grow from within your being and are nurtured by that quality that we have called love, the topic, the only topic, of all our humble words to you over the many years that we have been privileged to speak with you and through you. It may seem far too simplistic an attitude with which to move through your daily round of activities, yet we would remind you, my friends, that the one Creator is simplicity itself. Within your illusion much seems complex. It is as though the one Creator has played hide and seek with Itself and with love. And yet as each of you are a portion of that one Creator and as all creation is that same Creator, there is no place beyond your reach where love may be hidden that you may not find it. Persevere, my friends—and yet persevere with a light heart, knowing that all is truly well, that all things move in love, that you are an infinitely valuable portion of that love and of that one Creator and that you cannot err in your seeking of love. You may discover many and variant ways to seek, to find, and to experience and yet you shall make no mistakes, for all efforts are born of love, move within love, and in some fashion produce love.

We thank each of you for allowing us to speak our simple and humble words, and we shall be with each upon request in your meditations in order that you might experience a deeper vibration of that love of which we have spoken. We shall pause for a moment before leaving this group and move among each that you might experience our vibration. If that be your desire, mentally request that this be so and we shall be honored to be with each. We pause for a moment.

(Pause)

I am Hatonn. It has been our privilege to be with each of you. We leave you now in the love and in the light of the One Who Is All. We are those of Hatonn. Adonai, my friends. Adonai vasu borragus.

(Jim channeling)

I am Latwii, and we are also most happy to join you this evening, my friends. We have not had the opportunity to greet this group in love and light for some time and we take great joy in doing so at this time. We hope that you will be somewhat patient with us as we have been attempting for a portion of your time to work with this instrument in a slightly variant fashion. We are attempting to utilize the word-by-word type of channeling with this instrument in hopes that we might allow it to be somewhat more flexible in its perceiving of our contact. We shall attempt those queries which those present may have brought this evening and we would now ask if we might begin with the first query?

S: I have a question, Latwii. I'm sure that some of those present in this room this evening have dealt with this question before but I would like, if you don't mind, some information on the subject of what, if any, in your opinion, is the value and/or effects of using what could be termed as a crystal generator to heighten the transmission, perhaps, of this type of contact?

I am Latwii, and am aware of your query, my sister. We feel that we may be of the greatest aid by suggesting that the intention that motivates the use of any gadget of this variety is that which is the foundation principle that will determine the value of such use. There have been many gadgets, shall we say, which have been utilized throughout the history of your cultures upon this planetary influence that have had the purpose of enhancing the abilities of the initiate or the one who wishes to serve as an instrument in the service of others. The desire to serve in as pure a fashion as possible is that factor which determines whether a device such as the one of which you speak will be of any true assistance or not to any individual or group. There is with the use of such a device a potential temptation to see such devices as necessary for such a service to take place. There is also the temptation to utilize such devices for purposes of one's own gratification, shall we say, for it is true that such devices can be helpful and are indeed powerful when utilized with a strong enough intention. The polarization of the intention, therefore, is that which must be carefully achieved.

May we answer further, my sister?

S: Yes, please Latwii. Would you suggest a diagram of an apparatus such as this to be used? And you don't have to do it right now, it's basically a yes or no question.

I am Latwii, and we find that even if we were willing to produce such a drawing, we would be greatly hampered in doing so by the limitations of this instrument's mental configuration, for not only is this instrument quite untutored in this area, but this particular instrument has some degree of resistance, shall we say, to the use of such devices, and we would be hampered by this mental configuration. We remind you, my sister, that the use of such devices is much as the use of a crutch in some instances for those who have abilities that would remain untapped if there were such a device handy to rely upon.

May we answer further, my sister?

S: If I might ask one more question. I attended a meditation Thursday night. Latwii, I'm going to ask this because I need some outside affirmation, so to speak. Were the members of the Confederation actually present and in attunement with those that were present at that meditation Thursday night?

I am Latwii, and, my sister, it is our desire to be of the greatest service possible in this regard, but we find that the query moves within an area which is sacred unto your own seeking. It is therefore with some regret that we must refrain from giving any definitive response, for the decision as to the nature of the experience of …

(Side one of tape ends.)

(Jim channeling)

I am Latwii, and am once again with this instrument. To complete our response, my sister. This decision must be one which is achieved by your own efforts, for it is just this kind of decision that allows one to exercise one's own spiritual muscle, shall we say, and grow stronger in discrimination. If we were to give a definitive response, we would be removing from you the opportunity to accomplish that which you have set before yourself, and we would, in our humble opinion, not be serving as well as we can serve by refraining from a definite response.

May we answer in any other fashion, my sister?

S: No, Latwii. By your answer you have answered, and I thank you very much.

I am Latwii, and we thank you very much as well, my sister, for allowing us to speak. May we attempt another query?

J: Yeah. What was the cause of the disappearance of the colony of Roanoke?

I am Latwii. We shall attempt a response, though we are not certain that this instrument is capable of transmitting that which we shall give. We shall pause for a moment to deepen this instrument's state.

(Pause)

I am Latwii. We find that the entities of which you speak were those who had for many incarnations moved as a group in the service of the one Creator as those who partook in a, what you may call, tradition or mystery school which had the purpose of serving in the capacity of generating certain potentials in the consciousness of what you may call the racial mind of those about them. This was not completely a conscious function and moved within the subconscious realms of these entities in order that the work to which each was apprenticed might be accomplished in what you may call more of the mundane fashion than is normally ascribed to those operating within such a mystery school or tradition.

Thus, the approximate cause of the disappearance of these entities was their seeming capture by groups of other entities known to your peoples as various tribes of the American or Native American Indians who were themselves agents of this same tradition and who, by the seeming capture and removal to other locations of this colony were playing their roles in the mutually agreed-upon purpose that was the motivating factor for the incarnations of all those involved.

May we answer further, my sister?

J: Are you saying that they willingly disappeared? That they willingly moved to another location?

I am Latwii, and this is basically correct, my sister, although the willing choice was more preincarnative and subconscious than conscious. Yet as these entities adjusted to their new surroundings, the memory of this choice became more clearly defined within the conscious minds of each.

May we answer further, my sister?

J: May I ask where they went?

I am Latwii. We present to this instrument the picture of the area of your continent known as the southern portion of the Canadian provinces bordering the Great Lakes area as the final destination of these entities as they were moved by various tribes to a succession of locations, eventually ending in the southern province of the Great Lakes region in your Canadian area. This instrument is unable to transmit the precise location.

May we answer further, my sister?

J: No, thank you very much.

I am Latwii, and we thank you very much. Is there another query?

(Pause)

I am Latwii. We find that we have exhausted the queries for the evening, and we have been most grateful to be able to speak those words which were ours to speak. We hope that you will remember that we are but your brothers and sisters upon the same journey which you find yourselves and are most fallible as well. Take that which has value in your own seeking and leave that which we have spoken which does not ring true. We thank you for allowing us to join you this evening. We shall look forward with great glee and joy to our future experiences with this group. We are always happy to be called to your midst and rejoice with you in your songs, in your words, and in the love which each brings to the other. We are those of Latwii. Adonai, my friends. Adonai vasu borragus. ☙

Sunday Meditation
February 23, 1986

(Carla channeling)

I am Nona, and we come to this group due to the great cry of one of this group who is not here. We come to you in the love and in the light of the infinite Creator and are most grateful to this instrument for allowing us to, shall we say, speak or intone through her. Also, we are grateful to those of L/Leema who have allowed us to be first, for there is some urgency in this calling which, as we have said, is not of the group in this room but for another.

(Carla channels a healing melody from Nona.)

(Carla channeling)

I am L/Leema, and I greet you, my friends, in the love and in the light of the one infinite Creator. It is a great privilege to be called to your group and we thank you for the opportunity of being of service to you, for it is your service to us to allow us this great privilege. We shall speak tonight of the positive, the negative, and the neutral; of the proton, the electron, and the neutron; of serving, of receiving, and of being.

Of the positive and the negative and the neutral we feel that we need only say that each will have his own idea and an approximately accurate one it is of the meaning of these words. In metaphysical terms, positive equals that which radiates or gives, emits or shares. In metaphysical terms, that which is negative is that which attracts or takes or enslaves.

When we come to speak of what this instrument thinks of as fundamental building blocks—that is, atoms of your physical illusion—we find this instrument ill-equipped with the vocabulary sufficient for an elegant exposition of the subject. Metaphysically speaking, however, we ask you to consider the great starry sea of space and star which you view now if your eyes are open and gazing skyward, for it is the nighttime upon this portion of your planet at this time.

We do not wish to compare stars to that which is negative and positive, and yet we say to you that the one who looks into the heavens is gazing at a multiplicity of atoms in the larger sense. The model holds steady for the so-called atom and the difference between positive and negative will one day be found to be a part of your physics and is linked with what is now an incomplete and incorrect field, that being gravitation.

Let us look closer at some systems within galaxies. There in a sun system you may see several planets in an energy shell that binds them tightly to the star to whom they are attracted.

We say to you that that which is termed the neutron, which seems to take up a great and vast majority of the actual matter or energy of an atom, is that which is lost in love, or to put it more scientifically, it is that Thought or Logos which is uncreated, and thus is neither positive [nor negative] but remains at rest within the unmanifested mystery and personage, if you will, of the one infinite Creator.

Now let us carry this analogy more firmly into metaphysics, for we may assure you that far more of your own life within this illusion and far more of your seeking within that life is likewise lost in the Creator, safe within the Kingdom of Heaven, if you will, than any can realize while bound within the illusion, which makes it seem as though there is an endless series of things which are good and things which are bad. There may be things that do not matter, but it is seldom, my friends, that the value of the great majority of the self is ever seen, appreciated or used.

Now let us look at the energies about which we are speaking. Each of you is a spiritual atom. Life energy which is universal and nondirectional is drawn into the force field or energy field of the physical body, together with its mental, emotional and spiritual complexes, through the soles of the feet and rises upward. That which is positive and radiant is that which is sought, that inspiration, that truth, that knowledge or awareness that the seeker's heart yearns for and thirsts for and must have. The meeting place of that which some call prana, the life energy drawn up from the feet into the body and that light which radiates and which is brought into the body complex through the higher chakras, is that point at which you as an entity will function and from which you as an entity will learn your lessons, each being a lesson of love, yet each being completely unique as are you.

However, let it be known upon a dark Earth that the vast majority of the essential you has not left the creation of the Father, but dwells unmanifest and unpotentiated, full of energy, full of life, but without any need for outer expression, that need being a part of what it is to be in the illusion of positive and negative and lessons to be learned and journeys to be walked.

How wonderful each of you is, my friends, how full you are of the Creator, how at one with the Creator you truly are, how joyful is the greater part of you. Yet it is a part that cannot speak to your conscious self, it is a part that cannot be taught, it is a part that is not of time and not of space. Within it lies your future, for from its infinite regions, you yourself will require some small portion for each lesson which you accept the responsibility of undertaking and if possible, completing.

In other words, my friends, that which is neutral, that which is your neutron, that which is of the Logos within you, waits and waits without time. My friends, each of you has one or more things which are desired at this particular juncture, yet the time has not yet come for this lesson to be undertaken. We ask you therefore to take the lesson of the atom to heart. Sometimes it is time to wait, for that which is unmanifest cannot be pushed or pulled or bullied. The rhythm of the Father is such that only in the Creator's time, which is your inner time, shall your lesson emerge from timelessness and act out its drama upon your world's stage, and then you shall learn and know and you shall go on and again you will wait. But for each of you now, there is waiting to be done.

We suggest, therefore, that you wait happily, knowing that that which is necessary for you to do is single—that which you must do is ask, for is it not written in one of your holy works, "Ask and it shall be answered." Therefore, we always and ever caution seekers to be careful of that which they ask, for in good time that which is asked will be received. Be sure that you are asking for that which you truly desire.

We would say this in closing. Many are the notions that seekers have of the appropriate fruits of seeking. The products of seeking in many persons' opinions are quite visible, often dramatic and most astonishing. Each seeker naturally wishes to be of service, to advance in seeking, to develop as a spiritual personality, and so forth. And yet we ask you to look at some of those whose lives have produced a content of speaking and action which people have followed for many of your years.

Let us look at Gautama Siddhartha. This entity was a king among men. It sought the truth, and it gave its fruits most productively when, after many adventures, it ferried people from one side of a river to another. We ask you to look at the entity known to you as Jesus of Nazareth. This entity did not even start incarnation as a king, but was without pretension from [birth], living as a carpenter and a carpenter's son, walking about in the dust and heat of desert land, and dying along with two petty criminals.

Where are the fruits of these lives which were so dramatic? Put yourself in either of their places and attempt to define just when it would be that you would know that your life had become spiritually productive. The secret that these two extremely compassionate and wise entities shared was the secret of waiting, of metaphysical neutrality, so that one met each circumstance with spiritual freshness, with a vivacious love that pierced the seeming tension and dissolved positive and negative so that all was light and love.

Those lives which are dramatic are neither more nor less capable of being spiritually productive as those lives which seem to be prosaic and full of that which is daily and mundane. The eyes to see, the ears to hear and the hearts to understand lie in that part of yourself that has never left the Logos and that is waiting to be potentiated by your free will as co-Creator, for you are in God and the Creator is in you. We shall wait with you, my friends, in joy and without anticipation so that we may, as you, be surprised by the even greater joy of action within the love and the light of the One Who Is All.

Never attempt to spin your electrons or to gather your protons so that you may gain more electrons—no, no, my friends—this is not the way to spiritual productivity, for that is not a shell, it is a situation which you shall inherit when the waiting is over for now. It is something you shall experience in the moment, and then you shall wait again in joy, in peace. Know yourselves as powerful beings. There is no circumstance which was not given you by your own self for a reason. Wait. And the time shall be ripe and the lesson learned.

We would transfer to another channel within this group at this time. We leave this instrument as a galaxy within a galaxy within a galaxy, and so on to infinity, for that which is true in the microscope is equal to that which is true in the telescope. That which is true in your smallest experience is that which is true in the deepest sense. Life has much of illusion to offer and you wait in that blessed reality that is the Creator. We wait with you. We leave this instrument. We are those of L/Leema.

(L channeling)

I am known to you as L/Leema, and I greet you again, my friends, in the love and the light of the infinite Creator. We ask your indulgence at this time, for this is our first opportunity to speak to you through this instrument and desire a few moments that we might attune ourselves more efficiently to this instrument's capacity to communicate our thoughts.

We desire, my friends, not to lecture nor to teach, but simply to share with those present those thoughts which your questions generate, that together your seeking and our own might lead us both to greater perception. My friends, it is the way of the wanderer to arrive without acclamation, for in silence is much work done. Therefore, my friends, those who would act in the role of catalyst both for their own growth and that of their brothers should consider that their own efforts may serve only to influence unduly those about them, should those efforts be directed toward the turning of a brother or sister to a specific path. To be truly of service, the seeker, the wanderer, does not seek to teach, to lead, or to guide, for to do so would be to exert an influence upon a brother or sister much as those forces described earlier as positive and negative in the physical realm would exert a force upon other minute particles of matter …

(Side one of tape ends.)

(L channeling)

To truly serve, my friends, is not to pull or to tug but simply to exist, to be that which is immune to the pulling and tugging, which of itself seeks not to influence but rather to simply show. It is only in this manner, my friends, that one might purely help a brother, for one may only demonstrate attainment and the values of that attainment by example. We leave you now, my friends, in the love and in the light of that which you term the infinite Creator. We are known to you as L/Leema.

(L channeling)

I am Latwii, and I greet you, my brothers and sisters, in the love and in the light of the infinite Creator. My friends, it is a great pleasure to be here as we have been waiting quite impatiently for our opportunity to be with you again. It is always our pleasure to eavesdrop upon such erudite lectures as those provided by our brothers and sisters of

L/Leema, yet we also have the desire to be of service and are quite pleased that it is now our opportunity to do so. At this time are there any questions we may in our humble efforts attempt to answer?

M: Yes, Latwii. We have spoken before. I'm the one from the planetary [system] Kreeton, approximately 246,000 light years away. My question is, does Kreeton have more than one moon, and does it have a sun like ours, and does it support a third experience like unto what we share on the earth plane?

I am Latwii. I am aware of your questions. My brother, it is our desire to answer your questions, yet we feel that we would be somewhat remiss if we did not include within our answer the observation that few entities are capable of claiming only one previous address. However, we shall continue in our efforts to answer your question. My brother, there are two moons in the system which you describe and the solar disk to which you refer is quite similar in that most logi seem to originate from the same source.

May we answer you further?

M: Yes. Does the planetary sphere, Kreeton, support a third-density experience that is like unto the one here on the earth plane?

I am Latwii. My brother, the planetary system to which you refer has at a different point in time, as you would describe it, experienced a third-density collective existence. However, this particular entity, as you might describe it, is not currently at the previously mentioned address.

May we answer you further?

M: Yes. In comparison to Earth, how large is this planetary system Kreeton?

I am Latwii. My brother, we assume that you refer to a specific body as opposed to a solar system. The terminology "planetary system" we find somewhat confusing and would request that you clarify this as we are uncertain as to the correct answer to your question.

M: Yes. Assuming that Kreeton is a planet like Earth, would Kreeton be much, much larger than our planet Earth?

My brother, the planet to which you refer is of approximately the same dimension. However, as you are aware, one might equally well say that the planets Earth and Jupiter are also of approximately the same dimension. We would, however, further interject that such conjecture, while stimulating to the mind, might be of lesser importance than that existence within which one is currently occupied.

Is there another question?

M: No, thank you.

Carla: Is Kreeton a member of the Confederation of Planets in the Service of the Infinite Creator?

The former occupants of that planet are not yet of that status. It is currently supporting that which might be referred to as early second density in this point in time.

May we answer you further?

Carla: Is it possible that the term "Kreeton" refers not only to a planet but to an entire planetary system?

I am Latwii. That is correct, my sister.

Carla: Are there wanderers from one of the planets of Kreeton to this planet at this time?

I am Latwii. My sister, we feel it inappropriate to divulge such information for the reason that there are those known to individuals present who feel themselves of this particular status. Should this indeed be true, there are more appropriate manners in which this information might be attained for the individuals concerned.

May we answer you further?

Carla: No, I just suspected that in M's eagerness to get at his home he was remembering a planet which he had helped at a previous time rather than the planet from which he came. I don't need you to answer that—I was just figuring that since I knew another person who was a wanderer from Kreeton that there was probably another planet that was other than the one that was remembered by M. Thanks for your help.

I am Latwii. We thank you my sister. Is there another question?

M: Yes. In this planetary system, Kreeton, collectively, Latwii, can you tell me how many planets might be in total in the planetary system Kreeton?

I am Latwii. My brother, we would offer to you the number five.

Is there another question?

M: I felt Latwii, always, that I am a wanderer from the planetary system Kreeton. Is it possible to divulge the name of the planet that I may have visited at one time or helped?

I am Latwii. My brother, it is our desire to be of assistance at all times. However, we are sure that you understand that the information you seek is that which should be sought from within, for it is our desire to avoid interfering with an entity's path.

May we answer you further?

M: Yes. Do the five planets in the planetary system Kreeton, do they support densities one through six? Or maybe just one planet out of the whole group? Or all of them?

I am Latwii. My brother, the potential exists for all planets to support all densities, for as you [are] no doubt aware, the abilities of the Creator to adapt to specific situations are quite admirable and the potential always exists for any location to be successfully utilized by any of the logi. However, to attempt to answer more accurately your question, we would suggest that at this time there are two of the planets of this system currently occupied, and one of the two has recently been vacated, so to speak, by a third-density memory complex. As the conditions were suitable, the newly vacated planet was used for the continuation of the development of a second-density level of evolvement which had been initiated at an earlier point.

May we answer you further?

M: No, you have been most kind, Latwii. Thank you very, very much.

We thank you, my brother. Is there another question?

Carla: Yes. In your pattern of answers to the questions from the member of Kreeton, I detect a gentle nudging of the mind of the questioner away from that line of questioning and onto another. And I would like to ask the kind of question which might be another kind of question which you might be able to work with better. And that is, what are the central things for a wanderer to seek, to work on, to hope for, to aim for, within this illusion on planet Earth at this time?

I am Latwii, and my sister, we are quite grateful for the opportunity to attempt to challenge our brothers and sisters of L/Leema for the award of erudition. We shall, however, attempt to show our stuff, so to speak, in a less wordy manner. We would offer for your evaluation, therefore, the suggestion first that the role of the wanderer within any existence be examined, for as [in] the catalyst to which our brothers and sisters of L/Leema referred, the wanderer is that which is injected into a previously developed level of existence so as to increase the intensity of energy without by doing so necessarily being affected by their own introduction into the situation.

One must be aware that the wanderer is in a sense both protected and numbed in a sense, for the wanderer must not be initially aware of the wanderer's own origin and role. To do so would be to invalidate in advance the efforts to be made by that individual, much as introducing in one of your auto races a competitor who has three times circumscribed the racing field before those present have left the starting mark. In this manner, the wanderer is allowed to begin with the same level of confusion as those among whom he or she arrives, yet because of their previous attainment, finds it more in personal attunement to go within and to seek answers to questions not readily apparent to the society at large within which the wanderer has been injected.

We should point out at this time further that the role of the wanderer who desires to perform effectively is not that of a leader or of a savior but rather as one who single-mindedly follows a path of attainment, for to lead is to attempt to influence other selves. This from the superior vantage point of the wanderer is unacceptable and would cost in polarity, for it is what you would describe as a manipulative effort.

It is further observed that the adage often quoted referring to hiding one's light within a basket is also applicable, for to be effective as a catalyst, the wanderer must further make themselves readily available that their brothers and sisters might see their light and seek to attain it themselves. In this manner all become followers of that which truly leads rather than most becoming followers of one who is slightly in advance yet has to attain perfection, himself or herself.

May we answer you further, my sister?

Carla: No, thank you.

Is there another question?

A: Can you just reiterate something on … So you've got this wanderer. What kind of seeking do they do and questions do they ask?

I am Latwii. I am aware of your question. My sister, the wanderer, if we correctly construe your question, might be described as "at a loss for worlds[3]," and spends an early portion or perhaps of the entirely of their life in a state of confusion or puzzlement, the role of that which on your world is referred to as the "stranger in a strange land." The attainment of the wanderer's bearings, so to speak, is arrived at with the realization that one has landed oneself within an unfamiliar situation, and that there is no Scotty to beam one back up. At this point, should the wanderer decide to advance along the path of positive polarity, then the wanderer would tend to seek personal development.

We are aware that this seems puzzling in that the similarity between personal development and service to self will be readily available to the questioning mind. However, personal development is a path which might be characterized as the desire to develop positive polarity in a cautious manner that one might avoid unduly influencing their brothers and sisters to the extent of becoming themselves acclaimed as a messiah and becoming the object of veneration rather than one who seeks to venerate. As you may have guessed, this is quite a row to hoe.

May we answer you further, my sister?

A: So are you saying, in other words, that first of all, they tend to develop themselves cautiously, and in order to do that go within themselves to develop themselves in order to serve others more effectively?

I am Latwii. We would offer one correction, my sister, in that we would suggest that should the wanderer successfully arrive at that point described as "getting one's bearings," a successful wanderer *might* choose the path which you described.

May we answer you further?

A: No, that's fine. Yeah, I was assuming that they would go with service to others. Yeah, they could go with service to self.

I am Latwii. Is there another question?

Carla: Thanks for coming by.

We thank you, my sister. As there are apparently no further questions, we shall offer again our gratitude for the opportunity to join with you and to learn from you. And in the love and the light of the infinite Creator we shall bid you adieu. We are known to you as Latwii. ☘

---

[3] Carla: In this case, Latwii is perfectly capable of having made a pun. The stranger in a strange land is definitely at a loss for the right world!

Sunday Meditation
March 2, 1986

(Carla channeling)

I am Hatonn, and I greet you, my friends, in the love and the light of our infinite Creator. It is a great blessing for us to be invited to share our humble opinions with you. We thank you for requesting the sharing of these thoughts, and before we speak upon any subject, we wish to express our desire that each realize that we of the Confederation of Planets in the Service of the Infinite Creator are not infallible, but are, like yourselves, entities who are seeking the refinement of that which is loosely called the truth and which we often call the one original Thought or love. As you listen, keep what seems inspirational to you and leave the rest behind, for we do not wish to become a stumbling block upon your own path of seeking. With that said, we shall begin.

We are giving information to this instrument word by word, consequently, this instrument has no idea of what is to come next, and there will inevitably be pauses while the instrument has a fit of analysis and loses the contact. This instrument has yet to be fully confident of channeling in this manner and so it is a good learning technique.

As you look up at the stars, my friends, that which you see is inconceivable. Indeed, before your so-called science developed instruments capable of measuring and classifying that which the eye sees when gazing at the night sky, the majority of the inhabitants of your planet felt that they lived inside a dome through which there were tiny holes and therefore through which at night the great light beyond the sun could be seen. You are dwelling at this point in your experience within a physical vehicle which is inconceivable. Yes, my friends, you are very used to your bodies and therefore do not find them astonishing. Yet could you, without seeing a form, develop the intricate system of, shall we say, the most primitive internal combustion which is your body? The universe of man is a universe in which those things which are the true mysteries are often those things which are most taken for granted and unexplored while man turns his excellent mind to the creation of artifacts of his own making.

Although the instrumentation of science has long since altered humankind's view of the universe, yet still it is taken for granted. And although healers have plumbed the depths and examined through microscopes the tiniest cells and explored the many systems within the body which you wear as your garment within this illusion, yet still it is taken for granted. And although each entity within your illusion will age and the physical body die, life is for the most part taken for granted while the mind of your peoples turns to the distractions, the recreations, the amusements, and the creation of the artifacts of man.

We have said to you many times, please meditate, and in our saying this, we hope, without learning for you or guiding that which you may find within yourself, to offer to you the most efficient path towards the removing of the numbness of daily life, that numbness which keeps one from perpetual astonishment and transformational joy from moment to moment. There is a kingdom within you which those whom you call religious leaders have located far away from you. This instrument would call this kingdom the Kingdom of the Father. It is difficult to find names for the Creator which express the concept appropriately, for within you is the Kingdom of the Father and yet within you is the Father, Father and Kingdom being one.

This concept is too simple to easily grasp. It is just as difficult to grasp the concept of dwelling within the present moment. Any substance which is formed of the stuff of your illusion has a process of existence. This is a mechanical and measurable process. We speak not only of the progress within your physical bodies, but also the progress of aging, of gems, of planets in their courses, of great sun bodies, and of the physical universe as you know it.

In none of these processes does there indwell, to the casual observer, the concept of the present moment, for there is always the process that is going on and the feeling of time passing. We shall not overtax your rational minds this evening, for we wish instead to offer that which this particular group at this particular time requests and that is affirmation, confirmation and companionship as you attempt to enter into joy. It is possible within the processes of the body of rock, of star, to feel what could be termed joy, and yet because joy is so short-lived, there is great disappointment to each who dwells within the process. Instead of plucking yourself from the process, we suggest to you that that which is most real within you was in existence before any process began. That which is within you which is real is so full of joy that it is as though there were an unlimited, infinite and eternal orgasm which can be retrieved and experienced from within by meditation, by vision or by circumstance.

How we would like for you to be able to allow all those things which are illusory to fall away just now in this moment as we speak so that you may feel the heartbeat of the Kingdom within you. Why else, my friends, would you meditate except to find your true self? Why would you ever stop talking and studying and listening and looking and learning? Why would you seek silence that the world does not give unless you suspected that there was a Kingdom within and that Kingdom within dwelt more in that which was real than all of your experiences in manifestation upon the outer exoteric planes of human existence?

What is this Kingdom like? There are many hints, many clues, many messengers that come and offer to you the great abundance of joy, of peace, of wholeness. There is the grass that greens, the trees in their stately dignity that offer shade and beauty, blossoms that nod in the gentle winds of summer and sweet songbirds full of mirth that offer their tuneful anthems to the listening ear. There is the smile upon the stranger's face, the laugh of a child, the dignity of one grown old, the wisdom that one may find in certain places and with certain companions, inherent, unspoken. And there are those things which are offered to the self alone, meaningful to the self alone, subjective only and yet promising a reality full of love, full of joy, full of peace. Step-by-step you walk and you move from place to place within your body, within the illusion, and step-by-step in a metaphysical sense, you walk upon your spiritual path and seek to accelerate the rate at which you are able to develop that spiritual self.

We say to you that a coming into focus of the creation of the Father is that which will accelerate the rate of your spiritual development most efficiently. As you do this, you move from the dimension of physicality into the dimension of the present moment. The present moment does not go away, it does not turn into the future, nor does it leave the past behind. The metaphysical present moment is not at all the same as a physical present as indicated by your clocks.

It is often the approach of those who seek most earnestly to attempt to replicate the symptoms of one who is progressing, to attempt to feel joy, to attempt to feel love, to attempt to manifest the one original Thought, and yet those symptoms of spiritual growth are that—only symptoms. One may manifest them for a time, however the energy available to one seeking phenomena is limited. So we ask you to attempt this evening to step momentarily out of time, to allow yourself to enter the Kingdom within.

Let us speak with you as you enter that Kingdom. How beautiful and how fair, how full of glory is the face of creation. How shall we praise that which is love? How shall we come into true association with infinity? How limitless is the light. How full of thanks are we. Why are we not traveling, why are we not moving, for there is a great sensation of moving and traveling as we dwell in the present moment? We move, we dwell, we are. Motion and motionless, these things are one. All things are One. Oh, greet each other, my friends, and know each other as One. Know each other as the Creator, and now look and see how gracious, how gentle, and how profound the one original Thought is.

We are full of thanks to ourselves—for we thank ourselves—as we are the Creator and we are the Creation. Where can we go and be not in the creation? What can we see that is not the Creator? Let us move back into time. Let bliss drift like the waves of the sea moving back and forth and let us find ourselves seated within the illusion, within physical bodies, within all of those things which may seem to separate us from each other and from the Creator and from the consciousness of the Creator.

This, my friends, is travel without time. This is a kind of talking that attempts to describe that which is meditation and which is found in meditation. Felt you then the glory, the wonder, the beauty of the timeless present wherein the one original Thought expresses itself as reality? Then you shall be able to radiate that light and that love not by doing but first by being, for your worth is as infinite as the Creator. And that which you do shall always be an imperfect trace of the energy pathway of limitlessness.

We are so very pleased to have been able to share a few thoughts with you, and we rejoice with you that the creation of love is nearer to you than your breathing, closer to you than your thinking, more dear to you than your body. We would, if you wish, be with you in meditation in order to be able to aid you in the strengthening of that state. We are capable of offering a kind of carrier wave which can blend with your own energies to strengthen the process of meditation. There is no one who is unworthy, there is no one who is exempt by folly of any kind from the possibility of dwelling in love. May we join you in that unity of being which we have shared since that time before time and which we shall share beyond the end of creation as you know [it]. May we rejoice with you. Yes, my friends, the nature of reality is joy. Seek the Kingdom and allow yourself to rest in the present, in the infinity, in the light of the one original Thought.

We are those of Hatonn, and again we thank each of you and leave you enmeshed together by the nature of creation that you share. O beauteous love, o wondrous light, how can we leave you, for we are as you are, all that there is. Go within yourself and you shall find forever. We leave you now that our brothers and sisters may speak through another instrument. Adonai, my friends. Adonai vasu borragus.

(Jim channeling)

I am Latwii, and we greet you in the love and in the light of our infinite Creator. We are overjoyed to be asked to join this group this evening. We thank you for requesting our presence. We, as always, are eager to share our humble words in whatever manner may be of aid in your seeking. We would also remind each present that we are but your fallible brothers and sisters who have moved somewhat further, shall we say, upon the same journey which you find yourselves traveling on. We are available at this time to attempt to answer queries which those present may have value in the asking, and we will do our best to respond in a manner which is helpful without infringing upon your own free will and seeking. May we then begin with the first query?

Carla: I'll break the ice since everyone's being polite and waiting for the other guy. Last week we had a message about an …

(Side one of tape ends.)

Carla: We had this message last week that dealt with the function of the nucleus of the atom, and there were some connections made metaphysically with the unpotentiated Logos and the fact that most of the creation, most of the sun systems and stars that you see and so forth, and most of each cell within our body all dwell in unpotentiated, undifferentiated Logos or love, and that what we were experiencing we were experiencing with a very small part of our total capacity to experience.

I was thinking about that earlier today and I began wondering about how illness works because if each cell of the body is full of the love of the Creator and is dipped into only very slightly, then when the cells of the body become damaged or ill or attacked by some bug or whatever, it seems that the Logos is being used in a way that is not of service but is destructive of love. I couldn't get much further than that with it and I wondered if you could discuss the relationship between the cells and the nature of the cells, in other words, if each one is a living, conscious entity which mostly dwells within love, and illness.

I am Latwii, and am aware of your query, my sister. This is a large topic and one which is somewhat difficult to translate into your word system. However, as you look upon the cells of your physical vehicle, and, indeed, the nature of the illusion which you inhabit in general, you will see at the heart of this manifestation of love various patterns or frequencies of vibrations of the photon as you have called it. These patterns or fields of vibration are constructed in such and such a manner by the Logos under whose care we find ourselves in this portion of the creation. Within the frequency of the third density illusion that you inhibit there may be within your physical vehicle variations in the field of vibration chosen by each entity, either upon the conscious or upon the subconscious level of mind, for the purpose of experiencing a certain set of circumstances that will have as the end result, shall we say, the opportunity to learn certain lessons and to utilize these learnings in the serving of others. The diseased pattern of vibrational distortion, shall we say, is much like building various structures within one of your streams or rivers that serve to divert the movement of the water in its normal flow, thus creating swirls, pools, depths, eddies and so forth.

When an entity in its incarnational pattern experiences that condition that you know as disease, it has done the equivalent of blocking or causing an alteration in the normal pattern of vibratory frequency in order to provide itself with what may be called a teaching device. The seeming damage done to the pattern of vibration or manifestation of love is as illusory as the manifestation is in its original state of creation, shall we say, and will last for as long as is necessary for the opportunity to be grasped and the lessons learned and the services offered.

May we answer further, my sister?

Carla: Are you implying then that the state of health is as illusory as the state of ill health?

I am Latwii, and am aware of your query, my sister. In general this is correct, though the free and even flow of the life pattern is substantially more stable in its illusory manifestation than is the unbalanced or diseased or blocked configuration.

May we answer further, my sister?

Carla: Is there any way that we can use this knowledge to inform the cells of our desire that they become distorted towards health rather than ill health? Besides meditation?

I am Latwii, and we may suggest, my sister, that there are as many ways to look upon and utilize these configurations of health and disease as there are entities to perceive them. The configuration of the pattern of manifestation may be studied as the riddle in the attempt to discern the opportunity contained within the configuration, for each configuration that has become distorted has a symbolic value, shall we say, that serves to focus the attention of the individual upon the distortion in order that the purpose of the distortion might be understood and balance once again achieved.

May we answer further, my sister?

Carla: Thank you, no.

I am Latwii, and we thank you, my sister. Is there another query?

Questioner: Of what density is Latwii?

I am Latwii, and we are privileged to pursue our seeking of the one Creator within the illusion of the density numbering five, [which is,] as you are aware, the density of light.

May we answer further, my brother?

Questioner: Does the blockage which you mentioned concerning illness, can this blockage be eliminated through the use of kundalini meditation?

I am Latwii, and this is one technique of removal of the blockages when pursued with diligence and discipline, my brother.

May we answer further?

Questioner: No, thank you.

I am Latwii, and we thank you, my brother. Is there another query?

Carla: Why is it that some of us do have music in our heads all the time?

I am Latwii, and am aware of your query, my sister. We find that there is no simple or single explanation for this phenomenon, for the ears to hear the sounds of music that is not heard by all may reopened for any number of reasons. There are many whose inner seeking has taken the form that provides an avenue that is analogous to the mathematical relationships between sounds, and the desire to know what you have called the truth then is translated by the subconscious mind of the seeker into a constant refrain, as it were. This, then, is always present in such an entity and serves as a constant reminder to such an entity that it does seek that known as the truth and does also constantly receive answers to the seeking.

May we answer further, my sister?

Carla: No, thank you.

I am Latwii, and we thank you once again, my sister. Is there another query?

Carla: Okay, I'll hog the time just one more time and then I'll shut up. For some time I've been working with depression because of the death of a dear friend, and just recently I've felt that I was getting much better and began easing off the medication that was designed to keep me from becoming suicidal. As I ease off of the medication, I find that some of the really bad patterns of thought which are very destructive and not at all helpful and not true come back more than they did when I was on this medicine, and I've started having nightmares again. It seems that there should be a metaphysical way to work with these energies and to transform them, but although I meditate every day, that hasn't happened. Could you give me any kind of suggestion as to how to work with destructive thought processes and the expression of that destruction in nightmares?

I am Latwii, and am aware of your query, my sister. Though we may not speak with over specificity in guiding your own thinking and thus infringing upon your own free will, we may speak in a general fashion to suggest that those desires to utilize the lessons now placed before your notice may take the form of, shall we say, programming your own subconscious mind to release in the dream state the symbols of transformation that might be then in the conscious state interpreted by your own efforts in a fashion which attempts to achieve a wholeness of understanding. The difficulties which you experience in your waking state and in your sleeping state may be looked at for the deeper meaning and this meaning then used as the programming for further revelation, whether in dreams or in meditation, that will further enhance the piecing of the puzzle shall we say, thus to grasp the bull by the horns, to use a phrase, may enable your attempt to relieve the distortions in a fashion that utilizes both the conscious and subconscious experiences of sleep and waking.

May we answer further, my sister?

Carla: I don't think so. Thank you.

I am Latwii, and we thank you, my sister. Is there another query?

(Pause)

I am Latwii, and as we feel we have completed those queries which have been so graciously placed before us this evening, we shall thank each present for requesting our presence in this group of seeking this evening. We are always with you upon your request and rejoice in joining you during your seeking upon these evenings. We shall be with you again. We are known to you as those of Latwii. Adonai, my friends.

Carla: C, I feel Nona's energy. Do you want to try to channel Nona?

C: I'll try.

(C channeling)

I am Nona. We come to answer calls for healing from those present who have concerns for those here and those who are close.

(C channels a vocalized healing melody from Nona.) ♣

L/L Research

L/L Research is a subsidiary of Rock Creek Research & Development Laboratories, Inc.

P.O. Box 5195
Louisville, KY 40255-0195

www.llresearch.org

Rock Creek is a non-profit corporation dedicated to discovering and sharing information which may aid in the spiritual evolution of humankind.

ABOUT THE CONTENTS OF THIS TRANSCRIPT: This telepathic channeling has been taken from transcriptions of the weekly study and meditation meetings of the Rock Creek Research & Development Laboratories and L/L Research. It is offered in the hope that it may be useful to you. As the Confederation entities always make a point of saying, please use your discrimination and judgment in assessing this material. If something rings true to you, fine. If something does not resonate, please leave it behind, for neither we nor those of the Confederation would wish to be a stumbling block for any.

CAVEAT: This transcript is being published by L/L Research in a not yet final form. It has, however, been edited and any obvious errors have been corrected. When it is in a final form, this caveat will be removed.

© 2009 L/L Research

Sunday Meditation
March 9, 1986

(Carla channeling)

I am Hatonn. I greet each of you in the love and in the light of our infinite Creator. We thank you for the great privilege of being allowed to share our thoughts with you, for you are of great service to us by requesting our presence, for as you listen, so we learn and so the Creator continues to know Itself. Because this instrument is being overshadowed by another member of the Confederation, we shall first transmit the information which our brothers and sisters of Q'uo wish to transmit. There has been a request for the spelling of this entity's name, and we say to the one known as J that although naming is unimportant and therefore the spelling likewise unimportant, our brothers and sisters wish to share the spelling: "Q'uo." Those of Q'uo thank each of you that you were patient enough to allow remarkably uninteresting information to be received.

As the night sky opens, and as you come together in circle this evening, we find that there are questions upon some of your minds concerning a certain aspect of love which has to do with the interaction of entities who wish to express love for the Creator and to each other.

There are many, many ways in which separation betwixt one entity and another or one group and another can be apparently seen. There are differences in appearances between what you call your races. There is the difference between male and female, there is the difference between young and old, and there are many, many finer or shall we say, less obvious differences having to do with personalities, as you call them.

One of these differences especially has been the subject of much pondering by some within this group and by many others of your peoples as they contemplate the most appropriate way to share their lives with others. We speak of the various dimensions from which wanderers, as you call them, come. We shall elucidate.

Those of fourth, fifth and sixth densities, those being the densities of love and compassion, light and wisdom, and unification, all have some representation amongst your peoples at this time as there is a great call, my friends, a call which cannot be ignored, which comes from this planet in travail which you call Earth. Because wanderers are most often far different in their internal modes of thinking and their external modes of expression from those native to the third-density experience, wanderers feel and express a kind of loneliness which is born of being the stranger in a strange land. At times this difference seems almost nothing and the daily life flows quietly and with a nearly imperceptible difference from that of the native to this third density planet. However, it is the nature of the wanderer to find itself homesick. And out of this homesickness is born the desire for companions who more closely approach the native ways and modes of thinking and action of the density whence each wanderer has come.

The fourth density, being one full of love and compassion, has as its native way of living the banding together in groups within which are often many more than one mated couple. Many fourth-density wanderers moved within the Earth planes during those years which this instrument calls the baby boom years, thus many of the young of your peoples who were known within your culture as hippies who dwelt not in couples but in communities and who through memory yearned to reproduce the love and compassion that is a larger reality than the reality whose illusion you now experience within third-density incarnation.

Likewise, there have been wanderers from the sixth density which have been among your peoples for a more extended period of time but in far fewer numbers. Within the dimension of unity the common practice again is to dwell in large families whose members are related not by blood but by a commonality of thought.

At the same time, my friends, you have begun being visited by those of fifth density, the density of wisdom. The native of fifth density seeks solitude, for being wise, it is also without need for the company of others, for the essence of wisdom, my friends, is the knowledge that that which is to be sought is a grasp of the unity of all things. This part of the journey of the seeker must needs, then, be a solitary one. The most clearly understood and easily accepted forms of companionship within fifth density are those of teacher and pupil and those of respected equals.

We are aware that as each of you has thought of community, there has been the puzzle which did not seem to be able to be put together, some wishing one kind of community, some another, with no guidelines offered that seem universally acceptable. My friends, this is due to the mixture of fifth-density entities with those of fourth and those few of sixth, each of whom find a mated relationship somewhat confining, not because each wishes greater experience in mated relationships, but because each half-remembers the depth of friendship, companionship and caring possible, and indeed right, among groups larger than the mated pair. And yet those of fifth density must needs seek solitude within community; those of fourth density—loving, joyful and generous—have hospitality to offer as do children who play and welcome all to their games. Those of sixth density, though somewhat more reserved, nevertheless carry the half-forgotten and half-remembered memory of the larger family and the comfort found therein.

In addition, of course, my friends, there are many very close to graduation within third density who have come to grasp the possibilities of deep friendships and true companionship not limited to the husband and the wife as it is known among your peoples but instead offered to those of like mind. The chief reason for failure of larger communities among your peoples is the inability to bring the disparate memories of fourth and fifth and sixth-density wanderers into alignment, and further, the inability of all those who dwell in the present incarnational experience in third-density bodies in confusing love offered by the Creator from the Creator to the Creator and that love which among your peoples is termed romantic love.

My friends, we cannot offer you solutions, we can only offer a sort of diagram of the causes for miscommunication that contribute to that which is considered the failure of community when it occurs among your peoples. However, we feel that it is important at this juncture to speak to you about that concept of failure. My friends, each of you seeks the far country, if you will, the grass which is the greener. Each of you has gone to at least one far country and has been disillusioned. There is a kind of feeling of death, a death of spirit, of heart, of emotion, when the journey of community and of companionship seems to fail and there is the turning toward what seems to be a journey backwards, a journey to one's home, a journey to safe ground. And yet we say to you that there are no failures, for it is the attempt about which you shall be concerned. The attempt to share love is far greater than any manifestation which may seem to fall short of the ideal. And the journey home is not a journey backwards, for you cannot go backwards, and the home to which you come is eternal. And each time that you visit that home, you have been transformed. You have been dead but again you live and your spirit begins to soar once again and have hope for the morrow.

Those of you who feel that you are wanderers, take heed, for you came not only to share yourself with each other, you came primarily to share yourself with those of third density who may be helped by the sharing of experience with those whose consciousness includes a belief, a faith, and a hope in the ideals of love, compassion, wisdom, service to others, and the seeking of the truth. If you are indeed a wanderer, let it be incumbent upon you to remember why you offered yourself in service to the infinite Creator, and if some are sociable and others solitary, know you that each has the nature of its experience, of its memory, and of its birthright.

We close by speaking to those who approach graduation from third density. Look you, my beloved friends, not to the seeming failure of any ideal of love or community, any expression of family, tribe or clan, but look you instead to the ideal which has been shared. Manifestations shall die; the ideal which spurs man's spirits on, ever onward shall be, as they have been and as they are.

My beloved, have you any conception of the word "forever"? Beyond any dimension there is that which binds all in One. And we ask you to cease pondering your differences. Have you white skin and another black? Are you male and another female? Are you old and another young? Are you solitary and another sociable? Are you compassionate and another wise? My friends, this is all illusion. It is reality to you so that you may learn. And those within your midst who are wanderers among you are dealing with not one but two illusions: the illusion of their native densities and the illusion of the present incarnational experience. How easy it is to be the accountant and separate the lists of entities who are all the one Creator by this or that difference. We ask you instead to rest and be quiet within yourself and find that within you which is one with all that there is. We ask you to have eyes of trust that you may see the oneness of each other, of yourself. We ask that you may attempt the impossible, for we ourselves are still those unique, still those aware of our differences, although our differences are more easily made harmonious because of the vision given us by the density of love.

Yet, how can you exist as spiritual entities if you seek only that which is possible with this illusion, recognizing not the great mystery of the creation? We say to you only that mystery is a unity, though it is far beyond your comprehension. Just as the star is far beyond your reach, that reaching, that seeking for comprehension, that love of what seems to be impossible—the unity of all things—shall give you joy and power and bring you peace, not the peace of one who is dying, but the peace of one who is full of the Creator and fearless in the face of change, for as you interact with each other, whether it be between mated couples, between companions, or between friends, much shall occur which shall seem to be disharmonious. The peace of that which we speak is retained in the face of all disharmony, and indeed grows stronger and more powerful as experience seems to go awry.

Those who seek, my friends, place themselves upon a road which seems strewn with boulders and yet is very, very narrow. And as you clamber over the boulders and attempt to stay upon the path, many, many differences seems to present themselves. Count you then the coins of this plenty of difference and toss those coins away, for such riches shall only cause you unhappiness, and seek you instead that coin within yourself, that unity of self which is in little, the example of that which is in the macrocosm. You are all one, my friends. Please dare to love each other. We assure you that though you shall fall, you shall always be helped up again, if only you keep your heart and your mind in the belief, in the faith, and in the hope of unity with the one great original Thought of love.

We shall leave you now, greeting especially the one known as B. We confirm that we have been with this instrument at times, and it has been our joy to be one with this faithful instrument as it is our joy to be with each of you at your mental request. We leave you as an inspiration …

(Side one of tape ends.)

(Carla channeling)

I am Hatonn. We shall continue. We leave you as an inspiration that has no value except the value that comes from the resonance within you with the thoughts that we share. If there are any thoughts which are not pleasing to you, we most earnestly request that you ignore them and erase them from thought, for our only hope is to be of service to you and we do not wish to be in any way a stumbling block in the path of your seeking. We leave you, although we cannot leave you, for we are all One, in the love and in the light of our infinite Creator. We are known to you as those of Hatonn. Adonai, my friends. Adonai vasu borragus.

(Jim channeling)

I am Latwii, and we greet you, my friends, in the love and in the light of our infinite Creator. We are honored again to be asked to join your group, and we thank you for this privilege of blending our vibrations with yours. It is our hope that we might be of some service this evening by attempting to answer queries which those present may have value in the asking. Without further delay, then, may we attempt the first query, my friends?

Carla: M asked me to ask a question. He wants to know if there is any light you could shed on the phenomenon that he shares with some other people, of affecting metal and other materials so that they bend, and of affecting electromagnetic fields. Basically he wants to know why this happens and what he can do about it, as he has inadvertently managed to bend a portion of his brand new car, which he did not intend to do.

I am Latwii, and am aware of your query, my sister. We find in this instance that there is a general rule, shall we say, that applies to those who are able to demonstrate this type of phenomenon. The entity who seeks the nature of truth will in some fashion pursue this seeking in a disciplined manner. The discipline often is that not as much consciously constructed in some cases, especially [with] those known as what you have called wanderers, but that which is subconsciously remembered, shall we say.

Thus, there is in the electromagnetic force field or aura of such entities a certain configuration that is the result of latent talents having been tapped in some degree and having manifested by the contact of what this group has come to call intelligent energy or that energy which forms the matter or manifestations of the illusion which you inhabit. Thus, when this talent, shall we say, has not been consciously pursued but has become the outgrowth of a more general conscious pursuit and expression of a subconscious ability, the talent is often, shall we say, channeled in an uneven fashion, thus the occasional interference with the electromagnetic equipment that your society has developed within the last few decades and the occasional bending of the metallic substances that are in, shall we say, the range of an entity's unevenly surging abilities at the right moment.

The means of controlling or affecting these talents upon the conscious level involve conscious discipline of this unevenly surging energy through whatever means of discipline the entity may find value therein. The meditation upon the sensations that precede such surges is that which is helpful in all cases. The direct control or manner of control of this phenomenon is that which must be left to the free will of each entity.

May we answer further, my sister?

Carla: Does this also apply to the inadvertent disrupting of electromagnetic equipment which I experience frequently?

I am Latwii, and this is quite correct, my sister. We would add that the ability to discern the approaching surge of such manifestation is that which requires the subtlest of perceptions and sensitivities and may in many cases be more of a distraction than the pursuing of the heart of seeking the truth, and may be considered simply a nuisance, shall we say.

May we answer further, my sister?

Carla: No thank you.

I am Latwii, and we thank you, as always, my sister. May we attempt another query?

Carla: I'm curious. I went to a fiftieth wedding anniversary party last Sunday afternoon and thought about a couple that was still as romantically in love as it had had been when they were first married. This is not the norm among our people. Why is that?

I am Latwii. My sister, why is it that any excel in any field of study? There are those who seem to have talents in one area or another. Is it then not natural to expect that within the area of relationships there would be those who would excel in utilizing the relationship as a vehicle for sharing love, experience and growth more efficiently than do others?

May we answer further, my sister?

Carla: In other areas, some have to work very hard to get even a competence, say something like piano playing. Others have a natural or God-given or native talent that makes it possible for them to become concert pianists. Does this analogy carry over into the ability to love not only well but over a long period of time?

I am Latwii, and am aware of your query, my sister. This is in general correct, and to be more specific, it is often the case that such studies as the piano and even relationships may be undertaken through a series of incarnations. Thus one or two, in the case of a relationship, may find the fruit of the endeavor at a time within an incarnation that is the culmination of many, whereas others may be beginning the lessons at a relatively newer, shall we say, time within their overall experience of the lessons which your illusion offers.

May we answer further, my sister?

Carla: No, thank you.

I am Latwii, and we thank you, my sister. Is there another query?

(Pause)

I am Latwii. We find that the minds are quiet of queries as the hearts are full of peace and the enjoyment each of the other's company. In this enjoyment we are happy to join this group and shall only in name leave this group in that love and light in the hearts of each and of the One Who Is All. We are those of Latwii. Adonai, my friends. Adonai vasu. ☥

Sunday Meditation
March 16, 1986

(Carla channeling)

I am Oxal. I greet you in the love and in the light of our infinite Creator. We thank you for allowing us to come and share our thoughts with you. We would like to say to the one known as L that we are very grateful for his openness to our contact but found some difficulty in establishing our identity. We shall be most happy to use this instrument as he desires and will begin through this instrument.

We would speak with you this evening of joy, that quality which is beyond its name, that energy which creates in fire and yet in peace, that explosion which is yet a steady state, that translation of that which proceeds into that which is.

We would speak to you of history. Those among your peoples are fascinated with history, that which is past history and that which shall be future history, and we would point out to you that if you wish a specific remedy against joy it would be history that would take the first place among the active distractions of those who seek.

We speak to you of these things at this time because there are those among you who have spent a good deal of time as you call it in prayer and in meditation supporting what this instrument calls the great peace march. We would like to point out to you that the ideal involved is a part of joy and that the history of that effort is not. It is difficult to perceive the possibility of feeling joy when watching what could have been disintegrate, and we understand that among your peoples that which does not eventuate as a finished process is counted as failure.

Success and failure belong to that outward portion of yourselves which belong to history. The discipline of joy is the discipline of remaining outside of time, or to speak more precisely, within that womb from which time issues and towards which it shall once again be drawn in the great rhythm of the cosmos. To remove oneself from processes is to remove oneself from all of those things which seem real, beginning with the processes of one's own physical vehicle, continuing on with the processes of the daily living—the telephone that rings, the doorbell that rings, the visitor that knocks at your gate, the information that comes through the post and all those things which remind one again and again of the processes of dailyness.

Shall you then reject all of these things in order to remain joyful? We suggest to you that there is a portion of you which should do just that in order to achieve something which you may wish to nurture and that is the sense of humor, the light touch, the feeling of being seated within love and its expression—joy and laughter—regardless of outward circumstances. Processes, as all things which partake of time, begin and end, are successful or fail, and yet consciousness is variably affected by these processes.

May we suggest to you that by reserving a portion of yourself to be centered within that great womb of time where joy holds sway, one can experience differently the processes of living within the illusion which you now enjoy and from which you shall learn as you choose to learn, slowly or more rapidly, ineffectually or more effectively.

The more one throws the whole self into that which may be called petty, the more one allows oneself to worry and be concerned over seeming failures, the more one robs oneself of the opportunities for transformation, and yet transformation is what you have come to choose to do. It seems that that which is new becomes old, but we say to you to consider whether it is not one's interest that becomes old. When one perceives things from the standpoint of joy, nothing can escape the illumination which love brings.

We would at this time again attempt to communicate through the one known as L. I am Oxal.

(L channeling)

I am Oxal, and I greet you again, my friends, in the love and in the light of the infinite Creator. We are encountering slight difficulty in working through this instrument but will continue so that the instrument may become familiarized with our vibration and become more fluent in its ability to communicate our transmission. We of Oxal appreciate the effort displayed and request your patience as we work with the instrument.

It is our desire, my friends, to be able to be one with you in your pursuit—correction—in your efforts to seek awareness.

We shall relinquish our use of this instrument at this point as the instrument is fatigued and having difficulty with our communications. We are grateful for the opportunity to exercise this instrument and thank those present for their patience. We are known to you as Oxal. Adonai, my friends.

(Carla channeling)

I am Q'uo, and we greet you in the love and light of the One Who Is All. It is a great blessing to blend our vibrations with yours and to drink in the beauty of your beings. We would speak only briefly through this instrument, however there is a calling at this time for our particular bias in vibration and we gladly share it with you, knowing that the fellowship which we feel with you is only the surface of the service that you do us by allowing us to be with you.

We would give to you our encouragement and speak upon meditation for it is the key which unlocks the door to that which is within you—and that which is within you is nothing less than the one original Thought which is the Creator. You may call this Creator "Universal Mind," yet that is not precise, for the mind proceeded and precipitated from the Thought which was thought without mind, but only with consciousness. You are the Creator, and as you experience each other, the Creator gains experience.

We speak from the point of view that the Creator has made a great sacrifice in causing a portion of Its being to have mind and to become independent, for there is much effort in accepting the free will of portions of Itself which seem disharmonious with other portions of Itself. And yet the Creator has repeatedly made this sacrifice of wholeness without effort in order to bring Itself an expanded Self. The Creator, shall we say, takes the very, very long view and looks upon all that occurs through all the densities and dimensions, of which there are an infinite number, in order that It may key into Its own Self all of the selves that have become unique and learn all those things which each unique portion has learned. And you yourself are a sacrifice to your own mind, for without mind you would constantly be in a state of meditation and all things would be whole and entire unto themselves and one with you and acceptable in every respect. Yet you have sacrificed that awareness to come into incarnation and to be limited by your separation from those things about you—the material of the seat upon which you now bear your weight, of each other because you can touch but you cannot become in one in physical sense.

Separation seems to run very deep and one forgets that the stones sing, that the earth shouts with rejoicing, and that the trees skip in the springtime. How easy it is to feel oneself separate from life that indwells all things. How easy it is to feel separate from oneself, to feel that there are factions within the self which must be reconciled, to find oneself analyzing and reanalyzing to no avail. The only road from separation into unity is keyed with meditation. Some there are who benefit from meditating at great length. Some there are who benefit from meditating a brief few minutes in each day, and some there are whose meditations are in action and through action they are centered and one with all that there is.

Therefore, do not assume that you know what meditation is and what your goals should be towards it, but rather, as you meditate, listen to that voice which speaks within and meditate as that voice instructs you. There is no set time nor is there a set method. There is one thing however which we must emphasize and that is the fidelity to the practice.

We thank you. We are most privileged to have been able to speak through this instrument to this group. We ask only in that you treat our words as those of your brothers and sisters and not as those from, shall we say, on high. We are imperfect and most fallible, yet we have that to share which we have experienced, and so we shall with many thanks for the invitation. We would leave you now upon the many, many sounds that drift past your inner ear as the domicile rests in the chilly wind of springtime and the night sky sings with the songs of galaxies and stars. We shall drift away so that our voice is no longer heard, and yet we are always with you if you request our presence mentally. We leave you in the love and the light of the one infinite Creator. We are those of Q'uo. Adonai, my friends. Adonai, my children. Adonai.

(Carla channeling)

I am Nona. I greet you in love [and] in light and am so happy to share [this] evening with you. We shall say no more.

(Carla channels a lovely healing melody from Nona.)

Sunday Meditation
March 23, 1986

(L channeling)

I am Laitos, and I greet you, my friends, in the love and the light of the infinite Creator. My friends, we are pleased to speak to you tonight, for this is an occasion which we of the Confederation find beneficent for your planet. For we approach that time in which many of your planet celebrate the memory of the events of the life of one whom you call Jesus the Christ. We celebrate with you the efforts on the part of many to turn inward, to use this occasion as an opportunity, a stimulus to turn within and examine oneself, to reunite oneself with one's Creator, for in truth, my friends, is this not the significance of that which you call the resurrection? Consider if you will the similarities. The one whom you call Jesus led a life of quiet contemplation, of study, and of experience, and reached the point where he found the core of his existence lay not within the physical shell, but rather within his own source, and, in reuniting himself with his Creator, was sustained and nurtured through his period of hardship to the extent that he was capable quite literally of rising above that which is called death.

My friends, in his words, "I am the way," he left a clue for those [who] would hear to follow, that those who desire may follow a similar journey, may turn within in the face of any difficulty and find that which truly sustains. To rise again is simply to return to the illusion with this awareness and to again, so to speak, take up the cross that others may be reached, that others may see, and in seeing find the opportunity to wonder and to seek for answers.

My friends, why did the one called Christ choose to remain after this point in time? Has it crossed your minds to wonder? Upon reading the accounts following that event called the resurrection, and the nature of this man's physical existence afterwards, is it not true that his life thenceforth in the eyes of the narrators took on what may be referred to as a mystic hue, [as] that being who suddenly arrives from nowhere when the need is present and is no longer visible when the need has been filled? Consider the lesson he would share with you, my friends. Those to whom he spoke and those with whom he met were men and women such as yourselves, who faced with doubt the dangers and perplexities of their lives, who faced with a teacher those lessons they could but dimly grasp, found themselves [out] of their depth, or so they thought. Yet, my friends, they, like yourselves, were to discover that when the need was truly present, when the asking occurred, it was given to them, as it is given to you.

My friends, rejoice and celebrate not only the resurrection of one who has gone before, but also, my friends, celebrate your own, for you have truly learned to go within and to bring back that which you found. My friends, like the one known as Jesus, you shall find yourselves called at times, perhaps without your knowledge, to be in a situation where others have need of that light you bear. My friends, give freely and give without fear, for there is no way in which one who does so can fail to find their way safely home once again. In the love and in the light of the infinite Creator, I am known to you as Laitos. Adonai, my friends.

(Carla channeling)

I am Hatonn, and like our brothers and sisters of Laitos, we greet you in the love and in the light of our infinite Creator and we thank you for requesting our presence this evening. We too would speak upon that which is alive and beleaguered which faces the death and which through faith recognizes the greater reality of larger life.

It is clear that we know nothing, and we suggest to you that in all humility you examine that which you know and find its value. Intellectually speaking, you may well find in vigorous honesty that nothing is known. The framework upon which concepts which govern your life patterns are laid consist of theses, compositions, suppositions, adages, empirical observations, and unsupported opinions. And yet in this forest of unknowing which most of those among your peoples consider "knowing," the spiritual student must make his way.

Subjectively, a great deal is known by each of you. In the deeper portions of your being lie the faculties which empower your being—faith, compassion, love, hope, a seeking for the light, a thirst for truth. One of the basic subjective assumptions is that there is a Creator. Another is that the Creator is in relationship to you. A further subjective supposition is that the relationship betwixt the Creator and you is right relationship, one which abounds in fruit, in harvest, in bounty.

And yet the Creator subjectively seems to offer a great deal that is bitter. It is as if the Creator were handing you a cup full of bitter wine, and yet because the hand holding the cup is the Creator's, in faith we drink it and it is bitter. The faith in which you take the most bitter drink within this illusion is in essence the faith that the Creator, being in right relationship with you, shall give you that which shall seem bitter, but which is in the end sweet and rich.

You shall spend a very large portion of this creation's time/space and space/time dwelling upon the fruits of the bitter cup you take in faith now, for although there are heavier illusions than this one, this is the heaviest illusion for those beings which have become conscious of the self. This is the illusion in which we choose whom to serve. Therefore, we draw your gaze not only to the Kingdom of Heaven, as you would call it, where all the good is known and the subjective has become the objective, and that which is solitary within your soul has become common and shared among all souls. We ask you to turn to the illusion, for it is important that you spend these few moments of your infinite experience in compassionate scrutiny and the most honest reaction and interaction to and with the bitter cup which you may be asked to drink. We ask you not to flinch from this experience, but insofar as it is possible at any given moment we ask you to gaze without regret at all which seems bitter and difficult, for this has been given you with the greatest love and wisdom.

We did not choose this particular time to explore the paradox of a seeming other who gives you what you give yourself. Let us for the moment accept the intellectual necessity of dichotomy and assume that there is an other which has given you the opportunity to learn how that which is bitter may be sweetened by your reaction to it, by your working through it, and by your gradual acceptance and joy in it. To transcend that which grinds the soul into numbness is to shake off all suppositions of the unfairness and unjustness of the creation in its relationship to you. You may picture the greatest and most terrible torture. The limits of your imagination are all that limit the possibilities of difficulty within this most intense illusion. And yet it is the Creator's hand which has dealt you these bitter things and has asked you to taste them and accept them and to see through them into the graves of pain and agony and towards the transformation and purification of the self so that the relationship between you and your Creator grows ever more intimate and trusting, until finally the paradox of separation betwixt Creator and created is at an end and the hand that serves the cup is your own.

My friends, how happy we are to share this cruel and beautiful pageant with you and to rejoice with you not only in the vision of angelic rejoicing, at transformation and resurrection, but to rejoice with you also at the process by which transformation is chosen. We are those of Hatonn. We leave you in the love and in the light of the One Who Is All. Adonai vasu borragus.

(Jim channeling)

I am Latwii, and I greet you, my friends, in love and in light. We are very happy to be with you this evening. It has been a measure of your time since we were able to speak with this group. It is our honor and our privilege to join you in our humble capacity of entertaining your queries. We hope that we may be of some small service this evening in that capacity. May we then begin with the first query?

Carla: I have a question from S. She had a great difficulty when she was a child in speaking and the words "tongue-tied" didn't even come close to describing the agony of her difficulty. Sometimes she couldn't even talk at all. And although she overcame this in later years and can now say what she wants when she wants, she retains not only the painful memory of that but continues to be rather painfully shy underneath her acquired social abilities. Insofar as you can talk upon the subject, she would like to know what this childhood difficulty might indicate or what function this kind of difficulty might have in her learning.

I am Latwii, and am aware of your query, my sister. We shall speak as we are able upon this topic, and shall attempt to give that which is permissible without the infringement upon the free will of this entity. In the young portions of this entity's current incarnation there were the recognitions upon the conscious level of this entity that the world about it was most unusual in relation to this entity, that is, this entity saw the world or environment about it in somewhat of a threatening fashion. The desire of this entity, being most positively oriented, was to make itself available in the service of those about it in whatever way was possible. Yet, because of the seeming alien nature of the world about this entity, this entity felt great difficulty in moving itself and communicating itself in easy patterns, shall we say. There was the seeming natural resistance that presented itself immediately to this entity's perceptions. This resistance became somewhat internalized, causing a kind of blockage of what you would call communication from this entity to those about it.

Therefore, in the desire to be of service, and with the recognition that that which the entity wished to serve was seemingly hostile and alien, this entity then internalized to a degree that disharmonious nature of the world about it, and found that internalization to block the free flow of communication. Thus, the efforts were put forth upon the part of this entity from the early portions of its incarnation to the present time that would allow a free flow of communication to occur, and this the entity has accomplished to a large degree in its efforts to provide those services and to learn those lessons which this incarnation was designed to accomplish.

May we answer further, my sister?

Carla: I'll let S read this transcript and let her ask further. Thank you very much.

I am Latwii, and we thank you, my sister. Is there another query?

L: Yes, Latwii. I have difficulty trusting the one known as M. I've gone over it in my mind a number of times trying to understand it—apparently I'm missing something. Could you offer any suggestion of things I might examine within myself or in my past to help me understand this feeling?

I am Latwii, and am aware of your query, my brother. We shall attempt to respond to this query in an helpful manner though there is some difficulty with this instrument's own coloration of feelings concerning the entity of whom you speak, and we must needs work with these distortions in order that our concepts be as clearly communicated as is possible. We can suggest, in general, that at any time that you might find a difficulty with another of your other selves that you might look upon that difficulty as being symbolic in some degree or fashion of a portion of your own being which has yet to receive the full approval of your own …

(Side one of tape ends.)

(Jim channeling)

I am Latwii, and am with this instrument once again. For the world about you, my brother, and all those other selves which populate it, is in one respect a mirror for the opportunity to see the self in as many aspects as one is aware of. Each aspect then comes before the mind of the self to be discerned or judged, to use a more distorted term, to be accepted or to be rejected. To those who are conscious of the process of evolution then, this acceptance or rejection becomes the indicator of aspects of the self which yet remain to be balanced and accepted, for if you look to the heart of each entity and each experience and the illusion which you inhabit, you will find the underlying unity of all creation. You will find the Creator in all things, whole, perfect and balanced. That there might be perceptions other than unity, perfection and balance within the mind of any entity is the play of the illusion, the game in which each partakes in order that experience might be gained and the Creator might come to know Itself in ways that are richer, more intense, with greater purity and with far greater variety than if those individual portions of the Creator had not been flung from it at the beginning of your octave of experience.

May we answer further, my brother?

L: No, that gave quite a bit to look at. Thank you very much.

I am Latwii, and we thank you as always, my brother. Is there another query?

Carla: Well, this is a stupid question, I know that—but isn't it possible that one might not trust someone because of the simple fact that such a person is in some ways untrustworthy?

I am Latwii, and am aware of your query, my sister. That there is a degree of truth to what you say is not reason, shall we say, to trust or not trust another, for in truth all are the one Creator and are expressing aspects of that one Creator in distorted fashions which when followed to their source express patterns of learning and service that are whole and perfect. To focus upon that which is upon the periphery of an entity's being and to judge the entity itself from that distorted aspect is to miss the heart of the entity and the heart of the opportunity that the interaction between you and that entity presents to you.

May we answer further, my sister?

Carla: No, thank you.

I am Latwii, and we thank you, my sister. Is there another query?

Carla: Well, before we close up shop, I do have one more question which will try the instrument's abilities to be a channel. Is there any way open to us as we are now to receive the rest of the information having to do with the archetypes of body and spirit which Ra was giving in the trance state when Don was alive? And if so, how should we prepare for or approach that way?

I am Latwii, and am aware of your query, my sister. We find that there is one area in which we may speak, and that is to refocus the attention upon the use of your own instrument by those of the entities known to this group as L/Leema. In the pursuit of this information it is possible that after a sufficient amount of study has been accomplished of that information which is already available within these areas, that sessions could be had that would focus upon one archetypical image at a time, as you would say, and information could then be received of a somewhat more precise nature. We cannot speak as to the advisability of pursuing this information through the contact with those of Ra, for this is an area that lies most completely within the free will of your own making.

May we answer further, my sister?

Carla: Could you give a subjective opinion as to the degree of distortion from the information Ra might give which would be present in information from L/Leema? In other words, how watered-down or distorted would this information be?

I am Latwii, and we find that this query is one with variable possibilities of response due to the factors which would comprise each session. These factors would be variable according to the entities present, their interest in this kind of information, the general level of vital energy, of all present for the session and the preparations in the way of study, shall we say, that had gone into the, shall we say, mental and emotional computations prior to the sessions. In general, we may suggest that the degree of accuracy that could be hoped for would be seventy-five to eighty percent in relation to the accuracy that was achieved in the contact with those known as Ra.

May we answer further, my sister?

Carla: No—that's fairly high. Let me make sure I understand. This would have to be a special series, then, not the open invitations. You can just confirm that. And would you suggest any opening or ritual preceding the asking of the group question?

I am Latwii, and we find that you have discovered areas of importance that would indeed be of assistance if accomplished in a dedicated fashion. Yet this again must be respected as lying within the domain of your own choosing. We may suggest that it would be well to ascertain that each entity attending such a session was indeed interested in the information which was being sought, and that there might be an enhancement of the tuning process by the formation of rituals used for these sessions alone. The construction of such rituals and the dedication procedure must be left to your own discrimination.

May we answer further, my sister?

Carla: No, thank you.

I am Latwii, and we thank you, my sister. Is there another query?

Carla: Yes. Is the instrument in the Ra session of a deep enough stability of mind to resume the exercise of the [Middle Pillar] as a magical personality? This entity is unable to judge this for itself.

I am Latwii, and we find that we once again must not cross the line or Law of Confusion, for in these areas there is a great metaphysical charge or power, shall we say, that one is working with, and the work in such areas must be carefully guarded that it is a function totally of the free will of the entity seeking this power. Thus, we must refrain from specific response, my sister, and must once again apologize for a lack of information.

May we answer in another fashion or another query?

Carla: No, thank you.

I am Latwii, and again we thank you, my sister. Is there another query at this time?

Carla: Could you give me an idea of how much advantage in percentage it would be for the people involved in such special sessions to be dwelling under the same roof and living in harmony as opposed to dwelling apart and living in harmony?

I am Latwii, and am aware of your query, my sister. We can suggest that there would be a significant advantage to the type of companionship that produces harmony on a regular basis, for the constant interaction of entities provides for the constant refinement, empowering and enhancement of the harmony that is necessary in any undertaking of this nature.

May we answer further, my sister?

Carla: No, that is all. Thank you.

I am Latwii, and we thank you, my sister. Is there another query?

(Pause)

I am Latwii, and we thank you, each of you, for inviting our presence this evening. We have had a wonderful time and we hope that we have been of some small service to you who have been so gracious as to invite and accept our presence this evening. We shall be with you again upon your requests, whether in your private meditations or in group meeting. We rejoice at the ability and opportunity to praise the one Creator with you in the seeking of that one Creator. We shall leave you now in love and in light. We are those of Latwii. Adonai, my friends. Adonai vasu borragus.

(Carla channeling)

(Carla channels a vocal melody from Nona.)

I am Nona. In love and light I greet you. Adonai. ☥

Sunday Meditation
March 30, 1986

(Carla channeling)

(Chanting intonation, rising in pitch, then in volume.)

A-mi-ra, A-mi-ra, A-mi-ra.

I am Amira, and I greet you in the love and the light of the Father. My brothers and sisters, how I yearn to touch your hearts, how I have always yearned to move the hearts of people. Why are your heads turned to the burnt offerings which you insist upon offering to the Most High, for have I not said that the sacrifice of blood is to be offered no longer? And yet within your nations, instead of spreading the unity of the children of God and taking comfort in each other, you offer your first born again and again and so often do you do it in my name. I came to you as a servant and you have called me a king. And yet the words I humbly offer you as messenger of the Father, you have disregarded. When shall your burnt offerings cease and when shall you turn towards each other, nation to nation, people to people, in love?

My peace I leave with you. I am Amira. Farewell in the love and the light of the Father. Adonai.

(Carla channeling)

I am Hatonn, and I greet you also in the love and in the light of our infinite Creator. It is a great privilege to be with you this evening and to share our humble thoughts with you. As you know, no matter what our subject may be, we are speaking of some aspect of a life lived in love, and we would choose this evening to speak to you of the art of hope.

It is easy to confuse hope with faith. Yet faith is blind; faith does not have eyes that see, nor does it need them. Faith is an inner sureness and is an invaluable ally to the spiritual seeker. In no way would we discourage any from the cultivation of the faculty of faith, for it is one of the great tools of learning available to you upon the spiritual path. Yet there are situations in which a focused vision has its place and is far more effective than blind faith. That faculty is hope. Hope is the development of faith upon a specific area of intent or interest so that there is a vision which is developed which affirms all that is best in a situation, all that is requisite in an outcome.

Hope is that which, while the eagle soars, gazes towards its prey. Faith is that which causes the eagle to leap into the air. The eagle has wings, yet it does not cogitate upon its flying. It hopes for its prey and in its inner eye sees it long before the outer vision finds that which it seeks.

It is well to refine your inner vision, for that faculty of hope is a means whereby one may use one's deeper intuitions to envision that which is sought. This does not say that one attempts to predetermine an outcome. It is rather to say that through hope one may perceive a situation in such a way that the good can be seen and the rest can be seen to fall away, just as in the eagle's eye all that which is not the prey is seen, but is not registered as important. Hope has a way of clearing the mind, of strengthening inner vision, of pulling the cobwebs out of situations, of focusing that incredible strength within each of you which is will.

Do you think that you know what you desire? Is that desire intangible? Then sharpen that faculty of hope until within you you can almost taste and feel and see that which is hoped for. Then allow faith to set you winging upon the air and open your inner eyes wide as you fly. Focus *(inaudible)* is that which you seek, is that for which you truly hope. Your faith shall carry you—but where shall it carry you?

Sharpen that within you that hopes, for hope is a valuable tool and never more valuable than when it seems unlikely that that for which you hope shall appear. Sad indeed is the soul which is hopeless, for faith alone cannot turn the mind to the goal of love. Faith has no direction, but is a faculty which strengthens the spirit so that it may go forth and seek. Hope is the result of having found a direction in which to point the faithful self. We hope for you that which you hope for yourselves. And for ourselves, we hope we have been of service, and further we hope that we may continue to be of service to you, for, my children, you have become very dear to us. All entities in the Creation are dear to us, and yet those to whom we speak become especially dear as we appreciate the beauty of each vibration, the charm of each complex personality, the tune of each singer's song.

We do not ask you to hope for a wonderful, trouble-free, careless existence, although for some this is part of the environment in which lessons of love are learned. In your density it is to be expected, by the very nature of the lessons that you have set yourself to learn, that there will be confusions and difficulties. To put an end to these confusions is to limit your ability to learn the lessons you came to absorb into your very being, and yet we hope with you that you may penetrate the outer shell of experience and aim unerringly for the transformations which lie just the other side of understanding.

How we appreciate being able to speak with you. We ask as always that you remember that we, like you, are hopeful seekers, our feet dusty upon the path, and our knowledge incomplete. Yet we serve the same Creator, and we hope with the same beauty of seeking and purity of desire that lies within each of you. We leave you upon the path, your feet dusty, your bodies perhaps tired, and yet your goal always in your mind's eye. We are known to you as those of Hatonn and we leave you upon that path, yet we are with you and shall be with you in hope, in love, and in joy. In the love and in the light of our infinite Creator, we say to you, adonai. Adonai vasu borragus.

(Jim channeling)

I am Latwii, and greet you in the love and the light of our infinite Creator. We are happy to be with you again, my friends. It is our hope as well that we might be of some service to you this evening by attempting to answer those queries which you feel may point a clearer way in your seeking of the one Creator. May we then begin with the first query?

Carla: I have a question from S. Actually it's a question from me too due to the fact that her questioning has to do with something that happens to me also. She and I both have problems with short-term memory. We both can remember things that happened some time ago, but we have difficulty remembering what happened last week. We are not old enough to be senile and this has been going on with us as long as we can remember—which obviously isn't very long … no. As long as we can remember, we've had trouble with short-term memory. Things just pass us completely by. Could you comment on this in any way? Give us some idea of what it is we're dealing with? Are we freaks? Is there something wrong with us that we should go to a doctor? What is this a symptom of?

I am Latwii, and am aware of your query, my sister. We shall speak as concisely and clearly as possible given our desire to refrain from infringing upon any entity's free will. When one looks at the concept and functioning of the memory, one may observe that portion of the conscious self in this instance which is utilized for the storing of experiences which have value to the entity in its deeper sense, that is, the sense with which the entity incarnated. And this sense is that then which recognizes the, shall we say, purpose of the incarnation. This sense of self which collects about it those memories or experiences that are deemed of use in fulfilling the purpose of the incarnation may not be congruent with the consciously active self, that self which is formed around the central or deeper self and is much influenced by the society in which the self exists.

Within your culture or society at this time the ability to remember events, the nature of which you have described as recent or within the short term of experience, is deemed normal and valuable, for one may recount with another self mutual experiences of the recent past that may serve as the lubricator of conversation and social intercourse, shall we say. Yet to some entities the daily round of activities, especially those of the more trivial and mundane nature, do not hold the attraction to the central self which they do to others, for it is the case with many entities who have begun or have continued for some time the path of the conscious seeking, the daily activities are looked through or perhaps beyond for the meaning that may be contained therein, and frequently when little is found, the activity is discarded, perhaps without even a second thought:

Therefore, when there has been little attraction to [an] event and little thought given to its potential significance, the event may then be lost, for the deeper and more central sense of self recognizes that which is of use and drops that which is not deemed of such use in the seeking of the entity.

Also we must realize that some people are collectors of experiences and thoughts more than are others. For some it is helpful to remember much if not most of the recent experiences, perhaps not so much for the experience itself, but for the ability to comprehend the activities in which one finds oneself engaged. Others are not so much the collectors of the activities and experiences but instead glean the essence of a thing or event, dropping then the event while retaining the heart.

May we answer further, my sister?

Carla: No. I will await S's reading of this material and her own questioning further. Thank you.

I am Latwii, and we are most grateful to you and to the one known as S as well. And to the one known as S we send our heartfelt greetings, welcoming this entity in spirit with our joy. Is there another query?

Carla: Yes. It's from me. I feel like a "Johnny One Note" because I ask questions like this a lot, but I seem to keep experiencing *(inaudible)* most recently the problem is that *(inaudible)* when attempting to help Don the year before he died. I feel so very badly about this that eventually I have to seek time alone and talk out loud to Don, and sometimes I try but sometimes not. But I always feel quite awful about the various things that I wish I had done better or wish I hadn't done at all in that very confused time. No matter how many justifications are offered to me by my friends for all of the things that I did, it has no bearing whatsoever on the situation which is that I feel very, very sinful and guilty and I have a great deal of trouble forgiving myself.

When I talk to Don, I always receive his blessing and I feel better until the next morning when I wake up all over again with this same problem. How can I work to strengthen my ability to forgive myself and my ability to believe that it's possible for me to be redeemed from the kind of terrible sin that I feel I have fallen into?

I am Latwii, and am aware of your query, my sister. We feel that this subject is one which is of great value to you, for it is one in which you have found great difficulty. It is uncomfortably true, my sister, that value and difficulty frequently are companions within your illusion, for within your illusion, the perspective that one must assume in order to accomplish the tasks of the incarnation is necessarily limited in order that focus upon those tasks might be concise and pure. It is this very finely focused attention that allows for the possibility of learning in any area of one's choosing. If the focus were expanded to include all that could be included within the vision of the far-seeing entity, there would be little of worth within your illusion, little of learning that would be possible, for all would be seen as one, and would therefore be seen as well with no need to intervene or interfere in any direction for any reason.

Thus, each of you bravely and courageously and consciously limit yourselves as you enter this illusion in order that you might pursue the learning of love, acceptance, forgiveness, compassion, mercy, all of those facets of understanding in areas of your own choosing. Each learns it in a slightly different fashion, and in your case, my sister, we find that you have chosen, as it is well known to you, to learn a compassion and acceptance for the value of your own self as it moves through this illusion and experiences the Creator in many disguises. You have chosen to express love in whatever situation you may find your experience has led you.

Many situations have proven quite difficult. Yet, in each instance, your determination to love without stint and with a whole heart and to give totally of yourself in love has carried you through each challenge. And so you have moved through your incarnation with the knowledge that it is possible to love and indeed is really the only choice. Thus, there has come the opportunity for you to experience not only the ability to love but the opportunity to refine that love so that it may do its work in a realm beyond your conscious comprehension.

Thus, in the experience of which you speak, the challenge, or opportunity, shall we say, was presented to each within this group of three to experience …

(Side one of tape ends.)

(Jim channeling)

I am Latwii, and am once again with this instrument. We shall continue. To experience some facet of the learning and refining of the concept of love, for each had in some degree experienced the more fundamental lessons of love, and there was then seen the need to refine this expression with [the] quality which may be termed wisdom, and each attempted to do that which the moment required, yet each found …

(Inaudible)

This instrument is somewhat concerned that the device used to record our words is not functioning correctly and therefore has attempted to rectify the situation. We shall continue.

Thus, in the experience of which we have been speaking, the attempt to refine the love was placed upon the wings of faith and sent forth with the hope that the attempt would be successful. Yet it was made clear to each that the designs of the desires were beyond the control of any conscious mind and that the results of efforts must then also be accepted in love and in joy and the self which sent forth the efforts on faith propelled with hope would also must needs be accepted in love and in joy, for one could not, it was obvious in this situation, judge the self or the results in any manner that was understandable. All was quite beyond effort or desire, therefore the opportunity to accept that which was. And the self was accentuated.

In this situation, my sister, you have found yourself within the dilemma of your own being, for within the heart of your being beats the one desire—to serve and to love the one Creator in all, most especially in those to whom one has given love. However, also within your own being was the need and the desire to expand the ability to accept not only the situations in which you might find yourself tested severely, but also to accept the self and to give to it the same love that you have given to all those entities and situations that you have touched with your life.

May we answer further, my sister?

Carla: Thank you.

I am Latwii, and we are grateful to you, my sister, as always, for allowing us to attempt our humble service.

Might there be another query at this time?

Carla: No, thank you.

I am Latwii, and we thank each for allowing us to join this group upon this most special of occasions. Our hearts are full of joy at each opportunity to blend our vibrations with yours. We thank you, we bless you, and we rejoice with you that each day and each moment provides the opportunity for the One to be born again within each heart and each breath. We are those of Latwii. Adonai, my friends. Adonai. Adonai vasu borragus. ☥

Sunday Meditation
April 6, 1986

(Jim channeling)

I am Hatonn, and I greet you, my friends, in the love and in the light of our infinite Creator. We greet each of you this evening with a special joy for we are aware that there is a special kind of good feelings and camaraderie which this group has generated this evening, speaking upon those topics which are of special interest to the group. It is in such a manner that the vibrations of each are blended and then combined with others, and thereby provides us with the harmony of all with which we may blend our own vibrations.

This evening we would speak upon the topic of harmony, using the experience of this group this evening as a starting point, for though the topics of which you spoke upon were little concerned with matters spiritual, it was the desire behind the topic, shall we say, that allowed the work of blending vibrations together in a harmonious manner to occur. Each desired to share with the other what could be helpful in increasing the enjoyment of the group as a whole. Thus it is in your daily round of activities you will find yourselves, as you have countless times, engaged in conversations and activities with those about you in such a manner as might often seem tedious, confusing, inane and pointless, for the topics of daily interaction are frequently most trivial and mundane, having to do with the carrying on of endless rituals, regulations and so forth. Yet these tedious interactions, shall we say, bring together people such as yourselves, people who have hopes, dreams, fears, feelings, family, friends and so forth, just as you do.

When you are able through these activities to find the heart of the situation, shall we say, and share in an honest and loving fashion your point of view with those who share the situation with you, then the tedium of the moment may in many cases be forgotten and left behind as even the most minute and mundane of activities takes on the communication of heart-to-heart. It is in such instances that each entity has the opportunity to find more than is apparent on the surface of the moment, and is this not the case in each area of your lives, my friends? For if you will look upon those activities which have filled your previous measure of time which you call a week, how many of these activities would you guess were of more than a routine nature? Yes, my friends, the routine, the mundane, the seemingly trivial, is the fabric of the illusion in which each of your peoples move.

The illusion about you is well constructed to hide the unity of all people and events. In such a well formed illusion it is then the norm that entities shall move about in a seemingly endless array of irrelevant matters and have countless opportunities to interact with others in any fashion which those involved may choose to fathom. You may in your daily round of activities concentrate only upon the surface of appearances and pass each moment off as one more item completed upon the list that shall comprise your day. In this way entities, activities, days, years, and eventually one's life, may be measured by an unending string [of] check marks with activities being dutifully completed but without a harvest which gives meaning to the life.

One may, with a certain desire, persistence and attitude, however, look beneath the surface of the events which present themselves in a day, in a year, or in a life and see below that surface that which was hidden previously from sight due to lack of desire to find what was hidden or lack of knowledge in knowing that more is available in each moment for each entity, for each entity brings to each moment the entirety of its being. When you consider that each entity is a facet of the same Creator, moving within this illusion with you with the purpose of finding that which was hidden with you, you may see those about you in somewhat of a different fashion, for these entities, then, with such an attitude become more than functionaries or bureaucrats of the day, shall we say. They are those who with you travel this illusion in search of that which many are unaware exist. They search with you for the one Creator that exists in each moment, disguised as difficulty, as confusion, as jealousy, as ignorance, and so forth. And yet, when one can bring one's heart of seeking and desire to be of service to others to each moment that is shared with others, then one may see unfolding before one's eyes level upon level of richness of being, of desire and of potential for uncovering yet further treasures hidden within each moment.

Those about you may not exhibit the degree of desire to seek the heart of the moment as do you, and yet this need not be a hindrance in your own experience of the perfection, balance and joy that is available in each moment, for as you take that which is given, whatever has brought you together for any moment, and propel the activities necessitated by such a moment with your own desire to imbue that moment with love, with compassion, with wisdom, with a kind word, perhaps simply a smile—there are infinite ways to express these qualities—then you will discover that the other entities within your shared moment will feel that love which you have projected touching their own hearts and will perhaps without even thinking respond in kind in order that love may not go unrecognized, for love knows its own kind and leaps to rejoice when it finds another of like heart.

You will see moments, and entities within moments, transformed when you are able to imbue your portion of the moment with the honest sharing of yourself and your beingness which you bring to each moment, for always the truth of your nature is with you; though it may be seem to be lost within the mundane, yet it is within each portion of your being awaiting the call to be of service to another. And notice as you share the heartfelt feelings and the honest communication with a true concern for those about you, that the response is so overwhelmingly accepting and loving that the joy which you have cast upon the waters of the moment returns to you manifold, though it was your intention to give it away.

We realize that each within this gathering this evening is quite well aware of these simple principles, for each has experienced them in action, shall we say, yet we find from time to time that it is often helpful to remind each within these groups of that which is already known, for it is oh, so easy, my friends, to forget and to become again a seeming slave to the triviality of repeated routines in days that seem to be the same, one upon the other.

When we speak to your group and to others, we cannot speak upon topics which are unknown, for each of you, my friends, is a portion of the same Creator with an endless storehouse of knowledge that needs only from time to time to be repeated and shown again to the mind of the seeker.

We thank you for allowing us to speak this evening in this simple manner and hope that our words may have been of some small service. We shall relinquish this contact for the nonce. Before taking our leave, however, we would pause for a moment and move about each within this group that our vibrations might be felt and aid in the deepening of the meditative state, if this is mentally requested. We shall pause. I am Hatonn.

(Pause)

I am Hatonn, and am again with this instrument. Again we thank you, my friends for allowing us to speak with you this evening and to blend our vibrations with yours. We are most grateful. We shall be with you again. We are known to you as those of Hatonn. Adonai, my friends. Adonai vasu borragus.

(Jim channeling)

I am Latwii, and we are also most happy to join you, my friends, and we also come in the love and light of the one Creator. We have been patiently waiting for our turn this evening and are happy to be able to offer our services as well. We would, as always, attempt to answer those queries which those present may have value in the asking. We remind each present that we are not infallible, and will give that which we have found to be helpful in our own seeking with the knowledge that we are but your brothers and sisters who speak of our own experience in our opinions. May we attempt a query at this time?

Questioner: Can you tell me of the concept of soul mates?

I am Latwii, and am aware of your query, my brother. We find that this is a term which is most popular among many of those who seek the nature of truth among your peoples at this time, yet it is a term which has been somewhat misused, shall we say, in its most common usage. We find that the term of soul mates is reserved for those entities within your third-density illusion who have from incarnation to incarnation journeyed together and found the seeking of truth to be enhanced by joining in repeated incarnations in order that lessons begun and carried on at one time may be completed, as you might say, at yet another time. Those of the nature of soul mates may be many in number, not just two, and may be of many sexual natures in order that there might be the variety of the interaction between various entities in various incarnations.

May we elaborate in any further way, my brother?

Questioner: There's also the term "twin flames." Is that also soul mates or is this a different form of incarnation?

I am Latwii, and we believe that we might best answer this query by suggesting that the term twin flames is a term which is somewhat more specific in its use. Entities who are of this nature are, shall we say, somewhat more closely connected in the nature of their being and in the nature of their seeking. The entities will have found their individualization of consciousness as having sprung from the same root, shall we say. This is a concept which is somewhat difficult to explain in terms of your language, however, we shall attempt such.

The origin of the individualized nature of these entities is an origin which in many cases brings forth only one individualized portion of consciousness and sends it forth that it might gain further experience and continue through the process of evolution thusly. The twin flame concept springs from the dual aspect of the consciousness foci which then have the same origin within what you might call the upper levels of the second-density pool of consciousness. Thus, the entities who might fall within the designation of twin flame are somewhat like the Siamese twins that are the rare occurrence within your own illusion.

May we answer in any further way, my brother?

Questioner: Is there any way that one can tell if he has met his twin flame?

I am Latwii, and am aware of your query, my brother. We find that there are many ways one may know about the nature of another. In the case of which you speak, the recognition of such an entity could perhaps be first noticed in a certain unspoken feeling that is shared between the entities. The somewhat unconscious knowing of another might then expand in its expression to include what you may call the precognitive experience of another, that is to say, one may begin to anticipate the thoughts, words and actions of the other before they occur. Within the meditative or perhaps the dreaming state, one may discover certain experiences shared in other illusions making themselves known in symbolic fashion. The entities may then through continued interaction become aware that there is more to their current experience than meets the eye, and this may then be pursued in what you may call the hypnotic regression where the intent is to move into previous experiences in order to discover more of the shared experience which is, shall we say, magnetically drawn to this current experience.

May we answer further, my brother?

Questioner: No, thank you.

I am Latwii, and we thank you, my brother. Is there another query?

(Pause)

I am Latwii, and we thank each of you for allowing our presence this evening. We are happy to have been able to join this group, and we shall join you in what you would call your future upon your request. We shall leave this group at this time, as always in the love and in the light of the one infinite Creator. Adonai, my friends. Adonai.

Sunday Meditation
April 13, 1986

(Carla channeling)

I am Latwii, and greet you in the love and in the light of the one infinite Creator. We apologize for the pause between our contacting this instrument and her responding to our contact, but this instrument was concerned that we did not feel like ourselves, and, indeed, our vibration is a bit subdued for we recall the many times that we have caused this instrument to bounce up and down in the seat because we had not adjusted. We finally convinced this instrument when we began to sing "When the Saints Go Marching In." That did it. Therefore we thank you for asking our presence this evening.

My friends, we would speak to you about something somewhat seemingly different than the usual topic of love and meditation. We would speak to you of expenditures. The questions that bring you to a metaphysical group which is seeking the truth are basic. You wish to know who you are, you wish to know why you are here, you wish to determine where you are going. And somehow, philosophy often neglects that which may be called daily or ordinary life, expecting and hoping that the seeker will experience that more and more of the consciousness will be taken up with these deep and impenetrable matters so that as the life experience grows longer, the seeker will become closer and closer to the infinite mystery of the source of all that there is.

And yet each of you does live a daily life. That ordinary life is "grist for your mill[4]." It is the material from which you extract the answers to the most basic metaphysical questions. The fabric of this everyday life may seem banal, or at the very least, tame. And yet, if you have a listening ear and a watchful eye, that which is daily will also yield to you the most extravagant fruit in your seeking.

One of the things with which each entity in his or her daily life must consider is the expenditure of money and time. We cannot and would not attempt to be over-general on this subject, for each entity incarnates with a slightly different intention. Love is not a simple lesson, but is indeed a unified and single creative principle which has a million faces, and it is this unified yet infinite principle for which each of you sacrificed knowledge, memory and comfort in order that you might work more carefully and closely in your own seeking after that one great original Thought.

You do not each have the same time to spend; you do not each have the same money to spend. What you have in common is the ability to look inward and to discover consciously within yourself that about which you feel the most strongly. Some of you have incarnated with a special love for the second density of your planet. We suggest to you that this is

---

[4] Carla: A phrase made famous by Ram Dass' book of that title.

not only a chance for you to rejoice in the beauties of the outdoors but may well also be a suggestion made to your conscious self through roots of mind to aid the environment in which you find yourselves and in which you enjoy your days and nights. Some may have a special feeling for the plights of those who are hungry. One may then give thanksgiving that one has fed one's family, but more than that, one may discover the suggestion that stewardship regarding the feeding of strangers in need might be appropriated.

One may have incarnated with no strong interest in the world's problems but with a strong interest in seeking the presence of the Creator. For that entity, stewardship may be not the expenditure of money, but rather the expenditure of time. Usually both time and money are involved in spiritual expenditure or what this instrument would call stewardship. It is easy for us to feel very strongly that what you need to hear is the central information, that is, central to the metaphysical life. The centrality of meditation as a source for that flow of the love which each of you seeks is something about which we feel so strongly that we usually find within each entity present a particular way of speaking about the central subject so that we may hope to inspire the listener to turn inward, and yet tonight we would suggest that you turn outward and face the world about you.

It is important, in our opinion, that the awareness of unity with all things and co-responsibility for all that there is be sharpened. Your talents and gifts are for you to discover, but that environment which you enjoy hungers for your touch, for your caring, for your presence and for your expenditure of yourself. We could speak for hours suggesting the different kinds of involvement in your environment which serve to heighten your societal consciousness and awareness of love. And yet, it is far more accurate and far shorter to admit once again that each of you is a unique being, but that each of you has an appointment with your daily life with the turning outward, and it is well that that appointment be kept, for your incarnation is not your own—your incarnation is the Creator's gift to Itself and the Creator is in all things.

What portion of the creation disturbs you? Draws you? Concerns you? We ask you to ask yourself if you are spending enough of your riches on impersonal giving, and we do not mean only money, for we cannot emphasize enough that time is often far more of a sacrifice than your money. For those who do not feel the call to any particular part of the daily life, we urge that that being consider how active it is in its beingness. If what it has to offer is a determination to become closer and ever more close to the Creator, how often and how freely is that companionship given to the world? And not an exclusive world of people who already think as you do, but to a world of people whose faces are blank and whose names are unknown.

Now, of course, you understand that in order to be a good student, it is necessary first to determine that you seek the lessons of love, that you seek to serve, and that you seek to intensify your learning and your service through meditation, so you see, we have come back to our main subject after all. However, may we suggest once more that your daily life, your everyday life, is a veil beyond which lies fantasy, imaginary beings, wondrous dreams, terrible dragons, and the most amazing of stories.

When one [who is] dull of sight looks, one layer is seen; one layer of the illusion. But you are dreaming your own dream and you can look at as many dimensions and layers and parts of your dailyness as you wish. Miracles are exploding about you every second. Perhaps it is merciful that so much is veiled to you. Perhaps the overload to your senses would cause you to become unstable and unable to seek further. But we suggest that you can look a bit further, you can find hope in dark corners, and you can share that in whatever way is your way. We do ask that you consider carefully what [response] you are offering back towards your environment. Think carefully and if you are not satisfied with your answer, do not blame your community for the boring quality of your existence but ponder stewardship and value, both the fastidious attention which you pay to your own inner preferences and the faculty of imagination which allows you to see what it is you may do that is just precisely what you can do, want to do, and feel good about doing.

Much is written in your holy works, especially those best known to this instrument, that is, the books of the Bible, about the fruit of good works. We would like to distinguish between the traditional concept of good works and that which we are suggesting for you. Bow first to your inner nature, for there is a good work waiting for you. But it is the determined seeker who picks that good work up, imagines a way to further it, and finds the persistence and determination to accomplish it.

We are so happy to be speaking through this instrument and we would like to greet each of you. We are aware of the fatigue of each in the group, and yet we rejoice in the love for each other and for inspiration that brought you together. We hope that some inspiration which we may have in our poor words may return to your dwelling with you as you leave this domicile. May you be in love with life while you are in it. May you be in love with each part of your life, for there is nothing that is without beauty to the Creator. Yes, you may privately think to yourself that there are things about yourself or especially about your bodies that are less than lovely. You may think that there are many things about the world that are less than lovely and about which you can do nothing. But just as you cleanse your body and make it a holy place, regardless of how many times it becomes unholy and you must cleanse it again, so may you see the world in which you live. There is no spot too small and no problem too large for your attention and for your stewardship. Listen carefully to yourself and you will find that which you may do to give back to the world which is part of the Creator that love which the world has for you.

We leave you considering how we could ever think that the world is beautiful in the same week in which your government takes the tax money from your peoples, so that we may transfer to another instrument in order that we may catch any questions that may be flying our way. We leave this instrument. We are those of Latwii.

(Jim channeling)

I am Latwii, and I am with this instrument, and we greet you again in love and in light. We are hopeful that if there are any queries, we may increase our service in some small degree by giving our measured response. We remind each of you of that which you are undoubtedly aware—we are most fallible, but eager to attempt your queries. May we begin then, my friends, with the first query?

Carla: Are you aware from any third-density environment, any planet's third density that you've been familiar with, in which money was available as needed instead of extreme variations in richness and poorness and in fatness and in hunger that we have in this world?

I am Latwii, and, my sister, we are aware of a great variety of third-density illusions in which the means of sustenance is provided in many and various ways. The means by which your people have devised to provide the basic necessities of your daily existence are not unheard of in far reaches of this galactic system, and as portions of our social memory complex have traveled beyond this galaxy, we have through their experience discovered that the abstract means of measuring wealth which you call money has also found its roots in other systems as well, for the monetary system that may be controlled by a few yet utilized by almost all of a population is one seed of the service-to-self polarity which is sown wherever there is the opportunity to plant such a crop and gain an inroad into the conscious complexes of a planetary system.

It is, however, most usual that such attempts are made upon planetary systems such as the one which your peoples now inhabit, that is, those planetary influences which are housing many races of beings who have found the need to repeat the third-density illusion and who therefore call for assistance from those of the positive polarity in most cases. When such aid is given by those of the positive polarity, as you are aware, it is necessary that the opportunity for the negative polarity to be experienced is also realized. Thus, the implanting of the concepts of abstract wealth and the more basic concept that undergirds this concept, that is, of the separation of peoples and the exercise of rights over peoples by groups of others, are those concepts which give rise to the experience of the monetary system which you as a planetary population now experience.

In those planetary influences which have had less outside aid, shall we say, or need to call for such aid, it is more unusual that such a system of money exchange would develop. The ambiance, shall we say, of such a native and homogeneous and seemingly isolated planetary influence is that this influence shall remain somewhat naive in the area of wealth and shall instead look each to the other for the means of support and sustenance.

May we answer further, my sister?

Carla: Yes, let me just tell you the reason for my asking that and then perhaps you can comment. I was reading a book called *Genesis*, not in the Bible. It's a proposal for community by a British chap who wanted to start a community in New Zealand, and he felt that any money that anyone had should be invested in shares with the community. And even if one had an inheritance, that the income from that inheritance should be invested in that community and that everyone should be dependent upon the community, with perhaps a very small allowance for minor things a person might need, but that all clothing would be made by the community or won by the community, and so forth. And it struck me that this was a Utopian ideal which could probably not be mastered by humans brought up in the Western hemisphere in the twentieth century. And I was trying to ponder to myself, because we're thinking about community, where correctness lay—what people should agree upon, what people should expect from each other in community in the way of monetary support. It had me completely baffled. If you have any comments on it, I'd be glad to hear them.

I am Latwii, and we are aware of your query, my sister. We find that we are talking here of old dogs and new tricks. Well, this is not an easy subject, and we would not move too far within its reaches for we would not wish to influence the course that you might wish to take.

The course that is taken is one which must be both the product of those who take it, their thinking, their ideals, their capabilities, their limitations, and so forth, and must also be that which can be flexible and be able to change as new situations arise. The means by which a group of entities arranges, supports and governs itself is the binding influence for that group, and becomes the beginning of the shared consciousness of that group, and is that which shall be as the young child, newly born into a world of seasons. How this child is nurtured and fed will determine how it shall evolve in its own being and thinking. When you join in groups and share common purposes, you become more than you are as individuals. There is that which must be given in order that the group might be sustained. There is that which the group provides each other in order that the individual not be forgotten. The balance is the trick, my sister, and is that honor and that duty which the group of individuals must collectively assume.

May we answer in any other fashion, my sister?

Carla: No, thank you.

I am Latwii, and we thank you, my sister. We thank you especially for putting up with our somewhat oblique response, for we know that each seeks most earnestly for the guidelines and hints that might provide a means by which ideals can be realized. We must remain somewhat mysterious for there are great potentials for learning within this area and we must not take them from you. Is there another query at this time?

(Pause)

I am Latwii, and we are happy that we have been able to speak with this group this evening. It has been an unusual honor to be able to address the group with an opening message and …

(Tape ends.)

Sunday Meditation
April 20, 1986

(Carla channeling)

I am Hatonn. I greet you, my friends, in the love and in the light of the infinite Creator. It is, as ever, a great privilege and pleasure to be called to your group this evening, and we are most grateful for this opportunity to share our vibratory patterns with your own. We would greet especially those who have not sat in person, shall we say, with this group previously, greeting them most heartily and offering blessing and love from those of us who are unseen and yet ever near. And indeed we greet all and are with all and are one with all, for are we not all One?

We would like to take this opportunity before we speak to make a suggestion to this instrument, for it is necessary that we do some fancy footwork, shall we say, to maintain the correct bias in this channeling. Because of this instrument's sensitivity to direction, one instrument would do better to be facing to the north, and we would suggest this in the future.

There is within the heart of each of you, my friends, a pathway. There is within the heart of each of you, my friends, a home. These are one and the same. Very often because of your illusion the seeker believes that the journey he is on is of a certain nature which among other things leaves him homeless. This has been the description of the seeker's quest in many a spiritual metaphor—the road that stretches ever onward, the straight and narrow path, the craggy mountain trail, the dangerous, rock-strewn road, the endless desert. As these are all aspects of your own selves, these are aspects of the journey upon which you have set out by choice and from which you shall not return, therefore some feel homeless and others who know that they are in an oasis, comfortable, surrounded by support and love, almost feel as if they have left the path.

The first steps upon a journey are difficult, for to prepare the mind for a journey is most wrenching. One must decide what baggage to carry, what shall be left behind, and what shall be taken. Within the mind of the traveler too, there are furnishings that are chosen, attitudes that may be left behind, biases that are picked up and treasured. Much preparation is involved in the first step. This degree of concentration is necessary because any decision moves one through a barrier. It may be an invisible one, yet nevertheless it is the barrier between this path and that, this choice and that. Once having made the decision, once having gotten out of sight of the starting point, the journey changes its character. How upsetting this is to many seekers.

It seems too easy sometimes. One step, then another, and then another, all so logical, all so necessary. The journey becomes better understood, problems become challenges, and challenges become things to enjoy. Hardship becomes that which is not so bad and then becomes that to which one is used. And the seeker begins to wonder if he is still on the path.

For you see, my friends, it is impossible to go back to the you that you were before you began your conscious journey. Were you to go back, you would find yourself to be doing the equivalent of the things people do who have been on hard treks. They cannot sleep on hard beds, but seek the floor. They forsake their comfortable couches and stoop or squat or sit cross-legged as they have upon the trail. Yet when one is on the trail, such behavior is normal, has become comfortable, and one begins to think, "How can I be comfortable and be a pure and sincere seeker?"

It is easy to forget that your birthright was not to sleep but to seek, and that you as seekers will find the only comfort available to your deeper spirits on the seeker's path. And then, what is even [more] confounding—you reach an oasis. There are no stones; there is no desert; the path is not straight and narrow, but you seat yourself upon the greensward under trees and drink of the cool spring, and you say, "How can I be a serious seeker and be so very, very happy? Am I not supposed to suffer?"

My friends, you are supposed to seek. Not only is that your responsibility, it is your inevitability, for the choice, once made, is irrevocable. And there is as much patience involved in waiting to move from the oasis back to the desert to the relative discomfort and to the hardship of the punishing path ahead as there is upon the trail itself. Yet, you cannot hurry your journey, whether you are in the desert or high among the rocks or gently seated upon the grass, comfortable in your oasis.

In your illusion, suffering is almost inevitable. But so is joy. You must learn to accept the gifts that are given you. You may look at them, you may question their meaning, but do not put them from you. Whether they seem too hard or too easy, they are yours—no one else's. No one else can quite grasp your dilemmas or your joys. No one else can lift your next foot or tell you when to leave the waving palms of the oasis.

It is a good thing in your mind to allow the various myths and legends about the seeker's journey to evaporate from your minds, and to cease expecting and anticipating your journey's next day, your experience's next hour, for you are creatures of the moment and the journey lies within. And so, my friends, we suggest that you toss concern about your own sincerity to the wind and sing the songs of joy that are in your heart at this moment, or turn your face to the wind and moan and cry if that be your lot. Accept joy and sorrow as if they were the same thing. Accept the rocky place and the oasis as if they were equal gifts, for these are your home. You shall learn comfort in suffering, and you shall find the undertones of sadness in the most joyful moments, for that which is within you is whole and entire. You are not an experiencer of isolated events or a chronicle of segmented stories, but rather eyewitness to a present moment which this illusion shall suggest to you often to be more than one thing, longer than one moment, fragmented and broken. Yet if the road goes on forever, how can it be fragmented?

That which is forever is also One, and you are that One. All that happens of joy and sorrow, ease and unease, is happening to you simultaneously and offered to you for one reason only—that you may from it learn ever more clearly the lessons of love.

You who are in this circle, reach out within your minds and touch in love those next to you. Feel the joy of sharing love. Now reach out further, my friends, for you are in meditation and time is no longer important. Reach out to the many who are troubled, who are torn with strife and war. They are your brothers and sisters, and more—they are you, and you are all the Creator. Touch your planet with that love and let its being sink deep, deep into the Earth that lies beneath your feet, for the Earth is troubled and in need of healing just as each of you feel in need of healing. And now, move back within your own physical vehicles and allow that feeling of love united with the one next to you, with those who need you whom you do not know, and with the planet itself, to remain united in your heart, in your life, in your thinking, for my friends, you are each so very powerful in service of something. Shall you choose to be in the service of light? Shall you seek ever more quickly and ever more patiently?

We leave you in meditation, and, as always, encourage you to return to meditation daily, that it may cleanse you of the illusion and refresh you with life. We leave you on your journey and your home in the present moment of forever. We are known to you as those of Hatonn, and we leave you in the love and the light of our infinite Creator. Adonai, my friends. Adonai vasu borragus.

(Jim channeling)

I am Latwii, and we greet you, my friends, in the love and light of our infinite Creator. We also are most grateful to be able to join your group this evening, and we thank you for allowing us to do so. As always, we hope that we may be of some small service in attempting to answer those queries which you may have value in the asking. We remind each that we are but your humble and fallible brothers and sisters. Please take that which we offer that may have value and use it as you will and leave that which may have no value without a second thought. May we begin with the first query?

Questioner: Yes, I have a question. It follows closely with what Hatonn said, and it's really strange because I thought of this question before the session began. It has to do with coping and conquering. And by that I'm talking about, you know, a particular individual's life if they have a problem. In our culture we normally think of, if you have a problem, you're going to lick the problem. You're going to lick the problem; you're going to conquer it. You're going to work on it until you conquer it. But sometimes it seems that you work on something and work on it and work on it and basically all you do is cope with it. And when you don't conquer it, in other words, completely overcome the problem, you tend to lose sight of the fact that you are *coping* with the problem, and therefore maybe you don't learn what you should be learning as you cope every day with it. In other words, you learn from coping as well as conquering. And that doesn't sound like a question, I know—it sounds like I'm making a statement, and I guess I'm asking for some comment or corroboration on this. I have ideas about it—I'm looking for another opinion.

I am Latwii, and am aware of your query, my brother. We can suggest that you have stated a situation which is most common among those seekers of truth. However, it is also true that much of what one experiences is somewhat or [in] some cases greatly hidden from the eye. Therefore, when one looks upon a situation that seems to be in need of attention and provides the opportunity for mastering a new lesson and the mastering takes somewhat longer than the seeker's estimation of what it should take, there is, as you have surmised, within this process much of value which is hidden from the seeker's eye and which continues to draw the seeker onward as layers and levels of understanding evolve from the interaction between you and the situation which is seen as the problem or difficulty.

Within your cultures, the product of an effort is given much value and the process by which the product was achieved is relegated to lesser value and is oftentimes overlooked completely. However, we assure you, my brother, that the situation which you have described as the coping has much more to it than merely, shall we say, keeping one's head above the water. There is much work upon the metaphysical or inner levels which is accomplished at that time that may be likened unto the tempering of an instrument that it may probe yet further without bending or breaking.

May we answer further, my brother?

Questioner: When a person allows themselves to become very discouraged by seeming non-results, in other words, not conquering a problem, doesn't that tend to even more so cover up what you might get out of the coping process? In other words, to keep a positive attitude. I mean, these are things that I know—I know it sounds like—but I'm just looking for another comment on it.

I am Latwii, and am aware of your query, my brother. We might liken your statement to the situation of the entity who is attempting one lesson and who adds yet another lesson before the first has been completed. This, of course, is quite possible to accomplish, yet in some cases may make the situation somewhat more complicated or prolonged as the new set of lessons is added to the previous, that is as the seeming difficulty and the coping are joined by the dissatisfaction and what can be learned by one who becomes dissatisfied with one's own progress.

Within each situation is an opportunity to expand the limits of one's perceptions and understanding. To add unto the lesson by becoming that called dissatisfied then increases the opportunity, and according to the point of view of the seeker, may add more difficulty, more challenge or more opportunity.

May we answer further, my brother?

Questioner: No, thank you very much.

I am Latwii, and we thank you, my brother. Is there another query?

Questioner: Yes, I have a question please, Latwii. In self-analysis of my problem in my adult life, the greatest one seems to be communication with those that are most meaningful to me. And I was wondering if you could give me any sense of direction in improving this problem?

I am Latwii, and am aware of your query, my sister. In this instance, we may speak in general in a manner which we hope may be of value. To look upon the situation in which you engage in communication with another, with a perception that the other is one to be loved as are you, and to find within yourself the pure and undistorted love and acceptance of self and other self without expectation of any result for the communication is to give the heart of love, is to give the best which you are and which you seek. To love, my sister, with all of your heart both yourself and the other self is then to place the situation within the clearest light available. All else falls away. What remains is love giving love to love.

May we answer further, my sister?

Questioner: Yes, please. I feel that I am trying to do what you're describing but it isn't received that way. So, therefore, something's not operating well. I do feel that I'm trying to do what you described and perhaps you can give me a little more feedback—is not received as I mean to give it.

I am Latwii, and am aware of your query, my sister. To give the specific reasons would be to seem to judge another and would require that we look within the mind of another and would require that we describe the patterns in which another entity finds use in moving. May we say that all patterns are appropriate; all patterns are love. The perception that one may hold determines what one experiences. You may look upon the response of another to your gift of love as being completely unimportant. All that is of importance is that you love with no expectation as to how that love shall be received. That is beyond your responsibility. If you can love—you have fulfilled your own ability to respond to all that comes before your notice.

May we answer you further, my sister?

Questioner: No, thank you, because I was feeling that I should withdraw from giving love, but I see that I should still keep on, no matter what the results are—is that what you're saying? Keep on giving my love even if it isn't well received?

I am Latwii, and this is so, my sister.

Questioner: Thank you.

We thank you, my sister. Is there another query?

Questioner: Yes, I have a question. First, I would like to thank you very much for your love and your guidance and the sharing which is ongoing with you, Latwii. My question regards cellular memory, *(inaudible)* and its significance to entry into fourth density. Could you comment on that, please?

I am Latwii, and am aware of your query, my sister, and we thank you for it as well. The illusion in which each moves within the third density is one which …

(Side one of tape ends.)

(Jim channeling)

I am Latwii, and am again with this instrument. To continue our response. Your illusion is one made of love. The structure of the physical material of your illusion is one which vibrates at a certain frequency of what might be called motion or even understanding, for that which is moving moves in realms of grasping a certain portion of the nature of unity. The words are imperfect, yet we beg your forgiveness and shall continue. As each entity which is composed of the material of your illusion becomes aware of the nature of love, the awareness then interacts with the material of the illusion and the very physical vehicle itself. This interaction creates pathways or access one to the other between the entity and the material of which its vehicle is constructed. Thus, each teaches and learns from each, for each is a pattern of vibration and understanding, each seeking that which it is at its heart. Thus, the remembering or reconstructing of understanding accelerates the vibratory frequency or ability to further understand and love.

At this time we would ask if there might be another query that we could further refine this general concept by our response to it.

Questioner: I thank you very much for your information. There is so much given there that I would ponder and meditate upon it before further query. Thank you.

I am Latwii, and thank you, my sister. Is there another query?

Questioner: When you're speaking *(inaudible)* of the vibrations in reference to this previous question of love within the person, are you stating that it interweaves within the makeup of that person, that feeling of love, or am I misunderstanding what you were implying there? You're talking about love and vibrations and the vehicle.

I am Latwii, and am aware of your query, my sister. We were in our previous response attempting to describe in a general fashion the nature of evolution in the third density illusion which seeks to learn the lessons of love, and to describe how the seeker's ability to love is felt and responded to by the creation about it. More specifically, the physical vehicle by which the entity moves through this illusion, all of the illusion, the vehicle and the entity being composed of love at the heart of each cell of material, and of desire and of concepts, so that when the seeker loves, the entire creation sings in harmony, shall we say, and the eyes of the seeker look upon a new world.

May we answer further, my sister?

Questioner: No, thank you. That was very beautifully expressed. I shall treasure it.

I am Latwii. We thank you and we treasure our blending of vibrations with you. Is there another query at this time?

Questioner: How can we help Ra in his work?

I am Latwii, and am aware of your query, my sister. Again, without meaning to sound simplistic, we can suggest that to love and to give love freely is that which aids any entity or effort in service. That love then can be used by the entity in whatever way has meaning to that entity.

May we answer further, my sister?

Questioner: No, but love to you Latwii. Thank you.

I am Latwii, and we thank you, my sister. Is there another query?

Questioner: Latwii, could you please expand upon this statement for us: "To think with the heart and feel with the mind."

I am Latwii, and am aware of your query, my sister. We might suggest without infringement that the statement which you have made is one which provides the opportunity to blend love with wisdom and wisdom with love in order that one might serve with greater, shall we say, effectiveness, in that love be guided by wisdom and wisdom be ennobled and enabled by love.

May we answer further, my sister?

Questioner: Thank you.

I am Latwii, and we thank you, my sister. Is there another query?

Questioner: There is one more query, Latwii. It concerns the instrument. The suggestion of the facing to the north, should that be adjusted to the twenty degrees north?

I am Latwii, and am aware of your query, my sister. Our brothers and sisters of Hatonn took the opportunity this evening to suggest to the instrument known as Carla that it would be more helpful in her service as an instrument for her to face in the northward direction due to her increasing sensitivity or ability to receive the signal, shall we say, that those of Hatonn are privileged to send. The fine adjustment to the twenty degrees east of north direction may at a future date be appropriate. At this time, however, it would suffice to face in the direction of magnetic north.

May we answer further, my sister?

Questioner: I thank you. We are very concerned for the continued and improving wellness of the instrument. Is there any other information which you could offer that would be assistance in our helping her?

I am Latwii, and am aware of your query, my sister. We find that this instrument, the one known as Carla, is the beneficiary of great love, light and healing opportunities of which she is aware upon one level or another, and indeed has called upon these offerings on many occasions, and is most grateful for the giving. We find that the one known as Carla is improving in her state of what you would call health to the degree that we join each in rejoicing that her heart again sings a happy song, and we thank each who gives love, light and concern to this entity.

May we answer further, my sister?

Questioner: Thank you.

I am Latwii, and we again thank you, my sister. Is there another query?

Questioner: Could you tell us about your planet—where you come from, please, if you're not too tired?

I am Latwii, and am aware of your query, my sister. We do not tire of the joy of speaking and sharing our humble service with this group. However, this instrument is somewhat less sturdy. We shall speak briefly upon this topic, for it is not one which we find great opportunity in being of that which we would call service. We are a race which dwells within the density that you would call five, that of light, that of wisdom. Our experience upon our, what you would call, planetary influence is one which is of an unified nature of seeking. The vibratory nature of our planetary influence is one with which we move now in harmony and which we join in its progression to the One, for all creation is constructed of the one Creator, and in the unique fashion given to each, moves in a way which attempts to glorify the One in all.

May we speak in any other fashion, my sister?

Questioner: I thank you, and I too seek in this incarnation to aid in the unity of our soul growth here in this *(inaudible)*. I appreciate that you have given us this love and light and wisdom tonight from those whose goal is the same.

I am Latwii, and we join you in praise and thanksgiving, my sister. We find that there is enough energy within this instrument remaining for a short query, if there might be one with which we could close this gathering.

Questioner: One final question, Latwii. This instrument, Jim, is there anything that we can be doing to make him more comfortable. Should he also observe the facing to the north?

I am Latwii, and am aware of your query, my sister, and as regards this particular instrument, though its sensitivities are also making a steady progress, we find that there is less need for a heading of the northward direction, though due to its connection to the instrument known as Carla, we find that it shall also share this new direction if that be their choice, and shall at some point in its progress as an instrument also find benefit in that heading.

May we answer further, my sister?

Questioner: Thank you very much.

I am Latwii, and we thank each present for inviting our presence, and we are filled with joy at the opportunity to join this group in its seeking of love and light and the unity from which both spring. We shall at this time take our leave of this instrument and this group, leaving each, as always, in the love and in the light of the one infinite Creator. We are known to you as those of Latwii. Adonai, my friends. Adonai vasu borragus.

(Carla channeling)

I Yadda. I greet you in the love and in light of infinite Creator. We say "okay" to this instrument about challenging in the name of Christ. We so lonely for someone to say, "Do you come in name of Zoroaster?"—he was a good guy, you know. Why always the Christ, Christ, Christ? My goodness! Christ! You know there are many teachers, but one Source. Why you not challenge in name of Source?

But that okay. We go on to what we have to say. One, two, three four, five, A, B, C, D, E, you, me, you, me, you, ye, yah, yah, yah. Okay? You get the point. This instrument making nonsense, no sense whatsoever—but she doesn't care.

Why you so serious? Why, we ask you? If this instrument can be trained, seriously trained—yes she's very serious, you know, but she is a careful instrument so we can use her for example—and we did. This instrument willing to make a fool of herself because that's what we gave her to say. It not important to her to make sense.

Why you so serious? You are the people who have too many clothes on. You wear four coats, three sweaters, sixteen pair of pants. What you protecting yourself against in this seeking of yours? It is good to be naked against love. That all we have to say to you. Be a fool for love. Do what comes in your heart to do. And don't look back.

We Yadda. We leave you in joy and we hope that you may enjoy your seeking. We leave you in the love and light of infinite One. Adonai. Adonai.

Sunday Meditation
May 4, 1986

(Carla channeling)

I am L/Leema. I greet you in the love and in the light of the one infinite Creator. It is a privilege to have been called to your group this evening, for although none in the circle but the instrument had a question, this instrument has a pressing question and to this we shall address ourselves. The question this instrument believes it is asking is, "Am I a Christian?" However we shall approach the answer in a way unexpected to this instrument.

To be what you call alive, and what more precisely could be called within a certain type of chemical body that dwells in a third-density illusion, is to be concerned with death, for insofar as you have been born into an illusion, to that illusion you shall inevitably die, for that which begins shall also end. The question of what lies beyond the incarnation you now experience is a question central to an understanding of your own nature. We of the Confederation of Planets in the Service of the Infinite Creator have offered you in many different ways the message of eternal existence and infinite consciousness which is offered you not only by that which you call Christianity, but many other religions.

We would speak first of the love of death which distorts many among your peoples. This yearning for death may have many causes. Many have been uncomfortable within their incarnate bodies, dwelling in what seems to be an inhospitable atmosphere as long as they can remember, and consequently yearn for that which puts a period to this existence, an existence which is seen as inadequate, foolish. Others have had experiences devastating enough to have caused distortions toward the contemplation of removing the self from this illusion. Others, being of a warlike nature, find it deeply ingrained in their nature to seek risk, knowing well that death may ensue and welcoming that possibility in order to live what seems to be a more finely tuned moment by moment existence during the time of risk.

It is not coincidence but intention upon the part of the author who created the motion picture known as *Rambo* that that seemingly blood-thirsty and death-filled person has a name which is the Americanized spelling of a French poet, fascinated with the romance of death and capable of writing about it with ravishing beauty. However one comes at a fascination of death, it is as though one were making war upon oneself, for each of you came into this incarnation not to die, but to live. And to live, thinking greatly of death, is to live less well, and to live absorbed in, rejoicing in, and giving thanksgiving for each moment of beauty, love, and glory—for glory there is, all about you and within you.

It is the glory within that causes your peoples to seek some way of finding, exploring and expressing that articulated glory which, though gushing like a geyser from the deepest portions of being, comes into consciousness with a demand to be articulated. It is a rare being who can consciously love and serve the Creator without some structure. This is, however, by no means impossible, and, indeed, there is a minimum of distortion involved in the patient returning again and again to the daily practice of meditation and to the persistent analysis of one's own being, for it is within you and within each of you that the consciousness you seek lies, that the foreverness for which you hunger and thirst is seated.

To many there has been given a gift—that is, the gift of congruency and personality and character with an already established religion, as you call it. We call this a gift because it puts within the reach of the aspirant who finds himself congruent with an established religion many helpful tools for discovering the consciousness which constitutes the presence of the Creator. Now, there are semantics involved in the discussion of religion, and many who would wish to be Christians have found themselves unable to accept some of the wordings, phraseology and seemingly limited viewpoints of others who also call themselves Christians. In many cases, Christians are more vitriolic and judgmental of other Christians than they are of those whom they consider to be heathen. These things cause one who has been given the gift of congruency with a certain distortion of structure of approach to the one original Thought the feeling that one does not fit in, that one cannot possibly be Christian. And yet we say that if it is pleasurable and instructive and nourishing to study the teachings and to live the life of the Christ, then one shall not listen to those whose Christianity bears a different mark. However, in return, one Christian so judged as "not being Christian" is cautioned to refrain from making the same mistake about the challenging, for this word is a word and no more. The point in any approach to divinity is to discover and dwell in the presence of love, the one original and creative Thought.

You people have many idols. They include those things which your peoples think of as idols and recognize as dangerous, spiritually speaking. We may name money, power, and worldly addictions such as lust, gross eating, and other excesses as being those idols which the world recognizes very well. There are other less recognizable idols. One of these idols is the man known as Jesus. Another is the man known as Gautama Buddha, another, Lao Tsu, another Confucius, another Mohammed, and so forth. None of these men hollowed themselves out to be worshipped, but rather to become the messengers, channels and wayfarers sharing a consciousness, the consciousness of the Creator.

It is well to honor and respect the ruthless determination of such men as we have mentioned, the determination to listen and to follow the spirit within, that which may be called the higher self, the Holy Spirit, the comforter, the Paraclete, the counselor or inner guidance. We are not interested in semantics—we are interested in providing each of you with the freedom, the feeling of free inspiration, shall we say, to pursue the presence of Christ Consciousness, that is, that which was channeled through Christ the man [known as Jesus], Christ the Buddha, the Christ of Lao Tsu, the Christ of Confucius, the Christ of Mohammed, and so forth.

There is nothing that lies between a judging Christian and a judged Christian but semantics. To allow any outer influence to remove one's attention from the inner voice which speaks in silence and in thunder is folly, and we may strongly suggest to you that you be not dissuaded from what you feel to be so for you because of the judgment of others, although we urge each of you to consider patiently and in love each word spoken, whether in condemnation or praise, for each word that you hear from another is a mirror into which you may look and find yourself. One can only thank a mirror. It is but glass with a backing to show you to yourself. That backing may not think itself to be neutral, may not consider itself a catalyst, but rather an apostle of what is right. This is not important to one who listens, for the Creator is speaking to you in condemnation as well as in praise, and if there is a lack of patience when looking in the mirror, then perhaps the gaze may be, through the discipline of meditation, be found to become more and more easy as one comes into loving and compassionate unity with the one who judges.

It is not for any entity to follow another's path, for you have your own path. It is, rather, incumbent upon each seeker to be firm, stubborn, and inexorably persistent about listening to the guidance which comes from within. Your discrimination will tell you what feeds you and what does not. You cannot be competitive about spiritual unfoldment or enlightenment. You can be only your personal best. We ask you to follow each of you your own path, but to give it your personal best, for though it is not well to be fascinated with death, it is indeed well to recognize its inevitability, and to seek for what lies beyond, for until one dwells in mystery, one cannot have the energy and the motivation to seek the truth, to find a way to live that reflects the glory within.

Are you a Christian? Are you a Buddhist? Are you a Confucian? Does your path lie with the Sufis? Have you found the Confederation of Planets to be closest to your own path? Very well. Whatever your choice, acknowledge it and do not look back, for the choice of one path and the following of it faithfully are most important. We suggest that you follow it not only with energy, but with discrimination, gazing with joy upon the example of the entity or entities whom you have found to be fullest of Christ consciousness.

But we ask you to look always not only at the frail, brave suffering and hollowed out human which became a channel to be of service to many, but to spend time gazing upon the face of Deity, however you may find it and by whatever names you preserve it. It is a good thing to be what you are, and what you are will grow and change and transform, yet it is likely that one pattern or another is most likely congruent with your vibratory energy pattern. Thusly, not all of you will be Christians, not all of you will be Sufis, and so forth. Yet all these structures yield the same living water. All are channels through which this water may flow, and it is the discipline and devotion and firm intention to follow the example set before you that will open to you the consciousness which all have come to give—that one Consciousness of the one Creator. You have within you that one Creator, and, in fact, in the end you shall be that one Creator.

May your path be pleasant and light and may your voice be merry as you walk along it, for though you may be often cast down, yet the example set before you by whatever path you have chosen is always that of one who presses on, asking only to be more and more hollowed out, to become a more and more pure channel for the love and the light of the one infinite Creator. To take oneself too seriously is to stumble on a rock of your own making. So, reach toward the light as do your trees and flowers and clap your hands with joy, for you are here in the presence of Christ Consciousness. At this very moment it flows about you, within you, and between you, linking you with your deepest self and with each other. That moment is now, and all the nows that you shall ever experience. Encourage the faculty of laughter, for the face of the infinite invisible One is a face of ultimate joy.

We rest within your vibrations, lost in the joy of your presence within us, and we offer back to you our blessing and assure you that we are with you at any time you should wish to invite our presence. We shall leave this instrument now, hoping that the answer to this question is not obscure or confusing. It is difficult to cut through the semantics of emotionally laden words which signify different things to different people. We hope that we have been helpful. We are those of L/Leema and we leave this instrument at this time.

(Jim channeling)

I am L/Leema, and greet you once again through this instrument in love and in light. We would at this time offer ourselves for the answering of other queries that may be of importance to those gathered this evening. May we attempt any such query at this time?

Carla: Yes, L/Leema. I'd like to ask a question for S. This is the last of her questions. She would like to know if her off and on inability to remember to take in things that she sees and that she fears has anything to do with a condition which she calls Broca's aphasia. If you cannot answer that directly, I'm sure she would be most appreciative of any comments that you could have on that.

I am L/Leema. We look upon the entity and condition of which you speak and see that there is some latitude within which we may speak.

The condition that this entity has described and experienced may be labeled in any of a number of manners, including the use of those labels which you have mentioned. However, the true nature of the condition is one which is not definitely described by such labels and would not respond by the application of treatments which are usually utilized for such labeled conditions. The condition is unique to this entity in that its ability to remember that which it has noticed is a function of its changing desire to learn in a specific fashion. Thus, the entity within its subconscious mind and …

(Side one of tape ends.)

(Jim channeling)

I am L/Leema, and am again with this instrument. To continue our response. Within portions of both the subconscious and conscious minds of this entity, the direction of the learning is determined. That which is of value receives a focus of attention that does not forget. That which is forgotten is forgotten for a reason. The reason has to do with that which is desired. We may not speak more specifically in describing this reason or its function in the process of learning lest we take from this entity the opportunity that it has presented to itself.

May we answer in any further way, my sister?

Carla: Yes, it occurred to me to wonder whether this blockage was preincarnatively chosen?

I am L/Leema, and as we gaze upon the entity and the condition, we see that there are ramifications of this condition which trail backward, as you would say, through the incarnation to the early formative years at which time the more preincarnative choices were set in motion in certain fashions according to the young experience of the one known as S. Thus, the preincarnative choices were given first expression in a manner congruent with the abilities and opportunities that were developing in and about this entity.

May we answer further, my sister?

Carla: Just one question—after all, she's my mother, and I'm concerned, and I know, knowing her, that she will want to think about this at length. Would it be more instructive for her to dismiss it or to plumb the possible reasons for this preincarnative choice?

I am L/Leema, and without infringing upon this entity's free will, we may only suggest that the discernment of what is its heart's true desire be attempted. All else then shall fall into place, shall we say.

May we answer further, my sister?

Carla: It brings me to another question that I had, which was more general. I'll ask it on her behalf, and also on mine—on her behalf, because she has a growing family and, whatever her heart's desire may be, she wishes with all her heart to be a good mother and a good wife, and this will take at least the next fifteen years of her life—having to do with children, I mean. In our case, Jim and I have been questioning whether it is possible to be contented, harmonious and settled and still be learning. So the question is: Can one's circumstances, being settled and somewhat domesticated, offer enlightenment in the same way that suffering and traumatic change offer enlightenment in transformation?

I am L/Leema, and the query opens interesting possibilities. It is not one which can be definitively answered, for one must look to the entity about which the situation applies, shall we say. Each seeker brings with it a certain conglomeration of experiences, abilities and areas which are in need of refinement. The means by which an entity may increase and refine its understanding in any incarnation are determined by taking into consideration a great wealth and a variety of factors. The list is quite various and would include the family and friends with whom one would experience the incarnation, the culture within which the incarnation would be experienced, the point within the cycle at which the planet had progressed, the lessons and abilities thus far gathered, the desire to serve in such and such a fashion, and so forth. Thus, for some, one means of experiencing the illusion would be most helpful, whereas the same means would be far less useful to another entity.

To be more brief, each moment and experience offers the potential for enlightenment for any seeker with the desire that is sufficiently strong to penetrate the illusion and surface appearance of any moment. It is the unique quality of each seeker that determines what moments may be taken advantage of, shall we say.

May we answer further, my sister?

Carla: No, thank you, L/Leema.

And we thank you, my sister. May we attempt another query?

T: Yes, I'm not exactly sure how to put it, but I have a question. Recently I had a very serious argument, disagreement with my brother, my biological brother. It seems that part of the roots of this argument are in the way we treated one another when we were children, especially the way I treated him. And there seems to be the opinion on my brother's part that I really don't love him and this is something that during my life I have thought about a lot. Sometimes I don't feel as though I really do have the capacity or the capability to really and truly love. I guess my question is—to start with—is, how does one go about recog—I mean, in different people, is the—well, the capability to love, to show love and to feel love for others, seen different? I'm not sure what I want to ask. Could you just comment on that—or have I thrown such a hodgepodge at you?

I am L/Leema, and we believe that we may make comment from the information you have given. Within your illusion, the lesson is love. This lesson is begun when the conscious seeker becomes aware that it is the lesson. To begin the lesson, one may look at carefully the relationships and feelings that have developed within them that one has formed throughout the incarnation. Within each relationship, there will be a mixture of feelings and experiences that will sum into what you may call the core or foundation of feeling. Each entity seeking to love and to understand the concept of love will then compare what is felt with what is imagined to be love. And here we must state that few within your illusion are capable of truly loving and of knowing what love is, for there is only the ability within your illusion to begin this lesson. Yet, within most entities' experience, there is the remembrance of some, of a few, who have demonstrated what seems to be unquestionably that called love, for it easier to feel love from another at first than to give love.

Thus, the seeker throughout its experience of relationships with those about it begins to determine certain features or characteristics that seem to be a part of that called love, and then each seeker in some fashion takes that seed or facet of love and plants it as a desire within its own heart and mind, and waters it with attention, with care and with further desire that it might flourish and become a nourishment for those about it. At this point, those about the seeker begin to notice the quality that is developing towards love and begin to reflect back to the seeker other qualities more closely aligned with the developing concept and experience of love. This process then continues betwixt all those who are aware of the process.

Thusly is love born and does love become more and more seated or rooted, if you will, within each seeker's being. Yet, in most cases, such feelings of love are most nebulous and transitory, with moments of inspiration and brilliance to inspire the seeker onward. Yet, once again and once again and yet again, the seeker returns to the daily round of activities where it seems that love resides not. Undaunted in some cases, the seeker redoubles the desire and again the process is repeated. That which is felt is given and returns and is given and returns and love continues to take root. However quickly or slowly matters not—the process has been begun—and will continue as a direct function of the seeker's desire to penetrate the mystery of love, of loving, and of being loved.

May we answer further, my brother?

T: I have several things I'd like to say, but I think I'll hold them for another time. Thank you very much.

I am L/Leema, and we thank you, my brother.

Carla: I'll just follow up on T's, and let that be all because I know this has been a long session for you. What I heard him asking was, "Can I fall in love?" It seems that not everybody does. I think falling in love is different, is a different perception from universal love or compassion, and I think everybody yearns for it and you know a lot of people don't get the chance to fall in love. They don't meet the right person, the chemistry doesn't happen. Some people do fall in love—I've fallen in love. I count myself lucky, even though it's always turned out to be a painful experience too. Could you comment on the extreme chanciness of having the opportunity to fall in love in this illusion?

I am L/Leema, and shall attempt to speak to this subject. We find that there are many approximations of that which we would call love, the more universal compassion that one may eventually feel for all of creation. The concept of romantic love is what we would call an approximation of the more universal kind of love of which we have been speaking, and it is indeed true that few within your illusion are able to experience this type of love, though more, far more indeed, experience this type of love than experience universal compassion. The degree to which pain of the experience accompanies the experience is the degree to which, we would suggest, that the mind has formed the boundaries within which love is allowed to express, for if there are no conditions or boundaries to the expression of love, there can be no pain accompanying the loss of such love, for there will be no loss.

The love of which we speak is that which exists in all events, and, indeed, is the creative force that moves all entities and events. Thus, the condition of the romantic form or approximation of love is one which, shall we say, has tapped a certain path or channel to love and which forms certain boundaries within which the love may express. The boundaries are of mental construction and are not necessary except for the learning of certain lessons having to do with what may be seen both as a limitation of love from the universal point of view, or perhaps the expansion of love from the personal point of view.

May we answer further, my sister?

Carla: Thank you.

I am L/Leema, and we thank you, my sister. May we attempt a final query before we close?

T: Yes. It seems to be—and this is obviously not an original idea, but I've read it and I've heard it and it makes sense. In order to love another or to love everything, general compassion is love, you have to be able to love yourself. And since you are everything and everything is you, if you're successful in loving yourself, it seems to me that you have it whipped, or you at least have a real leg up on learning to love everyone. Could you comment briefly on that?

I am L/Leema, and we find that in general, this is correct, for as the entity which each is moves into this illusion, the first awareness is the awareness of self, and this awareness becomes the foundation upon which all experience is built. To learn to accept and love the self is to begin to build the foundation for loving others upon firm ground, for the self, in truth, is, in little[5], all that one will experience within the illusion, for through the eyes of the self, all experience must pass, and thus one will see and love the world in the same fashion that one sees and loves the self. Since for the self, all begins within the self, there first must love be found.

May we answer further, my brother?

T: No, thank you.

I am L/Leema, and we thank you, my brother. We would at this time thank each for offering us the opportunity to join this group this evening, and to offer that which is a portion of our humble experience in seeking and becoming that same love which draws each onward in the great quest for truth. We shall leave this group at this time, rejoicing with you in the experience of being and becoming. We are known to you as those of L/Leema. Adonai, my friends. Adonai vasu borragus.

(Carla channeling)

(Carla channels a vocal melody from Nona.)

I am Nona. We greet you in the healing love and light of the infinite Creator. Adonai. Adonai. Adonai. ☥

---

[5] An archaic usage that means "in miniature" or "in the microcosm."

Sunday Meditation
May 11, 1986

(Carla channeling)

I am L/Leema. We greet you in the love and in the light of the one infinite Creator and thank you for calling us to you this evening to consider the question, "What is the meaning of life?" This is not an inconsiderable question.

We will begin by pointing out the difference between "meaning" and "purpose." Meaning has to do with the nature of something; purpose has to do with its function. We shall address ourselves to the nature of life.

It is a glorious and mysterious thing that there is nothing in the infinite creation which is not full of life. The air itself is full of life, the earth beneath your feet, the stones, the rivers, the fires that heat you in the winter and the breezes that cool you in the summer. All the animals that delight your senses and provide you with birdsong, purrs and happy barking, the chattering squirrels, all of these things, all of these entities are full of life. Those of you who dwell within third density and are self-conscious are not only full of life, but know that you are alive. You are then self-conscious, and so, unlike rocks and fire and air and water and trees and small animals and the beasts of the jungle and desert, it is within you to ask, "What is the meaning of my being alive?"

In essence, that which has meaning in life is consciousness. That is the essence of life. All consciousness comes from the Father, the Creator of all things. Through those portions of Himself, thrown out into the vastness of the starry heavens, this infinite and invisible Creator offered the incredible opportunity for the Creator to be conscious of the Creator. In a limited way the stones are conscious of water, the fire is conscious of air. Small animals are far more conscious of each other but do not think abstractly, and therefore learn in a limited fashion about the Creator from those other beings which are around them.

However, those of you in third density have wisdom and questions upon your mind, those things that you would ask, and this makes you very meaningful to yourself and to the Creator within yourself. It is impossible not to be a meaningful person, for as you experience, record and change through catalyst, you are becoming aware in a unique way, in a brand new way, in a way valuable to the Creation, of some part of the creation. When you think a thought, you think it not only for yourself, but for all that lives. When you meditate and wish someone well, that wish has meaning and power. When you think a thought and wish someone ill, that wish also has meaning and power. When you decide to seek to find love, all that you do has meaning, for as you experience and as you record what you experience within yourself, you are adding to the store of knowledge of That Which Is. And so you shall do and cannot help but do, as long as you are in incarnation in this density. More than that, between incarnations, and as you go forward from density to density, you shall not for one instant cease to be [part of] the meaning of creation, for the meaning of life is an essence and that essence is the one original Thought of the Creator, that creative love which through light has created us all.

It may be difficult to accept that you need do nothing, you need accomplish nothing, you need have no worldly ambition in order to have meaning. Yet you as consciousness are meaning, and each entity that you see is the essence of creation. Creation is cut of one whole cloth—there is no division in meaning or in unity. As all are One, so each of you is a holograph of all that there is, containing within yourself the great circle and heart of the universe. In the interest …

(No more audio was recorded on side one of the tape. The recording resumes on side two of the tape.)

(Jim channeling)

I am L/Leema, and am again with this instrument. May we answer in any further way, my sister?

Carla: Well, yeah—it brought me to the other thing I did want to ask about tonight. I addressed a question to the Holy Spirit day before yesterday and got an answer and I was writing it down but it felt just like channeling. And I wondered if, is it exactly the same as the Confederation—is it different in any way? Could you enlighten me? I guess in a way I'm saying, is the Holy Spirit, angels, all the things that people pray to or principles that people pray to and the Confederation of Planets in one way, is that all one channeling and just different stations, different channels on that band of vibrations, communications?

I am L/Leema. The source of which you speak may be called the Comforter, for within the service of the Confederation of Planets in the Service of the One Infinite Creator are vibrational complexes which offer themselves according to the quality and nature of the call to those such as yourself who seek what may loosely be called an inner guidance. These sources of comfort move as they are called and speak as they are allowed in a fashion most likely to be understood by the entity who calls. In your particular case at this particular time, the form which this communication takes is the one of the expressing of a heartfelt concern and the awaiting of an answer that takes the form of writing upon the paper. Thus, it is correct to see this communication as a type of channeling, yet do not all entities channel the one Creator in one form or another, thus the form you have chosen is unique to the purpose that you have chosen.

May we answer further, my sister?

Carla: Yes. I guess I'm just curious as to the relationship between the Confederation channeling and channeling from the Holy Spirit, channelings from the Holy Spirit that have come down to us through the writings of the church fathers and the writings of the saints and people that have felt that they have gotten their words from angelic presences. And as a tag end to that question, do you feel that you yourself, and channeling such as I had from the Holy Spirit, are sources or are themselves channels for Deity—in whatever form you want to use that word—Creator or whatever?

I am L/Leema, and we find that direct answer to this query is both simple and difficult. All sources of information within or without the Confederation of Planets are the Creator and yet speak for the Creator as instruments. Yet as an instrument, each may utilize its own experience to give a richer, deeper and perhaps purer view to a specific entity which is of like vibration, shall we say. Thus, many, many upon your planetary surface throughout its recorded history have been touched in what may be called a sacred way, and have through such inspiration shared with others the words of wisdom and of nourishment which they themselves have found useful.

May we answer further, my sister?

Carla: No, thank you.

I am L/Leema, and we thank you, my sister. Is there another query?

(Pause)

I am L/Leema, and we perceive the gathering in its direction moving towards its completion for this evening. We thank each for inviting our presence in your seeking of truth. We remind each that we are quite fallible and desire no undue emphasis upon our words, but rather suggest that those which have meaning be utilized in whatever way has meaning to each. We shall be honored to join this group in your future, as you would call it. We are those of L/Leema. Blessings, my friends, to each. Adonai. Adonai vasu borragus. ☙

Sunday Meditation
May 18, 1986

(Carla channeling)

I am L/Leema, and I greet you in the love and in the light of the one infinite Creator. We greet each of you with great affection and thank you for calling us to your group this evening for it is your service to us to allow us to share our humble thoughts with you. And yet, you must know that in some degree we too are channels, and we pray, as does this instrument, that our words may have not only the meager understanding of our experience, but the inspiration of those who are our teachers as well, for are we not all channels of the one infinite Creator? And as we speak, do we not listen? And as you listen, does your heart not speak? We ask you these questions because the question has been asked of us, "What is the place of analytical thought upon the spiritual path of seeking the truth?"

The intellectual mind and the intuitive mind are two sides of one coin. Analysis is a form of speaking, intuition a form of listening. And yet, when one is speaking, does one not also have ears? And when one listens intuitively, does one not hear the voice of silence?

We shall not over-generalize and say to you that it is impossible to reach a significant degree of, shall we say, enlightenment, for want of a better word, through the singular pursuit of either course. However, it is safe to say that a total dependence upon either the intellect or the intuition leaves one open to the imbalance that might come to one in the physical body standing upon one foot. Each entity who seeks has an unique character and therefore an unique way of approaching knowledge.

Now we caution you that knowledge is a word which is constantly misused by us and by anyone who speaks of spiritual knowledge, just as it is only with regret that we use the term enlightenment. However, we use these terms because in your intellectually based society, progress is measured by units of knowledge or degrees of enlightenment. It is our opinion that this method of measuring the walk upon the path of spiritual unfoldment is vastly incorrect and without virtue.

This is perhaps the greatest single difficulty with an overdependence upon the intellect, for the presence of the Creator is an experience, not a knowledge. It cannot be gainsaid that there is such a thing as the consciousness of the Creator; nor yet would we deny in any way that you may attain it. We would not even deny that practicing this precedence, in other words, awaiting the experience, is repetitive and may indeed seem to improve with repetition. However, the Creator is always the same, is the singular, is the simple, and is not to be learned by degree, by method, or by rote.

Let us then swim into the sea of intuition. My friends, you will find that total dependence upon intuition is a total dependence upon a portion of your deep self which is unreliable. Much comes through the intuition which is of extreme merit. Much occurs by seeming intuition which is in fact a product of deep fears, experiences from previous incarnations which have not yet been worked out, and the phantasmagoria of static, shall we say, as if you were between radio stations, as this instrument would call them, and were picking up no clear signal, but a babble of varying messages. So you see that the mind is to be taken as a whole thing and not split, for the intellect and the intuition are both portions of the mind.

You are not your mind. Your mind is a kind of information processor which works for you as a tool. It is well to understand that the mind has great value in your seeking. It is well to balance your seeking, not shutting out the loud voice of intellect when it offers you new ideas, new questions, new waves of skepticism. It is wise to listen to your intuition, to quiet yourself, so that you may feel and be in a more whole and entire sense, for the heart of yourself is being—not thinking, not feeling—but being.

You are consciousness, and that consciousness creates. It has created this moment for you by the work it has done in the past. It will create what you call your future as the work that you are doing at this moment comes into manifestation. The tool of intuition is one which may be applied by the remembering and recording of your dreams and visions, by the listening to what this instrument would call the still small voice, the voice that says, "This is good; this is not so good. This feels right; this does not feel right." An intuitive person often has no verbalized reason for these feelings. It is always well to recognize them and give them respect. It is also well to use the tool of the intellect insofar as that skill is a portion of your native character, for the intellect can analyze dreams and visions, can examine thoughts and find from them the harvest of love therein, can temper the feelings of "should" and "could" and "yes" and "no" with sometimes an encouraging and sometimes a cautionary analysis of those intuitions. Many a baseless fear has been removed because of the work of the analytical portion of the mind.

However, neither analysis nor intuition can offer the heart of seeking, for the heart of your seeking is found in that fathomless portion of yourself which seeks and wills to know and has the faith that there is something to know. These things are gifts. The mind has been earned. It is a product of many, many incarnations, and it reflects your biases. Neither intellect nor intuition often reach deep enough to uncover faith and will.

So turn, then, from the consideration of clear minds and clear intuition long enough to gaze at the mystery of the [new moon]. You have the will to seek. And what do you seek? Many would say truth; many would say love; many would say the Creator. We say to you, there are no words, for the Creator is mystery infinite and invisible. It cannot be reached by analysis. It cannot be sounded through intuition. It is closer to you than that, for you are that which the Creator is, the one original Thought. That one great original and creative Thought is something that we can find no word for but love in your language. You are the consciousness that is love. The consciousness that you seek in knowing the Creator is love. You are what you seek and you seek what you are.

What you are doing in seeking is remembering and recapturing that which you knew before anything that is visible was created. For you are old. You are as old as this creation and you shall continue until its end, when at last you have achieved not only the presence of the consciousness of love, but that consciousness Itself in such totality that you know longer feel the need for individuality.

My friends, we have learned more, experienced more, and been exposed to more than you, and our yearning is just as strong. We seek our source. The tools of analysis and intuition, the tools of mind, are helpful, but the driving force that leads step-by-step, day by day in incarnation by incarnation and density by density back to the one infinite Creator are faith and the will, driven by faith, to walk that path.

We encourage each of you to find, ask for, and seek the grace to acknowledge within yourself the divinity of the consciousness of love within you, to seat that consciousness through meditation and so become a channel for that love which is the one great original Thought. There is no portion of your mind nor any portion of your experience that will enable you to continue seeking or to continue manifesting love. The seeking is too wearing and without the strengthening of love itself, found in the silence of meditation, the feet drag upon the path and one finds a stone which looks to the eye of the dusty traveler more comfortable than the road. One sits down and one pauses and the will fails.

And so it is with manifestation. If one works from one's human resources, in this illusion of yours, my friends, you are limited and you can only love so much, you can only give so much, you can only bear so much fruit. Therefore, seek to enrich faith and will that you may become instruments through which the infinite supply of love can come to you and through you that you may realize at last that you stand already upon holy ground and dwell in the consciousness and presence of the Creator.

We again thank each, especially welcoming one new to this group and greeting her with love. We would now transfer this contact that there may be an opportunity for queries to be asked. We are sorry to relinquish this instrument, however we are eager to greet the one known as Jim, and so we shall leave the one known as Carla. I am L/Leema.

(Jim channeling)

I am L/Leema, and we greet you each once again in love and light. We are pleased to be able to speak our thoughts through this instrument and hope that we may be of some small service in attempting to answer those queries which remain within this group. May we then begin with the first query?

C: In the field of Dianetics is the term "engram." As I understand it, it is those things that have been impressed upon the mind. Could you briefly speak about what exactly an engram is?

I am L/Leema, and we shall attempt to speak upon this subject. As we are aware of the use of this term, it is analogous to what one may call a blockage of energy centers or chakras which serves to distort one's perceptions and experiences in a fashion which is somewhat imbalanced. The desire of those who describe such blockage is to remove the blockage that the life-giving energy of the one Creator may move freely through the being, allowing it to manifest its fullest potential. We see these blockages or engrams as that which each entity has chosen before the incarnation in order that during the incarnation certain lessons may have the opportunity of being learned, certain imbalances may have the opportunity of being balanced, and certain services may have the opportunity of being offered.

May we answer further, my brother?

C: No, you gave me plenty to think on. Thank you.

Carla: I'd like to follow up on that because I listened to someone talk about Dianetics for about two hours one time, and the whole idea of Dianetics was for a person to become "clear." It all sounded very humanistic and unattached to any ethical perception. Could you comment on the goal of being "clear," that is, having no blockages? Without any ethic?

I am L/Leema. We see the use of the term "clear" in this context as indeed that which seeks the free movement of energy and potential through an entity without there being a choice of direction or polarity. The entity which attempts this process in this fashion is one which must utilize the analytical mind to a large degree. It is much as a ship attempting to move upon the sea from one part to another without the firm operation of the rudder. It is difficult, but not impossible to remove and balance the blockages programmed for learning and serving without a motivating force, or as it may be called, an ethical stance. We prefer to describe it simply as the making of the primary choice to be of service to others or to self. To have such a choice firmly in mind is most helpful to an entity which seeks to fully utilize the potential which it carries with it. Such a choice serves as the fuel, the primary motivation for accomplishing the work.

However, if an entity is indeed successful in achieving the clearing process, as it is called, then it will at some point become apparent to such an entity through its cleared perceptions that such a choice is necessary in order for its fullest potential to be realized, for though at a great and distant point removed from this third-density illusion, there will be the joining of polarities in a more neutral configuration, shall we say, within the illusion your peoples now inhabit, the making of the choice is quite necessary for progress upon the path of seeking the truth to continue.

May we answer further, my sister?

Carla: No, thank you.

I am L/Leema, and we thank you, my sister. Is there another query?

C: Then to be clear is to be in a static kind of state?

I am L/Leema, and we would describe in inadequate terms the state of being clear, as we understand its usage in this philosophy, as being likened unto what we could describe as an entity sitting within one of your automobiles after having perfectly cleaned and readjusted each portion of the engine and transmission so that the automobile would move perfectly upon your roadway if it had a direction in which to move. The choice of direction and the motivation for the choice then become necessary for the driving entity to make. Thus, the point is not so much static—in that movement is not possible—but is a point awaiting choice, that movement may then result.

May we answer further, my brother?

C: No, thank you.

I am L/Leema, and we thank you again, my brother. Is there another query?

C: With second-density creatures, with those far shorter life spans, when one lifespan is over, is there a very long period of time until they reincarnate if they reincarnate back into second density?

I am L/Leema. We look upon the great variety of creatures which inhabit your second-density illusion, from the tiniest single-celled creature to the greatest mammals, reptiles and beings which you call trees, and see that there is within these creatures a great variety of time span, as you would call it, which would separate one incarnation from another. For some there is a great portion of time, as you would mark it, that passes between one incarnation and another. For others the time is quite short.

Is there a more specific way that we may speak to this topic, my brother?

C: I feel that I'm getting a repeat as far as the second-density creatures that we have close to us in the family. More specifically, I feel the same entity is showing up in feline form …

(Side one of tape ends.)

(Jim channeling)

I am L/Leema, and am again with this instrument. The phenomenon of which you speak, my brother, is one which is found at the highest level of the second density, that is the phenomenon of what your peoples call the pet. It is indeed true that due to the process of investment of identity upon these second-density creatures by their companions which you call owners that they oftentimes will choose after one incarnation is complete to move again into the life pattern of those they have grown to love and who have invested them with their love. Thus, your perception that there is a returning to your family of an identity in second density is correct, and is often accomplished within your illusion in precisely the manner you have described in order that the second-density creature may be further invested and may eventually achieve its own graduation, shall we say, and begin an incarnation at some point within the third-density illusion, having received enough love and given enough love to have marked its own identity or self-conscious awareness, which is the beginning hallmark of the third-density creature that is known as the human being.

May we answer further, my brother?

C: No, thank you.

I am L/Leema, and we thank you, my brother. Is there another query?

Carla: Well, L/Leema, if I can read this, there will be another query.

L of Long Island, New York … I can't read it, so I can only ask one of the two questions, which is just as well. I'll ask the next one next week when I memorize it. The one I remember is this question—and I hope that I get it right. L has been experiencing people commenting to her about conversations that she had with those people, things that she said when she was with them and so forth, when in fact she has been someplace else. She always has the sensation of being in her body doing what she's doing where her body is and so forth, but having a "funny feeling"—she doesn't describe it any more than that, I think, and she knows that it's occurring. But she doesn't know whom she's seeing or what's she's talking about. She only finds that out later. Apparently, the advice that she gives is considered helpful. Her question is: Would it be helpful to her own spiritual development at this point for her to go more seriously and deeply into this phenomenon, and if so, how would it be spiritually helpful for her, and in what direction should she investigate?

I am L/Leema, and we are aware of this query. The phenomenon described is one which is common to those who have sought to be of service to others in the time/space or metaphysical portion of your illusion. Many there are who accomplish this service while in the sleeping and dreaming state, moving at that time to be of aid to others in a similar state. This is the means by which many healings are accomplished and the means by which many teachings may be presented that will nurture the being when the subconscious mind which has absorbed these teachings releases them in a careful fashion to the conscious mind at various times during the entity's waking experience.

There are also entities among your peoples who perform this service while conscious themselves, but are usually not conscious of accomplishing this service. Much interaction there is between entities while conscious that entities are not aware of. The communication network, shall we say, is always in place, and is utilized when the need is felt without the necessity of conscious awareness. The unconscious mind may call, may hear, may move, and may receive without conscious participation on the part of either the one who calls or the one who hears.

The one known as L has partaken of this service for a large portion of its incarnation and is now becoming conscious of the phenomenon in a small degree and seeks to enhance its service at this time. We appreciate greatly the desire to enhance this service, but can speak in no specific way as to how this may be accomplished, for it is necessary that such choices be made by this entity as a function of its free will. We may perhaps provide some comfort to this entity by suggesting that it serves well without conscious participation and that the unfoldment of its ability to serve moves in a sure and steady line of evolution.

May we answer further, my sister?

Carla: I wouldn't speak for L. I feel sure that when she reads this, she will ask further if she does have a question. On my own, I would like to follow up on when L was here. When I took a look at her hand, I discovered that although she had a strong line of protection in her birth hand, the hand that experience had lined had removed that line of protection and had confused what palmists call the line of destiny. And because of this mechanical way of looking at someone's path, it occurs to me to ask just on my own, in general, if one person is setting out to be of service and does not have native protection in a strong degree, what would be most helpful to do to ensure that as one polarizes, one is also protected?

I am L/Leema, and we would remind you, my sister, that the polarity of service to others is one which contains a great deal of protection. The fruit of service to others is that which is guarded by the light of those who observe the movements within your illusion from outside of your illusion. Within this general arena of protection, shall we say, the one who seeks to be of service to others may invoke this light at any time the need is felt. At all times it is recommended that for the greatest protection, the one who seeks to serve others may attempt with a full and joyous heart to see the Creator in all beings and events which come before its notice, to seek the light, to praise it and to rejoice in the opportunity to be of service. In this frame of being and attitude of seeking to serve, one bathes oneself in the armor of light, that which is, and that which is not, the darkness, then becomes illumined and becomes as that which is light. Thus, the light speaks to itself and knows no fear or foe for all is seen as one. The truth is known as the light is called.

May we answer further, my sister?

Carla: I think you're tremendously eloquent tonight, L/Leema. Thank you, no. I do have one for the road if the instrument still has enough energy to answer one question.

I am L/Leema, and we are happy to be able to utilize this instrument for another query or two.

Carla: I only have one, I think. And that is—okay, we've asked before about palmistry and things like that and the answer is phenomena are phenomena and that's cool and it's sort of a guideline thing, it doesn't mean that your fate is fixed, it's just sort of a general lay-of-the-land kind of way of looking at things. But I've been looking at peoples' palms for a long time. L had a very clear one—very few lines, very well marked. But I've seen this before in looking at peoples' hands, people that are seeking. Often the birth hand is very clearly marked with a line of destiny and a line of protection running right along side it happily, and then somehow, somewhere in life, the protection goes, and the destiny becomes a little bit cluttered or perhaps even broken. In L's case it was actually vanished. And she said it just vanished within the last six months.

That isn't the point. The question is: If one's protection is native from birth, it's in the birth hand, what in the world happens in the person's being or consciousness that blocks that innate, inherent, inborn angelic protection from showing up in the actual experience? Is it a choice made consciously that is athwart the intended lesson to be learned? And if it's not, could you comment at all on this phenomenon? If it's a stupid question, just say so and don't answer.

I am L/Leema, and we are happy to respond to this query which is not in the least lacking in sense. There are instances in which the incarnation and its purpose will be realized to a sufficient degree at a point within the incarnation that arrives sooner than expected, shall we say. When this occurs, a conscious choice may be utilized or a preincarnative parallel program may be invoked to, shall we say, up the ante, to make more opportunity for learning and serving available by presenting a greater degree of difficulty, shall we say, within the life pattern. The juggler may do quite well with both hands operating freely. However, by adding more objects for two hands, or by removing one hand, the difficulty is increased. The difficulty, however, is also that which offers greater opportunity.

Thus, the entity with great native protection surrounding its incarnational pattern, having achieved a large measure of its goals with such protection in place, may then seek to strengthen its will and faith by removing a significant portion of that native protection, as you have called it, in order that the will to continue to serve and the faith that means to serve shall be provided, are both strengthened, in a manner which would not be possible if the incarnation moved with the ease provided by the native protection.

May we answer further, my sister?

Carla: No, thank you. That's very helpful. Thank you.

I am L/Leema, and we thank you, my sister. Is there another query at this time?

(Pause)

I am L/Leema, and as it seems that we have exhausted the queries for this evening, we shall with great joy and thanksgiving take our leave of this instrument and this group. We thank each for inviting our presence and allowing us to serve in our humble way. We remind each that we are but your fallible brothers and sisters in the seeking of truth. Take those words that we have spoken that have value in your own journey and use them as pleases you, and if we have spoken any word which does not ring true, please disregard it without a second thought. We wish to place no stumbling blocks upon the path of another's seeking.

We shall be with this group in your future, as you call it, and look happily forward to that time. At this time we shall leave each of you in the love and in the light of the one infinite Creator. We are known to you as L/Leema. Adonai, my friends. Adonai vasu borragus. ✥

Sunday Meditation
May 25, 1986

(Carla channeling)

I am Q'uo. I greet you in the love and in the light of our infinite Creator. It is a great privilege to be with you this evening. We are using word by word channeling with this instrument, which requires more fine tuning on the part of the instrument, and therefore there may be pauses as this instrument is still at the stage where it is noticeably more comfortable with concepts as then it feels it has more control over the channeling process. However, the more flexible instruments we have found in working with those among your peoples who offer their services as vocal channels are those who are willing to speak complete nonsense, once the tuning and the challenging of instrument and source has been done. Therefore, we persist, as do others in the Confederation, in using this technique with those instruments which allow us to work in this manner.

That this instrument finds it more difficult to work word by word is a good example of the impatience that plagues those whose sight is as limited as is yours in the third-density illusion which you inhabit. It is often impossible to see the richly textured pattern which links events, situations and emotional states in coherent manner. In fact, it is far more logical to assume a stance of extreme skepticism when faced with the question of the "why" of existence and consciousness, for even the most patient among you must be patient to the point of silence, usually for many of your years, before the inner connections between all things, events, people, emotional states become evident or even partially so. Since much is obscured from your vision, it is logical to assume that there is nothing to be seen. Yet, there is that irrational, shall we say, impulse among all conscious beings to seek beyond that which can be seen, heard, felt and touched in any way, measured by any instrument, evaluated by any means whatsoever.

Of things for which there is no measurement, the mind can have little use, for the mind is developed as a specific tool for specific applications. Therefore, what your biological—and may we say somewhat atavistic—self presents you with is a vision of creation in which consciousness is not explained. Further, although a good case can and often has been made for ethical behavior in the face of an uncertain future, it is difficult rationally to assume any sort of continuance beyond the disintegration of the physical vehicle, even within the incarnation which you now enjoy. It is quite difficult for the rational mind to accept the probability that gifts may be freely given to conscious beings which are mysterious in their origin and palpable in their effect. Thus, when we speak to you, again and again we suggest meditation, that which takes one out of one's mind and into the realm of mystery.

It is well to know one's biological handicaps, my friends, for there is no deep instinctual yearning in your biological makeup towards truth, the betterment of others as opposed to the self, the cooperation between peoples or nations, or any kind of redemptive saving grace to life. That body which you inhabit will say to you time and time again that mysteries will come to nothing, that meditation and seeking are games which one plays to distract oneself from the certainty of one's own death, and that ethics are the luxury of men who have no needs which are not already met in the physical and material world. This is the material which will be thrown up before your vision time and again as long as you inhabit the dwelling place of your fragile physical vehicle. It is a wondrous machine, full of delights and folly, and it is well to know it and its limitations, and even to acknowledge before the magnificent rationality of that portion of the physical shell you call the brain that intense skepticism concerning the spiritual seeking is the logical stance.

Let us plunge then, into darkness. Let us become blind and deaf. Let us become aware of the something within us that is other. Other than what, you may ask. Perhaps a good adjective would be "other-worldly." And yet we do not mean other-worldly in the sense of absentminded—we mean something more basic.

And the body with which you are so familiar seeks and loves light. It basks in the summer; it delights in the fire, and the darkness is alleviated always by man's mastery of light, be that light a flickering candle or the most magnificent display of electricity. That within you which is other, that which is spirit, delights in the darkness which frightens the biological shell. It is the darkness of the seeker, for we do not seek in light, or we should most surely have a short journey to the end of our seeking. We seek in the shadowland where the only light is that of hope, the only star that of faith, the only flickering candle that of blessed will, the only electricity that of inspiration.

Your logical, rational, measurable shell is itself mutable, and, indeed, your environmentalists will be pleased that it is also biodegradable! That within you which seeks is immutable and unchangeable in its essence. It is eternal and is co-eternal with the Father. It is your source and it is your goal. You are the full circle of that which you seek. And yet, seek it you must and in some length, for an entire creation shall be spent with the seeking of one self for the Self.

If you attempt to seek, using the physical shell, you will truly be whistling in the dark. There will be fear, there will be much blockage, and information will not come easily. It is a very compassionate move on your part to allow yourself to free yourself from your perceptions of yourself within the physical shell so that you may go into the darkness of the unknown—intrepid, unafraid, fearless and eager.

We have said in a little while what the program of discovery may be [for] you for an infinitely long journey. It is far easier said than done. And yet you do not need to make the journey at once, for your journey is this step, this moment, this situation, the entities about you at this time, the emotions you feel at this juncture. The rational mind can stretch back into the past and into your future and oh, how it loves to do that. The heart of your seeking lies with that portion of yourself that is other, and that otherness dwells in an eternal present moment. As you would pick up a pencil from the blotting pad and scratch upon the paper, so you shall live the shell of your life. As you gaze into a blackness that opens and flowers, reveals and beckons, so you shall live the mysterious [zero] of the spirit. May your dance in the darkness be all that you hope and all that you seek.

We speak to you as representatives of the Confederation of Planets in the Service of the One Infinite Creator. We are your brothers and sisters and we extend ourselves to you in compassion and pity, for we know how you struggle against the bonds of measurability. Have compassion upon yourselves and turn inward, for there is no struggle, but only the dance in the darkness within.

We leave you in the blinding light of that darkness and in the creative love of that infinite [zero], that opening, that keyhole, unlocked and opened in silence. We are known to you as those of Q'uo. We would at this time attempt to make contact with the one known as Jim. We shall at this time transfer.

(Jim channeling)

I am Q'uo, and am pleased to greet each of you once again through this instrument. We are happy that this instrument has been willing and able to perceive our contact and we thank it for the opportunity to utilize it in continuing to offer our service which is both humble and, to this instrument, unique. Our contact, as we have stated before, is one which is most fruitfully expressed in the word by word mode of transmission. Thus, we shall attempt with this instrument to continue that method of transmitting information, resorting to the concept method only when the word by word technique becomes too difficult.

At this time, we would attempt to respond to specific queries which those in this group may have prepared for this portion of your gathering. May we at this time entertain the first query?

Carla: I'll go ahead and ask the other question that L asked. She wanted to know how the service-to-self path can use the light, and what role this path plays in the drama of creation. That's not word-for-word, but I did read the question, so it's in the instrument's mind more specifically.

I am Q'uo, and we feel that we have a grasp of this query and shall begin. The path of service to self is one which intensifies the illusion of separation which is inherent in all of creation, for when the one Creator divided Itself in order that It might further know Itself, the division which took place became likened unto an illusion, for the result was the creation and is moment by moment the creation as you know it and far beyond what you know.

As the Creator, which is simplicity itself, became that which seemed complex, the possibility of two means of traveling through the creation or each portion of the creation became apparent. That which moved in resonance with unity became that which you know as the service-to-others path, that which is radiant and expresses the light of the one Creator to all about it, for all is seen the same as self, that is, the one Creator.

The service-to-self path became possible when the first division in third-density consciousness occurred due to the placement of what you have called the veil of forgetting between the conscious and the unconscious minds. This intensification of the illusion of separation provided to the Creator a more intense and purified means for that portion of Itself which may be seen as magnetic to function. Thus, the service-to-self path is one which draws unto itself the light of the Creator in all portions of the creation about the entity which has chosen this means of knowing itself and of evolving towards the same Creator.

Thus, it is the same light which powers both paths in opposite fashion, or so it would seem within the saga of polarity, for as those of the service-to-others path give forth the light to all about them, it would seem that this action is in opposition to the service-to-self path which absorbs the light and uses it for its own purposes. Yet, in truth, it is the Creator which provides the light for both paths, and the same Creator which receives the light as a result of the action that is potentiating upon each path.

May we answer in further detail, my sister?

Carla: I'm sure that L will let us know if she wishes further answer. Thank you very much.

I am Q'uo and we are filled with gratitude at the opportunity to speak in response to this query. May we attempt another query?

Carla: I was wondering, what is the purpose of incarnating as a man and as a woman repeatedly? Is it necessary to know both male and female energies or to become balanced between those energies?

I am Q'uo, and we find that in essence you have begun to answer your own query. This is the nature of learning in general. The excellent query will draw forth from the questioner that which is sought, for indeed all entities are that unity which contains all things.

The incarnational patterns of experience within the third, the fourth, the fifth, and the sixth-density illusions offer an entity the opportunity of experiencing the dual nature of the one Creator which is found in all creation, that nature of which we have just spoken in the query preceding this one. The male and female principles of radiance and magnetism, of light and dark, of wisdom and of love, are those qualities which in dynamic tension provide all catalyst for experience to each seeker of truth, as you would call it. Thus, the giving and the receiving are means by which the Creator, shall we say, dances with Itself. Each seeker, then, reproduces this movement, and when done in an intelligent fashion this movement becomes an evolutionary journey which continues to gather together portions of the one Creator in accelerating frequencies for each seeker to glean those parts for which it has need in its own pattern of growth. Thus, within …

(Side one of tape ends.)

(Jim channeling)

I am Q'uo, and we shall continue with our response.

Within each evolutionary journey, within each density of illusion, within each incarnational pattern, each moment and each thought, there is the interaction and interplay of the positive and the negative polarity that is the fabric of all creation. Thus does each seeker recapitulate the essence of the one Creator, and when accomplished in a directed fashion, this process presents to each seeker the ever-expanding opportunity to grasp more and more of its nature as the one Creator.

May we respond further, my sister?

Carla: Yes, I'm going to take it a step further because the source of my concern is this. I've examined my own self and have found strong elements of assertiveness, aggressiveness—male characteristics—which suggest to me that I've been a male plenty of times as well as being a female. It has not caused me any suffering in this life. I have known several women who were considerably more yang, I suppose would be the term I would use, and it has not caused them any suffering. I don't know any female homosexuals, but I do have a friend who is a male homosexual and he is suffering a great deal because he has the same needs for love and nurturing that any other person has, but every instinct that he has puts him in a situation which is basically untenable in a sense of receiving a stable domestic environment which is full of support and genuine and continuing love from another human being.

This seems to be the fate of the homosexual, the male homosexual, very difficult to maintain companionship and affection over a long period of time. I don't understand why the higher self would choose to so unbalance the incarnational pattern that two-thirds or more of the incarnations would be as women and then the soul would move back into the male body and be terminally confused. If you could shed any light on this suffering and its purpose, I'd be appreciative.

I am Q'uo, and we may suggest that within your third-density illusion the limitations which are experienced, on every front, shall we say, are designed to allow the entity to learn how to free the self. There are experiences that are most needful of balancing that require what seems within the incarnation to be greatly distorted circumstances. The cumulative effects of previous, shall we say, incarnations often decree that the upcoming incarnation provide the arena in which these various distortions may find the opportunity for balance. The choice of one biological gender or another will be made according to these distortions in need of balance. It may be that throughout the full third-density pattern of incarnations an entity would find it necessary to choose one gender over the other more often than not in order to fulfill a larger pattern of learning. The difficulties, as you call them, associated with this choice, in this case, as it has been called, homosexual orientation, are then incorporated into the larger pattern and utilized in the overall growth of the entity. Within the third-density illusion, the great array and degree of limitation is utilized as, shall we say, a force against which to test the spiritual strength, for within your illusion one must rediscover the foundation or fabric of one's being time and time again.

May we answer further, my sister?

Carla: No, thank you.

I am Q'uo, and we are grateful to you, my sister. May we speak upon another subject?

T: Yes, I have a question. The reason I took so long, I was trying to figure out exactly what I wanted to ask. I read a book recently on channeling and utilizing and internalizing sexual energy. It seems that basically, from what I read, that it's a matter of developing this energy from a purely physical level, learning to control it, and then learning to internalize that energy, thereby increasing the inner power or chi, as they call it—this comes from a Chinese tradition, obviously. And this also ties in with physical exercise that is meant to do basically the same thing, which is Tai Chi, which does the same thing. Could you comment? Could you just—do you have any comment on this—I don't have a specific question, I guess, that's why I took so long before.

I am Q'uo, and we would suggest that the means of reinvesting one's own beingness with the essence of the energy produced by the physical vehicle in conjunction with the mental process which you have described is one which focuses the, as it has been called, chi, or prana, in a specific fashion which is then utilized in what may be called a sacred manner. The physical vehicle provides the foundation upon which all experience is built for an entity. The preservation of the vehicle and its ability to reproduce and its ability to serve as a triggering mechanism give to the entity the basic energy and environment of energy which it then may utilize in higher and higher, if you will, means. Thus, the creation and storing of physical sexual energies may be focused upon any of the succeeding centers of energy or chakras as we find them called of an entity. Thus, in this way any balancing of distortion or removal of blockages or accomplishing of magical workings, shall we say, may be carried out. The function then of the mental complex is to design the framework or channel through which these physical energies may be moved. When this framework has been firmly constructed within the entity, the power of the internalized physical sexual energy is then more and more available for use in the proscribed fashion.

May we answer further, my brother?

T: No, thank you very much. That's very good. Thank you.

I am Q'uo, and thank you, my brother. May we attempt another query?

Carla: I need to follow up T's question. The only thing I've ever read about … gosh, what kind of Yoga is it … Tantric, suggested—and this was in the magikal, with the "k," tradition, that one—and I think this was also written by a man, okay—that one move close to orgasm and then stop and do this repeatedly, was called magical chastity, but it also recommended that the partner be a stranger. This struck me as being potentially very negative in that you did build your own personal power, but you were not exchanging the opportunity with the partner. And I wondered if the same energy could be stored using the same magical chastity with two people working together with equally efficacious results and hopefully a more positive slant to that storage of personal power?

I am Q'uo, and we find your statement to be correct in general and specifically.

We would suggest a final query at this time for this instrument is somewhat fatigued as a result of the word by word contact method and is less and less able to maintain the depth of meditation necessary for this type of contact.

Carla: I'm torn between two questions. I'll ask … gee—I hate decisions. I'll ask you about yourself—no, I won't do that. That would detune the contact. When I was channeling earlier, I wasn't with it entirely, but I did catch the repeated distinction between the physical self and the spiritual self. A dichotomy seemed to be reigning in the kingdom of this particular discussion tonight, and yet, this body is what we use to manifest our spiritual selves in this incarnation. I wondered what special need there might have been to emphasize that dichotomy this evening. What purpose underlay the concentration on that concept this evening?

I am Q'uo. We have spoken this evening of the apparent and of that which is not apparent in order to share our understanding, simple though it is, that within your illusion you draw upon resources constantly that are far, far greater than you can imagine. And when you move within your daily round of activities, you are utilizing but the tiniest fraction of that which is at your disposal. Yet that very movement itself draws unto your limited self more and more of that which knows no limits in order to enhance your ability to experience within your illusion. Thus, we speak as we have spoken, of limitation and infinity being recapitulated within your own being and of this process being fueled by your will to seek and your faith that the seeking will bear fruit.

May we answer further, my sister?

Carla: No, thank you. I enjoyed you.

I am Q'uo. We have greatly enjoyed this evening with each of you, and we are happy to join this group at future times, as you would call them. And we look forward to the opportunity to blend our vibrations with yours. We shall take our leave of this group and this instrument at this time. Again, with gratitude and in joy, we leave you. We are known as Q'uo. Adonai, my friends. Adonai. ✣

Sunday Meditation
June 1, 1986

(Carla channeling)

I am L/Leema. I greet you, my friends, in the love and in the light of the one infinite Creator in Whose name we come to serve this evening. We thank you for calling us to your group for we are most grateful to have this opportunity to serve you and in serving you finding the most blessed service given to ourselves, for it is in service that we are able to move forward in our own refinement on the understanding of the ways of the one infinite Creator.

The request that has been made this evening is a layman's discussion of the concept of three-dimensional time.

We shall do a bit of talking through this instrument while we are settling our contact with the instrument and deepening the meditation to the point where the instrument ceases to have any concern whatsoever for the channeling that it will be doing. This instrument knows little or nothing of this subject, far less even than your scientists who have, shall we say, only fragments of the conceptualization of the universe as we are aware of it.

We would like to express our desire that as we speak, those concepts which do not seem helpful to you be put aside immediately, for we are your brothers and sisters and our opinion is as fallible as our natures. We are those with somewhat more experience than those of third density, yet there is much we have to learn before we come to the position of bidding farewell to the incompleteness of our own sense of searching. And indeed, when that completeness comes, we shall be once again a portion of time/space and therefore be uninterested in communicating, as we shall be being drawn back to the source of All that there Is, and at that stage of evolution, will have a strong enough gravitational pull, metaphysically speaking, towards that great central source that we would be unable to communicate.

You dwell, in your meeting this evening, in a domicile that is rich in time. Although it has stood still in space, it has endured through many of your seasons and is full of years. It has not gained in size, yet it has gained in time. Each of you sitting within this circle has ceased to grow in the physical sense. The space which you occupy is that which you shall occupy insofar as your bony structure and your organs are concerned. It is within this instrument's mind that poundage may be gained or lost, however, the point we are making is that as you dwell within your physical bodies in space/time, you dwell also in time/space, and as you grow more full in years, so you grow rich in time. This fullness of time is a characteristic of those who are seeking, and the sense of it and its wonder are most beneficial for the consideration of one who seeks the truth.

In a simplistic manner, we would use a description which we have found within this instrument's mind in speaking of the difference between the world of space/time and the world of time/space. You would, in your physical vehicles and in this illusion of space/time, think little of setting out for another city. When that trip had been accomplished, you would again think little of your next journey, and so you would travel geographically to and fro in space. Within this house there is a long portion of time/space and were the seeker sensitive enough, it could within this house become aware of this house's reality, shall we say.

In another year, a sensitive enough student would not think a great deal of moving back in time and experiencing in the stream of space the movement in time. Indeed, without reverting to the heart of the meaning of time/space, the mechanics of time/space are relatively simple. You call one of your planet's journeys about the sun a year, and you number them after that which is thought to be the birth of a master teacher. Your year 1929 would be as Cincinnati to Louisville, the year 600 BC perhaps equaling Australia or Madagascar. Just as we do not notice when moving in space that time is anything but simply a flowing river, so in moving through time, space is seen as a simply flowing river. One place is as easily arrived at as another, as all places are in the stream of space. This is an illusion which is useful for travel outside of the chemical vehicle which is your physical manifestation within the illusion of space/time. Each of you has also a physical vehicle of another kind which is inextricably intertwined with the space/time physical vehicle which can and does move in time/space.

Thus, it is quite possible for each of you to visit your past or your future, for this is the illusion represented by the mechanical time/space. There are physical characteristics to what we may term geometric or mechanical time/space which are polarized to space/time in such a way that space/time and time/space, perfectly matched, equal among other things, the speed of light and the energy of that which is eternal. Perfectly matched space/time and time/space are not available within illusion, for the perfect matching thereof is the removal of illusion.

It is the mismatching of spaced time which gives to your space/time physical bodies the experience of moving through an incarnation. You will notice that in space/time, it is time upon which one focuses, although it is space within which one moves. In mismatching of time and space so that time is predominant, it is space which is noticeable and important, and time which is moved about in carelessly and taken for granted. Thus the physical space/time trip to Cincinnati would be as miraculous to a time/space entity as time travel is to you who have asked this question. It is the simplicity of the concept that tends to confuse the mind, rather than its complexity.

We would now move to the heart of the nature of three-dimensional time, bearing in mind, of course, as this group has asked us to do, that your concept of time involves a request to us, who are known to be somewhat wordy, to limit our answers in time so that the listeners may eventually move about in space, once again being free from our lecturing. We will therefore attempt to be reasonably brief.

Often and often members of the Confederation of Planets in the Service of the Infinite Creator have encouraged each who seeks the one original Thought to move inward into silence and the listening. We ask this because it is, as far as we know, the single most efficient controllable method of achieving conscious experience of time/space, for within time/space dwells much of that which you call the mind. Much of what you experience goes unnoticed by the conscious mind which is dwelling in space/time, and which is a tool designed for use in space/time. All of your instrumentation of a scientific nature at this time, if you will pardon the misnomer, is given to the measurement of space/time phenomena. Time/space, when viewed from the standpoint of space/time, is completely subjective. Nothing which you experience in time/space can be definitively proven or reliably repeated, for the instrumentation for measurement of time/space phenomena is not in your present available.

Time/space is unknown territory. The word which perhaps more closely than any other in your language represents [it] is the numinal; another word would be the mysterious. To the space/time consciousness, time/space is shifting, illusive and unpredictable. And yet, the majority of your true mind dwells in time rather than in space, and is used for more efficiently processing that catalyst which is gathered during your incarnational experience in space/time. When you dream clearly, the portion of your mind which is dwelling in time—we will abbreviate time/space to time and space/time to space—speaks to you of that which you have not yet become aware in space.

Teachers, which are called by some, "angels," and others, "inner plane masters," speak within time and most often within sleep and often without memory. Yet still biases are formed and refined because of the interaction of the deeper mind with that world of three-dimensional time which serves, shall we say, as the backboard, if you wish to think of experience as a means of putting the ball in the basket. One's conscious experiences in space are such that one may learn lessons without recourse to the deeper mind which dwells in time only by extremely accurate observation, which in this analogy, would equal the action of the ball so thrown through the air that it moved through the hoop without touching the rim or the backboard. It is seldom that one of your sports players develops the skill of a basketball game without recourse to the use of the rim and the backboard. It would be an inefficient use of the tools which such an athlete would be given for this game. It is equally unlikely that an entity will move through an incarnational experience without the use, conscious or unconscious, of the backboard of the deeper mind.

It would be an intellectual game to speak of parallel universes, of space/time and time/space. We ask that you perceive that in our opinion, this mode of thinking, while accurate, has to do with the mechanical space/time and time/space which are polarities to each other. For the metaphysical seeker, it is far more interesting to work with the concepts of what the time/space portion of each being can offer to the spiritual development of humankind.

We move back now to the concept of the river, if you consider time to be the river, as one in your illusion is almost forced to do when they see that the river never ceases flowing, nor is it patently conceivable that the flow of time will cease. In the illusion called time/space, it is equally incongruous to suppose that the river of space, or may we say, physical manifestation of energy fields which are polarized electrically, will cease. The river is a foreverness, whether it be the river in space or the river of time. The work of the spirit, however, is most efficiently done through the river of space which takes its nature from the illusion of time/space. You were in time/space before you came into incarnation in this space/time incarnation, and to that river you shall return, and time then, as before, shall become static. It is the stasis of time which enables the spirit to do so much with that tool in seeking, for within the body which is your chemical vehicle, you are subject to and bound by the river of time.

In time/space that river ceases to flow and you may remain in an eternal present moment so long as you are seeking to use the tools of time and flowing in the river of space. In this river of space lies each experience, and without the prison of time one may, unbarred and free, search out the nuances of even the most complex and difficult situation so that one may find the Creator and love, which is the Creator, in each and every experience and situation. Throwing off the trammels of time, it is possible to use the tools of many portions of a deeper self. It is possible to dwell what may seem to be long upon the most brief moment, for that moment may hold a key for you and it may be important to dwell within that moment, using the deeper tools and doing the work of the spirit, that is, the seeking of the truth.

We wish you the joys of that search. Truly, your incarnation, were it lost to the freedom of metaphysical time/space, would be far too short, regardless of the years in it, to accommodate learning to any significant degree. This is why the majority of your minds are each of the nature that dwells in time/space. When you go into meditation, you can experience this stretching of time until the time slows and ceases to turn in its inevitable cycles. Remember, we are speaking here of illusions, for the reality is a timelessness and a spacelessness which precludes experience. The goal of your consciousnesses is to seek out experience and to process it in such a way that you add to the Creator's knowledge of Itself. Thus, it is necessary that space and time be mismatched.

In your illusion of space, time unbuckles and is undependable. All that is dependable about it is that it shall pass all too quickly and as more and more experiences come and are incompletely processed, time will seem to move more and more quickly, the river flowing faster and faster as more of time is needed to balance the space in which you dwell. In time/space it is space which is unpredictable and buckled. While you are dwelling as space/time beings, the movement into time is a movement into a freedom from time in the illusory sense. We encourage that movement, as it will with continued use facilitate the efficiency with which the seeker may process experience and transform itself, and through the transformation of the self effect the transformation of the greater consciousness which is that of family, society, nation, continent, planet and creation itself.

We realize that though we have used no words which are not familiar, we have undoubtedly given a less than adequate explanation of this simple concept, and for the deficiencies of language itself, and of illusions in general, we apologize.

(Side one of tape ends.)

(Carla channeling)

We feel that we can do no more than encourage and inspire the kind of indwelling [thought] process within each seeker which will lead each to a subjective grasp of this concept.

It is to be noted in this regard that the lack of time/space instrumentation is the cause of the inability of your intellectual minds, and more especially the minds of the scientific community, to encompass events which may be called paranormal. The events occur due to the spontaneous or conscious use of the combination of time/space energy in a space/time environment. The so-called subatomic particles which are so often discovered, disputed and researched by your scientists are the results of scientists poring so deeply into the nature of energy patterns that they become able to perceive time/space energy patterns in physical manifestation in space. These at least, being energy patterns, are reproducible, but inexplicable, and the discovery of them shall continue to be both inarguable and mysterious as long as discipline of the deeper consciousness is neglected by those among your peoples who wish to call themselves men of science.

This instrument is telling us that we have spoken overlong. We are sorry and beg your pardon. We are moved by the honesty and depth of seeking within the group to which we speak and would willingly speak further, yet for a general expression, this is undoubtedly more than adequate. Therefore we would at this time transfer the contact to the one known as Jim so that we may field whatever questions you may wish to ask at this particular time—if you will pardon the, shall we say, cosmic joke. We are those of L/Leema and in gratitude we now leave this instrument.

(Jim channeling)

I am L/Leema, and greet each of you again in love and light through this instrument. At this time it is our honor to attempt to answer questions which remain with those of this group, if we are able. May we begin, then, with the first query?

J: Did I understand correctly that we have a physical body in space/time and yet also a physical body in time/space?

I am L/Leema. In the time/space or metaphysical portion of creation, you have a metaphysical vehicle which is more, shall we say, filled with the substance of creation itself, that is, with light. The remainder of your statement is correct.

May we answer further, my brother?

J: When we experience physical death in space/time, do we then occupy this metaphysical body in time/space?

I am L/Leema, and this is correct, my brother. This vehicle has been called the etheric body by many of those adepts of your illusion which study the metaphysical nature of reality.

May we answer further, my brother?

J: Were the pyramids used in any manner to help those in experiencing space/time to experience time/space?

I am L/Leema. This is again correct, my brother. The nature of seeking the heart of evolution is of itself best described as a metaphysical process. That which is metaphysical is that which is of a primary or foundation nature. That which is physical springs from this foundation and is a manifestation of it, and through the physical illusion of incarnation upon incarnation, an entity distills certain attitudes and lessons that bias it toward further seeking of what you would call truth and the nature and purpose of life. The geometrical shape of the pyramid was designed to aid this process, and indeed did so by funneling the light of the Creator, which has been imbued with love and called by many prana, in such a way that the distortions and disturbances likened unto mental static fell away from the seeker and the pure desire to seek the truth was then intensified in such a fashion that a finely wrought pathway between the seeker and the greater truth or reality which it sought was then constructed which allowed the seeker to experience more and more of that which it sought.

May we answer further, my brother?

J: I don't want to hog all the time. Maybe someone else has a question.

Questioner: I have many questions. I really don't know where to begin. I primarily want to know what my next step might be. I don't know if that's too personal for right now. Is it?

I am L/Leema. My brother, we seek to be of service in whatever way is possible for us without infringing upon any entity's own free will choices. We view this query as one which offers the possibility of such infringement, for we do not feel it proper to look upon an entity's life pattern and to describe to it that which is most likely to become its next experience from among the many potentials that await each. We can, however, suggest to any seeker who is desirous of placing the foot upon the path most securely as its next step that within the meditative state one may take this desire and open the heart of one's being to the inspiration which the greater portion of yourself may move and speak to you who inhabits this illusion, and in such a manner may you then find for yourself the next appropriate step.

We would hasten to add, however, that to focus overly much upon what is next upon one's spiritual agenda, shall we say, is in some degree to deny the appropriateness and efficiency of the present moment experience which is in itself whole, complete and most appropriately suited for your journey at this time.

May we answer further, my brother?

Questioner: I'm afraid it would take up too much time for this group, but I've got lots and lots of questions. I appreciate your response to my question. Thank you.

I am L/Leema, and we thank you, my brother. Is there another query?

J: I was just wondering—the kundalini energy that we experience in space/time as individuals, is this a function primarily of energy in space/time or does it also have a component in time/space?

I am L/Leema. We may suggest, my brother, that all events which you experience within your space/time illusion are manifestations of, shall we say, greater or richer events within the time/space or metaphysical reality which undergirds all that you experience in your present illusion. The phenomenon of the rising of the kundalini, as it has been called, is most centrally related to the time/space nature of your experience, and is indeed a manifestation or fruit of work which has been accomplished upon the metaphysical level by your experiences within the physical reality.

May we answer, my brother?

J: If we could develop a tool of measurement of time/space in this illusion, what would it be like?

I am L/Leema. We may suggest that the most efficient tool for measuring the time/space nature of creation is conscious experience. As the point of viewing of the conscious seeker expands and penetrates the surface appearance of all things that surround it, then the seeker becomes more and more aware of the truer nature of all creation, and as its awareness becomes richer and deeper and broader, it then begins to encompass or measure more and more of the time/space nature of all that surrounds it. This measurement, as you may hypothesize, is unique to each entity and would be difficult to translate in literal, practical terminology. To another being, the communication of such measurement would be best accomplished by the communication of concepts, shall we say, and is that which is of the nature of the mind to mind or telepathic contact.

May we answer further, my brother?

J: At what density is L/Leema, and do you dwell in space/time or in time/space?

I am L/Leema, and it is our honor to inhabit that density that is of light, which in your system of numbering numbers five. Within each density of the creation, there is the phenomenon of dual existence, that is, of space/time and time/space, for each density within the creation recapitulates the dual nature of all creation, that is, the manifest and the abstract, the male and the female, the light and the dark, in general terms. These principles, then, are reflected within each density of creation.

May we answer further, my brother?

J: No, thank you.

I am L/Leema, and we thank you, my brother. Is there another query?

Carla: Yeah, I'd like to clear up something that J asked. Is time/space that which awaits, i.e., the female, and space/time that which reaches? Is that the polarity?

I am L/Leema, and in an attempt to clarify the use of terms in a very general manner, the time/space or metaphysical portion of any density may be likened unto the female polarity which, awaiting the reaching, provides when reached for much of that which shall become the experience that is shared betwixt the polarities. The space/time portion of each density, then, is analogous to that male principle which reaches, and in the reaching seeks the experience that will enrich it by enabling it to know itself more and more as a unique portion of the one Creator, and which enable it also to see that about it more and more purely as the same Creator experiencing Itself in infinite variety.

May we answer further, my sister?

Carla: That being the case, is that the reason for the fabled woman's intuition or the apparent relative thinness of the veil between the conscious and the unconscious mind of the female due to the fact that time/space has female characteristics?

I am L/Leema, and we find that this is a reasonably accurate analysis, yet is a function also of the manner in which your particular culture has nurtured the female quality or principle within the biological female entity, for it is unto this biological female entity that the access and use of such pathways to the deeper mind has been viewed as most appropriate, for these are indeed pathways which provide to the conscious mind much which is of a nurturing nature, that is, the insights which enrich the experience and perceptions of the conscious mind.

May we answer further, my sister?

Carla: No. I think I grasp the qualification that I realized that biological males have just as much capacity for intuition as women, it's just that the culture doesn't encourage it in men as it does in women. I believe that was your qualification, wasn't it?

I am L/Leema, and this is correct, my sister.

Carla: Thank you.

And we thank you, my sister. Is there another query at this time?

J: I have one more. Is the Urantia book familiar to you, and if so, is it of a valid nature, in your opinion?

I am L/Leema, and we are indeed familiar with this writing of which you speak, but we again do not desire to influence one's free will in an undue manner by seeming to judge the value of any work, for there are many who would find great value in this work and many who would find less value. The value is a function of not only the work but the one to whom the work is made available and the needs of that particular entity at that point in its evolution.

May we answer further, my brother?

J: That seems like it would hold true for many other written things that we have, such as the Bible and general written material. Is that true?

I am L/Leema, and this is correct, my brother. May we answer further?

J: One thing in specific. About the Urantia portrayal of the universe, the physical universe. Does that seem to be something that you could put your, "Yes, this seems like a reasonable approach," or, "It seems like an interesting approach to me, anyway"?

I am L/Leema, and without risking infringement, my brother, we may suggest that there are many, many points of viewing the infinite creation which each contribute a portion of truth and a portion of distortion, for those entities such as yourself and all which exist within this infinite creation are unique in their ability to experience, to formulate concepts and to move forward in thinking from those concepts, and thus there is a great variety of points or places from which to view the one creation of the one Creator. Each is true and each is false, for that which is the one creation is beyond all definitive description. And yet, each description reveals a portion of That Which Is.

May we answer further, my brother?

J: No, thank you.

I am L/Leema, and we again thank you, my brother. Is there another query?

Carla: L/Leema, how's the energy of the instrument?

I am L/Leema, and as we scan this instrument, we find that there is the necessary energy for another two or three of your queries. May we attempt another query at this time?

Carla: I've been reading a book which has a good deal of mythology in it and one of the realities it posits is the reality of a fairy world. It's a retelling of the King Arthur cycle of legends. I have always suspected that these worlds are real in another illusion. It's hard to say "real" when you know that it's all an illusion, okay, but it's another kind of illusion. Is that illusion co-equal with ours, just as male and female are co-equal energies, and space/time and time/space are co-equal and complimentary to each other? Is there a symbiosis is what I'm asking, a way in which that world helps us and we help that world, or are they simply two parallel illusions which happen to occupy the same space?

I am L/Leema, and we might suggest the term "available" to replace the term "co-equal," for as the story of which you speak has been recorded by its author and shared with those such as yourself, the possibility of its influence upon your perceptions becomes available, that is within your own experience, perhaps that of the sleep and dreams, then it is possible for you to enter this particular illusion and to partake within it in a manner that enriches your total beingness, for indeed this is much of what the nature of what the sleep and dream cycle provides in the healing and enriching of an entity's life pattern.

May we answer further, my sister?

Carla: Well, let me just try to put it together real quick here. So, just as you said we use time/space in processing space/time experience, so would time/space wherein the fairy philosophy is that the Earth is alive and to be worshipped in its entirety. It's as easy in a fairy world to rape the Earth by plowing it as it is to rape a woman who is a virgin. And this kind of reality then is basically a time/space conceptualization which would enrich our space/time understanding of the Earth as a living being. Is that what is connoted by your previous answer?

I am L/Leema, and we find that you have indeed grasped the heart of our previous response and have enhanced it by your own description.

May we answer further, my sister?

Carla: Do you have any suggestions as to how we can dwell more honorably with this Earth of ours which is alive?

I am L/Leema, and we might suggest, my sister, that each thought and action an entity entertains is an expression of love in some manner, whether it be love of others or love of self. To attempt in each thought and action to give freely that known as love is to place the life pattern upon what you have called an honorable stance, for to honor another portion of creation, or entity, is to give that which each by the nature of its being requires to continue in its being. And that force which enables and ennobles all beingness is that which is called love. Thus is all of creation moved by its power. And to consciously seek to give this love to that which surrounds one's incarnation is to …

(Tape ends.)

Sunday Meditation
June 8, 1986

(Carla channeling)

I am Yom. I greet you in the love and in the light of our infinite Creator. It is a great privilege to speak with this group and we thank you for calling us to you. It has been some time since I and my brothers and sisters spoke to this group, and we find that this instrument is apprehensive in its ability to be a useful instrument for us. However, we find no serious bar against using this instrument, for the vocabulary, if not the knowledge, of the instrument suffices for our purposes.

We would speak with you this evening about some applications of that which you call light. We shall begin with what may be seen to be a mechanistic description of the influences which light may have using various catalysts upon each entity. It is not known to your peoples the nature of light, for the necessary paradigm for grasping its nature is not available to your scientists. It is because of this lack of understanding that the nature of the crystalline structures have never been satisfactorily researched or understood by those you call men of science.

We find this instrument requesting that we amend this to men and women of science. We acknowledge the correction, realizing that within your biological illusion it is not obvious to you that all of you are men, that is, not sexually, but in the sense of being perfectly unified in essence so that there need be no dissension betwixt biological gender. We return to our subject.

Light itself, being alive and being the first creature created of love, forms all that there is. It furthermore in its creative freedom surrounds and interpenetrates in original form the structures which have been created by the influence of free will upon light. Thus, all that there is is not only made, mechanically speaking, of articulated light, but is also interpenetrated by limitless light, which some among your students of metaphysics call prana. We have, then, a vast array of crystalline structures, for you may term each atom an inchoate crystalline structure, that is, the active elements are inchoate, some being without the need to bond with other elements, are themselves articulated. Each element has the capacity to bond with other elements and form either non-crystalline or crystalline structures.

The nature of the crystalline structure—that is, the window or opening wherein limitless light may form an influence … We must wait while this instrument retunes. If you will be patient. We are Yom.

I am Yom. We have instructed this instrument to refrain from analysis, and we feel we have a better contact now, if the instrument can refrain from examining the words it uses. Unlike our fifth-density brothers and sisters, we do not have the ability to tune to a sufficiently narrow band of contact to enable this instrument to go deeply enough into meditation to lose the fear of speaking about that which it does not know. Therefore, the instrument must take conscious responsibility for being patient with us, as we give word by word that which we would that you could hear this evening, as many in the group have an interest in the applications of that which is called light. We continue.

The crystalline structures within your creation are many. Some crystals have properties in time/space, others in space/time, others in both. For example, galaxies, stars and planets have a time/space crystalline structure. Your own planet has such a structure. You yourselves are time/space crystalline structures. Those among you who learn to heal are manifesting in space/time that crystalline structure which is the essence of regularized light.

Therefore, light has many influences upon each entity, for the nearer stars and the planets of your sun system have regularized time/space properties which result in instreaming from planet to planet which in turn affect the crystalline entities of third density which inhabit the planet. It has often been questioned whether the art you call astrology has a basis. The basis, in fact, is most dry and scientific. It does not, however, yield to present measurement techniques, due to time/space properties inherent in the nature of crystalline structures. Thus, the orientation of your being at the time of conception shall affect the physical parameters of the illusory physical vehicle which you now enjoy. The orientation of this particular sphere towards the cosmos at the time of entry into incarnation has an effect over the mental, emotional, and to some small extent, the spiritual nature of the entity within incarnation, it being remembered at all times that each entity, though influenced within an incarnation, is as it is, was, and will be, changeless, unified with the Creator and completely whole.

However, in your illusion, you deal with the illusion of the state of the body and the state or nature of the personality. It is, therefore, interesting to observe that astrology is in fact the science of the crystalline properties of light in time/space, the influence of this upon the planet and the residual influence of entities in a particular place upon the planet of these crystalline structures.

The planet itself will influence entities to a varying extent, depending upon the development of time/space awareness in the entity as it moves through the incarnation, for not all Earth energies are the same as one would expect in a crystalline structure. Picture, if you will, the gem which is cut. If it is not properly struck by the tool which cuts it, it will shatter. If it is touched in a place which does not fracture, there will be no breakage, clean or splintered. So it is with your Earth. There are points of energy instreaming upon your planet, not only in your—we find this entity calls your illusion third density—but also first density, second density, third and fourth, all now activated to a large extent. In potential are also far more complex crystalline structures which will resonate when the planet achieves fifth, sixth and seventh densities. This particular planet has not yet done so, however, theoretical work may be done by those with the technical skill to pursue this field of study.

Thusly, there are instances where entities may desire to remove themselves from a given geographical location. In a sensitive entity, this well may be the result of an awareness in the deep mind that the particular location is not harmonious with the entity's nature, or is not a place which is live enough, shall we say, for the entity to achieve the maximum energy or power from the crystalline structure beneath the entity's feet.

Lest you find yourself believing in a mechanistic universe, we hasten to suggest that each cell within the physical vehicle has a great portion of its nature hidden in time/space and is in that portion in a crystalline structure which is open to influences from other crystalline structures. The greatest of these influences is that influence of the third-density entity which has achieved to some degree the manifestation in space/time of its crystalline nature in time/space. Such entities are often teachers, healers and leaders, those which serve as the watershed over which many entities will move and thereby be transformed, or in many cases, specifically healed.

The mechanical structure of space/time crystals is a good tool also, though not as efficacious as the crystalline being, for healing both physical and subtle or etheric. The use of crystals is an art rather than a science, because each entity using the same crystal will mesh its points of crystalline energy with the points of energy of the crystal itself in an unique fashion. Thus, one healer's crystal may work well for it, while being inefficacious for another. However, the more highly evolved crystals such as the ruby and the diamond are powerful enough that very nearly any somewhat crystallized being may efficaciously use the ruby and diamond for the healing techniques.

It is to be noted in this regard, that it is well to work, if one desires this service of healing by crystals, with the lesser crystals first in order that one's technique is able to keep pace with one's power, for there is a great deal of power in the more articulated crystals, and it is well not to experiment with the more powerful ones before having become sensitized to energy instreaming by using lesser structures.

The most powerful crystalline structure may be perceived to be the self. As we have noted, the nature of each self is consciousness or being which is co-eternal, shall we say, with love itself. Each of you was created before your planet was created and shall be a being after the planet has become uninhabitable for third density. Thus, the great tool of light, the one we recommend to you, is the conscious use of the unconscious and almost always sleeping powers of the crystalline self.

This instrument, and perhaps some of you, have made light of writers who advocate the use of affirmations. We would suggest to you that if one is not satisfied with any portion of the being, it is well to write or use another's affirmation repeatedly as a way of moving from conscious thought to concept to light to the sending of that light to the cells of the body or the brain or the subtle bodies in order that healing at the cellular level may take place. The light cannot infringe upon free will, therefore, if the—we find this instrument calls the etheric body the form-maker body, or the higher self—has prescribed an incarnational experience for the body in which one of the parameters is some physical dysfunction or mental dysfunction, the crystalline sendings will not cause the change the conscious mind may request. This is the only stop against the use of light by the self for the self for healing.

Consider yourselves stewards of the love that created you and the light that manifests you. In meditation, call upon the silence that you may hear the silence which speaks of love, and both in meditation and in contemplations such as the use of affirmations, offer yourself as instrument for the manifestation and realization of the limitless possibilities of creative light. We may note that while most affirmations find their benefit to people in the mental and emotional areas, physical healing is also quite available through the use of affirmations which, indistinct or poetic, prosaic or wondrously beautiful, nevertheless have the intent of focusing the light of the infinite Creator in such a way that it interpenetrates and enlivens each cell of each of your bodies.

Light is used in another way in your language and that is as the opposite of heavy. We would end by suggesting to you that to be full [of] light is to be light, that is, cheerful, joyful and resilient. This is not, shall we say, a characteristic encouraged by the catalyst of your illusion, and we are sure that time and time again each finds itself growing heavy. It is well, then, to recall the nature of illusion and the nature of time/space and its limitless love and light. While illusory, it is a far merrier illusion, and is as available to you as is the experience of difficulty after difficulty that the illusion of third density will offer you.

(Side one of tape ends.)

(Carla channeling)

I am Yom. We shall conclude. Therefore, my friends, when you discover heaviness within the heart, you have a choice. It is acceptable to the Creator if you wish to experience the heaviness or darkness of the illusion. This informs the Creator just as efficiently as any other experience, and you are being of service to the infinite Creator whom we all wish to serve, by feeling terrible, sorrowful, or in any way upset. You may, however, choose to turn to some affirmation, one of what you call your jokes, or any inspiration which yields realization of light. It is without you and within you, interpenetrating each cell of your body and your brain and it is a tool for your use in learning the truth in seeking the love and the light of the one infinite Creator and in becoming more and more a polarized instrument, designed to manifest the Creator's love and light to other beings.

We thank you for your interest, and as we have not said for so long, this is a good group and we thank you for requesting information that lies within our realm of inquiry. We have not previously contacted others in this group with the exception of making satisfactory, though limited, contact with the one known as A. We shall therefore attempt to make our vibrations known to the one known as L and the one known as Jim. We would now transfer this contact to the one known as L, asking this entity to feel free to express inner reluctance if it does not desire to be used at this time. We would then make this vibration available to the one known as L. We are those of Yom.

(L channeling)

I am Yom. I come to you in the love and the light of the infinite Creator and wish to express to you our appreciation for your attentiveness as well as for your consistent striving in your efforts to perceive beyond your illusion. It is our desire to be of assistance to those present whenever possible and we place ourselves at your disposal that you may call us as one would another self in moments of disquietment or confusion. We desire to be of assistance whenever possible and will respond if you simply open your self to our vibration and mentally request our presence.

We shall now transfer our contact to the one known as Jim. We are of Yom, in the love and the light of the infinite Creator.

(Jim channeling)

I am Yom, and am pleased to greet you again through this instrument in love and in light. We have quite a bonanza this evening in the utilization of three instruments, and for this we are most grateful. We realize that we have used a good deal of your time as you reckon it and your patience and [comfort] in speaking as we have spoken. We at this time would attempt to answer those remaining queries that you may find the value in asking. May we attempt such a query at this time?

L: I'd like to ask a question concerning affirmation. Frequently things or conditions which we desire to occur may be associated with our illusion and place us in a position of advantage in relation to our other selves. For example, one might be considered for a promotion in one's area of employment and using an affirmation to attain that goal is an act which places one in a position of advantage over others who are being considered for that position. Could you discuss the morality of using affirmation, because I have some qualms in that area.

I am Yom. We may note two points of possible interest. Firstly, within your illusion you are never certain as to whether one position or another is more or less advantageous in the metaphysical sense. This is determined by those lessons which you have chosen to undertake and the services which shall be the fruits of those lessons. As to the morality of such affirmations and desires, within your illusion it cannot be said that one act is more or less good than another, for indeed these judgments are reserved for the point of view that is far wider than that which is possible within your illusion.

Secondly, the general nature of the affirmation is to specifically focus the attention, the expenditure of personal energy which is always at your disposal. Indeed, the life pattern itself without such affirmations of a specific nature is an affirmation of a general nature, for whatever you seek and in whatever degree you seek it, you shall eventually discover within your life pattern, for it is indeed true that as ye seek, ye shall find. To bend the will and exercise the faith by forming them around a spoken or visualized affirmation is to make the specific use of those powers that are always yours. This is likened unto utilizing the scalpel of the surgeon as opposed to a more crude technique of achieving the same results.

May we speak in any further fashion, my brother?

L: No, that's given me a lot to ponder. Thank you very much.

I am Yom. Our gratitude to you, my brother. May we attempt another query?

Carla: I'd like to understand something, because I share L's concern about ethics. It seems to me that affirmations having to do with working on the self are what you were talking about, and affirmations resulting in power over others or something of that nature, although possible, would be along the negative path. Is this correct?

I am Yom. This is basically correct, my sister, for any tool may be utilized in the positive or negative sense. The tool, however, remains neutral. The choice of its use then lends the, shall we say, coloration of your ethical system.

May we answer further, my sister?

Carla: Yes, because I have known people that you could just say were lucky, but like L says, these are often people who say, "Well, I'm going to get that job—no problem—I'll get a job; it'll be a good job." Or they'll say, "Everything's going to be fine," or they'll say, "Oh, this cold will be gone in a couple of days." And they won't say, "Gee, I hope I get the job," and they won't say, "Well, I probably won't get the job." They'll just from within themselves have the buoyancy of spirit to say, "Oh—no problem—I'll get a good job, I just know it." And yet they're not attempting to be negative in any sense of the word. How do you draw the line ethically between that and the negative use of power?

I am Yom, and again we would suggest that we would not draw any line for any entity, but would rather suggest that each entity will determine for itself the motivation for its actions and thoughts. Much within your illusion is shrouded in mystery, including one's own awareness of one's own motivations. It is most difficult to untangle the life pattern of any being. One may observe such entities and make judgments for oneself, and yet the value of such judgment is personal unto yourself, for you cannot know the forces that are moving within another, their purpose and their means of manifestation. Each entity undertakes the journey of seeking these inner truths for itself and does well to begin to glean the nature of one's own experience. Therefore, it is well not to attempt to draw any line for any other being.

May we answer further, my sister?

Carla: Only in noting that in my own experience, the hardest entity to unshroud the mystery of is myself because I don't have the objective point of view that other people do. I wonder if that's a common experience?

I am Yom, and, indeed, this experience is shared by all within your third-density illusion, for the catalyst of thoughts, words and deeds that move through your being is colored in a unique fashion by your own preincarnative programming. Thus, what has charge in the emotional sense for you may carry little or none for another. Thus, the bias you have placed within your own being in order to learn and to serve in such and such a fashion is that coloration which you will use as your food and nourishment for your journey of seeking, learning to discover these biases, seeking their roots and then balancing each with its opposite so that your journey may be complete and your lessons and services fully expressed.

May we answer further, my sister?

Carla: No, thank you.

I am Yom, and we thank you, my sister. Is there another query?

G: I have one if no one else wants to speak up. The affirmation and the decree that I've heard, the understanding that I have, is that a decree is basically affirmation which is in multiples of three. Is there some reason or some explanation on why the multiples or repetitions of the affirmation being used is empowering? I don't know if that is clear or not, but that is my question.

I am Yom. We may respond in a general fashion by suggesting that the repetition of any affirmation is likened unto driving the nail deeper into the inner conscious awareness in order that the focus of attention be firmly affixed to that which is desired.

May we answer further, my brother?

G: Yes. Then you're saying the significance of the decreeing as opposed—with the thought in mind of three repetitions, this is not particularly significant itself, it's just that repetitions as such will help to deepen that state of [openness]. Is that what you're saying?

I am Yom and this is correct, my brother.

G: Thank you.

We thank you. Is there another query?

L: I have one more quick one for the sake of curiosity. In your discussion, you selected specifically diamonds and rubies as crystals that were specifically more effective. Is there a specific area of use that you would attribute to each of these two crystals? And if so, what are they?

I am Yom. These crystals were selected because of their purity of structure and what is seen in your illusion as the analog to this purity which is the hardness, shall we say, the sureness with which the structure is made, thus they lend themselves well to the general uses which one who is beginning in the study of crystals might begin with. The diamond and the ruby, then, would offer to the beginning student the greater ability to realize effects within the preliminary diagnosis of dysfunction and the basic treatment of such.

May we answer further, my brother?

L: Yes. Is there a capacity to perform in this manner due to their inherent qualities or due to our perception and value placed upon those qualities?

I am Yom. It is more nearly correct to say that their efficacy in diagnosis and treatment stems from the inherent qualities of the crystal. Yet, these qualities are combined with other qualities such as rarity of number and size which tend to make the crystals quite dear within your economic system of valuing.

May we answer further, my brother?

L: No, thank you very much.

I am Yom, and again we thank you, my brother. Is there another query?

J: I have read that the entities of Atlantis have used crystals in healing. If this is true, does that mean that they used space/time crystals such as the ruby and diamond? Or does it mean that they somehow tapped the crystals of time/space which were earlier discussed?

I am Yom. The use of the crystal by these entities or any who would seek to utilize crystals for healing is accomplished by using a third-density space/time crystal in such a manner that the aura, as you would call it, of the one to be healed would be interrupted long enough that the diseased configuration of mind, body or spirit could be worked upon by the time/space or metaphysical analog of the one to be healed. If the one to be healed was able to utilize the interruption of its auric fields, and accept the more balanced configuration of mind, body or spirit, it is at this time that such a healing would be accomplished within the metaphysical or time/space realms, then to be translated to the manifest space/time illusion.

At this time the one serving as healer would then allow the auric field to be closed once again in order that the new configuration of a more balanced mind, body and spirit would become a part of the one to be healed's experiential nexus.

May we answer further, my brother?

J: Is it true that the Atlanteans did use crystals for such purpose of healing? I'll leave the question at that.

I am Yom. This is correct. May we answer further, my brother?

J: Were pyramids also used in healing in Atlantis?

I am Yom. This is also correct, my brother. May we answer further?

J: Could we today in modern times learn how to use such crystals for healing?

I am Yom. This is correct, and, indeed, many of your peoples are presently rediscovering these abilities which have always been within the ability of the population of your sphere.

May we answer further, my brother?

J: Would the ruby be considered a solidification of the red-ray light?

I am Yom, and we find that this is much too narrow an interpretation of this crystal's full nature, for within each crystal, and, indeed, within the ruby lies the full expression of the spectrum of light, though in many cases there is the outer manifestation of one portion of this spectrum.

May we answer further, my brother?

J: No, thank you.

I am Yom, and we thank you, my brother. Is there another query?

Carla: Two real quick ones. First, would a spectroscopic analysis of a mineral, the colors of it, in any way correspond with the colors of the energy centers—question number one. Question number two, does the healing by the crystallized being, without the stone, work just as the healing through the stone?

I am Yom. We find that the analysis of the spectrographic qualities is relatively unimportant and not related to the crystal's ability to aid in providing healing catalyst. Indeed, to move to the second query, the most important portion of the healing process is the one to be healed's faith in the possibility of such, combined with this entity's realization of the fruits of the so-called diseased configuration.

Also to be considered of primary importance—beyond that of the crystal and short of that of the faith of the one to be healed—is the crystallized nature of the one serving as healer, for it is indeed the case that each energy center within any entity is likened unto a crystal itself, and when each center is properly balanced, then the one serving as healer may channel the instreaming prana or limitless light of the one Creator through its green-ray energy center and therefrom through the crystal being utilized, and therefrom to the one to be healed in order that its auric field might be momentarily interrupted.

May we answer further, my sister?

Carla: No, thank you.

I am Yom, and we thank you once again, my sister. Is there another query?

L: I have one more question, and this may be off the wall or completely off the mark, and if it is, a brief statement to that effect would be sufficient. Would it be correct to state that the individual who is acting in the role as healer attempts to maintain within himself as a crystal a balance of the various spectra of light and that the crystal itself acts in the manner of a capacitor, that the healer attempts to project a balanced spectra of light to the individual to be healed through crystal, the crystal in the manner of a capacitor delays that projection until a balance of the spectra has been attained and then allows it to project, thereby giving what is intended instead of the variations and fluctuations which would be existent in the human crystal at a specific instant?

I am Yom, and we may comment as follows. It is basically correct …

(Tape ends.)

L/L Research

L/L Research is a subsidiary of Rock Creek Research & Development Laboratories, Inc.

P.O. Box 5195
Louisville, KY 40255-0195

www.llresearch.org

Rock Creek is a non-profit corporation dedicated to discovering and sharing information which may aid in the spiritual evolution of humankind.

ABOUT THE CONTENTS OF THIS TRANSCRIPT: This telepathic channeling has been taken from transcriptions of the weekly study and meditation meetings of the Rock Creek Research & Development Laboratories and L/L Research. It is offered in the hope that it may be useful to you. As the Confederation entities always make a point of saying, please use your discrimination and judgment in assessing this material. If something rings true to you, fine. If something does not resonate, please leave it behind, for neither we nor those of the Confederation would wish to be a stumbling block for any.

CAVEAT: This transcript is being published by L/L Research in a not yet final form. It has, however, been edited and any obvious errors have been corrected. When it is in a final form, this caveat will be removed.

© 2009 L/L Research

Sunday Meditation
June 15, 1986

(Carla channeling)

I am L/Leema. I greet you in the love and in the light of the one infinite Creator. We are most privileged to and grateful for your call to us this evening, and are most pleased to blend our life energies with the stream of your own vibrations. We rejoice too in the unity of the circle, for it is larger than you may think, as there are many who join with those within this domicile in order to lend desire to the seeking and therefore more clarity to the material. It is, of course, to be noted, and we wish you to take special note of this in light of tonight's subject, that it is far more important, my friends, that you are together in the light, seeking the light, persistently, steadily, over and over again making of this sphere which you call your home a place where there does beam light even in darkness, than that any word of inspiration or information be transmitted. Were never another word to be transmitted through this light center, it is well to know as individuals and as a group that the love collected and given to the Creator in such group meetings and each by yourselves is what will make or break your society, shall we say, as a group.

The critical mass for achieving fourth density as a group is nearly reached. Therefore, each effort to add light to the planetary consciousness is by far the greatest service you can be at any time.

We now speak upon the subject of healing energy. The question put before us, if we may paraphrase, is this: if, as Dr. Andrija (Puharich) says, healing energy is eight hertz or cycles per second, how can one achieve that rate of vibration naturally and how can it be used?

It is to be noted that this group for the most part has much previous information about energy centers, therefore we shall speak of one heart energy center, or the green-ray energy center. Each ray and each combination of rays has at least one vibration, depending upon the combination of rays used for an activity within the undertones to a vibration. However, in the use of healing energy, one is not using healing energy as such. This must be emphasized, for it tells much about healing. The wave of what you would call the alpha state includes the eight cycles per second rate. In this state, the self is laid aside and the greater self is that which potentially the seeker can realize within the self. Therefore, there is an impersonal self which is far more pure, as you would say, than the waking conscious as it manifests itself. We say "clear" in the sense of vibratory tone.

This energy which is oblique and electrical in nature is brain wave activity, no more and no less. It is, however, that which occurs within the meditative state when an entity turns purely to the heart chakra and moves the brain wave energy in concentration to that locus. From that locus, then, enters a very pure love vibratory emanation, crystallized by the crystallized being which acts as a catalyst in the connection between the two green rays and in the interruption of the outer shell of the one to be healed in its auric sense. Once the auric shell has been pierced and the green ray opened in the one to be healed, the energy is sent forth and the one to be healed may choose healing at that time.

Love, my friends, is a creative, fiery, intelligent, and ever present source that is concentrated at the heart chakra of your beings and sent forth to nurture, to help, to encourage, to grow, and to transform. Such are the uses of protection. Many healings there are wrought by one who listens with a wide open heart. The listener may never speak, but the talker will feel the healing of green ray, which is love. The babe at the breast seeks green-ray nurturance. Milk is the second-density reason for the suckling. The green-ray exchange betwixt mother and child is the metaphysical reason for such nurturing as does take place in the suckling of an infant. Indeed, there is so much healing associated with the green-ray energy center that when something as far different, physically, from a person as your very planet is, is looked at in a nurturing sense, it is always described in terms of a breast, that is, putting one's head upon the breast of Mother Nature as one lays one's head upon the [mother's] breast. We retrieve this reference, which we discover to be somewhat obscure, from the instrument's reading of the letters of John Keats[6]. However, there are far more accessible instances of this as in other of your poetry.

As to how one may enhance the eight hertz center, we may say that it is not currently within the abilities of—we give this instrument the figure of 99.5 percent—cannot shield themselves from the effects of the transmissions spoken of, which vary. The human brain, you see, is able to manufacture only weak electrical charges and is therefore sensitive to similar vibrations. However, the use of this weapon is, may we say, less prevalent than was supposed and has only been used experimentally, and is not … we are sorry for these pauses, but we tread close to the Law of Free Will and we look for ways to avoid specificity.

This device is not what would be considered to be a life-threatening or quality-of-life-threatening problem for most probability/possibility vortices. That is, only in the event of a declared war would these devices be freely used.

As to how to enhance one's own brain wave energy, we may note, as always, the efficacy of persistent meditation and opening to the silence. Perhaps the attempt is never perfect or even near to perfect. Perhaps one's thoughts are led astray. This matters only insofar as the seeker allows this to discourage it from pursuing calmly and patiently the clearing mind. This is the work of a lifetime. However, the discipline of silence, not easily begun and not easily maintained, is all-important to the eventual and continued contact with intelligent infinity. This is the simplest and most important method of enhancing green-ray intensification and crystallization.

---

[6] From John Keats, "Epistle to my Brother George," 1884:

"These are the living pleasures of the bard:
But richer far posterity's reward.
What does he murmur with his latest breath,
While his proud eye looks though the film of death?
"What though I leave this dull and earthly mould,
Yet shall my spirit lofty converse hold
With after times. The patriot shall feel
My stern alarum, and unsheath his steel;
Or, in the senate thunder out my numbers
To startle princes from their easy slumbers.
The sage will mingle with each moral theme
My happy thoughts sententious; he will teem
With lofty periods when my verses fire him,
And then I'll stoop from heaven to inspire him.
Lays have I left of such a dear delight
That maids will sing them on their bridal night.
Gay villagers, upon a morn of May,
When they have tired their gentle limbs with play
And formed a snowy circle on the grass,
And placed in midst of all that lovely lass
Who chosen is their queen, with her fine head
Crowned with flowers purple, white, and red:
For there the lily, and the musk-rose, sighing,
Are emblems true of hapless lovers dying:
Between her breasts, that never yet felt trouble,
A bunch of violets full blown, and double,
Serenely sleep: she from a casket takes
A little book, and then a joy awakes
About each youthful heart, with stifled cries,
And rubbing of white hands, and sparkling eyes:
For she's to read a tale of hopes, and fears;
One that I fostered in my youthful years:
The pearls, that on each glist'ning circlet sleep,
Must ever and anon with silent creep,
Lured by the innocent dimples. To sweet rest
Shall the dear babe, upon its mother's breast,
Be lulled with songs of mine. Fair world, adieu!"

We need hardly offer the information that each attempt one makes to serve another is, when given freely and with no design other than to serve, a polarizing and crystallizing green-ray activity.

Thus, there is no time that is too insignificant of enhancing green ray and therefore becoming a nurturing and healing person. Each word that is spoken to mate or colleague, friend, stranger or seeming foe vibrates with intention. If the intentions are persistently compassionate, so you shall enhance development of green-ray crystallization and power as well as working oftimes upon higher energy centers.

We shall cease this discussion at this point, as we have noted in the past that we have spoken far too lengthily and we are attempting to clean up our act. We do enjoy your language and are very glad we are able to speak in your language, as it is very humorous with many idioms. We enjoy the American language very much. We are so grateful for having been able to speak to you on this subject, and would now leave this instrument with thanks, in order that we may transfer to the one known as Jim. We are those of L/Leema.

(Jim channeling)

I am L/Leema, and we are happy to greet you again in love and light through this instrument. We hope that we might continue our humble service by attempting to answer those queries which may remain within this group this evening. We remind each of you that our opinions are indeed opinions, though we may have experienced more of the journey than those present this evening, we wish no extra weight, shall we say, be given our words. Use them as they fit your needs. May we attempt a query at this time?

J1: Last week we had a session on the use of light and crystals in healing. Would the use of the crystal be then to magnify or intensify the green-ray healing frequency from healer to the one to be healed in some manner?

I am L/Leema, and your statement is basically correct in that the use of crystals by those offering the healing energies which they are able to channel is a use which may enhance these energies and their availability, shall we say, to the one to be healed. The one serving as healer through its own balance of centers of energy is likened unto a crystal itself and when it is able to channel energies of the green-ray nature, then it charges or potentiates the crystal in order that it might vibrate in harmony with the one known as the healer and amplify the energies which this entity channels.

May we answer further, my brother?

J1: If the heart chakra is the source of the green-ray healing energy from the healer, would the crystal then be placed in the proximity of the heart chakra for the most benefit to the one to be healed?

I am L/Leema, and this positioning is one fundamental position which any entity serving as healer may begin with, for its efficacy is most easily achieved for those who have worked for some time upon this path of service, but which have as yet not utilized the more finely tuned placements of crystal and techniques of use such as the use of the swung crystal which utilizes the transfer of the green-ray energy in a somewhat refined nature by allowing its movement through the right arm and hand and thereunto the crystal.

May we answer further, my brother?

J1: Could you repeat that, and describe further that technique and first of all, what is the "swan" crystal and how is it used once more?

I am L/Leema, and the crystal which is swung from the right hand of the healer is a technique which is somewhat advanced in that it utilizes the spiraling field of green-ray energy that emanates from the heart chakra or energy center in a precise fashion which allows the one serving as healer to transfer or transmit the healing energy in a more precise fashion than is accomplished with the use of the crystal from the chain about the neck which places the crystal at the heart chakra location.

May we answer further, my brother?

J1: Thank you. I understand now. Does the green ray—is that the only ray that vibrates at eight hertz? Does each ray, does each color of the spectrum vibrate with a different frequency?

I am L/Leema. The spectrum of colors which has its origin within the white light, shall we say, or prana, that is instreaming to each portion of creation may find a slight refinement as each color is filtered through the various centers of energy in the mind/body/spirit complex. Thus, the white light is instreaming in this basic fashion and may be utilized in a specific fashion by the one serving as healer. The use of this light by, shall we say, the usual configuration of energy centers of any mind/body/spirit complex then is according to a more widely diffused range of frequencies that center about the eight cycles per second, using this frequency as a foundation or background frequency which is then added unto by swings on each side of the eight cycles per second by each ray or energy center. The variation is not large, however, and is that harmonic vibration which enhances certain aspects of this basic frequency.

May we answer further, my brother?

J1: No, thank you.

I am L/Leema, and we thank you, my brother. Is there another query?

J2: Is it possible to use a charged crystal to transfer the healing energy from the crystal to water, so that water may be used for healing? And if so, could you give me an explanation of that?

I am L/Leema, and, though this is indeed possible, it is not necessary to utilize any crystal for such a transfer, for the water may be seen as a crystal itself and may be directly charged or affected by the conscious intent of any entity seeking to use the water crystal for the purpose of healing. The charging may take many forms. It is possible to charge this crystal water by the placing of the hands above its surface and imaging by the mind and intention healing energies being passed through the hands and into the water crystal.

May we answer further, my sister?

J2: Yes, please. Does it enhance the healing capability or is it necessary for this charged water to have healing effect for the person who receives it to understand and recognize the intent?

I am L/Leema, and though it is not strictly necessary that the one to be healed be aware of and consciously utilize such charged water, it is most helpful for the degree of utilization or efficiency for this entity to be aware of the opportunity and to consciously avail itself of this opportunity. For indeed, each entity is constantly bathed in such healing energies and according to the efficacy of any one to be healed in its desire to be healed and its opening of its own being to such healing, healing may take place, for the process of healing is one which occurs upon the metaphysical level as a direct function …

(Side one of tape ends.)

(Jim channeling)

I am L/Leema, and am again with this instrument. May we answer in any further way, my sister?

J2: Yes, please. If there were a group and they wished to send healing energies within the group and from the group to those outside, or were to use energy charged water and share the water, does one have more efficacy than the other?

I am L/Leema, and as we consider the many possibilities in utilizing these techniques of offering the healing energies, we note that though the sharing of the water may in many cases be more helpful, such is often the case because of the one to be healed holding the viewpoint that physical manifestations or vehicles of healing are more helpful than that which it cannot see. Thus, it is often helpful to ground the healing offering in whatever fashion has significance to the one to be healed. If, however, the one to be healed is not present, the sending of the healing energies by thought may be the means by which the most efficacy is achieved.

May we answer further, my sister?

J2: Thank you. I have just one more question on that subject. If the water which is used in this situation is placed in direct sunlight and receives the rays of the sun, preliminarily to receiving energies from the group, does this enhance its healing capabilities?

I am L/Leema. Again, upon the purely mechanistic level, the enhancement of the ability of the water to transmit the healing vibrations by such placement is small. Yet, if the intention of those seeking to serve as healers is to increase the water's ability to serve as such a transmitting medium, this intention itself will carry far more weight, shall we say, in determining the water's ability to serve as a medium of transmitting the healing energies. As you can see, we return again and again to desire, the focus of the will, and the intention of those seeking to serve as healers and the ones serving as the ones in need of healing.

May we answer further, my sister?

J2: Well, my observation is going to be, then, that essentially it is the intention. It seems to me from what you said that the intention and the strength of intention of the ones who want to heal is essentially the only thing, that the crystal or the water is really not necessary if the intention of the crystallized healer is there. Would you comment on that?

I am L/Leema, and one may see the use of the crystal as a step upon the path of service of that called healing. The intention of the one serving as healer is that which is paramount. It may be that at some point within this entity's progress that the use of the crystal shall be helpful in amplifying the fruit of the intention, that is, the ability to channel the intelligent energy through the green-ray energy center. It may be that the one serving as healer spends a great portion of its incarnation utilizing the abilities of the crystal in its service of healing. It is also possible that such an entity in its continued evolution of being shall be able to function without the need to utilize the crystal and shall in a more direct fashion channel those healing energies which it becomes more and more able to contact and transmit.

May we answer further, my sister?

J2: No, that's been very helpful. Thank you very much.

I am L/Leema, and we thank you, my sister.

Carla: I just wanted to check a couple of things. First of all, is the reason that we feel so instinctively more nurtured in the country than the city is because of all the second-density plant life which can't help but do anything but vibrate in total love at all times—it doesn't have free will yet?

I am L/Leema, and this supposition is basically correct, for within the natural environment, shall we say, the rhythm and pulse of the expressions of the one Creator move at a pace that is, as you have surmised, of an automatic nature, shall we say. The one Creator moves in a more clear and simplified manner, becoming more available to the third density entity within your urban environment. One may find that there have been various overlaid distortions which affect the natural rhythm available within your rural areas.

May we answer further, my sister?

Carla: Well, the other question was just another logical extension. It was that I've always noticed that salt water helps my arthritis a great deal or helps any wound to heal very quickly. And I imagine that there are perfectly good chemical reasons for that. But I also wonder if the water isn't magnetized? Is it magnetized by the sun that shines as a symbol of love, or is it magnetized, for instance, *(inaudible)* that run around the ocean sending love vibrations, or is it naturally magnetized? Or what? Or is there another explanation, and if so, what is it?

I am L/Leema, and you may see the waters of your oceans, lakes and seas as large crystalline structures which absorb much of the instreaming light or prana of the one Creator in what you have called a more natural fashion. Thus, when one immerses the physical vehicle in any body of water, one is utilizing the natural ability of the water to absorb and transmit that vibration of love which is light and to feel the healing energies then is more easily accomplished by any entity who is in need of or seeking such transfers of energy.

May we answer further, my sister?

Carla: No, thank you.

I am L/Leema, and we thank you, my sister. Is there another query?

J2: When one is in one's backyard and is being aware and conscious of and directing thought and attention toward the local inhabitants, the chipmunks, the birds, the squirrels and so on, and directing thought toward them in terms of communication, is there communication from us to them, and also is there communication between those backyard inhabitants?

I am L/Leema, and this is quite correct, my sister, though the communication that you transmit may be received in a much simpler form, the second-density creatures are quite aware of this communication and of communication not only from others of the second density within their vicinity, but of forms and sources of communication that originate from areas and entities not visible to your own physical eye. And these second-density creatures, then, respond to a great variety of communication, your own directed communication being one of many, many sources.

May we answer further, my sister?

J2: No, thank you. That was very interesting.

I am L/Leema, and we thank you, my sister. Is there another query?

J1: Well, on one seeking to be healed without benefit of the crystallized entity healer, is there a technique by which the one to be healed could use crystals to his benefit?

I am L/Leema, and though the response to this query is in the affirmative, we find that it is more probable that an entity seeking to be healed would utilize techniques other than the crystal, including that which may be seen as the attempting to achieve the crystallization of one's own being by utilizing the catalyst available daily in a fashion which penetrates to the heart of the entity's pattern of lessons which in some fashion become distorted in those experiencing the diseased condition. The use of the crystal or the crystallized healer or any external source of healing is but a step, shall we say, or crutch, as it were, for the one seeking healing.

In all cases of healing, the process is accomplished when the faith of the one to be healed has been activated to such an extent that it is able to accept a new configuration of mind, body and spirit that more closely resembles the balanced condition for this entity. The use of sources outside of the one to be healed is a kind of triggering device that is useful to many because of the shared belief of many that in order to be healed, one must seek an healer or healing device.

May we answer further, my brother?

J1: No, thank you.

I am L/Leema, and we thank you, my brother.

T: Yes, I have a question. It concerns healing somewhat, but more so, at least to me, it concerns the inner energy flow in a person's body, and meditative techniques for acquiring an even energy flow or removing energy blockages in the nervous system and the circulatory system. I'm specifically referring to … In order to heal or to achieve a balanced inner strength, this flow is necessary, I think—now I'm asking for a comment on that. And I'm also asking for comment on a meditative technique to achieve this specifically, the practice of Tai Chi Ch'wan. Could you speak on that please?

I am L/Leema, and we would comment by suggesting that indeed the one seeking to serve as the healer must first heal the self in order that the ability to channel the instreaming intelligent energy or light may be enhanced to the degree that it may then be offered to another. The technique of achieving this balanced flow of energy is as we have previously stated, that is, the continuing awareness of the entity of those portions of its experience which are less than harmonious and the placement of these disharmonious experiences or blockages at the proper energy center, and then the utilization of the meditative state in discovering the balanced configuration that the dysfunction or blockage points toward. This in many cases will necessitate the untangling of many physical and symbolic symptoms as well as mental configurations that have held the diseased or disharmonious state in place for the entity.

When the balanced view of any particular distortion is achieved and seated within the entity through meditation, contemplation or the prayerful attitude, then the blockage or dysfunction is removed in that it [is] enlarged in its scope, shall we say, making available a larger point of view and a lighter channel therefore through which the healing energies may eventually be channeled.

May we answer further, my brother?

T: Just one thing. Could you comment on the use of physical movement, specifically Tai Chi, as a meditative technique? It seems to me that for a person with nervous energy blockages that—it seems to me that it's easier to get into a meditative state if you can be in a concentrated movement type of meditation. It seems to work for me, maybe that's all I need to say. Maybe I don't need a comment, but if you have anything to say on that, I'd appreciate it.

I am L/Leema, and we would agree that such a technique is useful to some entities who are of a nature which can appreciate this type of meditation. Many, however, would find another technique more helpful in that the stilling of the mind would be more available as a result as a stilling of the body. However, this is quite variable among your peoples and we recommend that whatever technique feels appropriate be utilized and that the seeker remain alert to those refinements which shall naturally be drawn unto it as it achieves its purpose within the meditative state.

May we answer further, my brother?

T: No, thank you, that's fine.

I am L/Leema, and we would ask if there might be a final query before we take our leave of this group as this instrument is growing somewhat low on the energy necessary to continue its service.

(Pause)

I am L/Leema, and we are most happy to have had the opportunity to join our vibrations with yours this evening. We look forward to each opportunity with great joy. We leave each of you in that love and light which is ever present and available to all. We are known as L/Leema. Adonai, my friends. Adonai vasu.

(Carla channeling)

I Yadda. I greet you in love and light of infinite Creator. We not give instrument any trouble this time about coming in name of Christ because so many others have been giving her trouble about whether we do or not. We better tell her, "Of course we come in name of Christ—why would we send someone, we of the Confederation which cares so much for consciousness and its development, why would we send someone to live in Christ consciousness if we did not come in that name?" Our only gripe is that this instrument pick the one Jesus, who carried perfect Christ consciousness—so did some other good teachers—but we do not to argue that.

Of course we come in name of Christ. How else would we come? There is only one love and that love's consciousness is Christ. That what we show, pure compassion, you know.

Okay. We come to talk about shadows. You know, you all think you so vivid there in this room as you sit and watch the sky far into the beautiful evening. You think maybe you should even paint the face a little even, eh, you women? Heh? Make yourself more vivid? Well, we tell you, you are nothing but shadow. You know what you do in this incarnation? Heh! You build. You are architect. You know what you build? Something you cannot see. That why you don't know about it and you go about painting face and putting on funny clothes, eh heh!?

Now. What you build? First thing you build, you build something called you. What you gonna look like when you enter larger life? This instrument say "larger life," she means death. Okay. We not know if we larger, but we have more fun—eh heh! Anyway, we want you to know that you are building something called you. You build day by day by weary, weary day. It is weary—we know—we not argue that. What we encourage is that you know that the face you see in the mirror is not what you are doing here. What you are doing here is you are building behind the shadow world that whole person that you can, are and shall be.

Furthermore, second thing. You build other things. You have mate—yes? Then you build a person—not you, not me. It called "relationship." Okay. You not see that, but that what you building. What you putting into that building. You cannot control what your mate builds—you control what you build. Forget the shadows of your mirror. Forget what you can see and move to what you are building. You architects of the spirit.

We come to you in love and leave you in love. We come to you in light and so we leave you. We thank you for calling us. We getting our words better—heh?! We so glad to see you and we say good-bye. We Yadda of Confederation of Planets in Service to One Infinite Creator. Adonai. Adonai. ✺

Sunday Meditation
June 29, 1986

(Carla channeling)

I am Hatonn, and I greet you, my friends in the love and in the light of our infinite Creator. It is a great privilege and pleasure to mingle our energies with yours at this time, and we would greet especially the one known as L, as this entity has not sat in physical proximity with this group for some time. We send love and blessings to each of you and are most grateful to be able to share our humble thoughts with you.

The evening that spreads about you at this gentle, quiet moment glistens with beauty and throbs with the heartbeat of many lives as we experience it through the ears of this channel. We find it to be most wonderful, and we thank you also for this experience.

We would share some thoughts with you this evening upon the subject of freedom. Freedom is very much in each entity's consciousness at this particular moment in your solar year. Amongst you who call yourself Americans, you celebrate your independence and your freedom, the freedom that has been defined as "the pursuit of happiness." Indeed, my friends, the nature of freedom in third density is in large part social. We would emphasize that this is true in more and more full a measure as your cycle draws near to harvest.

How is this so? It would seem upon the surface of it that the nature of freedom is intensely personal and individual. One's inner freedom is to make one's own choices of thoughts and ideas, to choose the manner of one's agenda of living, and in all ways to pursue what shall enlarge happiness. And yet we would suggest to you that the deeper nature of freedom is no such thing.

You have heard countless times that the Creator manifested Itself as love—but what is love? You know that you are in pursuit of something called truth—but what is truth? The nature of love is such that it has created consciousness that is self-conscious. Each of you is love, thus each of you is the Creator. As the Creator is love, so therefore are you love. How then, we ask, does love seek truth?

Love chooses betwixt love of self and love of other self. We speak to those who are upon the path in which love is manifested as love of self and other self as self. If that were a mathematical equation, all the selves would be struck out and what you would have left with is the equation: service to others' self is love manifested towards other selves. We ask that you ponder this not once, but many times, for the truth in this statement is not immediately apparent. In no way do we suggest a lack of love for self; we suggest only that other selves are loved as the self.

And what does this have to do with freedom? You are given freedom in totality. There is no holding back upon the part of the Creator; there are no hidden loopholes or clauses. You are free. You are free to do nothing. You are free to work diligently upon a personal agenda which has no contact with other selves. You are free to create a rigid agenda in which things for the self and things for the other self are compartmented. You are free to throw yourself into service of other selves at every available opportunity, whether service is requested or not. And finally, you are free to leave yourself open to the potential for the opportunity of being of service to others whenever that opportunity is offered. We have found the more virtue in the latter course, and this brings us to freedom.

For what we are suggesting may seem upon the surface many times to smack not of freedom, but of slavery. Let us observe slavery among your peoples. There is no time, as you call it, in the history that you know in which humans have not been slaves. There is a reason for that and that is this. To some, happiness—that happiness which is the manifestation of freedom—lies in seeing a loved one happy, in tending a loved one's hurts, in tending and encouraging a loved one in distress. Many are those even now who are in actuality slaves against their will—this is not that of which we speak. We speak of those who love their masters and who are loved in return, and who therefore find happiness in service. Were slavery uniformly disagreeable to all, it would be attempted unceasingly, but it would be found to be counterproductive. It is those happy combinations which insure that slavery, whether traditional or untraditional, as in some marriage relationships, endures.

Now we are not suggesting that you choose a master and become a slave. Indeed, the scope is somewhat small in that suggestion, although it is not that learning and growth in the metaphysical sense would not be possible in this configuration of personalities. Rather, we are suggesting that freedom lies in the concept of oneself as a manifester of servanthood to any and all who cross the path.

Circumstances cannot be predicted by most among your peoples, and there are many surprises that await you, many unbidden and hitherto unheard of possibilities for service, and we would encourage you in this context to think of service in terms of slavery, for one of the great paradoxes of the spiritual search is that freedom and that service which approaches what you call slavery are both paradoxical and synonymous, for the totally dedicated entity, having heard the call to seek the truth, moves forth upon the path without looking back, and whatever the circumstances, looks for the opportunity to hear a call for help. When such an opportunity is perceived, it is then that the seeker offers itself in service, not condescendingly or patronizingly but as servant to all.

And if all are servants to all, then where shall be contention? And if all serve all—where is slavery?

The concept of service carries with it a semantic burden, a connotation of unhappiness or degradation of self. We ask you to consider the possibility that slavery, surrounded and infused with joy, is perfect freedom.

Service by itself shall always be a duty and shall not feel like freedom at all. Yes, you may learn many, many lessons without joy. It is the willing openness to the finding of peace and joy in the concept of the self as a servant which opens one to a freedom beyond that of human freedom. For in human freedom, you attempt to please yourself and gain happiness, and yet the happiness is caught up entirely in the pursuit and the goal is never truly attained. Not for those upon the path of service to others—and we again emphasize we are speaking to that group and not to those who follow the service-to-self path, against which we say nothing except that we are not those upon that path and do not presume to teach upon that path.

We ask you to glance back over your life experiences within this incarnation and look at the fruits of the seeking of personal happiness as "master of your fate and captain of your ship." We suggest that some of these fruits may include anger, frustration, jealousy, licentiousness, quarrelsomeness and dejection.

We ask you now to consider the many times each of you has indeed sacrificed the self seemingly as servant of another when that other was in need. Remember doing all that you could and more, and feel again the peace that comes from knowing that you have done all that you can and that you shall continue and the joy that comes when in any small thing another self turns to you and says, "Truly I have asked you and truly you have served." And so the fruits of service to others, though challenging to accomplish, are joy and peace that no man can take from you lest you take them from yourself, for you only can undo the work that you have done within yourself. And on that head, we would admonish you not to judge yourself when you have served to the best of your ability. If you feel you could have done better, remember then, you have done all that you can and be again at peace and allow joy to enter your being.

Spiritual peace is a terrible thing in the parlance of what you might call your culture, the ethos into which you were born, for it is a peace that comes from having exhausted oneself in an effort to serve others and setting again one's foot on the path, looking again for the next opportunity to serve, wherever it may be. Thus, one is at peace without having a spiritual contentment, shall we say, for you do not have a spiritual resting place in the sense that your body has a domicile. You are on a path. That path will continue and you will be where you were not and you will never be where you are now again. This is not so of those who do not attempt to become servants of others. The inner life for those who sleep is as stable as the outer, and a peace bound up in quiet dreaming is most glamorous and may take up an entire incarnation with no problem whatsoever for those who have not yet found the spark that sets them upon the path.

Spiritual joy can be a frightening thing, for it is a joy which has its roots in a love that is mysterious, for it is the manifestation of a sense of the Creator which is mysterious. You may experience joy, but it is an unknown joy, an unspeakable joy, a happiness which is both silent and creative. In this regard we encourage you to remember that anything at which you look is not only the Creator but is also less than the Creator.

We are fond of paradoxes, are we not? Let us clarify. The Creator is not only each tree, each stone, each bird, and each conscious entity. It is also the mystery that created these things. It is the invisible, the infinite. Why does it say in your holy works that the trees clap their hands and the mountains dance like rams? Does the Creator play so? You may look at it that way, but it is also possible to recognize the signs of worship and praise of a Creator that infuses all with love and joy.

My friends, you are far more complex than trees and hills, and within yourselves you have many, many beings interpenetrating each other, communicating with each other, and forming one whole and conscious hologram of the Creator. And yet there is also that mystery which you seek that is beyond and within your consciousness. As you approach what you call your Independence Day, we ask you to gaze many times at the concept of freedom, for there are many metaphysical systems which indulge in a hedonism that suggests that the Creator shall be used as a panacea to achieve happiness, prosperity, health and all manner of positive and comfortable things. We suggest to you that true happiness is often quite uncomfortable and yet so exhilarating that once having been experienced, it shall be the way you seek to manifest love.

Love one another, my friends. Serve one another. And find your freedom, your joy, and your peace.

We ask your pardon for causing what we so enjoy, the sensations of third-density incarnation. You are so rich, my friends. Feel it. Such a wealth of things to hear and see and taste and smell and feel and all things servants to you, there for your learning, your contemplation and your discretion. Open, then, the doors of your heart and love each other, and you will find yourself loving all manner of things and finding the life that you serve in the veriest blade of grass.

We are known to you as Hatonn of the Confederation of Planets in the Service of the Infinite Creator. We are, if you will, your slaves for the moment, and we are filled with great joy at the thought that we could have been of some service to you at this time. We do not know what you may be able to use from what we have said, and we ask you to discard anything that is not helpful to your development at this time. We do indeed hope that we have been of service, but we know only this we have offered, this channel has offered, and you have offered by listening. And all have been of service, one to another. We leave you in the love and the light of perfect freedom. Adonai, my friends. Adonai vasu borragus.

(Jim channeling)

I am Latwii, and we greet you in the love and in the light of our infinite Creator. We, too, are filled with joy at being able to join your group this evening, and we hope with our brothers and sisters of Hatonn that we may serve in some small way by attempting to answer those queries which each may find value in the asking. May we then without further delay begin with the first query this evening?

L: If I may be the person to read that, it would be a rather small inquiry from someone who isn't here this evening, but is concerned about carrying on some positive work. The sale of a violin—although I know this may sound a little enigmatic, the exact wording of the question merely says, "Concerning the expediting of the sale of my violin, any suggestions?" I just would offer that in behalf of that person not here. *(Inaudible)* The name of the person is J.

I am Latwii, and am aware of your query, my brother. We find in this instance an entity who has for a great period of your time attempted to be of service through those avenues which have been opened unto this entity and the construction of the instrument which has been described as the violin has been of an inspirational nature which this entity has become aware of in an increasing fashion as a result of certain discoveries or revelations, shall we say, which have made this entity likened unto an instrument itself.

Thus, as those inspirations become available to the conscious mind of this entity through its increased desire to seek the truth and to serve others, this entity shall find its own directions continuing to be placed before its inner awareness. Therefore, we find it most helpful, we feel on our part, that we speak only in these general terms and urge the entity to redouble its own desires to seek and to serve, for these motivations are the key factors that will release into this entity's awareness those actions, thoughts and attitudes that are most appropriate in providing the service through its own instrument and those which it manifests within the …

(Side one of tape ends.)

(Jim channeling)

I am Latwii, and am again with this instrument. May we answer in any further fashion, my brother?

L: I thank you for that reply. I think that certainly covers that question. If I may, I should perhaps, if I'm able, read the one other question from this same party that is perhaps more profound, difficult and complex to reply to. I will again read it as he wrote it so as to pass it along, and it reads as follows: "Is the technique of endocrine chakra stabilization and detoxification a suitable modality as I've developed it in the treatment of AIDS; if not a cure, possibly a palliative?"

I am Latwii, and am aware of your query, my brother. We scan the information and trace the implications and may without infringing upon the free will of this entity suggest that the technique which it has devised to treat the condition that is known among your peoples as AIDS as being that which is at the basic level of understanding, if you will, sound. This initial beginning is that which with further study may be refined so that the basic process of balancing the entity's centers of energy in the fashion described may be enhanced as the patterns of behavior are themselves traced into what you would call previous incarnational patterns.

Thus, the scope of treatment would include not only the current incarnation, but would stretch back, as you would say, to include patterns developed in previous experiences which are of a significant enough nature to be carried over into the current incarnation in a symbolic fashion which then, when unattended by conscious work, provides the opportunity for increased conscious effort by taking a form of a disease or disjunction which requires immediate attention.

Thus, one area which may be fruitfully investigated is the heart chakra or energy center as the entity sees itself in relation to the creation about it and more specifically as it sees itself giving and receiving love with the mate in the relationship which endures, shall we say. The relationship of mates, as you call them, is one which provides an entity with increased and intensified opportunities to learn and to teach, to give and to receive love. And when accomplished over a significant portion of what you would call time and experience with the dedication of each to the other to be of this service, the lessons and patterns of programs within each entity may be attempted in a manner which is far more efficient than the kind of relationships which are constantly in change and motion with little stability or dedication to service.

May we answer further, my brother?

L: Thank you. I think that is a very positive beginning on that question. I don't know what further to ask about it, it really is for another person and I'm glad for the reply that is provided as we have.

I am Latwii, and we thank you and your friend. Is there another query?

Carla: I have a question that may seem to be whimsical, but it's not, because I don't, spiritually speaking or metaphysically speaking, believe in coincidence. I've noticed for a long time that the word AIDS means "helps" in English, not as an acronym but as a word. Could you speak to the subject of how AIDS is an aid to spiritual growth?

I am Latwii, and am aware of your query, my sister. We may suggest that as with any disease, as you call these conditions, the condition of AIDS is that which focuses one's attention upon the most salient feature, shall we say, within one's being that is in need of the attention of the entity. When catalyst or the opportunity for growing and fulfilling those patterns designed before the incarnation by the entity has not been well used or appreciated sufficiently by the conscious mind, then that catalyst is given to the physical body in a symbolic form which then may be more successful in attracting the attention of the entity in order that its own desires to learn and to serve in such and such a fashion may be fulfilled. The physical disease, thus, is that which offers again the opportunity to accomplish certain lessons.

We may in general continue with the previous response by suggesting that one facet of the condition known as AIDS which many share, each in a unique way, is that of the fidelity, of giving and receiving love. That is to say, it is most helpful and efficient for most upon your planet to find the mate with which to journey upon the path of seeking the truth, as you have called it. For some, this efficiency in seeking is not only appropriate, but is by their own choice and design most necessary in order to complete patterns begun in previous incarnational experiences. Thus, there are, shall we say, training devices or aids, in this particular case provided by the entities themselves, that enable a more finely focused attention upon the symbol of the lessons and services that they have programmed before the incarnation.

May we answer in any further way, my sister?

Carla: Yes, in two ways. First, I would just like to clarify what I suppose to be correct from previous questions that we have had answered in this group. Can you confirm that in many cases the mate of a male biologically will be a biological male; the mate of a biological female will be a biological female? In other words, would you confirm that you are not suggesting that only the biological males and biological females can achieve a mated relationship?

I am Latwii, and this is correct, my sister.

Carla: Okay. The other question is typical of my rather pessimistic nature, but it seemed to me when contemplating AIDS that one of the things that it might help to do is offer a very unhappy person a rather rapid way of dying. This is one of the functions of disease, not to be sentimental about it. And further, not to be sentimental, but it is absolutely appalling how many ways homosexuals are beleaguered in this culture, not just in obvious ways, but in very subtle ways having to do with upbringing and self-image. Therefore, there is many a wretched homosexual just totally caught in the toils of human opinion, and I thought perhaps that that might be one of the reasons for AIDS would be a fairly speedy delivery from such an unhappy condition that could no longer be borne, but it would be an honorable way to die. Could you either confirm or correct this possibility, this supposition?

I am Latwii, and am aware of your query, my sister. We may suggest that the condition of AIDS is that which offers the choice. The entity may use the opportunity of the disease to discover those means by which it may find its own bearing, shall we say, with another and with that other seek in a fashion which unfolds life more abundantly as the condition is used and the catalyst is successfully processed.

There is, however, the choice of which you have spoken, and with the same opportunity the entity at some level of its being may decide to retire from this particular incarnation in order that that which has been learned may be seated within the totality of the beingness of the entity and that which has been left unlearned may be formulated in such and such a fashion so that at another time, as you would call it, another incarnation may be provided for the learning of those lessons.

May we answer further, my sister?

Carla: No, thank you.

I am Latwii, and we thank you, my sister. Is there another query?

L: Well, I'm tempted to ask one that's a sort of a difficult question, and I would be grateful for whatever reply could be given. In the fullness of my question, I think the core of it is I'd like to understand a little better what the difference is between different so-called levels of teachers. In the studies I've pursued, frequently a particular entity or source is referred as causal teacher or from the high Buddhic plane or providing perspective from the astral plane, and if you could, Latwii, comment upon this issue of discarnate teachers coming from different planes, perhaps giving an example of one from one or the other plane or what is meant by these planes and distinguishing the teaching thereby?

I could try to make the question clearer, but that's the general phrasing I can come up with.

I am Latwii, and am aware of your query, my brother. Within your planetary influence in those portions which are of the metaphysical realms, shall we say, those which are unseen, frequently referred to as your inner planes, there are various levels of understanding, shall we say, much likened unto what you could call a spiritual distillery. Light and love as realized in a pattern of beingness which you can call an entity or a mind/body/spirit complex, then, is radiated, for the positive path, in a more and more efficient fashion according to an entity's success, shall we say, at moving itself along the path of evolution and into greater and greater realization and unity with the creation about it.

Within your planetary influence there are then various levels of light beings which gather themselves in a fashion which is appropriate to their understanding or their ability to transmit the light through their crystallized beings. These levels of existence have been termed by many of your population in various and sundry ways and described differently by different groups.

That which is generally referred to as the astral level is that which itself contains seven basic frequencies of vibration, shall we say, with the lower levels comprising those entities which are of the grosser form of thought and which in many cases are creations of the darker thoughts of the population of your planet. As one proceeds through these lower levels which are of a darker nature, one may find that the efficiency of the light transmission by the inhabitants of each succeeding level grows greater and brighter until at the upper levels of the astral planes one finds beings of greater light which may move in service to others by serving as what you may call guides or angelic presences, and may or may not make themselves known through your spoken words, whether verbal or mental, but nonetheless, move in service in whatever fashion the entity they have chosen to serve can understand or perceive.

As one moves beyond the astral planes or levels of vibration one enters what has most frequently been called the devachanic planes of experience. These are also frequently called the heaven worlds of your planetary influence. Within these realms of vibration, also numbering seven at the basic level or in the basic manner of description, one may find that the population is somewhat reduced in number but is more efficient in transmitting the love and light of the one Creator to those whose seeking attracts or calls for their service. Again, service in this general level is that which is more of the specific call being answered rather than the constant guiding or watching over the incarnate entities of your third density as is the nature of the upper astral levels.

These beings which inhabit the devachanic planes in the lower levels of these planes, then, move to answer specific calls. Within the upper frequencies of the devachanic planes, there is less and less desire to serve in the manner of communication with the third-density incarnate population of your planet. The service at this level of vibration takes more the form of the sending and in some cases the providing of light, love and healing to the planetary entity itself and to larger portions of the population of your planet than one or two or a few of your entities which may call for service and receive it from other levels of either the astral or devachanic planes.

We would prefer not to name certain entities that may be placed in one level or another, for to do so would be to seem to judge, for many upon your planet view one level or another as being higher and therefore better than another, when in fact, each speaks with the voice of the Creator to the Creator which calls for that which is of the appropriate vibration of service.

May we answer further, my brother?

L: I think that's a very good reply, and I appreciate it. I don't think I could qualify the question further except that the Ra material makes a reference to the gateway to intelligent infinity and I wonder if that corresponds with other systems referring to what are called the Buddhic planes, and that would be the only final part, I guess, to ask you.

I am Latwii, and am aware of your query, my brother. We would suggest that the contact with what has been called intelligent infinity may be seen not just as that which contacts higher and higher levels of vibration within a planetary influence, but that which reveals unto the entity experiencing this contact the nature and unity of all creation and all that which lies beyond creation, all that from which creation springs. Thus the contact with intelligent infinity is the fully experienced presence of the one infinite Creator.

May we answer further, my brother?

L: No, thank you very much. That covers it.

I am Latwii, and we thank you again, my brother. Is there another query?

(Pause)

I am Latwii. It has been our great honor and privilege to blend our vibrations with yours this evening. We hope that each is aware that we share our own experiences and our opinions which are most fallible. Please take that which has value and leave that which has none in your own journey of seeking. We are your brothers and sisters who have traveled perhaps a bit further upon that same path which we share with you. We travel with you always, as does the great company of seekers both seen and unseen which moves in service, each to the other and all to the one Creator. We are known to you as those of Latwii. We bid you adieu for this evening. We leave you in the love and in the light of the one infinite Creator. Adonai, my friends. Adonai vasu borragus. ✦

L/L Research

Sunday Meditation
July 6, 1986

(Unknown channeling)

I am Q'uo, and I greet you in the love and in the light of our infinite Creator. May we thank and bless each of you for inviting us to share in your combined life-streams at this time. To be so invited to share our thoughts is a very great privilege, for it is by attempting to be of service to you that we gain in polarity and so advance along our own path. We ask that you remember, as always, when hearing any opinion whatever, that the truth is already seated in your own spirit and if you do not recognize it in our words, it is well for you to release it from your consciousness, for we would not be a stumbling block before you, to retard you in your spiritual growth. Indeed, that is far from our purpose.

We find the consciousness of those present this evening to be much aware of the day you celebrate in what you call your nation, as the birth date of your nation's independence and each is our personal freedom. We find the phrase, "All men are created equal," to be written large upon your hearts and your pride at this time. Thus, we would speak to you about how love and wisdom, to a lesser extent, function through illusion to facilitate and offer tools for the facilitation of individual spiritual growth.

Each knows that the phrase, "All men are created equal"—men, of course, meaning humankind, men and women alike—to be not only an ideal, but truth, for all have the same birthright, own the same godhead in potentiation, and possess all that there is within themselves. We would in no way argue with this truism and, indeed, wish to underscore its accuracy, in the sense that each of you is the Creator and thus do you each function as each other's catalysts. For each of you is a mirror in likeness, not similar but the same, so that your other selves may gaze within your glass and see what they need to see about themselves. Indeed, it is often among your peoples that you see things in other people not realizing that you are seeing the reflection of yourself.

However, this evening we would stress that in the illusion which is your so-called third-density reality all men are manifestly created unequal. In the illusion of personality each entity is unique. This illusion is a deep illusion which will continue to hold sway through several densities of existence and many millions of your years and far, far into your spiritual development and your journey back to the one original Thought. It is an important illusion. Why, indeed, does it seem so clear that in this illusion of personality each is unique and obviously different and therefore unequal to and from each other?

Let us consider one individual spirit. There are two basic influences which shall govern what occurs within the life experience of this individual. The first is, shall we say, the law of finished beginnings. This is not a law, but an influence. We use the term, "law," advisedly and ask that you understand it as a pervasive influence rather than an unshakable law. Your vocabulary does not have such a nice word, so we must use the closest in name. This pervasive influence is that which indicates that that which has been previously unfinished in an entity's experience in other lifetimes shall be once again brought before the attention of the entity in order that the entity may work, consider, meditate and do whatever seems to be valuable with these pervasive influences which are familiar.

Many difficult relationships are the result of previous unfinished beginnings and the difficulty of the relationship is much like the difficulty of a person that receives that which seems to be fresh from the grocery but which when taken home, though sweet and fresh to every physical sense, yet seems still somehow aging and putrefying. There is something ancient, something one cannot put one's finger upon, something which smacks sometimes of déjà vu. This is that with which you shall deal as lovingly, compassionately and may we say dispassionately with in this life experience in order to finish that which has been begun, that all may be balanced with that particular relationship or in regard to that particular point, that the entity has been attempting to learn and has as yet not completely gotten, shall we say, under the belt.

As each is familiar with the so-called karmic influence, we need not dwell upon this influence, but would note only that it is well to take such influences seriously, in that each entity gives such challenges careful and persistent consideration, but also that the entity employ the light touch, the laughter, the seeking of joy, the discovery of love within each difficulty and each challenge.

The other influence, although equally pervasive, is not an influence that is much noticed. However, it is equally important to your development and to your understanding of the process of development. You understand already that that which you seek will come to you. This follows the basic law of finishing the beginning. However, there is a balancing influence, and that is the influence of finding that which has least been sought. Each of you will repeatedly during your incarnation have a new experience, [an] experience to which you come as a virgin comes to her first love. You will have no previous experience to guide you within the incarnation or within your memory, for what is occurring is a balancing process.

If you have sought and sought and sought again that which is good and perfect it is a just balance and one with which the Creator is generous that that which is painful shall occur to you, not because you deserve it, but because the way to transformation is the way of balancing and for every familiar line of thought which you work upon in order to progress spiritually, there will be a brand new circumstance which has been not called for which shall occur to you also and for which you have no previously molded personal tools. This offers you the chance of assimilating new catalyst without incurring what you would call karmic responsibility or debt. If there are very difficult lessons in your life and one thing after another has been a half-remembered nightmare through which you wearily but determinately move in order to stop forever the wheel, as you would say, of karma or as we would put it, to finish that which has been begun, then it is that something utterly unexpectedly marvelous and wonderful shall occur, not because you deserve it but because a balance needs to be brought.

And so the Creator has gifts for you to aid in transformation, to surprise you and to offer you the opportunity to teach yourself that which you have begun to learn but have not yet finished; and that incalculable something which the balancing law offers as a teaching but which has been rarely spoken of and even less rarely grasped: that is, that there is such a thing as growth. There is that which rains when there is drought and which shines to brighten an interior dim landscape. There is an inborn keel which shall manifest itself within your life experience, not when you expect it but always as a gift, and whether these occurrences are happy or unhappy, you may find within yourself the blessing of lessons which are more simply learnt because you have been learning their opposite.

When you do not recognize in a situation or relationship any half memory of any past association, when you have no personal feeling of attachment to a challenge, then it is perhaps well to consider whether or not this may be a gift from the Creator that which you already have the tools to understand, if we may use a term that is incorrect in your density. Each of you has this balancing influence on hand at this time and we encourage each of you to look to such lessons with gratitude for grace which offers the easy lessons once in a while and with determination, for even though these lessons are easy because they come as gifts it is easy to waste them.

Therefore, be meticulous in acknowledging each gift in seeing the balance which is internal to your own development and no one else's. Thus shall you use the illusion which makes you seem unequal, one to another. We encourage you to rejoice in this seeming inequality, for the Creator so rejoices. You are the glory which the Creator could only realize by reflection, you are the manifest of that which is and always shall be unmanifest, and while you are manifest you are not only Creator and co-creator but also creation and the Creator finds you lovely.

We ask you, my friends, to allow all those concepts which you may be learning to become seated in your consciousness by the process and discipline of regular meditation. We encourage the daily meditation, for seeking within without words is analogous to returning once again to the truth that all men are created equal, for you move into that portion of your being which is co-equal not only with your brothers and sisters but with the Creator, and it is in this portion of your being that learning shall be seated or it shall be lost. That which skips along the top of the water does not influence the deep. Let that which you are learning sink as the stone shall do when it ceases its headlong flight across the top of the waves.

I am Q'uo. We would like to experiment with moving this channel in order that we may answer some questions, if there be any this evening. Therefore, we shall transfer this contact at this time, thanking each of you again for requesting this particular vibration and thanking this instrument for its service. We shall transfer. I am Q'uo.

(Unknown channeling)

I am Q'uo, and greet you once again in love and in light. We are pleased to have been able to make contact with this instrument and would at this time ask if we may be of further service to this group this evening by attempting to answer queries which those present may find value in the asking. May we begin with a query?

Questioner: Q'uo, you feel like a fifth-density contact. Are you?

I am Q'uo, and this is correct, my sister. May we answer further?

Questioner: Not unless you have anything that you wish to say about yourself or yourselves …

I am Q'uo, and we have little to offer as biographical information, as you would term it, for we are as you are, that which is and that which seeks the one Creator.

May we answer another query?

Questioner: What can you tell me about an event in our history known as the French Revolution?

I am Q'uo, and we would need to move with this instrument to deeper levels of its consciousness in order to speak in any detailed fashion concerning the event that you have called the French Revolution, for we are not historians and do not study this facet of your planet's history, as you call it. And in order to move beyond our abilities and desires to be of service in those ways which are ours to offer, we would need to be able to transmit information which was totally unfamiliar to this instrument.

That which is of the philosophical distortion, shall we say, is that which we are most able to offer, for the philosophy of one's existence and the attitude concerning the meaning in one's life pattern and life in general is that common factor which binds all who seek what you have called the truth. Therefore, we may speak upon this topic with far less difficulty than we would encounter should we move beyond these limits.

Is there some particular aspect of this event which you have called the French Revolution that we may speak upon, for, as you are aware, it is an event with many, many facets and to speak in even the most general of terms would be a great distortion of any one facet …

Questioner: Nothing at this time, I would prefer to withdraw the question. Thank you very much.

I am Q'uo, and we thank you, my brother, for your understanding and acceptance of our obvious limitations. May we attempt any other query?

Questioner: I would like to take up L's question and work with it a little bit because I think that there mat be something of substance which you could answer, so what I'll do is guess at the direction that he was going, supply you with some background and then ask a question that is philosophical if that is acceptable to you …

I am Q'uo, we are quite pleased to attempt our service in this manner …

Questioner: About the middle of the eighteenth centaury Europe rather exploded with revolutions having to do with freedom. Little European nations and, I suppose, England actually started it all in 1660 to 1680 with a civil revolution. It didn't work out but it started things off, and in the later 1700's America declared its independence and its freedom and the idea of liberty and freedom really took hold in people's hearts. And when this came to France it was in the 1790's and it was rather a bloody rendition of revolt, as I suppose revolutions tend to be, but there was a particularly nasty cast to this one. People got beheaded instead of merely having to go back to the old home countries. Nevertheless, the results were liberty, equality, paternity and it has often been surmised and has been stated by some Confederation members that some within the American revolutionary movement were very, very wise souls who had no home contact with Earth. This was not their home planet, they came here as wanderers. Jefferson, for instance, was one who was a wanderer and who came here in order to aid the entities of this particular part of the planet in effecting a transformation of thought. The same could be said, the same could be surmised of some entities within the French revolutionary movement, and certainly the goals were laudable.

The philosophical question is: there seems to be an interweaving of souls not of this planet who come to share an increased radiance of spirit with those who may still be sleeping and who will waken to a brighter beacon. I feel that wanderers have a far more organic tie with their adopted planet than is usually thought. In other words, that wanderers to this planet take from it as well as give to it and I wondered if you would like to comment upon the intertwining of energies of wanderers and those who are native or at least have spent many, many incarnations on this particular planet which we call Earth?

I am Q'uo, and we thank you for the opportunity to speak upon this topic, for it is one which is central to the lessons and purposes which each entity upon your planet's surface has incarnated to learn and to offer. The population of this planetary influence, being a third-density population, is one which attempts to learn the lessons of what may in general be called love; there is no better word in your language yet it falls short. This lesson as it makes itself apparent to those attempting to learn it manifests in differing degrees and through various stages that one may liken to the growth of the tree which produces a fruit and may also be likened within each human entity to the movement of light to higher and higher centers of energy within the mind/body/spirit complex. Thus, there is a season when the gardener, shall we say, may do its work and a season when the natural evolution of the tree may take its course. Those you have called wanderers, then, have incarnated in various periods of your planet's historical past in order to aid the overall growth of the tree of mind, or of your planet's population, as it has proceeded through those stages of growth which precede that aspect of love which may be seen as manifesting in the form of the ideals of liberty and freedom and equality.

We must pause … we …

(Side one of tape ends.)

(Unknown channeling)

I am Q'uo, and we shall continue. As [it has been that] been your planetary population has moved through the identification with groups and the giving and taking of energies between groups and has evolved in the individual sense as well to the appreciation of the ability to express one's own thoughts and actions without restriction, then this becomes the signal to those you have called wanderers that there is the need and the call for assistance in aiding those who have begun to appreciate the individual expression and who now are in need of finding within their being the ability to allow that expression within others as well, as the energies of the light move through the lower three energy centers and begin to approach the heart energy center or chakra, and that which is known as love or compassion begins to be activated within the individual and group consciousness.

The ideals of liberty and equality then become paramount in a form which begins in a distorted fashion for those who have long labored under the bonds of some form of slavery or have found themselves in a service to others which was not chosen but which was, shall we say, dictated to them. The desire for freedom and equality bursts forth in a fashion which first is quite gross and unrefined in its nature. Thus, the various tendencies towards retribution in the form of revolution begin to develop and within this framework of transformational change that is somewhat of a chaotic nature then those gardeners or shepherds, shall we say, that you have called the wanderers move in order to lend their assistance in a fashion which does not infringe upon the free will of those whom they have come to serve. Thus the incarnational entrance into your illusion is chosen in order that only the bias to serve be remembered and thus the service is offered as an equal to those who call for it. Thus, the concepts of liberty and equality are born in a season that is the result of a great span of experience of both the individual and collected consciousnesses of the peoples of your planet.

May we answer in any further way my sister?

Questioner: No, thank you.

I am Q'uo, and we thank you, my sister. Is there another query?

Questioner: I'll ask one more and then shut up. What is the nature of infatuation, compared especially with love, and what is its function?

I am Q'uo. We find that this concept, which you have called infatuation, is the mental and emotional analogue to the natural attraction of oppositely polarized biological sexes. This may be likened unto the magnet and the iron filing. There is no thinking required to bring the two together. Thus, when an entity notices an attraction to one of the opposite biological sexual nature, the entity may seek further contact in order that the attraction may be explored. When further contact reinforces the initial attraction then the mind and the emotions begin the processing of this catalyst and the beginning of what may later develop into that which you recognize as love is at hand.

The so-called infatuation period, then, serves the purpose of drawing entities of similar vibratory complexes together in order that they may proceed upon the evolutionary path in a manner which is efficient and appropriate to each, that is, in the utilizing of the daily round of activities as catalyst, that when pondered to a sufficient degree allows experience to be born and recorded within the significant portions of the self. Thus does the infatuation propel, or more correctly, provide the potential for the entities to propel themselves further along the path which each has chosen before the incarnation.

May we answer further, my sister?

Questioner: The portion of the question left unanswered, perhaps deliberately, was what is this relationship emotionally, to the emotions, the human emotions that we call love, although I understand that the creative principle love is not what we mean by the kind of love that people have in their eyes on their fiftieth anniversary. That's the emotion that I'm talking about.

I am Q'uo, and we see here a paradox, my sister, for in one way of looking upon infatuation it is a pure form of love, for it accepts totally another without condition. The other at this point in the relationship is so desirable that the one feeling the infatuation will, shall we say, go to any length to please the one with whom the infatuation is felt. All of the self and the attention of the self is given without reservation in order that the feeling of infatuation may continue. Thus, in this sense the period of infatuation is a pure form of love.

Pure, however, in the sense that it has not been tested; it as yet lacks the depth of experience. When the two who have become infatuated continue the relationship and begin the processing of the catalyst which is inevitable within any life pattern, the opportunities then arise for the love to gain in strength and depth and richness and purity, for there will be many, many times in the processing of catalyst that one or the other or both entities will feel less than acceptance of the other and will need to find within the self the ability to accept that which was previously not acceptable, to forgive that within self and other self that which was unforgivable, to have compassion for that which held little interest, or perhaps even dislike.

Thus, the lessons of love and acceptance make themselves known within the relationship born of infatuation and with the faith that the relationship will endure and that meaning may be found for both within it and the will to persevere in finding that meaning and growth. Thus does each entity grow in acceptance and in love and thus does the relationship do likewise and thus is love strengthened by testing true catalyst that each brings to the relationship. Thus, the love which results is a love which has greater strength and depth and variety of experience, shall we say.

May we answer further, my sister?

Questioner: No, thank you very much.

I am Q'uo, and we thank you, my sister. Is there another query?

Questioner: Yes. You basically covered this so please answer briefly, but you seemingly place more importance upon the broader definition of love which is compassion and I understand that as acceptance of people, situations and self as they are and allowing them room to grow in their own way. So for an entity who is attempting to develop love as we know it then probably the most expeditious way for them to do this would be to work on acceptance of others and themselves and this is something that I believe I know, but could you just give a simple yes or no, if that would suffice?

I am Q'uo. This is basically correct, my brother, for within your illusion of seeming separateness and limitation there is much which offers the challenge to be accepted, much which seems traumatic, tragic and filled with sorrow, distaste, horror, anger, jealousy and so forth. Yet, each entity and event is the Creator knowing Itself in a way mysterious to most. Yet, each in any portion of the experience may increase its evolutionary progress by finding the joy, the love, and the light of the Creator within that person, that moment, that event, that thought. When this can be done in a relationship then the relationship has served as a means by which the continuing ability to expand the point of view and the acceptance, the love, and the compassion for that which falls within the point of view then is also increased and the entity has moved itself further along its chosen path of evolution.

May we answer further, my brother?

Questioner: No, thank you. You answered quite sufficiently, thank you.

I am Q'uo, and we thank you, my brother. Is there another query?

(No further queries.)

I am Q'uo, and we find that we have exhausted those queries which have been offered to us this evening and for each query we are most grateful, for in our attempt to answer your heartfelt questions we find further ways to know and to serve the Creator in all. We are humbly grateful for this opportunity and we would remind each present that we are those who seek as you seek, fallible in many ways. Take those words and thoughts which have meaning to you and leave those which do not. Thus would we offer that which we have found helpful in our seeking to you in your seeking.

We shall take our leave of this group at this time, thanking each again for allowing our presence. We leave you in the love and in the light of the one Creator. We are known to you as Q'uo. Adonai. Adonai. ✣

Sunday Meditation
July 13, 1986

(Carla channeling)

I Yadda. I greet you in love and in light of infinite Creator. It our privilege to be with you this evening. We receive call with some puzzlement because we have to evaluate our audience. Here in this domicile we speak with unified group, unified in thinking and in tuning to this specific sparkle of light—heh!—I say that well, did I not? Yet also there is the somewhat larger audience of the metaphysics magazine which has requested our words. This audience not unified this particular moment in space/time. What we gonna do to speak to all the bozos instead of a few?

Well, you can't please everybody, so we decided not to worry about it, but to touch this group and through the concerns therein, touch all. So, we greet in thought all who may read these words, for we know that in the face of those in this room are all of your faces; within a few thoughts, all thoughts. For is there more than one path? Even though each has a unique way of taking it, in the end your feet move the same dust as spirits before you, and you leave the dust behind you as blessing for those after you.

So! We would speak this evening, and would thank you again for this great pleasure of the function of desire and of the tools that you may use to further your desire. Now you have desire [of] many things, but we speak of the strong desire for the truth that motivates the seeker. You do not want an answer as much as you want a clear understanding of the question.

The question, in our opinion, that each of you faces in your present incarnation in third density is, "How do I love? What is love? What has love to do with me?" This constellation of questions is the spearhead of your desire as a seeker.

Now we have gotten the question straight. That was easy—heh?! It is more difficult to clear away the stumbling blocks that have been placed before you by yourself than it will ever be to recognize truth. What are these stumbling blocks? There are two main stumbling blocks to the seeker. The first is the determination of seekers to think within the head without the slightest concept of how to go about the process of thinking. It is understandable that you should have this problem because your culture is fast and shallow, like a stream that has no depth, but moves very quickly.

So, your thoughts dart hither and yon but do not achieve the depth that you wish. Do you know why? Ah?! You know it is because you do not observe, you do not give yourself time. You cannot think until you have observed and gotten something to think about, you know. It is putting the cart before the horse, heh? To think right off the bat, you know—you cannot do that.

Now, what should you observe before you begin thinking upon the truth of love? What should you not observe, for everything speaks to you of love.

The second great stumbling block—that was a good one too; you hear those L's coming right out—to seeking the truth of love is your opinion of yourself. Now, you know you were born into "ihwusion." Wait—we gonna say that right, we gonna say it—il-*lu*-sion. You were born into an illusion. Your scientists tell you about this illusion, but you have known it was an illusion forever. Philosophers have told you this; masters and teachers have shared this with humanity always. This that you experience is to be observed, but it is not the answer—it is the way to the answer.

You are, as you look at yourself in the mirror, a system of electromagnetic vibration that is held together as a field so that the various elements within the cells of your body can work symbiotically to sustain a physical vehicle for experiencing of self-consciousness. Now we get closer. We begin to move around the stumbling block of self. If you see somebody in that mirror that is a certain age, weight, sex, makes a certain amount of money, has a certain number of degrees from learned institutions and a certain number of children, you are falling flat on your face, you are stumbling so much. You must lose all those provincial ideas about yourself if you wish to seek the truth of love.

For how can you love without any reservation? This entity that is so-many years old, and so-many feet high, has so-many names and letters after the name, and just and so-many children. If there was the ultimate love for this series of specified quantities, then you could not love others the same way. No, my friends—you must look in the mirror and see perfection. Now, how you gonna do that unless you remember that you are a collection of well-arranged atoms housing self-aware consciousness?

If you can remove prejudice from your gaze into the mirror and begin loving yourself not for what you do, not for what you succeed in, but for what you are, then you have opened the gate to learning the truth about love. For if you do not judge yourself because you have done this deed or thought this thought, or been this quality or that, but instead love yourself because you are the truth about love, you are the treasure to love which you seek to find, then you may begin to make "qweer"—we must try again. This instrument have trouble with our accent. We try to say—clear perception of other entities who may have more or fewer children, may have more or less money, may be older or younger, but have no consciousness, but unique experience. So you look into another perfect posit of the Creator each moment that you look upon any entity whomsoever.

When you can learn how to evaluate experience, and when you have gotten over the shock of having such an illusory identity, then you take off your mask, you put the intellect where it belongs, that is, as tool subservient to the widest observation of heart and spirit, then your path shall be more plain to you.

There is one last stumbling block that you now have because of a deeper reason than your culture. You are impatient because you have a physical vehicle which will not be with you long. So, you want to know everything now. You know you must let go of that desire and seek only to know this moment. Everything is in this moment, but this is most difficult for the mind to comprehend. And it is most unusual for an entity to become aware of it without spending much time seeking while standing right in the heart of the truth and not seeing it.

There is a process of waiting in faith and patience and hope. It may only last a moment for someone very close to the moment, very close to love, and in peace and harmony with those about it, but for most of us bozos we will have to wait on holy ground until that moment—and it may be years in coming when we see it for the first time.

Your best ally in this endeavor is meditation. We get each in this room saying, "I cannot meditate well, so how is meditation going to help me?" Well, my dear bozos, no one meditates very well, for the perfect meditation will remove all separation and restore all to unity. It is the force of the will that seeks meditation. It is the faith that moves a visible physical entity to seek the invisible and metaphysical. It is the discipline of doing so on a daily basis that will yield to you a continuing opening into your birthright, for as children of consciousness, are you not heirs to all of the truth? Are you not indeed embodiment of the truth?

Therefore, we ask three things from those who seek. We ask that you discount all conclusions, and instead begin to gather data. In other words, be a witness and remember what you see and hear, knowing that you are seeing and hearing illusion, but that this illusion was given to you by yourself as the experience that will yield to you the truth about love.

Secondly. We ask that you love not your mask, but yourself, and not the tasks about you, but the selves about you. If you must hate instead of love, at least hate that which is consciousness. But, my friends, you will have a hard time hating consciousness.

And lastly, we ask that you meditate and open yourself up to silence, never judging yourself because of the stray thoughts, but always seeking, seeking to be cleansed of all the dust of this path, that you may sit upon the stone, the hard rock of consciousness and be self-aware for the first and most holy time.

We wish you the joy of your journey and good courage in it. We have enjoyed ours and we hope that you do too—you might as well, for you are all on it. For our natures are bound up in our consciousness, and whether or not you try to seek the lessons of love, they will come to you. You might as well study, offer yourselves to each other as you would tasty food—for you are beautiful to each other and you can share love with each other. Hold your hands out to each other and hold all of your heart out to truth.

Before we leave this instrument, we wish to say in answer to this instrument's question when she challenged us, we did not give her hard time this evening. She was surprised. She said, "This really Yadda?" Well, you see this instrument challenge us in name of Christ, and then she say, "I find Christ in the master known as Jesus, and so I must ask you in name of Jesus the Christ. Do you come in name of Jesus the Christ whom I serve with all my heart," and so forth. She go through this long thing. Well, we so glad to hear that, because, you know, we do come in name of Christ and this instrument now ask the right way, becoming aware that any man can be love and any Christ can be worshipped, but that the Christ is so sacred that it is up to individual to say, "This is my Christ; this is how I see the face of the Creator, this is how I will follow to the death in order that I may learn the lesson of love." That why we so eagerly come. We wait long for this instrument to understand this, and we very happy that now we not have to give this instrument all that trouble.

It is a hard thing being a teacher, let me tell you. But we are so happy to be here and to be attempting with these poor words to say that which you all already know, but to say it in a way which you can recognize. He who has ears, let him hear. We Yadda. You know, we may be talking junk, you bozos, so if we talking junk, you throw it out—okay. If we talking in a way that seem good to you, that is a great blessing to us and we could ask for nothing more. As we abide upon our given task with regard to your planetary influence, we say to you—we beg you, "Love each other."

We known to you as Yadda, and we leave you in love and light—aheh!—of One Who Is All. May your cheeks be rosy with laughter upon the path, may your feet be strong, may your hearts be happy. And may your will to know the truth of love be your walking stick so that you may move gently, at varying speeds, responsive to wind and weather, inner and outer. And always, learn better to love. Adonai. Adonai. Adonai.

(Jim channeling)

I am Latwii, and we greet you, my friends, in the love and the light of our infinite Creator. It is our pleasure as well to join this group this evening and to follow those of Yadda. We enjoy their humor and light. We hope that we may be of some service this evening in attempting to answer queries if those present may find any value in so asking. May we then, without further delay, ask if we may begin with a query?

Carla: I have a question from R. She would like to know how she can tune in to people's vibrations when she is asked to do healing work or other psychic work, without picking up and empathizing with their pain, whether it be physical or emotional. She very much wants to continue healing and being of service as a psychic, but she finds it extremely draining to be in such pain for so much of the time.

I am Latwii, and am aware of your query, my sister. For an entity such as the one of which you speak who is beginning to become aware of the finer vibrations which always surround it …

(Side one of tape ends.)

(Jim channeling)

I am Latwii, and am again with this instrument. To continue. For such an entity, which is beginning to feel the inner sensations quicken within its own being in the developing of its ability to be of further service, the separating of the pain and disharmony of another from that which is less painful is a very difficult and delicate task, requiring usually a great deal of experience, for it is not the ability, shall we say, of the beginner to perform the more advanced task. The beginner is opening itself to all which comes before its notice and is such like the tuning fork, in that those vibrations which surround it begin to move it in a like or harmonic manner. If an entity should hastily begin to attempt the separation of that which is painful from that which is not, it is possible that it would become less able to perceive those vibrations about it and less able to serve in a manner which it has chosen.

We suggest as an initial step that this entity see itself in a certain fashion when it offers itself in the service of the healer. Rather than absorbing all those vibrations of various natures which impinge upon its notice, we suggest that this entity see itself as a portion of a river, that the feelings of all natures which are brought to it by the one seeking healing be allowed to move through its being in a manner likened unto the water moving through the bed of a river. The entity then may see itself as the bed and banks and the air surrounding the moving water, becoming aware of where there is the blockage, of where there are deeps, of where there are eddies, and the whirling of the waters. And when these characteristics of the moving water have been noted and worked with in order to aid in the process of healing, that they then be allowed to continue their movement through the being without needing to be absorbed in any way whatsoever.

May we answer further, my sister?

Carla: Yes. One of R's teachers suggested that there are different modes of perception and that she need not experience this empathic pain in order—to be able to diagnose, I suppose, and treat would be the medical way of saying it, but of course that would not be a good thing to say, so I guess one would say—in order to tune in to the vibrational pattern of an individual. That rang true to me, yet I have the same problem R does and I didn't understand what he meant—it just sounded right. I wonder if you could enlarge upon this concept?

I am Latwii, and in our previous response we were attempting to construct the framework by which an entity may move its conscious perception from the state in which it absorbs in an empathic sense the vibrations which are brought before it by the one seeking the healing so that the one serving as healer may then be able to be aware of these vibrations in order to serve as a healer without becoming affected in a manner which reduces its own ability to function in any sense. This framework which we suggested, that of seeing the self as the container of the moving vibrations that allows them to continue their movement, is a structured means whereby one may become aware of this means of perceiving which has been described to the one known as R.

However, we must add that this process of becoming able to utilize another level of sensing and perceiving is not available to each seeker in the same degree of quickening or awakening, shall we say. Many there are who will pass the entire incarnation without becoming aware of either manner of sensing. Others will find use in being that known as empathic, for within their own incarnational patterns, there is perhaps the need to be more aware of the feelings of others for whatever reason the entity has chosen before the incarnation. In still others, there is the pattern set out which draws unto the entity further levels or means of perception in order that its own pattern of lessons and services may be fulfilled. Thus, we must give our advice with some caution, for we cannot give general advice which is always applicable to a specific entity.

May we answer further, my sister?

Carla: Well, yes. I'm still working to try to get to the heart of what R and I really should be thinking about, and it seems to me that with your second response, you've shifted my mind around. Let me explain. When you described the idea of the riverbank and the riverbed and the air, I visualized that as being the same kind of technique that an instrument uses, visualizing itself as the pipe who is not responsible for the water, and all you have to do is be the best pipe you can be, in other words, doing something that I imagine R was already doing, which was giving her will over to the holy spirit, as R and I probably would both say, and saying, "Not my will, but thine be done." But this isn't what you were getting at.

It seems to me that the heart of what you were getting at more was, that there is a state of mind that sounds to me very much like the state of mind achieved during a hypnotic regression when a person has come up against something that makes that person fearful. And the hypnotist says to the person, "You are now an observer; you are watching it happen," and everything continues as before, but the person does not have any emotional reaction to it. I believe this was the heart of what you're suggesting as the state of mind to be cultivated, that of the entity, the mind/body/spirit complex staying in the physical body, but achieving a great degree of concentration, and then becoming the observer rather than the experiencer of what is happening to that person that is being seen. Is this by and large correct? And would you correct what I'm wrong on?

I am Latwii, and as we assess that which you have spoken, we find that you have discovered another means by which to describe the technique we have given. The heart, shall we say, of this technique lies in the pattern of lessons and services which an entity may have chosen. There is, indeed, the state of consciousness that is available in precisely the fashion you have described, that of the observer which is not affected by that which it observes. This is a state which comes to an entity not because it has done one exercise or another, but because it is the appropriate outgrowth of the efforts of the entity in seeking to be of service and in allowing those lessons it has chosen to bear fruit within its own being in a manner which then, as a natural process, produces the ability to serve in a continuing fashion of growth and refinement, shall we say.

Thus, the one seeking to be of service, the one in this case known as R, may undertake any technique in order to further amplify its ability to serve in such and such a fashion as described by its own inclinations, yet what will develop within its own being as an ability to serve will be a function not just of the conscious desire, but of those patterns set in motion before the incarnation began. Thus, [there is that] within the incarnational experience [which causes] what you may call predestination and free will [to meet]. Thus we cannot speak with specificity in this or any particular case, but may offer general guidelines which we hope are of some assistance.

May we answer further, my sister?

Carla: I will send a copy of this to R, and if she has further questions, I'm sure she'll write and ask. Thank you very much. And thanks for R.

I am Latwii, and we thank you, my sister. Is there another query?

J: I almost feel instead of asking the question, I almost feel I should ask you if there's something particular tonight I need to be told by you, particularly. Does anything come to mind?

I am Latwii. We appreciate the offer to speak without boundary, shall we say, but would choose to respond to those queries which are felt within your own heart to be of greatest need. We would not wish to inflict our opinions upon your free will without first finding the heartfelt query upon your part placed before us. We seek in each of these meditations in which vocal channeling occurs to guard as carefully as possible the free will of each entity. We, in our seeking to be of service, desire to serve in a manner which is congruent with the needs of the entity that we wish to serve. We cannot know those needs as purely or precisely as can you. Though we see with eyes that move somewhat further than do your own, we cannot feel what is of importance to you in the way which you can feel. Thus do we offer ourselves in service that you yourself determine.

May we answer further, my sister?

J: Okay. Tonight as the session started, I suddenly became terribly, terribly depressed, and it's so overwhelming that it's … almost the ability to think beyond that depression just doesn't seem to be possible. And I move back and forth between the feelings of possibly it's a cleansing of something, it's good for me to go through it, I'm releasing something I wasn't aware of, or it's just some stupid temporary weakness or fear of the unknown, of an all new sense of my immediate future, my move out west and the changing of my life, everything philogistically to whole new groups of people. And it was just so overwhelming that that's all I could think of was my depression, and I'm not quite sure what to ask about it. I'm just never quite sure how to deal with it. I don't want it to get the most of me, but possibly it's a cleansing, I don't know. Does that make any sense? I just can't get rid of it.

I am Latwii, and am aware of your query, my sister. We may suggest that the state of mind and emotions which you have described as the depression is that which offers an opportunity for that which you have called a cleansing, yet it is but the opportunity. If you, in your contemplation or meditation, can follow that feeling of depression and allow it to lead you to those areas within your own thinking and experience which are the source of anxiety, worry, fear, and which sum in that feeling you have called depression, then you will allow that feeling to show you the areas which may be consciously worked upon in order that a transformation or cleansing in these areas of your being may occur.

To remain with that state of feeling that you have called depression without moving with it in this case and allowing it to point the arrow, shall we say, is to remain in a somewhat dysfunctional state of being, You may in following this feeling discover that there are various beliefs which you hold in certain areas which are not necessarily so, certain fears which in time may dissipate, certain anxieties and certain guilts that may yield to transformation by the simple changing of what is believed to be true. Thus, you may find that widening the point of viewing in certain areas may allow the belief or viewpoint to include new concepts which, when seated within your being and manifested in your thinking and experience, will then remove the clouds of depression so that once again the rays of light may illumine the darker portions of your thinking and experience.

May we answer further, my sister?

J: Yes, please, Latwii, one more. Last month our dear friend M, whom you had contact with on our Thursday night meetings—I seem to be going through some changes, I think it's a combination of guilt—you see, as you're aware, she's blind and has other disabilities, and we've been very close, and I'm having a real sense of guilt and anger because I know I'll be going out west and I'll be leaving her and yet she relies so heavily on me. And I almost feel like there's something I'm supposed to teach her or make aware to her or bring forth in her that she's not aware of before I leave because, there's just not that much time left, and as I said, I get nervous about it, of the guilt and anger, and once I move out west, it won't be the same again and I'm just wondering why we were supposed to be together in the first place, and like I said, what it is that I'm supposed to teach her or maybe she's supposed to teach me something in the short time I have left physically at her side.

Like I said, with her being handicapped in so many ways, when she relies on you, she really, really relies on you, so I do have the guilt about leaving, but I feel there's something I should do in the short time I have left, and I just don't know what it is, and I just get this panic sense of—that it'd be very, very difficult for her once I've left, she's been able to rely on me so much in every way, and I wonder if you could help me on that. I just keep asking myself that or asking my guides that, and I'm just not getting the answer. And that was my question about myself and M.

I am Latwii, and you have now moved into a more specific portion of the area of inquiry that you covered in your previous query. Again, we would suggest that in your meditations or contemplations, you continue seeking the answer to this query. It is well to ask others, those you have called guides and presences for aid in such a matter, yet it is not to be wondered at overly much when the aid is of a nature other than one anticipates, for this dilemma which you now face is one which holds great opportunity for discovery upon your part, and if any guide or presence should give you the specific answer to this query, then your opportunity to gain in the spiritual strength required to solve this dilemma would be removed.

Thus, we can suggest that as you seek with growing intensity the answer to this dilemma, that at some point you will reach the, shall we say, critical condition within your own being that will call unto you the appropriate response. To seek and to seek and to seek is to amplify that pattern which is now in motion and to offer it fertile ground, shall we say, in which its seeds may be sown, its harvest made known. Thus, we can only suggest that you continue in your seeking, and at some point you may find it helpful within your meditation for the moment to give up the seeking and the questioning long enough to listen, for at some point, you will be ready to hear.

May we answer further, my sister?

J: No, thank you Latwii, I think I understand now. I'll see you soon. Thank you.

I am Latwii, and we thank you, my sister. Is there another query?

Carla: I have a very teeny query, and all you have to do is say yes, no, or I can't answer that. Something happened to me that's never happened before when I was channeling Yadda, and that was, in the middle of the channeling, everything stopped. I hadn't caused it to stop by analyzing. I was still focused, and I stayed focused, and there was nothing. I mean, it was an imposed nothingness. It's better than I ever meditate—nothing, total blankness, and then, bang, it popped in again, the channel began again, and it went on as if nothing had ever happened. Was this attack? [Or] was Yadda just making sure that I was staying in the position of channel?

I am Latwii, and we find in this instance that there was the need on the part of those of Yadda to determine your own state of readiness, shall we say, to continue with that particular work. The period of the silence was necessary to set your instrument, shall we say, in a fashion which is somewhat similar to a testing which, when passed, then readies the instrument for further service. Yet it is also more than that in that it included not just a readying of your own instrument, but a further blending of those of Yadda in their transmitting capacity with your own instrument. Thus, the period of silence was an opportunity for each to blend in a more harmonious fashion with the other in order that the concepts which those of Yadda wished to transmit might be more easily and appropriately transmitted.

May we answer further, my sister?

Carla: No, thank you. I'm always fascinated to learn more about the art of channeling.

I am Latwii. Again we thank you, my sister. Is there another query?

(Pause)

I am Latwii. We find that we have exhausted the queries for this evening, and we are most grateful for each opportunity to offer our humble words and opinions. We hope that each will remember to take only those which ring of truth and to leave the rest behind. We rejoice in each opportunity to join this group, and we thank each for inviting our presence. We shall be with you at any future request for our presence and will be happy to join each in meditation at any time. We are known to you as Latwii. We leave you in the love and in the light of the one infinite Creator. Adonai, my friends. Adonai.

Sunday Meditation
July 20, 1986

(S channeling)

I am Hatonn, and we wish to greet you, our brothers and sisters, in the love and in the light of the one infinite Creator. We again are most happy to be with you and we are glad that this instrument decided to let us work with him, for he has been a part of this group for some time. We wish to share on something that is most important [to many of you at this time] the ideas of *(inaudible)* and lessons …

(The rest of the channeling is inaudible.)

(Carla channeling)

I am Q'uo, and I greet you, my friends, in the love and in the light of the one infinite Creator. We too greet each in the name of infinite intelligence, and offer our thanksgiving that we may embrace your vibrations with our own. When we speak to you, we must ask you to take our words lightly, as if we were members of your family, close to you and loving you, yet full of errors. In no way do we wish to represent the Confederation of Planets in the Service of the Infinite Creator as an unimpeachable source of information. We offer what we know or think we understand, but we offer also that which we are, for we are as you—the Creator, made of love, and yet dwelling in illusion. The stuff of our illusion is fuller of light than your own and we enjoy more experience as souls, shall we say. We have made our choice and that is to serve others, and yet we find that there is much that we do not know and that which we do know we are continually refining.

Therefore, all that seems second-rate, unusable or incorrect to you, we ask that you discard. All that seems inspiring, we ask you to retain and use as you would, just as you would the loving words of a sister or brother.

We would speak to you about the manifestation within your incarnational patterns of the one original Thought which is the Creator. The one original Thought upon which all creation was founded and with which all creation redounds is love. Yes, my friends, love is a thought, a principle, a logos. You, by your very consciousnesses, are the Logos in a holographic representation, yet you are completely unlike any other holographic representation of the Creator, for your experiences are unique to your particular consciousness. Your field of energy is completely unique and precious to the one infinite Creator, and your greatest gift is your being, for by your mirroring of your perceptions, the Creator learns of Itself.

As each of you has to some degree or another already considered this present incarnation, like all in third density, yet none more so than this, is an incarnation of choice, the choice having to do with the one original Thought of love and your manifestation of it. There are two basic manifestations: one, service to others or love for others, and, two, service to or love for self.

You will note that in the service-to-others path, it is necessary first to love the self, that one may then love each other self as the self. Therefore, the service-to-others choice is one offering a more vast range of experiences than the service-to-self path in which others are loved only insofar as they serve a particular self, that being one's own self. Polarization then, takes place upon a more intense but smaller scale. It is therefore, a difficult path to follow.

We have chosen service to others, and would speak to you of it and would encourage you to consider not only making the choice, which as we have said, each of you to a greater or lesser extent have already done, but also to press forward, then, in investigating the ramifications of the one original Thought of the Creator, for how does that one original Thought think and manifest in the life of one who wishes to serve others?

Our brothers and sisters of Hatonn have spoken to you of peace. Love, of course, is the principle upon which the concept of peace rests. However, like many expressions of love, the achieving and maintaining of peace among brothers and sisters within third density is not made easy by the illusion which you now enjoy. Peace is perhaps best achieved by dwelling upon the nature and filling oneself with the presence of the one original Thought, and out of the love you bear for love itself, you then open yourself in love and as a channel for the Creator's love, for, my friends, your own love will fail you to those who are striving.

Now, to open yourself in love to those who are disharmonious seems to be an act of folly, and yet let us look at flowers. They open their faces in love to the sun which offers them the light of its countenance and the love of its radiation, and yet they do not withhold their perfume from any being. There is no judgment upon the part of [a] flower as to who shall receive its gifts of beauty.

You yourself are crystalline and many-petaled and capable of a great radiance. Yet, if you only open to those whom you already love, you are not a flower who has centered upon the one original Thought. Open, then, in love as a channel, for we do not recommend that you depend upon that limited supply of love which your illusory personality can offer you, and love those who seem to wish you, if not harm, then at least quarrelsomeness.

The nature of service to others is such that you will find again and again that you have nothing to offer except your very being. And yet, my friends, if you will investigate the nature of the one original Thought, you will discover that your consciousness, your attention, your sympathy, your compassion, your attempt to understand, is the most precious service you can offer.

It is not given you to act on instinct. That is where the analogy to the flower breaks down completely, for you are not preordained to do or be anything. All choices are yours, and you may make and remake them again and again, softening, firming, rearranging, adjusting. My friends, in this incarnation you shall go through many phases. You shall change your mind many times about the finer points of your spiritual search for truth, and yet we feel that it may well be that you will find that the heart of that journey shall remain as you first discovered it with the excitement and the joy of an explorer discovering a new continent or ocean.

The core of choice is love. There is nothing lukewarm about love itself, and as you refine your choice, remember the power of that with which you are dealing, for you deal with something that has created all that you can see and all that you cannot see. It has created all—from stars to relationships, stones to the concepts of beauty and truth. You would not wish to take such power and toss it casually here and there, a fire hose sprinkled hither and yon upon a town that is not burning. No, my friends, you wish to take something that you sense is at the center of light, that you wish to make the center of your own life. You wish to hone it, to sharpen it, to discover and rediscover the joy of it and to be channels for it, learning more and more about the original Thought as you manifest it to yourself by manifesting it to others.

You see, my friends, service to others is actually service to self, for as you serve others, you learn. If you serve yourself first, the learning is so much harder and comes so much more slowly. As you give, so you receive. As you put yourself into difficulty, so you discover peace. As you remain serene within yourself, so you maintain all of [the] peace that you can. Note, we did not say, "may." There is only so much that you can do in service to entities others than the self. This is due to the free will of each individual.

It may seem within the illusion that there are individuals who may have an inflated idea of the gravity and expense necessary in the demanding of free will choices. It may seem to you that another's fist has moved into your nose before it has said, "I stop—this is where your free will takes over." It may seem to you that you are injured. We say to you that it is impossible to be injured unless you allow that concept to enter your consciousness.

What is the worst that can happen in this illusion, my friends? You may lose your life. What is that to you who have your eyes set upon eternity? Fear not, therefore, a lack of freedom, for you give yourself freedom as you offer yourself in service to others, and this is your peace, that you may love others, that you can love others, and that all that you need to do to be effective beyond your hopes is to love.

Each of those within your illusion wishes and hopes for perfect harmony betwixt all, one way or another. It is a universal concept, for it is the birthright of each person of the consciousness of infinite intelligence. The nature of the one original Thought is unity. Therefore, how can any portion of that unity be disharmonious?

(Side one of tape ends.)

(Carla channeling)

It is a good thing to desire peace and to wish to serve in love, yet we encourage you to consider the possibility of remaining detached from solutions. When one wants a solution or outcome, when one thinks one has a right answer, one is often pulled away from the one original Thought of love and finds it difficult to allow other solutions, outcomes or answers to be in the end chosen by others.

Yet it does not matter what the result of your service is, in terms of your own growth and learning; spiritually speaking, it is important only that your pure desire was to serve. It is, of course, helpful if one uses the tools available to one in order to refine techniques of service so that they are as effective as possible. However, free will is so important a concept that if a service is abrogated, refused or denied, it should be as acceptable to the one who serves as the alternate outcome, that is, that one's service is accepted, enjoyed and in terms of the illusion, successfully manifested.

May you love each other, my friends, in joy and without demand insofar as it is possible on your end. To paraphrase one of your holy works, "Live at peace with all other selves." You are not responsible for them, but for yourself. When it is not possible to influence others to say they are at peace with you, it is always possible to become peaceful within yourself with others.

Do you demand to change the world, or do you ask of yourself that you become more and more one with the original Thought of creation? We suggest to you that the latter course is profitable. As you love each other, and as you love the one infinite Creator, so we love you, and so we love the one infinite Creator. We speak with Its voice, we think with Its mind, and you listen now with Its ears, and all of us dance one dance together in love, in seeking of peace.

Oh, my friends, may you have the joy of knowing love, of being in love with love and of serving as a channel, as a lighthouse, as a beacon for the love and the light of the one infinite Creator which bathes each of you, which shines through each of you, which is the essence of each of you and in which we leave each of you, with the promise that we shall come to you at any time you may request our presence mentally. We have nothing to offer you except our love. Perhaps we may help to deepen a meditation, perhaps we may be of comfort simply because there is an indefinable something about not being alone in one's perceptions, whether they be of happiness or sadness. Whatever your reason for calling upon us, know that we will hear you and will respond, for you are not alone, nor have you ever been nor shall you ever be.

We leave this voice, yet the Creator speaks in every breath of air that breathes through any entity or sighs through any tree or disturbs any blade of grass. We are known to you as those of Q'uo. Adonai, my friends. Adonai vasu borragus.

(Jim channeling)

I am Latwii, and we greet you, my friends, in the love and the light of the infinite Creator. It is our pleasure as well to join this group this evening, and we thank you most humbly for allowing us to do so. It is once again our honor and our joyful duty to attempt in some way to be of service by considering those queries which may be offered us, and sharing our opinions with you as each of you move yet another step forward upon the journey of seeking the one Creator. Please do remember that we are as you, seekers of truth, and fallible in our perceptions. Take that which we offer that is of value and leave that which is not. May we begin, then, with the first query?

Carla: What's the impact in terms of raising the consciousness of planet Earth of people attempting and seemingly failing in many ways to achieve a peaceful great peace march? What's underneath that illusion?

I am Latwii. My sister, so many times those of your peoples begin an effort, whether alone or with others, that is hoped will be of service to others, that will light a path that perhaps has not known light sufficient for its realization in previous times. Thus, an effort is begun, difficulties ensue, and perhaps the result is not as intended, and those who have attempted feel disheartened and wonder within where can be found this which was sought.

We look upon such efforts, my sister, and see the great light of intention that shines within all and this is what is the heart of all such efforts, for none within your illusion is wise enough to know how an effort can yield fruit. Within your illusion, you move within a darkness of knowing. It is a difficult illusion in which to find solid footing. Thus, each seeks in a unique fashion to find the one original Thought, and in a unique fashion manifests some portion of that Thought within the illusion life pattern which is apparent.

What is seen and what is registered and what has its effect is the intention, the intention that survives the struggles and the turmoils, the intention that does not die with seeming defeat or difficulty. This intention, then, my sister, is that which works in a way that affects each other person within the illusion in a way that adds a certain lightness and potential for finding greater light within the illusion as a whole.

Do not ever confuse results which seem magnificent with the intention that produced them, for your wisdom is small and little of it do you experience, yet what you can do is to desire, is to seek, is to intend and in this way do you set your compass upon that which is unknowable yet desirable. In this way does your own beingness radiate that which you have made available through your intentions and through your struggles to others who see in ways not always known or shown to the outward eye. Thus does that which truly inspires come from mystery and move through mystery to lighten the hearts of those within the mystery of this illusion.

May we answer further, my sister?

Carla: No, thank you.

I am Latwii and we thank you, my sister. Is there another query?

K1: I'm not sure this is an appropriate question at this time, and if it's not, please let me know. I'm wondering if it's possible to know if K2's son, D, is still alive, and if he is, if it's possible for us to find him?

I am Latwii, and we pause to scan. It is possible for us to speak in a limited fashion in order that there might be some small service offered that does not infringe upon the Way of Confusion. This entity of which you speak is one which has in its own pattern of movement through its incarnation embarked upon what within your illusion is seen as separation and trauma in order that it might, with the aid of others, provide for itself and the one known as K2 a balancing opportunity that has its roots in previous incarnational existence. To speak further in attempting to locate or predict the future location of this entity we find to be beyond the line of confusion or free will. However, we can suggest that this is not an accident, and that all is truly well.

May we answer further, my sister?

K1: Can you tell me if he is alive at this time?

I am Latwii, and we find as we look upon this entity that its current condition is one which we may not fully describe, but may suggest that there shall be a contact that will reveal the presence of this entity. We may not speak in greater detail and we must apologize for our lack of words for a situation which is of obvious concern to the one known as K2 and to your own self.

May we answer further, my sister?

K1: No. Thank you very much.

I am Latwii, and we thank you, my sister.

S: Can you tell me, if it's possible, of my last incarnation?

I am Latwii, and we greet you, my brother, in joy. We look upon the query and we must smile, for we see somewhat beyond this query and note that the experience which preceded your current incarnation is one which, if it were described even in general terms, would provide you with information which may be of such a staggering potential to your current way of thinking that it may in some fashion tend to bias that thinking unduly. We can, however, say that the experience which preceded this experience is one of light, and is one which moves through this experience because of your decision to allow it, in a time some small distance in your past of this incarnation, as you would call it. We encourage you, my brother, to find means within your own being which we see that you have developed to move your own consciousness to a place, shall we say, within, from which you will be able to view that which is of meaning to you from that experience. Though it may not be entirely possible to view it as the motion picture, you shall however find an ability to glean from it the emotions, the motives, and the attitude which was its fruit and which served as the seed for this incarnation.

May we answer further, my brother?

S: No, thank you.

I am Latwii, and we thank you, my brother. Is there another query?

C: If it is appropriate, could you elaborate and possibly help me understand the experience and the entity that is encountered by my friend W and I at the end of my road, which appeared to be living in my car at the time?

I am Latwii. My brother, we have been waiting for this query. We have scanned this instrument's mind, knowing that it does not mind, and have wondered if we would have this opportunity. We find this information both interesting, harmless and somewhat unusual within your illusion, therefore we shall attempt to speak, if this instrument is able to relay those concepts which we offer it, for as we have said this is a quite fascinating and unusual situation.

The entities of which you speak are indeed within your reality somewhat more than a thought form, as you would call them. They are a type of pattern of livingness which is neither a creature of your second nor of your third-density illusion. They are a possibility which becomes probable when a certain set of circumstances is achieved. This set of circumstances is that which we may have some difficulty in describing.

Within your illusion, time, as you know it, and that which you call space, move at a certain rhythm set in order that the third-density illusion may take on the character which you know as real. When there is a certain mismatching of that which you call time within an area that you know of as space that has been brought about, in this case by the condition not only of your automotive vehicle, but of your own frames of minds as well, and by certain points of instreaming energy within the location of your domicile, there may be transferred to your physical illusion entities of a playful and somewhat obnoxious nature in your way of thinking, from what you would call the lower astral planes, and these entities take up their residence in a form which they are able to construct from all of the patterns of energy of the foregoing parameters which we mentioned.

Thus, they find a residence within an environment which is most closely associated with their own patterns of expression upon the lower astral planes, and are on what you might call a vacation, skipping about your illusion in a way which is most perplexing and somewhat frightening to you, but most joyful and carefree to them. It is not likely that they shall be able to maintain their existence within your illusion for a very significant portion of what you call time, for the conditions which allow their presence are most tenuous. Therefore, you may not expect further interference with the performance of those automotive vehicles in care in what you would call your future.

(The telephone rings.)

I am Latwii, and we were at the completion of our query and waited with amusement as this instrument remembered what it had forgotten *(i.e. to unplug the telephone)*.

May we answer further, my brother?

C: No, thank you.

I am Latwii, and we thank you, my brother. Is there another query?

J: Yes, Latwii, this is J. I fell asleep there for a minute. Sorry about that, but my question is, tonight at the beginning of our meeting here with you, were you with me for a moment? Did you try to speak through me? I felt like you were, and at the end I wasn't quite sure what to do.

I am Latwii, and we greet you, my sister, in joy—ah.

(Laughter from those present.)

And we may suggest that we have been with each within this circle for the purpose of the aiding in the deepening of the meditative state. We do not intrude upon any potential instrument's consciousness by forcing an instrument to speak before it has clearly chosen that service and has been trained, shall we say, in some degree. We do not feel it is appropriate to do this for any new instrument, for we cherish each instrument and each opportunity to speak through yet another instrument and wish this opportunity to be given its fullest range of freedom of choice in order that the one serving as instrument may with as much confidence and assurance as possible begin that service with such as its foundation. To do otherwise would be asking overmuch of one which in its part desires to serve, yet in its mind knows nothing of how to do so.

May we answer further, my sister?

J: No, I understand. Thank you.

I am Latwii, and we thank you, my sister. Is there another query?

Carla: Well, before you go, old chap, do you have any suggestions, since we're on the subject, of how I might improve the training techniques for new channels?

I am Latwii, and am aware of your query, my sister. Ahh, now let us see. Reviewing all those venerable techniques of the masters of the past … three raps to the skull—no, that will not do. Silence—too, too perplexing. Written instructions—too boring. My sister, we are at a loss—it seems you do an adequate job. Seriously, now …

Carla: Is that Sirius the star or … oh, never mind!

… we do believe that we have been able to make somewhat of a breakthrough with this instrument this evening, and we ask your pardon for somewhat blowing its circuits.

(Laughter)

We find that your techniques are most appropriate, my sister, and will find their own additions as the opportunity to exercise them makes itself available to you.

May we answer in any further detail, my sister?

Carla: Oh, no—that'll be fine. If you think of anything, just drop me a paper napkin with the instructions on it.

I am Latwii, and we shall do so, my sister, and then you may guess who is coming to dinner.

Carla: *(Laughing)* Thank you.

Is there another query?

(Pause)

I am Latwii. We join with you in the appreciation of the sounds of your evening, and we thank each of you for inviting our presence to join you on such an evening and with such a seeking that we are aware of within this group is a joy that we cannot describe. We appreciate with you the silence between sounds, the difficulty in seeking the darkness and the light, and the joy in coming together with those of like minds to rejoice in the presence of the One that makes Itself known in each. We are those of Latwii, and we leave each of you in that joy, in that love, in that light, and in the peace of unity. Adonai, my friends. Adonai vasu borragus. ❧

Sunday Meditation
July 27, 1986

Group question: From J. It is: "There is a quote from the session of 15 June, 1986 from L/Leema as follows: 'The critical mass for achieving fourth density as a group is nearly reached.'

A) Expand, i.e. quantify, 'nearly,' time frame, etc.

B) How large is the group? Total population, harvestable entities, non-harvestable entities?

C) How does this affect planetary geological shifts?

D) Specifically, what should we do to maximize the harvest? What is the most important work that light workers can do at this time to maximize the harvest?"

(Carla channeling)

I am L/Leema, and I greet you, my friends, in the love and in the light of the one infinite Creator. It is our great privilege and blessing to be with you this evening and we thank you for calling us to your group.

You would wish to know more about a statement that we have made to the effect that the critical mass for harvest has been nearly reached. We are pleased to share with you what we can. Needless to say, there are those things which we are not able to share with you due to the Law of Free Will. What we have to offer, we offer with hope that you will, as always, assume our opinion to be just that, and in no way given the cachet of divine or irristible knowledge.

We would first extricate the question of the harvest of souls from an inevitable link with massive topographical changes which shall occur in what your geologists call the tectonic plate structure of your planet. It is understandable that you should link the many disasters which have been predicted by so many sources and the phenomenon of harvest which likewise has been predicted by so many sources. There is a relationship, and yet it is not a compelling one, and the relationship is one of interest more for its synchronicity than for its inevitability.

The relationship is one of cause and effect in that the thinking of the consciousness of this planetary sphere has been over a period of your time much confused. There has been hostility and anger amongst your people on a nearly steady-state basis for all of your modern, shall we say, time, and by that we mean that period of your time which is covered by written record. This has caused within your Earth a disease, a pressure, and what you may think of as a heat or fever which must be cooled. The venting of this energy must take place in some manner, and there are those, both in your inner planes and in your outer planes, which have for some time been attempting to withhold the time of greatest trauma to the planet until an area of space can be cleared in which the negative emissions following such a venting of negative energy may be consumed by those who prefer negative energy so that the free will of others in your celestial neighborhood shall not be abridged.

It is, it seems, among your people a matter of great interest to know precisely when this occurrence shall transpire. We note that it is as much a process as an occurrence, and has already begun to some extent. We are not at this time aware of a state of readiness for this event amongst those who are attempting to aid in the name of those whose free will would be abridged. Therefore, we would project the positive hope and faith that the greater magnitude of this event shall be between two and three decades of your time in coming.

It is to be noted in this regard that this does not signal the arrival of the so-called new age or fourth density. It is important, we feel, to note this, for many have linked the two as cause and effect whereas to the best of our understanding there is no direct cause and effect relationship—they are concomitant events or processes.

We feel that this perhaps frees us to speak about the true question, which is the coming of the fourth density. As we have said, your planet vibrates already in fourth density and the time does indeed draw near for entities with fourth-density physical vehicles to begin incarnating upon the level of physical manifestation. Indeed, many among your small children have incarnated with what you may call the double body of third density and fourth density, and by and large this hybrid doubly activated physical manifestation shall continue for some time in your probable future, the time extending somewhere between one and eight centuries.

You will note that we cannot pin down time. Firstly, we find it difficult to quantize that which occurs in time/space, for quantization is a space/time concept. Secondly, we cannot predict what entities in free will will accomplish or fail to accomplish during any very lengthy time period. It is not wise to make assumptions unless one has been given clear vision, and although we have opinions, they range more towards the probabilities involved than any specific knowledge. We would be less than acceptable teachers were we to offer to you that which even we know to be unsubstantiated opinion. All that we say is opinion, but we trust, substantiated opinion.

Therefore, my friends, the time frame for those in third-density physical vehicles attempting to graduate is perhaps as short as three decades, perhaps as long as fifteen. It depends upon how many entities are able to use increasing quantities of fourth-density light vibration, for as we said, this movement into the new fourth-density area of space/time which vibrates in a new fashion shall be one which is gradual and which takes much of your time to occur fully.

However, we feel that it is safe to recommend that each entity which has decided to attempt to increase the rate of spiritual, mental and emotional evolvement behave as if this were the last chance to achieve a harvestable vibration, for in that way you shall give to your effort all that it deserves.

Indeed, my friends, this is the only reason that the concept of reincarnation was removed from what you term the Christian church and its teachings. It was recognized that there was a human characteristic known as procrastination. It was recognized that a harvestable amount of love would take an utmost effort over several or perhaps many incarnations, therefore, if each entity who was within this structure believed that there was only one chance to achieve love, each entity would attempt with every fiber of his being to do so. Now, each of you has many incarnations already finished, and yet you know that you are here either to graduate or to help with graduation.

And if you are a wanderer, helping with graduation, yet also you must graduate, for you have put yourself within the physical vehicle in an incarnational experience and it is as much your duty as a naturalized citizen of your Earth to achieve harvest as it is any other person. Never think that wanderers are necessarily missionaries who may go home. My friends, you are now natives of Earth until you have graduated again to your native density. Therefore, under no circumstance assume that the lessons of love are not those which must be learned by you.

The question of the numbers of entities to be harvested and the number not harvested comes before those of the Confederation frequently and we hasten to remind each that because of free will, the numbers can only be approximate. Approximately eight to nine percent of your population at this time, that is, somewhere in the area of 360 million people—this instrument is telling us we may have slipped a digit. We do not scan that phrase, however, we understand percentage and that is percentage—may already be harvested, given that between this reading and the event of each entity's leaving incarnational experience and entering into the light, each entity remains at harvestable levels of service to others or service to self.

In addition, there are many, many entities who although they are aware that their lives in incarnation may not be very long, are willing and eager to make one more attempt to graduate. Thus, you have being born at this time many strong and sometimes disruptive entities who are old souls desperately in search of the lifting of a veil which is felt but not understood. As children, they will sometimes seem older, sometimes incredibly young, but always strong, willful and very much each his own person. These entities will polarize with the determination of steam rollers, and it should be an interesting generation upon your planet, interesting alike for those who bear them and for them themselves.

It is completely unknown, and, shall we say, even odds, that all of these entities shall or shall not graduate, therefore we give no percentage, but only advise each who considers the bearing of children that it is a service to many an old soul, and, in addition, a service to those pioneers of fourth-density vibration that shall be the nucleus of the beginning of fourth density on this planet, that being a positive fourth density as already determined by the fact that you are very near critical mass for a harvest.

Now we reach the heart of the question. When something achieves a critical mass, a given reaction begins. In this case, the mass necessary to be reached has as its desired result the formation of a social memory complex. An approximate ten percent of a population able to entrain vibrations to fourth-density levels within the self, and, moreover, able and willing to form a larger self and offering the self to the group identity are necessary.

We do not mean to suggest that the other entities hitherto unharvestable shall then be positively harvestable, for each entity chooses its own time of harvest and neither darkness or light shall be thrust upon any third-density entity any more than the darkness and the light shall be released from any entity in sixth density. However, what makes this planet remain populated by its natives of third density in the next density is this critical mass of natives which are able to form the nucleus of that group which then shall become the Earth, as you call it, social memory complex.

We do not mean to suggest that Earth has a name you do not know, although we call it Sorrows and others have called it many other things. It is a semantical thing to name a vibration or cluster of vibrations, and there is a vibration Earth which should be offered irrevocably should a native population from another system choose this planetary sphere for its fourth-density experience in the absence of a critical mass of native fourth-density entities.

Having said the above, it seems only logical to assume that each wishes to know what is best to do to create a harvestable condition within oneself and to manifest on behalf of others and for other's choice if they wish it, a way of suggesting the search for harvestability in each.

Now you know, my friends, that we have again and again suggested that you meditate. Meditation is not blank and lifeless in nature, but rather is a medium for transformation, enlivening struggle for clarity, centering, balancing, searching out from within the self those things which lie behind the veil of consciousness and yet are within the deep mind. We cannot speak to any excess about the importance of meditation. In this regard, it is interesting to gaze upon what you call the Lord's Prayer, with which this instrument opens each meditation meeting of this light group. As each of you says this, what this instrument would call ancient prayer, there are energies moving within which may or may not be felt be each. That is because it is true prayer and we would offer to you our understanding of the basic pattern of meditation or prayer.

The first action is a turning in praise, a statement that the Creator is hallowed, honored, set aside and venerated. As each is the Creator, this is the highest self-acceptance possible.

The second request is for authority to be given to those things of the Creator which are desired by, shall we say, the more polarized of outlook. When one says, "Thy kingdom come, Thy will be done on earth as it is in heaven," one requests that the little self listen to the greater self. It is an acknowledgment that humankind is not immune to mistakes or folly and a further acknowledgment of faith in a higher and more informed way of being, and further an affirmation that this way of being is knowable and may be revealed within each seeker's life.

There is a request for the so-called daily bread. Notice that the request is minimal. Within this request is an unspoken emphasis on demand. Note that there is no shame in asking for what you wish, for anything that you wish, as long as it is the will of the Creator, or to put it in more personal terms, the higher self.

Indeed, if one examines the portion of the holy book you call the Bible in which this passage occurs, you will find the parable of the man who knocks upon his neighbor's door in the middle of the sleeping period, in your nighttime, demanding food for a guest which has unexpectedly come. The neighbor does not wish to get up and answer the door, and yet because of the shameless continuing of the knocking upon the door, eventually the neighbor gets up and gives the host anything and everything that he needs.

This is the nature of that portion of yourself which you bring to meditation. There are things troubling you. Accept yourself in your troubled mode, and ask as you go into meditation that every load be dropped from you. Do not phrase it in pretty words, but speak clearly. And as you go into silence, expect, for you have demanded, that you shall be given that which you need wherewith to cause those burdens to be acceptable. It is not that the Creator does things for one who is honest about needs; it is that the Creator does things with the one who is in honest need and asks. Seek and you shall find is a true and succinct statement of this principle.

The fourth request is that each entity may be forgiven for being imperfect, just as each entity shall forgive any errors or debts made against him by others. This is simple bargaining. It is a simplistic way of saying, "Has it ever occurred to you seekers that you are all one, and that you have the power of forgiveness for all those about you, just as you feel the Creator has the power to forgive you?" You see, my friends, you are the judge of everyone you meet, and insofar as you hold people guilty, there is difficulty for that person as well as for you, and before you may remove this difficulty …

(Side one of tape ends.)

(Carla channeling)

I am L/Leema, and again we shall attempt to conclude this somewhat long-winded peroration. We thank you for your patience.

As it is written in the same holy work from which we discussed the Lord's prayer, the teacher known to you as Jesus instructed entities to be innocent as doves and wily as serpents. It is most important to be both of these things: innocent, loving, joyous, courageous and foolhardy; and at the same time, ruthless inspectors of the self to discriminate between those means which are acceptable to achieve an end and those ends which are unacceptable to achieve an end. For, my friends, it is our fixed opinion that no end justifies improper means. This is the area of temptation. Most of the temptation among your peoples has to do with what you call ego and what is in fact a complex of attitudes concerning the self with regard to other entities, to groups of other entities, and to large divisions such as nation states which have been useful and in the future shall be less than useful tools for learning.

Each of these five points are part of a pattern of attitudes which make up a framework for meditation. There is 1) a basic attitude of faith, 2) of praise, 3) of unashamed statements of needs, of conversation, in fact, 4) a request to be forgiven as one forgives and 5) a recognizing of the presence of temptation and of the strong probability that even though an entity may not know of any error, yet nevertheless, there may well have been in each entity's recent past an accumulation of unknown errors which are deliberately affirmed as forgiven.

So, there is 1) declaration of self and 2) its needs, 3) a recognition of the inevitable answer to each need, 4) a praise for existence and 5) for the source of consciousness which in some becomes a kind of cleansing that prepares an entity for the silence, for in the silence, you do not pose questions, but listen for inspiration. Indeed, sometimes the greatest result of meditation is a refining of the proper questions.

The greatest work that any can do at this time to maximize the potential for critical mass being achieved by harvest is, then, the personal dedication to the life of a contemplative who is also connected vitally with the environment with which he lives. That is, once gifts have been given to the seeker, it is then its responsibility to manifest those gifts in actions, in thoughts, and in intentions, not necessarily by dramatic efforts such as becoming a pilgrim upon a dusty path, for there are many, many entities whose lives have touched hundreds or thousands of people by the simple beauty of their presence. There are those who have chosen to be the mothers and fathers of very needful souls, and who have generated more positivity and light for the planetary consciousness by this activity, humble though it may seem, as the mother and father are doing the dishes, than the entrepreneur who goes upon the road feeling that it has found *the* answer.

Yes—those who speak to many, many people may well give their message to many, but that message, if impure, will slide off the back of those who are seeking a pure enough truth to be harvestable. Therefore, never judge yourself as not manifesting that which you have learned in meditation because you are not doing something dramatic. Remember that each person is the Creator and that you will do that which is give you by your higher self either well or poorly. If you do something poorly, you will do it again and again until you get it correct. This is the nature of the higher self's method of providing the catalyst which has been decided upon prior to incarnation.

However, take yourselves seriously, my friends, seriously enough to be serious about joy, to be serious about peace, to be serious about love. We hope that you may discover the joy that lies within tears and sorrow when one has the knowledge of greater horizons and greater cycles, that each one may experience the peace within difficult times as one discovers that one is not alone, but may share each burden, the love which is not cloying or sentimental, but creative and transformative, in other words, the state of divine unrest which is the ceaseless changing reality, shall we say, of one who is on the path and striving to realize Oneness with the infinite Creator. Never let the knowledge of your own seeming imperfections cause you to be cynical about your divinity or the importance of your self-realization of it. Look for it in yourself, not just in other people.

In conclusion, we shall say to those who are already light workers upon the path that in a more intensive learning situation it is most helpful first to achieve the ability to be solitary happily and then to work towards the sharing of your path with at least one other person. In the majority of cases, this one other person is the mate, and it was for this reason that so many entities have attributed in all honesty their achievements to the love of the mate, for, indeed, two who seek together shall always be more balanced than one who seeks alone.

And to go further, perhaps you have wondered why there is an almost unignorable call to live in community with others at this time, and, indeed, for two of your millennia? My friends, this is due to the nascent art to create the social memory complex, and it is again a very helpful mode to achieve harmoniously. It is very difficult for entities who have finally learned to be self-reliant, shall we say, to then make what seems to be a backward turn towards reliance upon others, and yet it is a celebration of the unity of oneself with others which impels sensitive entities towards a communal life. More hands mean more potential. More hearts and minds working in unison towards the same desire mean that each prayer, each praise, each thanksgiving is more powerful and holds more promise to those who are prayed for, who are loved, and for whom each community wishes to do its work.

We recommend contemplation of that which we have said before further questions are asked, as this is a large subject and we have compressed much material due to the limitations upon this instrument's speaking and your hearing and—this instrument just flashed to us in mind—her bottom. Therefore, we shall at this time wish you largely a more and more successful attempt to discipline the self to meditation, a recommendation that you observe the pattern with which you enter meditation, and a recommendation further, that you cultivate within yourselves a faith in the power of meditation and a hope, a knowledge, shall we say, of the promise which we suggest meditation and prayer and contemplation hold for you.

We are your brothers and sisters of L/Leema, and consider it a great honor to be asked to join you. Our blessings upon each of you, our love and the Creator's go with you. We leave you in all that there is, the love and the manifestation of love of the one infinite Love, which is the Creator. Adonai, my friends. Adonai vasu borragus. ❧

L/L Research

Sunday Meditation
August 10, 1986

(Jim channeling)

I am Hatonn, and I greet you, my friends, in the love and in the light of our infinite Creator. We are most honored to be asked to join your group this evening. Your seeking and desire to know the nature of your movement into unity with the one Creator is that which has drawn us to you this evening. We are privileged to be able to join you, for in sharing our humble experiences with you, do we also progress upon the same path which you tread. As we speak to you this evening, please be aware that we offer opinions and our experiences which are those of brothers and sisters who are like you, fallible and yet [who] desire to serve. Take that which has meaning for you and leave that which does not ring true without the backward glance. We do not wish to place any stumbling block upon your path.

This evening we have observed the questions and comments concerning the path of the seeker which attempts to serve others and to radiate the light of the one Creator to those about it. We have observed that in your discussion and in your concerns, there is the noting of those instances in the experience of any seeker which seem of a negative nature and which seem to provide obstacles, difficulties and deterrents to the continuation of the positive seeking.

We might add our comments to those which we have listened [to] this evening, for each seeker that sets out upon the journey of consciously determining that which is useful and that which is not for the pursuing of this journey is one which shall experience a wondrous adventure. The desire to know the nature of the creation in which you find yourselves and the desire to know the nature of the life force which makes you what you are and which propels you through this creation is that desire which you shall draw upon constantly as you make your journey day by day and moment by moment. This desire, then, is the central force through which you find your movement made possible.

As you observe the events within your life pattern unfolding, you will discover that some seem more helpful than others. This is due to that nature which is unique to you. You have the previous incarnational experiences brought with you into this experience, a collection of abilities, attitudes and interests which you have carefully gathered as those of significance through previous experience. These, then, are that with which you begin this incarnation and that which is the garden, shall we say, into which the seeds of your desire are sown and are grown according to the purity of the intentions that you focus this desire through.

Thus, you draw unto yourselves those experiences which shall provide you with the opportunities that you seek. These opportunities provide you the laboratory, shall we say, in which the lessons that you have designed for yourself may be attempted. The opportunities that form the fabric of your daily existence are of a variety of kinds, each colored by your desire to know more and more of the nature of yourself, the creation about you, and your movement through it. Each experience, then, provides what we might call a holographic miniature in which, if the intention and attention is focused finely enough, one can see the entire pattern of the incarnation unfolding within one's response to any situation.

As you note your own spontaneous and unrehearsed responses to those events in your daily round of activities, you will begin to note the various biases and attitudes with which you are currently armed, shall we say, for want of a better term. These attitudes and biases then form the beginning of your understanding of yourself. If you are able in the quiet moments of your daily round of activities to contemplate and meditate upon the manner in which you respond to those events placed before you, you begin to see a picture not only of your current being, as you manifest it in this incarnation, but also the potential which your attitudes and biases call to you.

Thus, if one can look at the honest and unreserved responses that become the pattern or nature of one's current being, one may without judgment, then, work with each in order that each might find its natural balance, and the experience then becomes broadening so that the point of viewing expands. What was once of a narrow focus, with contemplative and meditative attention begins to expand its boundaries as various attitudes and perceptions find a wider frame of reference within one's being.

For example, if one discovers within the being an anger or frustration, shall we say, that surfaces when one is unable to make its mark upon the world and the events in it in a fashion that is of one's own design, then one may see that there is a bias of frustration and disharmony that emanates frequently as a portion of the being when the events of the world do not fall in such and such a fashion. One might note other facets of being, such as impatience and the desire to control people and events, as being corollaries to the basic anger and frustration. If one is able to look without emotion and judgment upon this basic bias or distortion of anger and its corollary attributes, one may begin to discover the potential that is shut up within one's being by the presence of that known as anger.

It may be, for example, that an entity wishes to learn more of compassion, more of acceptance, and more of forgiveness, and wishes to place these concepts more firmly within the true self, that which you may call the soul. This may be done by programming the seeming opposite attribute within the incarnation in order to provide opportunity after opportunity after opportunity, one upon the other for the self to experience the lack of love, the lack of forgiveness, the lack of acceptance, and these are terms which describe that which you call anger, frustration, control and so forth.

Thus, by finding these attributes within the incarnational pattern, one may through conscious and non-judgmental study of the self become aware that in each release of anger there is the potential to accept, to love, to show mercy, and to have patience. As this becomes apparent, one then notes with more and more frequency and accuracy those moments in which this lesson is being offered. And as one is able to be more aware of the root or primary cause and potential set up by the expression of anger, then one is able to take advantage, shall we say, of that opportunity, and in a fashion to transmute or transform the situation in which anger might normally be generated, and instead generate the loving acceptance which was the original intention and which was achieved by constructing the basic personality to respond in the manner called angry or frustrated.

This is one common and simple example of how the lessons of an incarnation may be set up or provided for before the incarnation by utilizing the full range of what you would call human emotions so that these emotions then become a connecting link, connecting the level of understanding which has been achieved in previous incarnations to the potential which now awaits each entity.

Thus, within the incarnational pattern, one may discover that within even the darkest and most dimly lit moments of one's experience, great treasures potentially await. It is often easy for the conscious seeker of truth to look upon those times that are full of joy, peace and new learning as those times in which the greatest growth within the soul occurs. However, we would suggest that the moments of seeming difficulty and trauma not be overlooked, for it is within such moments that one's fiber of being is truly tested and given the greatest of opportunities to expand in its scope and strength.

The moments of difficulty and disharmony, then, are those moments in which the spiritual strength, to use a general term, of an entity may receive the opportunity for further strengthening. This is also true of those moments in which one feels that there might be negative, as you would call them, influences moving in one's life patterns and providing obstacles that make further progress difficult. If one can see such situations as analogous to simply placing more weights upon the bar, which then can be lifted with that strength which each has to lift, then there is greater chance or opportunity for one's spiritual strength to be enhanced as one looks at difficulties not as that to be denied, but as that to be welcomed in joy as a more intensive opportunity to progress at even a quicker pace.

(Telephone rings.)

We shall pause.

(Pause)

I am Hatonn, and we wish to transmit this instrument's apologies for failing to unplug the device which records your conversations.

At this time, we would desire to complete our portion of this contact in order that our brothers and sisters of Latwii may provide their service of attempting to answer queries of those present. We have found the need to somewhat shorten the normal length of the contact for this instrument is functioning in a solitary fashion this evening and would benefit by a reservation of some energy for the service of those of Latwii. Again, we thank each present for requesting our humble service, and we look forward to future, as you would call them, gatherings of this group in which we may be honored once again to offer our thoughts upon the journey which we share with you. We are known to you as those of Hatonn. We shall leave you at this time in the love and in the light of the one infinite Creator. Adonai, my friends. Adonai.

(Jim channeling)

I am Latwii, and we greet you, my friends, in love and light. We have been waiting in the wings, so to speak, looking forward to this opportunity to offer our service to this group. We of Latwii are those who are presumptuous enough to attempt to answer queries. We, however, remind you as did our brothers and sisters of Hatonn that we are also most fallible, and do not wish to have our thoughts and opinions weighted overmuch in your estimation. Please do not hesitate to disregard any word or thought that does not feel right to you. With that disclaimer aside, may we ask if we might begin with a query?

A: Yes, Latwii, I have a question. I was wondering—I do not understand the mechanism that happens when you talk through the instrument. Why does the instrument become of less energy as time goes on? When you come through the instrument, do you not energize the instrument? Or do you take from the energy that is in the instrument? How does this work?

I am Latwii, and am aware of your query, my sister. In many cases an instrument such as this one may indeed feel energized and much replenished of energy when the session is complete. This particular instrument is somewhat hard-headed, however, and in order to provide the service of the vocal channel, needs to concentrate to a degree which exceeds that of other instruments that may be observed. The focus necessary for this instrument to transmit our thoughts without analyzing them as to their content is a focus that is somewhat difficult for this instrument, for it wishes no distortion of its transmissions that it can avoid and therefore attempts to focus in a precise manner to receive our thoughts which appear just as its own thoughts, yet, when spoken in a continuous fashion, do tend to become apparently discernible as other than this instrument's.

Thus, this particular instrument finds it somewhat wearing to serve both as an instrument for the opening message, shall we say, and for the question and answer portion of the meditation as well. As an instrument becomes more able to allow the channeling process to flow freely through it, there is less of the wearing effect, although it is somewhat wearing upon any entity to maintain one position for a length of time, seated an hour or so, as we have discovered amongst your peoples.

May we answer further, my sister?

A: No, that was very good. Thank you.

I am Latwii, and we thank you, my sister. Is there another query?

L: Yes, I have a question, Latwii. Concerning the subject matter of Maldek, the planet which is no longer present, did this have any effect upon our planet when its disappearance was brought about and did this effect—is it recorded within our own history?

I am Latwii, and we see a variety of possible responses to your query. We assume that the first level of interest concerns possible physical effects that may have been noted upon this planetary sphere when the planet known to you as Maldek was, shall we say, destroyed by the use of the nuclear and crystal-powered weapons of this population. The physical influence upon this particular sphere may be noted by geologists or perhaps archeologists who are able to correlate various levels of strata of the Earth composition in its surface.

There was at the time of the destruction of the planet known as Maldek a spewing of its, shall we say, particles throughout the local vicinity. Your planetary influence being within that vicinity, there was then the coating of some portions of your planet with a, shall we say, fine dust-like substance that may be noted by those who seek such explorations of the composition of your planet's surface. There was also within the local vicinity of the planet known as Maldek a vibration of waves which traveled great distances and did effect some harmonic resonance, shall we say, with neighboring planets, causing momentary shifts in magnetic fields so that the core structure of the neighboring planets was somewhat altered, though not to a degree that may be noticed by any measurements which your current technology of instruments could record.

The most notable influence of the destruction of the planet known as Maldek upon your own planet was that after the population of the planet known as Maldek had recovered consciousness of their very being, there having been the melding of consciousness into a, what has been called, "knot of fear" following the destruction of their planetary sphere, these entities then found the need to take up residence upon your third-density planet in forms which were not normally used or available to third-density intelligence.

Throughout succeeding eons of your time and planetary experience these entities formerly of Maldek have been able to move into your more normal third-density physical vehicle in order to continue their third-density experience and to more specifically achieve a balancing action within their own consciousness that they have found necessary as a result of their actions upon their home planet which resulted in its destruction.

Thus, you may discover many of these entities in …

(Side one of tape ends.)

(Jim channeling)

I am Latwii, and am again with this instrument. To continue our response. Thus, these entities have found the need to reproduce the circumstances which upon their home planet resulted in its destruction in order that the balancing action may be achieved and the harmonious resolution of those energies set in motion long ages ago might find a more harmonious result.

May we answer further, my brother?

L: *(Inaudible)*.

I am Latwii, and we thank you, my brother. Is there another query?

A: Yes, I have a question which *(inaudible)* but there's been so much said that I need to review a lot of things to get straight in my mind. When we get up against an opposition in our life—and is the opposition there to tell us that we are going the wrong road, or is the opposition there to tell us to work harder at what we are doing to gain strength, to, perhaps—I'm not sure of, but sometimes when I seem to hit a brick wall, so to speak, in a certain area, I feel that perhaps I'm going down the wrong road, and it's saying, "Let's reevaluate this, is this what you really want?" Am I seeing this correctly or not?

I am Latwii, and am aware of your query, my sister. Our brothers and sisters of Hatonn were, in their way of speaking, speaking to the general run of events, the general outline which one may observe within the life pattern. When one looks at any specific instance, however, one may need to apply other concepts. This is to say that those assumptions which you have made may each be correct, each in its own time.

There is a great variety of lessons and messages that are available in any one situation. What will be most perceivable by you at any particular moment is determined by your needs at that moment. In general, it is quite helpful to look at any difficulty or opposition as an opportunity to learn a more intensive lesson. However, this lesson may be one which says to you, "Proceed with greater intention and vigor," or it may be that the message is to take another path which is more appropriate. The message may also say that you may take this path if you choose and learn what it has to teach you.

The means by which you decide what any situation has to offer you and the message which is most appropriate is a means which we might suggest achieving through the meditative or contemplative state of being in which you take that confusion that you feel with you into the meditation or the contemplation, study with the mind as well as can be studied that which stands before you, understand what is possible with the mind, then release that which is described in intellectual terms and allow only the desire to know what is most appropriate for you to remain. And allow that desire, then, to draw to you the inspiration, the hunch, the intuition, that still, small voice which speaks when spoken to and listened to.

In this way you will find, as you know, the path opens more fully and freely in whatever direction may be most appropriate for your feet to tread. Oftentimes it will be as you have suspected; other times it may be a great surprise. Listen always to that voice within.

May we answer you further, my sister?

A: No, you do a very good job. Thank you.

I am Latwii, and we thank you once again, my sister. Is there another query?

L: Yes, I have another question. Do we, speaking as an individual, when one gives thought to something that they desire to have manifested, is the individual in charge of, completely, the manifestation of that thought, or are there other entities or guardians or divine intervention that permits or does not permit the eventual manifestation of this or that particular thought?

I am Latwii. Again we find that simple response is not possible to this query, for there are many, many possibilities. The entity who attempts to form through thought an event or experience or situation that shall be a portion of its future experience, as you would call it, may be joined by others of its own groupings, that is, the family, the friends, the seekers of like mind, and this grouping then may focus its attention upon the same pattern of thought and aid in bringing this pattern into manifestation.

There are, as you have described, entities of an unseen nature which also observe the patterns of one's incarnation and attempt to guide and to protect where possible. You know many of these entities as angelic presences, as those called guides, as the quality known as the higher self or oversoul, as well. Each of these may in conjunction with your thought-forming process work to aid this thought in its formation in the physical reality.

There may, however, be a wider point of view available to these guardian entities so that possibilities for your reconsideration of this choice of pattern may be presented which will give you then the opportunity to decide whether to pursue with greater or lesser vigor that pattern of thought which you have begun to formulate. There may be events within your own subconscious mind programmed preincarnatively which move in patterns which seem to negate efforts to form thoughts of such and such a pattern in order that lessons of, shall we say, another nature may occur.

We hesitate to give further examples of the various possibilities and probabilities that affect whether or not a thought may eventually be formed within your life pattern, for the range of possibilities is so great as to lend more confusion than clarity to this very, very wide field of study. For, indeed, all that you experience within your incarnational pattern is a product of your own thinking, whether that thinking be conscious or unconscious, whether that thinking be done during the incarnation or previous to the incarnation, for it is the power of the mind to generate thoughts that, when focused upon for a long enough period of what you call time or experience, that these thoughts then become manifest within your life pattern to provide glorious opportunities for learning or for serving. Thus, all you experience is a product of thought.

May we answer further, my brother?

L: Thank you. Your response has been most helpful. I have no other question.

I am Latwii, and we thank you once again, my brother. Is there another query?

(Pause)

I am Latwii. It seems that we have exhausted the queries somewhat before we have exhausted this instrument. We wish to extend our heartfelt gratitude to each for allowing our presence and for inviting our humble opinions on those matters which are of interest to you in your journey of seeking. We shall also look forward to future sessions with this group as we enjoy very much the vibrations generated by those present this evening. We are known to you as those of Latwii. We shall leave you, my friends, at this time in the one glorious light and the ever-present love of the one infinite Creator. We are those of Latwii. Adonai vasu borragus. ✿

Sunday Meditation
August 31, 1986

(Carla channeling)

I am Latwii, and I greet you, my friends, in the love and in the light of the one infinite Creator. We are very happy to be here tonight. We are very happy to be speaking through this channel. We have not been able to use this channel for some time, as we usually work with questions and answers, but we decided to work with this channel this evening, for the call of your group lies within our vibratory range of ability to respond and we are most privileged to be able to be with you.

We send our blessings among you and hope that you may find a few words worth your while in what we have to say, mixed in with the many foolish ones. We urge each of you to use all discrimination and take nothing as if it were given to you by an authority. For though we have experienced more, there is no guarantee that we have made our deductions properly. We merely share our experiences as brothers and sisters of you all.

My friends, let us review what little we know, and find if we feel that it is enough. Perhaps we would all agree that we know that that which is seen is transient. We would perhaps agree that there is more than chance to the universe, its creation, administration, and creative embroidery. Perhaps we would all agree that the most important force in each personal life experience has been love, the love that creates and the love that destroys, the love that gives and the love that takes.

Perhaps we would agree that all of us are bound by the bond of being fellow travelers, for unlike many, we have not been satisfied with that which we can see and experience with our senses in the physical sense, but wish always to push our knowledge of a deeper reality a little further, just as your scientists have continued looking deeper into your cosmic space, though all they find is more galaxies. Just as your aeronautical engineers have pressed further and further against the envelope of the planetary atmosphere until man now can escape it, so there is a certain kind of seeker who is stubbornly convinced that there is something more.

Now, my friends, the rest is speculation. Indeed, all that we have assumed is speculation, but it is perhaps a speculation that all can agree upon. We wish you to understand that we understand—if we may use such a term—that none of us is dealing with a comfortable thing when we deal with that for which we seek. We know there are no definitive answers. We know that all of your experience will be processed subjectively, and that such events in your life as joy, peace, exuberance and radiance will be gifts.

You see, my friends, there is a mechanical science by which one may replicate mental and physical conditions so that states of mind are achieved which are the vibration in what you call your alpha range, giving you the feelings of peace and joy and freedom. We, however, are not interested in teaching you how to achieve an empty state of mind. We are interested in those who wish to make a conscious decision concerning the speed with which each wishes to progress in a spiritual fashion.

The spiritual transformation of humankind upon your planet is our area of interest and service, and if we can encourage any by what we have said, then are we most pleased, for in helping you, we ourselves find that we are helped a great deal as we become more and more knowledgeable of how to help, of what helps, and of how to avoid infringing upon your free will, my friends. For you see, all of this choice, including the choosing of making the choice, is yours, not ours. You are here in freedom, and you are no man's slave and we are but as you—if you would call us who are souls, men, that is acceptable.

We wish to verify for you to the best of our experience, which is considerably larger than your own, that that which you suspect is there, that which lies beyond the envelope of known things is indeed a finer illusion, more filled with light, and far more desirable than the state of non-choice which many of your brothers and sisters have chosen, "Yes," they seem to say, "I know I must wake up someday and think about life and death and who I am and what the truth is, but not today, because you only go around once in life and you have to grab some gusto."

My friends, we have looked throughout your culture for this gusto, but we have not been able to find an objective reference, and can only assume that your peoples, even in going for the gusto, are indeed searching for that which is called love. Nevertheless, we applaud you for attempting to make a conscious choice and to continue making choices regarding not only what you think, but what you do about what you think.

We would encourage you to step back from the feeling of any urgency regarding choice, and know that in choosing to meditate, in choosing to seek, in choosing to find the polarity of service to others, you have sown seeds that will take some time to grow. We do not use time in the planetary sense, but in the cosmic sense. It will take you millions of years to be harvestable to the Creator. It is a joyful journey and you have been on it for some time.

Thus, do not allow yourself to be full of a feeling of inner pressure regarding what you should or should not be doing in order to seek more efficiently or more quickly. Rely upon your own purity of intention and pray, indeed, for a continuation of that intention, for as you desire, so you shall have.

(Pause)

Forgive us for pausing for so long, but we became interested in the energy in this group. It is quite fascinating to us. As you know, we are most interested in the various colors of the subplanes of your density, and the halo about each person in your circle makes a beautiful necklace of many colors. We hope that you may, during this communication, realize that you are indeed one as you sit and seek and listen to our sometimes foolish words, for we hear many requests which we cannot answer all of. Yet in your diversity of needs, you are all one, one harmony, one chord of being, one consciousness to love and to serve. And as you love and serve, you shall be loved and you shall be served.

We would throw in for the entity which may need this at this time that the working place is as much an area under one's control as any other, in that the consciousness of love, sought most earnestly and persistently, can transform and has and will transform any situation. Again, that which you seek, you will create for yourself.

Now, we will not ask you to have a ten minute quiz, but we will review what we have said. Pardon us for a bad sense of humor, but it has been a long time since we were able to talk through this instrument, and this instrument is much more fun than the one known as Jim, due to the fact that the one known as Jim always wants to get things exactly right. This instrument is a little more loose—we use the word advisedly.

But, indeed, we do wish, my friends, to go back and view a few home truths. There is one original Thought, the thought of love. We know that that thought creates and destroys, and that destruction is another name for transformation. We each feel that we know that we are a continuing consciousness that was before the world began and shall be after this planet is no more. Indeed, much of our planetary vibration is no more already. And yet, we persist, being longer lived than rock, for we are consciousness.

We know that we bring this consciousness to bear upon a very heavy illusion, and yet, through this illusion of experience, we slowly learn and begin to realize that we have control over our incarnations, that we may choose not only what we wish to learn, but how quickly we wish to learn it.

The key to this learning is the seating of experience in meditation. We urge an attempt to meditate daily. Above all, we urge you to laugh and love generously. Ah, my friends, if you only could see that you love but yourself, no matter where that love is turned, it would be easy for you.

At this time we would request a group retuning, and then we shall transfer in order that we may answer whatever questions you may have the need to ask. We leave this instrument in love and light. We are known to you as those of Latwii.

(The group retunes by singing together several times, "Row, Row, Row Your Boat.")

(Jim channeling)

I am Latwii, and greet you again, my friends, in love and light. We are very happy to be able to continue our service this evening with an attempt to answer those queries which you may have upon your minds. Without further delay, then, may we attempt such a query at this time?

A: Yes, I have a question. As we grow more spiritual, is it advisable to desire the things that we want, or is it best to just wake up each day and say, "Thy will be done," and not mind. Do we have to desire in order for situations to come to us that we need to learn?

I am Latwii, and am aware of your query, my sister. There is, in the deeper sense, that which you have preincarnatively programmed, shall we say, for your incarnational experience. There are times during your incarnation during which you will be more aware of those patterns and opportunities that you have provided for yourself. It is helpful if one can balance the individual desire to learn and to serve others with the fruits of that learning with a total surrender to the knowledge that that which is appropriate for you will be brought to you.

Thus, in your desires of a personal nature, if you can build upon the simplest level of desire, that is, to be made aware of what is appropriate for you at that time, that which is appropriate may find an easier entry into your conscious perceptions.

It is a natural function of the conscious mind which seeks the keys to its own evolution to think that this or that knowledge, function, lesson or service might be helpful in the overall growth of the entity, and, indeed, in many cases through such desires one becomes aware of the larger pattern of one's existence. Yet, if one is dedicated to a certain path or outcome for any action, that dedication and desire of a strong nature for such an outcome may hinder the more appropriate pattern of experience.

Thus, to desire is helpful, if the desire can be general, and the surrender of the self as complete as possible, and if there can be the lack of dedication to a certain outcome.

May we answer in any further way, my sister?

A: No, you answered very beautifully. Thank you.

I am Latwii, and we thank you, my sister. Is there another query?

Carla: Well, if everyone's going to be quiet, I'll put one in from J. I believe he wanted to know about the historical Israel and whether it had a part to play, and if so, what part in what it prophesied for itself as Armageddon or the last days or the change of the cycle or the planetary change or whatever it's supposed to be a part of.

I am Latwii, and am aware of the query, my sister. We look upon this query with some concern that a full response would have the possibility of infringing upon the free will of many entities, the one known as J, especially. But we find that we may in a general sense make a response to this query.

The grouping of energies which has come to be known in your cultures as the nation of Israel is a grouping which has a certain flavor, shall we say, a certain purpose, and a certain means by which that purpose might be carried out. This is not to say that it is a purpose that is special only unto those known as the inhabitants of the nation of Israel, for each entity and grouping of entities upon your planetary surface offers its own character, purpose and methods to the total evolution of your planet and its population.

Those of the nation known to you as Israel—and may we say that not all that are a part of this nation are within its boundaries—are entities which have in a general sense found the need to incarnate in a situation which offers experience of a most intensive nature within this experience, that of forming what seems to be new out of that which is timeless and of great experience upon your planet, take this new formation and through it begin to express the possibility, the reconciliation of difficulties between entities, between religions, between nations, between beliefs.

This is not an easy task, my friends, for those within this general region have accepted the honor and duty of reenacting and continuing to enact patterns of energy that have had an ageless and difficult expression upon this planetary surface. This general region has been the focus of much, as you would call it, catalyst, for the humankind. It is within this region that many great teachers have walked and have found the need to express, each in his or her own way, the attempt to reconcile what may be best described as the lack of love within entities and states, beliefs and religions. For within the third-density experience as you know it, my friends, the basic lesson is that which is described by the word you know as love, that which is quite difficult to define, but which includes the ability to accept more of the creation without condition and to see it as the self and to see it as one thing, even though many portions of it present the illusion of separation, difference and disharmony.

Those of the nation and way of thinking of Israel have then taken upon themselves the opportunity and the duty of first experiencing these difficulties of reconciling seemingly opposite points of view. When the difficulties have been appreciated by a growing number of individuals, then this widened point of view that has found its place of birth within these individuals may begin to expand so that there is the general perception of the possibilities of reconciliation, of forgiving that which seems unforgivable, of accepting that which seems unacceptable, of loving that which seems unlovable.

When this opportunity, then, has been presented in a wider and more profound manner, not only within the boundaries of the nation known as Israel, but has continued its progress throughout the various populations, nations, religions [and] beliefs of the various portions of your planet, the opportunity for each person to experience the reconciliation of difficulties and disharmonies is increased, and the opportunity to learn those lessons of love are enhanced.

May we answer further, my sister?

Carla: Only in clearing up one point. You mentioned that not everybody that was of historical Israel was in Israel, and may I take it that you mean those souls from the planetary influence of Mars that Jehovah tinkered with genetically when they took third-density physical form here on the planet Earth are the ones that, regardless of whether they are geographically in Israel or elsewhere, that those are the people that you are talking about as Israel, in other words, the Jewish race rather than the Jewish nation Israel. Is that right?

I am Latwii, and, in general, my sister, this is correct, although we might also add that there are other entities that have through their experiences within this planet's influence joined themselves with these entities in the learning of lessons that were congruent enough to allow such a joining.

May we answer further, my sister?

Carla: Is there balanced karma between the entity that called itself Jehovah, then, and the third-density entities of Israel? Is that worked out now so that they can go on?

I am Latwii, and we must invoke the Law of Confusion, my sister, for to give an answer to this query would be to seem to judge a process which continues in its movements.

Carla: I see. Thank you.

I am Latwii, and we thank you, my sister. Is there another query?

T: Yes, I have a question. I'm reading a book now which *(inaudible)* and there are several things I'd like to ask you about. One of the basic things in the book that they talk about is "true knowledge," the only way to *know* things, to know anything, is through our feelings, through our emotions, and not really through the intellect. And, I guess everybody's had the experience with thinking they know something intellectually in reading it, and then have someone come along and push their button, and, zap, in that one instant they find out what they really believe as being how they react through their emotions. Could you comment on that, as far as knowing true knowledge through your feelings?

I am Latwii, and am aware of your query, my brother. We shall attempt a comment, although it is somewhat difficult to do so without the definition of certain terms, for various authors and authorities will choose terms which seem different in describing processes which are the same. We shall in our description take that which is called by this source "true knowledge" and define it as that which is true for a certain entity during a certain incarnation and not necessarily that which is ageless and timeless and that which any entity may refer to as a fundamental principle of the evolutionary process.

That which is true for an entity is that which reflects the preincarnative choices for learning and serving in as pure a manner as possible.

It is, in our humble opinion, generally correct that an entity may more clearly know what is true for it in its pattern of learning through that complex of the emotions, for this biasing or coloration of experience that is called emotions is that which is a direct line, shall we say, to the preincarnative choices, for the unconscious mind, preincarnatively programmed, will color a situation in such and such a fashion according to the preincarnative choice, and this coloration then becomes perceivable to the entity through that faculty of the emotions. It is in this way that the entity becomes aware of what is true for it at a certain moment, of what it truly believes or feels aside from that which it consciously or intellectually may wish to believe or may ascribe to.

Thus, the emotions are the barometer, or shall we say the temperature gauge for an entity, in that the emotions show to the entity the degree of feeling or bias that the entity has toward any thought, word or action, and by becoming aware of this biasing within the emotional self, shall we say, the entity then may take this biasing, this emotional coloration, and work with it in a fashion that attempts to balance the emotional charge so that the final product is that quality known as love or acceptance. Thus, the emotions point to that which is in need of balance and which when worked with in an efficient manner may then yield a lack of emotion, a lack of coloration, and may finally yield that quality known as love.

May we answer further, my brother?

T: No, thank you. You commented very extensively on one of the other major questions I would have asked. Thank you.

I am Latwii, and we thank you, my brother. Is there another query?

S: I have a question. What is it—you said *(inaudible)*. Is there something about this group, or for what reason were we able to greet you tonight?

I am Latwii, and am aware of your query, my sister. When a group such as this one gathers for the purpose of seeking what you may loosely call the truth, the desire with which that seeking is propelled blends the …

(Side one of tape ends.)

(Jim channeling)

I am Latwii, and am once again with this instrument. That desire, then, we perceive as a call. It is a call that has a certain vibration. The vibration then requires that a certain response be brought unto it, much as the magnet draws the filing of iron. Thus, this evening, the call that was put forth by the unique configuration of this particular group was most appropriately answered by those of our vibration. We find it a great honor and a great joy to be able to blend our vibrations with this group and we thank each for offering that call which has allowed us to respond.

May we answer further, my sister?

S: I don't know whether this is the right way to put it or whatever, but do certain entities have some specialty, like, are you a specialty group, or maybe that's putting it too much on today's doctor-type things, you know, but it would seem to me that maybe each, since you sound like a group, you may have some sort of a special mission, and what is it? With us, interacting?

I am Latwii, and I am one of those of our group consciousness which seeks within the vibration that you would see as light or wisdom. We of Latwii, then, having experienced the vibrations and the lessons of love, have attempted to refine those lessons in a manner which hopefully will aid our ability not only to speak more of what you may call the truth, but to be of service to those who seek it from the aspect of light or wisdom. There are times when the gathering within your group seeks more of the lessons of love, and at that time there are others of the Confederation of Planets in the Service of the One Infinite Creator who then answer that call. There are many of both vibrations, that of love and that of light, who are available for such opportunities to be of service.

We of Latwii have as an addition to our general vibration, biased toward wisdom, a certain bias or tendency to expand in a manner that you might see as the humorous aspects of the process of seeking the truth. We also consider the aspect of the sense of proportion or sense of humor that a group brings in its calling for the giving of information. Thus, when the sum of this group is seen by those which are available to it, then the entities most appropriate and able to answer the calling answer that calling.

May we answer further, my sister?

S: No, thank you.

I am Latwii, and we thank you, my sister. Is there another question?

J: Yes, I've got one. It's just out of curiosity mainly. Approximately three weeks ago, people all over the east coast and myself and my family saw what was termed as a luminescent cloud. And I was just wondering what this might have been? What significance it had, that so many people saw it? Nobody was able to identify it.

I am Latwii, and am aware of your query, my sister. We find that the mysterious nature of this object is that quality which has the greatest potential of being of service to your peoples at this time. Therefore, we cannot give a precise definition of the object, its source or purpose, other than to spark the interest in that which is beyond human knowledge.

May we answer further, my sister?

J: No, thanks.

I am Latwii, and we thank you, my sister. Is there another query at this time?

Carla: I was greeted by someone, and I don't wish to say anything about that except, if you would like to comment on such a contact in any way, I would be happy to hear it.

I am Latwii, and again, my sister, we find that we are within an area which must remain mysterious, but we may confirm your own suspicions without adding to them.

May we answer further, my sister?

Carla: *(Humorously)* I'll just keep my suspicions to myself, thank you.

I am Latwii, and we thank you, my sister. Is there another query?

J: Yes. I was going to ask if the entity or source known as Ramtha is a member of the Confederation, and then it occurred to me, I don't even know if individual entities are members of the Confederation, or only social memory complexes. So, could you answer both those questions, please?

I am Latwii, and am aware of your query, my sister. To take the last first. It is indeed quite possible and is the case that many, as you would call them, individualized portions of a social memory complex which has yet to reach the social memory level are members of the Confederation of Planets in the Service of the Infinite Creator. These entities are, shall we say, somewhat early in their joining if you look upon them as portions of that which will be, that is, the social memory complex of this particular planetary influence. Yet, within the realms of time/space, those of the metaphysical nature, there is a looser view of what you call time and its movement and expression as experience. Thus, many individuals, as you would see them, are able at a certain point within their evolutionary process to offer themselves as candidates, shall we say, for membership within this Confederation. They shall at what you would see at a future time be joined by others of this planetary influence and form what is more properly seen as the social memory complex.

Concerning the entity known as Ramtha, we find that we are unable to give a specific response, for to do so would be to infringe upon the free will of many who seek the information of this entity and may accept or reject that information according to whether or not this entity would be described as a member of this Confederation. Thus, we wish to preserve the free will of those who seek it and utilize it without our seeming to have judged in one [way] or another the affiliation of this particular entity.

May we answer further, my sister?

J: No, thank you. That was helpful. I have another question from R. He made the observation that the month of August has been a profound month of things coming together, of situations and people and events, and asked me to ask what is the significance, at least for him, of the month of August? And my addendum to that question would be, is there a general aspect to the time of the year which August represents—full and late summer—does that have any significance?

I am Latwii, and am aware of your query, my sister. As a general principle, one may see the cycle of the seasons reflected in each portion of the incarnational experience, whether that experience is of the individual or of larger groupings of individuals. Thus, within your latter portions of the time known as the summertime, you may see certain directions of energy, certain patterns of beginnings, find a kind of completion, a fullness of effort is realized, and during the fullness or ripeness of efforts, energies, entities and thoughts, there is the possibility of producing the fruit of these efforts.

Such fruits may be perceived in a great variety of manners by various individuals and groups of individuals. In some cases there will be the difficulty of the harvest. In others there will be the abundance of the harvest. In others there may be the continuation of the process which has yet to reach its full harvest within the normal time of such a process. Thus, though there are many times of completion and thus the harvesting for individuals and groups, the cycle of the seasons has its effects upon these energies and may be seen to offer more [of an] opportunity for such and such an aspect, whether it be the seeding, the growth, the harvest, or the consideration of that which has been and that which will be. Thus do the seasons have their influence upon the events within each incarnation.

May we answer further, my sister?

J: Thank you, that was helpful. But I really didn't pick out of that a specific answer to R and his particular life situation. Or can you answer that specifically?

I am Latwii, and am aware of your query, my sister. We cannot speak in a specific sense for any entity, for to speak in such a fashion would be to seem to judge, and if our words were weighted overly much by such an entity, then this weighting could infringe upon the entity's free will by affecting its perception of its own pattern of growth and thus its actions in what you would see as its future. Thus, we spoke in a general sense with the hope that this entity and others could take from the general principles those portions of our speaking which may have application in the personal pattern of experience.

May we answer further, my sister?

J: Thank you for that clarification. Yes. R has one other question and that is this: Did Halley's comet have any effect upon the population of planet Earth, possibly in performing a service? And, if so, could you describe what that might have been?

I am Latwii, and am aware of your query, my sister. And we find that the interruption of the second-density creatures *(playful cats)* is quite humorous, and we join with you in the laughter.

We find that the effect of that known as Halley's comet is not one which is easy to describe, for there have been many speakings concerning this phenomenon. In general, we may suggest that one may see as an analogy the face of the clock and when there have been many descriptions of the meaning of certain positionings of the hands of the clock and the time arrives when the hands are congruent to a certain positioning that has been previously spoken of, then many will note the position and will in some fashion experience the effect which was predicted.

The positioning of the hands, however, may have a meaning which is quite different than was described in the speakings. The hands may describe a time during which certain opportunities are made available to a population, in this case, the population of this planet, and it is not so much the hands of the clock which affect the population of the planet as it is the time that the hands signify. Thus, the passage of the comet known as Halley's comet may be seen more as the striking of a certain hour, the hour having the meaning rather than the comet or the hands having the meaning.

May we answer further, my sister?

J: No, thank you very much.

I am Latwii, and we thank you, my sister. Is there another query at this time?

Carla: Is the instrument becoming fatigued?

I am Latwii, and we find that though this instrument is becoming somewhat fatigued, there is sufficient energy for another two or three queries of normal length.

A: Yes, I have question about the second density we were watching, the cats. Do animals come to people by accident? Or do the animals that come, like those—I have three cats—do they come on purpose, pre-set up ahead of time before we come in this incarnation, to teach you certain lessons and for you to help them. I mean, is it an accident or do these animals happen to come to us, the particular ones that come to us?

I am Latwii, and we find that we may answer most effectively, we hope, by suggesting that though there are no accidents within your patterned incarnations, that there are certain general possibilities or opportunities that each may make available previous to the incarnation without making the opportunity of such a specific nature that one and only one fulfilling of it is possible. Thus, though it is possible for an entity to decide upon a certain second-density companion that will join it during its third-density experience, it is more likely that an entity will decide upon that general kind of experience in order to learn certain lessons and provide certain services, and leave the specific fulfilling of that decision to what may be seen as larger forces, that is, the providing of catalyst by the source that you would see as the Logos, that primal energy that is generally described as love or the Godhead, which provides the precise patterns of energy within all creation. However, there are many cases of the second-density creatures joining those third-density companions that have shared experience in previous times, as you would say. Thus, it is not possible to give one simple answer to this query.

May we answer further, my sister?

A: Is it possible for an animal that gets killed in this lifetime to reincarnate again in a year or so again to that same family to learn other lessons?

I am Latwii, and this is quite so. May we answer further, my sister?

A: No, thank you.

I am Latwii, and we thank you, my sister. Is there another query?

G: Yes, Latwii. As entities, individually, would you comment on an endowment or something that we may have been granted by the Creator that is indestructible, that which is eternal and everlasting and unchanging—is there that endowment in all living manifestations?

I am Latwii, and indeed this is so, my brother, for each seeker of truth has discovered in one way or another that that which may be seen as the stream of consciousness is without beginning and without end, and moves in many ways throughout all of the one infinite creation, for the one creation is held in its place by that one Thought of love, given birth ageless eons ago by the one Creator, that the one Creator might through the movement of various portions of Its own love come to know Itself in ways not available to It without such division of Itself into the infinite portions and expressions of love that move throughout this same creation in order that each portion may come to know itself by gaining the experience of evolution in a unique fashion that will, at its culmination, bring the harvest of experience to the one Creator, that all may again know the heart of being as love, and may continue the process of movement and growth and seeking and gaining the experience that will reveal each portion of the Creator to each portion of the Creator as the one Creator.

May we answer further, my brother?

G: On more small question that relates to that. Speaking of this earth plane, or this level of density, is there or has there ever been or will there ever be an entity that will have an expression or a manifestation of a divine endowment that is not of the same intensity or the same quality as all other life manifesting upon this density?

I am Latwii, and am aware of your query, my brother. Though to the eyes of those of third density there may seem to be endowments, as you may call them, that are of greater or lesser radiance and purpose, in the larger sense there is one endowment, the endowment of love that has free will to know itself as it will. Thus, each learns in a unique fashion, and all need not be the same to be equal in will and faith.

May we answer further, my brother?

G: No, that's fine. Thank you very much.

I am Latwii, and we thank you, my brother. Is there a final query for this evening?

Carla: Well, just to top that one off, I'd like to go for the jugular and look at those who declare themselves to be the one prophet, or "the" son of God, which I don't think Jesus precisely claimed to be—he said the "son of man," but it's certainly been claimed enough for him. This is the kind of thing where you are supposed to realize that because this person did all stuff which you then take on authority, the rest of us poor mortals can sort of muddle our way through to a secondhand redemption.

I'm a Christian, and a believing and worshipping Christian, but I have never been a fundamental Christian, and I have trouble buying that, and I pretty much go along with your answer. But the way that I have thought of it to myself is that the fellow known as Jesus, who was the Christ, was actually—had he actually had his Christ consciousness activated rather than in potential? That was the difference. It's very difficult for us to activate that consciousness fully in this third-density illusion—for all the cat fights *(an observation prompted by the cats scuffling in the room).*

But one thing Jesus did was to show that it is possible. And I wondered if that sounded like it could come under your canopy of "generally right"?

I am Latwii, an am aware of your query, my sister. And we would agree that you have struck upon the basic principle that was expressed by the one known as Jesus the Christ, and that as with the teachings of all teachers who have found a path to the One, was to describe in whatever way possible the nature of that path and what the requirements might be if one wished to set upon that journey. The one known as Jesus the Christ was one who had successfully traveled this path as many had before him and many have since his incarnation known to this population.

This entity was of great desire to be a most humble servant and wished to provide a means by which those who felt the need for love within the life pattern might be able to express that love in a fashion which could be utilized in the daily round of activities. Thus this entity claimed no Earthly kingdom and claimed nothing that was not available to all. This entity spoke of that which was the birthright of each and spoke in a manner which could be interpreted in a variety of ways, and indeed, such has been the case.

It is the honor and the duty of each who seeks such a path to discriminate between what one or another teacher or philosophy has said about that path, for though there is such a path, there are as many ways to travel this path as there are travelers upon it, and each teacher who has found his or her own way to that one Source which moves through us all knows full well the difficulty in attempting to describe in any definite fashion the nature of such a journey, for the journey will be unique to each.

But any who have traveled such a path and completed that journey at this level of being will find such an overwhelming desire to share the truth of that journey with others that it will not be able to stop itself from sharing its own perceptions in some way with those about it, for the fruits of such a journey are compelling enough that to share with others such fruit is the only possibility, even though one may know that there will be great distortion and confusion given to any such description.

May we answer in any further way, my sister?

Carla: No, thank you. May I put in a request that we end the meditation *(inaudible)*?

I am Latwii, and, my sister, you must have read our minds, for we have observed that this instrument's fatigue has increased to the point that it would be well that we took our leave of this instrument and of this group. We thank each present for offering that call which has allowed us to join you this evening. It has been our honor and our privilege to do so. We shall be with you in your future times, as you would call them, and we look forward to such opportunities with glee and joyful anticipation. We are known to you as those of Latwii. We leave you in the love and the light of the one infinite Creator. Adonai, my friends. Adonai vasu borragus. ✣

Sunday Meditation
September 7, 1986

Group question: What's the point of bad moods for human beings?

(Carla channeling)

I am *(sounds like)* t'Michael'h. I greet you in the love and in the light of the one infinite Creator. It is indeed an honor and a privilege to be with you this evening. We shall speak for a time before addressing the question, as we are adjusting to this channel.

This is our first appearance with your group, and yet we have been observing this group for some time for we are most appreciative of those who persevere in service to the light. Our energy we find to be very powerful for this instrument and we are attempting to step it down so that we are able to use the instrument with less distortion of the instrument's physical complex.

We find that due to the aural nature of our particular contact and this instrument's difficulties in the right ear, we must tilt the instrument's head, and we apologize to the instrument for this inconvenience. We trust that we shall gradually discover how to lessen this inconvenience. It does not seem to interfere with the process of communication to each of you through this instrument, and so with this instrument's permission we shall speak a few more words of little import while we are continuing to fit in with this instrument's comfort parameters.

We are not of the Confederation of Planets in the Service of the Infinite Creator. We are of the inner planes. We wish to be clear on this, for this instrument has a prejudice against inner plane teachers. Yet we have been drawn to this group because we are interested in questions which have to do with the power of polarity. This is our area, what you would call the disciplines of the indigo-ray work.

We are third density, harvestable for fourth, and we believe, and it has been agreed by the Confederation entities that are about you now, that we perhaps can give some information from a point of view helpful concerning the question of the function of the nature and the correction in time and space of the seemingly petty negative mood, the transient melancholy, the sudden irritation, the quick anger, that which does not last in the perception, yet lingers along in the perceptions of those about one and in the actual effect in a cumulative sense on the spiritual journey itself.

As do our brothers and sisters of the Confederation, we who make up the principle of power and polarity request that anything that we say be taken very lightly until it has been filtered carefully through your discerning processes, for we are indeed as you, and not even of another dimension, but of your own. And yet, my children, we are old in your years and we are most happy to share with you what we can.

The seemingly inconsequential mood is as the shutting of a door, indeed, a shutting of two doors, the door to positive polarity and the door to negative polarity, for polarity consists in the acceptance of a certain job description, shall we say. That which is in between may be considered self-employment. The spiritual path is something that can be talked about endlessly. Great systems of theoretical discussion can be constructed, and yet if one does not become involved in a personal sense, the path remains outside of oneself.

When one contemplates putting one's feet upon the path or getting back upon the path when one has stopped to rest, it is well to view that which is ahead and count the cost. One would not go on a physical journey without checking the availability of that with which a traveler must be endowed before beginning the journey. One must have the supplies one needs, a coin for a bit of food, good shoes for the walking, and a warm blanket for the sleeping.

The spiritual journey is a very expensive journey, one which in metaphysical terms none of you can afford. In metaphysical terms, each entity is too poor to afford the undertaking of the spiritual journey from one's own resources. It is a popular misconception in your culture that you can do anything. In a metaphysical sense, it is well to realize quickly that you are unequal to the task of transforming yourself, for that would be asking the purchase price of tools, the name of which you do not even know and the function of which you can only guess.

You see, my friends, you are stewards of consciousness, you do not own consciousness. The nature of consciousness is unknown to you, and will continue to be unknown to each of us. And yet that is the nature of your journey and your exploration. You will never have a map for this journey. You cannot buy it. And so how do people begin and maintain themselves upon this journey? For of course you know that you are on the journey, perhaps reluctantly, perhaps enthusiastically, perhaps intermittently, but on it, and basically committed to it.

In essence, when one accepts stewardship of consciousness, one accepts that one is working for another. Your salary is heightened consciousness, increased perception, and the pain, travail, peace and freedom of the road you wish to be on. In order to move along that road, it is well to acknowledge that you are working for that which is not within your conscious mind and not within your control. Polarity has as one of the secrets of its effectiveness the surrender to your employer—consciousness itself. Many have defined consciousness in another way and called it love or the Logos or the one original Thought.

To this you shall surrender if you wish to polarize, and in that surrender you shall find the ability to become a receiver of the knowledge that you need—not for tomorrow and not for yesterday—but for the present moment. Both those who polarize towards the positive of love for others and those who polarize towards the negative of love for self, surrender themselves to the consciousness that they not only are, but know not, and thus they become what they know not. And in becoming, know for the first time.

Now, my friends, when you are working for yourself, you may use your consciousness in many ways, and yet the more you exercise your will without asking for help, the less effective you will be until you lose contact with love and become only that which seems not good, not bad, not positive, not negative, but swayed by the cross currents of a shifting and uneasy sea of phantasmagorical appearances, and you become prey to all the minor ills of your illusion, and at the same time become less and less able to create a polarized alternative to what you feel and are in the illusion.

It is not a wrong thing or an evil thing to be as this instrument said—cranky, unhappy, irritable or angry. It is rather a waste of potential. Each of you has a certain amount of incarnational time. When you tire of carrying consciousness, you may choose to become distracted and indifferent. Yet, when you are healed, we suggest that you seek once again to know that which overshadows you, that which is the greater part of you, that which created you and that which empowers you.

There are two aspects to the sense of other. One may be termed the higher self. Some have called it the Creator. It is the aspect of the Creator which is personal and yet which is far richer in experience than are you and it is far more representative of you than your seemingly complete mentality and personality within the illusion. It is benign and helpful and full of information insofar as your consciousness empties itself of judgment and self-importance and asks to know and to serve.

The other portion of the other is that which this instrument would call grace, that is, the kindness of the Creator, of love itself, which offers to the one who surrenders its will the ability to manifest the greater will that is made known to it through the overshadowing influence of the higher self.

Thus, you have available to you, if you accept the surrender of self-determination, a more conscious and wise point of view which is filled with compassion and wisdom and a practical, imminent agent which in its ineffable way marks well your needs and sees that you have what you need in order to manifest what you receive in your life and in the fruits of your travel.

Thus, if you find yourself at the mercy of what is often termed "moods," realize that you are doing nothing wrongly; it is that you are not polarizing either towards radiance or towards magnetism but are instead allowing an impotence of consciousness to hold sway over the incredible potential of the present moment. We ask you never to be impatient when you find yourself in a bad mood, but to realize that the soul grows weary when it is out of tune, just as the stringed instrument makes a poor sound indeed when it has become unstrung. Never attempt to tighten the strings of perception with your own energy. Distract yourself while you are tired; allow yourself to sleep, and by sleep we mean not the physical sleep, but the sleep of one who does not carry the burden of consciousness, and when you are rested and ready to work, seek your employer, consciousness itself.

For you do not own your consciousness—it owns you. You are a fragment of a great consciousness and the struggle towards unity shall be long. And you who must be on your way will do well to turn to the source that has the provender, the outfitting, and the map for your journey. And when once again you open to the infinite consciousness that is available to you always and you are overshadowed by love, you will wonder why you stopped, why you shut away that awareness, why you put down your consciousness. Do not look back, but count yourself most fortunate to have turned again to the road ahead, to have emptied yourself of indifference and to be filled with the consciousness of life.

You are a people used to stimulation, and we suggest as a practical matter that when you become aware that you are impatient to take up consciousness once again and be on your journey, that you allow stimulus of a loving kind to replace casually received and uncontrolled stimulus. For it is difficult when one is stopped and caught in the illusion to listen to silence and be saved, though it happens quite frequently that consciousness comes in where there is any seeking at all, under the most adverse conditions.

But if you wish to accelerate the process of getting back on the road, use the principle of stimulation. Read that which is inspiring, listen to those musical sounds which appeal to the highest and best within you and give you the proper environment for the opening up to love. If silent meditations are not helpful, use music, reading and inspirational discussion with others to stimulate yourself as is your culture's custom. Realize that when you are stopped and indifferent, it is not all entities who have experienced incarnation in your culture who can be started easily on a diet of silent meditation.

We encourage you to persevere. For although it may seem that you are being insincere by striving for that consciousness of love when you feel anything but loving, yet as you seek, so shall you find. And if you are too tired today to remove the glamour of your illusion from your mind and the fog seems very thick between your eyes and what you wish to perceive, take heart and realize that it is well for you to rest and then strive again by seeking, by meditating, and by asking to start once again to polarize and become more and more that which you seek.

All that you wish is ahead of you. All that you wish is available in the consciousness of the present moment. Love is a perception away. May joy fill you, may peace flow from you. May these things happen to you because you have surrendered to the one master, the Creator, love, consciousness, that which you are and that which you will more and more perceive.

We are the principle, t'Michael'h. We have greatly appreciated your patience while we worked with this instrument and your great unity …

(Side one of tape ends.)

(Carla channeling)

… which allowed us not only to be called to you, but to remain with you. We relinquish this instrument at this time, thanking you and blessing you, my children. May you feel the power, the peace, and the love that are your true consciousness and may you shine that others may see the Creator in a natural, refreshing and clear way, a way that transcends all dogma, all belief systems, and all objections. We leave you as we found you, in the consciousness of love and in the divine puzzle of seeking and resting. Rejoice in that rhythm and persevere. Peace be with you.

(Jim channeling)

I am Latwii, and we greet you, my friends, in the love and the light of the one Creator. It is also our great privilege to be with you this evening, and we thank you for this opportunity. We would, as always, hope to offer our humble words and insights in response to those queries which those present may have value in the asking.

May we then begin with a query?

S: I have a question. What is the difference in the inner plane teachers? I guess I'm asking what is an inner plane teacher as opposed to the entity that you are?

I am Latwii, and, my sister, we may suggest that those that are of the so-called inner planes are those who are of this planetary influence, having evolved from its beginnings of life and moved into that consciousness which you know as the third density, but who have for the time that you know of as the present not chosen a physical body in which to incarnate, but remain within the inner or metaphysical realms serving as those known as teachers and guides.

We of Latwii, and others of the Confederation of Planets in the Service of the One Creator, are from planetary influences other than this that you know of as the Earth, and also offer our services as teachers and companions upon the journey.

May we answer further, my sister?

S: No, thank you.

I am Latwii, and we thank you, my sister. Is there another query?

Carla: Could someone from our own planet's future be in the Confederation?

I am Latwii, and we find that this is the case in a few instances where there has been a relatively significant graduation, shall we say, within a certain population or source of beginningness, shall we say, for as you are aware, those who comprise the population of your planet are from numerous sources that are, shall we say, exterior to your planet. Many other third-density planets have given their populations to your own in order that they might again experience the opportunity to choose between the radiance and the magnetism that has been spoken of previously this evening. Thus, when a significant enough portion of any such population has reached that level of purity of choice that allows for the harvest, then these may be held in, shall we say, a potential harvest which also includes the potential of joining that which is known as the Confederation of Planets in the Service of the One Creator.

May we answer further, my sister?

Carla: So, Confederation members, in terms of time travel back to the present from the future of planet Earth's population, is not a possibility or a probability?

I am Latwii, and this is indeed a possibility and in some cases a probability, my sister. May we answer further?

Carla: No, thank you.

I am Latwii, and we thank you, my sister. Is there another query?

S: I have another question. When you say you are Latwii, is that an entity, and are you a person or a personality or an entity or are you a group? I mean, are you someone out of that group, or are you answering as a sort of a conglomeration of consciousnesses?

I am Latwii, and am aware of your query, my sister. It is a portion, an individualized portion of what you may call a social memory complex that speaks to you as those of Latwii. We are one in our seeking with those that comprise our social memory complex. We exist in a manner which is difficult to describe in your terms, but we are a, as you have described, conglomeration of entities which have joined their seeking in such a manner that that which has been gleaned in learning by any is available to all, just as each memory from each year and experience which you have had in your incarnation is available within your mind complex, so does our complex of mind, body and spirit comprise all experiences and learnings which each portion of our complex has gleaned.

May we answer further, my sister?

S: No, thank you.

I am Latwii, and we thank you once again, my sister. Is there another query?

Carla: I have recently heard a good deal about an apparent miracle in which a young child, an infant who was sure to die, has begun normalizing. And this interested me in what the dynamics of the miracle of unexpected healing are. Could you comment in general about that?

I am Latwii, and am aware of your query, my sister. In many cases such as the one of which you speak, there is the disease which seems to defy description in that its uniqueness or rarity is such that little is known within your orthodox medical community concerning the dysfunction. In the metaphysical portion of such dysfunction, there may be the need for an opportunity of a certain nature to be presented to those who will share experience with the entity experiencing the dysfunction or disease.

Thus, a disease that seems in some ways recognizable to those of the medical community, as you call it, will appear and according to the opportunity provided and taken advantage of, will then begin to recede in a manner which may not be fully understood or understood at all. Perhaps it has been decided in a preincarnative sense that the entity with the disease shall galvanize those with whom it shares experience in such a manner that that quality which you know as love shall be generated in a fashion which not only serves to heal the disease, but to bring a greater sense of unity to those within the grouping of the entity with the disease. It may also be the case that such a generation of that quality of love will provide for each individual expressing this quality opportunities for enhancing the personal expression of this quality of love in a fashion that is congruent with the potential brought into the incarnation which has heretofore remained dormant.

May we answer further, my sister?

Carla: No, thanks.

I am Latwii, and we thank you, my sister. Is there another query?

Carla: What relationship, if any, does—I'm not sure I have the name right, it's hard to get names—but it sounds like "Tah-Mi-*Kel*-Uh" have with Michael?

I am Latwii, and we view your query with some hesitation, for we do not wish to predispose your thinking in a fashion that removes the mystery that motivates further seeking upon your part. As you are aware, there are many entities that have the identification of *(sounds like)* Mih-*chel*. Many are those upon your planet at this time who feel an identification of that nature and express it in a manner known as the vocal channel. Many seek such contact out of admiration for its content, yet their service is of another kind, and such contact is, shall we say, beyond their grasp. Yet the contact seems to occur within the mind and is expressed as a valid contact.

We are having some difficulty with this instrument, for it also has its own biases concerning this information. We ask your patience.

We feel that we may best respond to your query by suggesting that the entity with whom you have contact this evening is what it says it is and may have some tangential relationship to those who share its name.

May we answer further, my sister?

Carla: No, I think I'll let that lie. Thank you. I appreciate it.

I am Latwii, and we thank you, my sister, and apologize once again for difficulty in expressing a response which might both be illuminating and free of distortion concerning your free will.

May we answer another query?

S: You said—well something you said made me think that we are drawn to our names or called. Is there any great insight in what we're called? Like my name is S—is there some great insight in that or is that just an accident—my parents named me S?

I am Latwii, and am aware of your query, my sister. We find that there are, in truth, no accidents within your or any illusion of the one Creation. The influence of the vibratory sound complex that you call "name" may be either that of a preincarnative choice that allows one to express its identity in a manner which may be summarized by the vibration of sound known as "name," or the name may be given in a more general sense which allows, rather than a summary, a broader scope of possibility to be presented to the entity assuming the name. The name of any entity becomes to that entity the trigger which opens to it and to others certain recognitions of abilities and potentials and avenues for expression.

The name in itself may be seen as relatively neutral in the beginning. As an entity continues with the incarnation and gathers experience within it and associates this experience to the self and that self to the name, then the name becomes that which symbolizes the experiences, the abilities, and the range or reach which the entity continues to provide for itself as it expresses and experiences those lessons and services that were its preincarnative choices.

May we answer further, my sister?

S: Well, was mine a preincarnative choice or something to give me wider range?

I am Latwii, and am aware of your query, my sister. We are not of the opinion that it is an easily answered query for any entity, for the choices that are made previous to incarnation are always enhanced in some manner by free will during an incarnation. Thus, it is a matter of degree for any preincarnative choices including that of the name, and we see that this is so in your case.

May we answer further, my sister?

S: No, thank you.

I am Latwii, and we thank you, my sister. Is there another query?

J1: I have one. Is there any link between *(inaudible)*?

I am Latwii, and we assume that you refer to the first name as you call it, rather than the family name …

J1: Yes.

… and we see that again, though in general there can be seen in many cases a connection to one's ancestry, not necessarily of the Earth plane, but of the metaphysical realms, there is in some cases the choosing of the naming which will allow [new] possibilities. Thus, there is no general response which can be definitive in this instance.

May we answer further, my sister?

J1: No, thank you.

I am Latwii, and we thank you, my sister. Is there another query?

Carla: I take it, then, that names of power would be those names which one found would sum up the actual *(inaudible)* personality itself?

I am Latwii, and again, though this is also a possibility, it is also equally as possible that a name for any particular incarnation or portion of an incarnation may be chosen for, shall we say, a narrower focus or an aspect of the greater self which now finds it appropriate to be expressed in what you would call the current incarnation.

May we answer further, my sister?

Carla: No, that's enough, Latwii.

I am Latwii, and we again thank you, my sister. Is there another query?

S: Can you tell me if there was any significance in that last week after I left here and I saw just momentarily a small kitten in the road that disappeared?

I am Latwii, and we see in this experience that there was the demonstration of the ability of a thought to become a thing and to express to the one creating the thought the ephemeral nature of all things. There is, of course, more to this particular experience, but those portions must remain within the realm of that which you seek.

May we answer further, my sister?

S: No, thank you.

I am Latwii, and we thank you, my sister. Is there another query?

J2: Latwii, this is J2. For some time now, about two months, I've been having a strong pull towards the part of Kentucky known as Lancaster, of which I have no past history and knowledge of. I [think] of it quite often in my dreams, and in my dreams I see myself there. I think something there is to unlock my—I won't say mysterious—but my higher consciousness that I'm striving to obtain. And I only get bits and pieces of the messages. I feel very strongly about having to go there, and I feel certain I will be told the exact date in which I should go.

Again, I don't really know exactly where I am to go in Lancaster, but I feel I will be told once I get on the road. And my question is, is such a thing possible, to be told a general idea of where to go, and upon arriving there you acquire some sort of stage or to get some sort of knowledge? Why Lancaster, I haven't the faintest idea. But it just keeps staying with me that I have to go there, and I'm to learn something very important.

That's my question—about are we given specific cities or places to go to without being given the rest of the answer as to what we will find when we get there?

I am Latwii, and it is indeed possible and quite often the case, my sister, that when one has opened the desire within one's heart of being to know more of that which is appropriate for one's own seeking, that gradually more and more of that pattern of being and experience will become known to the entity. The process is one in which the deeper or subconscious mind begins to release portions of information that respond or correspond to that which the conscious mind has turned itself in seeking. The strength and purity of the conscious mind's desire to know that which is loosely called the truth or the self, draws unto the conscious mind more and more of these pieces, shall we say, of the puzzle, if we may use this term.

The process by which an entity follows these intuitive flashes or pieces of information is one which may be termed the Way of the Fool, for one may seem quite foolish at times as these pieces are interpreted and action then taken in response to the interpretation. The foolishness is that which is an openness and willingness to be the fool, that is, to rely upon that which seems quite unreliable for it cannot be proven, it cannot be seen, it cannot be touched. But one may follow this lightly-left trail, and by continuing upon the journey with the faith and will exercised to the utmost, continue in a manner which will eventually find that which feels to the self, the inner self, to be of substance and of undoubted value. There may be missteps or mistakes upon this journey, at least that which seems to be such. Yet the seeker who continues in the face of such detours and difficulties will discover that each provides further resources that fuel the journey.

May we answer further, my sister?

J2: No, thank you.

I am Latwii, and we thank you, my sister. Is there another query at this time?

J1: Just out of curiosity, if we were to see a view of you with our physical eye, what would you be like? Would it be different for different people?

I am Latwii, and am aware of your query, my sister. Since we have achieved the discipline necessary to form our physical vehicle in any manner that is appropriate, we would form it in a manner which would seem most comfortable to you, and thus would appear quite similar to any other entity upon your planet, since we would not wish to shock you in any way or cause any fearful response.

May we answer further, my sister?

J1: No, that's okay—you can shock me any day you want.

J2: This is J2. May I make a comment, Latwii?

I am Latwii, and we are happy with this, my sister.

J2: Okay. To give J1, if I may, an example of what I saw when you were speaking in another group I was attending. I said, "I see you as different color sound waves, almost as different frequencies one would see on a radio dial, AM/FM, some much higher, some much lower, and the sound waves themselves, the different beats, different pulsations or different colors." And at that time when I said is that what you look like, at least that's what J3 saw, I was told, "Yes." I just thought I would say that to J1 because that is what I personally experienced one day with you, Latwii.

I am Latwii, and we are happy that you have been able to perceive an aspect of our being.

Is there another query at this time?

Questioner: Can you take human form, for instance, would you take a human form and wear that a lifetime, you know, would you marry someone here, would you have children or would you just be a … like a, you know, an interlude, you would just come for awhile and then leave?

I am Latwii, and am aware of your query, my sister. The interlude of which you speak would not be seen by our group to be an appropriate means of experiencing the third-density illusion, for we would be without the native third-density qualities that are necessary in order to live and move upon your planetary surface. It is not appropriate for entities of the higher dimensions, shall we say, to be generally observably in any form that may be seen by third-density entities without becoming third-density entities. This is to say, if we wished to move upon your planet in service and be seen as third-density beings, we would need to incarnate in the same manner in which each of your population incarnates, that is, with the process of forgetting.

This process of incarnation, then, removes the knowledge of one's past, shall we say, in order that one may begin the incarnation anew and make choices during that incarnation that are not influenced by previous experience that is consciously known. Thus each experience, each service and each lesson is gained and offered in a pure sense without bias, shall we say. Thus do many of the Confederation of Planets in the Service of the One Creator chose to be of service upon your third-density planet by incarnating and going through that process of forgetting so that the incarnation is totally that of a third-density being that has chosen to be of service.

May we answer further, my sister?

Questioner: Well, would you ever know? If I were one of those people, would I ever know that until this incarnation was through?

I am Latwii, and this is, shall we say, variably possible Many there are upon your planetary surface of this nature who have an indication that they are not of this planetary influence, but are of another. Many there are who, being of another planetary influence, yet have no indication whatsoever as yet within the incarnation that they are anything other than a being whose source or point of origin is this particular planetary influence. There is within each such entity a, shall we say, preincarnative bias that serves as a kind of beacon …

(Tape ends.)

Sunday Meditation
September 14, 1986

(Carla channeling)

[I am Q'uo.] I greet you, my friends, in the love and the light of the one infinite Creator. It is a privilege to join in your group meditation and we thank you for this honor.

It is an interesting unity that all your energies make together, and we shall pause from time to time in our message in order to align ourselves with the shifting nuances of the group unity as it is more subtle than most within the harmony of those who seek. And perhaps it is to that diversity in unity that we would speak this evening, for although love is always the same and the one original Thought remains the mystery that it always has been and always shall be to the conscious rational mind, yet the codes of perception of this one original Thought of love are many and varied, not only from person to person, but in each person from moment to moment.

Each of you seeks the truth and yet the truth comes in different clothing at different times. This is not due to the nature of the truth, but to the complex rational mind's perceptions which have a rhythm of rate of permeability, shall we say, so that each entity is constantly shifting in its ability to perceive, not only because of physical, mental and emotional rhythms, and indeed not only because of the regular spiritual rhythm, but also and perhaps most importantly because of the irregular and unpredictable nature of transformative energy.

The irregularity of your own spiritual cycle can be maddening to the seeker, for the seeker knows the intensity with which he has sought for the truth, and when he knows that the intensity has been even, steady and strong for a significant period of time, there is a tendency for the seeker to take his own spiritual temperature and be disgusted at the result. This is inevitable, for it is only rarely and unpredictably that the mists of illusion can clear that extra amount and perception can be heightened.

It is one of the many paradoxes of spiritual seeking that although one can choose to seek and thus quicken the tempo of spiritual evolution to a great degree, one can never rule the moments of transformative realization. Therefore, one is much like the watchman who patrols night after night and year after year. But only once—and at the burglar's convenience—does he find the object of his ceaseless searching.

It is perhaps well to remember this when one has the tendency to feel different from those who do not seek consciously, for you and one who does not seek, though different in a great many conscious and rational ways, have precisely the same number of opportunities for transformation. The transformations are small and fewer in one who is not consciously seeking, firstly because one who is not consciously seeking may miss the potential of a transformative period by interpreting it as a completely negative circumstance and denying it any reality. Also and perhaps more importantly, the same opportunity for transformation not accentuated by the determination to progress spiritually produces a far more pale version of transformation, a small step rather than a large one.

We shall pause, as this entity is somewhat distracted.

(Pause)

I am Q'uo, and I am again with this instrument. We greet you once again in the love and the light of the one infinite Creator, and are sorry for this pause, but the instrument was losing depth of concentration necessary for this contact and we did not wish to give you faulty information due to mechanical problems. If we have faults—and I am sure we do, my friends—let it be because of true mistakes that we make and not because of faulty transmission. We would request that those in the circle, remain. If any in the circle wish to leave, we request that it be done now. It is far better for any instrument when the energies in the circle are unified and stable. We thank you for your patience.

There is much that we would say to you of courage and cheer and yet we know that those are empty words, and so we offer a feeling to you, and would ask you to feel with us the love that we have for you. We ask you to relax and to allow the truest self that you know to be vulnerable to the love of the Creator which we hope we reflect, for beyond all transformation is the creative power of love.

It is so easy, my friends, to take the spiritual temperature, to be critical of the self and judgmental, and yet, we ask you to consider whether it is most helpful to rely on the one strong point, the great forte of conscious seekers, and that is the love that they have felt and found and wish to know more about, whether that love is defined as the beauty of truth or that which created all that there is, or is personified in a religious sense according to the needs and distortions of any particular seeker. That love, my friends, whatever it be called, however it is perceived, is truer than other perceptions, for it is a distortion of that which is original, whereas all other things are distortions of that which was created by love. All other things, therefore, are the shadows of a shadow.

Focus, then, on love, a feeling, a non-thing. It cannot be grasped and yet all have felt it, have basked in its glow, and we come to you because you called to us and said, "Tell us of love, speak to us of light." My friends, would that we could inspire you with words as we can inspire you with feelings. Yet feelings lie beyond words, as their source is a deeper river of consciousness, closer to the source of love.

There is a breakthrough, shall we say, that lies ahead for you, and we encourage you to keep your eye fastened upon the goal as you move through transformation after transformation and may find yourself weary wondering if all that there are are changes. There is a point at which you may find it possible to perceive in a steady state. There is a point at which the rhythms of transformation are no longer relevant. It is far in your—may we use the word future, for want of a better one—for most of you, and the way may seem long. Yet there are always those who share your journey to keep you company along the way.

The more you allow naive emotions like enthusiasm, joy and laughter to pervade your experience, the more you encourage the innocent things in yourself, the quicker will be your progress in polarizing to a positive enough state where that which is love may be touched, not just when the fogs of perception lift, but between those times, because you have contacted enough of what this instrument would call intelligent infinity, what we call the one original Thought, that you are able to reproduce the vibration which opens perception to love.

May your meditations be regular and fruitful, and if you do not think they are fruitful, may they be regular, for my friends, you cannot accurately predict your spirituality. We have yet to find a third-density entity of sufficient objectivity within your illusion to assess the self accurately. Turn from criticism of the self to encouragement. Turn from negative and neutral to positive in your assessment and your directions to the self. If you are disappointed, be disappointed in one who has made an error, but let your positive affirmation be that you shall avoid error, that particular error, in your next experience. And with ill negative emotion washed from your self assessment, feel your load lighten and your step become more brisk, for all of you, as do all of us, rest in love, that love which has created you and all that there is, that love which makes all one, for all are holographs of the same Thought.

It is with reluctance that we listen to the mental request of this instrument that we "wrap it up," as she put it, so that questions may be asked. This is an interesting group, as we have said, and there is much we could share, and perhaps we shall at another time, but for the present, we wish to transfer to another instrument in order to offer the opportunity for questions. Therefore, we will leave.

(Jim channeling)

I am Q'uo, and greet you once again in love and light through this instrument. At this time it is our privilege to attempt to respond to those queries which those present may find value in the asking.

May we begin with the first query?

A: Yes, I have a question. It's about trees. When we go to trees and we recognize in our consciousness that they are a first density—I think they're first density—and that they were created by the one Creator, do the trees understand when we talk to them? In their own way? Do they give out love? If you hug a tree, do they feel the love that you give to them in a certain way? This I would be very interested in knowing the answer to.

I am Q'uo, and we find that your assumptions are correct except for the level of consciousness expressed by those that you know of as trees. The second density is the proper designation for this particular form of conscious expression, for it has taken that basic awareness of being that has developed within earth, wind, fire and water and has added unto it the form that expresses a simple movement and growth that is not available to the first-density expressions of the one Creator.

May we answer further, my sister?

A: Yes, I'd like to know how the trees know when to lose their leaves. Is this an inward intelligence? If the weather remained warm through December and January would they still change in fall, the leaves, or is it triggered, through the sun's rays? What triggers the trees to tell them when it is winter and when it is summer and when it is spring. Is it strictly the sun?

I am Q'uo. The entities that you know as trees are integral portions of the one creation, as are all individualizations of the one Creator who has set all that there [is] into motion. All of the creation moves in a rhythm with variations upon a theme, shall we say. All portions of the one creation partake in cycles of growth and [death], as you would call it, cycling again from one to the other, from the receiving to the giving, in order that each portion of the one creation might gain in what you may loosely term as experience, and through that experience come to know the self as an individualized portion of the one Creator and the one Creator as the source of all that there is.

Thus, those entities that you know as trees, moving with their own rhythms, are affected by a number of forces, as you would say, that cumulatively cause these entities to move in their own cycles and to produce a number of outward effects that are visible to your eye, including the dropping of the leaf forms, and when the new season begins in the spring, the development amongst those who have dropped their leaf forms, of yet another crop, shall we say, of these leafy structures. The sun, the rotation of your planet, the location upon the surface of the planet, whether to the north or the south of that line known as the equator that divides your planet in two, the internal programming of these entities known as trees which responds to these outward forces and other more subtle rhythms that are not as easily apparent as those we have mentioned, together work to cause the cycle of seasons to have its effect upon these entities that you know as trees.

Thus does each portion of the creation move in its own rhythm and affect each other portion of the one creation in a fashion which may be subtle or overt, inner or outer, small or large.

May we answer further, my sister?

A: No, thank you very much. You've helped me.

I am Q'uo, and we are grateful for this opportunity, my sister, and we thank you. Is there another query?

Carla: Can I follow from that? Talking about transformation, could I make an analogy to the trees by saying that maybe the reason in sometimes when you want to improve and you can't, is sort of like asking the trees to put out new leaves before they shed the old ones, and that the rhythm isn't right? Of course the weather, being internal, wouldn't be regular like it is on a rotating planet. Is that one reason why it's irregular, that you can't predict when a transformation's going to occur or cause it to come about consciously?

I am Q'uo. And we find that in the basic sense your query is correct in its assumptions, for as the third-density entity which each in this domicile sitting in this circle in meditation represents, expresses its beingness and responds to those inner cycles or rhythms of being, the conscious mind tends to assess and direct the thoughts and actions of the entity. This direction, when done in a spiritual sense and an attempt to move the self along the path of the evolution of mind, body and of spirit, often attempts to move more quickly than, shall we say, the feet are capable. To ask that one move in such a manner is, as you have correctly surmised, to ask the portion of the self that is much likened unto the tree to find another season to replace the one which is now *en route*. And though the conscious mind and the thinking being may move itself in many ways and find fruitful experience in any direction, there is great value in the lack of judgment for the self or others, and the surrender of the will in a basic sense to the greater will which moves through one's being and which becomes apparent to one who has done this and experienced the fruits of such surrenders, for there is a delicate balance between the exercise of the will and the surrender of the will that the seeker of its own evolution must achieve. There is, shall we say, a cycle or season for each and a purpose for each that may be determined by each entity, and a unique balance for each thus achieved.

May we answer further, my sister?

Carla: No, thank you.

I am Q'uo, and we thank you, my sister. Is there another query?

J: Yes, I would like to ask. I've heard it being expressed that each entity on this Earth plane set up for themselves before incarnation with other entities to work with them while they're on this physical plane, and I was wondering if you could speak a little bit about the workers that work with us and if that is so? *(Inaudible)*.

I am Q'uo, and we can speak upon this topic by suggesting that indeed each entity within what you have called the third-density illusion has entered this illusion or experience with a purpose that has been agreed upon, and in fact constructed before the incarnation has begun, and this construction has had many loving hands and hearts to add to its strength, to its purpose and to its potential means of implementation, for before each incarnation begins, an entity will assess those lessons that have been well learned in previous incarnations and will look at those which remain for the, shall we say, graduation from this particular level of experience.

Those lessons that remain then will be seen as that which is of most importance in the upcoming incarnation. Many will join the entity in the incarnation as incarnate beings and these before incarnation will also join the entity, and others who shall remain without physical vehicles and upon the inner planes and serve as those that you know as guides and teachers. Thus, there are many, many beings which partake in the process of planning that which shall be the pattern of experience for an entity within an incarnation.

Those who remain behind, shall we say, within the inner planes and who serve as unseen presences remain with the larger view, that which is not limited by the process of forgetting which each incarnate third-density entity must experience before the incarnation as the incarnation begins in order that …

(Side one of tape ends.)

(Jim channeling)

I am Q'uo, and am once again with this instrument. Those upon the inner planes who serve as guides and teachers, then, with the greater view and purpose for the incarnation may be of service to the incarnate entity by placing certain reminders, shall we say, within the notice of the incarnate entity. These reminders or guideposts may take many forms, the form being dependent upon the entity's ability to recognize one hint or another.

For example, within the state of consciousness that you know of as dreaming, many experiences are possible for the incarnate entity to share with those who have remained upon the inner planes. And during such times, an entity may find nourishment and sustenance in the reminders that are placed within the subconscious mind and which then during the waking state may filter into that conscious mind as one kind of hunch, as you call it, or inspiration or another. These are most often perceptible during the times of contemplation, prayerfulness or meditation, for at these times the conscious mind is stilled to the point where there may be the recognition of other information, shall we say.

When an entity has, to use another example, discovered the appropriate book, person or piece of information at the time which seems most appropriate to it, the entity may well assume that those who guide it have once again accomplished that which was agreed upon before the incarnation began. With these times of reminders, then, the incarnate entity receives a communication from those who have chosen to serve as the guides and teachers within the inner planes.

Those incarnate entities with whom the entity finds normal daily activities shared also play out those choices made previous to incarnation in an infinite number of ways, as the interactions between familiar entities multiply one upon another until rhythms and patterns of experience are established and set up the potential for lessons to be learned that were chosen together before the incarnation began.

May we answer in any further way, my brother?

J: No, thank you.

I am Q'uo, and we thank you, my brother. Is there another query?

Carla: Is there any value to knowing consciously who your guides are, or is it just as valuable to deduce their existence from their effects?

I am Q'uo. In responding in a general sense to this query, we might suggest that if there is value in being able to name or identify any guide, teacher or angelic presence that has been drawn to one for the purpose of service, then that naming or identification will find a natural means of becoming known to the incarnate entity. To attempt to discover this information for oneself past a certain reasonable point may cause for the incarnate entity a certain wasting of energy as the attention is placed upon that which may not have significant value in the entity's process of evolution, shall we say.

May we answer further, my sister?

Carla: May I gather that the reason that it may not be helpful is that angels, guides, whatever, consider themselves messengers rather than the source of the message?

I am Q'uo, and may again may agree with the basic assumption which you have stated. Entities who are at the heart desirous of serving others, first and foremost are frequently those who work in the unseen manner, and who desire the service to be that which receives attention rather than the servant. It is also frequently the case that such entities have not chosen a vibratory complex of sound that you would call name. Frequently these names are chosen for the incarnate entity's benefit when desired.

May we answer further, my sister?

Carla: No, thank you, Q'uo.

I am Q'uo, and we thank you, my sister. Is there another query?

J: *(The question is almost inaudible.)* Yes. I recently learned about a system in which the teacher, he called himself a *(inaudible)* process wherein one gets in a meditative state and calls for animals to appear at each of the chakra centers. After one receives, or is in touch with seven animals, and, I might state, the animals seem to be very focal to the level of the chakra centers, and a dialogue may be entered into with these animals and they give information about questions that are asked, mostly of the nature about the individual *(inaudible)* consciousness that needs to be learned. I'm wanting to know where this information comes from. It seems like the animals are able to give very accurate information about the person. And I'd just like to know where this information comes from, what level is it being received from.

I am Q'uo, and this is a large field of study which this question has entered upon. An entity may engage in whatever method of self-discovery is comfortable to it, whether that method might be associating, as you have stated, animals with the various chakras or energy centers, musical notes, colors, archetypes, archangels, guides or whatever. The source of information which is transmitted by making any such association again may vary according to the nature of information sought by the entity who is incarnate.

The source may vary from the entity's own conscious mind to various levels of the unconscious mind, to guides, teachers and other angelic presences that are drawn to the entity according to the nature of the information sought and the overall tone, shall we say, of the incarnation. Thus, the source may vary with the information sought. However, the information given will be in direct response to the information sought.

The usefulness of the information, in our humble opinion, is that which [is] of most importance, and the source, then, is of secondary consideration, for any entity consciously seeking the keys to its own evolution may find those keys and the doors which they open in any of many, many possible locations, both within the mind and outside of the complex of mind. The entity will draw unto itself those means of receiving information which have the greatest compatibility with the current frequency or level of seeking of that entity. Thus, the means change as the entity proceeds upon its own personal path of growth.

May we answer further, my brother?

J: No, thank you. That was very interesting.

I am Q'uo, and we thank you. Is there another query?

A: Yes, I would like to know at what time during an entity's being incarnated within the womb of the mother is the entity actually attached to the physical body. I've heard many, many different answers to this. And I want to know if the entity to be incarnated follows the mother around some time before the mother gets pregnant. Would you give me an answer to this?

I am Q'uo, and we might suggest that the possible reason for a great range of response to such a query is that there is a great range of possibilities that is uniquely realized in each entity's particular case. Indeed, the one about to enter the incarnative process who has in previous incarnations become aware consciously during the incarnation of the purpose of the incarnation may then in the succeeding incarnations choose those that will serve as what you call the parents.

In this case there may be the joining of these parental entities by the one about to incarnate before the incarnation begins, for in many cases these entities previous to any incarnation have joined their thoughts and desires in a manner which, as you might say, plans or programs the incarnation of each. And those which wait as what you would call the potential child and enter the incarnation at a later time, as you would call it, may often serve as a kind of guide for a period of your experience or time.

It is possible for such an entity or any entity that is about to join the incarnated process to enter that which will become its physical vehicle at any point within the portion of time that the vehicle is within the womb. Some entities choose to enter at an earlier time than others in order to gain more experience within that environment. Others wait, shall we say, for a later entry in order that work of another nature might take place in other dimensions, shall we say, that will enable the incarnation to proceed with the hoped for efficiency, shall we say. Thus, there is no one time at which an entity seeking incarnation enters the physical vehicle as it is prepared within the womb of the entity serving as the mother.

May we answer further, my sister?

A: Yes. When a woman receives an abortion, what happens to the entity that had been attached to that baby, whether physically attached or not? What happens, does the entity have to wait for another incarnation or was that meant to have come about? Is it also prearranged before the incarnation that the abortion would come about?

I am Q'uo, and am aware of your query, my sister. Again we find that there is no simple or general response that may be given to such a query, for as the universe is infinite in possibility, each moment and experience reflects that infinity possibility.

In some cases, for example, when that activity that you have called the abortion is to occur, this potential is seen upon what you would call the inner planes far before it is manifested within your third-density illusion, and in these cases it is possible that there has been no entry into the physical vehicle of a mind/body/spirit complex, and thus the aborted fetus, as you would call it, was never inhabited by a mind/body/spirit complex.

In other cases it is quite possible that such inhabitation did occur and was indeed chosen before the incarnation for that short period in order to complete a process of balancing that you might liken unto the karmic restitution, for again a great variety of possible reasons.

In yet another case, it might be that the aborted physical vehicle known as the fetus must be abandoned by a mind/body/spirit complex which had hoped that there would indeed be the possibility for a lengthier stay, shall we say, within the incarnative experience. In such a case the entity may seek other parents, as you call them, and find a successful entry into the incarnative process in that manner.

There are some few cases in which an entity which has found the opportunity for physical incarnation ended by the process of the aborted fetus, that such an entity will attempt to work upon those lessons that were desired for the third-density incarnation in another manner, that which does not partake of a third-density incarnation. However, these instances are quite rare, for within your third-density illusion the opportunity to learn and to progress in the evolution of mind, body and spirit is quite intense, and is not easily reproduced without the actual experience of the third-density illusion.

May we answer further, my sister?

A: One more question. I'm sorry I'm taking more of your time, but these are real important to me. Has it happened very often that an entity would agree with a certain other entity before incarnation that they would come to him as a child, and then, during the incarnation, the agreement is broken by the parents not wanting to have children even though there was an agreement beforehand?

I am Q'uo, and we look upon this possibility as one which, though an infrequent occurrence, is indeed possible within your illusion as the free will of all entities within your third-density illusion is that which is of paramount importance, for within your illusion occurs the meeting of free will and that which you may see as predestination, or the choosing previous to the incarnation of patterns that free will shall embellish upon during the incarnation. As the process of evolution, then, is always a function of this joining of free will that has its origin both before and during the incarnation, there may be that which you call the change of plans. However, in no case is there the loss of opportunity to learn and to serve. The opportunities may change, yet always they exist.

May we answer further, my sister?

A: You did a wonderful job. Thank you for all of your answers.

I am Q'uo, and we thank you, my sister, for the opportunity to respond. Is there another query?

(Pause)

I am Q'uo, and we rejoice with you and with the sounds and the silence and the creatures of the evening do we all blend our hearts with the seeking of the One within all that is. We thank each present for the opportunity to share our humble words and thoughts with you.

We remind each that we are but your fallible brothers and sisters who travel the same journey of seeking as do you. Though we may have moved some distance further upon that path, we would not wish that any word that we have spoken serve as a stumbling block to any on that path. If we have spoken a word that does not ring true, please disregard it without a second thought.

We look forward, as you might say, to future opportunities of joining with you in your circle of seeking. At this time we shall leave this instrument and this group in the love and in the light of the one Creator. We are known to you as those of Q'uo. Adonai, my friends. Adonai vasu. ❧

L/L Research

L/L Research is a subsidiary of Rock Creek Research & Development Laboratories, Inc.

P.O. Box 5195
Louisville, KY 40255-0195

www.llresearch.org

Rock Creek is a non-profit corporation dedicated to discovering and sharing information which may aid in the spiritual evolution of humankind.

ABOUT THE CONTENTS OF THIS TRANSCRIPT: This telepathic channeling has been taken from transcriptions of the weekly study and meditation meetings of the Rock Creek Research & Development Laboratories and L/L Research. It is offered in the hope that it may be useful to you. As the Confederation entities always make a point of saying, please use your discrimination and judgment in assessing this material. If something rings true to you, fine. If something does not resonate, please leave it behind, for neither we nor those of the Confederation would wish to be a stumbling block for any.

CAVEAT: This transcript is being published by L/L Research in a not yet final form. It has, however, been edited and any obvious errors have been corrected. When it is in a final form, this caveat will be removed.

© 2009 L/L Research

Sunday Meditation
September 21, 1986

(Carla channeling)

I am Hatonn, and I greet you in the love and in the light of our infinite Creator. It is a great privilege to speak with you this evening and we thank you for calling us to your group this evening that we may share our thoughts with you for whatever value they may have to you. We urge you to remember that we are your brothers and sisters and can only give our opinions. We do not have ultimate knowledge, but only more experiences than you to call upon. This we gladly share with you, for it is our way of being of service to the Creator and thereby progressing in our own spiritual evolution.

Our native home is the density towards which you now strive, the density of love, compassion or understanding. It is a density when lies are no longer necessary and masks may be tossed away, for our thoughts are all shared, and we accept and harmonize each other's characteristics and seek together to be of service. Each of you has many impulses to live in just such a way, and we assure you that it will be your native land too when you have finished learning the lessons that you have set for yourself in this density of yours, the density of conscious awareness. Your density, my friends, must learn that consciousness has a certain characteristic which is its original characteristic. Consciousness is not a neutral thing, but rather sprang from a creative force, that creative force we call love.

When the seeker decides that it is time to take the spiritual journey in hand and attempt to accelerate the rapidity with which it is pursued, the seeker gazes at his own awareness, his own consciousness. After he has asked the question of identity and said, "Who am I?" and answered himself, "I am Consciousness," the seeker must then turn [and] ask, "What is consciousness?"

It is easy for us in hindsight to tell you that the original Thought from which has sprung all consciousness and which is the nature of consciousness in whatever distortion you may find it, is love. All that you see about you manifested in whatever form, is made of a direct emanation of love which is called by your peoples the photon or light. Light in various rotations forms itself into all that you see, feel, use and call by name, all elements and combinations of elements.

And yet, my friends, your lessons involve something beyond this simplicity, for you are not simple, but complex, and you have made for yourself an illusion that is not simple, but complex. You have made this for yourself because you have found it helpful in learning the lessons of awareness and consciousness, to pose for yourself the seemingly impossible and insoluble problems in order that you may through meditation and contemplation and analysis discover the love that lies in all its simplicity at the heart of every tangle of illusion.

The seeker must gaze at all that passes before his eyes with a determination to see—that is, perceive—what he is looking at in the light of creative love, and so move from complexity back to simplicity, breaking the illusion and entering the density that is to come.

My friends, this all sounds as if we were recommending that you do very grand things, perhaps meditate a great deal or do something dramatic to bring mankind together. There are those who have planned to do something dramatic within an incarnation, but most entities within any density are working for the most part upon themselves. And so, what you are working with is the little things. Therefore, forget your impressions of spirituality, for you will work best upon your spirituality by paying close attention to the very small things of daily life.

We ask each of you to look at what you have done this day, at each word that you have said to another, at each gesture and smile and frown that you have shared with another consciousness. What intentions had you for service this day: service to others, service to self, and service to the Creator? How much of today was spent in fulfilling neutral needs without inspecting them for the joy that lies within the humblest task?

You see, my friends, the one who irons a shirt, praising it as part of the creation of the Father, dwells in the kingdom of the original Thought of love. And that kingdom is within him at that very moment that he wields the humble iron. The cook who praises the broth and smiles at the soapy dishes has garnered far more riches than good food and a clean kitchen, for the consciousness of joy and peace has come into the domicile and softened the neutrality of everyday things.

What little angers have you had today that pulled you away from consciousness into unconscious negativity? How much of this day did you lose? How much of this day did you fail to function because of confusion, anxiety, worry, irritation or distraction?

My friends, we realize that the questions that we ask cannot well be answered by any entity, for concentration fails, the best of intentions do not endure, and one must periodically start again. Yet, we assure you that there is no penalty, metaphysically speaking, for the wasted moments. Indeed, each mistake teaches, each misstep strengthens future steps. And when you must rest, then at the end of the rest, you simply put your foot on the path again.

That path to the consciousness of love does not go anywhere—it is always with you. Your perception of it may shift and change, but it is as near to you as your breath. You have only to calm the mind and feel the key turn within the door that opens your heart to that path. For you see, my friends, the path of spirituality is a path which is taken by the heart as well as by the mind, and, for the most part, it is a difficulty in feeling universal love that distracts the attention from the path.

We do suggest that you attempt to spend some minutes of your time each day in meditation. No matter what else you may do during the day, the silent meditation is the most efficient tool for seating within you the awareness of the love of the Creator. When you dwell within that consciousness, you are no longer working under your power, a power which fails much like batteries fail and which must be replaced by your sleeping periods. No, meditation is much like finding the electrical cord for constant power. It may flow through you, then, and not from you, and you will be far more radiant and able to dwell in the consciousness of the love and the light of the one infinite Creator.

When you have focused for enough days and weeks and months on the little things, you will look back and you will observe that the large things, even the great things, have taken care of themselves, for when you develop the discipline of faithfulness, the scale of that to which you are faithful does not matter and you will find the large things as easy as the small and as free from worry. We encourage each of you in your several journeys and would be very happy to spend meditative time with you at your mental request if you so desire.

We find this instrument is unusually fatigued this evening, and so we shall cut this message short, reluctantly but with thanks that we were able to use this instrument. We are those of Hatonn. We leave you in all that there is, the love and the light of the infinite Creator. Adonai, my friends. Adonai vasu borragus.

(Jim channeling)

I am Latwii, and I greet you, my friends, in the love and the light of the one Creator. We are also most honored to be asked to join your group this evening.

It is our privilege to attempt to answer those queries which you may find value in asking. As our brothers and sisters of Hatonn, we would remind each of you that what we have to share is our experience and our opinions and we would not wish to put ourselves forth as any source of infallible information. Therefore, take that which we give which has value to you and leave that which has none. With that caveat, may we begin with the first query?

M: Are Latwii and Hatonn located in the same place, same planet? And if so, what is the relationship of the position of such planet in relationship to our solar system?

I am Latwii, and am aware of your query, my brother. Those of the vibration known to you as Hatonn are of a planetary consciousness, much as your own planet would appear if each being upon it shared the mind of each other and thus had a great resource upon which to draw in seeking the light and sharing the light with others. Their vibration, shall we say, is that known to you as the vibration of love, the universal love and compassion that sees the creation as one thing, the one Creator in many parts.

We, of the vibration known to you as Latwii are also of a planetary mind quality, yet we have in our journeying moved into the next vibratory density of light, that known as wisdom, thus we seek at another level of vibration from either those of Hatonn or those of your own planetary influence.

We as well as those of Hatonn are not located within your own solar system, as you call it, but find ourselves some distance and experience removed, and seeking the one Creator in a system which is difficult to describe, yet which moves with its own rhythms of being.

May we answer further, my brother?

M: How long has Latwii observed the events of our Earth that we call our history or antiquity?

I am Latwii, and we have been consciously and carefully observing the conditions upon your planetary sphere for a period of what you would call time that you would measure as approximately twenty-five thousand of your years. We have information that is somewhat older, shall we say, concerning your planetary influence and its progression in evolution, that has been left to us in thought patterns or records which we have also perused in order to further intensify our understanding of your particular position as a population and as a planet within the evolutionary process.

May we answer further, my brother?

M: Can you tell me when the third-density experience first began on planet Earth and where?

I am Latwii, and we find that the third-density experience, that experience which is now reaching its culmination upon your planetary influence, found its origination some seventy-five thousand of your years in your past. However, there are many of your population now inhabiting your planetary influence which experienced previous third-density experiences upon other planetary influences in other solar systems, as you call them, and thus have within their memory banks or resources recall of third-density experience that far exceeds that of the seventy-five thousand year period that is the normal length of time necessary in order for the self-consciousness awareness to develop to the point that the possibility of experiencing universal love and compassion is available.

The point or place of the origination of the third-density experience upon this planetary sphere is not one point or place. We are attempting to show this instrument the mental image of your planetary influence and to describe those places which were among the first to be inhabited by the third-density population that was first upon your planetary influence. We show this instrument locations which are no longer in original configuration, for there have been land masses upon your planetary surface that have, as you would say, been swallowed beneath the seas in previous times.

One of these is known to you as that of Lemuria or the land mass of Mu. Within this area many of the first of your planet's population found their beginnings. We further attempt to give this instrument the picture of an area within your African continent, that area in the northeastern portion of that continent and further surrounding the body of water that you now call the Mediterranean Sea. Within this area many of the first of the population of your planet found their beginnings. Also we show this instrument a location in south central Asia, as it is now known, which was also a place of the origination of another of the first of your third-density population.

There were other beginnings that were at a somewhat later point in your planet's cycle that are located within the South American continent and within the continent known to you as Australia.

May we answer further, my brother?

M: Did those of the population of the Earth of the third density plan and construct the great pyramid at Giza? Or was there some influence from other entities?

I am Latwii, and we find that both of your suppositions are correct, for circling your entire planetary sphere is a pattern of the pyramidal structures that had as their origin sources exterior to your planetary influence, for at various portions of your planet's cycle of evolution, there have been times when the planet itself was in need of balancing or alignment and the cultures of your planet at that time in some few locations were of a level of advancement, shall we say, and openness to information from sources outside of their culture that it was possible for entities of other planetary influences to communicate certain information and to take part in the construction of certain of the pyramidal structures that would allow not only a balancing of your planet itself, but of individualized entities who would enter these structures for the purpose of healing and initiation.

In many cases the pyramidal structure at a later date, then, was copied and constructed by portions of your planet's population. Thus, the source of the pyramid form is twofold: that of your planet and that exterior to your planet.

May we answer further, my brother?

M: What did the process involve, the balancing that you mentioned—the pyramidal shapes performed some balancing for the Earth or within the Earth? Can you describe that further, please?

I am Latwii, and we shall attempt to give a general description of that which is somewhat complex in its nature. Each portion of the creation, and each planet in particular, is formed of and by that force which you may call love. Each entity of the third-density level of vibration which walks your planet and the planet itself receives a constant infusion of this intelligent energy which we have called love, and this infusion of love moves into the entity, whether it be one such as yourself or the planetary entity, through vortices of entrance, shall we say.

These lines of force that surround an entity or a planet, and which may be seen as analogous to an aura, move and cross in various patterns. Certain intersections of these lines of force permit an influx of the energy of intelligent infinity which we have called love. This love then invigorates, ennobles and enables the entity, be it an individual or a planet, to continue upon the evolutionary process.

When there has been a period of what you call disharmony amongst various portions of a planet's population and this period of disharmony, even unto the bellicose actions of war, has lasted a significant length of what you call time, then this heat of anger radiates into the planetary surface itself and seeks release in various ways.

As the release is sought, the spin, shall we say, of the planet itself as it moves in its orbit about that body that you call the sun becomes somewhat unstable. This instability makes the influx of intelligent energy or love somewhat more erratic than is optimal for the steady progression along the evolutionary path of the planet itself and of its population.

Thus, the pyramid structures are an aid in rebalancing this imbalance because they have the ability to influence the planet's spin, shall we say, or use of the intelligent energy of love. Thus, this type of balancing pyramid may serve not only the planet, but may serve individualized portions of a planetary population which have also found certain imbalances within the mind/body/spirit complex.

May we answer further, my brother?

M: It sounds like we're during another period in which the Earth is heating up. Would the construction of more pyramids help balance the Earth once again? Or is that possible?

I am Latwii, and am aware of your query, my brother. At this time, as you would call it, the population of your planet has by the phenomenon of the continued process of evolution found itself in a collective position where each entity with the conscious awareness of the evolutionary process may serve as what you may see as a portable pyramid. That is to say, the conscious intentions of those who would seek to heal the ruptures in this planet's electromagnetic field due to constant disharmony for a great portion of your planet's experience may take part in this balancing or healing of the planetary entity as a result of conscious choice and practice.

Thus, such an entity, and there are many, many now upon your planetary surface, may within the meditative state, see those …

(Tape ends.) ❧

L/L Research

Sunday Meditation
September 28, 1986

(Carla channeling)

I am Q'uo. I greet you in love and in the light of the one infinite Creator. It is a great privilege to be called to your group this evening and we thank this blended energy for offering us the invitation to attempt to be of service to you. We can only hope that we may in some way endeavor to further or inspire you upon the path of your spiritual seeking. If we say aught amiss, we ask you that you discriminate rapidly, forgetting any thought of ours that is not helpful to you, for we are fallible and bearers of opinion, not gospel.

There are times in each seeker's experience when the waters of life seem somewhat dammed up, and there seems to be the need for the guardianship of precious things. There is a sense that those things necessary to life must be conserved and guarded. This is the very purpose of the illusion which you have fashioned for yourself. Without the illusion, there would be no temptation to feel that one must guard what one has, there would be no experience of lack, thus there would be no fear of that lack.

Each of you finds it all too easy to experience the illusion and accept its apparent reality to the point where you are spending your time in counting and preserving your possessions. The dearest possessions of most entities are relationships, and so each of you may find yourself worshipping spouses and children, parents and friends, feeling that it is important to preserve and further these relationships. Surely there can be no harm in this, nor can there be harm in attempting to conserve physical possessions which it has cost one dearly to possess. The good will of others, one's reputation, [each] is a possession which many spend much time in guarding. None of these things in themselves are in the least bit inappropriate.

However, there is a function of your spiritual evolution which it is impossible to fulfill unless you are to a significant extent empty instead of full, and doing nothing instead of keeping all the balls in the air. Have you ever wondered why there are so many of your people who have turned to solitude, fasting and silence as means of spiritual growth? They are attempting to empty themselves, that there may be room in their lives for the fulfillment of the spiritual function of polarizing by turning the attention to the search for the perception of the infinite Creator.

How much of yourselves are you willing to empty in order that you may behold the perception that is possible for all of the infinite Creator? We assure you that it is not necessary to give up all the responsibility except the responsibility to engage in any specific spiritual activity, for many entities, having made contact with a consciousness of love, are then capable of keeping that relationship with direct perception of the Creator as a part of the point of view which is used to evaluate all those things within the illusion. May we suggest that this is indeed a worthwhile process. It will intensify experience from the point of view of generating more catalyst for your heart to digest than meditation in a cave would.

Yet the emphasis on something outside the illusion rescues one from unawareness of the process, therefore the process is accelerated, for you are able to manipulate it for greatest and most efficient learning. All entities that you meet are a portion of the Creator. Indeed, as the Creator created all that there is of Itself, each of you is an holographic representation of the Creator, and herein lies your great and fundamental equality, for each of you is in all ways perfect. That is your reality. You are channeling a distortion of your actual original self. You are dimly perceiving your true nature, and you are gaining in experience in this illusion so that you may refine your perceptions and more and more define yourself in terms of love and all others in terms of love until your perception becomes clear.

We ask that you think about some of these things and take all of your thoughts, offering them up in meditation daily, if possible, always seeking the truth with all that is within you. We are known to you as those of Q'uo. For the purposes of answering questions we shall transfer to another instrument. We wish to thank you again for calling us. It is a great pleasure and privilege to be in contact with each of your life paths. We thank you for the perfume of your thoughts. We now leave this instrument. We are Q'uo.

(Jim channeling)

I am Q'uo, and greet each of you again in love and light. We are happy to be able to offer the service of attempting to answer those queries which each may have brought this evening and to aid in some small degree in shining a light where perhaps there is darkness. May we begin with the first query?

J: I'm a little bit confused from the session tonight as to exactly how we should go about preparing ourselves to receive more catalyst into our lives and to basically make space for the true reality. Could you elaborate a little bit more on that for me, please, to clarify that?

I am Q'uo, and it is our privilege to do so, my brother. Each person will find that much is shared, yet much is unique in the pattern of life as one may see it compared with others and as one looks upon it in one's own experience. Thus, as one proceeds through this pattern and sees the daily round of activities repeating in a certain fashion, one may note how the learning of love which each attempts is proceeding in the life pattern.

As one becomes consciously aware that there are certain areas in which this lesson has found firmer root and other areas in which this lesson remains to be learned, one will become aware of how this particular lesson is being utilized in the overall sense in one's life. As one notices the areas of difficulty and gives to these areas added attention and attempts to discern that which is unknown and to resolve that which remains a puzzle, one will find various attitudes and procedures helpful.

Among these, a general suggestion may be made that a certain portion of the day be set aside as a quiet moment of reflection, whether it be meditation, prayer or contemplation. During this quiet portion of one's day, one may review the process of learning this general concept of love and acceptance that is ongoing in the life pattern. During this time, one may note those areas where added attention would be helpful. One may note those areas of success, shall we say, and attempt then to build upon these strengths and to utilize in some fashion what has been well learned there in the areas which yet lack the proficiency of loving without stint and accepting without condition those offerings of others about one.

May we answer further, my brother?

J: As was mentioned in the session tonight, there are those who have essentially dropped out of society and become reclusive for the purpose of accelerating themselves along the spiritual path. Is this a technique by which one can accelerate himself along the path, and is this recommended?

I am Q'uo, and am aware of your query, my brother. It is the ancient path of the seeker of truth to seek those high mountain caves where the isolation from the mundane nature of the illusion may be achieved and closer communion with the one Creator Who resides in all may be sought. Whether this journey is reproduced in actuality or in thought within the seeker of truth is a decision which each seeker shall make for himself.

In one sense, such isolation is a part of each conscious seeker's journey, for in truth, though one find oneself surrounded by many other beings and portions of the man-made culture, shall we say, the use of these experiences that are shared with others is quite a personal matter, though others may inform and inspire by their own opinions, gathered through their own experiences. Yet each seeker must choose for himself how any such information is to be utilized within that seeker's life experience.

Thus, this basic fact may be enlarged upon by any who seeks not merely to separate the self from that which is busy and mundane and random within the life experience, but through such potential outer separation seeks rather to move closer to the heart of each entity and all being through the careful and individual consideration in moments of solitude of each experience that may be examined for the potential of growth that it offers.

Thus, the heart of all is that which one moves closer to in such a movement and if such be the motivation for seeking the high mountain cave, then, indeed, such isolation may be an effective means of learning those lessons that one has set forth in the life pattern, all reflecting in some degree the general understanding of love. Yet such isolation is not in the physical sense necessary if one can find those quiet moments in the high mountain caves of one's own daily meditation.

May we answer further, my brother?

J: Did the entity known as Jesus Christ meditate, or did he seek the high mountain cave, as you have said?

I am Q'uo, and in our response to your previous query, we could also have stated that it is seldom the case that an entity will choose one path or the other, but that it is more frequently the case that one will, for a portion of what you call time, seek those moments of isolation and perhaps even seek to extend them into days or weeks or months, and having garnered the frame of mind and fruit of seeking, shall we say, from this experience, then move again down the mountain side in order that that which has been found helpful and fruitful within the seeker's own experience might then be shared with others.

The one known as Jesus the Christ was one who in the middle years of its incarnation sought those high mountain caves, shall we say, and learned from various teachers those techniques and understandings which it later shared as the bounty of its own harvest of seeking with those that had ears to hear, shall we say.

May we answer further, my brother?

J: There's very little known to us from the scriptures of the middle years, let's say, of the life of Jesus Christ. Would it be possible to essentially highlight some of the events that took place in those middle years for us tonight?

I am Q'uo, and it is possible only in a general sense, for to delve in depth into this entity's incarnation and to report those experiences which were of particular and singular importance in that entity's life pattern would require a great deal of focused attention of a nature on this instrument's part which would be quite fatiguing and lengthy. However, we may suggest that the one known as Jesus of Nazareth who became the Christed being dwelling in the consciousness of love, that this entity was from the beginnings of its life pattern one filled with the desire to penetrate the illusion of appearance and to seek the heart of all being, which it perceived as what you would call the power of love. This entity was greatly desirous of being of service to those about it by aiding their own journeys of seeking this same source of power, that called love.

From an early age, then, this entity examined the religion of its people, and at an early age became quite advanced in its own understandings of what had been written and what had been passed from mouth to ear in the tradition of teaching of the elders of its race and religion. Having found certain sustenance of a spiritual nature in this fashion then, and having questioned many others of its own religion in the structured church of that time, it found that there was, shall we say, a boundary to that which could be learned within that structure of thought.

Feeling in an intuitive way that there was more available to one who could seek with a purity of desire in other manner of thought and philosophical understanding, this entity then set out upon a journey to distant locations where teachers in various philosophical fields, shall we say, became available to this entity as a result of its intense seeking. Many were located in those high mountain caves that we have spoken of previously. The disciplines of study and philosophy which this entity engaged in were of greater variety than it had experienced in its early years, and each added further insight, breadth and depth to the understanding that was developing, not only within this entity's complex of mind, but, we should say, within certain channels of connected feeling that this entity had brought with it in a latent form into the incarnation, thus, using that which it had been taught as a discipline to reach that which it contained in a latent form, this entity was able to open certain doorways or passages that one may liken unto rivers of nourishment.

The entity thus having penetrated, as it desired, to the heart of the power which sustains that known as the creation, thus it was able to realize that that power which it sought and called love and the one Creator was available to each person as a result of this same process of seeking which the one known as Jesus the Christ had itself undertaken. Thus, having realized that which was its great desire, it then moved again to that area which was its place of birth and began the activities that are recorded in the holy work that you call the Bible.

May we answer further, my brother?

J: In the middle years, in the many travels made by Jesus, did he visit what is known now as Mexico?

I am Q'uo, and we look upon this query with some concern, for there is the possibility of the infringement upon the free will of those who feel there is value in the possibility of this occurrence having truly occurred. We would, however, suggest that this entity remained in the vicinity of the near and far east, and was also one who journeyed into various portions of the continent now known as Asia, but did not partake in any journeys which crossed the barrier known as the Pacific Ocean.

May we answer further, my brother?

J: One more question—well, one more statement, I guess, then you can please comment on it as to its correctness. In the session that we had last week, we basically established that the pyramids were for balancing the planet at that particular point in time. And then the question was raised, at this particular point in time, would it be advantageous to again construct pyramids for this balancing technique, and the answer was basically that there are those among us now who have evolved along the spiritual path to such a degree that basically in and of themselves they are portable pyramids. Could it be that these individuals have evolved such that they can use the chakra centers of the body much like the chambers within the great pyramid for this balancing procedure. Is there any validity in that statement at all?

I am Q'uo, and we find that your statement is in general quite correct, for as time and experience has passed since the times of the pyramids, as you call them, entities upon your planet have had more opportunities to process the catalyst of each incarnation, and by such processed catalyst gain the experience of a spiritual nature which allows the movement of consciousness to proceed …

(Side one of tape ends.)

(Jim channeling)

I am Q'uo, and am again with this instrument. To continue our response. Thus, the accumulated experience that has accrued to the population of your planet has provided each entity now incarnate with the opportunity to utilize the heart chakra in a fashion which is congruent with the King's chamber position and provides to each entity who seeks consciously the keys to its own evolution the possibility of utilizing the energy of what you would call love in a fashion which may balance and heal not only the self in further processing of catalyst and others about the self, but in visualized meditations may affect the balance of your planetary sphere itself. This potential becomes available to an entity when that entity becomes consciously aware that it is proceeding upon a path of evolution and undertakes to accelerate that journey in a studied and continual fashion, thus becoming what we have called a seeker, a pupil.

May we answer further, my brother?

J: No, thank you. I think I've dominated enough of the time.

I am Q'uo, and we thank you, my brother. Is there another query?

H: Yes. Is there any stimulant or whatever that I could use, as the word goes, or suggest to my wife Eileen that might get her started some way in realizing her spirituality, which seemingly is lacking?

I am Q'uo, and, my brother, we sympathize greatly with the desire of all such as yourself who seek with a full heart to inspire another to consciously set foot upon that path of seeking the nature of the life experience, and we would only suggest that though many inspiring words may be spoken and offered to such an entity with the hope that it will indeed open the eyes to new possibilities of spiritual sense, that each entity has its own pattern or rhythm of unfolding which, given sustenance, nourishment and support from those about it shall take place in its own time. Who can say what is appropriate for another's journey of seeking, when so such within your illusion is filled with mystery and when that which is truly important upon the spiritual level moves in ways often unseen and does its work beyond any man's understanding?

Thus, for one to truly be of aid to another, one can only desire to be of such aid and to reflect the love that one has found in as pure a fashion as possible, giving always with an open and cheerful heart without expectation of return so that the greater will of the one Creator which has been planted as seed within all entities might in its own time be nourished and grow in a fashion which, [while] perhaps not understood by those about an entity, yet is appropriate to that entity.

May we answer further, my brother?

H: Yes. One more thing, on meditation. It seems that when I try to meditate, I try to take every little thought as they come up and gently put them out of my mind, and the next little thought the same way and just push it aside, and then all of a sudden I am just in a blank, as you might say, not really thinking about anything. But yet I find myself, more often than not, falling asleep. Is that meditation?

I am Q'uo, and, my brother, we may suggest that your experience of meditation is indeed an experience of meditation which has opened unto you a level of perception and being which has been of such a soothing nature that you have followed a natural tendency and moved with it into the state that you call sleep, and though not always consciously aware of how the process continues in the sleep state, nevertheless you have in that state continued the meditation and the associations and possibilities that it has opened for you. As you become more able to grasp these perceptions and associations consciously, you will find less and less need to work with them in the state that you call sleep.

May we answer further, my brother?

H: Yes. There's many questions on my mind, but one more question this session. In any lives past was I of any religious order, possibly?

I am Q'uo, and though we do not specialize in reading those experiences that you call previous incarnations, we may in a general sense confirm the suspicion which is strong in your own mind that in various experiences you have pursued a ritualized and disciplined seeking of the nature of your life and the creation and have done so in a manner that allowed you to share it in a formal fashion with others.

May we answer further, my brother?

H: I think that's all tonight.

I am Q'uo, and we thank you, my brother. Is there another query at this time?

(Pause)

I am Q'uo, and as we feel that we have exhausted the queries for the evening, we shall thank each present for offering us the great privilege and honor of blending our vibrations with your own. We remind each that we are but your brothers and sisters in seeking the light and love of the one Creator. We do not wish that any word that we have spoken should be a stumbling block upon your journey. If any word has not rung of truth to your inner feelings, please disregard each such word immediately. We rejoice with each in the presence of the one Creator that moves within all creation, and in that rejoicing and in the love and in the light of the one Creator, we leave this group at this time. We are known to you as those of Q'uo. Adonai, my friends. Adonai vasu borragus. ❧

Intensive Meditation
October 1, 1986

(Jim channeling)

I am Laitos, and I greet you, my friends, in the love and the light of the one infinite Creator. We are very pleased to be asked to join your group this evening. It is not often, as you would reckon time and experience, that we have the privilege of working with new instruments. We are honored that another has chosen to learn the service of vocal channeling in order that it might serve as an instrument for our humble thoughts, for as each new instrument begins this process, we find ourselves in the joyous situation of having before us yet another opportunity not only to serve the Creator, and another who wishes our services, but to aid a new instrument in being of further service in its own life patterns.

There are many ways that such an entity as those gathered here this evening may seek to serve those about it. There are many, many ways that an entity may seek to enrich its own process of growth. We encourage a wide-ranging spectrum of choices for any who would seek to be of service in whatever manner, and most especially the vocal channeling, for in this process of transmitting our thoughts to you, we feel that it is most necessarily a part of the process to use those experiences and avenues of seeking that you have found of value in your own journey of seeking the truth. Thus do we ratify and call upon the validity of your own patterns of seeking and being and use them in these messages that have as their purpose the inspiration of others to walk yet further upon their own paths of seeking.

Thus, do not be surprised if during the process of receiving our thoughts, if we should use your own experiences, whether recent or distant, in our messages. We feel that a blend of our thoughts with yours in a ratio of approximately seventy percent ours and thirty percent your own is that ratio which maximizes both our and your abilities to be of service to those about you. It is well for any instrument to be able to share its own beingness in as clear, concise and open manner as possible with those about it.

For in truth, all are instruments. Each person channels from deeper and deeper portions of its own being at various times in the life experience and when the desire is found within entities to be of service in the vocal channeling manner, this basic nature of each entity being an instrument then becomes more finely tuned so that there is possible the infusion of words and thoughts such as our own upon that frequency or desire to serve instruments that the new instrument manifests in this effort.

At this time, we would attempt to make our presence felt to the one known as K, and would attempt to simply identify ourselves through her instrument. If she will relax and speak those thoughts that become apparent to her, we shall attempt to simply identify ourselves as being those of Laitos. We shall transfer this contact at this time. I am Laitos.

(K channeling)

I am Laitos.

(Jim channeling)

I am Laitos, and am again with this instrument. We are very happy that we have been able to make contact with the one known as K. We are pleased that this new instrument not only was able to perceive our contact, but was, shall we say, brave enough to speak that which was received, for it is almost always the case with a new instrument that this new instrument will feel that the thoughts perceived in the mind are simply its own, for we transmit in a manner which almost precisely matches the generation of your own thoughts. Thus do we speak to your mind as you yourself speak through your mind.

We at this time feel that this is a good beginning, and before we would attempt a final contact with the one known as K, we would open this session to queries so that the one known as K may be able to ask any point that might be of concern upon her mind. Is there a query at this time?

K: Not at this time, thank you.

I am Laitos, and we thank you, my sister. May we ask if there be a query from the one known as Carla?

Carla: The question that's on my mind, I believe I will ask K in person. Thank you.

I am Laitos, and we thank you, my sister. At this time, we would again attempt to transmit our identification to one known as K, and if the one known as K feels adventurous, we shall transmit another phrase or two. We shall transfer this contact at this time. I am Laitos.

(K channeling)

I am Laitos … and I greet you, my friends … in the love and in the light of the one infinite Creator.

(Jim channeling)

I am Laitos, and am again with this instrument. We are exceedingly overjoyed at having made our presence known to the one known as K, and we thank this new instrument for allowing us to speak a few phrases through her this evening. We feel that her progress is exciting and quite well motivated, shall we say. We look forward to working with this new instrument in what you would call your future. We thank each for inviting our presence this evening, and we shall be with you upon your request. We are those of Laitos. We leave this group at this time in the love and in the light of the one infinite Creator. Adonai. Adonai. ☥

Intensive Meditation
October 2, 1986

(Jim channeling)

I am Laitos, and I greet you, my friends, in the love and the light of the infinite Creator. We are again most honored to be asked to join your group this evening in order that we might, as is our way, work with a new instrument who seeks in her own way to be of service through the vocal channeling. As always, we remind the new instrument that while the contact is being sought, and while it is experienced, it is well to reserve analysis and judgment of process and content in order that both may move in their own way through the instrument and thus exercise it that it comes to know that vibration which signals the contact and that feeling of surrender that allows the contact to move through the instrument.

We are always hopeful that simple instructions such as these will suffice to allow an instrument to serve as an instrument, for it is not a difficult task and further complexity in explaining the nature of such contact is, in truth, unnecessary unless the questioning mind of a new instrument might be put to rest by further words. This is also acceptable, yet is not necessary when looking at the experience of vocal channeling itself, for the world in which you move and the incarnations which are your vehicles for movement through this world of illusion is one which by its very nature is formed of complexities.

Yet if any portion of the complexity of your daily round of activities be followed, the source will be found to be that which is quite simple. The love of the Creator enables all portions of the creation to move in their various dances and to play the parts that allow experience to ensue and allow contemplation of that experience to distill from it the crystal seeds of thought that are love in a simple form.

At this time we would attempt to make our presence felt to the one known at K. She will begin to feel a certain sensation which will signal to her our presence. At this time we shall attempt to transfer this contact and speak not only our identification through the one known as K, but also include a few simple phrases that might allow this new instrument to gain somewhat in confidence as she is able to perceive that which we transmit. Again we suggest the reservation of all analysis and the simple speaking of those thoughts and concepts as they become apparent with the mind complex. We shall now transfer this contact. I am Laitos.

(K channeling)

I am Laitos … and I greet you, my friends, in the love and in the light of the infinite Creator. We are happy to be able to be here at this time.

(Jim channeling)

I am Laitos, and am again with this instrument. We are indeed overjoyed to be able to speak those words through the one known as K that we were indeed able to speak. We are very happy with the progress of this new instrument and can only encourage her to continue in that attitude that might best be described as a combination of bravery and foolhardiness, for to speak words which seem to exist in a vacuum, shall we say, unconnected to others of their kind, puts a new instrument in the position of moving further, it would seem, out upon a limb with no assurance that the limb will support one's weight or that the words spoken will be followed by others which together shall make what you would call sense.

This is the heart of the nature of the vocal channeling process, for it is not possible for most of the population of your planet to receive a complete message which then would be dictated line by line, for the receiving mechanism of the peoples of your planet has not been developed to that degree at this point in the evolution process. Thus, in order to utilize the capabilities of the receiving instruments, we must provide small portions of a larger message and follow each portion with another portion of roughly equivalent length in order that the entire message may eventually be transmitted.

This makes the process somewhat more, shall we say, challenging for any instrument, and most especially for the new instrument. Yet it is well that such a challenge be presented, for the opportunity to serve as such an instrument and to be of service to others in this manner is one which requires to be the fool, shall we say, in many, many instances where one shares that of greatest value with others who may or may not share similar views. Thus does any entity who seeks to serve others by sharing what is within the heart without reservation call upon that quality of foolishness that does not ask any return for what is given, nor does it ask that what is given be accepted or acted upon. All that is asked is that the opportunity to serve be available.

Thus, we encourage the one known as K to persist in this foolishness, if we may call it that, for within the illusion which you find yourselves now placed, nothing may be known with certainty, for that which is the foundation of all creation and inspiration is shrouded in mystery and hidden from all but the most persistent inward-seeking eye.

At this time we would make a final attempt to contact the new instrument, and perhaps say a few additional words through this new instrument. We shall contact the one known as K at this time. I am Laitos.

(K channeling)

I am Laitos. We are with this instrument again. *(Inaudible)*. We wish to say that we are pleased [to be talking through] this instrument. [At this time we wish to] say …

(The rest of the channeling is inaudible.)

(Jim channeling)

I am Laitos, and am again with this instrument. We are very happy that we have been able not only to contact the one known as K and to speak a few words through this new instrument, but that we have been able with each contact to expand the abilities of this instrument, and we look forward to each opportunity to work with this new instrument and this group. Before taking our leave of this group, we would ask if there might be any queries that we might respond to in order to facilitate the process which is ongoing?

K: *(Inaudible)*.

Carla: *(Inaudible)* … trying to frame a question?

K: *(Inaudible)*.

Carla: I'd like to know if my perceptions are accurate. However, I don't want to make you infringe on our free will. Would it be possible to ask you if my perceptions throughout this period were accurate, and again answer, yes or no.

I am Laitos, and am aware of your query, my sister. Though we find there is some possibility of infringing upon your own free will, we find that due to the manner in which the query was fashioned that we may answer in the affirmative, and in general confirm the feelings that you have left in an unexpressed form.

May we answer further, my sister?

Carla: I dealt with the situation a certain way. I want to frame this so you can say yes or no. Was that the optimal way I could have dealt with the situation in terms of the welfare of all those in the group?

I am Laitos, and we find that this query is somewhat more difficult to answer than was the previous query. We may suggest that given the certain set of circumstances at the moment of which you speak, that the action taken was helpful, but to suggest that such action was more or less helpful than another would constitute infringement, in our opinion.

May we answer further, my sister?

Carla: No, but let me ask another question. When a person or a group—a person in a group or outside of a group—experiences a psychic greeting, say this person challenges the entity perceived and discovers that the entity cannot meet the challenge but is reluctant to leave, and mentally, verbally, begins snapping at the heels by discussing how much the meditator loves the Christ and the meditator begins singing a hymn in her mind, and this would presuppose certain assumptions that the meditator is making concerning the nature of attack or greeting and the nature of the kindest and cleanest and most loving way to illuminate it. Are those assumptions adequate, or are there other assumptions that would be helpful to consider?

I am Laitos …

(Side one of tape ends.)

(Jim channeling)

I am Laitos, and am again with this instrument. To continue our response. We find within this query greater possibility of infringement upon your own powers of discrimination and use of free will were we to give specific response. We may speak in general, and suggest that at any point in one's experience that one feels influences of a negative nature, that is, of a nature which seems to oppose the movement of one's free will, that the response which is most helpful is that response which moves with greatest freedom without distortion and with the widest possible view of the experience which has been encountered. That is to say, as one is able to see all entities, thoughts and experiences as portions of the one Creator and is able to bless and love these experiences, one then moves to their heart and at that point joins in love with them. If any outer expression by another entity, then, is not congruent to that heartfelt expression, such an entity will find it necessary to remove its presence from the mirror which reflects to it the heart of love which it itself has denied in order that it might progress upon that path which may be characterized by the phrase, "the path of that which is not"—separation.

May we answer further, my sister?

Carla: No, thank you.

I am Laitos, and we thank you, my sister. Is there any further query at this time?

Carla: I'm curious, Laitos. I miss one of your trademarks, and want to know why this group hasn't called it forth. And I keep waiting for you to say, "Be sure and meditate every day, even if it is only for five minutes." We haven't heard it once in two nights—what happened?

I am Laitos, and we might suggest, my sister, that we have attempted to speak to this topic in a more general fashion, weaving it into our overall message, with the feeling that this group is well aware of the necessity of meditation and the lighter touch, shall we say, would be more appreciated by those entities which comprise this group. However we do take requests. *Be sure to meditate each day.* Five minutes will suffice. Even five seconds.

Carla: *(Laughing)* That was great—thank you very much.

I am Laitos, and would be happy to respond to any further queries.

Carla: That's all, thank you—for me.

I am Laitos, and we thank each within this group for inviting our presence and for reminding us to remind you to do that which is most salient within the seeking of any entity who wishes to unravel the mysteries of being. Join yourselves at your hearts at any moment that is available, that you might remove that busyness of your daily lives and join the ever-present silence in appreciation of the might, the majesty, and the mystery of the one Creator. We are with you there, and upon your request we shall even join you in your busyness, for to taste of your experience is a delight to us. We relish the opportunity to find the Creator in yet another place of hiding. We shall at this time leave this group in the manner of speaking only, for always we are one with you. We are known to you as those of Laitos. Adonai, my friends. Adonai, in the love and the light of the One. ☥

Intensive Meditation
October 3, 1986

(Jim channeling)

I am Laitos, and I greet you, my friends, in the love and the light of the one infinite Creator. We are once again privileged to be able to join your group this evening. We greatly enjoy the opportunity to work with the one known as K in order that she might continue the process of becoming a vocal instrument.

We have listened with appreciation and affection to the conversation which you have shared prior to this meditation and we wish to express our gratitude at the careful consideration of this kind of service by each present. It is quite true that it is not a difficult service to perform, but that there is indeed a certain kind of caring that is difficult to find in many who would seek to perform this service. It is the desire to be of service to others and to do so in a manner which serves to the best of one's abilities, that is the most appropriate motivator, shall we say, in our opinions for this service.

For many of your people it is a service which seems somewhat glamorous, for it partakes of that which is unseen and yet felt by many of your peoples to be a portion of the underlying truth of the illusion that they see as the daily life. To many it speaks subtly yet convincingly of a greater reality, shall we say, that towards which all move in heart and mind, and to give voice to such a power seems to many to be that which must be reserved for the few. And yet in truth we say to you that each in some way contacts this same source of energy and power each day of the incarnation and chooses in one fashion or another to channel that power in a manner which may or may not be conscious, may or may not be understood, and yet surely is a reflection of the One through a portion of the One.

You who have gathered here this evening have chosen a more specific means by which this transmission of the power of what we have called love may be accomplished. It is no more or less better or worse than any other choice. It is simply a choice which will be useful to some and less useful to others. That it is offered in the desire to be of service to others is that which truly matters, shall we say. Thus, this desire is that in which we rejoice this evening and we share it with you.

At this time we would attempt to make our vibrations known to the one known as K, and after a few moments in which any needed adjustment may be made by mental request by the one known as K in order that our vibrations not be uncomfortable, we should then speak a few words through the one known as K. We shall now transfer this contact. I am Laitos.

(K channeling)

I am Laitos. I greet you, my friends, in the love and in the light of the one infinite Creator. I am with you now in order that you may understand what it is that we are doing.

We are adjusting our vibrations to this instrument.

We are here *(inaudible)* continue this contact.

(Jim channeling)

I am Laitos, and I am again with this instrument. We are very pleased that we have been able not only to make contact with the one known as K, but to reestablish that contact on the two occasions that she felt she had lost this contact. We feel that there has been great expansions of this new instrument's abilities, and would continue to encourage this new instrument to persevere with moving further and further out on the limb so that the contact might continue and further concepts be generated and it be truly found that the limb has no end.

At this time we would pause in this working in order for any queries that might be upon the minds of those present might be asked. May we respond to any queries at this time?

Carla: I'll give K time to think, and ask a question of my own. I'm writing a book on channeling. Not on the mechanics of channeling, but on every aspect of it that I can think of that might be helpful to people who want to channel and people who are channeling. Any comments or suggestions that you have would be appreciated.

I am Laitos, and, my sister, we are aware of the work upon this subject that you have undertaken, and in our way would choose to show our appreciation of this effort by observing that the process which you are utilizing in writing this book upon the topic of channeling is a process of channeling itself, and is one in which you are, again in our opinion, utilizing the most valuable tool of the instrument, and that is the personal experience of the instrument itself, for to speak upon any topic it is quite helpful not only to be familiar with the topic in an intellectual fashion, but to have made such a close identification with the topic that one truly draws it from the depths of one's own experience and responses to that experience.

Thus, the work takes on a life that is obviously of its own and is represented in a fashion which then is dynamic and in motion within the author so that the words might then convey this life force that is shared without reservation. That, in our experience and opinion, is the heart of any channeling process and we rejoice at the work which you have chosen to share in your own way.

May we answer further, my sister?

Carla: No, but I'd appreciate your help if you would please tell whoever is channeling this to me to use better English. I will too.

I am Laitos, and we can assure you, my sister, that the message has been received. Is there another query?

K: I have a question. The contact feels to me very tenuous and faint. I don't know if it gets stronger, but I was getting the feeling that I was supposed to be listening for it, somehow. Do you have any comments on that or suggestions as to how I might do that better?

I am Laitos, and we might comment by suggesting that, again in our opinion, you are perceiving our contact with unusual clarity for a new instrument, for, indeed, in the beginning of this practice it is usual that a tenuous feeling be associated with the perception of our thoughts. As you are able to quiet the inner conversations, the over-nervousness and any doubts that you may carry with you into the meditative state, you will discover that the signal, shall we say, seems amplified, and will eventually be as easily perceivable as any of your own thoughts. In the beginning of this practice we can suggest none too frequently that the new instrument simply be patient and continue with the process as if it were practicing its scales upon the piano. There is a certain amount of exercise that is necessary in order to develop the concentrative muscle, shall we say.

May we answer further, my sister?

K: When I start to feel like I'm losing the contact, is there anything that I can do at that point, other than to just continue to quiet my mind?

I am Laitos, and am aware of your query, my sister. We again would suggest that the quieting of concerns, thoughts and analysis is the most helpful thing that one might do in order to again begin to perceive the thread of the contact, and to, once having perceived it, await the next concept or phrase. Again, we might characterize this state of mind as a simple and quiet confidence, realizing that one is partaking in an event which is, as it has been observed, actually occurring.

May we answer further, my sister?

K: As you were contacting me during these practice sessions, is there a way that I would know when you have finished transmitting to me?

I am Laitos, and this query, my sister, we find quite easy to answer, and do not need to be facetious, but we will tell you when we are finished by suggesting that we are finished.

May we answer further, my sister?

K: No, thank you, that is very helpful.

Carla: You're such a wag.

I am Laitos, and we thank you, my sister.

K: I appreciate your sense of humor.

Carla: None from me—thank you, Laitos.

I am Laitos, and we are happy that we have been able to share a bit of the humorous nature of these beginning sessions, for the ability to laugh at oneself and the process of learning any new experience is an attitude which greatly enhances the learning of that new skill or experience.

We at this time would attempt not only to transfer our contact once again to the one known as K, but would attempt to close this contact through the one known as K, and in this manner she will know that she has finished the contact. I am Laitos.

(K channeling)

I am Laitos, and I am with this instrument again. We find your humor to be refreshing as well. We thank you for this as it is enjoyable to us. We wish now to say that this instrument is progressing satisfactorily. And we will now close this contact. I am Laitos.

(Carla channeling)

I am Laitos, and I greet you once again through this instrument in love and light. We were attempting to recontact the one known as K, and then the one known as Jim. However, we found each to be somewhat puzzled.

We wished not to give any further message except to note to the one known as K that it is well to observe carefully when the naming is done, to discern the sentiment of love, peace, joy, light and blessedness in some close conjunction with greetings and farewells, for we do not wish to leave any with a name alone, but rather with the name of that principle, as this instrument would say, in whose service we come to you, for we are but messengers, bearing news, news of complex things and news of the very simple things that underlie the complexities. We greet and bid farewell of that which is simple, that which is unified, that which we worship and are—love and light.

If those concepts do not rise in your consciousness, challenge immediately, my sister, for the source is questionable in that event. That is, it is certainly not necessary to question that it is not the Confederation which speaks. Thus settling into the night and enjoying this added few moments to hear the sounds of your katydids, we do bid you farewell in the love and in the light of our infinite Creator. We are known to you as those of Laitos. Adonai. ❦

Sunday Meditation
October 5, 1986

(Carla channeling)

I am Q'uo, and I greet you in the love and the light of the infinite One, the Creator of all that there is. We trust that all can hear this instrument's voice. We find this instrument to have a low supply of energy this evening, and so are attempting to conserve by speaking in a quiet voice. It is most pleasurable to be able to speak with you, and we thank you for calling us to you this evening.

It is but a moment for us to move through the densities to you, yet in terms of novelty of experience the moment is momentous for us, for us experiencing third density through third-density senses as you share them with us is a marvelously beautiful thing. We thank you for offering us this service and we hope we can inspire you in some way with what we say. All topics are a challenge in one way or another. A query from the group concerning the validity of [an] inspired set of writings certainly has a challenge for us, as we do not wish to seem to judge any source.

You must understand that we are offering information to you through an instrument. There was a source offering the one you know as Nostradamus information. It came through him and this entity recorded it. It may aid in your evaluative process to regard this very devout person as the same kind of instrument as the entity who is channeling our words.

The information is for you to use in order to effect the most spiritual progress. Each individual finds its own aids towards that task. Those things that you find helpful may mean nothing to another. Prophecy may inspire one and leave another with a cold heart and an indifferent curiosity. We hope that these comments aid you in the subjective evaluation of data concerning some aspects of the mystery which surrounds those things which you seem to know within the illusion. It is of course to the mystery that you will turn—that is why you have gathered this evening in light—to seek the truth. Would you have done so had you thought that all that you perceived was so and formed the sum total of all that needs to be known of ultimate causes?

We move now to a discussion of prophecy from another point of view, from the point of view of subjectivity versus objectivity.

Begin with the original Thought, the unified, ceaselessly eternal, all-encompassing Thought that created all that there is, creates all that is to become, and yet remains uncreated. The Logos—love—has no mate but the divine spirit of free will, and its creations are of itself. Thus, each portion of the creation is a hologram of love. Each portion of each illusion contains within it all that there is, all truth, all wisdom, and all understanding. Is it any wonder, then, that there is a marvelous amount of redundancy within the objects which make up your illusion? Is it any wonder that the energies of the atom mimic in miniature the very visible heavenly arrangements of planets, solar systems and galaxies?

And is it any wonder that there should always be occult or hidden knowledge of future disaster [or] a global war in days which are in your past—worldwide proportions. For you see, my friends, each of you has an illusion within your consciousness, the illusion to which you are tied by the chemicals and liquids of your heavy physical body. It is designed that one day you shall drop this body and your consciousness shall once again take wing and move into a more light-filled body.

This is known as the physical death. Subjectively, it is inevitable that the illusion which repeats and repeats patterns within the subjective self should repeat the death experience.

We are attempting to say some rather subtle things. Let us briefly recapitulate. We are attempting to say that your discriminative powers are being underrated by questioners who believe another's work over their own.

We have no bias, and therefore we do not speak. Were we biased, we might speak. The more we were biased, the more surely we would share our opinions with you, and yet, would you wish to take on faith the biased opinion? We ask you to take responsibility for the information which you assimilate. Digest it well, excreting those things which you do not find spiritually inspiring, and pursuing with a lively curiosity and interest those things which speak to you of mystery. Attempt to be swayed only on interesting technical points, shall we say, by anyone. Allow yourself to be swayed by anyone who can help you frame your questions better, but reserve your own right to perceive the information which comes when questions are asked. Reserve for yourself the right to choose that which feels inspiring to you, for the search for truth is not a cold building up of facts, but a journey to the heart.

As you live in your head, so you die to the passion that can burn within you, to the joy that can leap from your heart at simple things. If prophecy is to be inspiring, let its vision make you rejoice at that which is to come, or pray and offer yourself in dedication for any event you feel may come which may be sad.

Remember also to take yourself seriously enough to realize that this creation is more and more created by you as co-Creator, for during the third density man becomes more and more the true captain of the craft which is his consciousness, becoming more and more self-conscious, self-aware, self-sensitive and aggressive towards the environment which previously has been molded by love alone. More and more the third-density illusion becomes a metaphor for the self as you subjectively see yourselves to be. Thus, at this point in your third density, as it moves into fourth, you find yourselves at bitter odds, torn between compassion and comfort, between patriotism and peace, between love and anger. And your creation is reflecting this.

Nothing shall be so crushing to your physical being as your own death; nothing shall be more liberating. And so you have the subjective model for the new age. My friends, it is no more, no less than the larger life which awaits as you move through the gates of the death of your physical body and are able to release it and transform your consciousness into that of a more light-filled being.

In conclusion, we would say that your planet is indeed in travail and has been—is in—the middle of an ice age, has the potential for moderate destruction over a fairly lengthy period of approximately one of your centuries, or a much shorter period of extreme trauma. We will not give you the odds, as they change constantly. However, we will say that it appears that many who dream struggle now to awaken.

There is more movement in consciousness upon your planet at this time than any time since we have been working with your people. We do not despair, but hope, for there is a substantial reward for practicing the faculty of hope and faith. Remember that all is subjective. Your consciousness is greater than that of the planet in its delineation and fastidiousness of character. And that which man wishes the environment, the creation about man will reflect. The faculty of hope, of faith and positive outcomes will create enough light to vitalize a great deal that is now broken and without life within your planet.

Each time you send light to that entity who loves you whom you call Earth, the Earth changes. The question was a simple one, and we have commented on Nostradamus. However, my friends, we hope that we have turned your minds to a new consideration [of] prophecy, one that offers you room for praise and rejoicing, for excitement at new things and for hope in the future. As you mold your consciousnesses, so in echo will your growth mold itself.

We greet and send love to each present, and would prepare to leave this instrument, thanking her and you once again. We would now transfer. I am Q'uo.

(Jim channeling)

I am Q'uo, and greet you through this instrument in love and light. We are aware that there are some queries which those present might wish to ask, and we would be happy to attempt to respond to those queries through this instrument. We again remind each that we do not wish our words over-weighted, and suggest that each take those which ring personally of truth and use them as they will, leaving behind all those which lack this ring. May we begin now with the first query?

J: Our scientists speculate that great civilizations within what we call our past, our history, have vanished from the face of the Earth due to cataclysmic periods such as pole shifts, one being the civilizations of Lemuria and another being approximately six thousand years ago, or about 4000 BC. Was the latest that I've just mentioned, the one at approximately 4000 BC, was there a cataclysmic period at that time, and, if so, was it a pole shift that caused this cataclysmic period?

I am Q'uo, and am aware of your query, my brother. We look at this time of which you speak and can discern that at a slightly earlier time there was indeed the cataclysmic events that resulted in the removal of a large segment of land mass that had been home to a large population of your third-density beings. However, we find that the time was previous to that you have mentioned, and the source of the difficulties was not that of the natural catastrophe as you might call it, but was rather man-made and technological in its nature.

May we answer further, my brother?

J: Were these man-made difficulties have been—would they have to do with the use of nuclear devices in what we would call Atlantis?

I am Q'uo, and this is in general correct, my brother.

May we answer further?

J: We are told by our scientists that the buildup of ice in Antarctica is becoming almost at a danger level, in that it accelerates or increases the wobble of the Earth about its axis in space and as this wobble increases, the impetus alone as the mass of ice builds up in Antarctica will eventually lead to a pole shift. Does this logic sound correct to you? Can you comment on that?

I am Q'uo, and our opinion in this area is that which sees this possibility as being a possibility if it were only acting in, shall we say, a vacuum. This is to say that there are many other factors to consider, and this factor which you have mentioned is that which is affected by other geophysical phenomena, and even more to the heart the, shall we say, choices that the population of your planet makes and remakes on the metaphysical level of experience. These choices may be seen as a kind of indicator likened unto a thermometer, shall we say. As the choices obtain a more balanced character, the temperature recedes and less heat is given off in a metaphysical sense, to then be transmuted by the physical illusion in such and such a geophysical manifestation.

Thus, there are many, many factors affecting the potential for physical change which your planet exhibits at this time, and it is not possible to predict with any degree of accuracy what the final result might be at any point in your continuum of time and experience.

May we answer further, my brother?

J: Is that to say the collective consciousness of mankind then basically determines the destiny of the planet?

I am Q'uo, and this is a relatively accurate statement, my brother.

May we answer further?

J: We are constantly warned of impending earthquakes, especially on the west coast, which are basically inevitable, our scientists now tell us. Is it possible that through some metaphysical means that we could somehow avert this cataclysm?

I am Q'uo, and we might suggest that this is indeed correct, and is that formative feature of consciousness which is manifested within your illusion as events which occur in time and space.

May we answer further, my brother?

J: In the history of the Earth, how many times have civilizations been wiped out due to cataclysmic periods or upheavals within the Earth itself?

I am Q'uo, and at this point we would have some difficulty in giving an accurate response, for at previous periods of your planet's history populations were so few in number within any particular civilization and civilizations, if you would call them that, so isolated one from another, that it would be difficult to say whether one group of entities leaving the physical incarnation by geophysical means would constitute the destruction of a civilization. Of the more obvious or largely populated groupings of entities leaving the incarnation by such geophysical means, we note that there have been two, those of which you have mentioned.

May we answer further, my brother?

J: No, thank you very much. That's all for now.

I am Q'uo, and we thank you, my brother. Is there another query?

H: We know that the atomic bomb that we have today is very destructive, materially destructive. But yet though—I've read—I've kind of studied a little bit where certain people on Earth that have been informed by others outside this Earth not to drop the bomb, not to have the battle of doomsday war. I was wondering, does the bomb have something to do with the soul, with the destruction of the soul a possibility? Is there any connection between the two?

I am Q'uo, and we might respond by suggesting that there is the release of energy of such a nature within the process of detonation of one of your nuclear weapons that not only does the physical material of your illusion suffer great disfiguration, but it is possible that the mind/body/spirit complex which might be referred to as the soul, if you will, can also undergo a type of disintegration if there is not the immediate aid of those able to harness this released energy and other energies for the preservation of the integrity of the mind/body/spirit complex.

May we answer further, my brother?

H: I'm confused at what's a mind/body/spirit complex again?

I am Q'uo, and we have responded …

(Side one of tape ends.)

(Jim channeling)

I am Q'uo, and am once again with this instrument. Our choice of terminology was that most familiar to this instrument, and we apologize for using that which was not familiar to your own experience. The concept of the soul being affected by the release of the nuclear energy is that which we have described as the potential for the disintegration of those major components of what you have called the soul, and that is a being that is complex, a being which experiences the creation by means of utilizing the mind, the body, and the spirit. The effect of the release of the nuclear energy is to cause a disintegration, or an unbinding, shall we say, of mind, of body and of spirit, each from the other, so that the unified joining of them called a soul in your terms is no longer able to perceive experience and to focus conscious awareness.

Thus, there is the necessity for the healing or maintenance of the integrity or unity of these complexes during the release of nuclear energy. The maintenance of such integrity is the honor and duty of those who watch over the progress of your planet's populations, and these entities have moved in this service in previous times of your planet's experience in order that no soul might lose its integrity through the release of nuclear energy.

May we answer further, my brother?

H: Okay, the Nostradamus, in his prophecies, is it true that he foresaw maybe the doomsday wars, the nuclear holocaust? Did he actually foresee that?

I am Q'uo, and the entity of which you speak was one to whom information was transmitted in the form of visions which then this entity sought to transmit or capture in words that would then be preserved for use by future, as you call them, generations. This information which was transmitted and perceived as the series of visions was one point of viewing of one potential within the consciousness of this particular planetary influence. It is by no means the only potential. It was not then nor is it now alone in the possibility of occurrence, and in fact is that which is constantly formed and reformed by the choices of the populations of your planet, this in the metaphysical sense.

May we answer further, my brother?

H: No further questions at this time.

I am Q'uo, and we thank you for your queries, my brother. Is there another query at this time?

J: The asteroid belt, was that once a planet which was destroyed—which was once destroyed by the use of nuclear weapons.

I am Q'uo, and this is correct, my brother.

May we answer further?

J: Were entities who performed the service of healing of the mind/body/spirit complexes able to reunite these basic elements of the soul at that time?

I am Q'uo, and this is correct, my brother, though due to the magnitude of the destructive effects of that planetary influence and its previous experience, the healing needed to wait for a portion of what you would call time in order that the entities who had experienced this destruction might first as a group experience the immediate aftereffects and then become available for healing.

May we answer further, my brother?

J: When the bomb was dropped on Hiroshima, how long in terms of time did it take for the healing process of those mind/body/spirit complexes which were basically disengaged or dissimilated at that time?

I am Q'uo, and the healing is continuing for these entities of which you speak. The period of time is somewhat difficult to translate into your terms, for their current experience is within those realms where time is perceived in a far different fashion and measured quite differently than it is perceived and measured within your own.

May we answer further, my brother?

J: This separation of the mind/body/spirit complex, does this occur only, shall I say, at a ground zero type situation in a nuclear explosion, or is a large percentage of those entities which ultimately die as a result of a nuclear explosion, does the same separation take place in those entities?

I am Q'uo, and we find that, in general, as you would say, the most probability of the disintegration of the mind/body/spirit complex would be at that location you have described as ground zero, and would decrease as the distance from this point increased.

May we answer further, my brother?

J: Has there ever been a case in which the complexes of mind/body/spirit was beyond reorganization, as it was totally destroyed as a result of the nuclear device?

I am Q'uo, and we cannot answer as to yes or no, for we have not experienced all that there is to experience, and are unable to speak of that with which we are not familiar as either having observed or experienced such and such an event. We do not say that such is impossible. We can suggest that such is not probable, for always there are those who serve as observers, teachers and guides who take the necessary care for the preservation of those under their guidance.

We are aware at this time that it would be helpful if we concluded this contact, for there is a difficulty among one who is not comfortable at this time. We then will suggest that this meeting be brought to a close. We thank each of you for allowing our presence, and we look forward to each such gathering in joy and in praise of the desire to seek more of that which you call the truth. We are known to you as those of Q'uo. Adonai, my friends. We leave you in the love and the light of the one infinite Creator. ☥

Intensive Meditation
October 6, 1986

(Unknown channeling)

I am Laitos, and greet you, my friends, in the love and in the light of our infinite Creator. It is our privilege to join your group again for the purpose of working with the new instrument. We apologize for the interruption [to the one] known as K. We were, before contacting this instrument, attempting to initiate a contact through the one known as K. From time to time we use this technique with a instrument who has progressed to the point of being able to speak a phrase or two after identifying our contact. It is always helpful to be able to make one more step upon this journey by expanding the abilities whenever possible.

We do not wish to rush any new instrument past the point of confidence, yet we shall always provide the opportunity for a new instrument to continue to expand its abilities. This is true for all instruments, in fact, for even with an instrument which has practiced its art for many of your years, there is the constant opportunity to expand such an instrument's capabilities by presenting concepts of greater scope and, shall we say, intricacy, though we do not mean to suggest complexity.

At this time we would attempt to transfer our contact to the one known as K and when this new instrument is comfortable with the conditioning vibration which we offer, we would then speak a few words through this new instrument. Again we would remind the one known as K that we are happy to adjust our conditioning vibration, if it is not comfortable to begin with. As always, we remind this new instrument that refraining from analysis is most helpful in speaking those concepts which appear within the mind. We would transfer this contact at this time. I am Laitos.

(Kim channeling)

(Inaudible)

(Unknown channeling)

I am Laitos, and greet each of you again in love and light through this instrument. We are very pleased at the progress that the one known as K has made since our last session together and we continue to applaud this new instrument's efforts and willingness to take one further step and to move yet further upon the [ground] which continues to hold the instrument firmly. At this time we would pause for the opportunity to respond to any queries which those present may find value in asking. May we attempt any query at this time?

Questioner: I don't think I have any questions.

I am Laitos, and we thank each of you for affirming that which we had discovered ourselves. We are always happy when there are queries, for this allows us the opportunity to discover how the process in the new instrument's learning of vocal channeling is taking form, for queries are those gifts which we honor due to the new avenues of thought which they open. We are also pleased when there are no such queries, for in that situation we may assume that what we have offered has been utilized to its fullest and is ready for further expansion, shall we say.

At this time we would make one final contact with the one known as K in order that she might perhaps discover another facet of this ability. We transfer this contact at this time. I am Laitos.

(Kim channeling)

(Inaudible)

(Tape ends.)

Intensive Meditation
October 8, 1986

(Jim channeling)

I am Laitos, and greet you, my friends, in the love and in the light of our infinite Creator. We have been working with the one known as K in anticipation that she might be open to the possibility of initiating a contact this evening. We may suggest to this new instrument that the faculty of analysis is, though still somewhat significant within this new instrument, that which is far less of a difficulty in this new instrument than in most. We would therefore commend this new instrument for its ability to allow the analytical portion of the conscious mind to be put aside temporarily. This is a general faculty which this new instrument has utilized far better than most and though it has at this working presented somewhat of a difficulty in the overall sense, we are very happy that this new instrument has taken so quickly, shall we say, to the reservation of judgment and analysis. At this time we should attempt to contact the one known as K, and will transfer this contact at this time. I am Laitos.

(K channeling)

I am Laitos, and I greet you, my friends, in the love and in the light of the one infinite Creator. We are with this instrument again for the purpose of sharing ourselves with you in the mutual service of the infinite Creator. We ask [again] to remain open *(inaudible)* so that what we have to say will flow easily through this instrument, *(inaudible)* for indeed such is the work and service of the vocal channel, *(inaudible)* source, to its destination. My friends, let us be merry and [quiet]. [We may all be quiet] is not [really] very difficult *(inaudible)*. So too may the flow of your lives be with *(inaudible)* and difficulty, you can better accept that which comes to you *(inaudible)*. For it is in acceptance that *(inaudible)* that your path *(inaudible)* wise even though *(inaudible)* seeming difficulties, still you may confuse *(inaudible)* by accepting that which comes to you in going the way that is before you.

At this time we will transfer the contact again to the one known as Jim. We transfer this contact now. I am Laitos.

(Jim channeling)

I am Laitos, and greet each of you again in love and light. We are very happy with the progress that this new instrument continues to show and we would congratulate her on her ability to be just as the type of which she spoke. It is heartening to us to be able to work with one who is so receptive to the underlying attitude that supports the vocal channeling process. At this time we would open this session to those queries which those present may find value in the asking. May we begin with a query?

K: I don't have a particular question. I wish I did because I feel a sort of confusion, more an unsettledness about what the whole process—I guess I've been feeling more nervous, I guess, than I did before, and I don't understand the way I'm feeling. So, I don't have a specific question, but do you have any comments on that at all?

I am Laitos, and, my sister, we may reassure you that this feeling is not that which should alarm, for now, as you have become more firmly aware of the nature of this process of becoming a vocal instrument, it is becoming apparent to you both intellectually and emotionally that the process is indeed occurring, and that there is the transfer of information proceeding through your instrument. As you begin to realize that this process is ongoing and is a process in which you play a part, but a minor part, you now begin to feel something of what we might describe as a combination of excitement and anxiety. This is a natural response to a process which is quite unlike most experiences which you have had during your life and is one which tends to move toward the center of your being and resonate outward with a feeling of recognition that is not completely accepted by the conscious mind complex as yet.

We can recommend that you simply allow these feelings to move through you, much as you allow the information which we have to transmit move through you, without undue concern as you become more and more familiar with this process and are able to accept its validity completely within your being. As you gather those subjective verifications of which those present have discussed, you will become more comfortable at the emotional level, shall we say, and this shall then become more of an accepted experience for you.

May we answer further, my sister?

K: As you know, I'm still feeling the doubt, what Carla terms as the great conspiracy, the fear that I'm just saying things that are coming into my head from myself … I guess I still wonder, am I really vocalizing the thoughts that you're transmitting to me?

I am Laitos, and we would suggest that we in our work with any new instrument also play a part which tends to cause a new instrument to feel that this conspiracy, as it has been called, is indeed just that, and that the new instrument is providing material that is merely from its own resources, the conscious and the subconscious minds. This is due to our, shall we say, experience at working with new instruments and our finding that to be able to initiate contact through a new instrument most easily, it is well to use more of that new instrument's experience, both the current experience and previous experiences, and to utilize the new instrument's manner of phrasing as it communicates in its normal day-to-day life.

This is a process which we find enables a new instrument to speak the words which are given to it, and to allow the contact to remain open long enough that it is slowly being able to gather confidence, and this confidence will continue to build until new concepts are able to be offered through the new instrument. Always, however, do we continue to use, even with new concepts, phrases and words and experiences which the new instrument may be able to provide to aid the communication.

Thus, you are partaking in that which seems to bring up the possibility of a conspiracy within any new instrument's mind. We may assure you, however, my sister, that you have been quite accurately representing our thoughts, using, of course, your own words and means of phrasing.

May we answer further, my sister?

K: No, that's very reassuring. Thank you.

I am Laitos, and we thank you, my sister. Is there another query?

Carla: I wonder if you could shed some light on what it is I am perceiving when I say—because I don't have any words for it—that I can see the energy move when people are channeling in a room? I can see it move from channel to channel and so forth. I don't actually see a thing, but I feel it in some way that I don't know how to … I don't have any words. What is being generated? What *(inaudible)*?

I am Laitos, and am aware of your query, my sister. As you are aware, your abilities to sense the feelings of others have been present for most of your incarnation. We may suggest that you have utilized a form of this empathic ability in your ability to be able to sense the placement, presence and occasionally the nature of these contacts. You are much likened unto a being which has sent out from its heart tiny filaments of feelingness which permeate the physical and metaphysical space in which you reside at any given time. When there is a movement of energies, especially of the metaphysical nature through this lacework of filament, you are alerted that such is occurring, and it is as though the room in which you dwell has become an extended body for you so that the movement of energy of the nature of which we generate during these contacts is perceived by you as a movement within your own body or being. Thus, it does not feel precisely as though any particular sense is telling you of such movement, but that instead it is as though your entire body records movement through it much as though you are aware of the beating of your own heart.

May we answer further, my sister?

Carla: That was very helpful. I don't need another go at that one. It doesn't matter what level and [what at]. I have a way to understand it now. So it's an anomaly and it's nothing I have to write about in the book and that's good. Okay.

The other thing that I wanted to know is just why have you been stimulating me so strongly? I've been getting a lot of conditioning, and I haven't been getting any words or anything, just a lot of conditioning. Just a keeping the hand in? Every time I asked who it was, it was Laitos. That's you, right?

I am indeed Laitos, and have been working with you, my sister, as we have been working with each instrument within this dwelling. Each, however, receives a different kind of assistance, for each is working upon slightly different facets of the same phenomenon. With your particular instrument, we find that it is often helpful to stimulate, as you call it, the more experienced instrument in a manner which will allow it at any future time, as you would call it, to pursue the practice of vocal channeling with increased facility. In your particular case, we are working with the deeper levels of your mind complex in order to aid the transmission of word-by-word thoughts. We are, you might say, at once sensitizing your instrument and stabilizing it as well.

May we answer further, my sister?

Carla: No. I want to thank you for helping me. I'd like to be better very much.

I am Laitos, and we thank you, my sister, for allowing us to work with you in this capacity. Is there another query at this time?

Carla: I do have one more. Something I was thinking about writing in the book, and I'm just not sure whether I should cover it or not. So any comment would be helpful.

People have an incredibly array of ways of registering conditioning. A lot of the ways can scare people, even though they're harmless. The hair on the legs stands up, or people cry or their eyes water uncontrollably or they see a zigzag of green on the left side and a zigzag of blue on the right side. It just goes on and on. I will have to do a lot of listening if I try to write about it. And these things can scare you if you don't know that it is merely the side effect of another intelligence settling into your body, metaphysical physical.

What I fear is that people will start manufacturing these symptoms because I told them what they're supposed to feel. I don't want to give people troubles that they wouldn't otherwise have. Could you comment?

I am Laitos, and we may agree that your analysis of the conditioning phenomenon is basically accurate, that is, that any means by which our contact is perceived by an instrument is a means which is a by-product of both our actual contact with the instrument and the instrument's chosen—and this is usually of a subconscious nature—manner of perceiving such contact. Often an instrument will have a subconscious belief that any contact from entities that are unseen would be one which would cause a certain amount of fear or discomfort or a sensation in this or that location which then would signify such contact had been perceived. These beliefs are often difficult to trace to their origin, for within the subconscious minds of all entities of your density there resides what might be seen as a group consciousness that is aware upon the subconscious level of the ability to contact a great variety of entities which may be removed by distance and density from the one of third density who perceives this contact.

Thus, if such suggestions are made to those who might become new instruments that a contact with those who would speak through such a new instrument might be felt in such and such a manner, this then might indeed influence the manner in which such an instrument would perceive a contact if it were to pursue this type of service in its future.

This is not a great difficulty, but could in some cases confuse a new instrument in that it would be consciously overlaying a preconceived idea of how the contact would occur and this preconceived idea then might for a period of time interfere with the inborn, shall we say, choices or beliefs which the entity had provided for itself in the event that it would choose to serve as a vocal instrument. This confusion would at some point need to be resolved within the entity so that one manner or another of perceiving a contact such as our contact might be set upon as that way which becomes familiar and comfortable to the instrument, and becomes then an aid in its gathering of confidence and proficiency in serving as a vocal instrument.

May we answer further, my sister?

Carla: Yes, I would like to know how you would feel when I finished the rough draft of working with each chapter title, giving any comments of this sort of nature that you might feel appropriate in order that I may, in a book on channeling, use whatever thoughts I find helpful in your comments?

I am Laitos, and we would be happy to aid your effort in whatever way we could without influencing your own free will choices and we would be happy to present our opinions according to the way in which the information is sought, that is, we shall be happy to speak within the scope of your queries and the work which you have done, without adding to it that which you have not in some way touched upon as a result of your own creative efforts.

May we answer further, my sister?

Carla: I'll look forward to working with you. Thank you.

I am Laitos, and we are looking forward to this shared activity as well. Even though this instrument is somewhat dubious as to its ability to serve in this fashion, we shall look forward to working with this instrument as well.

May we answer further, my sister?

Carla: I merely say to the instrument, "Dooby, dooby, dubious." *(Laughs)* Thank you, Laitos.

I am Laitos, and we have been hoping that this instrument would allow us to speak just a few additional words without becoming too concerned about its future task, present confusion.

We can assure each present that this activity that is of the vocal channeling is one which shall be utilized in an increasing fashion throughout much of the work which is proposed in what you call your future. We are very happy to work with each instrument, as we have mentioned previously, in whatever manner each instrument requests, whether the request be conscious or unconsciously stated.

Therefore, we will seek to bring each instrument insofar as we are able to the current limits of its ability, and then provide an opportunity to extend those limits in some degree. Thus, the practice and the art of being that known as the vocal instrument is that which is dynamic in that the surrender of the personal will is that which is ongoing and is that which may continue for each instrument at any time that it is willing to open yet more fully to the opportunities which are naturally presented to any entity who seeks to be of service to others, no matter the vehicle chosen, whether it be vocal channeling, healing, or any other service.

We thank each present for allowing us to speak with you this evening, and to work with each as vocal instruments. At this time we feel that it might be appropriate to bring this time of working to its conclusion, and we shall do so, thanking each once again with our whole and happy hearts for allowing us to join you in yet another portion of your seeking. We are known to you as those of Laitos and we leave you in the love and in the light of the one infinite Creator. Adonai, my friends. Adonai. ✦

L/L Research is a subsidiary of Rock Creek Research & Development Laboratories, Inc.

P.O. Box 5195
Louisville, KY 40255-0195

www.llresearch.org

Rock Creek is a non-profit corporation dedicated to discovering and sharing information which may aid in the spiritual evolution of humankind.

ABOUT THE CONTENTS OF THIS TRANSCRIPT: This telepathic channeling has been taken from transcriptions of the weekly study and meditation meetings of the Rock Creek Research & Development Laboratories and L/L Research. It is offered in the hope that it may be useful to you. As the Confederation entities always make a point of saying, please use your discrimination and judgment in assessing this material. If something rings true to you, fine. If something does not resonate, please leave it behind, for neither we nor those of the Confederation would wish to be a stumbling block for any.

CAVEAT: This transcript is being published by L/L Research in a not yet final form. It has, however, been edited and any obvious errors have been corrected. When it is in a final form, this caveat will be removed.

© 2009 L/L Research

Intensive Meditation
October 9, 1986

(K channeling)

(K's voice is barely audible.)

[I am Laitos,] and I greet you, my friends in the love and in the light of the infinite Creator. It is our great pleasure to be with you again this evening for the purpose of working with the new instrument known as K and also the rest of you who are *(inaudible)*. We also wish to welcome the one known as S and are grateful for her presence [also].

As you know, my friends, it is our pleasure to be with you for the purpose of serving together with you in the process of your service as vocal channels. We ask [now] that each of you remain open and relaxed, putting aside any anxious thoughts that you may bring with you to this time, putting aside again your desires for analysis, and becoming simply channels as [we are meant to be].

At this time we will transfer the contact to the one known as Jim and speak a few words through him. We transfer the contact at this time. I am Laitos.

(Jim channeling)

I am Laitos, and greet each of you in love and light through this instrument. We are hoping this evening that we will be able to exercise each instrument in some degree, for it has been our experience that when a minimal level of proficiency has been gained in the vocal channeling process that is helpful to exercise the instrument wishing exercise and practice in a periodic manner. We feel that it might be helpful this evening if we should engage in a small story which would be accomplished by transmitting a few sentences through each instrument with no definite order given, so that each instrument would have some practice in both perceiving the contact and in transmitting a portion of it. We shall attempt a small story, therefore, with this goal in mind.

As most of your stories begin, once upon a time there was a young man living in a distant land who wished to know if there might be in the surrounding countryside others of his kind who thought as he thought, for this young man was somewhat isolated in a small village that had customs that were old and rigid. Yet he felt that there was something beyond custom and ritual which would fulfill his desire to know more of himself and the life that he lived. Thus he set out upon a journey in order to see how others lived their lives.

We shall transfer this contact at this time. I am Laitos.

(K channeling)

I am Laitos, and will continue our story with this instrument. The young lad of which we spoke journeyed first twenty of your miles to a village, known to only a few of the villagers with whom he had enjoyed his childhood. This village [was] set in a valley far amongst the trees, hidden and nestled between the hills of the surrounding countryside and there our aspirant of knowledge met an old man who spent much time conversing with our friend. He spent many a day under the bright sun and far into the moonlit night speaking, learning, his mind was a sponge, his heart growing ever fuller with the love which he perceived from this one who had spent many years upon this plane of existence. Until one day the old man would speak no more and the young one knew that at this point he had learned all from this lesson that he could. So he sadly took his leave of the old man and his village and continued his journey.

We will now transfer this contact to another instrument. I am Laitos.

(Carla channeling)

Onward traveled the lad, as quickly eating up the miles, his questing mind ever devising refinements in his question. Occasionally the dust of a certain village or the shape of a certain hill would resonate with his mood and there he would stop, looking about for ways to replenish his small supply of funds and for people that seemed to him to speak of those things he wished to know so that he might learn more and more about himself. He always found someone and he always learned. For three years he walked and asked, resting in the comfort of his own poverty and the ease of needing to impress no one but himself. At the end of that time he decided to take stock of all that he had learned.

We shall transfer. I am Laitos.

(K channeling)

I am Laitos. The young man sat and thought for a long time about all the things he had learned through his journeys. And as he sat, he saw before him a bird. He watched the bird and it flew away. He thought he must do as the bird and continued his journey *(inaudible)*. He thought he could learn no more from teachers [to whom he went] but rather his sojourn would be one within himself, that he would learn to be his own teacher. And so he sat some more and thought long and hard about his life and its meaning. He thought about things he learned from his teachers and he thought if he would return again to the native village. He began turning homeward, knowing for him it was a new journey and a new beginning.

When he got to his village, he learned a trade, a simple trade of making shoes, and in due time became the village cobbler. He became known as a quiet man and yet people came to him and sought him out, for his wisdom became known about the village. Thus he became known as a teacher in his own village and in due time there came to him other travelers to sit and learn with him as he had learned with others. Some learned the art of making shoes. Most sat and talked with him about life and he shared what he had learned from other teachers, but mostly what he had learned from the journey within himself.

We transfer the contact at this time. I am Laitos.

(Carla channeling)

And so the journey ended as it began. The young man had become old in his native village, living quietly. And yet the young man had also become what he sought, because he sought it. And so shall you, if you seek faithfully. For it is your creation. You are its creator and that which happens within your perception is as you perceive it to be. And that which you become is that which you have desired.

We urge you to desire carefully and steadily, carefully, because desire is a vacuum created in your future, causing that which is desired to be attracted into the empty space within yourself. In all your seeking, know the journey which never ends also ends. For although you will always be seeking, each transformation you undergo, each difficulty that you begin to perceive will move you as you desire, no matter what the outward pull of condition or a state of experience.

The inward form is malleable and will be brought into your consciousness in the shape and feeling it possesses due to your desires. May you crown each question you ask of others or yourself with the desire to know and serve the Creator, to know and serve love. For your journey shall end according to the shape of your desire. And in that ending shall be your beginning.

We would transfer the contact at this time. I am Laitos.

(S channeling)

I am Laitos, and we continue through this instrument. Each of you, my friends, has many desires, many goals. But the one that all has in common and that desire is the *(inaudible)* of the one infinite Creator, the one goal of love and truth. And this desire, my friends, and through this goal is the joy, our pleasure to help in whatever way we may. The journey each of you *(inaudible)* you put upon as you well know, may not be altogether an easy one, but it is the desire and the love, the continued strengthening of that desire which will soothe the rough places of your journey. [There are many,] my friends, there are many who walk the same path with you; you are never alone. Always [in the] one Creator is within, without, all-pervading, surrounding, protecting, always One. We leave you now, my friends, wrapped in this love, surrounded in joy [and] infinite good. I am Laitos. I leave you, my friends. Adonai vasu borragus.

(S channeling)

I am Latwii, and it is with great pleasure that we greet you, our friends, in the love and light of the one infinite Creator. It has been quite some of your time since we have worked with this instrument and are most grateful for her assistance. We are also very grateful, my friends to be with you once again and would like at this time to transfer this contact so as to exercise the other instruments in the room. I am Latwii.

(Carla channeling)

I am Latwii, and greet you once again in love and light. We come to you from the color of recompense. We find this instrument does not understand what we mean. There is, shall we say, the big payoff of colors which sums up a good deal about a planetary state of health. The compensated, shall we say, or paid or finished vibrations, the color of protected health, is a beautiful bright and clear magenta, a reddish purple. You planet has a good deal to study in this area and we have been doing so. May we say the health of your planet is increasing, which is most encouraging. We place the blame for that squarely at your feet, my friends, for you of the planet are those who must make any change and to see a positive indication of planetary well-being is a happy matter for us who attempt to be of service to your people. We are enjoying the contact with this instrument. Much of the difficulty that we were having in times past has been alleviated by a good deal of strengthening of this instrument's receptive mechanisms. Some people really put in the time and this entity seems to have done so. We thank the instrument for putting in that time and hope it will continue to do so. It is a good feeling not to be causing the instrument discomfort. We do miss the opportunity of sharing, especially since it always got a laugh. We will have to hope for quiet laughs from this instrument from now on. We think we have exercised this instrument enough and would again transfer. I am Latwii.

(Jim channeling)

I am Latwii, and greet each of you again through this instrument. It is a smorgasbord of delights this evening. We have many from which to choose in our speaking this evening.

We have been attempting to work with the new instrument known as K so that this new instrument might gain in experience in the perceiving of contacts. We are somewhat more noticeable, shall we say, in that our conditioning vibration is a more intense vibration that the new instrument will feel in a more obvious manner. We would suggest to the one known as K that she, as she has been learning to do, release the tendency towards analysis and simply speak those words that she becomes aware of, even though she may feel she is speaking that from her own mind, having anticipated what would be perceived. We are eager to acquaint this new instrument with our vibrations in order that we may be able to utilize this instrument in what you would call your future times. We enjoy greatly the opportunity to exercise new instruments and to speak the simple message which we have to offer in yet another manner through another instrument. We would at this time attempt to contact the one known as K, if this entity will relax and speak those thoughts that it becomes aware in the mind. I am Latwii.

(K channeling)

I am Latwii, and I greet you once again, my friends through this instrument. We are very pleased to be here this evening among you, having a chance to speak through so many different instruments. It is a pleasure for us, my friends, and we appreciate the opportunity to share it with you. It, shall we say, lightens our day. We are pleased also to have the opportunity to speak through a new instrument, for it is our pleasure to serve in the manner of speaking through vocal channels such as these. We are happy for each new opportunity to do so. We ask *(inaudible).* Rejoice with us in the opportunity for service to the one Creator.

(Side one of tape ends.)

(K channeling)

I am Latwii, and am again with this instrument. We thank you, my friends, for your faithfulness in pursuing the service of the vocal channel. It is a service which is greatly appreciated by us and by others who are here also who perform the same service of speaking through vocal channels such as you.

We speak through instruments such as this in order to share the simple message of love and light which is ever unseen and yet which is perceived in so many different ways. We are delighted for the opportunity of sharing our humble perceptions with each of you who have asked for it. At this time we transfer the contact once again. I am Latwii.

(S channeling)

I am Latwii, and I greet you once again, my brothers and sisters in the love and light of the one infinite Creator. We would speak only a few more words and then will leave you in that self-same light and love. We had only wanted to reaffirm to this instrument our vibration, for her tendency towards analysis have grown over the past months instead of diminished. We still love her the same, however, as do we love each of you within this domicile. The purpose with which you have gathered, the service to your planet, to your brothers and sisters, and to the one infinite Creator is indeed the most healing of all that anyone could find anywhere in the universes. And with that thought, our friends, we leave you now in the love and light of the one infinite Creator. I am Latwii. ☙

Intensive Meditation
October 10, 1986

(K channeling)

[I am Laitos,] and I greet you once again, my friends, in the love and in the light of the infinite Creator. It is our great pleasure to be with you once again for the purpose of working with the new instrument which is beginning to gain a little of what you call experience in the matter of vocal channeling. We are pleased to be working with this instrument, and indeed with each of you. It is our pleasure and our joy to have the opportunity of sharing this service with you. At this time we would transfer the contact to the one known as Jim. I am Laitos.

(Jim channeling)

I am Laitos, and greet each of you again in love and light. We have been working with each instrument present as each needs and requests such assistance. We have found that with each instrument there is a firm foundation which has been built of desire to be of service to others, and this foundation has been elaborated upon by each present as experience in this way of service has been gained. Each instrument, then, upon the same foundation of desire to be of service to others, fashions a structure, a framework, a channel, if you will, through which our contact and other contacts may move. As each of you is unique in the makeup of what you feel is significant, in the life experience in general and in the spiritual seeking in particular, the form that your structure or channel takes is completely unique unto each of you. In this uniqueness, we take our joy, for we are through such individuality able to impress our message which is always and ever the same.

Always do we speak of that great original Thought, that thought of love of the one Creator which binds all of the creation and all entities within it together as portions of that one Creator and that one great Thought of love. Each of you in your daily patterns and in the larger patterns and rhythms of your incarnation, and, indeed, throughout the many series of incarnations that you have experienced, gather to yourself biases in your thinking and experiences within your being which then serve as resources upon which you draw as you do all that you do, as you think all that you think, and as you serve as vocal channels in this particular manner.

Thus, from each we find a great library of resources of experiences, of thoughts, of joys, of sadnesses, of what you call success, and what you call failure, and much, much more that we may utilize in expressing the simplicity of the great Thought of love, the one Creator as a general principle which motivates all of the many complexities of your illusion and of others.

Thus, as you move through your incarnation you gather a certain kind of momentum, shall we say, that may be seen as the present moment's culmination of all that you have experienced. This is a very, very rich resource, my friends, and we rejoice in the uniqueness which signifies each of you one from the other, and yet is an emanation of the same Thought of love.

Thus, in the vocal channeling type of service, we feel that it is most important that each instrument feel as much acceptance and love for its own experiences and identity as it does for those of others, for in this way we are aided in our attempt to unify those many divergent thoughts and experiences which each of your peoples gathers about it, and as you serve as an instrument in this process and are able to see the love and joy—perfection—within your own experience, and as you are able to see it as equal to any other's experiences, then are we more able to utilize that which is yours to offer into this service by means of the transmission of thought.

We thank you, my friends, for offering yourselves in the full range and depth and breadth of richness which you have fashioned for yourselves, and which we find a most valuable portion of this manner of serving others. At this time we would continue in our attempts to give further exercise to the instrument known as K, for we are quite pleased with the progress that she has made and wish to offer her another opportunity to continue in that progress. Thus, we shall speak a few thoughts through the one known as K. We shall now transfer this contact. I am Laitos.

(K channeling)

I am Laitos, and I greet you once again through this instrument. My friends, it is important to us to know that your desires lie in the direction of service to others, and we see that each of you has evolved upon that chosen path and has proceeded for a great length of your incarnations. Thus, the foundation once begun has been built upon quite sturdily until a structure exists that will withstand the buffeting effects of time and the difficulties that you each encounter upon your journey [then]. The structures that you have built for yourself may also function as a refuge, shall we say, for you from these same buffeting effects *(inaudible)*, for you have built around yourselves *(inaudible)* protections, armories, as it were, of light, and thus shielded, you continue on your journey, taking refuge in your shelter as needed.

My friends, we urge you not to fear to take refuge in the shelter when you feel it is needed, for rest is a good thing and needful, and it is not well to push yourselves beyond your limits of strength, whether of physical complex or other portions of your mind/body/spirit complex. Nor is it wise to push yourselves beyond the protections of light which you carry with you at all times. [Yes,] my friends, to rest and take refuge in the shelter which you have built for yourself of yourself is not giving up. It is not retiring from the journey upon which you have evolved and are proceeding. Rather it is indeed a part of the process which, when ignored, can lead to further difficulties and obstacles. Thus, my friends, we encourage you to be merry, to be joyful. Do not concern yourself with great goals or ideas that you must pursue these goals at a certain pace, that you must keep up this anything, for what you need will come to you. So, my friends, you need only to take the experiences of your life as they come to you, but not worry yourselves with pursuing them.

At this time we would leave your group as we have encountered it, in love and in the light of the infinite Creator. Be merry, my friends, rejoice with us in the love and the light *(inaudible)*. We are known to you as those of Laitos. Adonai, my friends. Adonai.

(K channeling)

I am Latwii, and I greet you once again, my friends, in the love and the light of the one Creator. It is our great pleasure to be with you once again this evening, for we enjoy working with your group. It is our pleasure to be able to take part in the exercising of the instrument known as K for the purpose of her service as a vocal channel. We are pleased that she had adapted so easily to our vibration, for it is sometimes perceived as a little stronger than some other contacts.

At this time we wish also to exercise, as it were, the other members of the group also, and will transfer the contact at this time. I am Latwii.

(Pause)

(Jim channeling)

I am Latwii, and greet you, my friends, in love and light through this instrument. We apologize for the delay, but we were having some difficulty making a contact with either instrument, for both wished for the other to have the opportunity. We are happy that one was finally able to say yes. We would at this time attempt to answer any queries which may have been raised in the minds of those present this evening. May we attempt any such query at this time?

Carla: There was a perception that I had that I would like to talk to K about. Was it a correct perception?

I am Latwii, and we find that in answering this query we have to tread somewhat close to the Law of Confusion, but we are hopeful that we shall [be able] to accomplish this high wire act without falling upon the wrong side, shall we say. My sister, you have perceived a portion of that which you feel was in effect, and we would suggest that it might be helpful to converse with the one known as K in order that not only should you be able to share that which you have perceived, but that you should also be able to enlarge that which you have perceived.

May we answer further, my sister?

Carla: No, thank you.

I am Latwii, and we thank you, my sister. Is there another query?

K: I have a personal question. I've been told by a couple of people that they think I am what we call a wanderer, and I wonder if that's something that you can comment on at all?

I am Latwii, and it seems that we cannot move away from that Law of Confusion this evening. We find ourselves once again face-to-face with that great Law of Free Will which assures to each that that which is gathered about one in the incarnational pattern shall be useful to such an entity because it has been chosen and experienced through the process of free will choice. That of which you speak is not directly a portion of experience gained during an incarnation, but is that which precedes and perhaps even motivates an incarnation.

We attempt to respond to your query by suggesting that the feelings which you have concerning this subject are those signposts which are of most aid in determining whether this indeed be true. We would suggest that in your own meditations and within your own feelings there are contained the tones of feeling that will indicate to you in a clear sense the status or source of which you speak. We do not mean to be obscure, my sister, but we find that in this instance there is yet discovery of your own that might be helpful in laying a foundation that we may enlarge upon perhaps at a later time.

May we answer further, my sister?

K: No, thank you.

I am Latwii, and we thank you, my sister, for putting up with our verbiage. May we attempt a further query?

Carla: No, thank you.

I am Latwii, and we are very happy that we have been able not only to join this group this evening, but that we have been able to make our contact known to the one known as K. It is a joy to work with an instrument which is so eager to be the fool. We are also fools, my friends, and find great mirth and happiness in such foolishness, for in this way of being, one may see the creation as indeed being a joyful unity in which all may play any part that might be chosen, and these parts may be traded, may be enlarged upon, may be discarded, may be ignored, and may be enhanced in whatever way or manner has meaning to the entity. And indeed the play of each entity is that which glorifies the one Creator in a manner which is only possible because each moves as freely and as happily through the creation as foolishness allows.

At this time we would take our leave of this instrument and this group, rejoicing always in the love and in the light of the one infinite Creator. We are known to you as those of Latwii. Adonai, my friends. Adonai. ☥

Intensive Meditation
October 11, 1986

(K channeling)

I am Laitos, and I greet you once again, my friends, in the love and the light of our infinite Creator. As always, my friends, it is our great pleasure to be among you this evening for the opportunity of working with the instrument as well as with all those of your group, for we appreciate your service, my friends, for the work that you do as vocal channels is, shall we say, near to our hearts, for as you serve the Creator in your role of vocal channels, so you also enable us to serve by speaking through you.

It is our pleasure also to greet those of you who are not speaking this evening, but who are contributing by their presence. We acknowledge and appreciate this service also.

At this time we wish to ask if there are any queries with which we may help? Is there a query at this time?

R: Is this Laitos?

I am Laitos, and greet you, my brother. May we answer further?

R: No, I wasn't ready to form a question. I just asked that. I just wanted to say, "Hello." It's been a long time. It's good to hear you.

I am Laitos, and I thank you for your greeting, my brother, and we also return it to you. Is there another query at this time?

Carla: Hold onto that contact … Never mind … Thank you for waiting. I'm sorry, but I thought I had a list of questions here from someone, but I don't, and I can't remember what it was he wanted to know.

I am Laitos, and I thank you, my sister. Is there any further query at this time?

(Pause)

I am Laitos, and again we thank you, my friends, for the opportunity of speaking through this instrument. At this time we will transfer the contact. I am Laitos.

(Carla channeling)

I am Laitos, and I greet you in love and light through this instrument. We have greatly enjoyed working with the one known as K, for in this session we have been able to exercise the instrument to its, shall we say, full capacity so that the instrument may begin to have confidence in the limb upon which it sits. Or more properly we should say, since the instrument and each instrument jumps off of the limb each time it channels, that it is the experience of moving out of control that you may hope to get used to. It is a blessed thing to be able to blend our experience with yours at this time.

We can think of each other as the other torn half of a perfect shape, for each entity that you encounter is your other half. Each of you is [a] miniature of each group to which you find yourself belonging, to your culture and your race, your species and your archetypical souls, and finally the universe itself. Is it any wonder then, that you are all such good channels for each other, sharing with each other one universe in so many wondrously various facets that the picture seldom stales and wonder is but an eye-blink away?

We have been urging the new channel to open the mind, to let down the armor, to become vulnerable and without fear so that we may touch her mind with our own. Each of you could use this frame of mind that your mind may be touched by the thoughts and the hands of the Creator in every entity you meet.

We would transfer at this time. I am Laitos.

(K channeling)

I am Laitos, and am with this instrument again. We wanted to say a few final words through this instrument so that she would have the additional opportunity to gain confidence in this *(inaudible)*. We wish to remind you, my friends, that we are all bound together by love in the service of the one Creator, for love is all that there is. It is that which motivates us as well as that which enables us. It is also that which rewards us, shall we say, as the fruit of our efforts to serve. The message that we bring you is simple, my friends, and yet there are many words to fill that simplicity, and so we strive to ever share that simplicity with you in yet another way. We thank you again for serving with you, my friends—we correct this instrument—for serving with us, for our services are a means of journeying ever closer to the love and the light which is all things. At this time, we leave this instrument and your group, my friends, in that love and light of the one Creator. Peace be with you, my friends, this day and always. We are known to you as those of Laitos. Adonai, my friends. Adonai. ✣

Sunday Meditation
October 12, 1986

(Carla channeling)

I am Hatonn, and I greet you in the love and light of our infinite Creator. What a privilege it is to be able to speak through this instrument to you this evening and to share your life patterns for this moment. The blending of energies is most enhancing, each piece of the Creator enhancing the experience of each other portion. We are most grateful for your sharing of yourselves with us and only hope that our poor thoughts may be of some interest to you this evening.

We were enjoying the peaceful centering of the energy of your group in silence and left you in that silence because those of Laitos were working with two in this group. We try not to step on each other's toes, as it were, when one or more of the members of the Confederation, or indeed, when any other contact is working with the same entities we are.

It is rewarding to see that the concept of meditation in this group has not broken down to include only the concept of the channeled information, for, indeed, it is the silence that teaches, perhaps more than even the most inspiring words, just as it is the space between objects which allows objects to have dimension.

We hope that you may bring that silence with you as a tool to use not in the dark with your eyes closed only, but in the harshest of daylights and under the most trying of conditions, for if there is a portion of you that remains in the silence of that which is most precious to you, then all else is but a shadow which moves across the sun at the center of your being, and no cloud is large enough to blot out the joy you may take in living, and if the silence be gone from the noon day, then you are lost to the hustle and bustle of your conscious daily thoughts. It is difficult to love when one is busy. It is difficult to perceive or experience the consciousness of the Creator or to take part in the one original Thought which created you.

If you no longer have any silence in your heart, it is as though you were a king who could direct and control your kingdom in any way that you wished, and so you began to wish and one thing was added upon another, all things that at one time or another you had wished, all eventually manifesting in one way or another. And yet, as wealthy and powerful as a king may be, still there is a limit to what a king can perceive and enjoy, and so you end up being not the ruler of your life, but its servant, ministering unto your desires and moving through your days as your kingdom wills you to move. Your past desires have all come home to roost, and you have been trapped by your own snare.

None of you who feels that these words have truth is alone in this perception, for it is the nature of your culture to distract yourself from the consciousness of the love and light of the one Creator. It is difficult to turn [from] the riches of an earthly, shall we say, kingdom and choose the bright and shining ideals of an unseen kingdom. They do not glitter in the hand nor are they grateful to the touch. Pursued, they retreat. Those unseen values which you desire have no market value. It is difficult to explain the spiritual path to any who do not love the silence already or at least hunger for that which cannot be held in the hand or assessed for material wealth.

Yet, if you are dwelling in the silence to the extent that you can carry a small portion of it with you, it will not disturb you that many do not understand what motivates you. It will be enough that you have the opportunity to express yourself in love to other portions of the Creator. What entities may think of you is irrelevant to the excellence of your effort. Indeed, what you yourself estimate to be your excellence is irrelevant, for in the world of invisible things, where truth and beauty lie waiting to be found, all that is needed, all that is relevant is your seeking, that is your power and your peace. It is your very identification, for you are what you desire.

May your desires flow from you in a clean and pure stream, glittering and bubbling and moving in life into the great ocean of all that there is, that when all things are prepared as is necessary for you, each and every desire may be yours in full, your birthright claimed.

Before we leave this group, we would like to exercise the new instrument, and so we would close through the one known as K. I am Hatonn.

(K channeling)

I am Hatonn, and I greet you once again, my friends, in love and light through this instrument. We deem it a great privilege to be able to speak through yet another instrument who has offered herself in service as a vocal channel. It is our desire to share our humble thoughts with you for whatever help they may be to you on your various paths toward the One. We are ever grateful for additional opportunities for this.

My friends, the time is near when we will no longer have the need to speak through a vocal channel, for our thoughts will be known to you, but for the present, as we seek to aid your planet in its birthing pains, shall we say, it is our privilege and our service to share our thoughts with you through those who have offered themselves as vocal channels. We are glad to be able to be with you in these times, my friends, and are grateful for your desire to share with us those things which are eternal. Many are the distractions upon your paths, my friends. Many are the things of the moment which capture the attention, which pull you one way or another. There are many things of great interest which are of but transient importance. We know that you are aware of this, my friends.

We urge you to hone your awareness of those things which are transient and those things which are eternal. We watch your growth and we appreciate your efforts in focusing on those matters which you deem to be of true importance. We are glad of the opportunity to offer you our humble opinions, and, as always, my friends, we would urge you to take our words lightly, to take to your hearts only those words which you feel to be of value to you, for it is not our intent to lay on you heavy burdens. Your illusion is heavy enough, my friends and we would count a privilege to be able to lighten your load, not to add to it.

At this time we would take our leave of this instrument and your group, leaving you in the joy of the love and the light of the one infinite Creator. Let your hearts be merry, my friends and rejoice, for truly your path may be and your burden may be light, as it is written in your holy works. Farewell, my friends, in love and light. I am Hatonn.

(Jim channeling)

I am Latwii, and I greet you, my friends, in the love and the light of our infinite Creator. We are overjoyed to be able to join your group this evening, and we thank you for this opportunity. It is once again our privilege to be able to offer ourselves in the capacity of attempting to answer those queries which you may find of interest in your own seeking. We would repeat the suggestion of our brothers and sisters of Hatonn that you neither take our words too seriously or regard them as being more than our opinions. With that disclaimer, we would be happy to attempt to respond to those queries you may have.

C: Latwii, could you speak to me briefly about living within the moment?

I am Latwii. In brief, my brother, it is a good idea.

We shall perhaps elaborate. It is a common feeling and tendency among your peoples to look backward and forward as the present moment is experienced. The present moment then becomes a recapitulation of the history of one's existence, and when this is not occurring quite frequently the present moment becomes a consideration of the possibilities which the future might hold for one. Thus, the present moment is that which offers to an entity the opportunity to look backward and to assess that which has been accomplished, to look forward and to consider that which is possible to accomplish, and all that has been done and shall be done will be done within a present moment.

That present moment, then, is that which has power within one's experience. The power of that present moment may be harnessed in any manner in which you choose. Indeed, we affirm the efficiency of looking upon the experiences one has gathered and gleaning from them those attitudes and biases and considerations which are helpful in the process of spiritual evolution, for by such contemplation is one able to benefit from experience. We can also affirm the helpfulness of taking what one has learned from experience and projecting possibilities as to how future moments might be enhanced by applying these lessons which have been learned. Thus, one prepares oneself to share the harvest of one's experience in a helpful manner.

However, as you well know, my brother, the present moment is also that which is complete within itself, and in this light needs no addition from the past or from the future. The present moment may become, if it is one's desire, a finely focused experience of all that one is and all that one can be and all that one has been. In this focus of experience the full potential of one's being is brought to bear upon one's thinking and the boundaries or limitations of one's thinking or one's beliefs are offered the opportunity to expand. As one begins to create a space in experience in the present moment which is undiluted by the past or the future, one then harvests potential. One in this harvest may become inspired, shall we say, by that which is and that which exists within one's being. In such present moment experiences, one may fully appreciate the completeness which is the foundation of any entity's being.

Of course, my brother, you are aware that the meditative state is that state which offers the easiest access to such present moment experiences, for such experiences of the power of the present moment and the perfection of one's being are those which become available to an entity when there is no coloration of past or future or thought of any kind to form a filter through which the present moment must be perceived.

Thus, within the present moment experience one may, in a manner of speaking, not only recharge the battery of one's personal energy, but may discover that that battery is fully charged at all times, and in this discovery and from this discovery one may then move into the daily round of activities inspired and ennobled, shall we say, so that the ability to utilize what has been learned is enhanced and the ability to gather further lessons available in each present moment is also enhanced.

Thus, my brother, you see how the present moment is the moment of power within any seeker's experience. Within that moment, one may turn the eyes backward, forward and may also rest the eyes within the moment of one's being.

May we speak further, my brother?

C: Here of late I go through long spells where I have trouble remembering anything of the past. Things seem like this is how they've always been. And actually its been very peaceful to feel that way, but at times I will get a feeling of guilt, thinking that I should have more feelings than I do about the past. But they're just not there.

I am Latwii, and we perceive a comment upon your experience that may also benefit from a comment from our point of view, though we have not been queried specifically. We may suggest that when you have the ability to look upon those experiences that are a part of your history, shall we say, without a feeling of joy or sadness, you may assume that those experiences have been utilized in an efficient manner, for when there are emotional charges, shall we say, that are apparent and connected to any experience, then one may assume that there is work in that experience which one may undertake, for the emotional colorations that one feels for any thought, experience or entity are distorted perceptions that are distorted in such and such a fashion in order that an entity will be drawn into the process of balancing these perceptions so that the final product of all experience is a quiet acceptance that may in metaphysical terms be translated as unconditional love.

May we answer further, my brother?

C: No. That's reassuring, and I say thank you because I know that many times I'll ramble instead of putting a question together and you always pick it up for me. But I would ask you just this one last thing.

I find at this particular time an attraction to a person who I see as myself ten or twelve years ago—the person whose development is pretty much where mine was. Can you give me any indication on why I'm feeling pulled towards something like that?

I am Latwii, and am aware of your query, my brother. We find in this instance that the attraction of which you speak is one which has numerous—we search this instrument's mind for the proper terminology—components which are feeding in to the attraction. Some of these are those which we would rather allow your own discovery to bring to the conscious attention, for this is a part of your current experience which offers to you the opportunity for growth which we would not wish to take from you. We may suggest in one aspect of this experience that as you see a portion of yourself in another which you have yet to balance, shall we say, in your own experience, but for which you feel great affection, you may expect that this recognition of a portion of yourself in another has the potential to offer to each of you an opportunity to move from one point of viewing to another which is larger, shall we say, in scope.

May we answer further, my brother?

C: No, thank you very much.

I am Latwii, and we thank you, my brother. Is there another query at this time?

K: I have a couple of questions, Latwii. The first has to do with emotional charges attached to past experiences or people. I know there are a number of experiences in my life which are painful to me to remember, and I have some more feelings attached to a number of people, some that are very close to me. I wonder if you can comment for me on the balancing process that needs to be done in these situations?

I am Latwii, and am aware of your query, my sister. When one sees within one's emotional responses a charge which is significant, whether it be positively expressed or negatively expressed, one may look upon such charge as that which is one-half of the full point of view which, when attained, will represent balance within one's being. Thus, if one wishes to work upon this balance, one may in the meditative state or in solitary contemplation look upon that charge and examine its nature. If one can recall specific instances in which this charge was developed, these experiences then may be relived, shall we say, within the mind and may indeed be enhanced to the point that the charge is magnified to the greatest extent that is possible. This charge then may be likened unto the pendulum which has been moved …

(Side one of tape ends.)

(Jim channeling)

I am Latwii, and am once again with this instrument. We shall continue. The pendulum then may be seen as having been moved to the fullest position upon its arc on one side of the perpendicular, shall we say, so that there is now the potential of swinging in a full arc to the opposite side. The magnified emotion then may attract in one's mind the polar opposite. This is a natural process which one may then allow to increase within the mind until the opposite emotion is of equal strength. When both may be seen within the mind, you may then view each as a portion of a continuum, the entire continuum offering to you the opportunity of experiencing more of the one Creator. If you can accept yourself completely for containing within your being this range of opportunities for knowing the one Creator, then you have utilized the emotions that have guided your progress.

May we answer further, my sister?

K: Can you tell me if it's possible as a result of having a strong emotional charge attached to particular people or situations and having those remain unbalanced, is it possible to throw off the course of a planned incarnation? I guess I mean throw off to the point of it being a waste.

I am Latwii, and we feel that we are aware of your query. If our response does not reflect this, please query further. If you have emotional responses to any entity or event which become strong enough to be recorded in your memory and which have not found the resolution in balance, one may expect to see these types of responses repeated within the life pattern until work with them is sufficient to achieve balance. When an incarnation has been completed, there is seen those patterns which have achieved balance and those which yet await balance. The latter then become a portion of the work to be accomplished within the next incarnational pattern. Thus, we do not see efforts within any incarnation as being wasted, shall we say, but as providing further opportunity for learning and for serving others.

May we respond further, my sister?

K: If an entity has a particular planned service or mission, as it were, a plan for a particular incarnation, is it possible to miss that by failing to utilize catalyst efficiently or failing to learn a lesson prior to the time that this service was to be accomplished?

I am Latwii, and in general we would respond to your query by suggesting that such is possible, for within any incarnational pattern, there is the possibility and the freedom of ignoring or rejecting any catalyst that one may find within the incarnational pattern. Indeed, within an incarnation, the nature of free will is such that an entity may move in any pattern which it chooses, however, there is the momentum, shall we say, of the preincarnational choices which tends to bring before the entity's notice the catalyst which has been designed to provide the entity with the opportunity to learn and to serve in such and such a fashion according to the preincarnative choices. It is a somewhat difficult task to ignore or reject what one has placed within one's path. However, this is possible if a strong enough exercise of will is manufactured, shall we say.

There are lessons that then develop from this ignoring of preincarnational patterns which may have been totally unplanned, yet may also add to the entity's ability to learn and to serve, whether the service is that which was planned previous to the incarnation or not. The possibilities of any incarnation are infinite, for within the incarnation free will and that which has been predetermined mix and blend, weaving various patterns at various times so that there is a constant interplay of attraction and repulsion.

May we answer further, my sister?

K: No, thank you, that was very helpful. I have one further question, though. Can you comment for me at all on the nature or the cause of very strong positive attractions to various people or specific people?

I am Latwii, and am aware of your query, my sister. It is quite a large subject, for all things and people which come before one's notice within the illusion in which you experience your current incarnation are a portion of the self in one degree or another. The attraction of the self to the self is that which is a natural portion of the creation, for the creation, as you know, is of one thing, that great Thought of love which motivates all that is and is the fabric of all creation.

If you are able to perceive in a relatively clear fashion more of the heart of your own being within yourself and are able then to look with this same eye upon those about you and recognize a clearer reflection of that which each is, then you may feel an attraction which is unhindered by the disguises, shall we say, that are the personalities which allow entities to pursue lessons in a unique fashion. Thus, it is not so much the uniqueness of entities which attracts one to another as it is a clearer and clearer expression of that which is the same for all, that being the expression of the love of the one Creator.

May we answer further, my sister?

K: No, that's very helpful. Thank you.

I am Latwii, and we thank you, my sister. Is there another query at this time?

(Pause)

I am Latwii, and we find that for the moment we have exhausted those queries which those present have brought to our attention. We thank each of you for your gifts of the query which opens yet another avenue of seeking the one Creator. We have enjoyed our speaking with this group this evening. We always look forward to the opportunity to join this group, for it is a merry one which enjoys even our silly sense of humor. We can't get laughs in every bar in the universe, you know. We always hang out with our friends—we too have our attractions.

We shall leave this group at this time, rejoicing in the love and in the light that we have found here and in all portions of the one Creation. We are those of Latwii. Adonai, my friends. Adonai vasu. ☙

Intensive Meditation
October 13, 1986

(K channeling)

I am Laitos, and I greet you, my friends, in the love and in the light of the one infinite Creator. It is our great pleasure once again to be with your group for the purpose of exercising the new channel for a brief period of your time. We are quite pleased with the progress this instrument has made and glad of the opportunity she has had to work with other contacts as well as ours. We hope to continue working with this instrument in your future. At this time we would transfer the contact. I am Laitos.

(Jim channeling)

I am Laitos, and greet you again in love and light through this instrument. We are very happy to have the opportunity to speak through this instrument as well, for the process of working with new instruments provides those who are more experienced with an opportunity of expanding that experience and becoming a new instrument on another level, shall we say. We have been happy that this instrument has offered itself in the capacity of serving as somewhat of an anchor in this particular proceeding.

We look upon the vocal channeling type of service as one which offers increasing kinds and depths of service to all those with whom the process is ongoing. We choose in these kinds of sessions to offer information which is more useful to the people, as you call them, that have joined in the session in order that they might serve as vocal instruments, rather than offering information which is more general in its application, for these workings are those which have been set aside for the purpose of developing the instruments which will at a later time, as you would see it, [move] into the kinds of service that will move to a wider selection of your peoples.

At this time we are aware that there is the need to be brief, for there is the opportunity for some of this group to participate in another type of service, of praising the one Creator by singing of the sacred music. Thus, at this time we shall attempt to close this contact through the new instrument known as K. We shall transfer this contact at this time. I am Laitos.

(K channeling)

I am Laitos, and greet you once again through this instrument.

(Long pause.)

As we have said, my friends, we do count it a privilege to be able to serve with you in this manner, for there are many who are seeking and the call is great, so we are appreciative of any additional means by which you may seek to answer this call.

We thank each of you in this group for your faithfulness to this service. At this time we will take our leave of this group, for we wished only to say a few final words through this instrument. And so we leave you, my friends, in the love and the light of the one Creator. Be joyful, my friends, and peace be with you. We are known to you as those of Laitos. Adonai, my friends. Adonai. ❧

Intensive Meditation
October 14, 1986

(K channeling)

[I am Laitos, and] we greet you once again, my friends, in love and light. It is, as always, a great privilege to be with this group and to have the opportunity for working with the new instrument known as K. It has been a pleasure for us to work with this instrument over the past several of your days, and we do look forward to working with her again in the future. At this time we would transfer the contact. I am Laitos.

(Carla channeling)

I am Laitos, and I greet you through this instrument in the love and the light of the infinite Creator. This instrument is most surprised that contact transferred to her, for she intended to be engaged doing normal work rather than working as an instrument. However, we find a request in the one known as Jim that he be allowed another period of time to work upon the meditative state itself and we were happy to oblige, as this instrument, as was her wont, was prepared and needed only to ascertain our identity and challenge. We now address the new channel.

My sister, the new channel must be vigilant concerning the challenging of entities. There was less than perfect contact with our social memory complex. Although there was some degree of contact, there was less than the desirable strength of connection, and we would suggest that it is never as important to speak as it is to assure yourself of a strong contact. If there is a feeling of varying of energies, it is well mentally to request that the energy [be] regularized [and] that the identity be given in a stronger and more stable *(inaudible)*.

We realize that the new instrument is struggling still with the analysis of thoughts. We find no fault in this, as it is inevitable given the instrument's habitual method of ratiocination. There will be that personality trait to accept and manage regardless of how much experience this particular channel may gather. Therefore, it is not a negative but rather a challenge that can be turned to good use, for if one knows one's challenges, one may properly meet them.

Perhaps more than any conditioning which we have noticed to do with this channel and for which we are grateful, it would be better if the instrument were signaled to our presence not only by call to the instrument hailing it, but also by a certain feeling which pervades the inner seat of compassion when mind, body and spirit greet a loved acquaintance.

So we do to you when we contact you, and if there is not a certain comfort or sweetness in the call, it is well to ask for it mentally that you may know that there is indeed a contact, a contact of compassion and love, of spiritual truth and of peace. And when you feel the touch of that emotionally palpable contact, it is to you as conditioning [is] to others, for your area of sensitivity, your area of surety, your particular mental makeup, is circuited through the emotions, and it is in the emotional area that you may look carefully for conditioning.

We hasten to point out that many fifth-density entities who are of the Confederation do not have nearly as strong an emotional carrier wave due to the nature of wisdom and the wisdom density. However, many do and we feel that the one known as K has the sensitivity needed for this type of conditioning to work well for her.

We say all this because we are aware there was a certain amount of questioning on the instrument's part as to why the contact seemed to vary in strength to the point where the instrument was not *(inaudible)* receiving thoughts. It was a matter of having one foot in the door, my sister, and one on the porch.

We would commend both the new instrument and the new teacher, realizing that for both this has been partly duty as well as honor, partly responsibility as well as pleasure. In the realm of spiritual work, as in any endeavor, the two go hand in hand, for all that is alive has the question of what to spend the life upon, what to offer the life up in aid of. If it is an offering of pleasure that it is to be, then the responsibility remains small for most, the honor of pleasing the self by distraction equaled by the responsibility of polluting the physical vehicle by excess.

If an individual is polarizing either towards the positive or towards the negative poles, both the pleasures and the responsibilities increase and the life becomes, shall we say, enlarged in its proportions, not altering that entity inside which is the seat of consciousness, but rather enlarging those things which may impinge upon the recording, analyzing, processing and evolving entity.

As you evolve, we encourage each of you to continue opening more and more to honor and to responsibility, not more quickly than you are able happily to bear the burdens which you decide to lift, but in all comfort and with a feeling of correctness and appropriateness …

(Side one of tape ends.)

I am Laitos, and am again with this instrument. We would ask again of the one known as Jim of the possibility of transfer of this contact at this time. If we are unable to make a good contact, we shall leave this group that another contact with the vibrations more closely approximating those of the one [known as] Jim may be used. We make the attempt at this time. I am known to you as Laitos.

(Jim channeling)

I am Laitos, and greet each of you in love and light through [this] instrument. We are pleased to be able to make this contact and to be able to offer ourselves in service through this instrument in the capacity of attempting to answer what queries may be on the minds of those present. We would ask if there might be a query to which we might respond?

K: At other times besides today when I felt that the strength of the contact varied, can you tell me what the reasons behind that are and what I can do about it, if anything?

I am Laitos, and we might suggest, my sister, that the process of learning to serve as a vocal channel is as any other kind of learning which you might undertake in that there are rhythms and feelings of comfort and confidence that are not always conscious which yet affect the ability of the learner to demonstrate that which it is learning.

This applies to the vocal channeling process in regards to one's mental preparedness, shall we say. As you enter the meditative state, and as you prepare yourself to serve as a vocal channel, there is a certain centering, shall we say, which is necessary in order to perceive any contact in as clear a manner as is possible for you to perceive. The day's activities, the conversations, the thoughts, and so forth are with you as you enter the meditative state. In some degree they tend to remain unless one with care sets them aside or moves aside from them sufficiently enough that the ability to perceive is enhanced as much as is possible. Even the most pleasant of conversations and feelings can become a hindrance to the new instrument or any instrument if they are allowed to remain within the conscious mind and filter, shall we say, the contact which is offered the instrument.

Thus, it is well to focus one's desires as well as one's attention as fully as is possible upon the process which is being undertaken. The vocal instrument must always place the desire to be of service at the fore in one's mind so that the concepts which embody the contact might be perceived clearly.

In short, my sister, what we have been attempting through this instrument is that the concentration and the attention and the desire must be focused as cleanly and clearly as is possible, as well as must the challenging of spirits be conscientiously accomplished. In this manner the conscious mind gives itself over that it might become a part of the service which the new instrument or any instrument wishes to offer.

We do not mean to sound overly concerned, for this is a common experience of the new instrument. The focus of attention is that which can be learned more and more efficiently as one practices this art and the simple desire coupled with practice may then allow the new instrument to function in a way which is sure and purely offered.

May we speak further, my sister?

K: I don't seem to have developed much facility yet at ignoring my own thoughts that bounce around my head. Can you give me any ideas as to how I might better do that or how I might better practice on focusing my attention?

I am Laitos, and we are aware that there are many ways which peoples of your culture and others have devised that will be of aid to one who wishes to still the mind for the purpose of increasing the concentration of attention. We find that there have been useful suggestions made in this regard previously by those present this evening. We might suggest that as your thoughts become apparent to you that whatever technique you choose to still them or ignore them, that you not be overly concerned with the application of the technique, though technique is most helpful in refining the desire to do that which you seek, that is, the stilling of the thoughts. It is the desire to be of service and to focus one's attention which is most important in doing so.

The thoughts which move through your mind may be seen as a kind of momentum which has been built up during your daily round of activities. It might be helpful to spend some time in silent meditation before any contact and vocal channeling is attempted in order to allow this momentum to run down. This is an exercise, you might say, in which one does less and less in order to gain proficiency. Therefore, we might suggest that in order to practice this exercise that you develop some time or times during your day during which you give over yourself to a meditative session. It is completely your own design which will determine the manner of practice, that is to say, the choice of time and the length of time will be of your choosing and your progress will also be a function of your desire to accomplish this task.

May we answer further, my sister?

K: No, that's all. Thank you.

I am Laitos, and we thank you, my sister. Is there another query at this time?

(Pause)

I am Laitos. We find that we have been somewhat of a surprise to each of the instruments present this evening. This, we feel, is helpful, for as it has been mentioned previously this evening, the process of serving as a vocal channel is one which is continually surprising, shall we say. The instrument who has practiced its art for however long it has done so, at some point begins to gain a certain amount of confidence which at once assists further progress and can potentially inhibit it as well if the confidence is that which does not allow for the dynamic nature of serving as a vocal instrument. Thus, if one wishes to continue to progress in the ability to serve as a vocal channel, one may expect what seem to be anomalistic situations to occur within the practice of the art.

We would suggest that one who experiences such surprises and anomalies not be overly concerned that something is wrong, shall we say, but rather look upon each situation as that which can teach one further lessons that will enable a service to be enhanced, for, indeed, that which we have offered as our contact to each instrument this evening is but a portion of what is possible. Indeed, each of you and many, many others who serve as instruments of this nature contain the possibility of growing in the art of serving as a vocal instrument continually throughout the span of your incarnation. We can assure you that there is no end to what is possible to offer when serving as a vocal instrument.

At this time we would again attempt to contact the one known as K, and to speak a few thoughts as we close this session of working. We shall now transfer this contact. We are Laitos.

(K channeling)

I am Laitos, and greet you again through this instrument. We find this instrument to be in a much more cautious state, shall we say. It is not our intention to be overbearing, but we felt that our words of caution were necessary and appreciate this instrument's attention to them. We understand that perception is not always easy for you, but discrimination is a matter of practice. We see that this instrument's desire to serve is strong, and are confident that *(inaudible)* continues she will be able to master the tasks which she sets for herself.

(Carla channeling)

I am Laitos, and I am with this [instrument] briefly only to say to the one known as K—my sister, you have had our contact, however, we fear we have indeed overdone our cautions to you, for in the taking of care, there is also more analysis which is a handicap indeed to the process of channeling. We realize that this seems as if it is a difficulty at this time which is substantial. We assure the new instrument that these are inevitable stages. Perhaps we may say that it is a good illustration of the aid the experienced channel can be to the new channel, both in giving confidence and in serving as channel when some caution is needed.

We hope the new instrument will take courage and recover at least half of the former fearlessness which made its progress so swift. Even in the climate of the contact of varying strength, if challenging has been done correctly, the instrument will have the contact it has challenged. There may simply be pauses in the contact while the under or overloads of energy are regularized. This happens not only to new channels, but to all channels from time to time, and there is no criticism either from us or from those whom you will serve on account of pauses, for who would wish a channel to speak when the contact had not offered any food for thought?

Again we shall transfer to the one known as K in order to close this session of working. We are known to you as those of Laitos.

(K channeling)

I am Laitos, and am again with this instrument. We thank you, my sister, for your patience with us as we have attempted to share our thoughts with you. It is a privilege to work with you and with each in this group as your desire to serve is strong. At this time we will take our leave from this group, leaving you once again in the love and the light of the infinite Creator, leaving you in the comfort and peace of love. We are always with you, and are known to you as those of Laitos. I am Laitos. Adonai.

Intensive Meditation
October 15, 1986

(K channeling)

[I am Laitos.] We greet you, my friends, in the love and the light of the infinite Creator. We are pleased to see the conscientiousness with which this instrument has gone about the challenging process and are pleased to have established a firm contact with her. We are also pleased that she was able to perceive our greeting to her personally which helps strengthen her confidence in the contact.

We have enjoyed working with this instrument and feel that she has made good progress. It is our privilege to have worked with this group over many of your years for the purpose of working with new instruments and aiding their training, shall we say, as vocal channels in the service of the infinite Creator. We are pleased to be a part of this process with you.

At this time we wish to address a few words to the instrument, even though she will shortly be in Venice. *(Inaudible)*. It is our wish to be able to communicate clearly with this instrument and as she is uncomfortable with this taking place through her, we transfer the contact at this time. I am Laitos.

(Jim channeling)

I am Laitos, and we greet each again through this instrument in love and in light. We have been very grateful for being able to work with the instrument known as K, and we are aware that she is desirous of continuing her practice in the art of vocal channeling. We feel that there has been a good discussion upon this topic between those of this group and our comments are meant only to augment those concepts which have been presented thus far.

In general, it is a helpful thing for a new instrument to have periodic exercise in the presence of an experienced instrument so that those small and sometimes medium-sized difficulties which occur in the practice of vocal channeling might receive the attention of experience and a sure hand at the appropriate time. This is the ideal situation and one which we endorse whenever it is possible.

We are aware that the one known as K has moved quite a significant distance in her experience and practice in serving as a vocal channel, and has in many ways achieved enough proficiency and confidence that the exercising of her instrument would be possible in a carefully guarded situation, shall we say, in which there was not present the more experienced instrument.

However, we would also suggest as has been suggested that this guarding of the situation would take the form of utilizing the presence of at least two other entities who were not only in harmony of a stable nature with the one known as K, but also felt the open-hearted acceptance of this type of information and this means of its transmission. This kind of a situation is not that which is easily obtained, for the vagaries of the seeker's path and the choices that may be made upon it by any who travel it make gathering such a grouping of entities somewhat difficult.

Even if such a situation were available to the one known as K, it would also be our recommendation that this new instrument also avail herself of periodic contact with this particular group for the purpose of reinforcing those basic principles which she has gained in this period of study and for the answering of those queries which are undoubtedly a part of her practice of this part, for as the practice continues, new experiences arise and there is often confusion in the mind of the new instrument as to the most appropriate means of resolving each new experience, be it simply new and untested or a difficulty of some kind.

If the one known as K does not feel that there is available to her a stable situation of the nature which we have described, we might recommend that there is still work that can be done in the practice of a portion of the art of vocal channeling. That practice does not, however, take the form of the actual vocalizing of our contact as is ongoing at the present moment, but would rather take the form of setting aside regular periods of meditation on a preferably daily basis, during which our conditioning vibration might be mentally requested and we might continue to familiarize ourselves and our contact to the one known as K and allow this new instrument to refine her ability to perceive our contact though there would be no transmission of thought other than our identification. The experience would be primarily one of recognizing our contact and experiencing the conditioning vibration …

(Tape ends.)

Sunday Meditation
October 19, 1986

(Carla channeling)

I am Q'uo. I greet you in the love and in the light of the one infinite Creator whom we serve as we serve you. Such indeed is our intent. We wish to thank you for requesting information which called our group, for it is a privilege to be able to attempt to be of service to you. If there is anything which we say that speaks not to you with the voice of inspiration, disregard it please, for we are as fallible as are you, and as little likely to penetrate the mystery of the uniqueness of each entity's past. Take what is for you and leave the rest, my friends. Your powers of discrimination are one of your strongest tools.

When you request information on enlightenment and appropriate methods for attaining it, you are speaking of attaining a manifestation rather than an essence, for enlightenment can only be seen by its reflection. Just as light itself is the creature and creation of love, so also is enlightenment the creature and manifestation of the thought of love which an entity has made his own.

Let us turn then from the manifestation to the essence. How to achieve communion in the unity of consciousness and love is perhaps the most basic magical question which could be asked. Magical in the sense that any entity which desires power, whether on the positive or negative path, must form a congruency of a kind with the original Thought of love in order to create personal power. Each pilgrim which embarks upon the path of attempting to increase the pace of the spiritual journey …

We are sorry for the delay, but we are having difficulty with this instrument, due to its state of fatigue. While this instrument retunes, we would transfer to another instrument. I am Q'uo.

(Jim channeling)

I am Q'uo, and greet each of you again in love and light through this instrument. We are grateful to be able to utilize this instrument while the one known as Carla works upon receiving the conditioning vibration which we offer in a state which is more comfortable to her. We thank also the one known as Carla for offering herself as instrument on this particular occasion when her physical vehicle is quite depleted of energy, having expended a great deal of effort in this day's activities prior to this evening's gathering.

We would at this time attempt to recontact the one known as Carla and continue our speaking upon the topic of the seeking of that which you call enlightenment. We transfer this contact at this time. I am Q'uo.

(Carla channeling)

I am Q'uo, and am again with this instrument, greeting each of you in love and light once more. We apologize for precipitate haste in leaving this instrument in mid-thought. However, we became aware of its discomfort, and wished to give it a chance to—we find this instrument has a phrase—"shake up the troops." This instrument wished to shake up its troops, it being on the edge of sleep. We have shaken up the troops and will once again embark upon the question about enlightenment which is actually more interesting than we make it sound, it being what you are all trying to do.

This is where we left off. So … each student of metaphysics is also a student of magic in the most pure sense, not in the sense of enchantments, ointments, curses and blessings, but in the sense of developing personal power. Enlightenment is the manifestation of focused power given a coherent shape, a degree of desire which one has towards the achieving of spiritual goals.

The most basic tool for the achievement of a realization of a life lived in magic is meditation, for meditation introduces you to yourself. You may not like what you see. You may discover many, many, many thoughts, thoughts that do not stop, thoughts that do not seem important, thoughts that you do not control. You may find yourself ill-suited at first to meditation from a physical viewpoint, the body being perhaps not used to sitting completely still without falling asleep. And yet, if all you discover about yourself over and over is, as far as you know, that you are dissatisfied with your meditations, nevertheless the intent that sits you in a chair or on the floor or on the ground and puts you in the kingdom of silence is fulfilling completely its part in your development as a magical personality, for it is not only intent, but intent carried through with even and steadfast perseverance that creates personal power.

As to personal power, there are many distortions of the magical personality, and those who seek enlightenment are for the most part seeking positively polarized distortions of that one great original Thought. That is, the path to enlightenment is considered, by those to whom service to others is a goal, to be the service-to-others path. May we say we find it to be the preferable one, but do not wish to influence your thinking beyond a certain point.

Once you have meditated—frustratingly or pleasantly makes no difference—for long enough to perceive yourself differently than you did before you began to meditate, you will begin to experience outward changes in your perceptions. This is due to the fact that contact with the essence of love, the one original Thought of the Creator, causes a continuing shift in the point of view. The method of evaluation of data becomes far more regularized and polarized towards valuing those things which are considered to be of service to others and to the Creator and devaluing those things which are seen as unethical or service to self.

You will find many wars going on within yourself during this period and it is as though everything that you did know methodically becomes torn away. This is a necessary and a continuing part of the spiritual path, for distortions are all that we notice. It is difficult for the critical consciousness to perceive complete regularity in an infinite configuration. No, my friends, each of us notices peculiarities, and it is by emphasizing certain dynamic tensions that polarity itself takes place.

And so, you may go through a short or lengthy period during which you are seeking with your mind and your heart, you are offering yourself to meditation, and things basically are falling apart for you. If this does not happen to you in at least a small way, if you are not reevaluating your point of view after a certain amount of time, as you call it, meditating, it is perhaps for you to meditate a little bit longer or a little bit more regularly. Perhaps you have a high tolerance for the illusion and to awaken from it may take a little more.

In no way become discouraged because this may be so, for your intent will bring you that which you desire. The only variable is what you call time, and there are mysteries in each entity's life pattern having to do with the higher self's choice of lessons to be learned in any incarnation which may prohibit the apparent perception of enlightenment. Be patient with yourself at all times. Ask of yourself only that you be faithful once you have decided to seek the truth.

Once you have begun this journey, you shall never arrive, for part of you is always aware of what you do not know; another part is learning and is quite disorganized; and another part has learned something recently and is resting and is waiting to see what the next lesson may be. My friends, you are complex people. However, enlightenment is essence in importance, and your perception of enlightenment is the shadow of the reality of compassion. As you meditate, as you begin to widen your point of view, never rest, for there is always another refinement which may offer more beauty to your own consciousness of love, and for you to reflect that consciousness, for you to seem enlightened, a light to those around, is a most helpful thing to wish. Never suspect that enlightenment benefits the enlightened one. Enlightened entities, my friends, for the most part, work very hard and do not consider themselves enlightened.

No, enlightenment is for the benefit of lightening others' weary loads, lifting other people's spirits with an enlightened smile or a few soft words. Seek the essence of compassion. Seek the Creator which is all truth and all love. Enlightenment will be your harvest. We wish you a good appetite for meditation, my friends, for it will stand you in good stead.

We are always pleased to join you in your meditation if you feel the need to meditate, shall we say, with a group. We would be delighted to add our vibrations to your own if you would mentally request it. We do not, however, wish to speak with any privately, reserving that for the working sessions, my friends.

We would wish to greet with pleasure the one known as K who is new to this group and greet each again through this instrument before transferring to the one known as Jim so that any questions that you may have about this body of material you have been given could be answered or any other questions you may wish to ask. We would at this time transfer to the one known as Jim. We leave this instrument with the word love and the vibration light. I am Q'uo.

(Jim channeling)

I am Q'uo, and we are grateful to be able to greet you again in love and light. We apologize for the delay, for this instrument was desirous through its challenging of being certain that it was receiving our contact and no other. At this time it is our privilege to ask if there might be any queries to which we might respond more specifically than we were able to respond in our opening message. Is there any query at this time?

J: From tonight's lesson, do I understand correctly that the path to enlightenment is the path of positive polarity, that is, the path of service to others rather than service to self? Is this correct, first of all?

I am Q'uo, and we emphasized in our previous speaking that the positive polarity choice is, though in our opinion preferable, but one of two choices that those within your illusion may make in traveling the path that leads toward what you have called enlightenment. Thus, the negative choice, that of choosing to be of service to self first and foremost in one's life patterns, is as valid a choice as is the choice to be of service to others first and foremost in the life patterns.

May we answer further, my brother?

J: No, thank you, that cleared that up. Well, one other question. I know this has been asked before, but let me ask it one more time. What is the best technique for meditation?

I am Q'uo, and in this regard, my brother, we would have no specific meditational technique to offer above all others, for each shall find a particular way of seeking in the meditative state which shall be more efficacious than others. Yet the variety of choices is large. Each choice, however, to be most efficacious, in our opinion needs to be based upon the great desire to seek what you may call the truth within each portion of one's life, and then in a particular portion of the daily experience choose to reflect the light which one has received back to the Creator in a manner of communing with the one Creator which will allow the seeker then to become aware of the essence of all things within the life pattern.

That is, in the process and state of meditation, one begins to become aware of the unity of love which binds all things and which moves all experiences in intricate patterns which then offer the lessons of love to those of your illusion. The desire, then, to seek the heart of the life pattern is that desire which is most helpful to propel one into the meditative state, no matter what technique of meditation is chosen.

May we answer further, my brother?

J: No, thank you. I think it was about two weeks ago when Q'uo joined us once before, it was stated at that time that the Earth is at this time in the middle of an ice age. And we really didn't get the opportunity to question that particular statement. Could you comment on that now, please?

I am Q'uo, and we scan the previous transmissions and experiences with this group. We find that this particular information is in regards to the geophysical manifestations upon your planetary sphere at this time which affect the physical illusion. At the same time that the change in what you know as conscious awareness is occurring at the planetary mass mind level, the various physical geophysical patterns of your planet's expression of this change in vibration or consciousness are various side effects, shall we say, that seem to have a significant influence within your illusion, but which are in effect but rippled effects, shall we say, that fall by the wayside as a greater force finds its expression within the experience of each within your illusion.

Thus, you will in the years to come, shall we say, notice more geophysical changes occurring as the shift in the atomic core vibration of each particle of your creation continues in its progress. Thus, we do not feel that these side effects, as we have chosen to call them, are of particular influence or significance when one looks to the heart of the evolutionary process which is ongoing both within your planetary sphere, upon it, and within the life pattern of each entity which calls it home.

May we answer further, my brother?

J: I guess I'm still somewhat confused as to exactly what was meant by the "ice age." It's been my understanding that our scientists are now saying that we are beginning a so-called heat-up of the Earth and this seems somewhat in conflict to that. Could you comment on that?

I am Q'uo, and we find that there are many cycles of experience which in a physical sense are manifesting themselves within your third-density illusion. Some are consecutive and others are congruent with each other. When one looks at a wider view, shall we say, of your planetary influence and sees that which is occurring at various levels of consciousness and various positions upon your planetary sphere, there is an interplay or overlay of points of view that may be taken in both the practical and the metaphorical levels of viewing. Thus, there may be in some portions of your planetary experience the manifestation of increases or reduction in what you would call the planetary transfer of heat or manifestation of this transfer. These may be perceived for a relatively short period of your time or experience in one manner and be perceived in another manner at another time. Thus, we continue to refer to the relative unimportance of this type of research, for it is but the manifested reflection of the greater movement in conscious awareness that is at the heart of all manifestation upon your planetary influence.

May we answer further, my brother?

J: No, thank you. I think I understand now.

I am Q'uo, and we thank you, my brother. Is there another query at this time?

Carla: I was just curious if you were referring to the cycles that were referred to by a fellow named Hammaker—in his book? If you were, I could just give J the book.

I am Q'uo, and we have indeed been referring to many of these cycles, my sister, and others also which are not described within this entity's work.

May we answer further, my sister?

Carla: No. No, thank you.

I am Q'uo …

Carla: Wake up!

… and we appreciate the attempt to bring into conscious awareness each member of this group, for it is helpful to the group as a receiving mechanism and to any serving as instrument or transmitting mechanism to be focused upon that which is being shared from this group to our group and from our group to yours. Is there any further query at this time?

Questioner: Yes. I appreciate the information on meditation. Now tell me, is anything like a candle or incense when you meditate alone, is that beneficial in any way?

I am Q'uo, and we find, my brother, that there are many such items and portions of ritualized practice which one may utilize in practicing the art of meditation. You may choose any such item or practice that speaks to you of that which you seek in the practice of meditation. Thus, you make your own that which you include within your practice. Many have found these items to be of service in focusing the mind in a manner which does not waver and which serves as a stabilizer for the practice, shall we say.

May we answer further, my brother?

Questioner: That's fine. One more short question. Two or three times a week in my activities, out of the corner of my eye I sort of see an aura at the tip of one of my fingers. Is there anything to that? Just out of the corner of my eye, only, not looking directly at it.

I am Q'uo, and again, my brother, we find that you have in a unique fashion discovered one manner in which you may view a portion of your own auric field or the electromagnetic pattern of energy that your seeking creates about your physical vehicle. The ability to see in a new way is fundamental to sharpening one's visual perceptions that would allow the viewing of that called the aura. Your particular method has allowed your conscious perception to be averted in a fashion which then provides entry into your …

(Side one of tape ends.)

I am Q'uo, and greet each of you again in love and light. As we had completed our response to the query which was asked of us, we would then ask if we may respond in any further way, my brother?

Questioner: No more questions.

I am Q'uo, and we thank you, my brother, for your queries. Is there another query at this time?

J: If I understood correctly tonight from the session, it was mentioned that as we begin to meditate and seek the enlightenment, that many times we experience somewhat of a chaos either physically or mentally. And I didn't quite understand the reason for that. Could you comment further on that, please?

I am Q'uo, and am aware of your query, my brother. As one becomes consciously aware that the daily experience is that which contains the opportunity to progress upon the path of evolution, and as one begins within the meditative, contemplative, or prayer-filled state to consider the meaning of various experiences and thoughts within one's daily round of activities, portions of these experiences then take on a new light, as it were, for there is the desire to see beyond the exterior illusion within each experience. This desire propels one's perception beyond that exterior in order that more of what you might call the true nature of the experience might be made known to the conscious seeker.

As this process continues and feeds to the conscious mind more of the nature of the daily experiences, the seeker may for a varying portion of time or experience see that about it in a new configuration which tends to confuse or fuse together with that manner by which the experience [was] previously perceived. Thus, there is the fusing of perception, that which is more exterior, with that which is less exterior or more toward the heart of experience that is Love.

Thus, the seeker may find that its experience begins to change in configuration in the manner in which it is perceived, and, indeed, the manner in which it is experiencing. Thus, there is the continual, shall we say, transformation of experience and seeker as the process of seeking that which you have called enlightenment continues for each seeker.

May we answer further, my brother?

J: Although the meditator progresses along the path towards enlightenment, could he experience this transformation as possibly deep depression at times?

I am Q'uo, and we bring to this instrument's mind the image of the elephant which is perceived by the blind man, each portion of the elephant seeming different from the other, yet each portion being a portion of one entity or concept. The concept of enlightenment has many avenues of entry, shall we say. The journey towards its realization moves through mountains and valleys, across deserts and through jungles. At one time or in one experience, the seeker may perceive a portion of the entirety which is radiant with light, and the life experience is lifted high into that light. At another portion of the experience or the journey the seeker may find it necessary to move into the lower or darker regions where the valley of the shadow of darkness as it is called may be that which consumes the seeker's attention and seems the totality of its experience.

Yet each of these extremes, shall we say, and all points between are portions of one journey, and together may be seen as the entirety of that which shall be the total experience of a seeker throughout your third density illusion in order that each seeker may be provided with those opportunities for learning which are most appropriate with the current needs of that seeker.

May we answer further, my brother?

J: No, thank you. That analogy was very helpful.

I am Q'uo, and we thank you, my brother. We have been made aware through another manner of transmission, shall we say, that there is the need to bring this session to a closing at this time, for there is a great amount of fatigue which is limiting one of the members of this circle from contributing the necessary attention and rejoicing in the experience. We thank each for asking our presence, and for allowing us to join you in your own journey of seeking this evening. We look forward to joining this group at future gatherings as you would reckon your time, and we leave this group at this time in the love and in the light of the one infinite Creator. We are known to you as those of Q'uo. Adonai, my friends. Adonai.

L/L Research

Special Meditation
October 22, 1986

(Carla channeling)

I am Q'uo, and I greet each of you in the love and the light of the one Creator. It is a great privilege to be speaking with you, and because of the nature of this channeling we would pause at this time to move in the stream of time, as you call it, and blend our vibrations with yours at this time, in order that we may empathize and blend our energies with your own, for we wish to speak not only inspiring words, but also words inspiring and needful to you. We shall pause at this time. I am Q'uo.

(Pause)

I am Q'uo, and am again with this instrument. We are pleased to have shared in your life stream, and shall speak at this time about those things which are upon your mind. Although many are the concerns which you have, perhaps the one you hold most in common is the desire to know more about meditation.

Each of you has consciousness. That consciousness is greater than you may perhaps have perceived. You may associate consciousness with your ability to reason, analyze and think. Many are the questions which yield to the excellent tool of your waking consciousness. Yet, let us gaze upon the frontiers of rational thought with care to examine the ultimate nature of the knowledge gained through reason.

The rational mind is a calculator, and it calculates many things very well. Your race has built many gadgets, many beautiful and interesting artifacts, and yet, in all the complexity of the creation of man, there is no ultimate truth. All rational inquiry has ended thus far in mystery. Geniuses, as you call clear thinkers who are scientists, turn finally to appreciation, and even adoration, of the mystery which unifies all phenomena, never convinced that there is not an ultimate answer, but aware that it has not yet been found.

Consciousness is not only rational, and it is in using the rational mind alone, or the subconscious mind alone, that knowledge has become fragmented and incomplete. The mind functions with precision and elegance in the portion of your consciousness which most among your peoples shrug off as being that province of fools and dreamers—the subconscious or unconscious mind. And yet each of you well knows how many times you have known through intuition or hunch, because you saw it in a dream, or just knew it to be so, what would occur before it did. You have known when you would be visited or telephoned, what your friend or family would say to you. You have seen solutions that could not logically be arrived at. Without even intending to, you have used the deeper powers of your mind to simplify your life. You have managed your consciousness perhaps better than you think, yet there is far more improvement possible through meditation. Let each of us step back for a moment and look carefully at what we feel may be so about consciousness.

We suggest to you, my friends, that there is one consciousness, which in its original and undistorted form may be called love. The consciousness of love is the great original Thought, crystal clear and pure, and by its profound, generative nature, the Creator of all that there is.

Thus, the consciousness that is your identity and nature is some distortion, one representation of that one great original Thought of love which created all that there is. When the conscious mind of man is used without the aid of the deeper mind, very little of the consciousness of love can be channeled through you from consciousness to manifestation. The person who lives in mind and not in heart lives a dry and arid life, unrelieved by the beauty of love or the joy of passion, for, indeed, it is those with a passion and joy for knowing the truth, for celebrating friendship, and for seeking love, that creates the full potential of consciousness for each of you.

When you move from the conscious mind into the deep mind, you are moving from busyness and noise, distraction and sleep to a cool, clear pool of light, silent, profound and infinite. Infinity cannot be comprehended by the rational mind, for the mind calculates only the calculable, leaving mystery uncalculated. The deep mind is at home and comfortable in the endless sea of infinity, for [in] infinity it has its home, just as you have your home in infinity.

You are an eternal essence, part of the Creator, and before your planet hung, round and beautiful in its orbit, you existed, complete and perfect. It is your birthright to experience infinity. Your conscious mind keeps you limited. In meditation, you enter the eternal, and as you allow your mind consciously to run down and become quiet, you tap in more and more to the great stream of love and wisdom which runs underground, shall we say, in your consciousness

Perhaps you feel that in some ways you are not worthy to meditate and to seek understanding, but we assure you that all entities make what could be called errors in judgment. We ask you always, as you go into meditation, to release your previous perceptions of yourself, your identity, your faults, and your weaknesses, focusing only on that which you desire—knowledge of the truth. In meditation you shall become more and more aware of the true nature of the creation. You shall begin to see the unity that binds all in the Thought that created all.

If all whom you meet and all that you meet are love, then what shall your perceptions be after meditation? The more you meditate, the more you will discover the expansion of your viewpoint, the increase in tolerance, in awareness, in understanding, for, my friends, the creation is far other than it may seem to those who view the incarnation, the lifetime, as all that there is.

To the one who has no hope of eternity, the consciousness of love may come hard. However, we urge you to attempt to justify in any rational way the order of the magnificent and infinite universe without suggesting the unity of the creation under one Progenitor, one Father, one Principle which creates all. And as for eternity itself, we leave it to your hearts to validate the truth of the nature of the universe.

Turn then regularly—daily, if possible—from the endless wrangling, disputing, proving and disproving of the conscious mind, long enough to swim in the sea of eternity, so that you may cleanse yourself of dailyness and emerge clear, clean, spotless and perfect, resting in infinity, bathed in the love and the light of our infinite Creator.

My friends, you are experiencing changes as it is, and the more you meditate, the more changes you will experience in addition to that which by nature is changing in your perceptions. The path of one who seeks through meditation and opening to infinity is not always an altogether easy one, although it is a joyful one. There is often little peace in perceiving more love in situations than others perceive. Yet, may it be a joy to you, and may you always seek the truth.

We surround you with our love, which is only that channeled from the Creator through us, for all things are the Creator, and the Creator is in all things. If we have said any words which do not seem to ring true, use your discrimination in removing and forgetting those things we have said which are not for you, for we make as many mistakes as any other friend. Yet, we are your brothers and sisters, and we hope that we have been able to assist you.

Love each other, my friends. Care for each other, and experience the Creator in every face you meet.

We are those of Q'uo in the Confederation of Planets in the Service of the Infinite Creator. We do not ask you to take any note of our identification, for it matters not whether we are extraterrestrials, spirits or voices on the wind. If our words have truth and meaning for you, that is all and more than we could hope to desire from this service we humbly offer. We would leave you now in the love and in the light of the one infinite Creator. Adonai vasu borragus. ✣

Sunday Meditation
November 2, 1986

(Carla channeling)

[I am Q'uo.] Greetings in the love and in the light of the one infinite Creator. We are those of Q'uo. It is a great privilege to speak with you this evening. We would ask before channeling further that the instrument place her free hand in the free hand of the other instrument.

As both instruments have the hands crossed, we are now satisfied that there is adequate metaphysical or etheric protection for this contact. The physical energy level of this instrument is quite low, that is, we should say, in [the negative], and therefore there is some difficulty in working with such a small group. *(Inaudible)* this is satisfactory.

In answer to the queries of the instrument regarding the nature of prior contact, we may say that the previous messenger was not acceptable as a spirit filled with love of service to others, and we are pleased at the instrument's determination to name and dismiss the persistent contact. We ask that this instrument attempt to erase from the mind the name of this entity, as thought of the name is an attraction, forming a bond between instrument and contact.

We find this instrument in an unusually good state for contact, the mind being in repose with no curiosity as to what is about to be said. This is satisfactory.

The presumption of the seeker is that all parameters are to be understood and searched out and that there is trail of wisdom to the stars, a series of questions that will lead one to infinite wisdom. This is not so. Wisdom is born of suffering, dilemma, contradiction and pain. The so-called happy times that you experience within the illusion are useful as randomly as are the difficult times, and the intrinsic value of happiness is quite low.

Indeed, no experience has a great deal of value except as a part of a very large base of information from which the deeper mind may begin to draw intuitive conclusions about the way things are not. Each of you considers the self a fairly long-term, consistent and stable personality. Seekers tend to view the self as a kind of business to be managed—so much of this, so much of that, the proper conditions for growth, and behold: a well-managed and prosperous-looking metaphysical path. We realize that we are not speaking to those who are seeking reasons to commit themselves to the spiritual path, but rather that we are speaking to those who will live life within third density to its end, incarnationally speaking, moving as closely in accordance with metaphysical principles as intuition and reason permit.

Thusly, we wish neither to commiserate nor inspire. We wish to explain to you that you inspire us, for you cannot see any good that you do, nor can you know what you have learned within this incarnation. And yet you struggle onward, ceaselessly valiant, forever spraining your metaphysical ankles and breaking your bones, picking yourselves up, putting yourselves in traction and moving back into your search, your fruitless, hopeless search for a well-ordered, productive, maximally service-oriented expression and manifestation of love.

You seek to create a life. Do you know that you cannot help create life, or that the enormous bulk of that which you create was created before you got your rational hands on it? Did you know, my brother and my sister, and we speak also to our sister, J, that you move in a maze, working not on understanding but on prejudice? What are you seeking to be prejudiced for or against? You are seeking to be prejudiced against happiness and for suffering, against comfort and for discomfort, against social ease and for solitude, against peace of mind and for humble and disquieted thought, against law and for law. You are seeking to tie a knot so complex that it becomes unity, moving through complexity and dissolving. You are seeking the mystery you name but cannot describe and the doors to the mystery open most fruitfully when the attention is heightened, focused and intensified by loneliness, discomfort and suffering.

Would that we could teach those within an illusion to pay sufficient attention while peaceful and happy, for then discomfort and pain would have no spiritual use whatsoever, these being the two-by-fours which are applied to your foreheads by your higher selves in a loving effort to get your attention.

Why is it, my friends, that when it is noon, you think about what you shall do from noon 'til one and at one you think of what you shall do in the afternoon? And even if you hear a noise or are disturbed, you do not think to yourself, "I wish to take this time out of time. I wish to take this moment with utter seriousness"? Why do you skate on the pond of your life, never plunging into the icy waters that protect sleepers from wake ones?

There are techniques which may insulate you against the chill of pain, the discomfort of solitude. Some there are who gradually don these protections and move into a kingdom where all is wakeful, listening, full of light and conscious. In attempting to understand the surface geography about you, metaphysically speaking, you cut yourself off from the acceptance of those tools which you can use to move through the icy waters of wakefulness.

Things are simple, as our message always is. You may put on light; you may put on love; you may put on commitment; you may put on honest doubt. In all of these ways, you are declaring that your element is wakefulness and that your goals are not surface, not sleep-ridden, but further into the light, further into life, further into that which is conscious, for there is that within each life which is conscious, but hides beneath the waters, and the waters hide beneath the ice.

We shall transfer. It is a pleasure to speak through this instrument, and we thank both instruments for their fidelity to that service which they offer without regard for the outcome of that offer. This is satisfactory. I am Q'uo.

(Jim channeling)

I am Q'uo, and greet you again in love and light through this instrument. We are pleased that we have been able to utilize each instrument this evening, and at this time it is our desire to open our contact to queries which may be on the mind of either instrument. If there may be a way in which we could serve in this manner, we would be most happy to do so. May we speak to any concern or query at this time?

Carla: I was wondering if you could say what you just said so I could understand it. I didn't understand what you were saying, exactly. Something about the good times don't help and the bad times don't help?

I am Q'uo, and we feel that your ability to perceive that which was transmitted through your instrument is that which might be considered for one serving as an instrument, for if one is able to open oneself fully enough to a contact such as ours in order that it might move without resistance through the instrument there will be the tendency towards forgetting that which has moved through the instrument. This is as it should be, my sister, and we feel that you will be more able to grasp the concepts which we have transmitted through your instrument when you are able to view them upon the page, if all has gone well with the recording of these concepts, as we are aware there has been some difficulty in this area.

The core of the concepts which we were attempting to share this evening is that concept which we have discovered in our own experience and feel is quite applicable to each entity who [is] within your third-density illusion—the nature of that illusion. For, indeed, all you perceive within your life experience is made of illusion. That which seems good and favorable and that which seems bad or repugnant together form the mountains and valleys of the terrain of your life experience. And it is not from reading of such geographical configuration of land masses that one learns how to navigate such terrain, or is able to deduce any precept or final conclusion from such configuration. One must travel this terrain, moving between the peaks and the valleys, and remaining in various locations for a certain period of your time and experience in order to be able to grasp the effect upon one's thinking, that residing within a certain location of being and expression will affect the thinking.

By so experiencing these various geographical configurations, to continue, one may then, through this experience, fashion that which is truly born of wisdom and which may eventually produce a loving acceptance of all that one experiences within the life pattern, when one is able to utilize the experiences to their fullest extent.

May we answer in any further way, my sister?

Carla: I'll follow your advice and read it. It did seem a little—it took me aback to hear you say that nothing that we did is basically any account, there was no way we could learn anything. Sometimes I really do think that we're making progress. So, I guess I should not think that way.

I am Q'uo, and in this regard, my sister, we may only add that as one moves further along the path of evolution, and begins to feel a sense of accomplishment, that one in the true sense has begun to discover that there is much to learn, and what seems to have been learned will affect the thinking yet may not carry the impact upon the total beingness that the conscious mind imagines it will carry. Indeed, you make progress, my sister, as do all seekers of truth. Yet that progress is registered within your total being in a way which you cannot imagine, for you do not have the tools within your illusion to grasp the breadth, the depth, or the height or the intensity or any true measure of that which [you] have attained.

Doubt not that you have attained, but continue to doubt that you know what you have attained, for that which you seek is truly born of mystery and will continue to attract your seeking. Only one who is either unaware that such mystery exists, or is satisfied that the mystery is solved shall fail to make progress in moving closer toward the heart of that mystery. In time you will see with clearer eyes the nature of that mystery more and more clearly. Yet within your illusion at this time you must content yourself with continuing upon the journey toward mystery and accept that you do not know what you do or how to do it, but that you wish to do that which will make the mystery move within your life in the pattern that may only be described as love.

May we answer further, my sister?

Carla: I have a different question. Thank you for that answer. It helps a little bit—I'll read it. A couple of questions that have been on my mind and I'm glad to have this chance to ask them. Just personal.

Question number one on my mind. In writing the book on channeling, I've found more and more that I do have a fairly singular view of the nature of channeling and its context, and things that I really didn't know that I thought, in such an organized fashion. I've just been going along in my biases, I guess, and not really analyzing it. I find that I perceive channeling as a kind of ministry, like any other metaphysical or religious attempt to minister to people. Not in the sense of orthodox or unorthodox religion, but just in a sense of offering the best guidance that we can give and being responsible about and living according to metaphysical rules that produce some control over the phenomenon of channeling.

It has begun to concern me that by offering this view of channeling to people who are thinking about channeling or who are channeling, I would help a few but put off a great many more because of my perceptions of the basic nature of channeling. People are often put off by the thought of having to live a spiritual life according to metaphysical principles, and, you know, too much seriousness and discipline and so forth. Does my point of view have the best help I can give to the audience I want to offer this material to in it, or should I seek further for another expression of these principles?

I am Q'uo, and, my sister, in this regard, we may respond to your query by suggesting that that which is within you is that which you have to offer to others. Be not concerned that your own opinions will be given too much weight and will affect others overly much, for each will take from what you have to offer that which is appropriate to that entity at that particular point in its own journey of evolution. You have with your own desire to be of service to others sought within the depths of your own being, and experience that which you feel is the best which you have to offer regarding the channeling service and the preparation for such service and the maintenance for such service. What more can [you] do, my sister? To give that which is the best of one's being is to give all that one has. To attempt to fashion that which one has in a way which one feels might be more palatable, shall we say, to those who will share that offering, is to skew that which one has, and in that skewing, reduce the purity with which one shares one's own beingness.

There are many, many ways to view any particular topic that might be of service to others. We value each instrument through which we may speak, for our message is always and ever the same and gains in variety by being able to be transmitted through a variety of instruments, each with his or her own unique personality and experience to give another facet of this single message which we of the Confederation of Planets in the Service of the One Creator have to offer. Thus, we applaud your efforts to share your opinions and your experience and your thinking. They are yours to offer, freely given with no expectation of any particular outcome.

May we answer further, my sister?

Carla: The other personal question. That was a really classy way of saying, "It's up to you." I appreciate the classiness of that. The second question has to do with silent meditation and its possible value to our group. I was talking with the leader of the silent meditation group who never has channeling. She wanted to get together once every six weeks or so. I was thinking to myself that it has been literally years since this particular group offered the opportunity for silent meditation. In your estimate, would it be more helpful for the channeling always to be included in meditations, or for there to be an occasional silent meditation in terms of the inspiration there that the experience would offer to those who sit in the circle?

I am Q'uo, and again, my sister, the desires of the group are those considerations which will fashion that which is most appropriate for the group to experience as a group. We are aware that there are many ways for inspiration to be experienced. If meditation is chosen as one way in which inspiration may be experienced, then the further determination may also be made as to whether the vocal channeling shall be a part of that inspiration. We cannot decide for you …

(Tape ends.) ❧

Sunday Meditation
November 9, 1986

(Carla channeling)

I am Q'uo, and I greet you in the love and the light of the one infinite Creator. We greet each of you, and welcome especially the one known as D and the one known as B. Blessings to you and may you drink deep at the fountain of light that lies within the circle of consciousness at this time of meeting. We ask, as always, that any opinion which we offer to you be considered as opinion rather than fact, for we make errors and would not wish to teach were we to feel that each student did not have the power to take or to discard each and every thought, each and every concept that is discussed.

Those things which we say are the best we have to offer through a particular channel at a particular moment, and we would not deceive you, thus we speak as truly as possible within the limits of spoken language. Yet each word has many meanings, each concept can be heard with many ears, many attitudes, and many predispositions. Those things which do not seen appropriate for your growth at this time must needs be left behind without a backward glance. The answers lie within you, not within us.

We are those who would inspire each of you to seek, to ask your questions with more and more care and love for the search itself, for your answers, as all answers, shall turn out to be illusion and with each revelation and transformation you shall discover that you have pushed back the frontier of mystery, only to find that same mystery beckoning from the new frontier. There is no information so complete and so satisfying that it constitutes the ultimate answer, for if it can be said, it is not the truth and he who says it has pride, not understanding.

We ask you plainly to beware of answers and to focus upon questions, for as you seek and seek again, so shall the doors of your own consciousness open to you and you shall carry understanding deep within your heart, not to communicate except clumsily and incompletely, but only to manifest in your smile, your laughter, and the light of joy which you share with those about you.

There are civilizations in the creation who have become far more one with the concept of simplicity during the experience which you call third density. This civilization which you enjoy is far from simple, and because of the great expectations which you have forged by observing the many mechanical marvels available to you, you come to assume that a spiritual body of knowledge will be complex, articulate and serial, much like a detailed and philosophical list of directions for putting together an enlightenment kit.

And yet, my friends, although there are many enlightenment kits available to you, the instruction booklets need to be viewed with affection and misgiving, affection for the infinite desire of those upon the path of service to others to share in whatever fashion they may those things which have been helpful to them with others, and wariness and even dismay because there is not an intellectually acceptable set of instructions for studying, building, putting together or constructing enlightenment.

What you are after is a kind of simplicity that is not in fashion, a simplicity that is not dogma, doctrine or in any way complex. We are messengers of a simple and simplistic truth, a truth that cannot be put into words, a truth that each of those to whom we speak is already aware of.

We would seem to be talking ourselves into a corner. What do we have to talk about, if we do not have an understanding to give you that is complex and thereby rendered learnable? We are here to give you in words and by the essence of our vibrations more of a feeling for the immediacy and the value of this trip that you have taken in your heart, that you are on now, and that you wish to continue to be on until you dwell in eternity in the presence of the Creator.

To put that another way, and more simply, each of you falls headlong into a blazing white light, the white light of an infinite Creator whose very nature is love. You are falling unbelievably quickly, and you shall fuse and become one in your perception as you already are in reality with love itself. This is your destiny. And yet speed is such a relative thing. None of you knows how quickly spiritual gravity pulls you toward that great center, that great unity. Each of you feels you cannot possibly be moving quickly enough, you need to know more. And so you draw yourself along. Yet in reality, you could not hold yourself back if you tried.

We come with a simple awareness. We come to be with you, for although each seeks only for himself by necessity, for no one can seek for another, yet how much it aids each to meet together and form a circle of light, to consider, however imperfectly or incompletely, the Creator of all that there is.

We have spoken to few groups. However, the experiences that we have had with these upon the surface of this planet indicate that many are more than willing to be tempted by elegant reasoning, seeking in philosophy the objective security that forms the illusion of the scientific method of information gathering.

We urge that all consideration be given to the value of silence, of the focused mind. Lift your spirits, therefore, from the physical body which enables you to gather experience and share love within your incarnation, lift and shake the heart and heart free of the dust of dailyness and move with the solar wind, as this instrument would call it, until you are far, far from town or country or planet, until you indeed leave the solar system behind, voyage far, voyage until you do feel that you are indeed falling, and gaze at the white light towards which you fall. Glory is yours now if you can but release the demand to know, to understand, and to judge, and replace the desire to catalog with the desire to feel with head and heart in unison the light and the love that does not speak in words.

We would that you would stoke the fire of your desire to know the Creator by allowing knowledge to come into all of your being, for there is no cleverness in knowledge of the creation or love of the Creator. There is no right answer, there is no argumentation. If you have a longing, a yearning for the presence of the Creator, and if you allow that longing to persist and to grow, if you encourage that desire, the study and meditation, mind and heart both exercised, then shall that longing deliver you into the very presence you seek. Expect it, look for it, and when the moment comes that you feel that you have been given something you cannot describe or name, rejoice and let that go too.

There are questions in the group this evening. We encourage them and invite then. We cannot use this instrument for the questions and answers.

(Pause)

I am Q'uo. We apologize for the pause. This instrument began to analyze our information and we were unable to send more concepts through this instrument. May we say to the one known as Carla that we are indeed sorry that we cannot channel through her, however, we did not intend to cause her to break off her own meditation. Our apologies. We would at this time transfer this contact to the one known as Jim. We are most grateful for the desire, the longing, and the seeking that you share with us. Blending our vibrations with yours is a benediction to us, and we would only wish to be of as much service as possible to you. We leave this instrument. We are those of Q'uo.

(Jim channeling)

I am Q'uo, and greet each of you once again in love and light through this instrument. We are pleased that we have been able to make our contact available once again through this instrument, and it is our hope at this time that we might be able to attempt to respond to any queries which those present might find value in the asking. Again we remind each that our responses are our opinions and the fruit of our own seeking, which we would hope that each would weigh with the inner discrimination that speaks to the heart, taking that which rings of truth and leaving that which does not. At this time may we ask if there might be a question to which we could respond?

D: I have been in contacts associated with two other channeled entities, you being the third, each of whom has a vastly different perspective and approach to teaching and communicating. I wonder if you could clarify those differences, those various perspectives, those … why an entity seems to be, for instance, to emphasize information as opposed to another entity which might emphasize energy or intuition? This seems counter to my expectation that entities operating on planes above our own would have the facility to tailor their responses and their teaching more to the individual who seeks rather than to have so strong a predisposition on their own.

I am Q'uo, and am aware of your query, my brother. We find that there are a number of concepts within this query which are relevant. Each entity which seeks does so in a unique manner, from a point of view that is similar to many but unique unto itself, and calls for information that will be helpful in continuing to expand its scope of experience and understanding.

There are many, many ways by which a call may be answered. The vocal channeling is one of many potential responses to any seeker's request for aid. Within this phenomenon is found a great variety of sources and resources which may choose to be of service in providing information or inspiration or any kind of guidance which may answer a seeker's call.

Many upon your planet who seek in a conscious fashion the nature of their reality and their being assume that that which is yet unknown is also homogeneous, whereas it has been our experience that the portion of the creation which lies beyond the reach of your senses and your understanding is as varied and rich as that which you experience within your illusion, within your portion of the creation.

Those who would seek to move in service to seekers upon your planetary sphere, and who are seen by those within your illusion as being beyond or external to your illusion, are as unique as each on your planet and each offers itself as it is in full in the attempt to be of service. To be of the most service possible, we have found it is necessary to be what one has discovered in the way of uncovering mystery and moving along the path of unity with all that is. As one then offers the fruits of one's own journey, one offers that which is unique and colored by experience.

Each portion of the Creator, which each source and seeker is, moves likened unto a planetary body about a great central sun or truth. The sun shines equally upon each, yet each from a unique point of view sees that sun and is warmed by it according to the position from which one orbits and views that sun. Thus do we and all others who offer themselves in the service of the vocal channeling offer that which is ours to offer, that is, the fruit of our experience, that those who seek information or inspiration might consider that which is offered for its potential use in furthering the journey of seeking for the self and in sharing that journey with yet others who may benefit from such sharing.

May we answer in any further way, my brother?

D: I think my difficulty with the question stems in part from an assumption that those entities such as yourself and others in my experience who seek to serve in this way by virtue of their position at their level, so to speak, have attained a level of being—they include so much more than our minds can know while we are here—that from our perspective there should appear to be more uniformity than there is. I don't think I've worded that very well.

I am Q'uo, and we feel that we grasp the sense of your query and will respond in a manner which we hope will be of service. Please query further if we do not speak to the heart of your concern.

As we mentioned in our previous response, the experience which lies seemingly beyond that which is common among your peoples and toward which each seeker moves is an experience that, though it continues to move closer into the harmonious understanding of all that is, yet moves further into the mystery that undergirds all manifestation that is seen and experienced as creation. Though one may know certain things about creation and one's own being and movement through the creation, yet such knowing continues to discover more of the infinite mystery that lies at the heart of all creation and seeking.

We who have had the privilege of moving a short distance further upon this journey than have those of your peoples begin to grasp more of this mystery, yet we also understand that there is much which awaits our understanding. Thus, those who are what you may call "in advance" of the level of seeking of your peoples yet seek with the same diversity the one mystery which draws all unto it. Though all experience more …

(Side one of tape ends.)

(Jim channeling)

I am Q'uo, and we greet you again through this instrument. We shall continue.

Those who are in advance of your own level of seeking, shall we say, have yet the configuration of identity which perceives similar truths in various fashions, all seeking to refine the understanding, until all not only understand but become that which is sought. There will be variation for a great portion of your experience beyond that which you now experience. The journey of evolution, my brother, is one which extends far beyond your own illusion and contains that which is rich and varied enough to allow for an infinite variety of points of view, all pointed toward the same truths, but seen from different perspectives and shared in that fashion.

May we answer further, my brother?

D: Thank you very much.

I am Q'uo, and we thank you, my brother. Is there another query?

Carla: Thank you for explaining as much as you did, because I was wondering, having heard many a closely reasoned argument from you myself about the emphasis on mystery, but I think I grasp what you're driving at. Thank you.

I am Q'uo. We appreciate the opportunity to speak in any fashion which is requested, and we would ask if there might be any final queries to which we may respond before taking our leave of this group?

D: I don't really have a question—I've just kind of been wrestling quite a bit lately with the concept of self-love, attempting to understand a little more how to accept myself and how to love myself more, and I guess I don't really have a question, but do you have any comments that might provide any sort of illumination on that subject? Anything would be appreciated.

I am Q'uo, and, my brother, we can suggest that as one considers the daily experience and all who move through it, that one is seeing various aspects of the self when one notices and responds to any particular person, trait, word, deed or activity, for the manner by which one perceives the environment about one is congruent with the manner by which one perceives the self, and we have found that the opposite is also true—that as one perceives the self in a certain manner the environment about one is reflected in an equal fashion so that there is really nothing but the self, be it small or great, which comes before one's attention and upon which one may work.

As you are able to find qualities and experiences within the self and within the environment which you are able to accept more and more freely, then you are accepting further portions of the self and may then use that acceptance to find other portions of the self and the greater self about one which then move into the focus of attention for the work in consciousness which will allow further acceptance of the self within the self and within all other selves.

May we speak in any further fashion, my brother?

D: No thank you. That's fine.

I am Q'uo, and we thank you, my brother. Is there another query at this time?

D: Yes, if I can take a minute to formulate it. If thoughts are real and exist on a level of which we are relatively unaware, I would presume that you would be much more fully aware of that level on which our thoughts exist as things. If that presumption is correct, I'm curious to know in general with entities who teach such as you do, if there often is a clearer perception of our questions—such as I'm trying to form now—than I'm able to put into words. To what extent are our thoughts apparent to you though our words in communicating those thoughts are sometimes less than adequate?

I am Q'uo, and am aware of your query, my brother. In attempting to respond to those queries which are asked of us, we attempt to utilize the query itself and any appended emotions or unspoken considerations when it is possible to do so without infringing upon an entity's free will. This is to say that if we were able to read more precisely than one has been able to formulate within one's conscious mind that which was sought, there would be the risk of accomplishing work for an entity which the entity would better benefit in accomplishing for the self.

There is a very fine line, shall we say, between offering information which has been prepared for in the understanding of an entity by its own efforts and in giving information which lacks the preparation by the entity and which would remove from the entity the opportunity to gain what we might call a spiritual strength in fashioning for itself the foundation of understanding upon which we shall offer certain refinements that lie within the realm of what has been prepared by the entity requesting information.

May we answer further, my brother?

D: The protocols of this sort of communication and the assumptions that we can make about it concerned me and that answer was very much to the point. Thank you.

I am Q'uo, and we thank you again, my brother. Is there another query?

D: Are personal questions appropriate at this time?

I am Q'uo, and though we are not, shall we say, specialists in answering queries of a personal nature, we are happy to attempt such responses as long as our responses again do not risk the infringement upon an entity's free will by providing information which would affect its future choices, shall we say.

D: Well, with that in mind, I'll ask a question, seeking some help in making future choices. I have been working and accepting all the teaching I could in the area of channeling *(inaudible)* and simply wonder if—I seem to be running into blocks that I keep butting my head into. I wonder if there might be any insight that you could give that would be productive or helpful to me without taking away the lessons that I'm obviously in need of learning.

I am Q'uo, and we are aware of your query, my brother. We might suggest that when one discovers within the life pattern that which appears as a blockage and which repeats itself, that one might embrace such seeming blockage as an obvious opportunity to avail the self of a certain lesson, a lesson which might yet lie beyond the grasp of understanding and present itself in a manner which might seem to disturb or to be disharmoniously experienced, even confusing and contradictory.

Such repeated patterns may provide to the diligent student a kind of riddle which when moved about within the mind and seen from various perspectives begins to unfold itself when one has been able to work with the pattern in a fashion which at once cherishes the seeming difficulty and moves to penetrate the outer illusion and seeming configuration in order that a more basic understanding of the nature of the self and its manner of learning might be gained.

May we speak in any further fashion, my brother?

D: No, thank you.

I am Q'uo, and we thank you, my brother. Is there another query at this time?

Carla: Just to say good-bye. I do have a question. I wasn't going to ask it, but I think I will. If it doesn't infringe on my free will, please answer; if it does, don't. Is the concept that I lost when I started analyzing the contact have something to do with a tree? It would ease my mind, actually, to know that it was you that stuck a tree in my mind after—actually after I stopped channeling, because I did not get a solid name for that concept being stuck in my head. Was that you and was that the point at which I missed a concept?

I am Q'uo, and we may speak in response to this query by suggesting that that concept of the tree was a portion of our contact which we were utilizing to speak to the concern that sparked your analysis. We, however, will leave the meaning of the tree to your discernment.

May we speak in any further fashion, my sister?

Carla: No, thank you.

(A recorded telephone message is heard being played to an incoming caller.)

I am Q'uo, and we appreciate each person's patience as we have awaited the completion of the recording devices works. May we ask it there is a final query before we take our leave of this group?

(Pause)

I am Q'uo, and we thank each for inviting our presence this evening. It has been a great honor and privilege to join our vibrations with yours. We look forward to each opportunity to join this group in its circle of seeking. We shall at this time take our leave of this group and this instrument and leave each in the love and in the light of the one infinite Creator. We are known to you as those of Q'uo. Adonai, my friends. Adonai vasu borragus.

Sunday Meditation
November 16, 1986

Group question: What do you say to people who are considering a divorce, ending a commitment?

(Carla channeling)

I am Q'uo. I come in the love and the light of the one infinite Creator, and because we speak through this instrument, we say to this group alone, we do come in the name of Christ, for it is not your Christ only, but Christ, a love, the love, the love of the Creator. How could we not come in that holy name, for indeed we too hallow love as we would hallow our mother and our father, for love is mother and father of all of us.

We greet each of you and we thank you for the privilege of being able to speak with this group. It is a pleasure to be using this instrument. We note the roughened condition of the instrument's throat and will attempt to be less forceful than is our usual habit.

My children, we offer our answers in love and in hopes of being of service, and yet because your question is about divorce, as you call this custom, our points of view diverge dramatically, and in sharing with you our point of view, we so far wish not to influence any unduly that we ask most especially for each seeker's careful discrimination in using any part of what we say, for we would not wish you to act as you think you ought, but as you feel. It is your discrimination and your choice at all times, and the greatest teaching, the most ideal rule, the most exalted creed is as nothing if it is not the echo of your heart and your mind and your will. It is indeed doing damage to yourself to take concrete and irreversible steps which are not of your own choosing. It is less unfortunate if the choice is temporary, and yet we would wish not to be of disservice at all. Therefore, please take those things we say and weigh them carefully.

Our view. We pause due to the fact this instrument has ambivalence in her mind. We scan and find we understand. There are two situations—one in marriage, one a commitment without your marriage. This is not a substantive difference to us—we find it is to this instrument.

We shall, however, use our own frame of reference and thus we should say that we find the purpose of the mated pair to be increased efficiency in the gaining of catalyst, fellow aid in the processing of catalyst into experience and the supplying of a yokefellow for whatever service you have created for yourself, with the aid of your higher self and the Creator, for polarizing within your own incarnational experience.

In any density higher than your own, partners in catalyst are chosen with much clearer eyes, for the veil of the subconscious mind and the veil between minds are both alike lifted and each entity has a much advanced grasp both of his own nature and of the nature of others.

Those polarizing for service to [other] self will most always choose an entity whose vibrational nexus complements and enhances one's own. Those involved in polarizing towards service to self are unpredictable in their choices as regards vibrational compatibility, for other considerations having to do with those things which are of the illusion are more important.

To follow this line of reasoning back into third density, may we say that a persistent difficulty in speaking of your matings within your civilization is the great variety of motives for inaugurating and sustaining such a relationship. Almost never is it for the reason that is most closely aligned with the actual function and purpose of the mated relationship. Almost never is suffering, hardship and trouble used as the reason for choosing a future partner. And yet, this is the precise experience you wish to share, for your illusion is created in order that you may suffer and learn. That is the purpose of there being an illusion, for self-consciousness must be awakened. The third density begins with a sense of self asleep, and happiness and contentment do little to awaken the soul. It is the interactions with others that bring grief, suffering, loss and trauma which create the opportunities you most cherished before the incarnation.

Thus, it is well to choose the mate you want to suffer with and for the mate you feel will pull and pull as strongly as do you to carry equally the burden of illusion. Certainly it is well to choose in love, yet, my children, do you think you were given your physical vehicles, as they are, for play? We suggest that in the divine play that is your sexual network of responses, there lies the great wisdom of bonding and creating a reason to consider one particular mate over another. The choices are often too many, for one may seem good, and then another, and then another. And so we observe most sadly that the motives for your mating often include the interest of the physical red-ray center, and often also include desires for benefit. This is service-to-self in orientation, as is an unenlightened active red ray, and will lead to exactly the kind of catalyst for which each in actuality enters into a mated relationship.

However, there being no grasp of the function of the mated relationship, the trauma of catalyst is seen not as what you have come to experience, not as the reason for which you became mated, not as an opportunity to learn what you came to learn, but as an unacceptable inconvenience, discomfort and impediment, something to be shrugged off as if the mated relationship were a piece of clothing that could be shed.

You can see, can you not, that we find ourselves little able to answer in what seems to be a sympathetic way when we are asked what we would say to one who wishes to dissolve a mated relationship? Certainly, we could explain the theory of choosing a mate for the purpose of learning through suffering, but this may not seem very persuasive to one who is suffering and wishes it to stop.

We would suggest that there be made special time for meditation. What could be gained in meditation, you may ask, when the problem, the catalyst, is coming from another? And we do not give a sympathetic response this time either, for the only sphere in which any entity has power is the sphere of himself. True power is power over the self and the right use of power involves the self. There are in any difficulties which you experience, whether or not another has difficulties, problems of perception within yourself, my children. If you see anything except the face of love, you are having difficulties with perception. The distortions are understandable and unnoticeable relative to other entities within the illusion. You may even feel that you have a clearer picture than others, and indeed you may.

However, we are speaking of something that is removed from the illusion, and that is love itself. For each entity has as its core reality the face of the Creator, the heart of Christ, the mind of love. If you do not see that in your enemy, your mate, or the earth and sky itself, then you must polish your glasses and set yourself to study silence again. Do not be easy upon yourself here. For no matter what your actions, my children, it is well to have a bedrock within yourself where you have a metaphysical honesty that will give you strength. You may not be pleased with yourself, but it is well to attempt to continue to know and to bless the self in all its distortions.

Any experience may be reexamined at any time for the possibility that the catalyst has become too much for the flawed illusory entity that you experience to buckle under, and so, rather than destroy your body or your mind by allowing truly impossible abuse, it might, of course, be possible and even necessary that there be a mated couple which must spend some time apart. It is our admittedly biased point of view that it is well to persevere at all times with only one question, and, as always, that question is "Where is God (Love)?"

My children, if you or your mate find love in another, remember your own time of romance with gratitude and thanksgiving, and then wish the best and the highest and the most for your love regardless of what your mate wishes to do. If the difficulty is a difference of opinion, turn from defending self and begin defending your love, for does your mate not need you now more than ever? Is your mate not in pain? Words, gestures, any attempt at communication will heal much. And if they do not seem to be efficacious, that also is acceptable to us, for we expect the catalyst and do not attempt to rule its flow into our experience.

It occurs to us that before we leave you, or we should say this instrument and this question, we can make one point which may be more telling, although we consider it to be no more central than any other, and that is this. The one who believes that by changing the situation, he will change his experience, is following a false belief, for those lessons which each came to learn are for each, shall we say, a list of priorities. When catalyst comes to a seeker, it is a sure thing that there is a lesson connected with the learning of the nature of love which working through the catalyst will benefit so that you may become richer in experience and more conscious with the consciousness of love.

When a lesson is declined by moving out of a situation, the same lesson shall be presented to the student again. The lesson, however, will be made clearer so that there is less chance of a misunderstanding. Translated into the perceptive bias of your illusion, that means the lesson will be more painful and will take longer to work out. Catalyst will be more extensive for the same experience. The one who walks away from a mated situation is buying time but not changing the catalyst that he or she is bound to have one way or another.

To those who have divorced or been divorced, who have left commitments or have been left, we would say that there is no, what this instrument calls, "sin," and what we would call error or mistake, in moving from a situation. It certainly buys, shall we say, trouble, yet with the wisdom of survival you have chosen to heal so that you may throw yourself once more into your catalyst with a new zeal.

If you have been left, and you have found yourself acting in negative ways, ways demeaning to your mate or to yourself, we urge you to take hold of your will and your powers of love, for if you have not been tested again, you shall be. You will feel betrayal and rejection somewhere and somehow. Next time, my children, offer your love back to the situation.

To those of you who must leave or have left a committed relationship or marriage, do not weep for your past, but rather gird your loins, for your next impulse will give just as much catalyst as the one which gave the catalyst in the first place. This time attempt to infuse your actions with love, with a love that realizes compassion, with a love that realizes the reason for relationships.

Forgive and forgive again. Forgive yourself, forgive any who seem to have hurt you, remembering that you have faulty perceptions if you do not see love in every situation. You have the power to create children of your thoughts, daughters and sons of your heart by what you say and how open your heart and hands are. We ask you to create love. Love one another, my children. Always do what you must with no excuses and no need for recrimination, and always turn your face forward and use what you have learned. This environment which we have called third density is a gift. Every tear, every ache of the heart is precious.

We hope you can give thanksgiving in the hard times and find joy in tears, for truly enough, there is sadness in any joy within the illusion—should there not also be joy in any sadness?

We would transfer at this time, having greatly enjoyed talking with you. We are sorry not to have been more helpful, but, you see, we do not speak of right or wrong—we speak of love. And I am afraid that questions of mated relationships in your culture do not usually revolve about the love of which we speak which is not defined by red ray or any ray, but by that which comes through one and is more than one could ever be. For love has the power of infinity, and you who attempt to generate are generating a very finite version which will, as your red ray itself will do, die away.

We leave this instrument in love and light, and transfer at this time. I am Q'uo.

(Jim channeling)

I am Q'uo, and greet each of you again in love and light through this instrument. We are happy at this time to open our meeting with you to any further queries which those present may have upon the mind. May we attempt any such query at this time?

Carla: Well, one of the marriages that I heard about today that may be breaking up, there isn't another person, there's just a strong difference between the way two people have grown to be that wasn't there when they got married. I realize that in general, the thing is to stay together—I got that all right—but at what point does mental or physical abuse become intolerable? You know, if somebody were reading this, trying to make a decision, there really wouldn't be anything in there. I guess that's the way you designed it—there wouldn't be anything in there to make you decide, you'd just more or less get the lay of the land, is that right? You designed it so that people wouldn't use it as a basis for action, but just for thought? I mean you designed the talk that way—is that right?

I am Q'uo, and am aware of your query, my sister. We have spoken as we have spoken this evening with the hope that we may indeed provide the food for thought, as you have called it, which will hopefully provide an opportunity for many who are considering the severing of a relationship more carefully, for it is within your culture at this time quite an easy and common matter to break a relationship and the commitments made as its foundation, and then to move oneself into another situation that one hopes will again meet the imagined requirements set by the self for the perfect situation, shall we say. We, in speaking as we have spoken, hoped to provide a more basic point of view concerning the nature of relationships, their purpose, and means of fulfilling this purpose. If an entity can realize that the point of view that it holds may be somewhat narrow in the overall view of an incarnation or a series of incarnations, then the expanding of that point of view may allow for the more fully realized potential of an incarnation or a relationship to manifest within the life pattern.

In our speaking we have not overtly presented our own bias, but have attempted to describe the nature of the process of your third-density illusion. In so describing the nature of your illusion, it must be obvious to the perceptive student that to remain with a relationship that one has undertaken with the commitment that the relationship will endure is the most efficient means of pursuing those lessons and services that are the reason for the incarnation. Entities may feel that there are reasons enough to end a relationship, that it is appropriate to do so. Again we may only suggest that this conclusion is the result of a point of …

(Side one of tape ends.)

(Jim channeling)

I am Q'uo, and am again with this instrument. To continue our response. The point of view which has produced this conclusion is perhaps that point of view which has yet to avail itself of the wider scope of the potential for an incarnation. Perhaps the entity in reaching this point of view has found the more difficult point in the relationship in regards to its fulfillment and in the fatigue encountered, whether it be mental, emotional, physical or spiritual, [and] has found the possibility of ending the relationship the most appealing avenue of action.

This is a natural conclusion, my friends, for the fatigue that comes at any of these levels of experience is a very real thing, and within your limited third-density experience with its great potential for limiting the point of view it may seem to many a seeker of truth that such an alternative is obvious, appropriate and acceptable, when, indeed, it might be that if a slight alteration in perception could be achieved, another possibility for the relationship's continuance might present itself to the seeker, who could invest yet one more effort in this direction. The pearls of wisdom and love within your illusion are not cheaply or easily won, else there would be little value in that which those of third density seek throughout all incarnations.

To find the love of the Creator in any moment within your illusion is a challenge, my friends, for there is much that hides it, and to find it in those situations in which there seems to be great difficulty, trauma, stress, pain and suffering requires the dedication of one who looks beyond the moment of suffering and sees that which no outer eye may perceive—the love of the One that dwells in all, and the dedication of the seeker to find that love in each of its moments of all incarnations.

May we answer further, my sister?

Carla: How is the instrument holding up?

I am Q'uo, and we find that this instrument is in a relatively comfortable physical and mental state.

May we answer any further question at this time?

Carla: I'll beg off, and let H have a turn if there's still time.

H: Okay, concerning divorce, is it better if say they could work out a friendly divorce—it seems like that's a common phrase these days—where after the divorce they don't hate each other, that they just simply agree that they can't live with each other, and so they get a friendly divorce. This is definitely better than going through a court ritual and battling it out and all that to where the person is brought down to nothing almost. Is that not correct?

I am Q'uo, and we might suggest my brother, that not only is that assumption basically correct, but any action that is able to produce love and acceptance of another is an action more to be desired than one which produces less of that quality of love.

May we answer further, my brother?

H: Well, that satisfies that question, but what about when there's children involved in divorce? There's an old adage that the mom always got the kids. Is that the best normally, that the mother raises the kids?

I am Q'uo. We find that this questions lies within the somewhat narrow point of view of what is possible within your culture. Your culture has decided, or so it would seem, many things for you concerning how the life is lived and with whom. Within your culture there is the division between the male and female of your species of many of the behaviors which in truth may be shared if the system of belief allows such choices. Thus, to answer your query in a specific fashion, when in truth the generality fails to meet the needs of a specific response, is to be somewhat misleading.

We would respond by suggesting that we are not aware of a general response which would suffice in this case, for the male or female entity within a relationship may, because of its individuality and not because of its sexuality, be more able to carry out the nurturing function necessary for the raising of the small child. We apologize for our inability to give a more concrete response.

May we attempt another query, my brother?

H: Well, something totally different now. When we talk about past incarnations and stuff like that, is there any catalyst that, any practice that we could exercise to where we could experience past incarnations, or where I myself could?

I am Q'uo, and though we are aware of some practices, those of regressive hypnosis, the guided meditation, and the utilization of the dream state that have the potential of allowing an entity to move backwards, shall we say, and to experience some portion of a previous incarnational experience, it is not our recommendation that such is an important portion of either learning those lessons designed before the incarnation or providing those services also designed before the incarnation.

The higher self, as you call it, has gone to some lengths, shall we say, to aid your beingness in placing yourself within your current incarnation with the forgetting of previous incarnations firmly in place in order that your current incarnation might be a finer and more purely [made] effort at achieving certain biases of thinking or expansions of the point of view which will enable the experience of love to move more freely through your being. It is recommended that entities within the third density look primarily to the current experience of the daily round of activities to indicate those areas where work yet remains and opportunity presents itself for growth and service.

To become overly concerned with those activities and patterns of previous incarnations is in most cases a turning of the attention from that which is important and potentially useful in the life pattern to that which contains far less potential in aiding an entity in its chosen pattern of experience. The removing of the attention in such a fashion tends to blur, shall we say, the possibilities of the present moment of any incarnation.

May we answer further, my brother?

H: I don't know as there's any more questions on that. But what about the term we use as "unconditional love"? Is that the true love that we're supposed to have for everybody? When I look at my work mates, is that the intense level of love we're supposed to have for everybody we meet? And if it is, how do we go about that without people thinking that you're weird or something?

I am Q'uo, and this term, unconditional love, is a phrase, shall we say, which has been developed within your culture or a portion of it which describes a facet of the love which [is] the Christ consciousness, shall we say. If one is able to love without condition all entities and experiences which come before the notice, one is expressing the kind of acceptance upon the deepest of inner levels that is a—we search this instrument's mind for the proper term—hallmark of the love of the Creator which animates all creation, for the ability to love without condition or desire of return is the beginning of the Creator within the self to recognize itself within all other portions of the creation. For an entity of the third density to experience this kind of expression of love requires that the entity move in harmony with those choices which it has made prior to the incarnation that were made with the wider point of view easily accessible to the entity.

This is another means of stating that each within the third density illusion has programmed for the self a program of study which when completed to a sufficient level will allow that entity to experience this condition of love that has no boundaries and seeks no return. Thus, to work with those experiences which one finds in the daily round of experience and to attempt to find love in each moment is the means by which such love may be found. Each has the program most appropriate for the self, and, as that love is found, one need not worry as to how it might be expressed, for it shall find its own level and means of expression that will be as natural and appropriate for the entity as is drawing one breath after another.

Carla: So you're saying that love is not an emotion, but a consciousness. How we express it has to do with our emotional make-up and how we like the person that we're looking at. But whether we feel it or not has to do with a consciousness—unconditional love, I mean. Excuse me for butting in, but that's an important point to me.

I am Q'uo, and you are quite correct, my sister, and we appreciate your thoughtful and perceptive interruption, for it has concisely stated that which we were laying the groundwork for and which was not as concisely stated. We thank you, and ask if there might be a further query upon this topic from either entity present?

Carla: Not from me.

H: No questions here.

I am Q'uo. We would ask if there might be any further queries upon any topic whatsoever that we might address before leaving this meeting?

H: Is there any way that we could practice or meditate and see the different colors? I had an experience one time several years ago where I saw a bunch of blues and purples just coming, like being stirred up in a way, very beautiful to behold in your mind. I was just wondering if there was anything that you could do that would cause that to happen again?

I am Q'uo, and, my brother, we might suggest that as the student completes a certain portion of its course of study, there is usually the recognition of moving from one level to another, one grade to another, a graduation of a kind occurs. There is at that time an experience that is reserved for that time and that time alone. We might suggest that those experiences which you have described that manifested themselves to your physical sight as the experience of various colors are likened unto your completion of a set of lessons, and to attempt to experience this graduation again, shall we say, without having completed the necessary course requirements is to seek the reward before the effort has been made to achieve the goal. The experiences which you describe are not random, they have occurred as a portion of a planned course of your own experiencing and processing of catalyst and will repeat themselves when the conditions are appropriate.

May we answer further, my brother?

H: No more questions tonight. Thank you.

I am Q'uo, and we thank each present for allowing us to speak our humble words this evening. We have greatly enjoyed this opportunity and feel that the unity of seeking demonstrated by this group this evening was that which is to be commended, for as each within any relationship joins the efforts with the other selves within the relationship in a unified fashion, the efforts are multiplied one upon the other until that which is sought is more surely found. We are known to you as those of Q'uo, and at this time we shall take our leave of this instrument and this group with our gratitude that we have been able to join this group this evening and we, as always, leave each in the love and in the light of the one infinite Creator. Adonai, my friends. Adonai borragus. ✥

Sunday Meditation
November 23, 1986

Group question: How can I better utilize my being?

(Carla channeling)

I am Q'uo. I greet this group in the love and in the light of the one infinite Creator. It is a privilege and a blessing to be with you this evening as we extend special greetings to those who are here for the first time. This is a tremendous privilege for us and we thank you for it. We would ask you before we begin to aid us by telling us if that which we are projecting through this instrument is of sufficient sound vibration to be audible to you?

Jim: Yes.

We thank you, my brother. We are dealing with an instrument which has some blockage in the breathing, and we do not wish to cause the instrument to project more than it was necessary to do. We apologize for the pause, however this instrument had to request that the entity most suited to answer the query chosen this evening not communicate at this sitting due to the difficulty which the one known as Carla has had in receiving the contact of t'Michael'h because of soreness in the neck. The contact attempted to work with this channel to achieve more comfort, but it was feared that there would be some loss of clarity, and so we who have a closer vibrational relationship with this particular channel agreed to do our best to speak with you on the subject of being.

We ask, as always, that you understand carefully that that which we say is opinion and not gospel. We have a great desire to serve you, and so we come as you do to those who know perhaps less than you, with our helping hands extended, but we are not so naive as to feel that we have learned all the answers, for although we seek the Creator, yet we are not yet the Creator, and in our individuality lies error. Thus, we offer to you our experience and that which we have learned along the way, but always we ask that if that which we say is not helpful to you, please leave it behind without a backward glance or second thought. Conversely, if that which we say is helpful, please feel free to use it and to build upon it as your own.

Each of you has a concept of what beingness is, based upon your observations of yourself and other selves. The difficulty with attempting to observe consciousness is that one is observing consciousness by the use of consciousness. It is therefore difficult, though not impossible, to get a well-rounded, shall we say, view of what one is by observing what one does, what one thinks, and what one intends. Beneath the level of any thinking, doing or intention lies beingness or consciousness.

When one can surprise oneself in a state of unthinking beingness, one has the evanescent glimpse of the face of the Creator, for each of you is in the basic consciousness a holograph of All That

There Is. Just so can one observe the Creator's face in space or tree or idea or emblem. Whether one goes to myth or to observation of the smallest natural detail, one is working to gain a more rounded awareness of the consciousness of love.

You will notice that we use love in the same way that we use the word Creator. We are sorry to use words that pale besides the meaning they are intended to convey. However, channeled information has as perhaps its tightest stricture the clumsy limitation of words. We attempt to connote such by the word love, but we intend to convey a fiery, creative love which is far more primal than any sense of love which is used to express emotion. The use of the word Logos in your holy work known as the Bible is perhaps the closest to our use of the word love, intending a meaning of the Creator that we could approach within your language. Your consciousness, that which is the tune you hum before you have learned to song, is that of love. You share the Thought that created all that there is, all the worlds that there are, and all the beings that live upon them, between them, and, indeed, all the beings that are them.

Now what shall you use this consciousness for? You have experienced sleeping, waking and exalted consciousness. If we were to ask you which level of consciousness you found most useful, you would perhaps choose the more active state of consciousness, for within the illusion which you experience as third-density reality you must choose your state of consciousness in terms of that which can be done, thus one would automatically choose to be awake when there are things to do.

It is likely that you have a prejudice against those who distract themselves so that they shall not become aware of the full extent of their own consciousness, those who do not enjoy the thinking and the pondering, those who have not yet set their feet upon a path which seeks, if not answers to questions, at least a better knowledge of what questions are worth the asking. And yet consciousness is not measured in terms of conclusions drawn or actions taken, for it is our humble opinion that nothing can be known within the illusion which you experience at this time, and, indeed, the purpose of the illusion that you experience at this time demands that you operate without full knowledge of the consequences of your decisions, for consciousness is other than is most often valued among your people, and by that we mean what this instrument would call Western civilization.

There is a kind of awakeness of consciousness which is perhaps the best way to express in a short period of time—which this instrument informs me we have—a proper and appropriate goal in consciousness, and that is the state of present joy, for the consciousness of creative love, the consciousness of the Logos, is ecstasy. This instrument did not wish to express this word, yet we insisted. We do not mean to suggest that those who seek pleasure are moving necessarily in the correct direction for the best use of their beingness. We wish rather to suggest that the nature of love is a joy beyond expression, and we find that that is the definition of the word ecstasy. The Logos is orgasmically joyful; that is a steady state. That is our perception at this time, if you will pardon our use of that inaccurate word.

We suggest that the best use of beingness is a persistent attempt to approach a natural state of present joy. We include the word present because the key to being fully free of that which would keep one from being joyful is entrance into the present moment.

The seeker, no matter how sincere, cannot systematically decide to be joyful and have it be so, for the state of mind is intrinsically counterproductive to much that this density of vibration has to offer in terms of learning.

The approach to joy involves several series of experiences in which the seeker becomes confident through meditation and the analysis of experience that he has penetrated the key factors of spiritual seeking and now grasps the nature of seeking. There develops then a lack of openness to change which results in further discomfort and challenges, which then open up the seeker to the painful consideration of further refinements upon the choices he has already made.

The ultimate result of these choices is finally a bafflement and a frustration deep enough to cause the seeker to surrender the quest and leave the understanding of the quest in the hands of the Creator which the seeker wishes to know. The nature of being is such that one cannot know the Creator except by being with the Creator, or, more accurately, perceiving the being of self and Creator as one. This is done only through the surrender of the self to the great Self. Thus, the most efficient use of being is the surrender of that being to the higher will of the greater Self, the greater Being, the greater love, so that these things which the seeker does are channeled through the seeker from an infinite source of compassion and creative love.

The uses of creative love are subtle, and service to others has never been easy to penetrate. What seems to be of service is often not; what seems to be directly not of service sometimes is. What seems to be worth doing, may not be—and vice versa. Creative love has an infinite capacity and patience and may burn long after human energy has given out.

We do not suggest that you go immediately towards a surrender, for first you must discover for yourself the nature of your journey and your quest and a great enough respect for your own being and for the Creator that you place your being and the Creator's together. We would not have you do these things because we suggest it. However, if we can inspire you to meditate and seek the experience of your own being and the further experience of placing your beingness in the presence of the consciousness of love, then perhaps you can make your choices with some awareness that will enable you to penetrate the nature of the journey that you are upon more quickly.

For that is what we are here to help you do, my friends. We are here to help you accelerate the course of your spiritual evolution. We are, if you will, the health food of the spirit, the mind, and the emotions, the yogurt, shall we say, of pilgrims. There are many things that you can put into your mind having to do with who you are and where you are going that may not enable you to be of service to yourself or to others or to the Creator whom you wish to know and to serve. We hope that we are somewhat helpful.

Move slowly, and turn always to meditation, for it is within the silence within your own being that you shall contact the source that lies deepest and truest within the universe that is your own being, for the greater part of your own being you shall not within your incarnations within this illusion fully experience, yet you shall see the reflection of them more and more as you meditate and dwell more and more comfortably with the deeper portions of yourself.

At this time, aware as we are that there are some questions that you would like to ask, we would transfer this contact. We are most grateful, as we have said, to be able to speak with you. We would now transfer. We are known to you as Q'uo.

(Jim channeling)

I am Q'uo, and greet each of you again in love and light through this instrument. We are hopeful at this time that we might be of some further service by attempting to answer those queries which may be upon your minds at this time. May we begin, then, with the first query?

H: Yeah, I have just one question. Just reflecting back on today, I noticed that I had entertained many negative thoughts through my chores. Just one negative after another one all evening. Could all these negatives have taken their toll and caused back discomfort that I'm experiencing?

I am Q'uo, and am aware of your query, my brother. We may suggest that it is possible that some burdens of mind are so heavy to carry that the physical vehicle may represent this burden to the mind in the fashion which you have described. This, indeed, is possible. We, however, in observing your current condition, would not speak in any more specific terms, for we find that the beginning you have made in your own understanding according to your own intuition and conscious analysis is that which shall be most fruitful to you, rather than listening to a description which we may give. Therefore, my brother, we commend you to your own thoughts and feelings upon this subject, for it is within your own capacity to understand that you will find the greatest illumination.

May me answer in any further capacity, my brother?

H: No, that's all for tonight, thank you.

I am Q'uo, and we thank you, my brother. Is there another query?

Questioner: Q'uo, will I make the ascension in this lifetime?

I am Q'uo. My brother, as we look upon your beingness, we smile, for within each entity, including your own self, there lies a roadmap which has as its destination the complete realization of one's nature, origin, purpose and destination, if you will. There is an infinity of possibility which resides not only within your own life pattern, but that of each seeker within your illusion.

For us to speak as to whether one particular outcome shall result in place of another would be foolishness upon our part, and would presume much, for the Creator that is within each entity has far greater depth, breadth and variety of possibilities and purpose of being than our limited vision could ever hope to encompass were we to speak in a definitive manner upon this subject. We would be assuming that which cannot be assumed or predicted.

But we can assure each seeker of truth that that which is necessary for the continued progression of one's life pattern will constantly be presented to one in each day and each experience, for each day and each experience that comes before your notice contains in symbolic form layer upon layer of understanding that is available to you as you penetrate it with your conscious perception and your meditative and prayerful desire to seek beyond the outer appearance of all illusion and penetrate to the heart of being.

May we answer in any further way, my brother?

Questioner: How may I best tune or raise my vibration?

I am Q'uo. Again, our response is that which is of a general nature, and that which any seeker may be able to apply to the life pattern. Know that all you experience is the Creator. See in each face that greets your own the Creator. Seek in each experience the source of light and love that forms experience. Seek beyond the illusion of separation that which binds all that you experience. Look, in other words, my brother, beyond the outer appearance of the illusion which surrounds you, for it is in its own way that which teaches you that the source of all creation and experience within it is the one Creator which moves by the power of Its love, and reveals by the power of Its light the unity of all things.

May me answer further, my brother?

Questioner: No, thank you.

I am Q'uo, and we thank you, my brother. Is there another query?

Carla: I'd like to re-ask a question that B asked. I was dissatisfied with my answer to it, and I would like you to tackle it.

Are the contacts that we have with densities more conscious and more easily obtained but less accurate at lower densities and with more of a tendency towards a deeper state and finally trance and more accurate information at higher densities, or what is the situation with regards trance, accuracy and density?

I am Q'uo, and we look upon this query as one which is more complex than its brevity of statement would suggest. We might indicate a direction for thought in suggesting that the term accuracy is that which somewhat befuddles understanding in this instance, for what seems accurate to one may not seem accurate to another. There is one truth, and many applications of that truth. That truth we see as unity of all things. There are refinements of understandings of various sources that would choose to communicate to those who call for their aid in the evolutionary process. Thus, as various entities within your illusion continue upon their path of seeking, their continued seeking and desire to know that which you call the truth calls unto them assistance from those who are able to respond in a manner which satisfies the call.

The level of understanding of any particular entity will determine, then, that which is called for as a further addition to that understanding, a further refinement to that which has been gained in experience and in thought. Those such as we and others, who respond to these calls for assistance in gaining a wider understanding of self and creation, provide information which is fitted to that call, and provide it in a manner which is also suited to enhancing the greatest amount of understanding on the part of those who call.

In the specific technique of response known as vocal channeling, this being one among many techniques of communication, there are further refinements as you have noted in this manner of response, those which utilize the more conscious type of channeling such as we utilize with the instruments present this evening, and moving toward the less conscious, as you call it, and more passive, or, as you have called it, trance level of communication. This allows the source or transmitter to provide information of a more refined nature.

The accuracy, however, of such information is dependent upon the information sought and the perspective of the source which responds. The use of greater or lesser degrees of trance allows for the possibility of a more refined type of information to be transmitted.

At this moment, we shall pause in our response to ask if there may be a further refinement of the query, if we have not been clear in our response.

Carla: I believe that what you're saying is that you have such a simple message that the most conscious channeling is accurate if it talks about love, and I accept that understanding. I do have another question—if that is wrong, please interrupt me.

The other question has to do with the reason that R asked the question that you responded to this evening. Since I was channeling, I didn't catch all of it, but listening to what I could, it seemed to me that R will still have many questions, because her perspective is that of a person who lived for a goodly number of years, like thirty-five, maybe …

(Side one of tape ends.)

Carla: R lived for at least thirty years as a relatively garden variety person, and then her psychic abilities opened up very rapidly and very undistortedly, from everything that she's told me and all that that I've observed. Tremendous amounts of phenomena are occurring with her, everything from spontaneous hearings at long distances to many, many prophecies, visions and the ability to see everyone's electrical body, whether she wants to or not. It's a very uncomfortable situation; it's changed her life a great deal. Her consciousness has suddenly become a very packed bunch of phenomena happening one after another, and she wants to know, really, I think, how to direct all of this. The answer that you gave simply had to do with surrendering to a greater will, a greater love, a greater way. Is there anything that you can add, having to do specifically with phenomena, with psychic abilities and the use of clear metaphysical senses for the good of others or service to others?

I am Q'uo, and am aware of your query, my sister. In addition to that which we have transmitted previously this evening, we might suggest that as the eyes of one become opened to a degree where the experience becomes enriched with phenomena which are somewhat incredible and unexpected and continuous in nature and therefore unsettling to one's personal experience, that there not be given to such phenomena too great a consideration or importance, for the eyes which have lost some of the blinders that caused the focus to move within a narrower realm and which now see with a wider perspective, it must be remembered at all times that one views portions of the one Creator.

When these phenomena tend to overwhelm the senses, it is well for the one experiencing this greater view to exercise that quality known as faith, faith that the one Creator moves before the newly opened eyes from patterns of perfection that yet lie beyond understanding, yet move in a manner which fulfills the desire of the Creator to know Itself. The faith that all is well, no matter what any part of the vision may tell the conscious mind, then must be powered by the will to serve the one Creator in as pure and unconditional fashion as is possible, for the greater sight brings the greater responsibility to use that vision in a manner which is of service to others. Yet with that responsibility, it well not to be overly concerned with the nature of the phenomena which present themselves in the life experience.

May we answer further, my sister?

Carla: No, thank you.

I am Q'uo, and we thank you, my sister. Is there another query?

Questioner: Yes, Q'uo. In the personality split within the individual, the higher self apparently operates without the conscious knowledge of the person. Does it read that road map that you spoke of for us and help guide us, or is it simply out there and responding to whatever the conscious person does?

I am Q'uo. The relationship of that portion of your being which you have called the higher self to that which is your conscious self within this illusion is one in which guidance is offered where possible, realizing that the free will of the conscious entity is that which is paramount in the evolutionary experience of any seeker of truth.

However, it must also be realized that the guidance which the higher self offers to you during each incarnation is a guidance which not only occurs during the incarnation, but is that which with your intention and agreement before the incarnation, sets out the possibilities that are analogous to what you have called the roadmap that would be available to the conscious entity during the incarnation. Thus, the incarnation is the point at which the predetermined purpose and direction of the incarnation meets the free will exercised by each entity during the incarnation.

There are points within each incarnation where the higher self will be more able to guide and at times even protect the conscious seeker. When the conscious seeker provides what may be seen as a call for assistance, such a call may be generated in many ways. The most usual means of generating such a call is a rededication upon the part of the seeker to move in a manner which suggests the desire to serve others has been increased and the conscious will of the seeker is surrendered so that what may be seen as a greater will may move through the seeker's incarnational pattern and allow it to fulfill that which is its desire to serve others as the one Creator.

May we answer further, my brother?

Questioner: Thank you. That seems to be satisfactory.

I am Q'uo, and we thank you, my brother. Is there another query?

Questioner: Yes, Q'uo. When will the United States currency be changed? And what will be the change, rate of exchange? And will gold and silver at the same time go up, and how high?

I am Q'uo, and am aware of your query, my brother. We look upon this type of information as that which is of the moment's interest, if you will pardon the pun. We are aware that many seek answers to these queries, yet we are also aware that knowing this kind of information lends little to the spiritual understanding, shall we say, that does the actual work in one's consciousness.

There are many events occurring upon your world stage, shall we say, that seem interesting and even at times important. Yet we might suggest that these are but training aids that will allow the seeker of truth to penetrate beyond the appearance of importance to the heart of all things, which is love, and which binds all entities together, whether their part upon the stage of the world may seem that of the villain attempting to control those about it with the tools of your cultures. Each seeks in a more or less distorted fashion to serve the one Creator in its own way. Many are the side roads upon this journey.

In our attempts to speak to those gathered within this circle of seeking, we seek to point the attention of each to the main thoroughfare, if you will, which leads beyond the illusion of appearance and in our humble opinion allows the seeker to gain that which is of truer value [than] any currency could hope to equal. Thus, we do not mean to be shy of information in this kind of seeking, my brother, but we might suggest that such information lies outside of our purpose in speaking to groups such as this.

May we respond in any further way, my brother?

Questioner: No, thank you.

I am Q'uo, and we thank you, my brother. Is there another query at this time?

Questioner: Yes. It's indicated that in each incarnation the soul to a certain extent picks and chooses its next physical body and at the same time its environment. At what point in development of the fetus, roughly, does the soul enter the fetus?

I am Q'uo, and in this area we may suggest that there is a variety of nexi of entrance that is possible. Some there are who enter at the point of conception, some there are who are more reluctant, shall we say, at the last moment, as you would call it, and wait the entry until shortly after the birthing process. Within this range lie the many possible points of entry, each uniquely variant according to the soul entering.

May we respond further, my brother?

Questioner: I wonder if this would have a basis because of this varying time period, for the Catholic religion's concept of the necessity of baptizing the baby immediately, even just prior to an after birth death in order to save that soul?

I am Q'uo. Many are the perceptions of the point of entry and the necessary rituals to seal and secure that entry of the soul into the physical vehicle. Many have been codified through the various religious and cultural practices of your peoples. That religion of which you speak is one which views the sanctity of the relationship of soul to physical vehicle in such a fashion that the immediate recognition of the validity of any life, no matter how short, is that which is paramount in the practice.

May we respond further, my brother?

Questioner: Thank you, that's satisfactory.

I an Q'uo, and we thank you, my brother. Is there another query?

Carla: Is any soul ever lost?

I am Q'uo, and in our range of knowledge which is admittedly limited, my sister, we are aware of no soul which has been lost to the point of being unable to be found or redeemed.

May we respond further, my sister?

Carla: Does that include those who are aborted? After they have chosen a body? Is there indeed murder in abortion?

I am Q'uo, and we find that our response will be perceived according to the point of view which one holds according to the physical vehicle's relationship with the spirit which enlivens it.

We may respond to the first portion of your query by suggesting that there is no soul lost, if by lost one means unredeemed and not capable of being able to continue its evolutionary journey when that process you have called abortion occurs. However, in such an instance there is the removing of vitality from the physical vehicle which within most of your cultures' definitions would equal that you have called murder. However, we suggest that the spirit which may inhabit any physical vehicle is not lost or irretrievably blunted in its search for incarnational experience by the act of the aborting.

May we answer further, my sister?

Carla: No, thank you.

I am Q'uo, and we thank you, my sister. Is there a further query at this time?

Questioner: If no one else has one, I'd like to ask another one. If I recall correctly, Edgar Cayce indicated that some of the records from Atlantis have been placed in, I think, an area in Egypt, perhaps one of the pyramids. One set of the records apparently had gotten destroyed and he indicated, I recall, that another set of records were still available and probably would be found. Can you comment on this?

I am Q'uo, and we might suggest that the recovering of these records is a possibility which exists for the current population of your planetary sphere. We, however, can speak in no way whatsoever as to the means of this discovery or its carrying out, for we do not wish to infringe upon the free will of any.

May we respond further, my brother?

Questioner: Do I understand that by your answer you are in the affirmative that the records do exist?

I am Q'uo, and this is correct, my brother. May we respond further?

Questioner: Thank you.

I am Q'uo, and we thank you once again, my brother. Is there another query?

(Pause)

I am Q'uo, and as it appears that we have exhausted the queries for this evening, we shall at this time give our heartfelt thanksgiving to each for allowing us to join your group this evening. It is an honor which we cherish to be able to speak our humble words to those who seek to know more of that which is the creation, the Creator, and the love which ennobles and enables each seeker to move through the one creation. We remind each once again that our words are but opinions. Weigh each with your own discrimination, taking that which has value and leaving that which has none for you. At this time we shall take our leave of this instrument and this group, leaving each in the love and in the light of the one infinite Creator. We are known to you as those of Q'uo. Adonai, my friends. Adonai vasu borragus. ❧

Sunday Meditation
November 30, 1986

Group question: Concerns the harvest and the nature of the harvest, whether there is a physical death of the vehicle, and the types of entities that go through the harvest, the effect upon wanderers that have come here from elsewhere to be of service during the harvest. And so forth.

(Carla channeling)

I am Q'uo, and I greet you, my friends, in the love and in the light of the one infinite Creator. It is a privilege and a blessing for us to share the vibration of your meditation with you this evening and to join our beings with yours. We greet and bless each of you and especially those who have traveled far to hear our humble words.

It is a great privilege to be called to your group and to behold your light among all people, for those who seek are indeed the light of your illusion, and your call and desire establish within your illusion those sources of light which may be shared with others who seek that they too may find, and that they in turn may shine for others with the effulgence of the Creator whom we all serve and Who offers through any channel that will open itself to light a radiance that is much desired by those upon your Earth plane at this time.

You have asked about the harvest and so we shall speak upon that subject, first begging you to grasp the fact that we are not without error, but are in fact as you, seeking upon a path which takes us into mystery, and when we understand that which we did not understand before, then we find a greater mystery. So we have studied mystery upon mystery, and study still, and there is great mystery before us. How could we be infallible, we who are seekers upon a path as you, we who are your brothers and sisters? Just as you reach your hand to teach those who request the teaching, so we come to you with our experience and our thoughts, yet we would not be a stumbling block before you, and we ask you to use all discrimination in listening to our words. Accept those concepts which have use for you, and leave without a second thought those which do not.

You have chosen a large subject for this evening, and we will attempt to be tidy and brief in our discussion. However, we hope that you will forgive us if we ramble a bit, for there is some ground to cover, for the subject of harvest is not one subject, but two, and we would discuss the concept of physical change separately from the concept of harvest in the metaphysical sense.

You who dwell within the illusion of chemicals are very fond of your chemical arrangements, and, indeed, feel a great dependency upon them, as you should within the illusion. Yet you are confusing yourselves when you wonder what will happen to your physical bodies at harvest. We of the Confederation of Planets in the Service of the

Infinite Creator are concerned with the harvest of your spirits, that is to say, your mind, your body, and your spirit in their most unified and true form, this you call the spirit or soul.

Your physical Earth has moved at this time into an area of space which is fourth density in vibration, and your Earth is having some difficulty, due to thought implantation of tension and stress moving into the planetary mind, accepting fourth-density vibration. It is possible that there shall be geological disruption and meteorological confusion which exceed even the state of discomfort you have achieved at this time. This is a mechanical manifestation of changing energy web patterns and does not have significance insofar as your soul's harvest time.

The third-density chemical body can for limited amounts of time, according to the unique vibration of an entity, exist for some portion of your time and experience within fourth-density space/time. Consequently, your physical bodies shall not all be removed in a trice, for harvest is a process rather than an event. Barring the use by your peoples of hostilities which could indeed destroy a large portion of your planet's entities' bodies, your incarnations and your children's incarnations shall move to their conclusion in a physical sense, although you have already seen and will continue to see evidence of the difficulties which physical bodies have to finer vibrations, for the density which with your third-density eyes you cannot see yet impinges upon you more and more and represents an unseen but very real source of light which may indeed be too full of life energy for portions of your physical vehicle and of those about you.

We move now to discussion of harvest, a subject more nearly central, we feel, to that which may be of service to those who may listen to us.

How do you prepare to *be*, my friends? Is there any preparation for *being*? Perhaps you can see that there is indeed no preparation possible, for you are being at all times. We are here to inspire you not to be, but to take yourselves seriously as beings, in order that you may be more and more conscious of the value of your basic vibratory patterns, for it is your consciousness which shall be harvested, the consciousness that has striven and learned and borne fruit, the fruit of adoration and service and giving to the Creator and to the face of the Creator in all that there is.

The concept of an instantaneous harvest has not been helpful, we have observed, and we would discourage each from contemplating harvest as an event, for although we who are not within your illusion see your harvest as what seems to us to be, shall we say in your terms, an afternoon's excitement, a cause for rejoicing that is all too short, yet we cannot translate our time to yours, for your time is that of planets revolving about a sun, and it is not the time of the timeless One which dwells in infinity and moves in light. Your time is a separator out of time, a unifier. How greatly you desire to know when you should be ready, when you should be prepared, and yet we say to you, it is this moment that you must be prepared and that you must be ready, and if you be not ready now, then you must work now, pray now, meditate now, surrender now and ask now to be channels for the love and the light of the one original Thought of love which is the Creator.

Let us look at this in a slightly different way. Each of you moves down streets and into buildings through your work, your chores, and your social life, meeting one entity after another, entities which hope to receive something from you or avoid you, entities which may ignore you. It is unknown to you in advance whom you shall meet, and what that entity may wish from you, yet that entity may be desperately looking for love, not the love of the glad hand and the pat on the back, but the total and accepting love of compassion, the love without judgment, the love that flows through rather than from, each of you.

You may have only one moment to be a channel of love for the infinite Creator, to show His face to this entity. One moment, my friends, no more. Shall you be a channel for love, then? We know that you hope so. Yet if there is a moment when you are not a channel for love, then we ask you to go into mind and heart to search out these things which have kept you from being such a channel, and do your utmost to bring your consciousness to the consciousness of love. You do not know when your harvest shall come, yet we have been speaking with you and urging you to understand that these are indeed the final days of your third-density experiences.

Are you eager for fourth density, and do you wish to graduate? Then rest your anxieties and your burdens about the future, a future which may never come, and gaze instead upon your being that you may channel love now, for if you are not ready for harvest at this moment, perhaps the next moment may be too late. We do not wish to suggest, as this literal-minded channel wonders within her all too analytical mind, that we may be hinting that the harvest is now. No, my friends, not even next Tuesday, not next month or next year. We are not able to suggest these things to you, for when one moves from dimension to dimension, when one describes events that are indeed processes, when one speaks from time to time, the translation is at best approximate and fuzzy and unsatisfactory.

We wish only to train your mind upon your mind, upon the goal, to urge your legs to be strong to run the race, to urge you to actual present effort, not for others, but for yourself, for you cannot harvest another, but only yourself. Yet the harvest of yourself depends upon your relationship with the Creator and with the face of the Creator in yourself and those about you. And so in order to be more and more of the consciousness of love, it is well to pay great attention to the way you perceive your other selves, your own selves, the Creator incarnate all about you.

There are many who have incarnated among you from higher dimensions due to the lateness of the hour and the nearness of what you would call the midnight of the last day. There is much distress among your peoples and among those you call wanderers who have come to aid you, for we see that many are taking the concept of the harvest and turning again and again back to the illusion in order to express their desire for love. One cannot, among your peoples, mate two pears and receive an orange, nor can one improve outer things and receive inner blessing. Those things which you feel may make you comfortable and content, loved too dearly and valued too highly, may create for you a wavering of attention which denigrates and diminishes your being.

Try, then, to focus your energy, your desire and your seeking upon those things which are eternal, upon those values which are infinite, until you are so full of praise and adoration for the Creator, that you are indeed a channel for love. It is well not to be dispassionate about your consciousness, nor about the Creator of that consciousness. Do you not love your parents, are you not grateful for the opportunity of experience that has been given you? Think, then, upon the value of knowledge, realization and understanding, if it does not end in love for the one infinite Creator and in a grateful desire to be for your Creator the hands that express love and the mouth that speaks of joy.

As we understand your time, the harvest shall be an event which is in process for many of your years. You shall come to it naturally, unless by your own artifacts you remove yourselves from your bodies. Be ready to die now. Be ready for harvest now. And then you are free to live for the Creator and in His service for however long you draw breath within the physical vehicle which loves you and has given itself to your use. Love it also, and see it as the helpful thing it is, but do not be its slave.

We rejoice with you that you experience third-density illusion at this time, that you have these choices to make, that you seek realization in darkness, in unknowing, and in great mystery. Know that no matter how rocky the road may seem and how blind may seem your choices, you are never without aid. You are never without comfort. You are never without confirmation. For the source lies within. The entire infinite creation exists within each of you. Each of you bears all that there is within the universe, for all its illusion is a thought, and you have thought it. And as you think it, so it shall be, from the smallest to the greatest. Let your universe be as kindly as the Creator, as full of love.

You cannot do this upon your own, for you are finite within your density at this time. Yet infinity lies within you, and you may choose to channel an infinite love which does not fail. The more you are in contact with this infinite love, the more you may manifest it and so bear fruit, not fruit that you may judge as fruit, but fruit which adds to your beingness which the Creator shall see, bless and amplify.

Go into meditation regularly and faithfully and never condemn yourself for your lack of skill therein, for one instant's tabernacling with the infinite One is all time and all space insofar as your deep mind is concerned. It is not length of time in meditation, but intensity of desire to seek the face of love which will draw to you a deeper and clearer perception of that one great original Thought.

Sunday Meditation, November 30, 1986

You have companions along the way, my friends, and you were given them for a reason, for those who seek together may help each other, exhort each other, admonish, encourage and praise each other by turns, and every mistake that is made by one who is admonished or by one who admonishes falsely is made up for by the love which prompts the caring, the giving, the sharing, and the supporting.

Above all things, my friends, love each other, for you shall feel love only as you love others, only as you truly love yourself, not that which you see about yourself or others, but that which is beingness in yourself and others, that which is by definition perfected and whole, without flaw. You are acceptable to the Creator, for you are the Creator, my friends. Each of you carries the creation within consciousness. Your vibratory pattern, unique to you alone, is a unique holographic representation of the face of the Creator. How distorted is that face, how close to love has your perception, your beingness, your consciousness, come?

Within the holy work you call your Bible, there is the parable of the maidens who await the bridegroom, who watch and pray and trim their lamps. Some there are who think perhaps they have a little time before the stroke of midnight, yet midnight comes, and the lamp, the light—the love—has not been lit, and it may be a long day before that midnight comes again, though come it will and there is no shame in studying a bit longer.

Thus, now is your harvest time. Now is when you shall be ready. And when you are ready, you shall be free, truly free in the service of the one infinite Creator as are we. We wish you the joy of that happy realization that you are through preparing. Celebrate your consciousness. Affirm it in all that is good, and if you feel that it is amiss, amend it, but do not prepare as for that which is in the future. Prepare as though, if we may use the same metaphor, the bridegroom knocked upon your door this minute, this hour, this night.

We have greatly enjoyed speaking with you upon this subject and would be glad to speak further, however we feel there are questions within the group, and would transfer the contact at this time in order that we may speak through the one known as Jim. Therefore, we would leave this instrument with thanks for its service. We are those of Q'uo, and we would transfer at this time.

(Jim channeling)

I am Q'uo, and greet each of you again in love and light through this instrument. At this time we would ask if we might be of further service by attempting to answer those queries which may have risen into the minds of those present. Is there a query at this time?

H: Yeah, I have a question, and that is, what happens to all the soul/mind complexes that are not ready to be harvested into fourth density, who after the, really, the end of the 75,000 year cycle?

I am Q'uo, and of these entities we may say that there is an infinity of time to utilize in the progression into fourth density. These entities small at the completion of their experience upon this planetary sphere find another planetary sphere which is beginning its third-density cycle of evolution and move there upon that sphere and within its influence …

(Side one of tape ends.)

(Jim channeling)

I am Q'uo, and am again with this instrument. May we answer in any further way, my brother?

H: That's all right now.

Questioner: Q'uo, in the moving to another planetary existence, would these third-density persons feel that they were still on the so-called planet Earth and feel as though they were remaining on the same planet that they are acquainted with?

I am Q'uo, and we may respond to you query in two ways. The first is to suggest that the lessons provided by any third-density planetary sphere are those which are ever and always the same, the learning to give and receive that which you call love without condition. Thus, the lessons will cause a remembrance and a familiarity of remembrance within the mind/body/spirit complex as it is called of each entity during the incarnational portion of each entity's experience. In the inner realms, shall we say, which are inhabited between the incarnational experiences, these entities will be aware that the entity they now inhabit as a planetary sphere is unique unto itself, and is that which provides the new environment in which the lessons of love may be attempted.

May we answer further, my sister?

Questioner: Thank you.

Questioner: I would like to ask a question about the so-called "star children," if they are different from wanderers, and in particular those who have a fourth-density body in actuation, what is the difference? Is there a difference in their energy?

I am Q'uo, and of these entities we may suggest that there is inherent in their incarnational experience a greater depth of resources which may be called upon to fuel the incarnation, shall we say. These entities would not properly be called that which you know as the wanderer, for this sphere, your own Earth as you call it, is their home vibration for the fourth-density experience. They, however, are entering this planetary influence at an earlier time, in your terms, than is usual for a population which is to begin a fourth-density experience.

The honor of an early entry is for the purpose of aiding those of the planetary population who have yet to achieve the level of ability to give and receive love without condition. The atmosphere, shall we say, or nature of experience which is now available upon your planetary sphere as it nears and experiences its own harvest is of such an intense level that these entities may not only aid others in their progression towards third density, but say also greatly accelerate their own beginning into that density of love and the perfection of that love.

May we answer in any further way, my sister?

Questioner: Yes, please. Are they, then, entering just now into the fourth density themselves for the first time?

I am Q'uo, and am aware of your query, my sister. This again touches upon the entire concept of the harvest for your planet and its population. This process is one which is in its beginning stages, and you may see your planetary sphere as that which is being born into the fourth density at this time, as you would call it. Thus, this illusion begins to take on new properties where thoughts tend more to become things and the power of the mind to influence the environment about it is more obvious and is of an increased nature. Thus, these entities of which you speak, those who have moved through a harvest from another third-density sphere and who have joined your own planetary sphere as the beginning population of its fourth-density experience, have entered the beginning of this experience which coincides with the completion of the third-density experience. Thus, the experiences overlap and it becomes somewhat of a semantic difficulty to describe whether it is of one nature or another. We have chosen to describe it to you this evening as the beginning of the fourth-density experience.

May we answer in any further way, my sister?

Questioner: No, thank you very much.

I am Q'uo, and we thank you, my sister. Is there another query?

Carla: I'd like to follow up on a previous question. There was a question about that when third-density people went to new planets, would they know that they were on a new planet, or would they think they were still on Earth. And I thought I heard in the answer that there would be some awareness of newness, and I was confused because, who knows, you know, where we were before this, because of the veil [of forgetting] and I would have thought that there would be the same veil on the same feeling that, you know, that this is just the way things are, then as there is now, regardless of what planet it would be on, it would [be] home, you know? And I wondered if you could clarify that for me, because I was a little puzzled.

I am Q'uo, and we have attempted to describe this experience as one which has a dual type of recognition of the experience of third density, that is, the recognition which partakes of the broader point of view available to those who await the incarnation within the inner realms …

Carla: Oh, *before* incarnation—thank you.

I am Q'uo, and if this point has been recognized, we shall discontinue the description. May we ask if there might be a further point upon this process to which we may speak?

Carla: No, thank you, my friend. I do have one further question which is on another subject. It came up tonight and I was rather interested in it, and didn't know the answer, really—I was guessing. Are you a representative of Q'uo, having all of the information available to the group consciousness, or are you an impersonal principle, representing the best of the group consciousness in this service to Earth?

I am Q'uo, and as an individualized portion of a larger grouping of beings who seek in an unified fashion—which you may understand as a social memory complex—we have the honor of speaking to this group. When the concept of social memory complex is described in your terms, there arises the difficulty in distinguishing the singular individualized entity from the group of which it is a part. Therefore, the terms "I" and the term "we" are used interchangeably and each describes that of which we partake.

May we answer further, my sister?

Carla: No, that's fine. I understand what you're saying, but I'm glad that there is an individualized person representing the social memory complex because I feel a lot of love from you, and I like to be able to return it, seeker to seeker. Thank you very much.

I am Q'uo, and we thank you, my sister. Is there another query at this time?

H: I've got one more little question. Well, actually it's two questions, but, for instance, if I should die tonight, and, you know, my soul/body complex was harvestable to fourth density, would that, that would indeed take place, I assume without having to be reincarnated back into the third density. Okay, I assume that is right, but now, if that is, then what if I wasn't harvestable, and I needed to be reincarnated again, or I was chosen to be reincarnated one more time, at what point, then, would I cease to be reincarnated as the third density itself ends?

I am Q'uo, and as the third-density experience upon your planet moves to its completion, there are available to those yet seeking the harvest to fourth density the opportunities to enter incarnation for as long as third-density conditions, for what you call the life patterns and physical vehicles available, pertain. We cannot give a specific length of time, for this is unknown depending upon the choices made by all those who currently inhabit your planetary sphere and its influence. We can assure you however, my brother, that there is as much time and opportunity available for any entity's progress through the third density which would culminate in harvest as any entity may need. The specific location or choice of planetary sphere is, shall we say, incidental to that overriding fact of evolutionary possibilities.

May we answer further, my brother?

H: Maybe what I should have said a while ago was, say like the third density, say like it ended one year from now. Okay, and add that in the meantime, would I go back and be reincarnated again just for a few brief months possibly?

I am Q'uo, and am aware of your query, my brother. We might suggest that this is possible, as are many opportunities of various natures possible. We suggest that one not worry overmuch as to how the specific functioning of the ending of a cycle occurs, for all movement of experience is enabled and ennobled by the love of the one Creator which exists within all things. Within your illusion, much is hidden from sight, yet if one may remember and have faith that all is truly well, for all is, indeed, one, then one may move most easily in harmony with all cycles which provide the opportunity to know the one Creator in each moment that presents itself to your notice.

May we answer further, my brother?

H: No more questions. Thank you.

I am Q'uo, and we thank you, my brother. Is there another query?

Carla: Well, you spoke about service to others and the importance to others and having just one moment to show love to somebody else, but a lot of times people don't react at all consciously to any kind of love that you show them or anything like that. You have absolutely no control over whether somebody's ready to see love or whether his mind is somewhere else, you know. It's really rare that you're reflecting love and really in the groove and the person sees it that way all at the same time. Does that matter? I mean, when you were talking about bearing fruit, I thought to myself, "Well that's tricky." Could you comment on that?

I am Q'uo, and we may suggest, my sister, that you cannot know the result of any action or the fruit that shall be born from intention. That which is of importance in your own evolutionary process is your intention which motivates any thought, word or deed. To cast the bread upon the waters, then, without regard for whether they shall return in one form or another, or return at all, is that which is of most importance, for within your illusion, you only begin to see, and much is mystery. And that which you call faith, powered by that which you call will are the truest guides one may call upon, and all action and thought and word then which is activated by the intent to be of service and to share that which you know of as love become ennobled by that intent to love without condition. This cannot be affected or changed in any way whatsoever by how another might view that thought, word or action.

May we answer further, my sister?

Carla: No, Q'uo, thank you very much.

Questioner: Q'uo, in the knowing that we are all one, that the love for all creates the One, does that not seem to be, does that not put an insurmountable load or cause for us to be very active or to be—it's very difficult for me to say this, because it comes so unusual. To accept all as One, how can we thus aid all as One? How can we be of assistance in our love? How can we bring love to all as One?

I am Q'uo, and, my sister, since all are indeed portions of the one infinite Creator and move in harmony with that Creator, whether the harmonious pattern of movement is known consciously or not known consciously, one may have faith that the life pattern has been described and conceived in a fashion which will bring to one those opportunities to be of service to all which come before one's notice and to share what you call love in a fashion which is most appropriate for each moment. Thus, it is not necessary, my sister, to look past the present moment and wonder at how it shall be possible to be of service and to radiate that love which one seeks in one's life pattern, for that has been given to you to recognize in each moment if one will but turn the desire to seek the truth toward each moment and continue to find the face of the Creator in each face which meets yours, and, indeed, within your own face and within each portion of the environment which supports and surrounds you at all times. Thus, you have as a life pattern that which has been designed to provide you with opportunity after opportunity to give that which is possible and to find that love which is there.

May we answer further, my sister?

Questioner: Thank you. I think you have answered it. It seemed to me the suffering on the Earth was more than I could handle, because I could seem to do nothing about it. And I think you perhaps you have given me a clue as to how to think on those things.

I am Q'uo, and we hope that we have been of some small service in that direction, my sister, for we realize the difficulty that any seeker of truth meets when looking upon the illusion which is your world.

There is much of sorrow and suffering which seems without just cause and even more seemingly tragic without a possible resolution. We can only suggest to each that one attempt to look beyond the outer appearance of any situation and see the heart of all entities and events as being the one Creator knowing Itself in yet another way that might seem incomprehensible, yet in such mystery lies infinite potential for love to be found, for, indeed, there is no thing or being made of any other substance.

Is there another query at this time?

Carla: I'd like to know the condition of the instrument.

I am Q'uo, and we find that this instrument is available for another query or two before the fatigue removes its concentrative abilities. Is there another query at this time?

Questioner: Yes, I'd like to ask a question. I'd like to know what differences the fourth-density body would have compared to what we know as our third-density physical vehicles?

I am Q'uo, and we may describe in somewhat insufficient terms the nature of the fourth-density vehicle as being that which in your terms would be far lighter and more mobile, shall we say. However, in terms of the light which is contained within such a vehicle, we may say that it is more densely packed with this light, which gives it then the ability to demonstrate greater flexibility in travel, shall we say, and in the ability to project and receive thought impulses. This vehicle is one which will resemble the third-density vehicle which itself is patterned after a certain portion of your second-density population, that is, the ape form, which moved from the quadrupedal positioning of limbs to the erect position, and then achieved further modifications that enabled the further and fuller development of the mind complex. The fourth-density vehicle will continue in providing the opportunities for the development of the mind complex so that the effect of the mind will be more immediate and will provide a more instant feedback, shall we say, to an entity so that its learning experience will be greatly accelerated.

May we answer further, my sister?

Questioner: Yeah. It sort of touched on that veil forgetfulness. When we enter the fourth-density bodies, will that veil then not be so? Would we be able to look backwards and see more of where we came from and possibly even forwards as well?

I am Q'uo, and, indeed, this ability—which we may describe as the far-seeing ability—shall be greatly enhanced, and the removing of that which is called—we find in this group—the veil of forgetting, is that which proceeds as a conscious process whereby the veil, having a large tear, shall we say, now allows the movement of consciousness through this tear so that the conscious efforts of an entity may continue in the dismantling of that which seems to separate one from another and the one Creator from the self, so that all begins to be put into a more unified perspective as a result of conscious efforts.

May we answer further, my sister?

Questioner: No, thank you, but I wish to say that I really appreciated your answers and your love. Thank you very much.

I am Q'uo, and we thank you, my sister, for the honor of responding to those queries. Is there a final query before we take our leave of this group?

Carla: I'd like to be really rude and ask the last question. I feel like the person at the banquet that takes the last roll. But I'd really like to ask this question because we're thinking about bodies and I've wondered this before and forgotten to ask it.

I've noticed that we're discovering a lot of subatomic particles like quarks and charm and nobody knows exactly what to do with them all, and there are all kinds of hare-brained ideas going around right now in physics. I know that the photon is a sub-sub-subatomic particle, and I was wondering, in fourth density is it possible that instead of a body being made out of atoms and molecules of elements and inorganic compounds, the way these bodies are, is it possible that fourth-density bodies are made of subatomic particles, held in the infinitely many graduations of electromagnetic fields that make a body, that hold a body together? Is it possible that the interpenetration of the fields is nothing more than the particles which make up those fields, being quite a bit smaller so that they interpenetrate because of the huge holes left by the distances the magnetic fields have between them in the third-density physical universe, seen from the perspective of a subatomic universe in a higher density?

I am Q'uo, and am aware of your query, my sister. We find that with this query you have moved into an area that partakes not only of the metaphysical realm, but of that which your scientists refer to as the physics of creation. We have a difficulty finding the proper terminology that we might transmit through this instrument to properly respond to your query. We find within the query such which is perceptive and which has begun to grasp more fully the nature of the construction of the fourth-density body.

The photon, which is the describable portion of light which makes up each portion of creation, within the fourth density begins a rotation and frequency of rotation which is stepped up from that which was experienced within the third-density illusion. The increased vibration, then, of the subatomic particles or photon, as we may generally refer to these particles, allows for what you have called an interpenetration of particles. The more dense placement, then, of these particles within a vehicle causes that vehicle to be more expressive of the properties of light. In your terms you would see this to becoming more radiant and more able to funnel or channel the intelligent energy of the one Creator in a specific fashion as a result of conscious intention.

May we speak in any more specific fashion, my sister?

Carla: No, I won't strain the instrument at this time. It really helps to see that I'm on the right track here, because it's always puzzled me that fourth was described both as lighter and denser. But I can see where if it were subatomic particles as opposed to atomic particles and molecules and chains of molecules, getting rather large there, that it would be a lot easier, a lot lighter to—a lot lighter matter. And also a lot easier to move around, which would explain the fourth density's ability to create things by thought much more easily than we can. It explains a lot and thank you for your answer, and—I know I speak for all of us—thank you very much for coming.

I am Q'uo, and we thank you, my sister. We indeed thank each present for inviting our presence this evening. It has been a great honor to be able to blend our vibrations with yours. We again humbly remind each that we are your brothers and sisters who move upon the same path as do you. Take that which we have given which has value to you and leave that which has no value, for we do not wish to place upon your path any stumbling block to it. We at this time shall take our leave of this instrument …

(Tape ends.) ❧

Sunday Meditation
December 14, 1986

Group question: Has to do with the season, more specifically, the birth of Christ, the life of Christ, and whether there may be any discrepancies in the time, place and what he had to teach, and a couple of side queries along the line of virgin birth, how it was accomplished, and the meaning of Christmas to Jesus.

(Carla channeling)

I am Q'uo, and I greet you in the love and in the light of the one infinite Creator, in whose name and in whose service we answer your call. We greet each of you this evening and thank you for the privilege of being allowed to share our thoughts with you. We urge you, as always, to remember that we offer our personal opinions and our beliefs, not infallibility. Therefore, listen to us in good will, but lay down those thoughts that do not seem helpful.

We find that in speaking about the subject of Jesus the Christ, we must be more careful than usual to guard against infringement upon free will, for this entity is centrally important to some of those present, and we wish our words not to be stumbling blocks nor to be paths into an unproductive wilderness, but rather helpful disclosures for neutral information. There are some levels of understanding above that which you in third density enjoy which are necessary for the grasp of the full nature of Jesus the Christ for you who seek this entity shall be in part a mystery to the conscious mind, not because there was an intention to be mysterious, but because the nature of Christ is mystery.

We take this somewhat slowly, as we are working with this instrument for a more delicate balance with less control from us and more surrender from the instrument which enables a lesser amount of energy to be adequate for transmission of adequate thoughts. This will eventually, we hope, enable the instrument to work at a deeper level while still conscious. We thank you for your patience.

To continue. The entity known as Jehoshua, whom Greeks called Jesus, or rather, Jesu, was born closely upon the heels of midsummer, very few years before that year suggested by your histories, approximately five and one half years. We believe this is the correct measurement. We only may only say it was in the middle of the seventh month. We are sorry, but your numbering does not make enough sense to us. We understand your moons, but not your numbers.

We cannot speak about what this instrument calls the virgin birth, and invoke the Law of Confusion, saying only that each new soul first awakened to its perception of itself as an eternal being has experienced the virgin birth. The event was difficult, and the birth was indeed humble, though brightened by an optical illusion, shall we say, a most unusual configuration within the heavens, which caused there to appear to be for some of your months an unusually bright cluster of light in the night sky.

The combination of the Christ with a serviceable life channel was powerful, and many psychic events occurred before and after the event as well as at the time of it. Astrologer kings did indeed journey following the star, however the arrival was approximately a year and a half later. That, indeed, is a spiritual adventure you would do well to ponder as you approach your own stable looking for the newborn, guided by hope, the brightest star of you being.

The entity Jesus was loved and loved in return, but his mind drove him to be alone, for though too young to have established to his own satisfaction the nature of his being, he had tremendous hunger for wisdom. You would call this entity a child prodigy. The entity taught many, many more things than are written, and could continue teaching for an eternity, yet what has been recorded is typical enough of the teaching's content in general that we do not choose to take this opportunity to adjust the teachings that are recorded. It is not only that there is some infringement upon free will, although that is part of our caution; we also do not wish to sway those who have not become interested in the Christ to alter their viewpoints.

For above and apart from any writing about the Christ, there is the Christ, and that which this teacher, channel and representative of the Creator called the Holy Spirit, call it what you will. There are many, many avenues in which the Christ speaks to each whenever the inner ear is opened and the ear harks, not listening passively, but leaning forward and truly harking.

The concept of the Christ was this—that intelligent infinity as experienced by the Logos and with the bias of the Logos would enter a third-density experience, not erasing the one known as Jesus' personality or being, but coming into the closest possible harmony with that being. There needed to be one who wished to sacrifice an incarnation to the ever-increasing pleasure and agony of the Creator, experiencing what this instrument would call the slings and arrows of outrageous fortune, for it is the nature of the Christ and the nature of third density that the two, perceiving each other, should react— the third density with a lack of understanding, and the Christ with wonder, joy and sacrifice. Such is the sorrow of your illusion and the joy of sensation and communion.

In the end, Jesus the man became so able to bear both joy and agony that this entity stopped experiencing the Creator and for long periods of time became the Creator experiencing third density. Such is the perfect channeling of love. The achievement of the perfect channeling was the mystery of union between Creator and illusion.

After this bonding, the burden of channeling rather rapidly began to tire the master teacher, Jesus. At the time of the crucifixion, as this instrument calls it, there were almost no tears left, there were no bones unbroken, there was no companionship that had not been betrayed in one form or another. Nevertheless, Jesus the Christ lived well and did not stop the channeling until the breath left the physical vehicle. We witness to this Christ with thanksgiving and joy, not suggesting that any worship or not worship, but celebrating the Creator poured into a channel who could share in full the nature of the Logos, the nature of love, the Creator's powerful, terrible love.

You ask what Jesus the Christ would think of the way your people celebrate Christmas. My friends, Jesus is very pleased. He is pleased [to see] all that is given and received of love, generosity and cheerfulness. This entity never confused the personal life that he lived with the Christ he channeled and in the end gave way to completely, but always knew the source and called it the Father. Call it what you will. We have no dogma or doctrine, but celebrate love.

It is the Creator who is pleased that those who do celebrate the spiritual advent of light into the darkness. Yet that Creator will also celebrate the same event on another level in each of your lives, whatever your season of Christmastide may be, whenever your star beckons.

We find that the concentration has caused this instrument to become fatigued more rapidly than usual, thus we shall cease speaking through this instrument and attempt to transfer the contact, with apologies, to the one known as Jim, who is at this moment announcing to us in no uncertain terms that we are making the wrong move. We do not think so. We leave this instrument in love and light. We shall now transfer. We are Q'uo.

(Jim channeling)

I am Q'uo, and greet each of you again in love and light. To finish that which we had begun through the one known as Carla.

We have come to the point in our discussion of the one known as Jesus in which we wish to share some information concerning the perceptions which the one known as Jesus would perhaps make upon the patterns and rituals of observing this occasion that is known as the Mass of Christ's birth. Indeed, within each entity who seeks answers to the mysteries of life there is a season during which the activities of the entity cease and the focus of attention is pointed inward.

The fruitful time in the sense of experience gained is considered within the inner being to be likened as to a foundation for that which is to come. Within each entity that seeks these truths of experience there comes the time when there will be a new beginning. This is often preceded by the trials which test that which has been known and applied to experience. From these trials, then, the entity moves to the limits of its being, and through a sacrifice of its own knowing and unknowing, and a surrender of these to that force which is paramount in the life pattern, call it the one Creator or love or the Christ Consciousness, if you will.

With this surrender, then, comes the possibility of a new seeding of awareness and experience within the seeker. As each of your peoples then take part in the celebrations in the name of the Christed Jesus, each then does also partake in some fashion of this ritual of renewal and eventual resurrection of the Christed consciousness within each manifested vehicle which has the Logos as source and motivator in the great experience of evolution which each of you undertakes.

There are, of course, many distractions to any life pattern and celebration, such as the one which this season has provided once again.

At this time we feel that we have shared that which is congruent with our perception of your call. We would then at this time ask if we might speak upon any further topics or attempt clarity with regards to that which we have shared this evening. Are there any queries at this time?

J: Did I understand correctly that the birth of Jesus occurred in midsummer, or did I hear incorrectly on that?

I am Q'uo, and we spoke thusly, my brother. May we speak in any further fashion?

J: And the birth of Christ was approximately five and one half years prior the time our historians believe to be the actual birth of Christ. Is that correct?

I am Q'uo, and as accurately as we can perceive your measurements of time, this figure is relatively accurate.

May we answer further, my brother?

J: What was the name of the entity that gave physical birth to the baby Jesus?

I am Q'uo, and we find that the literal translation of this entity's naming, as you call it, is not possible, but is approximated by the sound vibratory complex that is known among your peoples as Mary.

May we speak further, my brother?

J: From tonight's lesson I think I understood that Jesus, before incarnating in third density, chose to incarnate into third density, but somehow was granted the ability not to go through the veiling process that normally third-density beings go through prior to incarnation into this dimension. Is this correct?

I am Q'uo, and we find that this has correctness to it, though we see some difficulty in a full explication of the nature of the awareness that was experienced by the one known as Jesus. This entity was able to retain pathways of perception, shall we say, in its incarnate state that were easily activated in a sequential fashion according to experience gained throughout the incarnation so that at a latter point within the incarnation this entity was able to channel and experience the love of the Father which you would call the Logos in a fashion which was in harmonious resonance with the personality, shall we say, of the one known as Jesus without obliterating that per …

(Side one of tape ends.)

(Jim channeling)

I am Q'uo, and am again with this instrument. Since we had completed our response, we shall ask if there might be a further query upon which we could speak, my brother?

J: Why was it necessary tonight for the ones doing the channeling to do a deeper state of concentration, shall I say, in order to bring about this channeling tonight?

I am Q'uo. The reasons were two. Firstly, the topic queried upon was one which is central to the incarnational patterns of some within this group, thus there was some added risk in the possible infringement upon free will. Secondly, the nature of the queries was of a specific enough focus that in order to respond with the appropriate information there was the necessity of the ones serving as instruments to move to deeper portions of the conscious mind so that less static, shall we say, would be likely to interfere with the concepts being transmitted.

May we speak further, my brother?

J: Thank you very much. That cleared that up. I have just one more question. Well, first let me ask you this. Have there been further incarnations of the entity known as Jesus upon the planet Earth?

I am Q'uo, and we find that there have not been, my brother. May we speak further?

J: Will there be another incarnation of this entity on the planet Earth?

I am Q'uo, and we find that it is not the entity known as Jesus that shall appear again, but the Christed consciousness which shall move through those of your population which have prepared a place for this consciousness.

May we speak further, my brother?

J: I'm a little confused. Can you explain further about a place for this event?

I am Q'uo. We began speaking of such a preparation in the final portion of our opening message for this evening when we spoke of those seekers of truth who retire to the inner portions of the self to stand upon the foundation of what has been gained of experience and reach for that which is cloaked in mystery and attempt to bring forth within the incarnational pattern the proper conditions that will allow the same channeling of love which the one known as Jesus accomplished in its life pattern.

This "ritual of celebration," as we called the process, is one which each entity observes in some fashion in this season during which the birth of the one known as Jesus is celebrated. The process was demonstrated by the incarnation of the one known as Jesus, eventually culminating in the resurrection of the Christed consciousness within the life pattern of the seeker residing within the third-density illusion. Thus, by such seeking and exercise of faith does the seeker prepare a place within the life pattern for this resurrection, shall we say.

May we speak further, my brother?

J: No, I think I understand. That's all the questions that I have. Thank you.

I am Q'uo, and we thank you, my brother. Are there further queries at this time?

H: I have a couple—maybe just one. Immediately after Christ resurrected from the tomb, was his body solid, or would it pass through doors, like a vapor?

I am Q'uo. The entity known as Jesus at the time of that known as the resurrection was able to channel the love of the Father or the Logos to such an extent that it was able to affect the structure of its physical vehicle in a way which filled it with light so that it was able to manifest both the characteristics of your third-density illusion when appropriate, and able also to refine its focus of light to the point of being able to move through what you would see as solid material of your third-density illusion.

May we speak further, my brother?

H: No, that cleared that up quite well, and the second question too. That's all the questions. Thank you.

I am Q'uo, and we thank you, my brother. Is there another query at this time?

J: Could you explain the configuration of which you spoke, in the skies, that created the optical illusion of illumination or a cluster of light at the time of the birth of Christ?

I am Q'uo, and we pause in order to allow this instrument to move somewhat more deeply. The patterns of light that became obviously apparent to the physical eye of those within the vicinity of that known as the Holy Land were produced by an unusual alignment of both planets and constellations of stars that seemed to focus their brilliance upon a point which seemed far nearer your Earth planet by far than even your moon, so that there was projected from this alignment of celestial bodies a focus for their light that approached this planetary sphere at a focal point which was seen as a sign to those who studied the skies and more especially the stars.

May we speak further, my brother?

J: Was this configuration or alignment of the celestial bodies coincidental, or was it to fulfill the prophecy of the birth of Jesus the Christ?

I am Q'uo, and we may note that this alignment was a cyclical event which was an integral portion of the evolutionary cycle of your planetary sphere which provided a doorway of a kind through the metaphysical realms, shall we say, that was the signal for the opportunity for the one known as Jesus to begin its service in the fashion which became known as its incarnational experience.

May we speak further, my brother?

J: If this configuration is cyclical, when will it occur again?

I am Q'uo, and this particular configuration or opportunity for refining the focus of consciousness is that which appears near the ending of what we find many of your peoples call a major cycle of evolution, that which numbers approximately 25,000 of your years. This opportunity allows those of a planetary population who ready for the harvest or graduation, as we find you call it, to begin the final lessons that will allow such graduation. The refining of the focus of consciousness is the general opportunity which is provided to each in a unique fashion for each.

May we speak further, my brother?

J: Thank you. That clears it up. Have we pinpointed the exact spot of the birth of Jesus?

I am Q'uo, and we find that this location remains yet a mystery to your peoples.

May we speak further, my brother?

J: Would it be possible for you to tell us approximately where the exact location is, then?

I am Q'uo, and we are not able to move this instrument deeply enough in its own tree of mind for the transmission of this information, and we apologize for this limitation. Indeed, we find that the focus required for this particular transmission has begun to waver somewhat within this instrument.

May we attempt another query at this time?

J: No thank you, that's all the questions that I have.

Carla: I'd like to ask one last question and then, with thanks, encourage you to go on, because it does seem like the instrument's really tired. I know this was tiring for me, too. But I thank you for coming. First of all, two things. Just yes or no. Did you mean a 25,000 year cycle or a 75,000 year cycle, because you said "major cycle"?

I am Q'uo, and we meant to use the term "major" to signify the 25,000 year cycle, reserving the term "master" for the addition of three 25,000 year cycles.

Carla: Okay. The last question is just yes or no, but I have to go on for just a little bit because I've been pondering what you said earlier about mysteries. And the real mystery, I mean, you didn't decline to answer that much, but there was one thing that you hinted at, but it was a real mystery. I mean, it was a contradiction, which of course is the nature of spiritual things, and that was this. That you had me thinking for awhile that Jesus was—well, we've gotten in other information—a wanderer that decided he was up to doing this job and came here, and in other information we've learned, he was awakened to some lifting of the veil and it kept happening and kept happening until he was real aware. So basically, he channeled the Christ throughout his life, but there's always a distinction between Jesus the man and the Christ.

Now there was something that you said that hinted at the mystery, and that was, you said ultimately the Christ became Jesus, which would suggest more of like a walk-in situation where the Christ comes in and basically takes over the consciousness. Yet at the same time, you said that the one known as Jesus never forgot that it wasn't he, it was the Creator that he was channeling. Is this the heart of the mystery that you cannot in any satisfactory way explain to third-density minds?

I am Q'uo. This is indeed the mystery, my sister, for within the third-density illusion, each seeker of what you call the truth places itself in a position of receptivity to that truth by the intensity of the seeking, the strength of faith and will, so that at some point within the cycle of incarnations, it is possible for such a seeker to not only discover that which it seeks, but to become that which it seeks. Thus is the meaning of the resurrection within third density. The seeker builds with mortal hands a manifested life that may be constructed in such a fashion in metaphysical terms that that known as love may move through the being in such a pure fashion as to shine as that which it is, the pure and virgin consciousness of the one Creator, moving to gain the experience of the creation which it has made of Itself, and doing this within the life pattern of incarnate third-density beings who have prepared this place within their life patterns and, thus, not only receive that which was sought, but become that which was sought.

May we speak further, my sister?

Carla: No, that's food enough for thought. Thank you very much for an elegant answer.

I am Q'uo, and we thank you, my sister. At this time, we shall ask if there might be a final short query before we close this working?

T: Yes. This is the true meaning, what you just stated is basically to my way of thinking—I'm asking if this is true—the true meaning of achieving Oneness, becoming One, in other words, the physical and the higher self in very simplistic terms, truly become One, when this point is achieved that you just described? Is that basically correct?

I am Q'uo, and this is correct, my brother, for the inheritance of each portion of the one Creator is the one Creator. Much there is that shall be learned during that time of incarnation within the third-density illusion where the veils of forgetting are moved into place to enable that experience within this illusion to be of an intensity that provides each portion of the Creator the fullest range of opportunity to know the power of love to redeem and resurrect even the tiniest portion of the one Creator. Thus, when each seeker moves to the point at which it may so perfectly channel the one Creator in its love aspect, then each portion of the life pattern takes on an holy appearance and all is seen as sacred.

May we speak further, my brother?

T: No, that was fine, thank you.

I am Q'uo, and we thank you, my brother. At this time, we shall take our leave of this instrument and this group, with our great and joy-filled thanksgiving to each for allowing our humble thoughts to be projected through words to each heart and mind. Again we remind each that we seek as do you, hopefully, faithfully, yet fallibly. Take those words with meaning and use them as you will, leaving those with none. We are known to you as those of Q'uo, and we leave you at this time in the love and in the light of the one infinite Creator. Adonai, my friends. Adonai vasu borragus. ♣

L/L Research

San Francisco Meditation
December 20, 1986

(The quality of the recording is low, and thus the transcription is not entirely certain.)

(Carla channeling)

[I am Q'uo,] and I greet you, my children, once again in love and in the light of the one infinite Creator that moves within each heart and within each creation. We thank you for the gift of your calling to us, for it is in serving entities such as you that we are able to work towards our own progression, our own further understanding of the one great original Thought of love. Our consciousness is full with the joy of your company.

You ask us about the companionship of money and spirituality. It is written in one of your holy works that the love of money is the root of all evil. We would like to point out that it is the love of money, as it is any idolatry, which is at the root of separation, whether it be the separation of true worship of the great divine mystery because of pieces of wood and stone or the separation of one's focus from that same mystery because of the love of counting. It is not the money itself which is contrary to a life led with a spiritual center, but the idolatrous love of that which is builded by man in imitation of the Creator's abundance.

The love of power is understandable within your illusion, for quite purposefully did you design your physical vehicles to be nearly powerless in any natural sense, shall we say, against the greatly powerful forces of your illusion's environment. Indeed, you were given both the instinct for survival and the challenge of survival as the foundation for your learning in third density. The love of money is a sub-type for the idolatry of power, for among other things, the having of this artificial substance which mimics true prosperity causes one to be able to manipulate the environment about one in a simple arithmetical formula: more money equals more time.

You will note that those who have experienced the having of large amounts of your money have virtually no consciousness of idolatry towards that substance, but instead, having become fully aware of the ramifications of the having of artificial abundance, seek instead for truer reality, a clearer picture of the nature of the self. It is not that the fear of the loss of power is not there in potential, for all alike [out of] true sheer [habit], even artificial abundance can create a consciousness of prosperity which automatically generates abundance. However, because this removes a large portion of catalyst from the illusion, most souls which choose to incarnate upon the Earth plane elect to manifest in situations in which a consciousness of true abundance is absent and concern for survival creates consciousness of lack. How easy, how understandable, how logical to love money when the lack of it has caused numberless discomforts in one's person and vivid experience. Thus, we say to you that you must not waste time being concerned that so many have the love of money fighting with the realization that true prosperity does not equal the idol called money.

Perhaps the most helpful thing we can suggest is that through meditation the consciousness of abundance may be encouraged, and as truth always drives out falsity, as love always drives out fear, so true abundance drives out the false idol. The consciousness of abundance does not mean that all that one wishes will come immediately, or at all, within any particular length of time or any incarnation. It means rather that there is an awareness that that which is to be shall come to one through natural plentifulness.

Observe those who have found abundance. Some may be wealthy and some quite poor, but what they have is an awareness of the excellence not only of life, but of the very life which is being lived by them. This is most often earned rather than given to them, especially among your people who are perturbed with great earnestness by their consciousness of lack. There are those whose happiness lies in children, those whose peace lies in love, others who find satisfaction in learning, still others, those who have the gift of being who they are. It takes a certain level of comfort to achieve the consciousness of abundance for most. It is difficult while starving to death to rejoice in the plenty all about one, yet there be spirits who have done so and gone to their graves singing in praise and thanksgiving for all the blessings which abounded in the creation of the Father.

Perhaps the second thing that we can offer to those who wish to be free of idolatry is a consciousness of other's needs, for if stewardship of any gift and talent is expressed, then the gates of abundance open and one is flooded with plenty. We do not ask that you see money as a means to an end, we do not ask that you stop thinking about money. We do not ask any system of intellectual training whatsoever—we ask only that it be recognized that worship of that which is known is idolatry and is not a satisfactory way in which to polarize one's path or to accelerate the pace of one's journey upon it.

Seek first the consciousness of love through meditation and analysis of action and thought, and that which is needed shall be given unto you according to the circumstances needed by you in your own opinion before this incarnational experience. All shall be given to you, for you see, no matter what the illusion of manipulation and manifestation may be, all this can be given unto you. All is indeed free. And that which is not, will not be. Each has designed for himself a special incarnation offering powerful experiences of lack and plenty, pain and peace. If you have little money, think not that you do not deserve more. If you have much money, think not that you deserve less. But whatever your environment, fill it with your love of the Creator and allow that love to reach to the infinity of the Creator's laughing face, that His light may shine infinitely through you that you may become plenty to others.

Money is relevant in your illusion. Enjoy it if you have it, seek it if you must, disregard it if you can, but manifest plenty and the consciousness of love.

My friends, we are most pleased to speak with you and thank you for this great privilege, asking only that you take our voice lightly as brothers and sisters and not as authorities. We would leave you for now in the love and in the light of the one infinite Creator. May all shine upon you, through you, and from you in plenty. Adonai. Adonai. We are those of Q'uo.

(Tape turned off and then on again.)

Carla: Well, let's have a batch of questions.

L: What I would like to know is everything and anything pertaining to the facilitation, both for myself and then passing it on to other people, having to do with the process of [writing down] all of the work having to do with contacting intelligent infinity, getting instructions, getting the, if [that takes any] guidance, having to do with the advanced work of enlightenment.

Carla: Okay. You don't want much, do you?

(Carla channeling)

I am Q'uo, and I greet you in the love and in the light of the one infinite Creator. We are most grateful to this instrument's sensitivity to our needs, for there is some difficulty as has been mentioned within the group.

As each moves closer to the seeking of light, there will be the equal opportunity given for those who wish to give a darker message and the sadder one. And of ourselves, we can only wait and hope and ask that those who act as instruments for the forces of light may be vigilant. This instrument does not see into the darkness of this particular visitor, for it is not this instrument's visitor, and so we are grateful that the instrument paused and responded to our request by tuning the group. With your strong and unified dedication to light, with your unified consciousness of love, there flows betwixt us and you an impregnable road, a highway of light through which information may flow. We ask that you guard that highway for us and for this instrument. Be vigilant in your consciousness and channel this to the best and truest that you know. We shall proceed, thanking the instrument also for not losing the contact when we told her a private joke, for this instrument is given to fits of giggling and it would have broken the contact which we had just reestablished.

The question of how to achieve contact with intelligent infinity for oneself and for others is certainly an interesting one. Perhaps we should begin with a story.

There was once a woman among your people whose life was too filled with luxury and too barren with desolation and [non-physical] deprivation. This entity hungered for all the things for which young women hunger—admiration, beauty, the camaraderie of friends, and the achievement of those goals prescribed by your peoples as needful for an adequate experience of prosperous and normal adulthood.

Yet this entity found herself in love, in love with someone she knew better than her mother or her father or herself or any friend or enemy. This entity called this man her savior, and knew that for this man, who was more real to her than flesh and blood, she would live and would gladly die. The entity joined a convent and worked at menial tasks as do those who adopt the bridal ring of poverty, chastity and obedience. That for her was the knowledge of the scholar. Yet, as she touched, she healed, and so she was sent to be a nurse.

The order to which she belonged was not a rich one, except in ideals, and so it turned itself to the aid of the most poor. The entity found itself upon the streets of cities in India, as you call that portion of your planet's surface, kneeling day and night in the streets where homeless have their homes and the hungry ate no bread except death and ruin. The entity touched faces half-eaten by vermin, scabs and pestilence and saw the face of her savior husband. This entity walks among you. This entity could be you. And each of you knows that.

Yet each of you knows, too, that it was not given you to love the face of the Savior more than flesh and blood. We say to you, my friends, that if you wish to make contact with intelligent infinity, you must know what you love more than flesh and blood and your own life. Look deep in the ideal for the mysterious One whom you may call a savior. And when you find that face that you can love and love [wholly], then you shall find the gateway to intelligent infinity. There is no knowledge or understanding that will move you upon the journey to behold the face of the One who will save you from death, the death of limitation in consciousness.

Thus, you must examine day after day, and in meditation seek endlessly day after day, love itself. You cannot serve others and find the face of love—first you must know love, you must have subjective validation. Light and love must become real to you and more precious than all those things which you shall be asked to surrender and give up for the sake of that which you cannot see and never shall, that which is closer to you than your own breathing, dearer to you than any anything of which you may think. How can you love a face you shall never see? How can you personify the unfathomable mystery of creation? Love has as many faces as there are consciousnesses to behold love. Your savior will come to you when you have sought with [it]. Each day, each moment is pregnant and fecund with the infinite possibility of the full realization of the love for which you would gladly surrender all. Yet it is not known by any what moment you shall choose to open at last to love itself.

We can say that if you can think only in terms of action, by all means seek the face of love in action, but know that each hour that you spend acting in manifestation of the search for love needs to be matched in twice or four times the intensity, whether in duration or in simple caring, by the seeking within of the silence. For in developing your consciousness, in disciplining your personality, you shall at last draw near to an irresistible infatuation of puppy love, an innocent, crazy calf-mooning after the Creator. If you are not capable at this moment of falling in love, then the gateway of intelligent infinity is not yours at this moment, for you are not extravagant enough to know of love. Love is folly, for only folly could create the wonder that you see all about you. Only folly would wish to know itself. Only love can see life.

We are sorry to have no techniques to offer you, save one. Seek, and seek, and seek again, patiently, persistently and extravagantly. Find ways to laugh and bless your tears. Attempt to see love in everyone and everything and forgive yourself when you do not. Never let any seriousness, guilt or unhappiness divide you from your seeking for the love of love. Knowledge is not of your illusion. You [seek] to choose fully, to know the face of the Creator by a love that is full of compassion and service to others, a love that is radiant unto them, and so you must love and enjoy and cheer each other and know that if you bring each other to the resting place another may desire, it is love that has lead the way and not your knowledge. Seek, my friends, love, in love, for love's sake. All else will follow.

We find that this instrument grows fatigued, and we would suggest that the instrument rest before continuing any more channeling. The instrument informs us that this is intended. We are pleased. We wish all of you a …

(Side one of tape ends.)

(Carla channeling)

Thus, the consciousness that comforts lies everywhere and you are not alone, that wherever you are upon the path and whatever lonely thing you must do, there are these seen and unseen who witness and offer comfort at every turn and who pillow your head upon the *(inaudible)* of infinite patience, for it is a kindly universe in which the Creator has only [one] Thought and that is love. The gateway to intelligent infinity is the seeking of that love.

We are those of Q'uo, humble messengers and friends. Never confuse us with those who know something, for we are only your brothers and sisters. Yet insofar as we have any poor opinion, we share it with you gladly, thanking you for the privilege of the call you give us. We leave you in the love and the infinite light of the One Who Is All. Adonai. Adonai vasu borragus.

Year 1987

January 4, 1987 to February 22, 1987

Sunday Meditation
January 4, 1987

Group question: "Q'uo: We would speak with you this evening about that event with which some of your group have been involved and about which they are now curious, that is, the recent global day of peace. We shall not speak specifically about this one event, but rather about the mass spiritually based event in general and its nature."

(Carla channeling)

We are known to you as those of Q'uo, and we greet you in the love and in the light of the one infinite Creator. It is a great privilege to be asked to speak with your group this evening and we especially would wish to extend our love and blessing to the one known as N. It is most enjoyable to blend our lifestreams with your own. We would thank the instrument for the care taken and the challenging, as there was interference which was effectively sorted out.

We would speak with you this evening about that event with which some of your group have been involved and about which they are now curious, that is, the recent global day of peace. We shall not speak specifically about this one event, but rather about the mass spiritually based event in general and its nature.

We come to you not only as individuals, but also as a group, a cultural or societal mass consciousness which we use as an extended series of tools and resources in order to be able to speak to groups such as yours, and to serve as comforter to many who seek the Creator in a way which is complementary to our ability to function on behalf of the extended Self of all creation, reflecting the principles of faith, hope and trust, which then illuminate momentary difficulties for those whom we offer to comfort. Therefore, we have a sympathy for the impulse which birthed each day of prayer for whatever cause that has ever been organized and carried out among the peoples of your planet.

The nature of such an event is only partially that lightening of the planet which is intended, for there is a large portion in any such attempt of those energies which are more associated with societal and cultural movements, in other words, those energies which emerge from the solar plexus energy center and which this instrument calls yellow ray.

If one were to look upon your planet as a house, the special spiritually oriented events could be seen as the attempt to clean house in one day. Moreover, because of the complexities within your planetary subcultures, the belligerent actions and intentions of many among your peoples served as those who caroused, drank and destroyed the very house which was being cleaned. Further, these same aggressions continue each of your days. Long in your history is the march of days in which shots and missiles have been fired in anger and hatred, whether the missiles be of lead, stone, mud, or those subtle missiles called words.

We have said to you often that one entity's light is visible amongst the darkness of the whole planet, and so our modest estimate of spiritually oriented events must be confusing. Yet it is a question of bad news and good news, for we would not wish you to think that the running sore which constitutes your planet's yellow ray propensity for aggressive action can be healed by the application of one day's bandage. However, it is only through not only such events as these, but any other well-intentioned events whatsoever that your people's consciousness can be transformed, so there is no discouragement in our assessment of the actual event. Rather, we encourage each to focus upon that fine instinct which lead to the decision to commit time and energy to a light-filled purpose so that each entity which included peace, love, light and brotherhood in consciousness for one day may begin to include it in consciousness for all, for it is in the persistent turning of the perceptions toward one tenor of thought which eventually will transform consciousness, although consciousness is in great part a matter of one's perception of it. Nevertheless, by an effort of will and faith, consciousness can be taught to reverberate to the sounds of hope and peace, love and light.

We encourage each to turn again and again to the image of the world and of the self as a house, a dwelling. Each of you is a creature divinely designed to experience and reflect the Creator. The totality of consciousness upon your sphere is so designed as a whole, and one day, within a land which is only a promise to you now, you shall have the consciousness of the whole, you shall see your brothers and sisters as your true kin, and your heart shall not be torn between those you feel you understand and these you do not. Peace shall reign, yet always there is a greater peace; always in the journey of the seeker there is the restlessness which underlies all peace which causes those who seek to go on and on seeking the truth. As you see yourself upon that journey, see yourself also as a dweller within a structure which you have built so that it may contain that spirit within you which is of the Creator and which is the Creator.

Yes, you seek peace for your planet, but is your spiritual dwelling place strong enough for peace to reign therein? Is your heart and mind a place wherein the Creator may dwell and where you may be one with infinite intelligence?

My children, in order to build your house strongly from within, it is well for you to reflect deeply upon the nature of each portion of your being, for you are not only those who wish for peace, but also those instinctual creatures which cause war and aggression because of those instincts for survival which your body complex has inherited and which shall always color your perceptions and your consciousness while you dwell within your physical vehicle. You cannot legislate peace by prayer or any grand tours of the watchtower of your consciousness, for there is more to you than the top floor—there is the first floor and the basement. You must reckon with each and every instinct, each and every influence of the body complex, accepting, celebrating, and becoming a proper steward of each impulse which affects your consciousness. If each could do this for the self, then there would be peace.

We urge you to go within your mind into each and every corner of consciousness, examining, accepting and blessing every disharmony which your body complex seems to fit you for. Herein is the cradle of destruction: man's heart and mind, when the full consciousness of your kind is not acknowledged and disciplined. We do not urge you to behave in what you perceive as a dark or selfish manner, but only to perceive the logic of such behavior. You shall find peace to come more easily when the enemy which is within you is carefully understood.

We are giving this instrument some tuning at this time and we thank you for your patience. We are known to you as those of Q'uo, and are sorry for the delay, but this instrument is quite receptive this evening and we are winding her coil, although she does not understand what we are doing. It is a helpful thing for us and the instrument will find it helpful also. We thank you for your patience and would at this time transfer the contact so that we may indeed speak with the one known as N. We leave this instrument with thanks and would transfer now. We are Q'uo.

(Jim channeling)

I am Q'uo, and greet you again in love and light. We thank this instrument for allowing us to speak through it this evening, and we are hopeful that we might be able to be of further service by attempting to answer those queries which each may find value in the asking. We remind each that we are but fallible seekers, your brothers and sisters, who wish that our words not be given too great a weight. Take those which have meaning for you and leave those which do not. May we begin with a query at this time?

N: My question to you is the question, if a so-called dangerous weapon, such that a gun could be—[could] draw to the entity using it danger, also, or a negativity because of possessions that could be used for harm?

I am Q'uo, and we respond by suggesting that there is no artifact of your culture, including the weapons of which you speak, which in itself may bring to an entity a situation which you would describe as dangerous or negative, rather one may look to the intentions of the one who possesses the artifact and query as to the nature of those intentions, for though your world is one composed of many things and seems concrete and solid about you, indeed, that which moves it and has effect upon it is of the world of thought. As you direct your thoughts, so you draw unto you that which resonates in harmony with those thoughts.

This is a general principle which, of course, has many exceptions, but one may look to it as what you may call a rule of thumb. We may also add that the intentions which motivate any action are intentions which are themselves a product of what an entity has thus far learned within an incarnation and the efficiency with which that learning has been accomplished. Thus, the frame of mind and mood of emotion become the motivators for further actions and further thoughts as they themselves are products of the experience of the entity, so that an incarnation builds a certain momentum, shall we say, and it is within this field of thought energy that an entity will draw unto itself those experiences which are most likely to provide it further opportunities for learning and for being of service.

May we answer in any further way, my sister?

N: No, that was quite sufficient. Thank you.

I am Q'uo, and we thank you, my sister. Is there another query?

Carla: Am I to know anything about what "winding a coil" means? And does it have anything to do with the high degree of contact that I felt earlier in the day?

I am Q'uo. We find, my sister, that in responding to this query we must first lay a certain groundwork by suggesting that the receptivity which became apparent to you at an earlier portion in this day is a product of many energy patterns or rhythms which are known to your peoples as the biorhythms and their coincidence in your pattern of living. The coil of which we spoke is most easily described as the pattern that intelligent energy, or the love/light of the Creator, takes as it moves through your energy centers, both the primary centers and secondary centers as well. There is a rhythmic spiraling of energies that are, when seen, closely approximating the shape of a coil or spiraling light.

The pattern that is traveled in this spiraling of intelligent energy is a pattern determined by the openness and brilliance of each energy center in turn, so that the intelligent energy begins its movement at the lower center and is then spiraled upward in a fashion which, when meeting no resistance, becomes intensified as the energy passes into the higher centers and their secondary components.

When we spoke of winding or rewinding your own coil of intelligent energy, we were speaking of the effect which we are able to cause by intensifying the energy which moves through the spiraled centers of energy. Thus, we in effect complement work which you have accomplished by shooting an extra dose, shall we say, of energy through this spiraling coil of intelligent energy.

May we speak in any further fashion, my sister?

Carla: Yes, Q'uo. Was this service that you performed as a result of my praying before I channel each time to receive the highest and best that is possible for me to receive? Or would it occur in the development of any channel, regardless of the tuning? Due to the contacts to your own sense of service to others?

I am Q'uo, and we find that the answer to this query is not a simple one, for the entity serving as instrument provides much of the framework or foundation upon which any contact such as ourselves may then attempt to build a certain kind of structure or channel through which information may be transmitted. The prayer of which you speak is that tuning device which is most helpful in your own experience to ready yourself for this service. It is a crystallization of the life pattern which you have chosen in your daily round of activities, and this life pattern itself lends a significant portion of beingness to your tuning, so that the tuning then becomes a magnifier of the desire to be of service through the vocal channeling.

Added to this is the experience that any instrument gains as it practices its art, and in your particular case we have been able to work with your instrument for a long enough portion of your time that we are able at this time to move your conscious awareness somewhat more deeply into the meditative state in order that we might transmit concepts in a word by word fashion, thus hopefully acquiring the ability to be more precise, as you would call it, in describing one concept or another.

At this time we shall ask if there might be any further way in which we might respond to your query or if there might be further queries that you wish to ask to elicit further information upon this topic.

Carla: No, thanks.

I am Q'uo, and we thank you, my sister. Is there any further query at this time?

N: Well, now that you mentioned it, I have a question. I work at a place among deceased people, and my question would be, I try to look at each person and send good energy to them, and I was wondering, I don't know if you would call it the soul, but the energy of the deceased person, would they feel my energy going to them? I'm wondering if their soul would linger or any feelings or type of communication through the senses would linger after death is what I'm trying to ask.

I am Q'uo, and we find that among the population of your planetary sphere, being of the third density, it is often the experience of one who has recently made the transition from your earthly existence to the inner realms that the entity will for a portion of your time remain in the vicinity of its physical vehicle which it has now shed, and will also visit many of those with whom it has been close in the incarnation now complete.

The communication upon your part of love and good feelings to those who have departed their physical vehicles is a blessing which is greatly appreciated in most instances, for it is a reassurance to such entities that they indeed live still and receive interaction from others, even though they may feel themselves somewhat between worlds, shall we say. They are quite sensitive to the expression of love and affection and utilize these good wishes as they prepare to begin a journey that will finally take them into another density of existence in which they shall begin a study of the incarnation now complete and preparation for that which is to come.

Thus, it is quite helpful for all those who have recently known one who has passed through the door of death to send to that entity the heartfelt love and joyful farewell in order that the entity might be speeded upon its way and find the path through …

(Side one of tape ends.)

(Jim channeling)

I am Q'uo, and am again with this instrument. May we respond in any further fashion, my sister?

N: No, thank you. I sort of felt your answer before and I feel that that's *(inaudible)*. Thank you.

I am Q'uo, and we thank you once again, my sister. Is there another query at this time?

Carla: Only if you can make lemonade out of lemons. I have been asked too many times lately not to ask you once more for any help, any helpful concept that you could give me in responding to people who have a problem with spirituality and money. It's a basic question of ethics and supply and the consciousness of plenty or supply versus the consciousness of need. People who offer spiritual gifts to others seem to have the feeling that they shouldn't ask for money, and yet many people who want to offer spiritual gifts to others have to charge something, or at least they feel they do, in order to pay for their way in life. Is there any concept that I could take into my own thinking to work on in responding to people who ask me these questions?

I am Q'uo. We shall attempt to be of service in this regard, my sister, but we are somewhat unsure of our abilities, for this instrument has biases in this direction of inquiry which may be somewhat difficult to overcome. We may suggest that the planning to the last degree for any service to be offered is often an hindrance which makes the free offering of the service difficult, if not impossible.

What we mean to suggest in this regard is that for one who wishes to be of service to others in any particular fashion, it is recommended that that desire be the foundation upon which all further thought and action be built. The desire is that which shall form the framework that will allow the service thus to intensify and refine this desire. It is most helpful in that when the entity is able to remain in the full flush, shall we say, of this desire to serve, then it is often the case that the way to serve shall be made clearer and smoother for such an entity as the entity is able to call upon its own inner resources through the subconscious mind, and is also aided in its desire to serve by those friends and teachers of the inner realms who watch over each third-density entity.

Thus, the synchronistic events, as you call them, begin to have impact within the entity's life pattern so that the way to provide the service becomes apparent as the entity is propelled to it and through it by its desire to be of service.

Whether the entity sets a price upon its service and the amount or degree of that price is determined in a fashion which is most difficult to describe, but which is primarily the function of the entity's ability to gather its own inner resources in a fashion that allows their full and free expression, and as an analog, then, draws unto the entity the most appropriate manner by which the services may be provided to others.

As a general rule, we may suggest that the charging of a fee or price of any kind for such services is basically unimportant if the entity is able to look upon such a fee or charge or price as that which is not rigid, and is not that which shall become an obstacle to the providing of the service if the one desiring the service cannot pay the price.

Thus, the service is always offered, with the desire to serve being the motivation. The fee or price that may be decided upon, then, is that which is flexible and is secondary to the service.

May we respond in any further fashion at this point?

Carla: Just one related question. My apologies to the instrument who hates this, okay? It has been said to me, sincerely, by good people, that the giving of money or some fee, some gift, constitutes a necessary part of a metaphysical bond between giver and receiver of metaphysical information, and that without the payment of some kind, you are basically giving your service with a deep metaphysical request to the person receiving it not to pay any attention to it. Whereas, by accepting a fee, you are also accepting that you are going to give this entity something and the entity is agreeing to take it in and consider it, that it is a sort of metaphysical contract, so that the price of it becomes an important part of the gift that is received, the price of it, that is, becomes an important part of the gift.

Would you care to comment on this concept? Does it have any substance?

I am Q'uo, and we find in this instance that it is for most of the population of your planet a case of the cart before the horse, as we find your saying has put it. The situation which has developed upon your planetary sphere as a result of the development of monetary systems and their predecessors of the bartering systems is the root to which the principle which you have stated may be traced, and we find that in many cases, due to the belief of many of your peoples that each may own a portion of the creation that is separate and apart from that which is owned by others, that many do indeed need a crutch, shall we say, upon which to lean when seeking assistance of a metaphysical or physical nature, one from another. Because of these beliefs, it is often necessary to pander to them, shall we say, and to, if we may use yet another phrase, "throw the dog a bone," so that it shall lie quietly as the study goes on …

Carla: May I interrupt to ask a question?

I am Q'uo, and this is quite acceptable, my sister.

Carla: I'm concerned for the instrument. I'm concerned because of the emotional load of these questions. Would it be satisfactory to you if I withdrew this question and allowed the instrument to stop channeling?

I am Q'uo, and this is quite acceptable my sister, yet we are also willing to continue, as is this instrument.

Carla: That's okay. Not necessary. I get the drift. I'm concerned for the instrument personally.

I am Q'uo, and we shall continue. We are having some difficulty due to the confusion in this instrument's mind. It is unaware that it has any difficulty, yet it has consented to allow the questioning to cease for the evening. Is there any short query before we close this evening?

Carla: No. Just our thanks.

I am Q'uo, and we thank each for inviting our presence this evening, and we apologize if we have caused any discomfort to this instrument or to any present this evening. We are somewhat clumsy at assessing the vital energies of those serving as instruments, and hope that we may gain in a facility in this regard in your future.

We have greatly enjoyed our sharing of your vibrations this evening and we look forward to attempting to be of some small service to this group in what you would call your future. We are known to you as those of Q'uo, and at this time we shall take our leave of this instrument and this group, leaving each, as always, in the love and in the light of the one infinite Creator. Adonai, my friends. Adonai vasu borragus. ✤

L/L Research

L/L Research is a subsidiary of Rock Creek Research & Development Laboratories, Inc.

P.O. Box 5195
Louisville, KY 40255-0195

www.llresearch.org

Rock Creek is a non-profit corporation dedicated to discovering and sharing information which may aid in the spiritual evolution of humankind.

ABOUT THE CONTENTS OF THIS TRANSCRIPT: This telepathic channeling has been taken from transcriptions of the weekly study and meditation meetings of the Rock Creek Research & Development Laboratories and L/L Research. It is offered in the hope that it may be useful to you. As the Confederation entities always make a point of saying, please use your discrimination and judgment in assessing this material. If something rings true to you, fine. If something does not resonate, please leave it behind, for neither we nor those of the Confederation would wish to be a stumbling block for any.

CAVEAT: This transcript is being published by L/L Research in a not yet final form. It has, however, been edited and any obvious errors have been corrected. When it is in a final form, this caveat will be removed.

© 2009 L/L Research

Special Meditation
January 10, 1987

A question from S regarding this statement by Q'uo: "Q'uo: We would speak to you this evening about love. The call this evening circles around many concerns, yet there is only one response to the many-sided concern of illusion, and that is gently, cleanly and with grace to suggest the turning of the attention always to that which is the unity, the mystery, the love which is behind all the many scenes that shine, as if each part of the illusion were a sequin sewn on to an almost unimaginably large structure or model for the delight and benefit of all, that all could walk around and behold the beauty of the illusion."

(Carla channeling)

I am Q'uo, and I greet you in the love and in the light of the one infinite Creator whom we serve with our whole mind and heart. We thank each for requesting our presence during this meditation, and offer to each face of the Creator our own face, Creator to Creator and love to love. It is a great privilege to share being with you at this time. We thank both the one known as Carla and the one known as S for relaxing and ceasing to be concerned about what we have to say. It is well that each remember that all views are fallible and that none is teacher except to the self in any final capacity. We would not wish that our words mean too much or be taken with ultimate seriousness, but only used if helpful and discarded if not.

We would speak to you this evening about love. The call this evening circles around many concerns, yet there is only one response to the many-sided concern of illusion, and that is gently, cleanly and with grace to suggest the turning of the attention always to that which is the unity, the mystery, the love which is behind all the many scenes that shine, as if each part of the illusion were a sequin sewn on to an almost unimaginably large structure or model for the delight and benefit of all, that all could walk around and behold the beauty of the illusion.

Yet how easy it is, my friends, to come too close to these glittering false sides, never seeing the stitches that hold illusion to illusion, never seeing the bare chicken wire beneath the papier maché, never seeing the hollowness of the interior of illusion. Because illusion, like an onion, peels to nothing. It cannot be assumed that there is nothing beyond the illusion. Indeed, we suggest that it is that very marked nature which illusion carries which suggests equally markedly that a mystery lies beneath that which is seen.

Thus, we wish to speak with you this evening about love, for it is not helpful to speak of that which is not, unless we are able to inspire within those who seek some feeling for a direction of further profitable inquiry.

We ponder within this instrument's mind the direction that we shall take in this speaking, for this instrument is clearer than is its normal wont and is not aiding us, We have two separate points to make, so we shall make first one and then the other. We would suggest to this instrument that in the future this instrument trust its clarity to a greater extent than it is at this moment, for without this instrument's aid, we are not as able to offer inspiration. Pure channeling may well be full of clarity, yet it is the color and fire of personality and poetry which only the channel can offer which sparks and enlivens our simple messages. We shall proceed.

Firstly, we would like to suggest that there is only one arena for the true study of ultimate things—that is, one's own consciousness. Thus it is that meditation remains always the one discipline that is not to be ignored, avoided or shortened beyond a reasonable point. Its dailiness is a majority of its virtue, although any attempt at meditation is always encouraged. The benefits of cumulative meditational time are far more than the simple addition of day-to-day, week-to-week, and year-to-year might suggest. The meditation held daily is a commitment to the sacramental nature of the temple of the body, mind and spirit that is the self.

It is not known to an entity within the illusion when each moment for realization or transformation shall occur. However, one who meditates on a daily basis with intent to open to whatever transformation there may be in the silence is expecting and seeking on a daily basis the opening of the doors within the consciousness which are to some extent openable in a random manner, so that a great view which might be seen past one particular door might be missed entirely were meditation not to occur upon the appropriate day. He who watches shall not be surprised. He who does not watch shall perhaps not know the surprise that has been missed.

This is true not only of the meditative state itself, but of the meditative view of the present moment. The very sunlight, the white-capped sea, and the waving long-leafed branches of summer burst with the vitality of realization, for they dwell as do all things within the consciousness of love and are part of the one original Thought. Thus, one who is in a contemplative state, watching not the shiny face of illusion, but the face of the Creator within each illusion, may see that one original Thought in color after color, distortion after distortion. Some distortions may seem horrible and some wonderful, yet all are the Creator and realization lies within each moment's burden of love which is infinite to the discerning spirit.

Love cannot be seen by those who are not willing to open and call upon the consciousness of love. Thus, there is always the leap, shall we say, of faith that states as a necessary assumption that the mystery behind all the things that are not is in the end the one thing about the illusion which cannot be denied—that is, love. We may talk about the terrible distortions of love, we may drag the name of love through the dirt of every battle and war that has ever been fought, we may deprive love of every satisfaction it has ever been given by poet or musician, yet there is not one honest spirit that can deny the palpable effect of love within the life experience.

Thus, the leap of faith is not so great, but only an optimistic telling of what each entity knows is the most creative and powerful force, illusory or real, within the creation.

There is always something in the present moment to spark the heart and engage the passion of a seeker, for there is always a chance for adoration, forgiveness or some expression of the love of the one infinite Creator. This is one thing which we wish to say, for when many things are in doubt about one's perceptions, it is well to move to the only perception which has a central part in the evolution of spirit.

The other thing we wish to say, we apologize for not being able to work in in a clever way, but we do not believe it is central. It is only that we perceive that there is a difficulty which we may address, and thus perhaps be of service. That difficulty which we perceive is the acceptance of anyone's point of view, including one's own, as being of an importance which loses sight of the perspective of eternity.

My children, many are the things which shall pass through your conscious minds in the infinite amount of, what you call, time that exists for you as a conscious being. Many are the arenas you shall enter and leave, many are the life experiences which shall store up for you ten things which you have learned which will help you become of greater service and ten million things which you have learned which are of no use whatsoever once the incarnation has been processed.

Thus, it is well to care not more, but rather less about the thinking, the rightness, the probabilities, the future and all the many, many things which go into the intricate design of creating a lived life day by day. Turn, rather, to questions such as, "What is the motive? What service am I performing? What gift may I give? What consolation may I offer?" for consolation, justification, and all human gratification, if we may use that term, whatsoever shall come not from seeking, yet but seeking rather to offer aid to others. This is unfortunate from the standpoint of these within an incarnation, but we may suggest—and again this is not a central point—that from the standpoint which we hold as those called to offer inspiration, that …

(Pause)

I am Q'uo, and am again with this instrument. We apologize for the delay, but this instrument was unwilling to proceed due to its own concern that it was becoming too great a portion of the message.

And again we say to this instrument, if we may take the time, and we thank you for allowing us to do that, that it is well for this instrument to focus upon the contact and to accept the responsibility for a portion of conscious channeling, rather than to refrain from allowing any organizational abilities which this instrument has in profusion to be allowed to surface. It is not helpful to the contact, and, indeed, we are having some difficulty with the instrument. Perhaps this instrument needs to listen to this message, for if it is true that all seekers need to focus not on what is not, but upon what is, and to judge not the self or others, but seek only the best intention and service. Then is this not particularly so for those who seek to serve by offering the service of vocal channeling? Is pride or humility, indeed, any stance regarding the illusion, acceptable or as acceptable to the self as the allowing of freedom to the self in faith that that which is is, that love is not only true, but infinitely powerful; light, not only verity, but infinitely capable of anguish and darkness?

Where is there room for fear in a life lived in faith? And if there is no fear, then there is freedom. You see and deplore fear in others. Take it not upon yourselves. Limit not yourselves, but in true humility take upon yourself the yoke of one who serves, and serve in the name of the infinite Creator—no finite creator shall you serve, my children, for why would you? You seek infinity, power, truth and eternal peace, the peace of unity, and all those things are yours only as you manifest them, only as you believe them, thus manifesting to yourself, only as you open your eyes in faith and thus shine not your light, but your greater Self's light to others. Why should you accept human limitation and lack? You are channels for the infinite Creator and infinite things are your birthright and ours.

We apologize that we have had to stop and go in this channeling, yet we are grateful for your patience, and would at this time transfer to the one known as Jim. I am known to you as Q'uo. We transfer.

(Jim channeling)

I am Q'uo, and greet each of you again through this instrument. We are pleased at this time to be able to offer ourselves in the attempt to speak to any query which those present may desire to place before our consideration. Again, we remind each that our words are but our humble attempt to be of service, and we wish their fallibility to be well known. May we now ask if there might be a query with which to begin?

S: Yeah, I have one. If you are sending out what you think is your love to someone, and it is perceived as causing harm, what do you do? You can't send out more love, because it is perceived as something that will harm, and yet to stop sending that love is not good for the person who is the sender. What do you do in that space and in that time until some perception, some something is changed?

I am Q'uo. We consider your query carefully, my sister, for to speak in general terms to a query which has specific implications can be misleading. We ask that each seeker which desires to give that known as love as the finest of its gifts to another or others be made aware that there will be misperceptions in each effort to serve, for within your illusion you move in a darkness of knowing that seeks light, and you move in this darkness in order that light might be brought into it in a manner that is free and powerful, pure and ever-flowing.

By this we mean to suggest that the nature of one's being begins in mystery, moves through darkness, and seeks light, for all portions of the Creator which find themselves conscious and pursuing a path of service seek this light that is the one Creator, and seek to manifest it in the form that you know as love. And each portion of the one Creator, then, that partakes of this journey is unique in its seeking, in its being and in its sharing. That which is yours to give is yours to discover as well. Much may be discovered in seeking to give, and yet if that which is discovered be true, then one can do none else but give what is one's to give.

We find that in your holy works there is the phrase, "Bread cast upon the water," that is appropriate in this instance. When one gives with the pure desire to be of service, one also assumes that that giving, in order to be purely of service, must be given freely, with no desire or dedication to a particular return or outcome for the giving.

This means that the giving and the desire to continue in the giving will find the tests, shall we say, in which the query shall be asked in symbolic form to each who desires to give that of love, and the query shall be, "Do you wish to give when the giving is not well received or is even refused, perhaps ignored?" In this way the heart of love, shall we say, is offered the opportunity to give under what you may call adverse circumstances which offer the opportunity for strengthening the desire to give.

Thus, the movement through your illusion will oftentimes find the difficulties which may seem to be insurmountable and which will confuse the seeker at many a turn. Yet we remind each that what is provided within your illusion is the opportunity to give without consideration of return. This shall, in many instances, provide a blessing which is not seen as such at the moment it is provided, for many within your illusion feel the goal of the incarnation is a peaceful harmony in which misperceptions are removed, and yet we might suggest, my sister, that it is in the difficult times in which misperceptions abound that the work of the incarnation proceeds rapidly apace, and in these situations the ability to give is strengthened and will provide resources that will allow the giving in what you would call your future to be refined by the continued kindling of the desire to serve and to know love in order that it might be shared ever more freely.

May we respond in any further fashion, my sister?

S: Well, there's two things. I may be splitting hairs and getting caught up in analyzing, but to me there is a difference between freely giving of love without any expectations of it falling on gravel or fertile soil or anything else, and freely giving of love and knowing, because you have been told, that it causes pain, so that your consciousness knows and your subconsciousness knows now that what you give causes pain, then it is no longer a gift freely given, but pain freely given.

Carla: Isn't that kind of like "pearls before swine?" Just put that on the end of her question.

S: To me there is something about that that seems somehow tied in with a very distorted view of martyrdom. It gets very tangled, and I may be confusing things that shouldn't be confused, although if I am thinking them, then they exist. But I feel so incredibly caught between knowing that I want to give because that is how I am, without any sense of martyrdom, just simply how I am, and yet causing pain which is something that destroys me, that thought of causing pain. I don't know what to start doing. It is difficult to just wait. I am caught in a very peculiar time/space frame warp like I've never felt before in my life and I don't know what to do about it.

I am Q'uo, and we might hopefully without infringement, my sister, suggest that the situation of which you speak is one which has presented the tangle …

(Side one of tape ends.)

(Jim channeling)

I am Q'uo, and am again with this instrument. The puzzle for the moment confuses much of that which is desired and that which is possible for you to provide in the service to another. We cannot speak in a specific fashion to direct your footsteps or your mind in a way which would work the puzzle for you, for this puzzle, as well as all others that are encountered within an incarnation, are a portion of that which you have chosen to solve as a part of the incarnation and your desire to be of service to others.

We might suggest that, when one is convinced that the efforts one has given in love and the desire to serve seem to produce that which is painful and deleterious to continued growth together, that the gaining of a perspective upon the interaction and the relationship is that which may allow portions of the puzzle to become more clearly delineated and allow a working at a time which you would call your future, for the life pattern contains the constant opportunity for those services that are possible and those lessons that are desired, to find the full range of movement and realization for each seeker, the perspective that one may [have] at such moments as you now experience. This perspective may be gained in a variety of ways and it may be necessary that both time and space be placed between your current experience and the future resolving of the puzzle.

(Pause)

We find some difficulty in speaking here, for it is our desire that we not infringe upon the free will in providing our point of view. We apologize for the delay. This instrument is having some difficulty maintaining its concentration. We shall attempt to continue.

The perspective is not that which may be considered a product of the intellectual realm, but is that which might be pursued most fruitfully within the meditative state during which the effort is bent toward receiving the insights from the subconscious mind which await release as the conscious mind in its daily round of activities ponders that which is the puzzle.

We might, therefore, recommend that the meditative state be utilized to build a pathway to the subconscious mind, and that this pathway be traveled on a regular basis with the intent to retrieve those pieces of the puzzle which await discovery within. This process may be enhanced by combining the dreaming state and the information that can be gained in that state with the fruits of the meditative state so that the working of the puzzle becomes primarily a subconscious process that is aided by the conscious mind only in the providing of the more and more intense desire to know where one's feet may find love in the daily round of activities.

Thus, we might suggest, my sister, that the conscious mind has provided that which is its to provide in this instance, and may now be joined in the effort by the seeking to fashion the pathway to the subconscious mind for the directions that will allow the appropriate piecing of the puzzle which you now find yourself searching for.

May we respond further, my sister?

S: Would you care to give me any particulars on how to build the pathway using the dream state?

I am Q'uo, and we might suggest the general use of the dreaming state is that which allows the seeker to use the subconscious mind such as one of your computer programmers would utilize the computer. The conscious mind is aware of the situation that presents the puzzle. It then, through its desire to solve the puzzle, provides that which it has gained of knowledge to the subconscious mind, and that information, when charged with the desire to find the path of love for the seeker, shall return to the seeker in what you call dreams that are coded in a symbolic fashion,

To become aware, then, of these messages from the subconscious mind is the goal of remembering the dreams. One may learn this skill by reminding the self upon retiring for the evening that each dream shall be remembered and recorded as soon as possible upon its completion. These dreams and their coded messages then may become the topics, shall we say, for the meditation of the day. In this fashion, the subconscious mind is programmed to release information which may serve to reveal more and more pieces of the puzzle so that the feet may be placed more firmly upon the path of love.

May we speak further, my sister?

S: No, thank you.

I am Q'uo, and we thank you, my sister. Is there another query at this time?

Carla: No, thank you.

I am Q'uo, and we are greatly appreciative of the opportunity for joining with this group this evening. We are aware that there is much which concerns each within the group and we share the concern of each to find the fullest expression of love and service within the life pattern that is possible at any moment. We feel a great sympathy for each, for we are aware of the difficulties that each experiences within the illusion that seems overwhelming and confusing for a great portion of the incarnation, and yet we encourage each to remember that this trial and testing is that which each has come to experience, for by experiencing the confusions and difficulties and moving through them with faith that there is a purpose for each that can be realized within the life pattern, each may then go forth with the strength of this knowing and continue the search for love in each moment, knowing that, indeed, the one Creator has made each moment of that fabric of love, and the greater the confusion that seems to separate the perception of the seeker from that love, the greater the opportunity to gather an abundant harvest of love within the incarnational pattern. If there were no difficulties, my friends, there would be no opportunities to find and to share that of love, for it would be obvious to all that love was the only choice.

We join each of you in your seeking and remind each that we are available in your meditations for the deepening of your meditation as each seeks to seat the love which has been found within the being, and as each seeks to make sense of that which is confused. We seek with you in the simplicity of love and in the unity of light. We shall leave this group at this time. We are known to you as those of Q'uo. We leave you in the love and in the light of the one infinite Creator. Adonai. Adonai vasu borragus. ❦

Sunday Meditation
January 11, 1987

Group question: "Q'uo: You have asked us to discuss the paradox of opposite emotions. 'Why,' you ask, 'is there both joy and sorrow?'"

(Carla channeling)

I am Q'uo, and I greet you in the love and in the light of the one infinite Creator. It is a great blessing to share your meditation with you, and we humbly thank you for allowing us to partake in the vibrations which are so beautiful a part of the creation, for each of you creates a beautiful harmony and symphony with all of the colors and tints, hues and shades of emotion, thought and action with which you weave the tapestry of your lives. In meditation, each energy center, as this instrument calls it, flows more and more, and clearly, colorful and beautiful to our perception, with the aura sharing so beautifully that unique gift which is each entity's to offer to itself, for each which sees beauty is also of that beauty, and we thank you for the rare privilege of seeing so lovely a reflection of the Creator we are, all as you sit in the light of your circle, radiant and at peace.

Yet, what makes you at peace at this time is not what you have asked us to discuss. You have asked us to discuss the paradox of opposite emotions. "Why," you ask, "is there both joy and sorrow?"

As we gaze at each beautiful glittering aura, at the amazing complexity of shading, shape and brightness, each entity quite perfect and unique, we can only praise the Creator for such spiritually helpful paradoxes, for it is through the stress of unacceptable things that the finest and most extreme emotions, thoughts and actions may be brought out of an entity. And as the Creator can only become Self-conscious by gazing at the infinite numbers of reflections that are the consciousnesses given free choice, the Creator sees brighter, deeper and ever more glorious faces. And once again, each time an entity chooses to use the experience of joy in a productive way or to use a difficult experience productively, the greater self of that entity cheers, knowing that the Creator has again chosen to express Itself in a more coherent and unified manner, for all of evolution in the spiritual as well as in other senses seems to us, in our opinion, to move in a purposefully positive way, each choice for crystallization moving and polarizing the entity more and more.

This is our attempt at explaining why there is joy and why there is sorrow, but not why there is a paradox. In order to grasp the necessity of paradox in any limited expression of the inexpressible, one must first realize the profound mystery of the Creation itself. In terms of grasping an ultimate mystery, those who use words, and, to a great extent, those who use concepts to communicate, are completely unable to grasp truth. There is no polarity, nor is there sense. Sense consists of the organization of random effects so that coherence may be established. This is indeed the discipline of the personality.

The mind of your conscious self is able only to deal with sense. Therefore, it is extremely common among your peoples to see the Deity Itself in a polarized fashion. All of your illusion depends upon polarity, and not yours alone, but a large portion, indeed, a considerable one of the total experience of which we are at this present moment aware. Thus, the physical and metaphysical laws, shall we say, or descriptions of the way things are arranged, must include polarity of all kinds and the concept of oppositeness. The either/or nature of your experience is designed to enable the decision-making process that, as each entity moves through the density of choice, each choice has the chance of being a firm and serious choice, one highly polarized, making one a more conscious person.

Thus, all of the emotions may be found to have the opposite, and, indeed, in some way, include and evoke the opposite shadow, for has there been pure joy without sorrow? Or unadulterated sorrow without some fond or joyful shade?

As the seeker becomes able to grasp the intended use of both joy and sorrow, the seeker may then balance joy with sorrow and sorrow with joy, sickness with health and health with sickness, in all experience of polarized nature whatever, finding in any polarity of seeming catalyst a free choice for the emotion expressed in experience. It is rare for seekers to find it easy to master this discipline, but the problem of polarity being a central lesson for love and wisdom and balance between them shall be with you for a long portion of experience, and it is well to begin the process of either/or so that in each choice you may become a bit more balanced, a bit more compassionate, and a bit more aware of the full consciousness of love which created both joy and sadness and polarity itself, for in the end, if we can find joy an occasion to worship and sadness an occasion to praise, we shall once and for all have learned a central lesson of consciousness.

We leave you, delighting in the joysome and riotous symphony of planets, stars, galaxies and infinite constellations. We are grateful for the intensity of your seeking, and shall be with any which shall request our presence during meditation, that we may in silence kneel within the heart and bow before the perfect whole and unified creation which is All and in All.

We are those of Q'uo. We ask, as always, that you take no thought for any idea which may have been offered by us which you find unhelpful. We are far from infallible, and are imperfect and most humble in our offering to you of our opinions. We thank you again and again, and must reluctantly leave this channel. We would transfer at this time. I am Q'uo.

(Jim channeling)

I am Q'uo, and greet each of you again in love and light through this instrument. At this time it is our privilege to attempt to be of service by asking if there might be any queries?

H: Yes, I have just a small question, you might find, but this aura that keeps coming up, that can be seen with certain photography, is this aura related or connected to the soul as we understand the soul?

I am Q'uo. We might suggest that the aura, as you have called it, is a reflection, shall we say, not only of an entity's current ability to blend mind, body and spirit in its present incarnation, but is also a reflection of an entity's seeking throughout its entire series of incarnational experiences so that that quality which you call the soul brings into incarnation certain abilities and propensities that then become the foundation, shall we say, of the current incarnation's study. Therefore, when one looks upon the manifestation known as the aura, one may see a register of a seeker's current and previous attempts to blend the evolution of mind, body and spirit.

May we speak further, my brother?

H: No, that does it pretty good. Thank you.

I am Q'uo, and we thank you, my brother. Is there another query?

R: Yes, if you please. We are learning from various sources that perhaps the end of an age or the end of a civilization could be transpiring, and it seems as though we need perhaps words of encouragement as to how to consider this and how to accept it, not perhaps what to expect as such, as how do we as seekers of light, how do we respond so that we can remain strong, steadfast? What can we do?

I am Q'uo, and, my sister, you have queried upon a large subject which each seeker may find it shares with all others, yet which it might also find is reflected in the personal pattern of experience in a unique fashion. In general, we might suggest that each seeker remember the one Creator in each daily experience by spending time communing in the meditative state with the source of all cycles, all changes, and all movement in the evolutionary process. Such time spent in meditation allows the seeker to fashion a regularized channel, shall we say, through its own subconscious mind to those sources of power, shall we say, which manifest themselves as love and light, or compassion and wisdom in the metaphysical sense, and when contacted in a regular fashion become an unseen foundation upon which each day might be constructed.

For some the meditative state is aided by prayers, by the giving of praise and thanksgiving for that which is the seeker's to share with others that day, and perhaps with the study of information which the seeker finds of inspirational and instructional value. Thus, with this regularized framework of study and inspiration, the seeker prepares the incarnational self to receive those lessons and to provide those services which are its to experience, and to share, not only for the day, as you call it, but one after the other for the entire incarnational experience.

Thusly prepared, the seeker may move through its incarnational experiences empowered by the faith that there is purpose and direction to the life pattern, and that that which comes before the seeker's notice is appropriate and full of purpose and opportunity to learn and to serve. Thus, no matter what experience might find its way into the incarnational pattern, the seeker thus empowered by faith and the desire to learn and serve may look upon each experience as being yet another opportunity for the Creator to know Itself and to be served and glorified by the seeker that has the will and faith to penetrate the outer appearance of things and to find at their heart the love and the light of the one Creator.

May we speak further, my sister?

R: That is very, very explanatory. I'm quite inspired. Thank you.

I am Q'uo, and we thank you, my sister. Is there another query?

Carla: I've got one I'd like to stick in because of hers. I have a theory, which I haven't asked about yet, that I'd like to, that the reason that the Confederation contacts keep urging us to look on the praise and thanksgiving side of things, and not to go get mountain camps where the disasters won't happen, is that positive energies go into the planet, just like all of the negative energies went into it that made it what it is today. And if enough people are afraid and start preparing, they might hasten the day. Is that possible? That we actually heal the planet a little by trusting it?

I am Q'uo, and, in general, my sister, we find that you have begun to uncover the basic nature of your illusion, that is, that one within the illusion will perceive the experiences of the incarnation in a manner which is congruent with what one believes about the experience that it has. This is to say that as one moves through the incarnational pattern, all experience that comes before the notice of the seeker has the potential to be viewed in either, what you may call, a positive or radiant fashion, or the negative, magnetic fashion. This assumes that all events contain the unity of the one Creator and therefore will be perceived in the fashion which the perceiver chooses.

Thus, if one's mind is filled with the fear of a certain event, and this fear has power enough within the being of the entity, it will begin to color, shall we say, the way in which the entity perceives more and more of its illusion and experience within the illusion.

Thus, it becomes necessary at some point for the seeker to choose the manner by which it will view those experiences of which it finds itself a part. These perceptions, then, have the power to transform experience. This is why the messages which we and others of the Confederation of Planets in the Service of the One Creator [offer] always stress the benefit and necessity of regular meditation in order that the nature of the illusion in which each finds itself moving might be made more clear and coherent to the inner eye, and thus be seen as the infinite manifestation of one Being, the one Creator.

May we speak further, my sister?

Carla: No, that was quite beautiful. I thank you very much.

I am Q'uo, and we thank you, my sister. Is there another query?

H: I have a query, one more. At the end of [the] cycle we're in right now, the seventy-five thousand year cycle, just how gradual will it be? Will it really be noticeable among the population, that something is definitely wrong with the world?

I am Q'uo, and, my brother, we might suggest that the transition, as you would call it, has already begun and the perceptive eye may continue to notice that as your time continues to move, and events within the personal environment and the worldwide environment continue to transpire, that the general quality of thoughts having more effect upon the material world will be noticed, for the density of compassion, towards which you now move, is one in which the effect of the mind is immediate upon the personal experience and the environment. Thus, as one thinks, one experiences the effects of thought in a much quicker fashion. The movement has begun toward the vibrational change and is anticipated to continue for a greater portion of your time and experience than many who study this phenomenon have assumed.

We might suggest that it is a process rather than event, and, therefore, due to the cumulative effect of the free will of the population of your planetary sphere, the culmination of this process cannot be ascertained with any degree of accuracy, but may be understood to be expressing itself in each entity and event upon your planetary sphere so that those who have begun to become sensitized to the evolutionary process that each partakes of, each entity then will begin to notice that events and experiences seem to be filled with more intensity and potential for transformation.

May we speak further, my brother?

H: No, that explains that all right. Thank you.

I am Q'uo, and we thank you once again, my brother. Is there another query at this time?

T: Yes, I have a question, dealing with something a little bit different than the general line of questioning had to do. It has to do with manifesting either things or situations, people, or even a state of mind, a state of feeling about various things in our lives. I've been doing some study over the last year about how to manifest various things, various situations that you desire in your life. And most of the things that I've studied and read basically agree, and I would just like to get your comments on how we can manifest something in our lives that we desire.

I am Q'uo, and, my brother, we might suggest that desire has brought each into the incarnation. The power of the desire to experience your third-density illusion and the potential for transformation which it provides all within its boundaries is that which [each] present upon your planetary sphere has desired. The power of desire is that which moves each entity through each incarnation and each density or dimension in the eventual returning into unity with the one Creator. For, indeed, it is desire that has set the creation in motion, as the one Creator expressed the desire to know Itself and to do so by sending portions of Itself into the far reaches of what you know as the creation to experience all that may be experienced and to bring this experience as a harvest to the one Creator that It might know Itself in ways not available had it not desired to know Itself through Its many portions.

Thus, each entity within each density of the creation carries within it the same power of motivation and direction that empowers the entire creation—the desire to know, the desire to be, the desire to grow, to serve. This desire manifests itself in a workable fashion within your illusion as the qualities of what we may call will and faith. As an entity focuses the power of the will in any particular direction and empowers that will with the faith that what is willed or desired may be obtained, the entity then unleashes the power of desire to move itself in a certain direction for a certain purpose.

Thus, it is not a question of what is possible, but what one desires, for each entity may utilize the power of the will and the sustenance of faith to move itself in any direction which it chooses by its own free will choice.

May we speak further, my brother?

T: I have a comment—hopefully you'll comment on it. You're saying basically, then, that we are all the Creator and that whatever we focus our desire on we can bring to fruition by sustaining that desire …

(Side one of tape ends.)

T: … a lot of emotion behind a desire for a certain thing or situation or state of mind, then, is that a gauge by which we can gauge our own desire? I mean, I think I want something, but then if I'm not able to sustain a high level of emotion behind wanting it, can I pretty much take that as saying, well, I don't guess, at another level of my being, that I really do want that? Does that make any sense?

I am Q'uo, and we apologize for the delay, my brother. We might suggest that situation of which you speak is basically perceived correctly, for each entity is a complex expression of a variety of desires both preincarnatively chosen and chosen during the incarnation. These desires may have more or less power or focus of attention for each entity. Thus, if an entity has decided before the incarnation that it wishes to learn a certain set of lessons and provide a certain set of services, shall we say, and during the incarnation by the action of free will choosing decides that there are other areas in which it wishes to move its attention and focus its desire, there may arise a conflict within the subconscious mind of the entity so that that which has been chosen more recently works at cross currents, shall we say, to those basic qualities of choice made previous to the incarnation.

Thus, it is sometimes the case that an entity will find itself somewhat confused and unable to realize certain desires that it has chosen for itself. In such cases, the realigning of the entity's choices and their priorities is often a process which is speeded by the careful inward searching of what is truly of most value to the entity, for it is indeed so that the power of desire focused through the expression of will and faith provides an entity the ability to move itself as it chooses if its choices are fundamentally in harmony, shall we say, with its truest nature, that which has been brought with it into the incarnational experience.

Thus, for the most efficient expression and fulfillment of desire, it is well to know the self and those qualities which have become the foundation stones of the entity and which provide it a base upon which it might stand as it views the universe about it and chooses its path of moving through that creation.

May we speak further, my brother?

T: No, thank you very much.

I am Q'uo, and we thank you, my brother. Is there another query?

Carla: I'll give you one last question since nobody else has one. This is from J. I'll try to paraphrase it from her letter. She said it had occurred to her that the channel seemed a lot like the contact, and she wondered if those who channeled weren't wanderers channeling their true density selves.

I am Q'uo, and we find that though the supposition is one which may be correct in some cases, yet it is far too general in its application, for many instruments upon your planetary sphere at this time are from densities and portions of densities not available to their present incarnational experience and ability to contact in a reliable fashion. It is more nearly correct to suggest that those who offer themselves in service to others as vocal channels are able to provide information of a nature which is congruent with their own current level of seeking, thus attracting to themselves that which is in harmonic resonance with the nature of information which they have been utilizing within the life experience. Thus, as one learns, one may share that which has been found helpful to the self with others.

The most dynamic type of instruction is the personal experience, thus instruments may find that that which they have to share in the vocal channeling is oftentimes a reflection of the personal experience, and thus becomes a teaching and learning tool not only for the self, but for others within the evident reach of the self which serves as instrument.

May we speak further, my sister?

Carla: Not any further tonight. Thank you so much. Anybody else have questions?

R: Yes. Q'uo, I have heard and read and chanced to meet an entity by the name *(inaudible)*. By any chance are you teaching it or know of or of a form of that energy?

I am Q'uo, and as a grouping of entities into what you would call a social memory complex, we are of an origin which is exterior to your own planetary sphere. We are aware of many of the nature of the one of which you speak which have successfully moved through the various planes of experience which your planetary sphere offers as its third-density illusion. Many are those such as this entity who have learned well what is within this illusion and now offer themselves as teachers and guides, as you would call them, who are able to be of service by making contacts with vocal channels similar to the experience which each within this circle of seeking shares this evening.

May we speak further, my sister?

R: No, thank you. That answers it.

Carla: Is there any intention to the similarity of the two names. I noticed it too. Is there some *sympatico* vibe between you?

I am Q'uo, and there is no conscious intention upon our part to emulate or simulate the vibratory sound complex of another, yet all who seek to be of service in this manner share the desire to give that of love and light which it has been our privilege and honor to gain in our own journeys of seeking the truth. Thus, we find that the naming, as you call it, is a process by which we make ourselves more comfortable to those whom we contact, and do so in a manner which in some fashion represents our nature of being. Thus, the nature of our beingness may be similar to many who choose to be of service by establishing the mind-to-mind contact which is known among your peoples as the vocal channeling.

May we speak further, my sister?

Carla: No thank you.

I am Q'uo, and again we thank you, my sister. Is there another query at this time?

(Pause)

I am Q'uo, and we find that we have exhausted the queries at approximately the same time as we have exhausted this instrument. We are greatly appreciative at the opportunity to blend our vibrations with your own in this circle of seeking. We again remind each that we are but your fallible brothers and sisters who walk the same path as you, and we do not wish our words weighted overmuch. Take those which ring true and leave those that do not. We shall take our leave of this group at this time, leaving each as each is in the love and in the light of the one infinite Creator. We are those of Q'uo. Adonai, my friends. Adonai vasu borragus.

L/L Research

Sunday Meditation
January 18, 1987

Group question: "Ahbout Dey: … a Tibetan, and I greet you in the love and in the light of the One Who Is All. I thank you for allowing me to speak with your group. I am not a member of the Confederation of Planets in the Service of the Infinite Creator, nor am I a social being, but an individual as are each of you. I speak from an icy fastness far from humankind, and wish to contact this instrument for the purpose of sharing the joy of experiencing what I would call the end of the personal trail of my life. I have placed myself in my final resting place and will soon be gone from this Earthly habitation. My path has been strange, and I am most honored to be able to share with those who may share sympathy with me and wish me well, the story of my life."

(Carla channeling)

… a Tibetan, and I greet you in the love and in the light of the One Who Is All. I thank you for allowing me to speak with your group. I am not a member of the Confederation of Planets in the Service of the Infinite Creator, nor am I a social being, but an individual as are each of you. I speak from an icy fastness far from humankind, and wish to contact this instrument for the purpose of sharing the joy of experiencing what I would call the end of the personal trail of my life. I have placed myself in my final resting place and will soon be gone from this Earthly habitation. My path has been strange, and I am most honored to be able to share with those who may share sympathy with me and wish me well, the story of my life.

When I was a very young boy, I wished very much to be a girl, and my father was ashamed of me and gave me to a monastery near the *(sounds like)* Potulla. This may seem hard, yet it was my salvation, for in the monastery I saw good masters and bad masters but all sought not only the things of the world, but also and more importantly, the things of the spirit. And so, being young, ashamed and hoping for amendment with life, I blended quickly into the ceaseless prayer wheel of monastic existence. For thirty years I held a subservient place in the monastery, wishing for nothing more, for the simple things were more and more nourishing to me, and as I learned the discipline of myself my own company became more and more desirable.

When I was thirty-nine years old I was allowed to become a retreatant, one who contemplated constantly and alone.

When I was fifty-five I awoke one morning with itching feet and left my cave and started out walking. I desired to study more than I had studied in the monastery, for although I had contemplated for many years, I had not satisfied myself that I was free from karmic responsibility for my sexual aberration. I walked into China but did not find satisfaction there nor did I find satisfaction in India. But in India, in Singapore, I found a missionary who spoke to me of redemption, and so I studied redemption, and as I die, for I am now old, I am glad in my heart as if I were a still a young man that I have come to see redemption in all that lies around me.

Thank you for listening to my unremarkable story. I give you my name. *(Sounds like)* Ahbout Dey. This is not quite correct. We are sorry—the instrument is not capable of repeating correctly our syllables. It does not matter, for I have been alone, neither Buddhist nor Christian, for many years.

For thirty-three years, to be exact, I lived the incarnation of a solitary man. I witness that the Lord of my life is far more vivid than the sweetest tastes, sounds, feelings, thoughts or objects that are possible in the world. I rejoice at the dissolution of old bones and await the freeing of my perfect spirit. Neither Buddhist nor Christian, yet loving the sun of my day and the moon of my night, I come to my death as a bride to the wedding night, fearful yet full of gladness. It has eased my heart and mind to have one last human touch, and I bless you for having hearts that respond and understand that all humans are one together. When we are together, I will make myself known to you and we shall rejoice together as we do now. The Christ in me acknowledges and rejoices in the Christ in you. Farewell. Namaste.

(Carla channeling)

I am Q'uo, and I greet you in the love and in the light of the one infinite Creator. It is a privilege and a blessing to speak with you this evening, and we especially greet the one known as S. We wish to add immediately that the one known as Latwii wishes to greet this entity also through this instrument and through the instrument known as Jim at a later time. We had to say that to get the one known as Latwii off our collective backs.

The consideration which a seeker must do when faced with a question of service to another can be of necessity expensive, for true service is not an easy proposition. When one speaks of true service to another, it may be seen that free will is paramount. However, we would break down service-to-others questions into two kinds. There are service-to-other questions having to do with being of spiritual aid to another; there are service-to-other questions that have to do with aiding another in a non-spiritual fashion, at least in a surface or appearance sense. In no case is it acceptable for one who wishes to be of service to others to infringe upon free will. Thus, any service which is not requested by another is a service which may be suggested but not properly fulfilled without permission.

The question of service to another in a non-spiritual category such as the diet is, as the questioner may have surmised, not particularly important, for it is indeed the intention of being of service which is important metaphysically. Thus, if the choice be between carrots and cake, it is a matter of judgment and discussion.

We would emphasize always the value of communication. If there has been adequate communication on the subject of carrots and cake, for instance, the one doing the serving shall have the guideline of the entity's preference who is to be served. If the entity wishes to be aided but also wishes to be rewarded, it is then that the request has been made that one be the nurturer of the other, much as the mother would be to the child. It is acceptable for mothers to be very indulgent at times and very strict at other times, depending upon judgment. Thus, if the agreement has been made that one entity shall nurture another, the one who wishes to be of service may simply use its best judgment. If the agreement has specific instructions but it would be violating your own free will to fulfill the instructions, then the instructions must go unfulfilled, for your own free will is as valuable as that of the one whom you wish to serve.

We now move to the question of true service to another, that being that service which aids another entity in its spiritual evolution. It is helpful to see all events, situations and questions of service as having the potential for some spiritual aid. Take each service under brief analysis and evaluation to see if there can be an overriding metaphysical principle which may be of some help to the one whom you wish to serve. If that be so, and if free will is not abridged, then it is well to act according to your best perception of spiritual aid to another's evolution.

The life experience contains multitudinous small decisions which fade as does new dye into the soft pastels of remembered actions. As you gaze back upon those millions of things that you have done for others, attempt to remember those times when service had a metaphysical slant and realize that these are the important decisions to make, these are the services to value and carry out with the utmost of dedication.

Other questions are questions of nurturing. The mind complex of your peoples in your culture carries many, many demands which are not important. Once that is understood, if we may use that term, it becomes easier to give a priority to the importance of the decisions that you are making. There is the quantity of life within an incarnation to be considered, and quality of life within an incarnation to be considered. There is virtue and there is the joy of licentious behavior in celebration of the comedy of existence. One who does not enjoy iniquity may find it difficult to enjoy virtue, and we urge that those who nurture sprinkle rewards amongst the carrots.

Yet, if the entity whom you serve has other requests, and a fit of virtue comes upon it, then shall you enter a season in which the smallest service, the giving of the carrot instead of the cake, has new metaphysical meaning. Gauge the mood and the intention of the one whom you seek to serve by communication and agreement and value your own self and your other self as spiritual beings above all, who are acting within the illusion in such a way that outside of the illusion they will see that progress has been attempted during the life experience.

This instrument remains open, yet we find a lack of vital energy, and would at this time bless you and thank you for the great privilege of being allowed to give our poor opinions and to share the beauty of your vibrations as you sit in meditation this night. How we love each of you, yet the love pours through us, not from us. We ask that you take our words lightly, for we are fallible beings. We leave this instrument and this group in love and the infinite light of the one infinite Creator. We are known to you as Q'uo. Adonai. Adonai vasu borragus.

(Carla channeling)

I am Latwii, and I greet you in the love and in the light of the one infinite Creator whom we serve. We are so glad to be with your group this evening. We cannot tell you how long it has been since we were able to use this instrument. We speak to the one known as S frequently, but we are glad to do it through this instrument, and we also greet the one known as Jim and the one known as Carla, and even the one known as J. This is what is called a "tape letter." This instrument thought it was funny. We have nothing to say through this instrument, but only wish to keep working at adjusting our vibration so that eventually we may contact this instrument without discomfort. We have not gotten there yet, but will keep working on it as long as our patience and the instrument's neck hold out. For now, we will transfer with much anticipation to the one known as Jim. I am Latwii.

(Jim channeling)

I am Latwii, and greet each of you again in love and light. We are grateful to this instrument for allowing our contact. It has also been quite some time since we have been able to contact this instrument and we are overjoyed that we are able to speak our humble thoughts through this instrument and to this group. We thank each for allowing our presence and we hope that we might be of some small service by offering ourselves in the attempt to answer those queries which those present may feel worth the asking. May we at this time begin with a query?

S: Hello, Latwii. It's so good to hear you. I do have a question from R. When we first asked questions about the donuts it was some time ago and he has forgotten a lot, so he asked me if I would ask you about sweating. What it does for his illness and is more always better?

I am Latwii, and am aware of your query, my sister, and the query of the one known as R. We send our greetings to this entity as well and we may suggest that the exercise of the sweating is that which is most beneficial to one which wishes to remove from the physical vehicle those toxins which may accumulate in the daily round of your activities which include much that is of the deleterious nature in the foodstuffs, the waters, the air intake and the finding of the self within an environment which is altogether quite disharmonious from time to time.

The toxins which the physical vehicle stores in various of its organs are best released by the sweating technique when the sweating is undertaken in a manner which is regular and extensive, yet which does not exceed the body's ability to function. To be more specific, might we suggest, my sister, that the care be taken that the body fluids be not drained in such a manner that dehydration occurs for the entity who simply desires to remove the toxins yet desires to maintain the vitality of the physical vehicle. This amount of exercising of the sweating technique is that which each shall find the need to determine for the self, for there is the unique quality to each entity, and most especially to each physical vehicle, that requires that experimentation be undertaken to determine the amount of the sweating that might be tolerated without the dehydration and weakening of both physical and mental complexes.

May we speak further, my sister?

S: No, thank you Latwii, I'm sure that will be helpful.

I am Latwii, and we thank you and the one known as R. May we respond to another query?

Carla: This Ahbout Dey or whoever, is he going to tell us any more about his life? Or do you know any more about that? Can I know anymore about that?

I am Latwii, and the one of whom you speak is one which has for some time, as it is reckoned within your illusion, moved within a realm which is metaphysical in nature yet the entity has dwelt within your physical illusion for the greater portion of its physical incarnation. This entity has for a period of your time desired to make a contact with a physical group or entity upon this planetary sphere in order that it might satisfy the yearnings of its soul, shall we say, to have touched and to have been touched by those with whom it shared existence, though its sharing of existence was from a distance, shall we say.

The seeking of the one Creator for this entity has taken the form of finding that Creator within the silence and solitude of the personal experience of this illusion. However, this entity is aware that in order to complete the Earthly portion of its experience within this planetary influence, that it needed, in its own estimation, to ground that which had been learned by simply speaking of the experience that has allowed it to progress to its point of departure, shall we say, from this illusion. There is the possibility that this entity may desire further contact, although we might suggest the possibility at this point is small, as you would term it, for the entity moves rapidly toward the entrance to the larger life experience in which it shall find its abilities and desires focused in other dimensions.

May we speak further, my sister?

Carla: Would it help this entity if we read the *Tibetan Book of the Dead* for it?

I am Latwii, and we scan the entity and …

Carla: Let me finish the question, come to think of it, because he spoke of not being Christian or Buddhist. Would it help if …

(Side one of tape ends.)

Carla: To finish the question, would it, since he's sort of half Tibetan and half Christian, would it help to do either/or or both the *Tibetan Book of the Dead* reading or the *American Book of the Dead* reading or the Christian burial service from my Episcopal Church? Would that give him peace? The second part of the question on the other subject is, would he want to speak with us after he dies?

I am Latwii, and we apologize for the delay. This instrument found the need to accomplish that of the challenging and we now are free to speak again through this instrument, and in response to your query, my sister, we find that the entity of whom you speak is one which is not in need of the guidance for those whose eyes do not penetrate beyond the veil. This entity, for a great portion of what you would call your time experience, has been well aware of the metaphysical nature of the illusion in which it moved its physical vehicle, and has for a great portion of your time found a home within both the physical and the metaphysical realms, and therefore is quite conversant with the passage through which the metaphysical realm shall become its greater and complete experience.

We are unable to determine as to the future desires of this entity in regards to making contact with groups such as your own. We are, however, aware that this entity is greatly pleased with the contact which it has been able to share with this group, and wishes that each be aware of its gratitude and joy at this blending of energies for the brief period this evening.

May we speak further, my sister?

Carla: Just on the service of commemoration. Would this soul wish to have its death celebrated and sent on its way rejoicing which is pretty much what the Episcopal service does?

I am Latwii, and we find that the contact which was made this evening with this group by this entity was indeed a portion of that entity's commemoration of its incarnation, shall we say. The further commemoration of this incarnation by your own desires is that which is completely left to your own discrimination.

May we speak further, my sister?

Carla: No thank you.

I am Latwii, and we thank you, my sister. Is there another query at this time?

Carla: Does that mean that funerals as a whole are not appreciated by the dead person, but are held, indeed, for the comfort of the living? Pardon the nomenclature—I'm sure you understand.

I am Latwii, and we are indeed aware that there is a certain means by which the commemoration of the passing from an incarnation is described. Indeed, there is the multiple purpose to such commemoration. The entity moving through the doors of transition is frequently touched and moved and sent in joy upon its journey by such experiences as the funeral, the wake, the prayers, the singing and the placing of the physical remains within a certain location designated for such receptions. We are also aware that there is the need upon the part of those who remain to come together in the grieving for that entity which has gone on in order that the relationship with that entity be brought to a culmination and not be left, shall we say, hanging with the consciousness of those who remain.

The entity who goes on moves towards an existence which is a continuation of a larger pattern of being and the completion of a smaller portion of that pattern is a service, shall we say, to this entity and fills a need upon the part of those who remain to find their own completion.

May we speak further, my sister?

Carla: I'll have to read that. Thank you.

I am Latwii, and we thank you, my sister. Is there another query?

S: Well, Latwii, I have what may be a query. I've been feeling lately that in the *(inaudible)* years, R and I have made what seems to be several surprises—I know they weren't mistakes. It really gets aggravating, and I guess what I'm really hoping for is a shot in the arm here. Do you have anything up your sleeve?

I am Latwii, and we feel that we grasp the gist of your query, my sister. Indeed, many there are within your illusion which find surprises, as you call them, from time to time within the life patterns. Indeed, only those who have failed to rouse the self from the slumber of the third-density illusion to any degree whatsoever are those who live a life devoid of surprise, for those who seek in the conscious fashion the riddles to the evolutionary process and the movement into mystery the discovery of the surprises will become an experience that is repeated time and time again. For though little is truly understood within your illusion, all moves in a pattern of completeness and wholeness, and in a pattern which before the incarnation was quite apparent to each, and which each willingly placed the self in in order that certain tendencies and biases might be either balanced or accentuated according to the overall needs of the development of the soul.

Thus, the illusion is entered with the desire to progress in a manner which is not possible without the experience of the illusion. Those times of difficulty, of confusion, of the traumatic occurrence, and of the totally unexpected nature of the manner in which events fall in the pattern of the life are those times which before the incarnation are seen as treasures, my sister.

It is known that during the life experience within the third-density illusion that quite the opposite point of view shall be experienced, and it is known before the incarnation that one shall have to work carefully with this point of view, for it sees through a glass quite, quite, quite darkly, and what it sees is most often out of focus at least 180 degrees, for that which is of difficulty during the incarnation is seen as that which hopefully shall be minimized, perhaps even avoided. However, prior to the incarnation these difficulties are seen as those experiences which will allow the entity to test its own ability to perceive and to bring forth into the incarnation those qualities which it wishes to develop, much as you would develop a muscle of your physical vehicle by exercising it time and again. The difficulties then exercise a spiritual muscle which in the realms of harmony and joy tends to grow somewhat lax and loses its tone, shall we say.

Thus, if you should during an incarnation attempt to measure your experience and your progress in worldly terms, you shall become disillusioned and fail to see the overall perfection, humor and harmony of that experience which may seem difficult and confusing within the incarnation. Thus, we suggest judging not the self or another self or the progress of any, for as you judge, thus you are yourself judged by those worldly measurements which cannot begin to encompass the nature of the illusion in which you move and the purpose for which you have entered it and the goals that you have set for yourself.

Thus, the ability to retain the light touch, my sister, and to accept that which seems unacceptable are the attitudes that are most helpful, we have found, in dealing with those times which seem to be less than desirable. If this incarnation and this illusion were all that existed for any entity, then each would truly be in, shall we say, the hottest water. However, we may suggest that there is a stream of beingness that moves before, through and beyond this third-density illusion, and it shall carry you further and further toward the source of all being as you are able to accept in joy each experience that comes before your notice, for each experience is that which you had hoped for and planned for and girded your loins for and is that which shall tone and test your spiritual muscles and perceptions.

May we speak further, my sister?

S: Thank you, Latwii, for that two-by-four. It felt wonderful.

I am Latwii, and we thank you, my sister, and we hope that we have not given you any splinters.

Is there another query at this time?

Carla: Well, it did bring up something I had been meaning to ask about before I get the book out that I'm writing, and that was something I put in the book was that I felt that people who meditate go through more changes more quickly than people that don't meditate. It's a problem if you have a couple where one meditates and one doesn't because the one who meditates is going to start changing faster and there's going to be all kinds of problems there. And I wondered if that were true?

I am Latwii, and, indeed, my sister, we have found that this is so, most especially within your third-density illusion, for within this illusion, as we have previously spoken, the perceptions are clouded by that which is of unknowing to such a profound degree that when one utilizes the tool of meditation and begins at the deeper levels of the subconscious mind to clear the way of beingness in order that it might make itself known and felt and begin to undergird the incarnation, then the entity thus engaging itself within the meditative state upon a regular basis begins to be powered by a source of being which is far more subtly profound, shall we say, within the incarnative pattern than any influence within the illusion, that the entity is changed, shall we say, in its basic perceptions so that the general run of experience in the life pattern is perceived in a fundamentally different fashion from those whose primary focus is within the mundane reality.

Thus, the entity engaging in a sincere and dedicated fashion in the practice of meditation and contemplation and the prayerful attitude is an entity which is less moved by the turbulence, shall we say, of the daily round of activities, and will see these activities in a manner which begins to penetrate beyond the outer appearance of things and moves towards the heart. This type of perception differs markedly from that perception which does not move beyond the exterior shell of the daily round of activities and which focuses instead upon the seeming importance of mundane details.

May we speak further, my sister?

Carla: No, thank you, Latwii.

I am Latwii, and again we thank you, my sister. Is there another query?

Carla: Not from me, thank you.

S: Well, I've got a million, but I didn't bring my list so I'll save them for another time.

I am Latwii, and we are most happy to have been able to speak to this group this evening, and we look forward to each of the million queries which remain, for this means that we shall be able to speak many, many more times to this group, and hopefully be able to crack a few more jokes through this instrument, and perhaps apply another two-by-four or two. We hope that each will remember that our words are not infallible in any degree. We are your fallible brothers and sisters of Latwii—you know us well, we can't kid you. We leave each of you at this time in the love and light in which we have found you and in which each at all times dwells. There we dwell with you. We are known to you as those of Latwii. Adonai, my friends. Adonai vasu borragus.

(Carla channeling)

I am Nona, and would sing of love and light and healing. We come in the power and love, the light and joy of the infinite Creator.

(Carla channels a vocal healing melody from Nona.) ❧

Sunday Meditation
January 25, 1987

Group question: What style of life makes one more adaptable to the spiritual journey, whether it might be the more community oriented lifestyle of the Communist China where the individual is programmed and taught to think of the welfare of the group, or the type of lifestyle of the hermit who lives secluded for years contemplating the Creator, or the style of life that we ordinary American citizens enjoy where we have many temptations and ability to express ourselves in whatever way we choose?

(Carla channeling)

We are known to you as Q'uo. We greet you in the love and in the light of the one infinite Creator whom we as you do serve. With the Creator's blessing do we bless each and greet each and with our own love may we also greet you as brothers and sisters.

The question that you have asked poses an interesting problem to us, for in answering we must change your question. We cannot speak to you concerning the structure of your communism as opposed to the structure of your capitalism in regards to the spiritual benefits of either because government is not of the ray wherein spiritual concerns are addressed.

The nature of spiritual programming is that it overrides all other programming, changing the perceptions of the entity which is working within spiritual programs of thought, so that regardless of the experiential catalyst which greets the seeker the seeker perceives a spiritual question and attempts the appropriate spiritually motivated action in response.

The key to understanding why communism, which is a direct mundane analog of your religiously based community—for example, the Essenes, the Christians, and the Hindus—is nevertheless placed in the position of governing. The tools of the government are persuasion and force. It is hoped by governments that emotional responses such as patriotism shall encourage a spiritual response to a mundane and illusory web of social structure. In many spiritually oriented people this patriotism does indeed lend a harmonizing, solidifying influence to any government.

However, the communist can experience either complete freedom or complete slavery within the communistic way of life, as can the capitalist. The perceptions govern the experience, not the catalyst. Similarly, though it may seem that the communism offers a simpler life, in actuality it is the rural nature of life lived under any governmental system, with its shorter lists of places to go and people to see, which enable the spiritual oriented seeker to nurture the spiritual orientation which he may wish to aid.

When any rule of life becomes a law within the life experience, but not one with the consciousness of those metaphysical principles which are eternal, one has removed [it] from the system, from the range, of spiritually reliable, useful tools for spiritual growth. It is to be noted that the so-called monasteries are responses to the felt need of those who have begun working upon spiritual energies to the point where the choice is made to sacrifice all portions of the life experience which do not feed into the greatest possible spiritual content of life. Thus, the sacrifice is the cornerstone for the development which ensues. Few monasteries are located within your cities, and even these few maintain an artificially simple lifestyle. Thus, you may see that the spiritual choice is to retreat from both the world and the government.

When one gazes at the communist experience, one may find many groups of shamanic and other entities which without the approval of the government meet to attempt some spiritual seeking. Thus, neither can government can aid in spiritual seeking nor shall any government which may govern humans, if we may use that word, in the third-density state of unpolarized experience, also hope to govern a reliable promotion of spiritual seeking. The choices for social government by law must rely upon the lowest possible level of excellence, shall we say, the greatest possible swing of error, so that whatever action is undertaken amongst humans, there shall be a governing principle.

The law which is interesting and profitable to the spiritual seeker is a law which the seeker hopes shall become more and more able to be perceived by all seekers, and certainly by all seekers within a spiritually oriented community, as one law so that spiritual government is government by complete individual consent. Thus, any one entity would be able to help such a government. This is considered unacceptably inefficient by those whose energies turn to the government of your peoples, and understandably so.

There is one element, we may say, of the concepts involved in capitalism which is to our opinion a metaphysical principle of some degree of excellence. That principle is not fully respected at this time among your peoples, yet we observe that the concept of freedom is indeed valued by each which dwells within your capitalistic society. It is excellent that freedom is taught, yet, for spiritual seeking, it is to be remembered that one is always free, for the world, indeed the creation, lies within the mind and the heart, and there is no government which may interfere with the polarizing done by the spiritual seeker except if the government destroy the physical body of the seeker. This may, for a particular seeker, be a great aid since, taking the larger view, that seeker may have completed the lessons it was to learn and may, by being a sacrifice to a principle, inspire others as is the way of spiritual seekers of excellence among your peoples.

We ask each of you always to turn your gaze at last from the creations of humankind, however lofty and beguiling they may be, however intellectually precise and fascinating, for that which lies within you is a dimly perceived holographic representation of one great original Idea, an idea which is a mystery. In the end, turn aside your face from gazing in the mirror of the world about you, and, in order to know yourself, seek the face of the Creator.

Why do you look within illusion for your true nature? Do you not wish to know the truth? The truth lies not among the fallow fields of men's imaginations and actions, nor within fine words or great governments, although great ideas and great philosophies both communism and capitalism feed. The truth about you lies within the mystery of the face of God, if we may use that term. The one thing which you have been taught is constant in a shifting and relative world is light itself, and yet we say to you that light is only the physical manifestation of an Idea that created all that there is. It is within the mystery of the Idea of love that the truth about you lies. There is no government that may help or hinder in the seeking of that face.

We would at this time transfer this contact. We thank this instrument for making itself available. We are known to you as Q'uo, and we transfer at this time.

(Jim channeling)

I am Q'uo, and we are pleased to greet you again in love and light through this instrument. At this time it is our privilege to offer ourselves in the service of attempting to respond to any further queries which those gathered may have value in the asking. We remind each that we offer but our opinions and ask that these be taken as such. May we begin with a query?

Carla: What would you say to someone who is having physical difficulties that make it kinda hard to get around and feel some despair over the future? Besides "don't do that"?

I am Q'uo, and we are aware, my sister, that this question has special meaning to your own experience. And we would suggest that it be remembered at all times that one moves within the limitless love of the Creator within this illusion in order that through your experience the Creator might become aware of the possibilities for love to be placed in situations that will require an increased experience of Itself in order to uncover that love which has been carefully hidden. Thus does the Creator find Its beingness expressed in your experience in manners vivid and pure as a result of the constant effort to uncover Its own face through your efforts.

Thus does the Creator move within the tiniest, the grandest, the most joyful and the most difficult of circumstances in order to enable each seeker at every portion of its journey to both become aware of the ever-present sustenance of the love of the Creator when appropriate and also to find those times within the experience of an incarnation when the price, shall we say, for such joyful discovery is far greater in order that that discovery might be imbedded more deeply and securely within the seeker's total being. Thus, one may see a relationship evolve in which the more difficult seeking provides the opportunity for the more deeply experienced and securely seated revelation of love and unity which ever underlie all experience. Thus, that which is cheaply bought is easily forgotten; that which bears the greater price is that which remains as sure foundation stones upon further experience and service of the One is possible.

May we speak further, my sister?

Carla: No. Thank you very much, Q'uo.

We thank you, my sister. Might there be another query?

H: Yeah, I have something I've been thinking about for a few months now. In our Bible, it's got in the last days that there will be the final conflict or the final war, the war of all wars. And after that it said there'll be something like a thousand years of peace. Could you elaborate on that statement?

I am Q'uo, and within this work of which you speak, we find the beginning recognition of the quality of existence that shall fall unto those who remain within the loving guidance, shall we say, of the free and joyful expression of love, one for another. Those who shall find their own experience producing the fruit of love and compassion shall enter upon a journey which, within the work you have described, was able to be perceived as the thousand years of peace.

Yet in truth, my brother, we might suggest that this time has no such shortened boundaries, but refers to a level of existence in which the love of the Creator becomes ever more apparent and powerful within the personal incarnation and is seen without doubt to be that which undergirds all creation and experience within the creation. Each entity within this level of experience shall find that the doors of perception are swung wide until the heart is filled full of the creative and compassionate energy of the Creator and is given freely to those about one in a fashion which knows no boundaries and is the result of the simple beingness and natural expression of that beingness for each seeker.

May we speak further, my brother?

H: No, that answers that quite well. I just have one more comment on the same statement. Would the seventy-five thousand year cycle actually end upon the end of this era, then?

I am Q'uo, and this is correct, my brother, for the cycle which is now reaching its culmination upon your planetary sphere has provided the opportunity for those within its boundaries to move the conscious perception of the creation far enough to allow a greater experience to follow. The ability of each seeker within your illusion has been developed to the point during its seventy-five thousand year cycle where it is now possible for each seeker to welcome and enjoy the greater intensity of light that shall be presented within the fourth-density experience.

May we speak further, my brother?

H: No, I think that took care of that. Thank you.

Carla: Okay, one last one for me. I wondered if you could comment on just what the spiritual impact of Shirley MacLaine's TV special was on the consciousness of this planet?

I am Q'uo. And we look upon the event of which you speak as that which is likened unto a great and shining light in a sea of darkness. Yet, if one perceives carefully this sea of darkness, one begins to note many lights flickering in various portions of the darkness. Each light burns of an intensity which each seeker has produced according to the desire to know that which you know as the truth. Events such as the airing of the program of which you speak are seen within the metaphysical realm as a great and shining light which for a brief period of your experience illuminates the darkness to the extent where all inhabiting that darkness are able for that moment to perceive carefully outlined shadows of truth. In this momentary perception and possibility for perception, the light which burns either dimly or brightly within all who inhabit your illusion finds a greater intensity possible for that moment that may, if empowered with personal desire to continue the seeking, allow the light to burn more brightly after the event has passed.

Many there are who find within the incarnation for the first time the opportunity to experience the birthing of desire to know what lies beyond the boundaries of previous perceptions. Many others who have felt this yearning begin are reinforced in their seeking to move their own consciousness beyond their self-made limitations of perceptions. Others who have yet to discover the desire to move beyond such boundaries consider for a moment that such might be possible, and though the thought passes quickly, each shall within the deeper being remember that moment in order that the momentary interest which was experienced might, at what you would call a future date, find another potential for birthing. And when enough of these opportunities have been noticed by the entity, there may in that entity be born that same desire to know the truth, and the light of that entity then will begin to glow ever more brighter, fed in even a small part by each experience which has been provided the entity within its incarnation to spark the beginning yearnings to know the meaning of the incarnation and of experiences such as the program of which you speak.

Thus, there can only be greater light result from light which is freely given. Its work moves at its own pace as is appropriate within each seeker's incarnation. When the student is ready the teacher, in whatever form, appears, be it a book, a person, a television program or experience within the daily round of activities.

May we speak further, my sister?

Carla: No, thank you.

We thank you.

H: I have one more question concerning Shirley MacLaine, about the gentleman named David. Did he ever have contact with Maya again, what he was so much seeking?

I am Q'uo, and am again with this instrument. We find that this entity has experienced the presence of the one of whom you speak in a fashion which is not the person-to-person physical vehicle contact, but which is that more of the nature now being expressed as we communicate our thoughts through this instrument. The entity, David, has satisfied itself that this is the most desirable form of contact for this time within its incarnational pattern. However, we cannot speak as to the future as you call it, for this [we] see as an infringement upon free will.

May we speak further, my brother?

H: No, thank you, that's all.

I am Q'uo, and we thank you, my brother. Is there another query at this time?

(Pause)

I am Q'uo, and we thank each for allowing our presence this evening. We have been very honored to be able to join this group and to respond to those queries which have been placed before us with loving care. We ask that if our presence be desired in your meditations that a simple request will find us joining you there. We shall leave this group at this time, rejoicing and giving praise that we are able to join you on your journey of seeking. We leave each in the love and in the light of the one infinite Creator. We are known to you as those of Q'uo. Adonai, my friends. Adonai vasu borragus. ❧

Intensive Meditation
January 28, 1987

(Carla channeling)

I am Laitos, and I greet you in the love and the light of the infinite Creator. It is a pleasure and a privilege to meet the one known as W. It is our function as members of the Confederation of Planets in the Service of the Infinite Creator to work with those who wish to be aided in their attempts to be of service as vocal channels, and it is a double privilege to be able to work with the channels already within this group.

We wish to create for the one known as W a protected space of time at this time in which this entity may safely dwell in silence while being willing to be made aware of the presence of those forces and principles which lie under the shelter and shadow of the name of Love and through Love may be able to aid in the funneling of energies into the appropriate configuration for the new instrument's most desired pattern of welcoming vibrations. With this aid more firmly in consciousness, it is then a matter of a shorter period of seeking until the moment patiently waited for occurs and one new piece of the puzzle is added, one more thing about the self is learned and one more portion of life experience may then be committed and dedicated in the service of humankind and of the infinite Creator of which all created things are but the reflection and image.

Thus, we would pause for a time that the one known as W may sit in the quiet and feel the loving company of those portions of the consciousness of love which are available for her comfort and expanded information. We now pause. We are of those known to you as Laitos.

(Pause)

(Carla channeling)

I am Laitos, and am again with this instrument. We greet you again in the love and the light of the infinite One. We are aware that the one known as W is alive to the energies of which we spoke and for this we are most grateful. We confess that we also have been working a bit with the instrument attempting to make our first contact with the instrument a comfortable one. For now we shall thank the one known as W and each in the group for the privilege of sharing the very essence of each being in the circle of love and seeking. We are happy to meet with any who request our presence during meditation, but we shall not speak. Our aid in deepening the meditative process is sometimes appreciated, as is the feeling of having company, and we certainly enjoy this service also. We leave each of you in the love and the light of the infinite Creator. We are known to you as Laitos and we leave you for now. Adonai. ✦

L/L Research

Intensive Meditation
February 4, 1987

(Carla channeling)

[I am Laitos, and] I greet you in the love and in the light of our infinite Creator. It is a privilege and a blessing to be called to this meditation, that we may offer our service of working with new instruments that they more and more fulfill their desire to be of service to the infinite Creator and to its reflections upon your sphere, the other human beings. The service of vocal channeling is one among many and we encourage each to evaluate it not only for the comfort with which each may offer this service, but also in terms of an honest opinion as to its relative degree of service, for there are many, many ways to be of service in a creation of love of which you are a part.

Love has many faces. And though the Confederation of Planets in the Service of the Infinite Creator comes always in the name of love and through the manifestations of light, yet nevertheless we value and treasure each new instrument whose mind and heart we may plunder of its many treasures of experience and previous knowledge. For our message is so simple as to go almost inevitably unnoticed and ignored, for all we have to offer is our opinion and belief that the Creator is all that there is, that each is the Creator, and thus all who dwell in the creation are not only part of the Creator, but a holographic representation or miniature of the Creator, thus becoming co-creators with the Father.

The unity of all things suggests many pleasant conditions which should be prevalent among all peoples, yet you will find that the value of channeled information in general is that it looks at the illusion of your experience with an eye which sees beyond the experience to the reality which lies behind the illusion, for it is our opinion that most of a life experience of an entity which dwells in your density consists in those things which are not visible to the eye.

We have been working with each to attempt to make as comfortable a connection as possible with each of you and would request that any experience of discomfort of any kind be mentally noted at once that we may work to mitigate whatever the problem may be. Do not let a stiff neck or an odd position cause discomfort, when the request will bring adjustment. It is not necessary to make the request in the manner this instrument is speaking—a mentally projected thought is all that is necessary.

We are concerned as we begin working with each that each realize that we are as you, seekers after truth, lovers after love. Our eye is fixed upon the ultimate, thus we are enveloped and fascinated by mystery. We do not know the truth, but have only approximated our opinion as to some of the truth's characteristics. Our words are not meant to be stumbling blocks or replacements for other beliefs, and if anything which we have to offer is unwanted, we ask that it be rejected without further thought. We wish only to serve.

We ask that the one known as N continue tuning, for we are having difficulty sustaining a contact with this instrument. If the instrument would cease observing and analyzing and for the duration of this experiment merely react as seems appropriate, the difference in the concentration level would be great and we would be far more easily able to make suggestions of concepts which need to be transmitted at any given moment.

We make the same request of the one known as W, noting that this instrument is at a more calm level but there is always the tendency to analyze within any channel and this instrument is all too aware of the difficult influences that analysis can create within the service of channeling. Thus, we ask that the one known as W also attempt a more automatic and non-thinking attitude for the experiment, realizing of course that discrimination is very important and that there shall be time after the experience thoroughly to assimilate and gauge it.

We shall begin with a period of attempting to make our name known to the one known as W. If the instrument will relax and refrain from analyzing, we shall at this time transfer contact to the one known as W. I am Laitos.

(Pause)

(Carla channeling)

I am Laitos. We thank the one known as W for working with us and would attempt once again to speak with this instrument clearly enough that this instrument may conceptualize and repeat the name by which we are known to those among your people. We feel that we are making good progress in achieving a stable and comfortable contact and are sorry about the minor difficulties. We are working to make the experience a comfortable one. We thank the entity for attempting the challenge and encourage the one known as W in the fearless use of its own ideals. We now transfer in love and light to the one known as W. I am Laitos.

(Wendy channeling)

I am Laitos. *(Inaudible)* I am Laitos.

I am Laitos, and greet you once again in love and light and great joy for we have a good contact with the instrument known as W and are most grateful to this entity for allowing us to work with her. We realize there are many metaphysical side-effects, shall we say, which may result and thus we do not attempt to repeat this experience any more than we would give two overdoses of a strong drug in one session. One will do. We can only assure the one known as W that the experience which comes from releasing a portion of the self to an opening in which the contact can be made will be mitigated by experience and time so that it will no longer seem like an incredible rush, but will merely be a settling in of a comfortable and established relationship between two personalities who love each other and respect each other.

We now turn to the one known as N. We thank the one known as N for working upon the meditative state. This entity has a great deal of capability in this area and is in a partial state of meditation often. However, it is not as comfortable with the terminology of meditation, shall we say, as the experience itself. We encourage one known as N to think of this state as one of free joyfulness, a joyfulness that does not demand any results, but merely exists for its own state. This joyful spirit which we experience in the one known as N shall surely be an entity which has the potential for a stable service and we welcome this opportunity to work with this new instrument.

Again we request that the one known as N lay down the tools of discrimination and thought and become the listening ear hearing in silence those thoughts too deep for words, which yet echo somehow within the consciousness. It is not in our control to compartmentalize the contact in such a way that we can know for all people what experiences shall occur with contact. We do not know how each new instrument will perceive our thoughts. The beginning instrument is not predictable. Thus we cannot tell you to listen for a voice or to recognize a presence, but can only say that whatever thought occurs immediately after the contact has been recognized and challenged is to be spoken forth without thought. Thought is left at the threshold of the contact after challenging and is picked up in all of its discriminative power upon the surcease of that same channeling. During the channeling the instrument is just that. Portions of the instrument's mind, opinions and heart are used to form the contact, yet the contact is a creation of cooperation, offering something that neither we nor the instrument could offer by ourselves. The instrument's position then is one of passive yet anticipatory readiness. Thus we ask the one known as N to put aside thought, refrain from analysis, and allow us to speak our simple identification through her instrument. We shall greet the one known as N as we leave this instrument. I am Laitos.

(Nancy channeling)

I am Laitos. Greet you entities. This instrument wants to share of her knowledge with the entities on your planet. She had contact before her regression [trance] and was not aware of that [experience]. I will leave this entity as not to overstress her. This entity known as N. I leave you entities. I am Laitos.

(Carla channeling)

I am Laitos, and greet you once again in the love and the light of the infinite Creator. Before we transfer to the one known as Jim, we would speak briefly through this instrument upon the subject of challenging.

This instrument is fond of saying that it is a crowded universe and the one known as N has had an experience with a crowd other than the Confederation of Planets in the Service of the Infinite Creator. It is salutary that such has occurred to this excellent instrument so that the point may be made that in challenging lies the strength of the instrument's ability to discriminate between possible sources of information.

The use of a name is either magical or non-magical. It is difficult for most entities to repeat a magical name that does not belong to them, however it is by non-magical names that almost all contacts are known among your peoples and this is certainly true among the Confederation of Planets. For we do not wish to use words of power unless the situation requires it. The names by which we are known to you, therefore, are not acceptable in and of themselves, for they may be repeated by others who are not of the Confederation of Planets. Given the negative polarities' perceived virtue in lying, it is a powerful aid to a negatively oriented entity to be accepted as an entity it is not.

There are signs for which one may watch. When one is evaluating the usefulness and worth of information which has been channeled, one characteristic of mixed contact, that is negatively oriented entities which channel using a positive name, is the tendency to make a personal connection with the channel and so make the channel feel more and more important. This occurred during the particular communication which the one known as N experienced. However, there are positively oriented contacts which have had personal contact by thought or thought form with a channel, thus far better it is to rely heavily upon the challenging and only after a declaration has been accepted and agreed upon can the channeling be done in the most confident and trusting manner.

We would at this time transfer to the one known as Jim. Without first giving thanks to the ones known as W and N, we could not leave this instrument, for it has been a marvelous experience for us and we feel very blessed to have been able to share love and meditation with each of you and with this instrument. We now transfer to the one known as Jim. I am Laitos.

(Jim channeling)

I am Laitos, and greet each of you again in love and light through this instrument. At this time it is our privilege to offer ourselves in the capacity of attempting to answer those queries which may be upon the minds of those present. Therefore may we ask if there might be a query with which we might begin?

N: Yes, Laitos. It was a most incredible experience. I felt like I was in touch with the same feeling I had when the entity known as Jim was trans …

(Side one of tape ends.)

(Jim channeling)

I am Laitos, and am again with this instrument. We apologize for the delay, but this instrument found the necessity of reinstituting the challenging after completing its duties with the recording device. My sister, we are aware of the feelings which you have experienced in the just previous contact and in the hypnotic regression of which you spoke and might suggest that to the entity first experiencing a contact with what you might call discarnate beings, beings of thought, that this kind of contact is of such an initially profound nature that all such contact may seem similar upon first examination.

We might suggest that the experience of the hypnotic regression was an experience during which you were able to move into deeper levels of your own being and experience there the resources of your deeper mind which are available upon request when there is a need for your understanding in a specific area relating to your own growth and evolution. These resources are quite similar to what you may experience and have indeed experienced through a contact with beings residing within the world of thought and which seem to be quite exterior to your own self.

However, we might suggest that the means by which you may discriminate between these kinds of experiences is that which we suggested by the reexamination of the challenging technique. The gathering of the self about an ideal or principle for which one lives in a fundamental sense, and would indeed give the life if necessary, is the beginning of this principle and its exercise when contact with thought entities is noticed and felt. Then it is necessary to speak in the strongest mental terms to such perceived contacts and to challenge them with the full force of your belief and the core of your being in order that those of the positive nature may be discerned from those of a negative nature and the nature which might attempt to trick or confuse a contact in any way. Thus, we might suggest that contemplation and meditation upon the core ideal, by which you shall in future times challenge such contacts, be instituted upon a regular basis in order that you may increase your ability to discriminate between contacts in what you would call your future.

May we answer in any other way, my sister?

N: No, thank you, I will try that. Thank you very much.

I am Laitos, and we thank you my sister. It has been an honor to work with you and we commend the openness of your particular channel. Is there another query at this time?

W: Yes. I wondering if I was doing the challenging properly, and if not what I can do to change that?

I am Laitos, and am aware of your query, my sister. We find that the means by which your challenging has been exercised is one which is quite efficacious at this time, but may also suggest that the strengthening of the sense of self and the ideal about which one orbits the life pattern is most helpful in strengthening the ability to offer the challenge and to make the discriminations necessary in order to begin the vocal channeling process.

May we speak further, my sister?

W: No, I think I got everything.

I am Laitos, and we wish to express once again our joy at working with your instrument, my sister. Is there another query at this time?

N: Yes. I'm curious about the entity that I channeled in August. Can you give me any information about that?

I am Laitos, and in this regard we must speak in general terms, my sister, for many are the experiences which the seeker of truth will encounter that offer insight to that entity and that entity alone by that entity's own examination of the experience and the gleaning from it of that which is there to teach.

We do not wish to intrude upon this process overly much, but may suggest that there are various locations upon your planetary surface which have through ages past been imbued with certain vibratory nexi of experience presented by what you would call various tribes and cultures. These areas having thus been invested with a certain vibratory level or frequency then continue to attract entities of this vibratory frequency both in the physical and in the metaphysical realms. Thus, the area in which you found yourself at that time had, through previous experiences, drawn unto itself entities of a nature which we find are described in your culture as the medicine man or woman, the shaman, which is of a powerful nature and which operates largely in the world of thought in order to effect changes in the manifested illusion that are in a fundamental sense metaphysically empowered. Thus, the area and its history was presented to your sensitive inner feelings and amplified by the group of entities with which you shared this experience so that your instrument became available for the use of the entity which indeed made contact with this group through your instrument. Thus it was a coinciding of various circumstances that allowed this experience to ensue.

May we speak in any other fashion, my sister?

N: No, that is sufficient. Thank you.

I am Laitos, and again we thank you, my sister. Is there another query at this time?

(Pause)

I am Laitos, and at this time we wish once again to offer our heartfelt gratitude to each present for inviting our presence within your circle of seeking. We are full of the joy of the light and harmonious vibrations that emanate from this group and we thank each for offering us this gift.

At this time we shall take our leave of this group and remind each that we are available upon request for the joining in meditation and the deepening of the meditative state at any time you should request it. However, we remind each that the attempt to work upon the vocal channeling is best reserved for this particular gathering in order that the process might continue with the most efficacy and the least confusion. We are known to you as those of Laitos and we leave this group at this time in the love and in the light of the one infinite Creator. Adonai, my friends. Adonai vasu borragus.

L/L Research

L/L Research is a subsidiary of Rock Creek Research & Development Laboratories, Inc.

P.O. Box 5195
Louisville, KY 40255-0195

www.llresearch.org

Rock Creek is a non-profit corporation dedicated to discovering and sharing information which may aid in the spiritual evolution of humankind.

ABOUT THE CONTENTS OF THIS TRANSCRIPT: This telepathic channeling has been taken from transcriptions of the weekly study and meditation meetings of the Rock Creek Research & Development Laboratories and L/L Research. It is offered in the hope that it may be useful to you. As the Confederation entities always make a point of saying, please use your discrimination and judgment in assessing this material. If something rings true to you, fine. If something does not resonate, please leave it behind, for neither we nor those of the Confederation would wish to be a stumbling block for any.

CAVEAT: This transcript is being published by L/L Research in a not yet final form. It has, however, been edited and any obvious errors have been corrected. When it is in a final form, this caveat will be removed.

© 2009 L/L Research

Sunday Meditation
February 8, 1987

Group question: What do you say to people who have cancer and are facing the possibility of death?

(Carla channeling)

I am Q'uo, and I greet you in the love and the light of the one infinite Creator. It is a great privilege to be with you and to be called to offer our humble service during your meditation. We are honored that you choose to ask us questions which those who seek to know the truth would surely ask. It is good to share the vibratory energies of those who seek as we do the one Creator in each aspect. For we, as you, have no greeting but love and light, for there is no impulse but thought and no manifestation but light.

Yet few are those who may greet each other in the comradeship of shared seeking and under the banner of the one infinite Creator. And may we say to you that it is our opinion that it is the experience of dwelling in trust with those who are from elsewhere who yet share the same Creator, they are the true center and have the true value that we have to offer as we answer your questions and that you have to offer as you ask them of us. For the trust we place in each other is a symbol of our attempt to grasp our unity, one with another and our common identification as the Creator.

The sharing of beingness and consciousness is indeed a powerful thing and we take this opportunity to thank you; nor should you fear if your numbers are small and your meditation circle is not vast, or even if you sit alone. Yet still, if you know and claim the witness of unseen friends, the light that you may raise in meditation is enormously powerful. We hope this has set up that which we wish to say about advice to those who must speak to cancer victims.

My children, it is difficult to penetrate the illusion of life or death while living in such an artificially delicate and cumbersome mechanism as the physical vehicles which you enjoy during your Earthly experience. The nature of experience is interestingly mazed. Seemingly positive and happy experiences are oftentimes of little depth, times when thought processes are slowed and intellectual, spiritual and physical senses dulled, whereas difficult times and crises, seemingly so appalling as experiences, often produce excitement, revivification of heart and mind and soul, rededication and renewal of stewardship and service commitments.

When you receive the news of a known killer which has been found within your physical body, you are naturally going to spend an ocean of tears wept or unwept, a ton of words said and unsaid, railing against and being angry about the cessation of life. Yet in the crisis of possible death lies a tremendous opportunity for the rededication of the life. For news of a possible death is a creative disturbance, a freeing mechanism which allows the one experiencing it to consider a wider variety of options with more seriousness than when the entity thought he was perfectly healthy. There is an opportunity not to be afraid. There is the opportunity to turn into one who celebrates the life lived in the present moment.

Such an entity, having found a center of joy and peace in the appreciation of many blessings, notes with keen accuracy the difficulties of the present moment without becoming discouraged because of the debit side of the balance sheet. Thus, refraining from dwelling upon possible futures, yet inspired by the possible future of depth to the amendment of the attitude at the present moment, the seeker who wishes to transform the experience of cancer may begin by affirming and celebrating each day as it awakens. This is not an exercise to use merely during periods of potential death. It is an exercise for life, not for death, for each day may be lived far more fully and with far more enjoyment and freedom, spontaneity and humor than most among your peoples are able to manifest. For the negative emotions and blockages color and bias the experience in negative ways. Any entity may choose to begin to shape the life experience for the self and by so choosing may become a more and more polarized entity.

We turn to look at some practical matters. We realize that, as we scan this instrument, we look at two providers whose families are dependent upon money earned by one potentially not able to provide. We would speak to those who fear that there is not a plentiousness of all things—the remembrance of friends, strangers who smile, individuals who unpredictably but generously may aid an unknown person. It is well to put one's thoughts not on the lacks of one's incarnation, especially when these lacks are beyond one's control, but to focus one's interest and energy upon the assets of the same situation.

If one needs not worry about money beyond a certain point, in other words, if one values one's life and feels that the environment of the livelihood has contributed to the illness, then it is time to use the creative energy of difficult situations to view the needs, the true needs of the social unit of which the entity is a part. It is well to meditate and find out for the self whether the lesson is to stay and learn to love or to move towards a greater love and faith, but with small practical and earthly expectations.

We are not those who advise reckless moves for the sake of testing the faith, yet deep within each entity there lies a sure knowledge of the rightness of each step of the life plan. Within each at this moment lies a knowledge that the entity is on the path which has been set or not. To arrive at contact with that level of self-awareness is a blessing and it usually earned. You must seek to know yourself as if you truly and honestly like and respect yourself. You cannot plunder the self anymore than you would insult a high priestess. In each other area of practical earthly endeavor, think, meditate and discuss with the family unit which you have made those things which are for and not for you.

And then, when the thinking has been done, the centering and the clearing and the grasping of the feelings of the self have been accomplished, put aside the consciousness of the dying, and realize that that which is in a disease such as cancer is allowed because your emotional and mental complex were not able to love and instead blocked love in some situation. This is a mechanical rather than a judgmental description and refers to the fact that illness in general results when the body reacts to a loss of electrical and chemical balance within the body complex. The body then, as manifesting illness, is attempting to heal itself and so-called illness is indeed a process of health by positive and affirmative attention to the present moment the many blessings which are experienced in that moment and both the wonder and the terrible mystery of life and death.

One may transform the experience of serious illness into the beginning of a new consciousness, one which is closer to that which may be held within the illusion you now enjoy and after you leave that same illusion. Would you wish to change personalities because you change bodies? Or would you prefer to be more and more truly yourself, more and more fully a manifestation of the truth about yourself, more and more an opening through which the love and the light of the infinite Creator shine forth, not to impress, but to make joyful?

Perhaps we have rambled a bit this evening, my children. At times it was necessary that we say a few things quickly through this instrument that we might keep her at an appropriate level. We thank you for your patience and it is our hope that each may see the centrality of affirming and celebrating the Creator in the self and the self in the Creator. Who each of us is is hid complete in who the

Creator is and the truth of us is the truth of the Creator.

Let us all turn then to that great light that shines in the darkness of ignorance and chaos which is much of the illusion about you, and seize hold of the central search. Life and death mean very little compared to the song of the present, for to breathe is to sing. Each soft rustle of inhalation and exhalation makes a melody in the ether of creation and sends motes of light in millions of directions with each breath, moving and moving the particles of light. Each intentional prayer is a lovely song and each silence a poem.

Who you are is not how you feel, what the condition of your body is, what your bank account is or where you live. More deep ties are those of family, friend and companion. Yet in the end, the seeker stands alone with the truth and each seeker is as infinitely great and potentially infinitely impeccable as that great warrior, the creation Itself.

We are those of Q'uo and we humbly thank you for having asked us to be with you this evening. We leave our blessing and love with each and with each about whom questions were, asking, as always, that it be understood that we are not infallible. We would attempt to open the group to questions, and shall transfer to the one known as Jim. We leave this instrument with thanks and in love and light. I am Q'uo.

(Jim channeling)

I am Q'uo, and greet each again in love and light through this instrument. We would at this time be honored to respond to those queries which those present may have for us. May we begin with a query?

J: Is it not true that before our incarnation into this life that we choose our own death and it could be the case that we would use cancer or some other illness as the means of our death?

I am Q'uo, and we might suggest, my brother, that there are correctnesses and incorrectnesses in the assumptions which you have made. We shall attempt to speak to this topic. It is true that those who are aware of the process of incarnation and its purpose, due to a conscious discovery of this incarnative process during an incarnation, take a more complete role in the planning of the incarnation which is to come before the incarnation. The framework for attempting certain lessons that will enrich an entity as a whole is determined as are those services which might be shared as fruit of the effort of learning with others. There are many possibilities for each incarnation in these two general realms of endeavor, that of learning and that of serving.

Because free will is paramount within the incarnation, and indeed before, the planning must take a general form with many potential specific aspects, be they events or entities, programmed, shall we say, as possibilities and perhaps even probabilities. Many are dependent upon other choices and agreements made between entities for various times and purposes, thus there is much that is fluid and flexible, shall we say, within any incarnation that will allow for the learning of the lessons and the offering of the services.

That graduation, shall we say, from the incarnation that is called the death, in many instances is the subject of just such planning, which is to say, there is a variety of possibilities for each entity that may occur according to the completing of the overall plan for the incarnation in a more or less successful fashion. It may be said that the lessons shall continue for any entity within an incarnation until their weight grows too heavy, at which time the entity shall have planned for one means of bringing the incarnation to its culmination.

This general means of ending the incarnation may be seen as a continuing effort to gain in the polarization in consciousness which has been chosen, thus when an entity is more successful, shall we say, in the overall plan and has achieved much of that which was laid out before the incarnation, it may be that one or more potential death, as you call them, experiences are presented to the entity who by its efficiency in continuing to utilize the catalyst may yet continue within the incarnation by successfully utilizing the catalyst which could have brought about that termination of the incarnation called death.

However, it may be that an entity finds some difficulty within some portion of the incarnation, perhaps through attempting to learn too rapidly certain lessons, and may take advantage of an earlier potential terminating of the incarnation through specifically planned catalyst which when unsuccessfully processed, may result in that which you call a disease and which then might end the incarnation. Each disease, as you call them, is a symbolic representation for a certain entity or perhaps a grouping of entities, of a certain kind of lesson, thus the ending of the incarnation shall come for each within your third-density illusion. Yet the ending is not necessarily that which has been chosen to unfold in one fashion only and one time only and by one means only, yet may be that which is possible after a certain point and may be possible in a continuing fashion according to the entity's ability to continue to process the catalyst which it has provided for itself within the incarnation.

May we speak further, my brother?

J: Thank you for that answer. Why is it that some cultures on this planet are virtually [free] of the disease known as cancer?

I am Q'uo, and we find that this disease is one which is late to join the experience of your peoples upon this planetary sphere and, being of recent influence, has found its first roots within those cultures which are of a more individualized nature, shall we say. By this we mean that those entities which comprise the cultures which are most susceptible to utilizing this disease are those cultures in which the identity of the individual is more firmly fixed and exercised, so that the relationships which develop from such strongly characterized traits that form the personal identity are those relationships which partake less fully of cultural or tribal or primitive traditions and more fully of those situations in which emotional exercise, shall we say, is determined and amplified by individual choice. Thus, the difficulties, as you call them, which bring about the heated feelings of anger and the venting of that emotion in an uncontrolled fashion and the failure to heal those wounds which it brings about are those conditions which are most salubrious for the fostering of the condition which you call cancer.

May we speak further, my brother?

J: No, that's all the questions that I have for now. Thank you.

I am Q'uo, and we thank you, my brother. Is there another query at this time?

Carla: Thank you, no questions tonight, Q'uo. Nice to hear your voice.

I am Q'uo, and we are most grateful to those present for inviting our presence. We greatly enjoy the opportunity to join with this group and to speak our humble words and we hope that we have been able to provide some small insight into those mysteries which are so great a portion of the illusion in which you find yourselves moving ever onward in the seeking of the one Creator. We shall be with you in what you call your future and look forward to each such sharing. We shall leave this group at this time, rejoicing always in the unity of thought which binds each seeker of truth. We are known to you as those of Q'uo, and we leave you in the love and in the light of the one infinite Creator. Adonai, my friends. Adonai vasu borragus. ☙

Intensive Meditation
February 11, 1987

(Jim channeling)

I am Laitos and I greet you, my friends, in the love and in the light of the one infinite Creator. We are honored to be able to join your group this evening in order that those who are new to the service of vocal channeling may work upon that service and make it ever more fully a part of their own being and a portion of the way in which they are able to share that of inspiration with others about them.

We commend each for giving careful consideration to this manner of service and for looking deeply within for those guideposts which point the inner direction and which reveal self to self, for this is the journey that you are upon, my friends. You are discovering ever greater portions of your own being and taking those discoveries as that which shall be the impetus for yet further journeying into the self, and by journeying into the self, discovering that one has a unique and intimate connection with all of the creation about one and with the one Creator, which through the power of It's love has set all of the creation in motion.

We thank each present for giving the most care possible in the consideration of how to approach the service of vocal channeling. We remind each that we are but your brothers and sisters who have moved somewhat further along upon the journey which you find yourselves traveling upon as well. We offer our opinions and what we have found to be of value in our own seeking to you freely with the hope that you will take that which is of service to you and leave behind that which has no value to you at this time.

At this time we would attempt to make our contact known to the one known as W. Again, we remind this entity that it is helpful after the contact has been perceived and successfully challenged to refrain from analysis while the contact is ongoing in order that the channel which is open might remain open and be available for the transmission of thoughts. We shall speak our identification and a few words in addition to that through the one known as W, if she will relax and speak our thoughts as she becomes aware of them. We shall transfer this contact at this time. I am Laitos.

(W channeling)

I am Laitos. This entity has successfully challenged and [remains] at our [conditional] level. It has succeeded in establishing a good channel. We are pleased with her efforts and are happy with her progress. I am Laitos.

(Jim channeling)

I am Laitos, and am again with this instrument. Indeed, we are pleased that we have been able to make our contact known to the one known as W and we might suggest that the challenging which the one known as W has successfully accomplished be followed by the opening of the self to the degree that not only our identification be perceived, but that in the future experiences this entity consider allowing the channel to remain open for a longer period, even if there is no apparent communication occurring in order that we might begin to expand the abilities of this new instrument and introduce further concepts through this instrument. We are pleased with the progress which the one known as W has demonstrated, and are hopeful that we might continue to strengthen the good contact which we feel with this new instrument.

At this time, if it is the desire of the one known as N, we shall make our contact known to this new instrument and shall simply attempt to speak our name through this new instrument in order that it might become familiar with our vibrations. Again, we remind this entity that after the challenge has been offered and successfully passed, that it might also refrain from analysis and simply speak our identification as it becomes apparent to her. We shall now transfer this contact. I am Laitos.

(N channeling)

I am Laitos. I greet you in love and in light. This entity is [sleepy] us as, as *(inaudible)* vocalizing our *(inaudible)* We leave this entity at this time and in *(inaudible)*.

(Jim channeling)

I am Laitos, and am again with this instrument. We are very happy to have been able to make our contact known to the one known as N and to speak a few words through this new instrument. We apologize for any discomfort which the one known as N has experienced during our contact. We advise this new instrument to make a mental note of any adjustments which we might make in order to allow the one known as N to experience our contact in a more comfortable and stable manner. We are very pleased with the ability of the one known as N to perceive our contact. This new instrument has the potential to develop quite rapidly and in this regard we would suggest to the one known as N that the challenging is an especially important portion of this type of service in order that this new instrument be able to discern the nature of the contact which she is experiencing. At this time we would open this session to queries which any present may find of value or of necessity in asking.

May we begin with a query at this time?

W: Laitos, my head feels as though it's been pulled backward and is very impossible to move. Is this just a temporary discomfort or can you give me some explanation?

Carla: I would request Laitos, that you adjust [her].

I am Laitos, and we are making adjustments with our contact with the one known as W in order to relax the muscles of the neck, the upper shoulders and the rear of the skull. We might suggest to the one known as W, as we have suggested previously to the one known as N, that any discomfort in the experience of our contact be immediately noted so that we might make the necessary adjustments. We are not skillful at making new contacts which are immediately comfortable, for the blending of our vibration with yours requires that we be able to perceive your vibration in a stable manner and become as familiar with it as you are with ours. This takes practice and patience on both our parts and we welcome any mental requests for adjustment which any instrument might need. We would also suggest as a general rule that the ability to relax not only the mind but the physical vehicle as completely as possible prior to contact and especially during contact is most helpful. It is sometimes the new instrument's stance, shall we say, that it prepares itself for contact in the same manner as one might prepare for a cold shower, shall we say, and brace the self in order to withstand contact. We would suggest that the relaxation of the physical vehicle through mental suggestion is most helpful to any instrument and most especially to those new instruments experiencing contact for the first time.

Is there a further query, my sister?

W: No, thank you.

I am Laitos, and we thank you, my sister.

N: Yes, Laitos, I have a few questions. First, when you were saying that she felt her head being pulled backwards, I felt a weight on my neck and head pulling me forward. I do not feel that that is the discomfort as you call it. I feel that to me that is more of a sign that I have a contact with an entity. Is, as time progresses and I continue channeling, is this alleviated? Or it should it be considered not good to have a pressure in my head?

I am Laitos, and we might suggest that this sign or indication of contact is just that, my sister, and is that sensation which is most helpful to you at this time in order that you are made aware that there is a contact which is about to occur and is indeed occurring. You, through your own level of comfort, may request that the indication be made more or less apparent. You will through your own needs in future experiences make this determination and through mental suggestion allow our contact then to become adjusted in whatever manner serves to both make you aware that the contact is available and to make you comfortable as well. There are many different ways in which new instruments may experience the contact with our group and we are happy to work with any manner of alerting a new instrument that has meaning to the new instrument.

May we speak further, my sister?

N: Yes. You're saying you mean that perhaps if sitting in an upright position you have to strain to either to hold your back straight or your neck. Would it be okay for a channeling entity to perhaps lie on the floor and have the whole body relaxed?

I am Laitos, and though this holds promise for the relaxation of the physical vehicle and the removing of strain upon its various portions needed, as you have mentioned, in order to maintain a certain posture, it is not a position which we recommend for the new instrument, for it is a position which through years of experience one of the third density such as yourself has associated with the activity of sleeping and the tendency to move into the sleeping state in that position is somewhat pronounced. Thus, we would suggest for the new instrument that the sitting in an upright position with the spine held reasonably erect is most helpful for the meditative state and the attempt to offer the service of vocal channeling through that meditative state.

May we speak further, my sister?

N: No, thank you very much. That's what I've come upon.

I am Laitos, and we thank you, my sister. Is there another query?

N: As a matter of fact, I have another question. You were referring earlier to yourselves being our brothers and sisters which made me feel quite good and closer to you, seeing that you are like us. My question is, as in emotions of entities of the third density, do you experience emotions as we would, perhaps like happy, sad, jealous, emotions more I consider of our entities? I was just curious if you experienced the same type of emotions?

I am Laitos, and in our experience of the one Creator, we have greatly simplified the emotional complex so that the overriding emotion which comprises our experience is one which you may see as love or compassion. It is our experience that all beings are a portion of the one Creator and this perception is aided greatly by having far fewer veils that hide the unity of all things from our sight and sense. Thus, it is ours to offer that called love in as pure a fashion as is possible for us. We work with the refining of this love or compassion at this time by attempting to imbue it in some degree with that quality which you might see …

(Tape ends.)

L/L Research

Sunday Meditation
February 15, 1987

Group question: About the "mark of the beast," as mentioned in the Bible, what it might be, what it means to people and so forth.

(Carla channeling)

I am Q'uo, and I greet you in the love and in the light of the one infinite Creator. It is a privilege to blend our vibrations with yours as you sit in meditation, and we thank you for calling us to join you, and offer our faulty and error-filled thoughts.

Upon the subject of the mark of the beast. This instrument wished us luck before she gave over control of the speaking mechanism to us, and we do indeed feel lucky to be able to speak with you about evil, for surely, the mark of the beast is only a symbol for that which is evil. Indeed, the mind often thinks in symbols rather than turning to the essence of things.

To be literal, which is of course one level of answering the question, the mark of the beast, it being 666, is a triple number, rooted in the Cabalistic traditions of your Eastern peoples. Within that tradition, the number six refers to the house of mundane things. The number six has connotations concerning finances, wealth, security and survival. If one has a penchant for luxury, the number six might be expected to figure in a numerological analysis of such an entity's name or birth date. When a number is doubled, it is the same number but stronger, and when it is tripled, it is very strong, thus the number 666 is literally, "the things of this world." Thus, the mark of the beast is symbolized by a number which connotes your present experience.

Lift your thoughts with me and let us look at this world of yours that is full of symbols of the evil of the beast; here a daisy, there a lark, here a thinking youth, and there a smiling woman. These things do not seem outwardly evil, yet for those who gaze upon the beast, the mark can be found, for the illusion is yours and each of you may choose to interpret what lies before you as you will. It is possible through description to cause the same scene to appear quite wonderful or quite the opposite by the careful use of detail. We might point out, for instance, instead of a flower, one of your refuse heaps; instead of a smiling woman, a hungry child. The choice of symbols is always yours, nor is the beast strong within one who chooses positively oriented symbols to facilitate the interpretation of catalyst.

What we are attempting to do is to indicate to you our feelings concerning prophecy. The mark of the beast is one of many symbols used within an inspired work of channeling done by the one named John. Much of this entity's effort was involved not in offering universal symbology, but rather in sending covert information concerning specific events and entities to those known to the one known as John.

The work has inspired and over-awed many, yet seldom has the deeper symbology been penetrated to discover the balance of the present moment. Such is the greatest danger of prophecy and symbology. Whatever one thinks about evil, one must cause one's thinking to become twisted and biased in order to accommodate the eccentric symbology of the beast, its mark, its unusual body design, and its various foes. Perhaps this has kept some from gazing upon the essence of the beast.

The essence of the beast lies within each heart and within each mind. The essence of the beast is the power of denial. Just as the essence of love is the power of acceptance, so the essence of evil is the perfect ability to deny what is true and believe what is false. Thus, evil has far less to do, for instance, with money than with less-than-straightforwardness in gathering, keeping and spending money. One who is seeking the essence of the positive seeks more and more to offer the self in service. One who wishes evil may seem to offer service to others, yet always there is some denial of free will, some rejection of some aspect of universal love, some implied or stated separation between you and some other. The one who looks for advantages at another's expense is a far clearer symbol of the beast than a number.

It has been said among your group this evening that as you sit in meditation, you live in the experience of the age of the beast, the age of universal credit and the rule of many by numbers. Remember that it is not the symbols that have power, but the essences that give the symbols power. The evil which lies within your monetary systems is an evil—that is to say a lie—which has been with you since the first money was used to make money rather than trading being done between two entities which had use of each others' surplus. Thus, the essence of money being artificial power is an evil essence by definition. However, the technology of your age, my children, is neither good nor evil, but a tool used for good or ill.

Would that we could guide you to one writing which made all things clear, one set of symbols in which there was no doubt of clear meaning, no confusion as to extraneous detail. We cannot, for there is no construction made of words and concepts which is not also a group of symbols, and in the end that which you know of good and evil abide not in symbols but in essences. Essences are felt by the deepest heart and mind of an entity so that there is recognition and knowingness of that which is, shall we say, morally pleasing and morally distasteful.

As you gaze upon this age which many find full of lies and therefore evil, look upon the essences of people, relationships and the stewardship of that which is seemingly evil—money—and find within yourself the positive truth affirming, life-affirming characteristics and attributes of people, relationships and stewardship which can be brought to bear upon each and every situation. For this is not an age—this, my children, is your age, and no mark of any beast can shape the rhythm of your own creation. That there are highly motivated, negatively oriented angelic spirits is as true as that there are highly polarized and motivated positive angelic entities.

We have no desire to play down the loyal opposition which challenges us and makes us learn to be strong. We wish only to correct any tendency towards feeling that one is in the grip of evil or in any way limited or governed by the apparent world view. To many, this is indeed the age of the beast. We find this among the peoples, this attitude of many greatly disturbed, greatly in pain, but accepting many symbols as essences. Knowing that love created all and that the great original Thought of love forms the heart of all that there is, we ask you to be satisfied only with the essences of things.

Thus may you find sunshine in dark places, and thus may your discrimination steer you from unexpected shadows which others may not see. It is your experience, your creation, your living we ask you to join with us in seeking the Creator, without fear and with an ever-mounting desire to touch again and again the wonderful light-filled mystery of consciousness. And now, because we have talked about a heavy word, a weighty, sad word, this symbol of despair that is evil, let us lighten our meditation before we move on. Let us release this question, for it troubles this instrument and may trouble others.

Let us turn to gaze upon the mark of the angels. What would that be, my children—except a smile. What is the truth and symbol of the truth—except a look of joy, for that which is, is love. We leave you in that love and in the light, and would speak with you further through the one known as Jim. We are those of Q'uo.

Intensive Meditation, February 15, 1987

(Jim channeling)

I am Q'uo, and greet each of you again through this instrument in love and in light. It is our privilege at this time to open this meeting to queries which those gathered may have brought for the asking. May we begin with a query at this time?

J: Is the basic denial that exists on this plane, is that basically just the denial that we are God and that our own will is one and the same with the will of God? Is that the basic denial that's kept us separated from the one God all this time?

I am Q'uo, and we find that the query which you have asked is one which covers a great deal of territory and experience within your illusion. If we may look upon the population of your planet's third-density illusion, we see that the great veil of forgetting which separates the conscious from the unconscious mind is that which effectively brings about a condition which you may in your terminology call a denial of sight. This sight is that which is most inward and outward seeking for the nature of the creation in which [an] entity finds itself.

If we are to look upon the primary means of perceiving the creation and its meaning for those of your third density, we might take that denial of which you have spoken and describe it rather as the inability to perceive the unity of all the creation, the infinity which is the foundation, the current reality and what you would call a future experience for all those of the third-density illusion. Thus, this inability to see the connected nature of all things, all thoughts, is a denial which, indeed, allows an entity to consider itself separate from and outside the influence of that power which you call God or the Creator. This seeming separation or denial or lack of perception creates a condition in which an entity may learn a variety of lessons which will eventually provide an opportunity for the integrating of each individual lesson with the wholeness of not only the greater self, which resides beyond the veil of forgetting, but the selves of all creatures and things about one in the creation and indeed with the Creator Itself.

Thus, the perception is limited, in order that work might be done within limited boundaries that would not be possible should the boundaries not exist and the sight penetrate infinity and thus make the experiment of limitations that which is obvious to those who see with far-seeing eyes. With the impossibility of such limitation there is also the lack of opportunity for the experience of the Creator in an individualized form. This individualized form is that which each third density takes up in order that there might be a greater experience and glorification provided for the one Creator through each individual.

May we speak further, my brother?

J: No, that was excellent, Thank you.

I am Q'uo. We thank you, my brother. Is there another query?

H: Yeah, I have one thing, one ideal on this thing, and that is this. If we entertain thoughts of this mark as such and all that, would that actually prevent or hold us from being fourth-density material? I assume that this is right, if we continue to entertain bad thoughts or evil thoughts rather than positive thoughts. Is this right?

I am Q'uo, and, my brother, though there is the tendency towards correctness in your supposition, the simplicity of its statement is that which we would hesitate in accepting as correct, for it is indeed true that the focus of one's attention determines where one shall find the opportunity for lessons and services. The focus of one's attention, in a general context, if it rests upon the appearance of things, is destined to move from that which seems separate and perhaps threatening to yet another portion of experience that seems separate from the self and perhaps again threatening to the self, for all the creation about one within your illusion seems to be quite removed from the individual experience without cohesion, without rhythm, and without harmony.

Yet, if one directs the attention and the desire to known the nature of things beyond the exterior appearance of things and begins to move into the heart of all things and thought and activity, one may with such a focused attention begin to harmonize the individual perception of each portion of the creation which surrounds one, thus bringing into a coherent pattern various portions of the creation which with renewed dedication of seeking begin to fit as one part of a puzzle fitting into another and another and another, so that the creation one [perceives] begins to take on a form and a feeling and a purpose, and an experience of unity becomes more and more possible for such a seeker and such a focused point of viewing the creation about it.

Thus, my brother, when looking upon any portion of the creation which surrounds one, it is well to note not only the exterior appearance and action of things, events and peoples, but to begin to move beyond those appearances within one's thinking and perceiving so that the common features and feelings and rhythms and tones may become apparent as well and as layer upon layer of meaning is discovered, the simplicity and unity of all portions of the creation become more apparent to one who seeks in this manner.

And thus, as the unified nature of the creation becomes apparent to such an entity, and the entity begins to move in harmony with the power, the creative power of love which is found to move all things, then one more and more readies the self for the graduation, as you have called it, into that density of love and understanding where the veils are removed and the Creator more clearly stands before the entity in all experience.

May we speak further, my brother?

H: No, that was very well explained. I have a much better feel for it now. I appreciate it and I thank you.

I am Q'uo, and we thank you, my brother. Is there another query?

Questioner: I have a question in reference to the number six, pertaining to numerology as in a person's name. If there is an absence of six, is this significant? And if so, in what way?

I am Q'uo, and we are not completely sure if our grasp of your query is sufficient Please requery if our response is not sufficient. The numbering that is apparent within any entity's naming or date of birth is a symbol which opens, shall we say, the road map in a certain area of the entity's life to the entity's viewing in order that perhaps the wide and narrow portions of the road might be seen and given appropriate attention. Whether one or another number is present or missing is a portion of the entity's roadmap, the presence or absence of which adds or subtracts certain characteristics or possibilities for that entity. Thus, the numerological understanding of an entity's significant nature provides the symbolic form that the entity has chosen in order to express certain characteristics and to allow opportunities for certain lessons within a certain incarnation.

May we speak further, my sister?

Questioner: I think that answers it. Thank you.

I am Q'uo, and we thank you, my sister. Is there another query?

Carla: Well, if everybody's all finished, I did have one. Q'uo, I wonder if you could help me in my teaching. I suspect one of my students, a girl named W, of having an entity present. I've challenged the entity, it seems to be a positively-oriented entity. It's not of the Confederation and I can't get its name, but I expect W could. Now, can I help this channel to develop in such a way that the entity has the best chance of making a good, safe, positive contact with this entity, which seems to be a helpful entity, without setting her up for it? You don't have to tell me how to do it without setting it up for it, if that's something I have to figure out, but any tips that you could give me on how to work with this situation would be helpful because I haven't run into it before.

I am Q'uo, and with this query we find that we must step carefully in order that we do not cross the line of free will choices which is reserved in a sacred fashion for each seeker to move within itself. The entity of which you speak, the one known as W, has as you have surmised both the ability to serve as a vocal instrument in a pronounced fashion and the opportunity to do so in a manner which is moving towards its appropriate expression. As to your role in this process …

(Side one of tape ends.)

(Jim channeling)

I am Q'uo, and am again with this instrument. We can only reaffirm, my sister, those techniques which you have utilized in a successful fashion in previous teachings, combined with the greater reliance upon the intuition which we find that you have also exercised in the recent meditation sessions with this entity. This is an opportunity not only for this new student to learn its service, but also is an opportunity for the teacher to expand the abilities in the teaching. The techniques are familiar to you. The reliance upon the intuition is that which is newer in your experience and that which we might suggest holds the greater opportunity at this time for your service, not only to this particular new instrument, but in your service as a teacher of the vocal channeling service as well.

May we speak further, my sister?

Carla: I'm going to read over what you said, but I believe I understand. Thanks a lot.

I am Q'uo, and we thank you, my sister. Is there another query at this time?

Carla: I have just one question that I've always wondered about and never had a satisfactory answer to. Why is everybody so fascinated with the mark of the beast? I mean, people are, anywhere in this culture. People from all different Christian and non-Christian viewpoints, very extreme, are actually interested in that.

I am Q'uo, and, my sister, we find that the simplicity of the query moved into an area which is not as simple to provide an answer for. The feeling for power and the ability to affect events and people is that which fascinates many of your population. Your population exists within an illusion in which many individual entities move and participate in the rituals of gathering wealth, position, respect and power of various kinds. It seems to many of your population that the gathering of power in whatever form and for whatever reason is an activity in which all wish to excel in some manner, whether the power be social, financial, religious or spiritual or simply the power over entities in one's own family or neighborhood. There is the feeling within many of your population that in some way, greater and greater power may be had by those who know certain secrets that will reveal unto them procedures or techniques for gathering such power unto themselves.

Many see the power of well known figures, or the power that is spoken of in many of your holy works, and make connections between the events of your world and the events that seem to be quite beyond the mundane experience. It is felt by many that the life which is lived upon this planetary sphere is a life which prepares one for a greater life that shall become apparent when the Earthly life is finished. And yet, the power-filled nature of the creation and those who move within it continues to fascinate many who wish to feel not just a glimpse, shall we say, of such power, but wish to partake fully in it themselves. Thus, when speakings of greater and greater powers are heard, entities begin to connect these speakings with the feelings that such powers are available only to a few who have certain secrets revealed unto them.

Thus, the concept of the dark force that is embodied within speakings of the beast, as it is called, bring not only to the conscious mind images of the very nature of creation itself, but draw through the subconscious mind the faintly remembered connection that each entity has with the entire creative power of love of the one Creator. The experience within your illusion for each entity is one in which there is in some form the attempt to reconcile the powers of light and the powers of darkness in order that a unified perception of all the creation might be achieved. The darker expressions of power, being by their very nature secret and separate, seem more fascinating than the obvious brilliance and power of light manifested as love, and through such mysterious and secret fascination attract the attention of many, such as the latest gossip attracts the attention of those who speak over the backyard fence, shall we say.

We apologize for the difficulty we have had in transmitting these concepts through this instrument, but we find that this instrument's mind is somewhat furnished with information which prejudges that which we have to offer, and we have not been overly successful, shall we say, in providing a response to your query which we felt was possible. May we speak in any further fashion, my sister?

Carla: No, I think you're giving yourself a hard time. I was fascinated with that. Thank you very much.

I am Q'uo, and we thank you, my sister. Is there another query at this time?

(Pause)

I am Q'uo, and we wish to thank once again each present for inviting our presence in your circle of seeking this evening. We are greatly honored to be asked to speak our humble words to a group of seekers which is as faithful as those gathered here this evening. We wish to remind each that we offer but our opinions which are fallible and filled with error. Do not hesitate to leave those behind which do not ring true.

At this time we shall take our leave of this group, thanking each once again for allowing us to join you.

We are known to you as those of Q'uo. As always, we leave each in the love and in the light of the one infinite Creator. Adonai, my friends. Adonai vasu borragus.

(Carla channeling)

I am Nona. I *(intoned single tone held on vowel sound "I")* greet you in the love and in the light of the One Who is All. I *(musical tone on two notes)* wish each of you to join with us in mind as we sing healing tones, for there is the need within this group at this time.

(Healing melody channeled through Carla.) ❧

Intensive Meditation
February 18, 1987

(Unknown channeling)

I'm in the love, I'm in the light of our infinite Creator. It is a privilege and a blessing for me to be with you this evening, and to behold the ongoing work of those upon your planet who wish to aid and lighten the planetary consciousness. We thank you for this attention, which more than any one thing which your people can do, heals the planet. The simple intention to heal, the desire to make well *(inaudible)* of law. Down in the stable in a persistent manner there is no greater service. That those within incarnation *(inaudible)* can perform *(inaudible)*. We are here to work with you, in the capacity of spoken channels. We've been very pleased with the progress made, however, we feel that in the case of the one known as W we still have work to do in adjusting the contact so that it is both comfortable and *(inaudible)*.

(Long pause.)

(Carla channeling)

I am Laitos, and am once again with this channel. We apologize for the pause, but we believe that the phrase "we pause (paws)" may be quite apt in this case, as the instrument was being sat upon in a most indelicate manner by one of the *(inaudible)*? Now the small "paws" have been readjusted and we may proceed. We request that the one known as W continue offering us an accurate assessment of the comfort of the contact, for we wish to strike just the right balance between comfort and the reassuring feeling of contact being available to make the contact supremely comfortable as possible, but we find that most instruments prefer to have some small conditioning, a name which has been used by this instrument before to describe some physical manifestation of our presence. This includes pressure and movement upon the head, neck and various portions of the jaw as well as certain other visual and bodily experiences.

As to the one known as N, we feel that we have made good contact with this instrument, and only request that we be given accurate information mentally. Here the one known as N desires an alteration of any kind in the conditioning which she is receiving. We would like to work now with the one known as W. We shall speak with a little bit more of a length of message than previously. We request, as always, that the instrument refrain from analysis and merely produce words which convey the concepts received. In all humility we request this not because our message has a sophistication or eloquence, but because we attempt to speak of the truth, knowing that we can only give opinion. We trust that it is your desire also to seek and to speak whatever part of the truth you may see. We shall at this time leave this instrument and transfer to the one known as W. I am Laitos.

(W channeling)

I am Laitos *(inaudible)*. We are pleased with the contact which we have obtained in the one known as W. We would like to request that she refrain from analysis and *(inaudible)* comfort in the knowledge that her efforts are being rewarded by this excellent contact. We would caution her from becoming too involved in the process and instead recommend that she merely observe that which is occurring. We would like to thank her for her efforts in continuing to remain open as a channel, and appreciate her efforts. It is our desire to continue working with the one known as W so that she may be *(inaudible)* this receptive to receiving our information at this time.

We will now leave the one known as W in the love and the light of the infinite Creator. We would like to thank *(inaudible)* I am Laitos.

(Carla channeling)

I am Laitos, and am again with this instrument, and greet you through this instrument once again in love and light. We find a lively energy in this room this evening, the product of happy souls and sensitive ones. Indeed, we find your feelings to be most happy this evening and enjoying the company of their favorite humans. We congratulate the one known as W for maintaining concentration throughout periods of kitty-cat deprivation. We wish now to work with the instrument known as N. May we thank the one known as N for working with us and may we commend this instrument for its care in challenging at our last meditation. It is much appreciated, for we who wish to serve the Creator by being of service to others have no desire to reduce our polarity by wrestling with any other who may wish to contact an entity. When the challenging and tuning are done there is no need, for one by one the less desirable, in terms of the channel's own tuning, contacts are simply removed so that in the end your choice as a channel is either singular or a very good selection of energies or vibrations from which to choose.

We operate upon what you may call a carrier wave which is much stronger than some vibrations used by Confederation members. We are what this instrument would call a broadband contact, and therefore are relatively easy for your instruments to perceive. We are of your fourth-density vibration moving upon vibratory patterns of love seeking wisdom. We wish you to know a bit about ourselves as we grow to learn more about each of you. At this time we would transfer to the one known as N and say a few words about love if this instrument would also refrain from analysis and simply produce words which express concepts which come into the mind. We now transfer. I am Laitos.

(N channeling)

I am Laitos. *(Inaudible)* to increase *(inaudible)* know about *(inaudible)* this *(inaudible)* as well as do not feel *(inaudible)* those who *(inaudible)* seek knowledge of those entities who do *(inaudible)* I am Laitos. I leave you in the light and the love *(inaudible)*.

(Carla channeling)

I am Laitos, and am again with this instrument. We gladly accept this instrument's query that we do come in Christ consciousness, in the consciousness of love. We have not established a fully sturdy contact with the one known as N, and the one known as N therefore is experiencing some surges of good contact and some periods where the contact is difficult. This is normal and we shall be continuing to adjust as the instrument continues to attempt to make meditation a daily habit, so that the necessary concentration of mind for channeling on a steady state basis may be more dependably possible. The amount of concentration necessary to carry a channeling is not necessarily great, but persistence is extremely helpful, for only through practice can one develop the confidence necessary to begin speaking without knowing the whole of what one has to say.

At this time we rejoice that we have been able to exercise each new instrument and would like to transfer the contact to the one known as Jim. Again we leave this instrument with thanks and transfer. I am Laitos.

(Jim channeling)

I am Laitos, and greet each of you again in love and light through this instrument. At this time it is our privilege to offer ourselves in the capacity of attempting to answer those queries which *(inaudible)* Therefore, may we begin with the query at this time?

Questioner: Are you making adjustments on us during the—during our meditations?

I am Laitos, and where it is appropriate we have in some few cases adjoined each of those present in the meditative state without making our presence consciously known or identified. We have chosen to simply offer the service of aiding the meditative state by harmonizing our vibrations with it in a manner which offers the possibility of deepening the meditation. In this manner we familiarize ourselves with the vibrations of each new instrument and increase the probability that we will be able to utilize the new instrument in a manner which is more comfortable to that new instrument.

May we speak in any other fashion, my sister?

Questioner: Is there a best [place] of meditation for the *(inaudible)*?

I am Laitos, and we find that though there are various aids to meditation which are generally comfortable, we cannot say that there is any best way for any particular entity to engage in the meditative practice. The intention of the meditation we find to be the most important quality that one may bring to the meditative state. To intend to meditate and to offer the self as a receptive instrument to the instreamings of love and light that are possible to perceive in a meditative state and to do this upon a regular basis we find to be most helpful, indeed. It is also helpful to find a time of the day which may be utilized, a regular [time] and a place which is used for this purpose, and to use the place for the purpose of meditation and for no other purpose is also a manner in which a place may be invested with intentions and a practice of meditation. To choose a time which is full of the quietness is helpful as well, and it is usually recommended that the spine be kept vertical so that the instreamings of love and light, or the prana, as it may be called, may find an easy entry into the energy centers, or chakras, as you may call them.

With these general parameters in mind, one may then adapt one's own desires and inclinations in a manner which feels comfortable to the instrument or to the one meditating so that the meditative state may allow the entity to be nourished in the most efficacious manner possible.

May we speak further, my sister?

Questioner: No, thank you.

I am Laitos. We thank you, my sister. Is there another query?

Questioner: Laitos. We know that you—are you the teacher of new instruments?

I am Laitos, and, indeed, this is correct, my sister. When the opportunity is presented in which we might introduce a new instrument to the beginning practice of the vocal channeling service, we are able to realize the most active form of service that is ours to offer to the third-density population of your planetary sphere. In a less active manner, we also are honored to be able to perform the service of sending the vibrations of what you would call love and light to those entities of your planetary surface of third density which are in need of such emanations in the personal incarnative pattern.

These emanations are sent without any identification on our part, and are most usually perceived as a general feeling of well-being, if they are perceived in a conscious manner at all. It is quite frequently the case that such vibrations shall do their work in a manner which is not noticed by the conscious mind of those receiving such sendings of love and light. In these rays we are privileged to be able to be of a small service to the population of your planet.

May we speak further, my sister?

Questioner: Yes. Does that mean that when I meditate and send love and light to individuals that it's sent through you or that you—or could be sent through you, or do you just send love and light to those who you feel a need?

I am Laitos. In many instances, our sendings of love and light are joined and blended with many other sendings of love and light which emanate both from outside of your planetary influence and upon your planetary surface. However, we do not have the function of, shall we say, a gathering of various sendings from entities such as yourself and then serving as a postman of a cosmic kind and then delivering such sendings. Such sendings are quite able to speed on their way and make themselves felt without any such aid.

We are also able and honored to join any entity in the meditative state when the entity has meant or requested that we do so. This, however, is a service which we provide to far fewer upon your planetary surface than we enjoy when we are sending the emanations of love and light as a general blessing, shall we say. To all those requesting such aid we would hasten to add that we are not alone in this service and are joined by many, many other beings that are not upon your planetary surface and who also send their emanations of love and light to those requesting such.

May we speak further, my sister?

Questioner: No. I wasn't thinking so much of the—but, if I wished to increase the amount of love and light or to join you and others in sending love and light to someone upon this planet, is that, would that have a greater effect or amount of love and light sent to that individual?

I am Laitos, and if our understanding is correct, my sister, the words suggest that your sendings are of an urgency which is quite equal to our own, for we each are a portion of the Creator, and the conscious incarnative intention to make the gift of love and light to another is a sending which is most propitiously potent, and in no need of addition. However, we might suggest that all such sendings tend to attract each to the other as likened vibrations so that there is a harmonic resonance that is set up when such sendings are offered, and this resonance then blending the sendings of many and all which make such offerings then increase the vibrational frequency of such sendings in order that those requesting such shall have a greater opportunity to be bathed in the love and light vibrations, and to be nourished in the metaphysical sense by them.

May we speak further, my sister?

Questioner: No, thank you. I appreciate your answers.

I am Laitos, and again we thank you, my sister. Is there another query at this time?

Questioner: Yes. Are you involved on a physical plane?

I am Laitos, and am indeed an individualized portion of that which you have called a social memory complex power. Our population of souls is of the fourth-density vibrational frequency in which we have the honor of pursuing the understanding of compassion, the offering of love to those whose call equals our ability to serve. We have, as you have surmised, evolved from a planetary influence similar to your own in that it was a third-density planetary sphere. During which …

(Tape ends.)

Sunday Meditation
February 22, 1987

Group question: Concerning the uses of anger, how anger can be used in the metaphysical search.

(The rest of the tape is blank.) ❖